Understanding
Human Communication

Understanding
Human Communication

ELEVENTH EDITION

Ronald B. Adler
Santa Barbara City College

George Rodman
Brooklyn College, City University of New York

with **Carrie Cropley Hutchinson**
Santa Barbara City College

NEW YORK | OXFORD
OXFORD UNIVERSITY PRESS

Oxford University Press, Inc., publishes works that further Oxford University's
objective of excellence in research, scholarship, and education.

Oxford   New York
Auckland Cape Town Dar es Salaam Hong Kong Karachi
Kuala Lumpur Madrid Melbourne Mexico City Nairobi
New Delhi Shanghai Taipei Toronto

With offices in
Argentina Austria Brazil Chile Czech Republic France Greece
Guatemala Hungary Italy Japan Poland Portugal Singapore
South Korea Switzerland Thailand Turkey Ukraine Vietnam

For titles covered by Section 112 of the US Higher Education Opportunity
Act, please visit www.oup.com/us/he for the latest information about pricing
and alternate formats.

Published by Oxford University Press, Inc.
198 Madison Avenue, New York, New York 10016
http://www.oup.com

Library of Congress Cataloging-in-Publication Data

Adler, Ronald B. (Ronald Brian), 1946–
 Understanding human communication / Ronald B. Adler, George Rodman, with
Carrie Cropley. — 11th ed.
    p. cm.
 Includes bibliographical references and index.
 ISBN 978-0-19-974738-2 (alk. paper)
 I. Rodman, George R., 1948- II. Cropley, Carrie. III. Title.

P90.A32 2012
302.2—dc22
                            2010046858

Printing number: 9 8 7 6 5 4 3 2

Printed in the United States of America
on acid-free paper.

BRIEF CONTENTS

Also Available:
Optional Chapters

Mediated Communication
Communication and
Service Learning

CONTENTS

PART TWO Communication Elements

CHAPTER 6   Nonverbal Communication 165

PART THREE   Interpersonal Communication

CHAPTER 7   Understanding Interpersonal Relationships 195

PART FOUR Communication in Groups

PART FIVE Public Communication

CHAPTER 13   Informative Speaking   379

CHAPTER 14   Persuasive Speaking   403

ALSO AVAILABLE: OPTIONAL CHAPTERS

Mediated Communication

Types of Mediated Communication
Mass Communication
Mediated Interpersonal Communication
Converging Communication Media

Theories of Media Effects
Flow Theories
Social Learning Theory
Individual Differences
Cultivation Theory
Agenda Setting
Cumulative Effects Theory

Manifestation of Effects

Cultural Studies
Gender Analysis
Political Economic Analysis

How We Use the Media
Media Consumers as Active Agents
Types of Uses and Gratifications

Different Theories, Different Observations

Communication and Service Learning

Service Learning: What and Why

Elements of Service Learning
Connection to a Field of Study
Shared Control
Collaboration
Reciprocity
Reflection

Benefits and Risks of Service Learning
Benefits of Service Learning
Risks of Service Learning
Managing Risks

Communication Strategies for Successful Service Learning
Communication Behaviors to Avoid
Communication Behaviors to Practice

Finding and Creating Service Learning Opportunities
Finding Opportunities
Creating Opportunities

PREFACE

Y ou can understand the philosophy that has shaped *Understanding Human Communication* by trying a simple experiment. If you're a professor, take a few moments to jot down all the courses you recall taking as an undergraduate. If you're a student, make a list of all the courses you can remember from high school. Next, circle the courses that have an ongoing benefit in your life.

If you're like most people, you only recalled a fraction of the courses where you spent so many hours. Of the courses you *did* remember, it's likely that only a few of them made a lasting positive impact.

Our intention in writing this book has been to insure that the course in which it's used will be one of those memorable ones that change your life for the better. Beyond understanding and appreciating how human communication operates, we hope that this book and the course in which it's used will help you communicate more effectively in the situations that count, and with the people who matter to you.

We remain convinced that the best way to measure this book's value is to ask three questions: Is its content important? Is the material clear? Is it useful? Our goal has been to focus on topics that are absolutely essential and present them so that every sentence delivers an informational payoff worth the space it occupies. You are the best judge of how well we have succeeded.

New in This Edition

Given our quickly changing world, the reasons for this updated edition are compelling. Several structural changes reflect how communication operates in contemporary society.

- Most noticeable is the **all-new Chapter 2, "The Changing World of Communication."** True to its title, this chapter reveals how the nature of communication and the discipline that focuses on it have changed in the opening decades of the twenty-first century. Major sections deal with demographic and cultural influences that shape and reflect how we interact with others, and with the ways in which technologies have created both new opportunities and new challenges. The chapter also presents a snapshot of the academic field of communication and shows how it has evolved to reflect the changing nature of human interaction.

- New **"@Work" boxes** in every chapter show you how key concepts from the text operate in the workplace. Topics include how multitasking can interfere with face-to-face interaction, building social capital for career enhancement, dealing with sexual harassment, and working in virtual groups.

- A **new appendix, "Communicating for Career Success,"** provides a wealth of information to help students launch and grow in their chosen careers. Sections cover both preemployment strategies designed to help you get the job you want and strategies for communicating in ways that enhance advancement throughout your career.

We suggest to our students that the value of this material alone can justify keeping *Understanding Human Communication* long after finishing the class in which it was used.

- The **streamlined and reorganized Part Five** gives students a quicker and more efficient entry to the art and science of public speaking. The new Chapter 11, "Preparing Speeches," synthesizes material on choosing and developing a topic (from the previous edition's Chapter 10) as well as managing communication apprehension (previously in Chapter 12). After completing this chapter, students will be ready to deliver their first classroom speech.

In addition to improvements like these, material has been updated throughout the book to **reflect the latest scholarship.** For example, Chapter 3 explains how we perceive strangers differently in mediated and face-to-face communication. Chapter 4 explains how cultural identity is reflected in linguistic labels by which we describe others. Chapter 5 introduces research describing how hearing loss affects relationships. Chapter 6 provides new information on nonverbal cues to deception. A new section in Chapter 7 describes how dealing with conflicts online differs from doing so in person, and Chapter 8 contains new information on how gender influences conflict style. Chapter 11 now offers guidelines for citing information gathered from web searches.

Finally, we have made some changes to the test bank for this edition, adding 20% more questions, revising others, and including more challenging questions.

Basic Approach and Special Features

This eleventh edition builds on the approach that has served over one million students and their professors. Rather than take sides in the theory-versus-skills debate that often rages in our discipline, *Understanding Human Communication* treats scholarship and skill development as mutually reinforcing. Its reader-friendly approach strives to present material clearly without being overly simplistic. Examples on virtually every page make concepts clear and interesting. A fresh design makes the material inviting, as do interesting readings, amusing and instructive cartoons, and stimulating photos that reinforce concepts in the text.

Along with the text proper, several features aim to make teaching and learning more effective:

- **Invitation to Insight** boxes offer readings that show how the elements of communication operate in contemporary society. Articles focus on topics as diverse as the dangers of broadcasting personal information via "sexting," social standards for using profanity, and the limitations of free speech when civil listening is absent.

- **Understanding Diversity** boxes address subjects including managing identity during the process of "coming out," the potential for misunderstandings during translation from one language to another, and how lessons from other cultures can enhance listening skills.

- **Understanding Communication Technology** boxes focus on topics including how new social media can meet a variety of communication needs, the etiquette of revealing what you've learned about others online, the dangers of being overly connected via the Internet, and the ethical principles for using and acknowledging information gleaned from the Web.

- **Media Room** reviews use examples from popular television shows and films to illustrate important communication concepts in every chapter. The entries represent a wide array of approaches: drama (*Precious, Up in the Air, Friday Night Lights*), comedy (*The Invention of Lying, Four Christmases, He's Just Not That Into You*), and documentaries (*The Cove, The September Issue, Good Hair*).

- **Ethical Challenges** invite readers to ponder subjects including whether honesty is always the best policy, the acceptability of presenting multiple identities, the tension between allowing free speech and the acceptability of hateful language, and the challenge of dealing politely but effectively with obnoxious group members.

- **Critical Thinking Probes** encourage students to consider their own actions in light of communication concepts covered in the text. Students might consider current debates among communication theorists, or test their own skills of perception or use of emotive language.

Pedagogy

For most students, the immediate objective is demonstrating mastery of material to professors. Recognizing this imperative, *Understanding Human Communication* contains tools that, along with the traditional Key Terms and Activities, help make learning more effective.

Case Studies now open each unit, presenting real-life communication challenges on the job, in school, and in personal relationships. Each chapter provides thought-provoking questions about the case students have read, encouraging them to apply the information they have studied to understand and solve the problem.

Within the margins of each chapter's text, Cultural Idioms help nonnative English speakers understand American colloquialisms, while they demonstrate to more proficient speakers how supposedly everyday speech can be misunderstood by listeners from other cultures.

At the end of each chapter, a wealth of resources help enhance student success. Along with the familiar Summary and Key Terms, new Activities help readers understand and apply material to their own lives. As noted earlier, questions regarding the unit-opening Case Study help apply principles in the chapter to a real-world challenge. Media Room entries highlight films and television shows that illustrate materials from the chapter. Finally, students are directed to online resources that will enhance learning.

Supplements

As the world has changed, so has the need for learning materials that support this textbook. Adopters of *Understanding Human Communication*, eleventh edition, will be pleased to find a complete suite of supplements—online and print—for students and instructors.

Online

This edition of *Understanding Human Communication* now offers two opportunities for online learning:

- **ClassMate:** (*Access Code Required*) A nationally hosted online homework system that gives professors the ability to manage digital content from this book and its supplements in order to make assignments, administer tests, and track student progress. With ClassMate, students receive access to a variety of interactive study tools designed to enhance their learning experience. ClassMate is perfect for distance and online classes as well as blended courses. Available Fall, 2011.

- **Companion Website:** (*Free*) An open-access student website with practice quizzes, flashcards, and other study tools. This companion site is perfect for students enrolled in traditional classroom courses who are looking for a little extra study material online. For instructors, there is a password-protected part of this site that includes the Instructor's Manual, PowerPoint lecture slides, and links to supplemental readings and films: www.oup.com/us/uhc11.

Contact your OUP sales representative or call **(800) 280-0280** for more information on these two options for online learning.

For Students

- **Student Success Manual** (print) is packed with tips that will guide students to mastering the course material. It includes a primer on effective study habits as well as chapter-specific information such as outlines, summaries, key terms, review questions, and critical-thinking exercises. Available free in a package with a new copy of the book.

- **Now Playing** (print) looks at contemporary films through the lens of communication principles. Conceived and written by Russell F. Proctor II of Northern Kentucky University and regularly updated by Darin Garard of Santa Barbara City College, *Now Playing* illustrates how communication concepts play out in a variety of situations, using a mass medium that is interactive, familiar, and easily accessible to students. Available free in a package with a new copy of the book.

For Instructors

- The **Instructor's Manual and Test Bank** (print) provides the largest, most comprehensive package of support of any text for this course. The Instructor's Manual includes teaching tips and course information, chapter-by-chapter overviews, objectives, critical-thinking and classroom activities, and suggested readings and films. The comprehensive Test Bank includes an average of sixty exam questions per chapter in multiple-choice, true/false, matching, and completion formats. The questions have been extensively revised for this edition, and new questions of slightly higher difficulty have been added.

- **Instructor's CD-ROM and Computerized Test Bank** includes the full Instructor's Manual, a computerized test bank, and pre-built, editable PowerPoint-based lecture presentations with selected tables and figures from the main book.

- **Instructor's companion website** at www.oup.com/us/uhc11: Instructors wishing to access either the companion website for materials or ClassMate (the nationally hosted online homework system) should contact their OUP sales representative or call **(800) 280-0280**.

- **Now Playing, Instructor's Edition** (print), includes an introduction on how to incorporate film clips in class, as well as even more film examples, viewing guides and assignments, a complete set of sample responses to the discussion questions in the student edition, and a full list of references.

Acknowledgments

Anyone involved with creating a project as comprehensive as *Understanding Human Communication* knows that success isn't possible without the contributions of many people.

We owe a debt to our colleagues whose reviews helped shape the book you are holding:

Brett N. Billman
Bowling Green State University

Ironda Joyce Campbell
Pierpont Community and Technical College

Dee Ann Curry
McMurry University

Amber N. Finn
Texas Christian University

Mikako Garard
Santa Barbara City College

Kara Laskowski
Shippensburg University of Pennsylvania

Jennifer Lehtinen
State University of New York at Orange

Kurt Lindemann
San Diego State University

Bruce C. McKinney
University of North Carolina–Wilmington

Daniel M. Paulnock
Saint Paul College

Kelly Aikin Petkus
Austin Community College–Cypress Creek

Russell F. Proctor
Northern Kentucky University

Shannon Proctor
Highline Community College

Elizabeth Ribarsky
University of Illinois at Springfield

Gerald Gregory Scanlon
Colorado Mountain College

David Schneider
Saginaw Valley State University

Robert W. Wawee
The University of Houston–Downtown

Rebecca Wolniewicz
Southwestern College

We continue to be grateful to the following professors for their input on previous editions:

Pete Bicak
SUNY Rockland

Beth Bryant
Northern Virginia Community College, Loudoun

Jo-Anne Bryant
Troy State University–Montgomery

Patricia Carr Connell
Gadsden State Community College

Heather Dorsey
University of Minnesota

Rebecca A. Ellison
Jefferson College

Gary G. Fallon
Broward Community College and Miami International University of Art and Design

Samantha Gonzalez
University of Hartford

Lisa Katrina Hill
Harrisburg Area Community College–Gettysburg Campus

Emily Holler
Kennesaw State University

Maria Jaskot-Inclan
Wilbur Wright College

Judy Litterst
St. Cloud State College

Jim Mignerey
St. Petersburg College

Kimberly M. Myers
Manchester College and Indiana University–Purdue University Fort Wayne

Catriona O'Curry
Bellevue Community College

Emily Osbun-Bermes
Indiana University–Purdue University at Fort Wayne

Doug Parry
University of Alaska at Anchorage

Cheryl Pawlowski
University of Northern Colorado

Dan Robinette
Eastern Kentucky University

B. Hannah Rockwell
Loyola University Chicago

Thresa Rogers
Baltimore City Community College, Liberty

Michele Russell
Northern Virginia Community College

Cady Short-Thompson
Northern Kentucky University

Patricia Spence
Richland Community College

Sarah Stout
Kellogg Community College

Curt VanGeison
St. Charles Community College

Princess Williams
Suffolk County Community College

Many thanks are due to colleagues who developed and refined the package of ancillary materials that will help instructors teach more effectively and students succeed in mastering the material in this text. **Ironda J. Campbell** of Pierpont Community and Technical College thoroughly updated and revised the Instructor's Manual and Test Bank, making it a useful and efficient teaching tool for instructors. **Valerie Hennen** of Gateway Technical College created the array of online tests and quizzes for both the ClassMate site and the companion website, providing excellent study guidance and learning assessment for students. **Dan Rogers** of Cedar Valley College enhanced **Jeanne Elmhorst**'s work on the Student Success Manual with major content updates and additions. This edition features newly designed and revised PowerPoint presentations for each chapter, created by **Ellen Bremen** of Highline Community College. These slides offer excellent visual guidance for both in-class and online settings. **Darin Garard** of Santa Barbara City College continues to craft useful content for the annual *Now Playing* film supplement with a keen eye for movies and scenes that offer relevant commentary for students in communication courses.

In an age when publishing is becoming increasingly corporate and sales-driven, we are grateful for the privilege and pleasure of working with the professionals at the venerable Oxford University Press. Led by John Challice, they blend the best "old school" practices with cutting-edge thinking. We salute our longtime friend and editor Peter Labella. We also thank Frederick Speers and Josh Hawkins for their editorial talents and good cheer, and Paula Schlosser for managing the design process skillfully and tactfully. We are grateful to the hardworking and talented Caitlin Kaufman for doing whatever was necessary to keep the project on track. We are indebted to Lisa Grzan for guiding the process that transformed a digital manuscript into the book you are now reading.

We also thank the freelance professionals on the UHC team. We are grateful to Sherri Adler for selecting the striking and unique photos the book contains; Teresa Nemeth for copyediting this manuscript, and Susan Monahan for her indexing talents.

Finally, we thank our partners for their patience and support during the time we spent working on this edition. They may be the best judges of how well we've practiced the communication skills this book preaches.

Ronald B. Adler
George Rodman
Carrie Cropley Hutchinson

ABOUT THE AUTHORS

Ronald B. Adler

Ronald B. Adler is Professor of Communication Emeritus at Santa Barbara City College. He is coauthor of *Interplay: The Process of Interpersonal Communication*, Eleventh Edition (OUP, 2009), *Looking Out, Looking In* (2011), and *Communicating at Work: Principles and Practices for Business and the Professions* (2011).

George Rodman

George Rodman is a professor in the Department of Television and Radio at Brooklyn College, City University of New York, where he founded the graduate media studies program. He is author of *Mass Media in a Changing World*, Fourth Edition (2011), *Making Sense of Media* (2001), and several books on public speaking.

Carrie Cropley Hutchinson

Carrie Cropley Hutchinson is a professor in the Department of Communication at Santa Barbara City College, where she directs the Interpersonal Communication and Business Communication programs. She also teaches Intercultural Communication for the college's study abroad program. Professor Cropley is the author of *Interpersonal Communication: Navigating Relationships in a Changing World* (2010).

PART ONE

Fundamentals of Human Communication

About the Americans

Y ou have been approached to contribute to a blog titled *About the Americans*. This website is designed for travelers from other countries who will be visiting the United States, and who need to understand how Americans communicate.

The blog will be a compilation of observations by a large number of people who have lived in the United States, both native-born Americans and visitors. The publishers believe that insights of keen observers will reveal a great deal about how communication operates in this country.

The publishers have chosen you because you are a student who has systematically studied communication. They will pay handsomely if your observations set the right tone by showing how the principles covered in your communication course operate in everyday life.

Use the activities and questions at the end of each chapter to structure your observations. Give specific examples of communication in the United States to illustrate each of your points.

You can find the questions and activities involving this case study on page 25 (Chapter 1), pages 54–55 (Chapter 2), and page 91 (Chapter 3).

This isn't our grandparents' world. Technology and demographics make communication different today than it was for previous generations. But despite the changes, some principles of human communication are timeless. The chapters in this unit introduce both the constant, underlying elements of communication and the factors that make relating effectively with others more complex and challenging than ever before.

After studying the material in Chapters 1, 2, and 3, you will understand better

- The elements that operate in every communication transaction.
- Some common misconceptions about the process of communication.
- What distinguishes competent communicators from less effective ones.
- How communication technology has changed the nature of communication and relationships in today's world.
- The cultural and cocultural factors that influence communication in contemporary society.
- How our notions of self shape the way we communicate with others.
- Perceptual factors that influence—and often distort—our understanding of others.

CHAPTER 1

Human Communication: What and Why

Chapter Outline

After studying the material in this chapter . . .

YOU SHOULD UNDERSTAND:

1. The working definition and characteristics of *communication*.
2. The types of communication covered in this book.
3. The needs satisfied by communication.
4. The characteristics of linear and transactional communication models.
5. The characteristics of competent communication.
6. Common misconceptions about communication.

YOU SHOULD BE ABLE TO:

1. Define *communication* and give specific examples of the various types of communication introduced in this chapter.
2. Describe the key needs you attempt to satisfy in your life by communicating.
3. Use the criteria in this chapter to identify the degree to which communication (yours or others') in a specific situation is competent, and suggest ways of increasing the competence level.
4. Identify how misconceptions about communication can create problems, and suggest how a more accurate analysis of the situations you describe can lead to better outcomes.

Communication Defined

Because this is a book about **communication**, it makes sense to begin by defining that term. This isn't as simple as it might seem because people use the term in a variety of ways that are only vaguely related:

- A dog scratches at the back door, signaling its desire to be let out of the house.
- Data flows from one computer database to another in a cascade of electronic impulses.
- Strangers who live thousands of miles apart spot each other's postings on a social networking website, and they become friends through conversations via e-mail, text messaging, and instant messaging.
- Locals approach a group of confused-looking people who seem to be from out of town and ask if they can help.
- In her sermon, a religious leader encourages the congregation to get more involved in the community.

There is clearly some relationship among uses of the term such as these, but we need to narrow our focus before going on. A look at the table of contents of this book shows

The Many Meanings of Communication

Few words have as many meanings as *communication*. The term can refer to everything from messages on T-shirts to presidential speeches, from computer code to chimpanzee behavior. Communication has been the professional concern of philosophers, scientists (social, biological, and physical), poets, politicians, and entertainers, to name a few. Responding to this diversity, Brent Rubin asked, "How does being interested in communication differ from being interested in life?"

There are several reasons why the term *communication* has so many different meanings. Understanding them will help explain how and why this word refers to a broad range of subjects.

Interdisciplinary Heritage   Unlike most subjects, communication has captured the interest of scholars from a wide range of fields. Ever since classical times, philosophers have studied the meaning and significance of messages. In the twentieth century, social scientists joined the field: Psychologists examine the causes and effects of communication as it relates to individuals. Sociologists and anthropologists examine how communication operates within and between societies and cultures. Political scientists explore the ways communication influences governmental affairs. Engineers use their skill to devise methods of conveying messages electronically. Zoologists focus on communication between animals. With this kind of diversity, it's no surprise that *communication* is a broad and sometimes confusing term.

Field and Activity   Sometimes the word *communication* refers to a field of study (of nonverbal messages or effects of televised violence on children, for example). In other cases it denotes an activity that people do. This confusion doesn't exist in most disciplines. People may study history or sociology, but they don't "historicate" or "sociologize." Having only one word that refers to both the field of study and the activity that it examines leads to confusion.

Humanity and Social Science   Unlike most disciplines, communication straddles two very different academic domains. It has one foot firmly planted in the humanities, where it shares concerns with disciplines like English and philosophy. At the same time, other scholars in the field take an approach like their colleagues in the social sciences, such as psychology, sociology, and anthropology. And to confuse matters even further, communication is sometimes associated with the performing arts, especially in the area of oral interpretation of literature.

Natural and Professional Communication   This is a natural activity that we all engage in unconsciously. At the same time, there are professional communication experts whose specialized duties require training and skill. Careers such as marketing, public relations, broadcasting, speechmaking, counseling, journalism, and management all call for talent that goes far beyond what is required for everyday speaking and listening.

Communication and Communications   Even the name of the field is confusing. Traditionally, *communications* (with an "s") has been used when referring to activities involving technology and the mass media. *Communication* is typically used to describe face-to-face and written messages, as well as the field as a whole. With the growth of communication technology, the two terms are being used interchangeably more often.

Brent Rubin
Communication and Human Behavior

that it obviously doesn't deal with animals. Neither is it about Holy Communion, the bestowing of a material thing, or many of the other subjects mentioned in the *Oxford English Dictionary*'s 1,200-word definition of *communication*.

What, then, are we talking about when we use the term *communication*? As the reading on this page shows, there is no single, universally accepted usage. This isn't the place to explore the differences between these conceptions or to defend one against the others. What we need is a working definition that will help us in our study.

As its title suggests, this is a book about understanding human communication—so we'll start by explaining what it means to study communication that is unique to members of our species. For our purposes we'll define human communication as the process of creating meaning through symbolic interaction. Examining this definition reveals some important characteristics of human communication.

> Human communication is the process of creating meaning through symbolic interaction.

Communication Is a Process

We often talk about communication as if it occurred in discrete, individual acts such as one person's utterance or a conversation. In fact, communication is a continuous, ongoing process. Consider, for example, a friend's compliment about your appearance. Your interpretation of those words will depend on a long series of experiences stretching far back in time: How have others judged your appearance? How do you feel about your looks? How honest has your friend been in the past? How have you been feeling about one another recently? All this history will help shape your response to the friend's remark. In turn, the words you speak and the way you say them will shape the way your friend behaves toward you and others—both in this situation and in the future.

This simple example shows that it's inaccurate to talk about "acts" of communication as if they occurred in isolation. To put it differently, communication isn't a series of incidents pasted together like photographs in a scrapbook; instead, it is more like a motion picture in which the meaning comes from the unfolding of an interrelated series of images. The fact that communication is a process is reflected in the transactional model introduced later in this chapter.

Communication Is Symbolic

Symbols are used to represent things, processes, ideas, or events in ways that make communication possible. Chapter 4 discusses the nature of symbols in more detail, but this idea is so important that it needs an introduction now. The most significant feature of symbols is their arbitrary nature. For example, there's no logical reason why the letters in the word *book* should stand for the object you're reading now. Speakers of Spanish call it a *libro*, and Germans call it a *Buch*. Even in English, another term would work just as well as long as everyone agreed to use it in the same way. We overcome the arbitrary nature of symbols by linguistic rules and customs. Effective communication depends on agreement among people about these rules. This is easiest to see when we observe people who don't follow linguistic conventions. For example, recall how unusual the speech of children and nonnative speakers of a language often sounds.

To most North Americans, nodding your head up and down means "yes" (although this meaning isn't universal).

Animals don't use symbols in the varied and complex ways that humans do. There's nothing symbolic about a dog scratching at the door to be let out; there is a natural connection between the door and the dog's goal. By contrast, the words in the human utterance "Open the door!" are only arbitrarily related to the request they represent.

Symbolic communication allows people to think or talk about the past (while cats have no concept of their ancestors from a century ago), explain the present (a trout can't warn its companions about its close call with a fishing hook), and speculate about the future (a crow has no awareness of the year 2025, let alone tomorrow).

Like words, some nonverbal behavior can have symbolic meaning. For example, to most North Americans, nodding your head up and down means "yes" (although this meaning isn't universal). But even more than words, many nonverbal behaviors are ambiguous. Does a frown signify anger or unhappiness? Does a hug stand for a friendly greeting or a symbol of the hugger's romantic interest in you? One can't always be sure. We'll discuss the ambiguous nature of nonverbal communication in Chapter 6.

Types of Communication

Within the domain of human interaction, there are several types of communication. Each occurs in a different context. Despite the features they all share, each has its own characteristics.

CULTURAL IDIOM
tune in:
focus on

Intrapersonal Communication

By definition, **intrapersonal communication** means "communicating with oneself."[1] You can tune in to one way that each of us communicates internally by listening to the little voice that lives in your mind. Take a moment and listen to what it is saying. Try it now, before reading on. Did you hear it? It may have been saying something like "What little voice? I don't have any little voice!" This voice is the "sound" of your thinking.

We don't always think in verbal terms, but whether the process is apparent or not, the way we mentally process information influences our interaction with others. Even though intrapersonal communication doesn't include other people directly, it does affect almost every type of interaction. You can understand the role of intrapersonal communication by imagining your thoughts in each of the following situations.

- You are planning to approach a stranger whom you would like to get to know better.
- You pause a minute and look at the audience before beginning a ten-minute speech.
- The boss yawns while you are asking for a raise.
- A friend seems irritated lately, and you're not sure whether you are responsible.

The way you handle all of these situations would depend on the intrapersonal communication that precedes or accompanies your overt behavior. Much of Chapter 3 deals with the perception process in everyday situations, and part of Chapter 13 focuses on the intrapersonal communication that can minimize anxiety when you deliver a speech.

Dyadic/Interpersonal Communication

Social scientists call two persons interacting a **dyad**, and they often use the term **dyadic communication** to describe this type of communication. Dyadic communication can occur in person or via mediated channels that include telephone, e-mail, text messaging, instant messages, and social networking websites.

Dyads are the most common type of personal communication. One study revealed that college students spend almost half of their total communication time interacting with one other person.[2] Observation in a variety of settings ranging from playgrounds to train depots and shopping malls shows that most communication is dyadic in nature.[3] Even communication within larger groups (think of classrooms, parties, and families as examples) consists of multiple, often shifting dyadic encounters.

Dyadic interaction is sometimes considered identical to **interpersonal communication**, but as Chapter 7 explains, not all two-person interaction can be considered interpersonal in the fullest sense of the word. In fact, you will learn that the qualities that characterize interpersonal communication aren't limited to twosomes. They can be present in threesomes or even in small groups.

Small Group Communication

In **small group communication** every person can participate actively with the other members. Small groups are a common fixture of everyday life. Your family is a group. So are an athletic team, a group of coworkers in several time zones connected in cyberspace, and several students working on a class project.

Whether small groups meet in person or via mediated channels, they possess characteristics that are not present in a dyad. For instance, in a group, the majority of members can put pressure on those in the minority to conform, either consciously or unconsciously, but in a dyad no such pressures exist. Conformity pressures can also be comforting, leading group members to take risks that they would not dare if they were alone or in a dyad. With their greater size, groups also have the ability to be more creative than dyads. Finally, communication in groups is affected strongly by the type of leader who is in a position of authority. Groups are such an important communication setting that Chapters 9 and 10 focus exclusively on them.

> Public speakers usually have a greater chance to plan and structure their remarks than do communicators in smaller settings.

Public Communication

Public communication occurs when a group becomes too large for all members to contribute. One characteristic of public communication is an unequal amount of speaking. One or more people are likely to deliver their remarks to the remaining members, who act as an audience. This leads to a second characteristic of public settings: limited verbal feedback. The audience isn't able to talk back in a two-way conversation the way they might in a dyadic or small group setting. This doesn't mean that speakers operate in a vacuum when delivering their remarks. Audiences often have a chance to ask questions and offer brief comments, and their nonverbal reactions offer a wide range of clues about their reception of the speaker's remarks.

Public speakers usually have a greater chance to plan and structure their remarks than do communicators in smaller settings. For this reason, several chapters of this book describe the steps you can take to prepare and deliver an effective speech.

Mass Communication

Mass communication consists of messages that are transmitted to large, widespread audiences via electronic and print media: newspapers, magazines, television, radio, blogs, websites, and so on. As you can see in the Mass Communication section of the *Understanding Human Communication* website, mass communication differs from the interpersonal, small group, and public varieties in several ways. First, most mass messages are aimed at a large audience without any personal contact between sender and receivers. Second, many of the messages sent via mass communication channels are developed, or at least financed, by large organizations. In this sense, mass communication is far less personal and more of a product than the other types we have examined so far. Finally, mass communication is often controlled by many gatekeepers who determine what messages will be delivered to consumers, how they will be constructed, and

CULTURAL IDIOM

operate in a vacuum:
operate independently of outside influences

when they will be delivered. Sponsors (whether corporate or governmental), editors, producers, reporters, and executives all have the power to influence mass messages in ways that don't affect most other types. While blogs have given ordinary people the chance to reach enormous audiences, the bulk of mass messages are still controlled by corporate and governmental sources. Because of these and other unique characteristics, the study of mass communication raises special issues and deserves special treatment.

Functions of Communication

Now that we have a working understanding of the term *communication*, it is important to discuss why we will spend so much time exploring this subject. Perhaps the strongest argument for studying communication is its central role in our lives. The amount of time we spend communicating is staggering. In one study, researchers measured the amount of time a sample group of college students spent on various activities.[4] They found that the subjects spent an average of over 61 percent of their waking hours engaged in some form of communication. Whatever one's occupation, the results of such a study would not be too different. Most of us are surrounded by others, trying to understand them and hoping that they understand us: family, friends, coworkers, teachers, and strangers.

> The amount of time we spend communicating is staggering.

There's a good reason why we speak, listen, read, and write so much: Communication satisfies many of our needs.

Physical Needs

Communication is so important that it is necessary for physical health. In fact, evidence suggests that an absence of satisfying communication can even jeopardize life itself. Medical researchers have identified a wide range of hazards that result from a lack of close relationships.[5] For instance:

- People who lack strong relationships have two to three times the risk of early death, regardless of whether they smoke, drink alcoholic beverages, or exercise regularly.
- Terminal cancer strikes socially isolated people more often than those who have close personal relationships.
- Divorced, separated, and widowed people are five to ten times more likely to need hospitalization for mental problems than their married counterparts.
- Pregnant women under stress and without supportive relationships have three times more complications than pregnant women who suffer from the same stress but have strong social support.
- Socially isolated people are four times more susceptible to the common cold than those who have active social networks.[6]

Studies indicate that social isolation is a major risk factor contributing to coronary disease, comparable to physiological factors such as diet, cigarette smoking, obesity, and lack of physical activity.[7]

Research like this demonstrates the importance of having satisfying personal relationships. Remember: Not everyone needs the same amount of contact, and the quality of communication is almost certainly as important as the quantity. The important point here is that personal communication is essential for our well-being. To paraphrase an old song, "people who need people" aren't "the luckiest people in the world," they're the *only* people!

Identity Needs

Communication does more than enable us to survive. It is the way—indeed, the only way—we learn who we are. As you'll read in Chapter 3, our sense of identity comes from the way we interact with other people. Are we smart or stupid, attractive or ugly, skillful or inept? The answers to these questions don't come from looking in the mirror. We decide who we are based on how others react to us.

> We decide who we are based on how others react to us.

Deprived of communication with others, we would have no sense of identity. This fact is illustrated by the case of the famous "Wild Boy of Aveyron," who spent his early childhood without any apparent human contact. The boy was discovered in January 1800 while digging for vegetables in a French village garden.[8] He showed no behaviors one would expect in a social human. The boy could not speak but uttered only weird cries. More significant than this absence of social skills was his lack of any identity as a human being. As author Roger Shattuck put it, "The boy had no human sense of being in the world. He had no sense of himself as a person related to other persons."[9] Only after the influence of a loving "mother" did

Understanding Communication Technology

Social Media Meet Communication Needs

As handheld devices become more powerful, communication technology can help address your needs wherever there's a Wi-Fi or phone signal. One popular source of tools is Apple Computer's App Store. The store offers over one hundred thousand inexpensive or free applications. Here are just a few.

Physical Needs

- Global SOS: Contains telephone emergency phone numbers in more than 150 countries.
- Bio Journal: Track biorhythms to schedule critical encounters when at your best physically, emotionally, and intellectually.

Identity Needs

- Photo Makeover: Adjust photos to improve appearance, including enlarging eyes and tweaking face shape.
- CLIPish: Customize messages with millions of images: animations, emoticons, clip art, wallpapers, symbols, and more.

Social Needs

- Loopt Mix: Lets you connect with nearby strangers whose interests match yours.
- Friend Mapper: Displays the geographic location of nearby friends.

Practical Needs

- Translate: Translate words and phrases between many popular languages.
- Career Builder: Search for a job from any location.

the boy begin to behave—and, we can imagine, think of himself as a human. Contemporary stories support the essential role that communication plays in shaping identity. In 1970, authorities discovered a twelve-year-old girl (whom they called "Genie") who had spent virtually all her life in an otherwise empty, darkened bedroom with almost no human contact. The child could not speak and had no sense of herself as a person until she was removed from her family and "nourished" by a team of caregivers.[10]

Like Genie and the boy of Aveyron, each of us enters the world with little or no sense of identity. We gain an idea of who we are from the ways others define us. As Chapter 3 explains, the messages we receive in early childhood are the strongest, but the influence of others continues throughout life. Chapter 3 also explains how we use communication to manage the way others view us.

Social Needs

Besides helping to define who we are, communication provides a vital link with others. Researchers and theorists have identified a range of social needs we satisfy by communicating: pleasure (e.g., "because it's fun," "to have a good time"); affection (e.g., "to help others," "to let others know I care"); inclusion (e.g., "because I need someone to talk to or be with," "because it makes me less lonely"); escape (e.g., "to put off doing something I should be doing"); relaxation (e.g., "because it allows me to unwind"); and control (e.g., "because I want someone to do something for me," "to get something I don't have").[11]

> Some theorists have gone as far as to argue that communication is the primary goal of human existence.

As you look at this list of social needs for communicating, imagine how empty your life would be if these needs weren't satisfied. Then notice that it would be impossible to fulfill them without communicating with others. Because relationships with others are so vital, some theorists have gone as far as to argue that communication is the primary goal of human existence. Anthropologist Walter Goldschmidt terms the drive for meeting social needs as the "human career."[12]

Practical Needs

We shouldn't overlook the everyday, important functions that communication serves. Communication is the tool that lets us tell the hair stylist to take just a little off the sides, direct the doctor to where it hurts, and inform the plumber that the broken pipe needs attention *now*!

Beyond these obvious needs, a wealth of research demonstrates that communication is an important key to effectiveness in a variety of everyday settings. For example, a survey of over four hundred employers identified "communication skills" as the top characteristic that employers seek in job candidates.[13] It was rated as more important than technical competence, work experience, or academic background. In another survey, over 90 percent of the personnel officials at five hundred U.S. businesses stated that increased communication skills are needed for success in the twenty-first century.[14]

Communication is just as important outside of work. College roommates who are both willing and able to communicate effectively report higher satisfaction with one another than do those who lack these characteristics.[15] Married couples who were identified as effective communicators reported happier relationships than did less skillful husbands and wives.[16] In school, the grade point averages of college students were related positively to their communication competence.[17] In "getting acquainted" situations, communication competence played a major role in whether a person was judged physically attractive, socially desirable, and good at the task of getting acquainted.[18]

Modeling Communication

So far we have introduced a basic definition of *communication* and seen the functions it performs. This information is useful, but it only begins to describe the process we will be examining throughout this book. One way to understand more about what it means to communicate is to look at some models that describe what happens when two or more people interact. As you will see, over the last half-century scholars have developed an increasingly accurate and sophisticated view of this process.

A Linear Model

Until about fifty years ago, researchers viewed communication as something that one person "does" to another.[19] In this **linear communication model**, communication is like giving an injection: a **sender encodes** ideas and feelings into some sort of **message** and then conveys them to a **receiver** who **decodes** them. (Figure 1-1)

One important element of the linear model is the communication **channel**—the method by which a message is conveyed between people. For most people, face-to-face contact is the most familiar and obvious channel. Writing is another channel. In addition to these long-used forms, **mediated communication** channels include telephone, e-mail, instant messaging, faxes, voice mail, and even videoconferencing. (The word *mediated* reflects the fact that these messages are conveyed through some sort of communication medium.)

> Ending a relationship by sending a text message to your lover's cell phone would make a very different statement than delivering the bad news in person.

The channel you choose can make a big difference in the effect of a message. For example, a typewritten love letter probably wouldn't have the same effect as a handwritten note or card. Likewise, ending a relationship by sending a text message to your lover's cell phone would make a very different statement than delivering the bad news in person.

The linear model also introduces the concept of **noise**—a term used by social scientists to describe any forces that interfere with effective communication. Noise can occur at every stage of the communication process. Three types of noise can disrupt communication—external, physiological, and psychological. *External noise* (also called "physical") includes those factors outside the receiver that make it difficult to hear, as well as many other kinds of distractions. For instance, too much cigarette smoke in a crowded room might make it hard for you to pay attention to another person, and sitting in the rear of an auditorium might make a speaker's remarks unclear. External

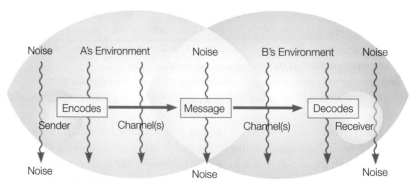

FIGURE 1-1 Linear Communication Model

noise can disrupt communication almost anywhere in our model—in the sender, channel, message, or receiver. *Physiological noise* involves biological factors in the receiver or sender that interfere with accurate reception: illness, fatigue, and so on. *Psychological noise* refers to forces within a communicator that interfere with the ability to express or understand a message accurately. For instance, an outdoors person might exaggerate the size and number of the fish he caught in order to convince himself and others of his talents. In the same way, a student might become so upset upon learning that she failed a test that she would be unable (perhaps *unwilling* is a better word) to understand clearly where she went wrong.

A linear model shows that communicators often occupy different **environments**—fields of experience that help them understand others' behavior. In communication terminology, *environment* refers not only to a physical location but also to the personal experiences and cultural backgrounds that participants bring to a conversation.

Consider just some of the factors that might contribute to different environments:

- A might belong to one ethnic group and B to another;
- A might be rich and B poor;
- A might be in a rush and B have nowhere to go;
- A might have lived a long, eventful life, and B might be young and inexperienced;
- A might be passionately concerned with the subject and B indifferent to it.

Notice how the model in Figure 1-1 shows that the environments of A and B overlap. This area represents the background that the communicators must have in common. As the shared environment becomes smaller, communication becomes more difficult. Consider a few examples in which different perspectives can make understanding difficult:

- Bosses who have trouble understanding the perspective of their employees will be less effective managers, and workers who do not appreciate the challenges of being a boss are more likely to be uncooperative (and probably less suitable for advancement).
- Parents who have trouble recalling their youth are likely to clash with their children, who have never known and may not appreciate the responsibility that comes with parenting.
- Members of a dominant culture who have never experienced how it feels to be "different" may not appreciate the concerns of people from nondominant cocultures, whose own perspectives make it hard to understand the cultural blindness of the majority.

Differing environments make understanding others challenging but certainly not impossible. Hard work and many of the skills described in this book provide ways to bridge the gap that separates all of us to a greater or lesser degree. For now, recognizing the challenge that comes from dissimilar environments is a good start. You can't solve a problem until you recognize that it exists.

A Transactional Model

Despite its simplicity, the linear model doesn't do a very good job of representing the way most communication operates. The transactional communication model in Figure 1-2 presents a more accurate picture in several respects.

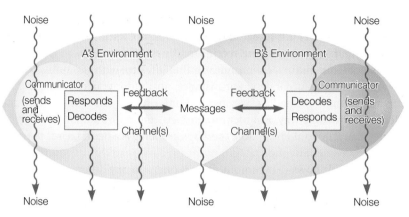

FIGURE 1-2 Transactional Communication Model

Simultaneous Sending and Receiving   Although some types of mass communication do flow in a one-way, linear manner, most types of personal communication are two-way exchanges.[20] The **transactional model** reflects the fact that we usually send and receive messages simultaneously. The roles of sender and receiver that seemed separate in the linear model are now superimposed and redefined as those of "communicators." This new term reflects the fact that at a given moment we are capable of receiving, decoding, and responding to another person's behavior, while at the same time that other person is receiving and responding to ours.

Consider, for instance, the significance of a friend's yawn as you describe your romantic problems. Or imagine the blush you may see as you tell one of your raunchier jokes to a new acquaintance. Nonverbal behaviors like these show that most face-to-face communication is a two-way affair. The discernible response of a receiver to a sender's message is called **feedback**. Not all feedback is nonverbal, of course. Sometimes it is oral, as when you ask an instructor questions about an upcoming test or volunteer your opinion of a friend's new haircut. In other cases it is written, as when you answer the questions on a midterm exam or respond to a letter from a friend. Figure 1-2 makes the importance of feedback clear. It shows that most communication is, indeed, a two-way affair.

Some forms of mediated communication like e-mail and text messaging don't appear to be simultaneous. Even here, though, the process is more complicated than the linear model suggests. For example, if you've ever waited impatiently for the response to a text message or instant message, you understand that even a nonresponse can have symbolic meaning. Is the unresponsive recipient busy? Thoughtful? Offended? Indifferent? Whether or not your interpretation is accurate, the silence is a form of communication.

Another weakness of the traditional linear model is the questionable assumption that all communication involves encoding. We certainly do choose symbols to convey most verbal messages. But what about the many nonverbal cues that occur whether or not people speak: facial expressions, gestures, postures, vocal tones, and so on? Cues like these clearly do offer information about others, although they are often unconscious and thus don't involve encoding. For this reason, the transactional model replaces the term *encodes* with the broader term *responds*, because it describes both intentional and unintentional actions that can be observed and interpreted.[21]

> Silence is a form of communication.

Communication Is Fluid, Not Static   It's difficult to isolate a discrete "act" of communication from the events that precede and follow it. The way a friend or family member reacts to a sarcastic remark you make will probably depend on the way you have related to one another in the past. Likewise, the way you'll act toward each other in the future depends on the outcome of this conversation.

CULTURAL IDIOM

pin the blame:
blame on other(s)

Communication Is Relational, Not Individual   The transactional model shows that communication isn't something we do to others; rather, it is something we do with them. In this sense, communication is rather like dancing—at least the kind of dancing we do with partners. Like dancing, communication depends on the involvement of a partner. And like good dancing, successful communication isn't something that depends just on the skill of one person. A great dancer who doesn't consider and adapt to the skill level of his or her partner can make both people look bad. In communication and dancing, even two talented partners don't guarantee success. When two talented dancers perform without coordinating their movements, the results feel bad to the dancers and look foolish to an audience. Finally, relational communication—like dancing—is a unique creation that arises out of the way in which the partners interact. The way you dance probably varies from one partner to another because of its cooperative, transactional nature. Likewise, the way you communicate almost certainly varies with different partners.

Psychologist Kenneth Gergen captures the relational nature of communication well when he points out how our success depends on interaction with others. As he says, ". . . one cannot be 'attractive' without others who are attracted, a 'leader' without others willing to follow, or a 'loving person' without others to affirm with appreciation."[22]

Because communication is transactional, it's often a mistake to suggest that just one person is responsible for a relationship. Consider the accompanying cartoon. Both Cathy and Irving had good intentions, and both probably could have handled the situation better. As the humorous outcome shows, trying to pin the blame for a disappointing outcome on one person or the other is fruitless and counterproductive. It would have been far better to ask, "How did we handle this situation poorly, and what can we do to make it better?"

The transactional nature of communication shows up in school, where

Source: CATHY © 1992 Cathy Guisewite. Reprinted with permission of UNIVERSAL PRESS SYNDICATE. All Rights Reserved.

teachers and students influence one another's behavior. For example, teachers who regard some students negatively may treat them with subtle or overt disfavor. As a result, these students are likely to react to their teachers' behavior negatively, which reinforces the teachers' original attitudes and expectations.[23] It isn't necessary to resolve the "who started it" issue here to recognize that the behaviors of teachers and students are part of a transactional relationship.

The transactional character of communication also figures dramatically in relationships between parents and their children. We normally think of "good parenting" in terms of how well children turn out. But research suggests that the quality of interaction between parents and children is a two-way affair, that children influence parents just as much as the other way around.[24] For example, children who engage in what social scientists call "problematic behavior" evoke more high-control responses from their parents than do cooperative children. By contrast, youngsters with mild temperaments are less likely to provoke coercive reactions by their parents than are more aggressive children. Parents with low self-esteem tend to send more messages that weaken the self-esteem of their children, who in turn are likely to act in ways that make the parents feel even worse about themselves. Thus, a mutually reinforcing cycle arises in which parents and children shape one another's feelings and behavior. In cases like this it's at least difficult and probably impossible to identify who is the "sender" and who is the "receiver" of messages. It's more accurate to acknowledge that parents and children—just like husbands and wives, bosses and employees, teachers and students, or any other people who communicate with one another—act in ways that mutually influence one another.

> A transactional model of communication should be more like a motion picture film than a gallery of still photographs.

By now you can see that a transactional model of communication should be more like a motion picture film than a gallery of still photographs. Although Figure 1-2 does a fair job of picturing the phenomenon we call communication, an animated version in which the environments, communicators, and messages constantly change would be an even better way of capturing the process.

Communication Competence: What Makes an Effective Communicator?

It's easy to recognize good communicators, and even easier to spot poor ones. But what are the characteristics that distinguish effective communicators from their less successful counterparts? Answering this question has been one of the leading challenges for communication scholars.[25] Although all the answers aren't yet in, research has identified a great deal of important and useful information about communication competence.

Communication Competence Defined

While scholars are still working to clarify the nature of **communication competence**, most would agree that effective communication involves achieving one's goals in a manner that, ideally, maintains or enhances the relationship in which it occurs.[26] This definition suggests several important characteristics of communication competence.

There Is No "Ideal" Way to Communicate   Your own experience shows that a variety of communication styles can be effective. Some very successful people are serious, whereas others use humor; some are gregarious, whereas others are quiet; and some are straightforward, whereas others hint diplomatically. Just as there are many kinds of beautiful music and art, there are many kinds of competent communication.

The type of communication that succeeds in one situation might be a colossal blunder in another. The joking insults you routinely trade with a friend might be insensitive and discouraging if he or she had just suffered a personal setback. The language you use with your peers might offend a family member, and last Saturday night's romantic approach would probably be out of place at work on Monday morning. For this reason, being a competent communicator requires flexibility in understanding what approach is likely to work best in a given situation.[27]

Competence Is Situational   Because competent behavior varies so much from one situation and person to another, it's a mistake to think that communication competence is a trait that a person either possesses or lacks. It's more accurate to talk about *degrees* or *areas* of competence.[28] You and the people you know are probably quite competent in some areas and less so in others. You might deal quite skillfully with peers, for example, but feel clumsy interacting with people much older or younger, wealthier or poorer, or more or less attractive than yourself. In fact, your competence with one person may vary from one situation to another. This means that it's an overgeneralization to say, in a moment of distress, "I'm a terrible communicator!" It would be more accurate to say, "I didn't handle this situation very well, even though I'm better in others."

Competence Is Relational   Because communication is transactional, something we do with others rather than to them, behavior that is competent in one relationship isn't necessarily competent in others.

A fascinating study on relational satisfaction illustrates that what constitutes satisfying communication varies from one relationship to another.[29] Researchers Brent Burleson and Wendy Sampter hypothesized that people with sophisticated communication skills (such as managing conflict well, giving ego-support to others, and providing comfort to relational partners) would be better at maintaining friendships than would be less skilled communicators. To their surprise, the results did not support this hypothesis. In fact, friendships were most satisfying when partners possessed matching skill levels. Apparently, relational satisfaction arises in part when our style matches those of the people with whom we interact.

The same principle holds true in the case of jealousy. Researchers have uncovered a variety of ways by which people deal with jealousy in their relationships.[30] The ways included keeping closer tabs on the partner, acting indifferent, decreasing affection, talking the matter over, and acting angry. The researchers found that no type of behavior was effective or ineffective in every relationship. They concluded that approaches that work with some people would be harmful to others. Findings like these demonstrate that competence arises out of developing ways of interacting that work for you and for the other people involved.[31]

"I SAID, 'I have trouble developing close relationships with people!' For cryin' out loud, clean out your ears, fathead!"

Source: CLOSE TO HOME © John McPherson. Reprinted with permission of UNIVERSAL PRESS SYNDICATE. All Rights Reserved.

CULTURAL IDIOM

keeping closer tabs on:
paying closer attention to

Competence Can Be Learned   To some degree, biology is destiny when it comes to communication style.[32] Studies of identical and fraternal twins suggest that traits including sociability, anger, and relaxation seem to be partially a function of our genetic makeup. Fortunately, biology isn't the only factor that shapes how we communicate: Communication is a set of skills that anyone can learn. As children grow, their ability to communicate effectively develops. For example, older children can produce more sophisticated persuasive attempts than can younger ones.[33] Along with maturity, systematic education (such as the class in which you are now enrolled) can boost communicative competence. Even a modest amount of training can produce dramatic results. After only thirty minutes of instruction, one group of observers became significantly more effective in detecting deception in interviews.[34] One study revealed that college students' communication competence increases over their undergraduate studies.[35] Even without systematic training, it's possible to develop communication skills through the processes of trial-and-error and observation. We learn from our own successes and failures, as well as from observing other models—both positive and negative.

> Communication is a set of skills that anyone can learn.

Characteristics of Competent Communicators

Although competent communication varies from one situation to another, scholars have identified several common denominators that characterize effective communication in most contexts.

A Wide Range of Behaviors   Effective communicators are able to choose their actions from a wide range of behaviors. To understand the importance of having a large communication repertoire, imagine that someone you know repeatedly tells jokes—perhaps discriminatory ones—that you find offensive. You could respond to these jokes in a number of ways. You could:

- Say nothing, figuring that the risks of bringing the subject up would be greater than the benefits.
- Ask a third party to say something to the joke teller about the offensiveness of the jokes.
- Hint at your discomfort, hoping that your friend would get the point.
- Joke about your friend's insensitivity, counting on humor to soften the blow of your criticism.
- Express your discomfort in a straightforward way, asking your friend to stop telling the offensive jokes, at least around you.
- Simply demand that your friend stop.

With this choice of responses at your disposal (and you can probably think of others as well), you could pick the one that had the best chance of success. But if you were able to use only one or two of these responses when raising a delicate issue—always keeping quiet or always hinting, for example—your chances of success would be much smaller. Indeed, many poor communicators are easy to spot by their limited range of responses. Some are chronic jokers. Others are always belligerent. Still others are quiet in almost every situation. Like a piano player who knows only one tune or a chef who can prepare only a few dishes, these people are forced to rely on a small range of responses again and again, whether or not they are successful.

CULTURAL IDIOM

common denominators:
feature common to several instances

counting on:
depending on

soften the blow:
ease the effect

Ability to Choose the Most Appropriate Behavior Simply possessing a large array of communication skills isn't a guarantee of effectiveness. It's also necessary to know which of these skills will work best in a particular situation. Choosing the best way to send a message is rather like choosing a gift: What is appropriate for one person won't be appropriate for another one at all. This ability to choose the best approach is essential because a response that works well in one setting would flop miserably in another one.

Although it's impossible to say precisely how to act in every situation, there are at least three factors to consider when you are deciding which response to choose: the context, your goal, and the other person.

Understanding Diversity

Call Centers and Culture

In a sleek new office building, two dozen young Indians are studying the customs of a place none of them has ever seen. One by one, the students present their conclusions about this fabled land.

"Americans eat a lot of junk food. Table manners are very casual," says Ritu Khanna.

"People are quite self-centered. The average American has thirteen credit cards," says Nerissa Dcosta.

"Seventy-six percent of the people mistrust the government. In the near future, this figure is expected to go up to 100 percent," says Sunny Trama.

The Indians, who range in age from twenty to twenty-seven, have been hired to take calls from cranky or distraught Americans whose computers have gone haywire. To do this, they need to communicate in a language that is familiar but a culture that is foreign.

"We're not saying India is better or America is better," says their trainer, Alefiya Rangwala. "We just want to be culturally sensitive so there's no disconnect when someone phones for tech support."

Call centers took root here during the 2001 recession, when U.S. companies were struggling to control expenses. By firing American customer service workers and hiring Indians, the firms slashed their labor costs by 75 percent.

At first, training was simple. The centers gave employees names that were acceptable to American ears, with Arjun becoming Aaron and Sangita becoming Susan. The new hires were instructed to watch *Friends* and *Ally McBeal* to get an idea of American folkways.

But whether Aaron and Susan were repairing computers, selling long-distance service, or fulfilling orders for diet tapes, problems immediately cropped up. The American callers often wanted a better deal or an impossibly swift resolution and were aggressive and sometimes abrasive about saying so.

The Indians responded according to their own deepest natures: They were silent when they didn't understand, and they often committed to more than their employers could deliver. They would tell the Americans that someone would get back to them tomorrow to check on their problems, and no one would.

Customer satisfaction plummeted. The U.S. clients grew alarmed. Some even returned their business to U.S. call centers.

Realizing that a new multibillion-dollar industry with 150,000 employees was at risk, Indian call centers have recently embarked on much more comprehensive training. New hires are taught how to express empathy, strategies to successfully open and close conversations, and above all how to be assertive, however unnatural it might feel.

"We like to please," says Aparajita Ajit, whose title is "head of talent transformation" for the call-center firm Mphasis. "It's very difficult for us to say no."

Originally, the ever-agreeable Indian agents had a hard time getting people to pay bills that were six months overdue. Too often, says trainer Deepa Nagraj, the calls would go like this:

"Hi," the Indian would say. "I'd like to set up a payment to get your account current. Can I help you do that?"

"No," the American responds.

"OK, let me know if you change your mind," the Indian says and hangs up.

Now, says Nagraj, the agents take no excuses.

David Streitfeld

Skill at Performing Behaviors   After you have chosen the most appropriate way to communicate, it's still necessary to perform the required skills effectively. There is a big difference between knowing about a skill and being able to put it into practice. Simply being aware of alternatives isn't much help, unless you can skillfully put these alternatives to work.

Just reading about communication skills in the following chapters won't guarantee that you can start using them flawlessly. As with any other skills—playing a musical instrument or learning a sport, for example—the road to competence in communication is not a short one. You can expect that your first efforts at communicating differently will be awkward. After some practice you will become more skillful, although you will still have to think about the new way of speaking or listening. Finally, after repeating the new skill again and again, you will find you can perform it without conscious thought.

Empathy/Perspective Taking   People have the best chance of developing an effective message when they understand the other person's point of view. And because others aren't always good at expressing their thoughts and feelings clearly, the ability to imagine how an issue might look from the other's point of view is an important skill. The value of taking the other's perspective suggests one reason why listening is so important. Not only does it help us understand others, it also gives us information to develop strategies about how to best influence them. Because empathy is such an important element of communicative competence, much of Chapter 5 is devoted to this topic.

> People have the best chance of developing an effective message when they understand the other person's point of view.

Cognitive Complexity   Cognitive complexity is the ability to construct a variety of frameworks for viewing an issue. Cognitive complexity is an ingredient of communication competence because it allows us to make sense of people using a variety of perspectives. For instance, imagine that a longtime friend seems to be angry with you. One possible explanation is that your friend is offended by something you've done. Another possibility is that something upsetting has happened in another part of your friend's life. Or perhaps nothing at all is wrong, and you're just being overly sensitive. Researchers have found that the ability to analyze the behavior of others in a variety of ways leads to greater "conversational sensitivity," increasing the chances of acting in ways that will produce satisfying results.[36]

Self-Monitoring   Psychologists use the term *self-monitoring* to describe the process of paying close attention to one's behavior and using these observations to shape the way one behaves. Self-monitors are able to separate a part of their consciousness and observe their behavior from a detached viewpoint, making observations such as:

> *"I'm making a fool out of myself."*
>
> *"I'd better speak up now."*
>
> *"This approach is working well. I'll keep it up."*

Chapter 3 explains how too much self-monitoring can be problematic. Still, people who are aware of their behavior and the impression it makes are more skillful communicators than people who are low self-monitors.[37] For example, they are more accurate in judging others' emotional states, better at remembering information about others, less shy, and more assertive. By contrast, low self-monitors aren't even able to recognize their incompetence. (Calvin, in the nearby cartoon, does a nice job of illustrating this problem.) One study revealed that poor communicators were blissfully ignorant of their shortcomings and more likely to overestimate their skill than were better communicators.[38] For example, experimental subjects who scored in the lowest quartile on

Calvin and Hobbes   **by Bill Watterson**

joke-telling skill were more likely than their funnier counterparts to grossly overestimate their sense of humor.

Commitment to the Relationship   One feature that distinguishes effective communication in almost any context is commitment. People who seem to care about the relationship communicate better than those who don't.[39] This concern shows up in commitment to the other person and to the message you are expressing.

Clarifying Misconceptions About Communication

Having spent time talking about what communication is, we ought to also identify some things it is not.[40] Recognizing some misconceptions is important, not only because they ought to be avoided by anyone knowledgeable about the subject, but also because following them can get you into trouble.

Communication Does Not Always Require Complete Understanding

Most people operate on the implicit but flawed assumption that the goal of all communication is to maximize understanding between communicators. Although some understanding is necessary for us to comprehend one another's thoughts, there are some types of communication in which understanding as we usually conceive it isn't the primary goal.[41] Consider, for example:

- *Social rituals.* "How's it going?" you ask. "Great," the other person replies. The primary goal in exchanges like these is mutual acknowledgment: There's obviously no serious attempt to exchange information.

- *Many attempts to influence others.* A quick analysis of most television commercials shows that they are aimed at persuading viewers to buy products, not to understand the content of the commercial. In the same way, many of our attempts at persuading another to act as we want don't involve a desire to get the other person to understand what we want—just to comply with our wishes.

- *Deliberate ambiguity and deception.* When you decline an unwanted invitation by saying "I can't make it," you probably want to create the impression that the decision is really beyond your control. (If your goal was to be perfectly clear, you might say, "I don't want to get together. In fact, I'd rather do almost anything than accept your invitation.") As Chapters 4 and 7 explain in detail, we often equivocate precisely because we want to obscure our true thoughts and feelings.

"My wife understands me."

- *Coordinated action.* Examples are conversations where satisfaction doesn't depend on full understanding. The term **coordination** has been used to describe situations in which participants interact smoothly, with a high degree of satisfaction but without necessarily understanding one another well.[42] Coordination without understanding can be satisfying in far more important situations. Consider the words "I love you." This is a phrase that can have many meanings: Among other things, it can mean "I admire you," "I feel great affection for you," "I desire you," "I am grateful to you," "I feel guilty," "I want you to be faithful to me," or even "I hope *you* love *me*."[43] It's not hard to picture a situation in which partners gain great satisfaction—even over a lifetime—without completely understanding that the mutual love they profess actually is quite different for each of them. The cartoon on this page reflects the fact that better understanding can sometimes lead to less satisfaction. "You mean you mostly love me because I've been there for you? Hey, a *dog* is there for you!"

Communication Will Not Solve All Problems

"If I could just communicate better . . ." is the sad refrain of many unhappy people who believe that if they could just express themselves better, their relationships would improve. Though this is sometimes true, it's an exaggeration to say that communicating—even communicating clearly—is a guaranteed panacea.

Communication Isn't Always a Good Thing

For most people, belief in the value of communication rates somewhere close to parenthood in their hierarchy of important values. In truth, communication is neither good nor bad in itself. Rather, its value comes from the way it is used. In this sense, communication is similar to fire: Flames in the fireplace on a cold night keep you warm and create a cozy atmosphere, but the same flames can kill if they spread into the room. Communication can be a tool for expressing warm feelings and useful facts, but under different circumstances the same words and actions can cause both physical and emotional pain.

> Communication is neither good nor bad in itself.

Meanings Rest in People, Not Words

It's a mistake to think that, just because you use a word in one way, others will do so, too.[44] Sometimes differing interpretations of symbols are easily caught, as when we might first take the statement "He's loaded" to mean the subject has had too much to drink, only to find out that he is quite wealthy. In other cases, however, the ambiguity of words and nonverbal behaviors isn't so apparent, and thus has more far-reaching consequences. Remember, for instance, a time when someone said to you, "I'll be honest," and only later did you learn that those words hid precisely the opposite fact. In Chapter 4 you'll read a great deal more about the problems that come from mistakenly assuming that meanings rest in words.

The explanations on pages 21–24 make it clear that communication is not a panacea. Explaining yourself and understanding others will not solve all problems; in fact, sometimes more communication leads to more problems. Think of an occasion (real or hypothetical) where more interaction would make matters worse. Imagine that the other person (or people) involved in this situation is (are) urging you to keep the channels of communication open. You know that if you do communicate more the situation will deteriorate, yet you don't want to appear uncooperative. What should you do?

Communication Is Not Simple

Most people assume that communication is an aptitude that people develop without the need for training—rather like breathing. After all, we've been swapping ideas with one another since early childhood, and there are lots of people who communicate pretty well without ever having had a class on the subject. Though this picture of communication as a natural ability seems accurate, it's actually a gross oversimplification.[45]

Many people do learn to communicate skillfully because they have been exposed to models of such behavior by those around them. This principle of modeling explains why children who grow up in homes with stable relationships between family members have a greater chance of developing such relationships themselves. But even the best communicators aren't perfect: They often suffer the frustration of being unable to get a message across effectively, and they frequently misunderstand others. Furthermore, even the most successful people you know probably can identify ways in which their relationships could profit from better communication. These facts show that communication skills are rather like athletic ability: Even the most inept of us can learn to be more effective with training and practice, and those who are talented can always become better.

More Communication Isn't Always Better

Although it's certainly true that not communicating enough is a mistake, there are also situations when *too much* communication is a mistake. The "@Work" box on page 24 illustrates how technology contributes to information overload. Sometimes excessive communication simply is unproductive, as when we "talk a problem to death," going over the same ground again and again without making any headway. And there are times when communicating too much can actually aggravate a problem. We've all had the experience of "talking ourselves into a hole"—making a bad situation worse by pursuing it too far. As two noted communication scholars put it, "More and more negative communication merely leads to more and more negative results."[46]

There are even times when *no* communication is the best course. Any good salesperson will tell you that it's often best to stop talking and let the customer think about the

@Work

When More Communication Isn't Better: Declaring E-mail Bankruptcy

Last month, venture capitalist Fred Wilson drew a lot of attention on the Internet when he declared a twenty-first-century kind of bankruptcy. In a posting on his blog about technology, Wilson announced he was giving up on responding to all the e-mail piled up in his inbox.

"I am so far behind on e-mail that I am declaring bankruptcy," he wrote. "If you've sent me an e-mail (and you aren't my wife, partner, or colleague), you might want to send it again. I am starting over." College professors have done the same thing, and a Silicon Valley chief executive followed Wilson's example the next day. Last September, the recording artist Moby sent an e-mail to all the contacts in his inbox announcing that he was taking a break from e-mail for the rest of the year.

The supposed convenience of electronic mail, like so many other innovations of technology, has become too much for some people. Swamped by an unmanageable number of messages—the volume of e-mail traffic has nearly doubled in the past two years, according to research firm DYS Analytics—and plagued by annoying spam and viruses, some users are saying "Enough!"

Those declaring bankruptcy are swearing off e-mail entirely or, more commonly, deleting all old messages and starting fresh.

E-mail overload gives many workers the sense that their work is never done, said senior analyst David Ferris, whose firm, Ferris Research, said there were 6 trillion business e-mails sent in 2006. "A lot of people like the feeling that they have everything done at the end of the day," he said. "They can't have it anymore." So some say they're moving back to the telephone as their preferred means of communication.

The term "e-mail bankruptcy" may have been coined as early as 1999 by a Massachusetts Institute of Technology professor who studies the relationship between people and technology. Professor Sherry Turkle, who estimated that she has 2,500 pieces of unread e-mail in her inbox, is one of those people. A book she has been working on for a decade is coming out soon. Turkle joked that it would have taken her half the time to write it "if I didn't have e-mail."

Mike Musgrove

product. And when two people are angry and hurt, they may say things they don't mean and will later regret. At times like these it's probably best to spend a little time cooling off, thinking about what to say and how to say it.

One key to successful communication, then, is to share an *adequate* amount of information in a *skillful* manner. Teaching you how to decide what information is adequate and what constitutes skillful behavior is one major goal of this book.

Summary

This chapter began by defining communication as it will be examined in *Understanding Human Communication*: the process of creating meaning through symbolic interaction.

It introduced several communication contexts that will be covered in the rest of the book: intrapersonal, dyadic, small group, public, and mass. The chapter also identified several types of needs that communication satisfies: physical, identity, social, and practical.

A linear and a transactional communication model were developed, demonstrating the superiority of the transactional model in representing the process-oriented nature of human interaction.

The chapter went on to explore the difference between effective and ineffective exchanges by discussing communication competence, showing that there is no single correct way to behave, that competence is situational and relational in nature, and that it can be learned. Competent communicators were described as being able to choose and perform appropriately from a wide range of behaviors, as well as being cognitively complex self-monitors who can take the perspective of others and who have commitment to important relationships. After spending most of the chapter talking about what communication is, the chapter concluded by discussing what it is not by refuting several common misconceptions. It demonstrated that communication doesn't always require complete understanding and that it is not always a good thing that will solve every problem. It showed that more communication is not always better; that meanings are in people, not in words; and that communication is neither simple nor easy.

Key Terms

channel Medium through which a message passes from sender to receiver. *p. 12*

communication The process of creating meaning through symbolic interaction. *p. 4*

communication competence Ability to maintain a relationship on terms acceptable to all parties. *p. 16*

coordination Interaction in which participants interact smoothly, with a high degree of satisfaction but without necessarily understanding one another well. *p. 22*

decoding The process in which a receiver attaches meaning to a message. *p. 12*

dyad A two-person unit. *p. 7*

dyadic communication Two-person communication. *p. 7*

encoding The process of putting thoughts into symbols, most commonly words. *p. 12*

environment Both the physical setting in which communication occurs and the personal perspectives of the parties involved. *p. 13*

feedback The discernible response of a receiver to a sender's message. *p. 14*

interpersonal communication Communication in which the parties consider one another as unique individuals rather than as objects. It is characterized by minimal use of stereotyped labels; unique, idiosyncratic social rules; and a high degree of information exchange. *p. 8*

intrapersonal communication Communication that occurs within a single person. *p. 7*

linear communication model A characterization of communication as a one-way event in which a message flows from sender to receiver. *p. 12*

mass communication The transmission of messages to large, usually widespread audiences via broadcast means (such as radio and television), print (such as newspapers, magazines, and books), multimedia (such as CD-ROM, DVD, and the World Wide Web), and other forms of media such as recordings and movies. *p. 8*

mediated communication Communication sent via a medium other than face-to-face interaction, e.g., telephone, e-mail, instant messaging. Can be both mass and personal. *p. 12*

message A sender's planned and unplanned words and nonverbal behaviors. *p. 12*

noise External, physiological, and psychological distractions that interfere with the accurate transmission and reception of a message. *p. 12*

public communication Communication that occurs when a group becomes too large for all members to contribute. It is characterized by an unequal amount of speaking and by limited verbal feedback. *p. 8*

receiver One who notices and attends to a message. *p. 12*

sender The originator of a message. *p. 12*

small group communication Communication within a group of a size such that every member can participate actively with the other members. *p. 8*

social media Communication channels that allow for mediated interactions between one person and an infinite number of receivers for the purpose of information exchange and social interaction. *p. 10*

symbol An arbitrary sign used to represent a thing, person, idea, event, or relationship in ways that make communication possible. *p. 6*

transactional communication model A characterization of communication as the simultaneous sending and receiving of messages in an ongoing, irreversible process. *p. 14*

Case Study Questions

Instructions: Reread the case study on pages xx–1 to answer the following questions in light of what you have learned in this chapter.

1. Describe an incident that illustrates how communication is a symbolic process.

2. Using your own experience, describe two to three examples of each type of communication (intrapersonal, dyadic/interpersonal, small group, public, and mass) in everyday life.

3. Discuss one or more typical communication transactions that aim at satisfying each type of need: physical, identity, social, and practical.

4. Use an incident from everyday life to illustrate the transactional process of communication, as described on pages 13–16.

5. Use the characteristics of competent communication (pages 18–21) to evaluate one transaction you have observed or experienced.

6. Show how avoiding common misconceptions about communication (pages 21–24) can make relationships more satisfying.

Activities

1. **Analyzing Your Communication Behavior** Prove for yourself that communication is both frequent and important by observing your interactions for a one-day period. Record every occasion in which you are involved in some sort of communication as it is defined on pages 5–6. Based on your findings, answer the following questions:

   1. What percentage of your waking day is involved in communication?

   2. What percentage of time do you spend communicating in the following contexts: intrapersonal, dyadic, small group, and public?

   3. What percentage of your communication is devoted to satisfying each of the following types of needs: physical, identity, social, and practical? (Note that you might try to satisfy more than one type at a time.)

   Based on your analysis, describe five to ten ways you would like to communicate more effectively. For each item on your list of goals, describe who is involved (e.g., "my boss," "people I meet at parties") and how you would like to communicate differently (e.g., "act less defensively when criticized," "speak up more instead of waiting for them to approach me"). Use this list to focus your studies as you read the remainder of this book.

2. **Choosing the Most Effective Communication Channel** Decide which communication channel would be most effective in each of the following situations. Be prepared to explain your answer.

   1. In class, an instructor criticizes you for copying work from other sources, but the work really was your own. You are furious, and you don't intend to accept the attack without responding. Which approach(es) would be best for you to use?

      a. Send your instructor an e-mail or write a letter explaining your objections.

      b. Telephone your instructor and explain your position.

      c. Schedule a personal meeting with your instructor.

   2. You want to see whether the members of your extended family are able to view the photos you've posted on your family website. How can you find out how easily they can access the website?

      a. Demonstrate the website at an upcoming family get-together.

      b. Send them a link to the website as part of an e-mail.

      c. Phone family members and ask them about their ability to access websites.

   3. You want to be sure the members of your office team are able to use the new voice mail system. Should you

      a. Send each employee an instruction manual for the system?

      b. Ask employees to send you e-mails or memos with any questions about the system?

      c. Conduct one or more training sessions where employees can try out the system and you can clear up any questions?

   4. You've just been given two free tickets to tomorrow night's concert. How can you best find out whether your friend can go with you?

      a. Send her an e-mail and ask for a quick reply.

      b. Leave a message on your friend's answering machine asking her to phone you back.

      c. Send an instant message via your computer.

3. **Increasing Your Communicative Competence** Prove for yourself that communication competence can be increased by following these steps.

   1. Identify a situation in which you are dissatisfied with your present communication skill.

   2. Identify at least three distinct, potentially successful approaches you might take in this situation that are different from the one you have taken in the past. If you are at a loss for alternatives, consider how other people you have observed (both real and fictional characters) have handled similar situations.

   3. From these three alternatives, choose the one you think would work best for you.

   4. Consider how you could become more skillful at performing your chosen approach. For example, you might rehearse it alone or with friends, or you might gain pointers from watching others.

   5. Consider how to get feedback on how well you perform your new approach. For instance, you might ask friends to watch you. In some cases, you might even be able to ask the people involved how you did.

   This systematic approach to increasing your communicative competence isn't the only way to change, but it is one way to take the initiative in communicating more effectively.

For Further Exploration

For more resources about the nature of communication, see the *Understanding Human Communication* website at www.oup.com/us/uhc11. There you will find a variety of resources: a list of books and articles, links to descriptions of feature films and television shows at the *Now Playing* website, study aids, and a self-test to check your understanding of the material in this chapter.

MEDIA ROOM

For more resources about communication in film and television, see *Now Playing* at the *Understanding Human Communication* website at www.oup.com/us/uhc11.

Meeting Needs Through Communication

Up in the Air (2009, Rated R)
Ryan Bingham (George Clooney) is a self-described "Termination Facilitator." He travels around the country giving employees the grim news that they are losing their jobs due to corporate downsizing. He is also a part-time motivational speaker, encouraging his audiences to jettison the baggage that clutters up their life—including all personal relationships.

Like all of us, Bingham seeks to satisfy his needs via communication. He earns his living conveying information, and by most measures he is a success. At first it appears that Bingham is an equally skillful communicator in his personal life. He makes his preferences clear to friends and strangers, and seems to be living his dream of a life with no entangling relationships. His affair with fellow road warrior Alex Goran (Vera Farmiga) is a commitment-free relationship, at least at first. But over the course of the film, Bingham begins to question the assumptions that have ruled his life. By the end, he—and we viewers—are reminded that no person is an island, and that we all need close relationships.

Communication Competence and Incompetence

The Office (2005– , Rated TV-14)
Michael Scott (Steve Carell) is a boss who believes he is funny, lovable, and a fountain of business wisdom. In actuality, Michael's misguided sense of humor and bumbling management style make him an object of ridicule among his staff.

Sideways (2004, Rated R)
Two clueless friends suffer the consequences of their communicative incompetence during a road trip to the California wine country. Neurotic Miles (Paul Giamatti) describes his favorite wine grape, pinot noir, as "thin-skinned and temperamental," but he might as well be referring to himself. Jack (Thomas Haden Church) would rather make another sexual conquest than tell the truth—most importantly, that his marriage is less than a week away. It's easy to laugh at the blunders of this odd pair of friends, but it's clear that Miles's hypersensitivity and Jack's dishonesty doom them to a life of failed relationships.

Misconceptions About Communication

Rachel Getting Married (2008, Rated R)
Recovering addict Kym (Anne Hathaway) is on furlough from rehab to attend the wedding of her sister Rachel (Rosemarie DeWitt). Kym and Rachel love each other, but they are incapable of managing expressions of their feelings. Their father (Bill Irwin) loves too unconditionally, and their mother (Debra Winger) is self-absorbed. Several scenes highlight the family's communication problems. The most memorable occurs when Kym attempts a toast at Rachel's prewedding celebration. Taken together, these moments show that communication isn't always a good thing, and that more communication isn't necessarily better.

CHAPTER 2

The Changing World of Communication

Chapter Outline

After studying the material in this chapter . . .

YOU SHOULD UNDERSTAND:

1. The ways in which communication technologies have changed over time.
2. How the field of communication has evolved to reflect changes in the way we communicate.
3. How culture affects communication.
4. The ways in which social media are different from mass media and face-to-face communication.
5. How, why, and by whom various forms of social media are used.

YOU SHOULD BE ABLE TO:

1. Identify the cultural and cocultural groups to which you belong.
2. Explain how the cultural values and norms outlined in this chapter affect your communication.
3. Use the guidelines on pages 39–43 to assess your own intercultural communication competence and suggest ways you can enhance it.
4. Describe how the characteristics of mediated communication apply in your life.
5. List the ways in which you use social media, using the "uses and gratifications" categories on page 43.
6. Use the guidelines on pages 48–53 to assess your competence in using social media and suggest ways you can enhance it.

Most schoolchildren learn the story of Rip Van Winkle, the eighteenth-century New Yorker who awoke from a decades-long nap to find his familiar world had changed dramatically. Imagine the amazement of a latter-day Rip Van Winkle, awakening in the early twenty-first century after slumbering for a hundred years.

Understanding Change

Our contemporary time traveler would scarcely recognize much of the new world. When he fell asleep, relationships were limited by geography: Most people lived and died within a short distance of where they were born. Those who moved far away were rarely, if ever, seen again.

At the dawn of the twentieth century, telephones and telegraph were the most advanced technology for personal communication. The first commercial radio programming had not yet been broadcast. Encounters with people from other cultures were few. Strangers were likely to be regarded with fascination and perhaps a degree of suspicion for being different.

Thinking about these differences gives you a sense of how much the nature of communication has changed in just a few generations. Today it's possible to interact with people from different backgrounds who in the past would have been the subject of uninformed conjecture. We are equipped with a range of communication technologies that, even a few decades ago, would have been the stuff of fantasy and science fiction.

Along with the opportunities in today's world, communication challenges also abound. How do we use the tools of communication in ways that make life richer and more satisfying instead of harried and confounding? How can we deal with people whose communication practices differ dramatically from our own, often in ways that are frustrating but hard to pin down? This chapter will provide some tools to help answer these questions.

Changing Technology

For most of human history, face-to-face speech was the primary form of communication. Writing developed approximately five thousand years ago; but until the last few centuries the vast majority of people were illiterate. In most societies a small elite class mastered the arts of reading and writing. But books were scarce, and the amount of information available was small. Speaking and listening were the predominant communication "technologies."

By the mid-eighteenth century, literacy grew in industrial societies, giving ordinary people access to ideas that had been available only to the most privileged. By the end of the nineteenth century, affordable rail travel increased mobility, and the telegraph made possible transmission of both news and personal messages over vast distances.

CULTURAL IDIOM

pin down:
identify clearly

face-to-face:
in each other's presence

The Accelerating Pace of Communication Innovation

3000+ BC	Sumerians and Phoenicians invent writing	1936	London Television Service begins regular broadcasts
900	China institutes world's first postal service	1963	First communications satellite launched
776	Homing pigeons deliver news from Olympic Games to Athens	1969	ARPANET (internet's forerunner) established
300	World's first great library established in Alexandria, Egypt	1972	First e-mail sent using "@" in address
200	Fire signals and human messengers relay messages across Egypt and China	1973	First cell phone call
		1975	World's first microcomputer, the Altair 8800, goes on sale
105 AD	Paper invented in China	1981	IBM announces its first Personal Computer
868	First surviving printed book (China)		
1450	Printing press with moveable metal type makes mass communication possible	1991	World Wide Web begins
		1992	First text message sent
1605	First newspaper printed in Germany	1994	Personal blogging begins
1620	Spain develops sign language	1996	Instant Messaging developed
1843	Long distance electric telegraph begins	1997	SixDegrees.com, the first social network, becomes available
1876	Telephone first demonstrated	2005	YouTube.com appears online
1920	First commercial radio broadcast	2006	Twitter launches
		2009	Smartphone sales top 170 million units
		2010	iPad enhances mobile computing and communication

The first half of the twentieth century introduced a burst of communication technology. Telephones shrank distance, expanding the reach of both personal relationships and commerce. Radio and later television gave mass audiences a taste of the wider world. Information was no longer a privilege of the elite class.

By the dawn of the twenty-first century, cellular technologies and the Internet broadened the ability to communicate beyond the dreams of earlier generations like those pictured in the 1930s cartoon on this page. Pocket-sized telephones made it cheap and easy to talk, send data, and exchange images with people around the globe. Now, new fiber-optic technology allows for over 150 million phone calls every second.[1] Videoconferencing adds even more channels through which to connect long distance and on the fly, allowing us to see each other's facial cues, body movements, and gestures almost as if we were face-to-face.

The accelerating pace of innovations in communication technology is astonishing: It took thirty-eight years for radio to reach 50 million listeners. It only took television thirteen years to capture the same number of viewers. It took less than four years for the Internet to attract 50 million users. Facebook added 100 million users in less than nine months.[2]

Changing Discipline

The study of communication has evolved to reflect the changing world. The first systematic analysis of how to communicate effectively was Aristotle's *Rhetoric*, written 2,500 years ago.[3] The ancient philosopher set forth specific criteria for effective speaking (called the "Canons of Rhetoric"), which still can be used to judge effective public communication. In various forms, rhetoric has been part of a classical liberal arts education since Aristotle's era. Today it is commonly taught in public speaking courses that are offered in most colleges and universities.

In the early twentieth century, the study of communication expanded from the liberal arts where it had been housed for over two thousand years and began to capture the attention of social scientists. As persuasive messages began to reach large numbers of people via print, film, and broadcasting, scholars began to study how the media shaped attitudes and behaviors. During and after World War II, the effectiveness of government propaganda was an important focus of research.[4] Since then, media effects has become one of the most widely studied areas in the field of communication.

In the 1950s, researchers began asking questions about human relationships in family and work settings, marking the beginning of research on small group communication.[5] The analysis of decision making and other small group communication processes emerged as a major area of study in the field and continues today.

In the 1960s, social scientists expanded their focus to study how communication operates in personal relationships.[6] Since then, scholars have studied a wide range of phenomena including how relationships develop, the nature of social support, the role of emotions, how honesty and deception operate, and how new technologies affect interpersonal relationships. Other branches of the discipline examine communication in organizations, the influence of gender on interaction, and how people from different backgrounds communicate with one another. The list on page 33 suggests the scope of topics studied in the discipline, showing that the focus of the field has expanded far beyond its rhetorical roots.

CULTURAL IDIOM

on the fly:
quickly, spontaneously

set forth:
present for consideration

Children, Adolescents, and the Media

Communication and Technology

Communication History

Communication Law and Policy

Ethnicity and Race in Communication

Feminist Scholarship

Global Communication and Social Change

Game Studies

Gay, Lesbian, Bisexual, and Transgender Studies

Health Communication

Information Systems

Instructional/Developmental Communication

Intercultural Communication

Interpersonal Communication

Intergroup Communication

Journalism Studies

Language and Social Interaction

Mass Communication

Organizational Communication

Philosophy of Communication

Political Communication

Popular Communication

Public Relations

Visual Communication Studies

Divisions and Interest Groups of the International Communication Association

Changing Demographics

In today's global village you don't have to be a world traveler to encounter people from different places and cultures. Thanks to immigration, we meet people from diverse backgrounds every day. In fact, demographers predict that by the middle of the century, one in five residents of the USA will be an immigrant.[7]

Cultural groups that were once considered minorities are now the majority in many places. The population of Miami is two-thirds Hispanic, and one-third of San Franciscans are Asian Americans.[8] By the beginning of the twenty-first century, virtually half of Toronto's population was foreign born.[9] The Latino population of the United States is expected to triple, making up almost 30 percent of the country's population by 2050.[10]

TABLE 2-1   Changing Population Trends

	2008	2050
Non-Hispanic whites	66%	46%
Hispanics	15%	30%
African Americans	14%	15%
Asian Americans	5%	9%

Source: U.S. Census Bureau

Not surprisingly, interracial contacts naturally cause cultures to combine. The 2008 Census Bureau noted that almost 5 million Americans reported belonging to two or more races, and that group was increasing in number ten times faster than white Americans.[11]

Globalization has made the workplace more diverse than ever before. Over ten thousand foreign companies and their subsidiaries operate in the United States.[12] Immigrants will account for all of the working-age population growth between 2016 and 2035. General Electric, an American company, operated in more than one hundred countries in 2007.[13] One way or another, you are likely to meet people who are different from you at work, whether on home soil or foreign territory.

You are also more likely than ever to meet diverse others at school. There were 671,616 international students studying in the United States during the 2008–2009 academic year, an all-time high in the history of international education.[14] In the next few years, ethnic and racial minority students are expected to make up almost 50 percent of the college student population.[15]

> In the next few years, ethnic and racial minority students are expected to make up almost 50 percent of the college student population.

Work and school aren't the only places where you're likely to encounter people from diverse backgrounds. Online social networking makes it easy to develop friendships with almost anyone, anywhere. Video game systems now include an online feature, allowing you to compete with players around the world. Although 96 percent of Americans born after 1974 have joined a social network, online socializing isn't limited to U.S. citizens.[16] China's QZone is the largest social network in the world, with over 300 million users.[17] Russia has the most engaged social media audience, with visitors spending 6.6 hours and viewing 1,307 pages per visitor per month.[18]

Online communication has also taken over the world of relationships, dissolving the boundaries that used to limit whom we date, marry, and have children with. One out of eight couples married in the United States in 2005 met via social media.[19] This is not our grandparents' world!

Communicating in a Diverse World

In earlier times, communication was a simpler matter than it is today. Most of your interaction was likely to be with people similar to you. The demographic shifts you've just read about make communication much more challenging in today's diverse world. In the following pages, you'll read more about how culture shapes communication, and how you can communicate most successfully with people from different backgrounds.

Intercultural and Intergroup Communication

Defining **culture** isn't an easy task. One early survey of scholarly literature revealed five hundred definitions, phrasings, and uses of the concept.[20] For our purposes, here is a clear and comprehensive definition of *culture*: "the language, values, beliefs, traditions, and customs people share and learn."[21]

When you think of cultures, you may think of different nationalities. But *within* a society, differences also exist. Social scientists use the term **coculture** to describe the perception of membership in a group that is part of an encompassing culture. The sons and daughters of immigrants, for example, might be immersed in mainstream American culture while still identifying with the customs of their parents' homeland. Members of cocultures often develop unique patterns of communication. The academic term that describes interaction between members of different cocultures is **intergroup communication**.

Cocultures in today's society include

- age (e.g., teen, senior citizen)
- race/ethnicity (e.g., African American, Latino)
- sexual orientation (e.g., lesbian, gay male)
- physical disability (e.g., wheelchair users, deaf persons)
- language (e.g., native and nonnative speakers)
- religion (e.g., Church of Jesus Christ of Latter-Day Saints, Muslim)
- activity (e.g., biker, gamer)

Membership in a coculture can shape the nature of communication. Sometimes the influence is obvious. For example, children who are native language speakers will have a very different experience in school than nonnative speakers, and gay men and lesbians can find it awkward, or even dangerous, to discuss their romantic relationships in a heterosexual environment.

In other cases, though, cocultural communication practices aren't so obvious. For example, ethnic background can influence what people consider the most important qualities in a friendship. One study found that Latinos were most likely to value relational support and bonding with friends. By contrast, Asian Americans (as a group, of course) placed a greater value on helping one another achieve personal goals. For African Americans in the study, the most important quality in a friend was respect for and acceptance of the individual. European Americans reported that they valued friends who met their task-related needs, offered advice, shared information, and had common interests.[22]

> Ethnic background can influence what people consider the most important qualities in a friendship.

Intercultural Communication: A Matter of Salience   Intercultural and intergroup communication—at least as we'll use the terms here—don't always occur when people from different backgrounds interact. Those backgrounds must have a significant impact on the exchange before we can say that culture has made a difference. Social scientists use the term **salience** to describe how much weight we attach to cultural characteristics. Consider a few examples where culture has little or no salience:

- A group of preschool children is playing together in a park. These three-year-olds don't recognize the fact that their parents may come from different countries, or even that they don't speak the same language. At this point we wouldn't say that intercultural communication is taking place. Only when cultural factors become salient (diet, sharing, or parental discipline, for example) do the children begin to think of one another as different.
- Members of a school athletic team—some Asian, some black, some Latino, and some white—are intent on winning the league championship. During a game, cultural distinctions aren't salient. There's plenty of communication, but it isn't fundamentally intercultural. Away from their games, the players are friendly when they encounter one another, but they rarely socialize. If they did, they might notice some fundamental differences in the way members of each group communicate.
- A husband and wife were raised in different religious traditions. Most of the time their religious heritage makes little difference and the partners view themselves as

CULTURAL IDIOM
take place:
occur

a unified couple. Every so often, however—perhaps during the holidays or when meeting members of each other's family—the different backgrounds are more salient. At those times we can imagine the partners feeling quite different from each other—thinking of themselves as members of separate cultures.

These examples show that in order to view ourselves as a member of a culture or coculture, there has to be some distinction between "us" and "them." Social scientists use the label **in-groups** to describe groups with which we identify and **out-groups** to label those we view as different.

Cultural Differences Are Generalizations   It's important not to overstate the influence of culture on communication. There are sometimes greater differences *within* cultures than *between* them. Consider the matter of formality as an example: By most measures, U.S. culture is far more casual than many others. But Figure 2-1 shows that there may be more common ground between a formal American and a casual member of a formal culture than there is between two Americans with vastly differing levels of formality.

Furthermore, within every culture, members display a wide range of communication styles. For instance, while most Asian cultures tend to be collectivistic, many members of those cultures would identify themselves as individualists. It's important to remember that generalizations—even when accurate and helpful—don't apply to every member of a group.

Cultural Values and Norms

Some cultural influences on communication are obvious. You don't have to be a scholar or researcher to appreciate how different languages or customs can make communication between groups both interesting and challenging.

Along with the obvious differences, far less visible values and norms shape how members of cultures think and act.[23] This section will look at several of these subtle yet vitally important values and norms that shape the way members of a culture communicate. Unless communicators are aware of these differences, they may see people from other cultures as unusual—or even offensive—without realizing that their apparently odd behavior comes from following a different set of beliefs and unwritten rules about the "proper" way to communicate.

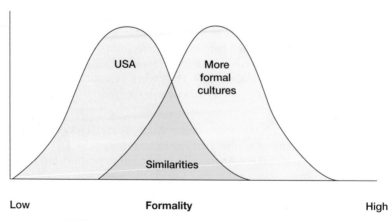

FIGURE 2-1 Differences and Similarities Within and Between Cultures

High- and Low-Context   Social scientists have identified two distinct ways that members of various cultures deliver messages.[24] The first deals with context, the set of circumstances that surround a situation and give it meaning. A **low-context culture** uses language primarily to express thoughts, feelings, and ideas as directly as possible. By contrast, a **high-context culture** relies heavily on subtle, often nonverbal cues to maintain social harmony. Rather than upsetting others by speaking directly, communicators in these societies learn to discover meaning from the context in which a message is delivered: the nonverbal behaviors of the speaker, the history of the relationship, and the general social rules that govern interaction between people. Table 2-2 summarizes some key differences in how people from low- and high-context cultures use language.

Mainstream culture in the United States, Canada, northern Europe, and Israel falls toward the low-context end of the scale. Longtime residents generally value straight talk and grow impatient with "beating around the bush." By contrast, most Asian and Middle Eastern cultures fit the high-context pattern. For them, maintaining harmony is important, so communicators avoid speaking directly if that threatens another person's "face," or dignity.

High- and low-context differences also operate within domestic cocultures. For example, researchers presented European Americans and people of color—Asian American, African American, and Latino—with examples of racist messages.[25] Some of these messages were direct and blatantly offensive, while others were indirect and less overtly racist. Leets found that European American participants judged the directly racist messages as more hurtful, while Asian American respondents rated the indirectly racist comments as more damaging. The researcher concluded that the traditional Asian tendency to favor high-context messages explains why Asian Americans were more offended by indirectly racist speech.

It's easy to see how the clash between directness and indirectness can present challenges. To members of high-context cultures, communicators with a low-context style can appear overly talkative, lacking in subtlety, and redundant. On the other hand, to people from low-context backgrounds, high-context communicators often seem evasive, or even dishonest.

CULTURAL IDIOM
beat around the bush:
approach indirectly

TABLE 2-2   High- and Low-Context Communication Styles

LOW CONTEXT	HIGH CONTEXT
Majority of information carried in explicit verbal messages, with less focus on the situational context.	Important information carried in contextual cues such as time, place, relationship, situation. Less reliance on explicit verbal messages.
Self-expression valued. Communicators state opinions and desires directly and strive to persuade others to accept their viewpoint.	Relational harmony valued and maintained by indirect expression of options. Communicators abstain from saying "no" directly.
Clear, eloquent speech considered praiseworthy. Verbal fluency admired.	Communicators talk "around" the point, allowing the others to fill in the missing pieces. Ambiguity and use of silence admired.

Individualism and Collectivism   Some cultures value the individual more than the group, while others place greater emphasis on the group. Members of **individualistic cultures** view their primary responsibility as helping themselves, whereas communicators in **collectivistic cultures** feel loyalties and obligations to an in-group: one's extended family, community, or even the organization one works for.[26] Individualistic cultures also are characterized by self-reliance and competition, whereas members of a collectivistic culture are more attentive to and concerned with the opinions of significant others. The consequences of a culture's individualistic-collectivistic orientation are so powerful that some scholars have labeled it as the most fundamental dimension of cultural differences.[27]

> Individualistic cultures also are characterized by self-reliance and competition, whereas members of a collectivistic culture are more attentive to and concerned with the opinions of significant others.

The United States is one of the world's more individualistic countries, along with Canada, Australia, and Great Britain. Latin American and Asian cultures are generally more collectivistic.[28] Table 2-3 summarizes some differences between individualistic and collectivistic cultures.

Individualistic and collectivistic cultures have very different approaches to handling disagreements. Individualistic societies are relatively tolerant of conflicts and use a direct, solution-oriented approach. By contrast, members of collectivistic cultures are less direct and more accommodating.[29] Collectivistic societies produce team players, while individualistic ones are far more likely to produce and reward superstars. Some research suggests that collectivist groups have a higher sense of teamwork and are more productive than groups of individualistic members.[30]

Power Distance   **Power distance** refers to the extent of the gap between social groups who possess resources and influence and those who don't. Cultures with low power distance believe in minimizing the difference between various social classes. Rich and poor, educated and uneducated groups may still exist, but there's a pervasive belief in low power difference cultures that one person is as good as another regardless of his or her station in life. Low power difference cultures also support the notion that challenging

TABLE 2-3   The Self in Individualistic and Collectivistic Cultures

INDIVIDUALISTIC CULTURES	COLLECTIVISTIC CULTURES
Self is separate, unique individual; should be independent, self-sufficient.	People belong to extended families or in-groups; "we" or group orientation.
Individual should take care of himself or herself and immediate family.	Person should take care of extended family before self.
Many flexible group memberships; friends based on shared interests and activities.	Emphasis on belonging to a very few permanent in-groups, which have a strong influence over the person.
Reward for individual achievement and initiative; individual decision encouraged; individual credit and blame assigned.	Reward for contribution to group goals and well-being; cooperation with in-group members; group decisions valued; credit and blame shared.
High value on autonomy, change, youth, individual security, equality.	High value on duty, order, tradition, age, group security, status, and hierarchy.

Adapted by Sandra Sudweeks from Triandis, H. C. (1990). Cross-cultural studies of individualism and collectivism. In J. Berman (Ed.), *Nebraska symposium on motivation* (pp. 41–133). Lincoln: University of Nebraska Press; and Hall, E. T. (1959). *Beyond culture*. New York: Doubleday.

authority is acceptable—even desirable. Members aren't necessarily punished for raising questions about the status quo. U.S. and Canadian societies have relatively low power distance, though not the lowest in the world. Austria, Denmark, Israel, and New Zealand proved to be the most egalitarian countries. At the other end of the spectrum are countries with a high degree of power distance: Philippines, Mexico, Venezuela, India, and Singapore.[31]

On-the-job communication is different in low and high power distance societies.[32] In countries with higher degrees of power distance, employees have much less input into the way they perform their work. In fact, workers from these cultures are likely to feel uncomfortable when given freedom to make their own decisions or when a more egalitarian boss asks for their opinion: They prefer to view their bosses as benevolent decision makers. The reverse is true when management from a culture with an egalitarian tradition tries to do business in a country whose workers are used to high power distance. They can be surprised to find that employees do not expect much say in decisions and do not feel unappreciated when they aren't consulted. They may regard dutiful, submissive, respectful employees as lacking initiative and creativity—traits that helped them gain promotions back home. Given these differences, it's easy to understand why multinational companies need to consider fundamental differences in communication values and behavior when they set up shop in a new country.

Uncertainty Avoidance   Uncertainty may be universal, but cultures have different ways of coping with an unpredictable future. The term **uncertainty avoidance** is used to reflect the degree to which members of a culture feel threatened by ambiguous situations and how much they try to avoid them.[33] As a group, residents of some countries (including Singapore, Great Britain, Denmark, Sweden, Hong Kong, and the United States) are relatively unthreatened by change, while others (such as natives of Belgium, Greece, Japan, and Portugal) found new or ambiguous situations discomforting.

A culture's degree of uncertainty avoidance is reflected in the way its members communicate. In countries that avoid uncertainty, deviant people and ideas are considered dangerous, and intolerance is high. People in these cultures are especially concerned with security, so they have a strong need for clearly defined rules and regulations. It's easy to imagine how most relationships in cultures with a low tolerance for uncertainty—family, work, friendships, and romance—are likely to fit a predictable pattern. By contrast, people in a culture that is less threatened by the new and unexpected are more likely to tolerate—or even welcome—people who don't fit the norm.

> It's important to have a wide range of behaviors and to be skillful at choosing and performing the most appropriate ones in a given situation.

Developing Intercultural Communication Competence

What distinguishes competent and incompetent intercultural communicators? Before we answer this question, take a moment to complete the Self-Assessment on page 40 to evaluate your intercultural communication sensitivity.

To a great degree, interacting successfully with strangers calls for the same ingredients of general communicative competence outlined in Chapter 1. It's important to have a wide range of behaviors and to be skillful at choosing and performing the most appropriate ones in a given situation. A genuine concern for others plays an important role. Cognitive complexity and the ability to empathize also help. Finally, self-monitoring is important, since the need to make midcourse corrections in your approach is often necessary when dealing with strangers.

What Is Your Intercultural Sensitivity?

Below is a series of statements concerning intercultural communication. There are no right or wrong answers. Imagine yourself interacting with people from a wide variety of cultural groups, not just one or two. Record your first impression to each statement by indicating the degree to which you agree or disagree, using the following scale.

5 = strongly agree   4 = agree   3 = uncertain   2 = disagree   1 = strongly disagree

_____ **1.** I enjoy interacting with people from different cultures.
_____ **2.** I think people from other cultures are narrow-minded.
_____ **3.** I am pretty sure of myself in interacting with people from different cultures.
_____ **4.** I find it very hard to talk in front of people from different cultures.
_____ **5.** I always know what to say when interacting with people from different cultures.
_____ **6.** I can be as sociable as I want to be when interacting with people from different cultures.
_____ **7.** I don't like to be with people from different cultures.
_____ **8.** I respect the values of people from different cultures.
_____ **9.** I get upset easily when interacting with people from different cultures.
_____ **10.** I feel confident when interacting with people from different cultures.
_____ **11.** I tend to wait before forming an impression of culturally distinct counterparts.
_____ **12.** I often get discouraged when I am with people from different cultures.
_____ **13.** I am open-minded to people from different cultures.
_____ **14.** I am very observant when interacting with people from different cultures.
_____ **15.** I often feel useless when interacting with people from different cultures.
_____ **16.** I respect the ways people from different cultures behave.
_____ **17.** I try to obtain as much information as I can when interacting with people from different cultures.
_____ **18.** I would not accept the opinions of people from different cultures.
_____ **19.** I am sensitive to my culturally distinct counterpart's subtle meanings during our interaction.
_____ **20.** I think my culture is better than other cultures.
_____ **21.** I often give positive responses to my culturally different counterpart during our interaction.
_____ **22.** I avoid those situations where I will have to deal with culturally distinct persons.
_____ **23.** I often show my culturally distinct counterpart my understanding through verbal or nonverbal cues.
_____ **24.** I have a feeling of enjoyment toward differences between my culturally distinct counterpart and me.

To determine your score, begin by reverse-coding items 2, 4, 7, 9, 12, 15, 18, 20, and 22 (if you indicated 5, reverse-code to 1, if you indicated 4, reverse-code to 2, and so on). Higher scores on the total instrument and each of the five subscales indicate a greater probability of intercultural communication competence.

Sum items 1, 11, 13, 21, 22, 23, and 24 = _____ Interaction Engagement (range is 7–35)
Sum items 2, 7, 8, 16, 18, and 20 = _____ Respect for Cultural Differences (6–30)
Sum items 3, 4, 5, 6, and 10 = _____ Interaction Confidence (5–25)
Sum items 9, 12, and 15 = _____ Interaction Enjoyment (3–15)
Sum items 14, 17, and 19 = _____ Interaction Attentiveness (3–15)
Sum of all the items = _____ (24–120, with a midpoint of 48)

Permission to use courtesy of Guo-Ming Chen. G. M. Chen and W. J. Sarosta, "The Development and Validation of the Intercultural Sensitivity Scale." *Human Communication* 3, 1–14.

"Excuse me. We're Americans. Would you give us your table?"

But beyond these basic qualities, communication researchers have worked long and hard to identify qualities that are unique, or at least especially important, ingredients of intercultural communicative competence.[34]

Increased Contact   Over a half-century of research confirms that, under the right circumstances, spending time with people from different backgrounds leads to a host of positive outcomes: reduced prejudice, greater productivity, and better relationships.[35] The link between exposure and positive attitudes has been called the *contact hypothesis*.

The connection between exposure and positive experiences with people from other backgrounds has been demonstrated in a wide range of contacts: between gays and straights, people from different cultures and cocultures, and people with and without disabilities.[36]

By itself, exposure isn't enough. In order to make contacts successful, some other conditions are important. The first is a genuine desire to know and understand others. People who are willing to communicate with others from different backgrounds report a greater number of friends from different backgrounds than those who are less willing to reach out.[37] Other conditions also contribute to positive relationships: They include equal status, a low-stress, cooperative climate, and the chance to disconfirm stereotypes.

Along with face-to-face contacts, the Internet offers a useful way to enhance contact with people from different backgrounds.[38] Online venues make it relatively easy to connect with people you might never meet in person. The asynchronous nature of these contacts reduces the potential for stress and confusion that can easily come in person. It also makes status differences less important: When you're online, gaps in material wealth or physical appearance are much less apparent.

CULTURAL IDIOM

in the end:
ultimately

Tolerance for Ambiguity   When we encounter communicators from different cultures, the level of uncertainty is especially high. Consider the basic challenge of communicating in an unfamiliar language. Pico Iyer captures the ambiguity that arises from a lack of fluency when he describes his growing friendship with Sachiko, a Japanese woman he met in Kyoto:

> I was also beginning to realize how treacherous it was to venture into a foreign language if one could not measure the shadows of the words one used. When I had told her, in Asuka, *"Jennifer Beals ga suki-desu. Anata mo"* ("I like Jennifer Beals—and I like you"), I had been pleased to find a way of conveying affection, and yet, I thought, a perfect distance. But later I looked up *suki* and found that I had delivered an almost naked protestation of love. . . .
>
> Meanwhile, of course, nearly all her shadings were lost to me. . . . Once, when I had to leave her house ten minutes early, she said, "I very sad," and another time, when I simply called her up, she said, "I very happy"—and I began to think her unusually sensitive, or else prone to bold and violent extremes, when really she was reflecting nothing but the paucity of her English vocabulary. . . . Talking in a language not one's own was like walking on one leg; when two people did it together, it was like a three-legged waltz.[39]

Competent intercultural communicators accept—even welcome—this kind of ambiguity. Iyer describes the way the mutual confusion he shared with Sachiko actually helped their relationship develop:

> Yet in the end, the fact that we were both speaking in this pared-down diction made us both, I felt, somewhat gentler, more courteous, and more vulnerable than we would have been otherwise, returning us to a state of innocence.[40]

Without a tolerance for ambiguity, the mass of often confusing and sometimes downright incomprehensible messages that impact intercultural interactions would be impossible to manage. Some people seem to come equipped with this sort of tolerance, while others have to cultivate it. One way or the other, that ability to live with uncertainty is an essential ingredient of intercultural communication competence.

Open-Mindedness   Being comfortable with ambiguity is important, but without an open-minded attitude a communicator will have trouble interacting competently with people from different backgrounds. To understand open-mindedness, it's helpful to consider three traits that are incompatible with it. **Ethnocentrism** is an attitude that one's own culture is superior to others. An ethnocentric person thinks—either privately or openly—that anyone who does not belong to his or her in-group is somehow strange, wrong, or even inferior. Travel writer Rick Steves describes how an ethnocentric point of view can interfere with respect for other cultural practices:

> . . . we [Americans] consider ourselves very clean and commonly criticize other cultures as dirty. In the bathtub we soak, clean, and rinse, all in the same water. (We would never wash our dishes that way.) A Japanese visitor, who uses clean water for each step, might find our way of bathing strange or even disgusting. Many cultures spit in public and blow their nose right onto the street. They couldn't imagine doing that into a small cloth, called a hanky, and storing that in their pocket to be used again and again.
>
> Too often we think of the world in terms of a pyramid of "civilized" (us) on the top and "primitive" groups on the bottom. If we measured things differently (maybe according to stress, loneliness, heart attacks, hours spent in traffic jams, or family togetherness) things stack up differently.[41]

Most people acknowledge the importance of treating others from different cultural backgrounds with respect. But what obligations do you have when another person's values are completely different from yours on fundamental matters, such as the sanctity of life, or gender equity?

Either on your own or with a group, craft a set of guidelines that cover communication in cases like these. How should you behave when confronted with views you find shocking or abhorrent?

Ethnocentrism leads to an attitude of **prejudice**—an unfairly biased and intolerant attitude toward others who belong to an out-group. (Note that the root term in *prejudice* is "pre-judge.") An important element of prejudice is **stereotyping**—exaggerated generalizations about a group. Stereotypical prejudices include the obvious exaggerations that all women are emotional, all men are sex-crazed and insensitive goons, all older people are out of touch with reality, and all immigrants are welfare parasites.

CULTURAL IDIOM

shift gears:
change what one is doing

out of touch:
lacking understanding

Knowledge and Skill   Attitude alone isn't enough to guarantee success in intercultural encounters. Communicators need to possess enough knowledge of other cultures to know what approaches are appropriate. The rules and customs that work with one group might be quite different from those that succeed with another. The ability to "shift gears" and adapt one's style to the norms of another culture or coculture is an essential ingredient of communication competence.[42]

How can a communicator acquire the culture-specific information that leads to competence? Scholarship suggests three strategies for moving toward a more mindful, competent style of intercultural communication.[43] *Passive observation* involves noticing what behaviors members of a different culture use and applying these insights to communicate in ways that are most effective. *Active strategies* include reading, watching films, and asking experts and members of the other culture how to behave, as well as taking academic courses related to intercultural communication and diversity.[44] The third strategy, *self-disclosure*, involves volunteering personal information to people from the other culture with whom you want to communicate. One type of self-disclosure is to confess your cultural ignorance: "This is very new to me. What's the right thing to do in this situation?" This approach is the riskiest of the three described here, since some cultures may not value candor and self-disclosure as much as others. Nevertheless, most people are pleased when strangers attempt to learn the practices of their culture, and they are usually more than willing to offer information and assistance.

> How can a communicator acquire the culture-specific information that leads to competence?

Social Media in a Changing World

Until recently, when people heard the word "media" they most likely thought of television, radio, and other forms of mass communication. But today, not all media are aimed at mass audiences. The term **Web 2.0** is often used to describe how the Internet has evolved from a one-way medium (rather like old-style publishers and broadcasters) into what one scholar called a *masspersonal* phenomenon[45] where individual users interact in a host of ways that include social networking sites, video- and photo-sharing services, and blogs.

As the name suggests, people use **social media** for personal reasons, often to reach small groups of receivers. You're using social media when you text message with friends or coworkers, exchange e-mails, texts, and instant messages, and when you use social networking websites like Facebook or MySpace. As mentioned earlier, the number of social media technologies has exploded in the past few decades, giving communicators today an array of choices that would have amazed someone from a previous era.

Social media are different from the mass variety in some important ways. Most obvious is the *variable size of the target audience*. Whereas the mass media are aimed at large audiences, the intended audience in social media can vary. On one hand, you typically address e-mails, text messages, and IMs to a single, or maybe a few, receivers. In fact, you'd probably be embarrassed to have some of your personal messages circulate more widely. On the other hand, blogs, tweets, and other postings are often aimed at much larger groups of receivers.

Unlike mass media, social media are *interactive*: The recipients of your messages can—and usually do—talk back. For example, nearly nine in ten teens who post photos online say that people comment at least sometimes on the images they post.[46] This figure reflects the difference between traditional print media, in which communication is essentially one-way, and far more interactive web-based social media.

Unlike traditional forms of mass communication, social media are also distinguished by *user-generated content*. You decide what goes on your Facebook or MySpace page and what topics are covered on your blog. There aren't any market researchers to tell you what the audience wants. No staff writers, editors, designers, or marketers craft your message. It's all you.

"Last tweet?"

Despite these characteristics, the boundary between mass and interpersonal communication isn't as clear as it might first seem. Consider, for example, YouTube and other streaming video websites. They provide a way for individuals to publish their own content (your graduation, baby's first birthday party) for a limited number of interested viewers. On the other hand, some videos go "viral," receiving thousands, or even millions, of hits. (Since first appearing in 2006, the exploits of "loneygirl15" have been viewed over 100 million times.)

Twitter is another example of the fuzzy boundary between personal and mass media. Many people broadcast updates to a rather small group of interested parties. ("I'm at the concert—Great seats!") On the other hand, millions of fans follow the tweets of favorite celebrities like Ashton Kutcher, Britney Spears, and Ellen DeGeneres. Twitter offers an interesting blend of messages from real friends and celebrities, "strangely intimate and at the same time celebrity-obsessed," as one observer put it.[47] "You glance at your Twitter feed over that first cup of coffee, and in a few seconds you find out that your nephew got into med school and Shaquille O'Neal just finished a cardio workout in Phoenix."

Blogs also straddle the categories of mass and social media. Some are highly personal: You can set one up and share your opinions with anybody who cares to read them. Others (like the Huffington Post, Gizmodo, or Daily Kos) are much closer to traditional mass media, published regularly and reaching audiences numbering in the hundreds of thousands.

Mediated Versus Face-to-Face Communication

In an age where social media are as common as face-to-face communication, it's important to understand how these two approaches compare. In some ways, mediated and face-to-face communication are quite similar. Both include the same elements described on pages 12–13: senders, receivers, channels, feedback, and so on. Both are used to satisfy the same physical, identity, social, and practical needs described in Chapter 1. Despite these similarities, the two forms of communication are different in some important ways.

Message Richness   Social scientists use the term **richness** to describe the abundance of nonverbal cues that add clarity to a verbal message. As Chapter 6 explains in detail, face-to-face communication is rich because it abounds with nonverbal messages that give communicators cues about the meanings of one another's words and offer hints about their feelings.[48] By comparison, most mediated communication is a much leaner channel for conveying information.

To appreciate how message richness varies by medium, imagine you haven't heard from a friend in several weeks and you decide to ask, "Is anything wrong?" Your friend replies, "No, I'm fine." Would that response be more or less descriptive depending on whether you received it via text message, over the phone, or in person?

You almost certainly would be able to tell a great deal more from a face-to-face response because it would contain a richer array of cues: facial expressions, vocal tone, and so on. By contrast, a text message contains only words. The phone message—containing vocal cues but no visual ones—would probably fall somewhere in between.

Because most mediated messages are leaner than the face-to-face variety, they can be harder to interpret with confidence. Irony and attempts at humor can easily

@Work

Can You Be *Too* Connected?

Today's array of communication technologies means that it's possible to be connected to others virtually all the time. This connectivity has led to a dramatic growth in *teleworking*—flexible work arrangements in which employees do their jobs outside the office.

The growth of teleworking has uncovered a paradox. Along with their benefits, the technologies that keep workers connected have a downside. When your boss, colleagues, and customers can reach you at any time, you can become too distracted to tackle necessary parts of your job.

Communication researchers Paul Leonardi, Jeffrey Treem, and Michele Jackson discovered that remote workers developed two

strategies to reduce contact and thereby increase their efficiency.[49] The first simply involved *disconnecting* from time to time: logging off the computer, forwarding the phone call to voice mail, or simply ignoring incoming messages. The researchers labeled the second strategy *dissimulation*. Teleworkers disguise their activities to discourage contact: changing their instant message status to "in a meeting" or posting a fake "out of the office" message online.

It's important to note that these strategies weren't typically used to avoid work but to get more done. These findings show that too much connectivity is like many other parts of life: More isn't always better.

CULTURAL IDIOM

jump to conclusions:
make a hasty judgment

be misunderstood, so as a receiver it's important to clarify your interpretations before jumping to conclusions. As a sender, think about how to send unambiguous messages so you aren't misunderstood. (We'll discuss the value of "emoticons" and other text-based cues in Chapters 4 and 6.)

Synchronicity   **Synchronous communication** occurs in real time. In-person communication is synchronous. So are phone conversations. By contrast, **asynchronous communication** occurs when there's a time gap between when a message is sent and when it's received. Voice mail messages are asynchronous. So are "snail mail" letters, e-mails, and Twitter postings.

The asynchronous nature of most mediated messages makes them fundamentally different from synchronous communication. Most obviously, asynchronous messages give you the choice of not responding at all: You can ignore most problematic text messages without much fallout. That isn't a good option if the person who wants an answer gets you on the phone or confronts you in person.

Even if you want to respond, asynchronous media give you the chance to edit your reply. You can mull over different wording, or even ask others for advice about what to say.

Permanence   What happens in a face-to-face conversation is transitory. By contrast, the text and video you send via hard copy or mediated channels can be stored indefinitely and forwarded to others. You can save and share the smartphone photos of your once-in-a-lifetime encounter with a celebrity. And if your boss e-mails saying it's okay to come in late on Monday morning, you're covered if she later complains about your tardy arrival.

Even with precautions like restricting your privacy settings and requesting that your personal material not be shared, the safest approach is to only share information that you are willing to have seen and read by anyone with an Internet connection.

Mediated Communication in Society

Now that you understand some characteristics that make mediated communication unique, let's look at who uses various social media, and how they use them.

Who Uses Social Media?   If you visualize the typical social networker as a teen, you'd be only partly right. At the beginning of 2010, almost 75 percent of American teens used social networking sites.[50] Use for young adults under age thirty was virtually identical. By contrast, about 40 percent of adults age thirty and older were social networkers.

Text messaging has grown just as dramatically as social networking websites. The first text message was sent in December 1992, and by 2005 the number of text messages sent every day exceeded the Earth's population.[51] The vast majority of texts are exchanged between teenagers. According to one leading researcher, a big strength of texting is efficiency:[52] You can quickly send and receive texts almost anywhere. The asynchronicity of texting also means you can send a message whether or not the recipient is available at that moment.

The use pattern for Twitter is different than for other social media.[53] Only 8 percent of teens use this medium, while four times as many young adults do so. Use is roughly equal across all income groups and education levels. The majority of Twitter fans use multiple wireless devices (such as smartphones, netbooks, iPods, and e-book readers), with the largest group owning four or more of them.

E-mails have been around longer than other forms of online communication, and they remain popular: The number of messages sent daily exceeds 200 billion. Almost 68 percent of adults online use the Internet for e-mail.[54] By contrast, teens are much less likely to use this medium. In one survey, only 14 percent of teens reported sending daily e-mails to their friends.[55]

> E-mails have been around longer than other forms of online communication, and they remain popular: The number of messages sent daily exceeds 200 billion.

CULTURAL IDIOM
up to:
engaged in doing
track down:
locate

How People Use Social Media   In the mid-twentieth century, researchers began to study the question "What do media do to people?" They sought answers by measuring the effects of print and broadcast media on users. Did programming influence viewers' use of physical violence? Did it affect academic success? Family communication patterns?

In following decades, researchers began to explore a different question: "What do people do *with* media?"[56] This branch of study became known as *uses and gratifications* theory. In the digital age, researchers continue to explore how we use both social media and face-to-face communication. Table 2-4 shows the findings of one study. The uses listed there fall into four broad categories:[57]

- **Information**
  What do people think of a new film or musical group? Can anybody trade work hours this weekend? Is there a good Honda mechanic nearby? Can your network provide leads on getting your dream job?

- **Personal relationships**
  Seeing what your friends are up to. Tracking down old classmates. Announcing changes in your life to the people in your personal networks. Finding a romantic partner.

- **Personal identity**
  Observing others as models to help you become more effective. Getting insights about yourself from trusted others. Asserting your personal values and getting feedback from others.

TABLE 2-4 Satisfaction Scores for Selected Communication Media

| | (1 = LOWEST, 5 = HIGHEST) | | | | |
NEED	INSTANT MESSAGE	E-MAIL	LANDLINE PHONE	CELL PHONE	FACE-TO-FACE
To communicate easily	4.20	3.95	2.49	4.61	4.41
To feel less lonely	3.18	2.05	2.09	3.48	2.88
To pass the time away when bored	3.89	2.9	2.2	3.65	3.87
To provide information	3.62	3.67	2.49	3.93	4.04
To get to know others	3.58	2.54	2.25	3.60	4.38

Adapted from A. J. Flanagan, "IM Online: Instant Messaging Use Among College Students." *Communication Research Reports* 22 (2005): 173–187.

- **Entertainment**
  Gaming online with a friend. Sharing your music playlists with others. Joining the fan base of your favorite star. Finding interest or activity groups to join.

Communicating Competently with Social Media

Perhaps you've found yourself in situations like these:

- You want to bring up a delicate issue with a friend, family member, or at work. You aren't sure whether to do so in person, on the phone, or via some mediated channel like texting or e-mail.

- You're enjoying a film at the theater—until another moviegoer starts a cell phone conversation.

- A friend posts a picture of you online that you would rather not be seen by others.

- Someone you care about is spending too much time online, crowding out real-life encounters.

- Reading a text message while you rush to an appointment, you bump into another pedestrian.

- Even though you know it's a bad idea, you answer a cell phone call while driving and nearly hit a cyclist.

- You are copied on an e-mail or text message that was obviously not meant for your eyes.

CULTURAL IDIOM

bring up:
mention

crowd out:
exclude without the other's consent

bump into:
encounter unexpectedly

bound to:
certainly

None of these situations would have existed a generation ago. They highlight the need for a set of social agreements that go beyond the general rules of communicative competence outlined in Chapter 1. The following pages offer some guidelines that have evolved in recent years. While they won't cover every situation involving mediated communication, they can help you avoid some problems and deal most effectively with others that are bound to arise.

Choose the Best Medium   A generation ago, choosing which communication channel to use wasn't very complicated: If a face-to-face conversation wasn't desirable or possible, you either wrote a letter or used the telephone. Today's communicators have many more options. If you want to put your thoughts in writing, you can use e-mail, text messaging, instant messaging . . . or the traditional pen-and-paper approach. If you want to speak, you can either use a landline telephone, a cell phone, or an Internet-based system.

CULTURAL IDIOM
on the road:
traveling

Sometimes the choice of a medium is a no-brainer. If a friend says "phone me while I'm on the road," you know what to do. If your boss or professor only responds to e-mails, then it would be foolish to use any other approach. But in many other situations, you have several options available. Table 2-5 on this page outlines the advantages and drawbacks of the most common ones. Choosing the best channel can make a real difference in your success. In one survey, managers who were identified as most "media sensitive" were almost twice as likely as their less-savvy peers to receive top ratings in performance reviews.[58]

Choosing the right medium is just as important in personal relationships. Anyone who has been dumped via text message knows that it only adds insult to injury. Just because there is an option that allows you to avoid a difficult conversation doesn't mean you should take the easy way out. Many difficult conversations are better when conducted face-to-face. These types of conversations include, but aren't limited to, sharing really bad news, ending a relationship, and trying to resolve a conflict.

> Many difficult conversations are better when conducted face-to-face.

TABLE 2-5   Choosing a Communication Channel

Choosing the best communication channel can make the difference between success and failure on the job. This table offers guidelines for choosing the channel that is best suited for a particular situation.

	SYNCHRONICITY	RICHNESS OF INFORMATION CONVEYED	SENDER'S CONTROL OVER MESSAGE	CONTROL OVER RECEIVER'S ATTENTION	EFFECTIVENESS FOR DETAILED MESSAGES
FACE-TO-FACE	Synchronous	High	Moderate	Highest	Weak
TELEPHONE, TELECONFERENCING, AND VIDEOCONFERENCING	Synchronous	Moderate	Moderate	Moderate	Weak
VOICE MAIL	Asynchronous	Moderate	High	Low	Weak
E-MAIL	Asynchronous	Low	High	Low	High
INSTANT MESSAGING	Almost synchronous	Low	High	Varies	Weak
TEXT MESSAGING AND TWITTER	Varies	Low	High (given briefness of message)	Low	Good for brief messages
HARD COPY (E.G., HANDWRITTEN OR TYPED MESSAGE)	Asynchronous	Low	High	Low	High

Adapted from R. B. Adler and J. M. Elmhorst, *Communicating at Work: Principles and Practices for Business and the Professions*, 10th ed. (New York: McGraw-Hill, 2010), p. 29.

CULTURAL IDIOM

tuck away:
hide

come up:
happen unexpectedly

In situations like these, a useful guideline is what's been called the "platinum rule": treating others as *they* would like to be treated. Ask yourself how the recipient of your message would prefer to receive it, and act accordingly, even though it's difficult.

Be Careful What You Post Most of us cringe at the sight of old yearbook photos, hardly believing that we are the same person as the adolescent looking out from those glossy pages. Older adults can safely assume that most of their questionable, odd, and rebellious behavior is tucked away in those dusty yearbooks, never to be seen by their current friends and coworkers. This isn't the case for modern teens, however, who may be forever haunted by adolescent mistakes in the form of digital text and photos posted online.

As a cautionary tale about how your digital goofs can haunt you, consider the case of Kevin Colvin, the young intern at a Boston bank who e-mailed his boss saying "something came up at home" and he would need to miss a few days of work. A Facebook search by his boss revealed a photo showing Kevin's true location during the absence, an out-of-town Halloween party with the missing intern dressed in a fairy costume, complete with wings and wand. Besides seeing his pixie-like image plastered over the Web, Kevin found that his indiscretion was not a brilliant career move. (To see the photo and read the boss's reaction, type the words "Kevin" and "cool wand" into your search engine.)

Some incautious posts can go beyond being simply amusing. As the reading on this page shows, "sexting" can have serious consequences. One survey revealed that 10 percent of young adults between the ages of fourteen and twenty-four have texted or e-mailed a nude or partially nude image of themselves to someone else, and 15 percent have received such pictures or videos of someone else they know.[59] Perhaps even more disturbing, 8 percent reported that they had been forwarded nude or partially nude images of someone they knew.[60] The consequences of sexting can be much worse than embarrassment or legal problems. In July 2008, eighteen-year-old Jesse Logan hanged herself after months of torment from classmates who were forwarded a sexually explicit photo she sent to a boy. The tormenters were other girls in her class.[61]

"Sexting" Surprise: Teens Face Child Porn Charges

Six Pennsylvania high school students are facing child pornography charges after three teenage girls allegedly took nude or semi-nude photos of themselves and shared them with male classmates via their cell phones.

The female students at Greensburg Salem High School in Greensburg, Pa., all 14- or 15-years-old, face charges of manufacturing, disseminating or possessing child pornography while the boys, who are 16 and 17, face charges of possession.

Police told the station that the photos were discovered after school officials seized a cell phone from a male student who was using it in violation of school rules and found a nude photo of a classmate on it. Police were called in and their investigation led them to other phones containing more photos.

Police Capt. George Saranko indicated that authorities decided to file the child pornography charges to send a strong message to other minors who might consider sending such photos to friends.

"It's very dangerous," he said. "Once it's on a cell phone, that cell phone can be put on the Internet where everyone in the world can get access to that juvenile picture. You don't realize what you are doing until it's already done."

MSNBC

Be Considerate   The word "etiquette" calls to mind old-fashioned rules that have little to do with today's world. But whatever you call them, mostly unspoken rules of conduct still keep society running smoothly. Most of us don't shove or cut in waiting lines. We return others' greetings, say "please" and "thanks," and (mostly) let others speak without cutting them off. By acting appropriately, we feel good about ourselves, and we're more effective in getting our needs met.

CULTURAL IDIOM

cut in:
intrude

cut off:
interrupt another's activity

Mediated communication calls for its own rules of etiquette. Here are a few.

Respect Others' Need for Undivided Attention   If you've been texting, IMing, and e-mailing since you could master a keypad, it might be hard to realize that some people are insulted when you divide your attention between your in-person conversational partner and distant contacts. As one observer put it, "While a quick log-on may seem, to the user, a harmless break, others in the room receive it as a silent dismissal. It announces: 'I'm not interested.'"[62]

Chapter 5 has plenty to say about the challenges of listening effectively when you are multitasking. Even if you think you can understand others while dealing with communication media, it's important to realize that they may perceive you as being rude.

Keep Your Tone Civil   If you've ever posted a snide comment on a blog, shot back a nasty reply to a text or instant message, or forwarded an embarrassing e-mail, you know that it's easier to behave badly when the recipient of your message isn't right in front of you.

The tendency to transmit messages without considering their consequences is called **disinhibition**, and research shows it is more likely in mediated channels than in face-to-face contact.[63] Sometimes communicators take disinhibition to the extreme, blasting off angry—even vicious—e-mails, text messages, and website postings. The common term for these outbursts is **flaming**. Flames are problematic because of their emotional and irreversible nature. Once you've calmed down, the aggressive message can continue to cause pain.

> The tendency to transmit messages without considering their consequences is called disinhibition.

Flaming isn't the only type of mediated harassment. Ongoing "cyberbullying" has become a widespread phenomenon, often with dire consequences. More than four in ten teens report being the target of online harassment. Recipients of cyberbullying often feel helpless and scared, to such a degree that one report found they are eight times more likely to carry a weapon to school than other students. There are at least four reported cases in the United States where a victim of cyberbullying committed suicide,[64] a sobering statistic in light of reports that 81 percent of cyberbullies admit their only reason for bullying is because "it's funny."[65]

One way to behave better in asynchronous situations is to ask yourself a simple question before you send, post, or broadcast: Would you deliver the same message to the recipient in person? If your answer is no, then you might want to think before hitting the "enter" key.

Respect Privacy Boundaries   Sooner or later you're bound to run across information about others that you suspect they would find embarrassing. If your relationship is close enough, you might consider sending out a "for your information" alert. In other cases, you may intentionally run a search about someone. Even if you uncover plenty of interesting information, it can be smart to avoid mentioning what you've discovered to the object of your searching. See the reading on page 52 for more about the etiquette of Internet "stalking."

Understanding Communication Technology

The Etiquette of Internet "Stalking"

Christine Reus is a self-professed stalker—a "Facebook stalker," that is. "I meet new people, and that's the worst, because I've seen them on Facebook. I know all about their life and who they're dating, but I have to pretend I know nothing about them," says Reus, 21, a Vanderbilt student from Birmingham, Alabama.

In this age of ubiquitous social networking sites such as MySpace and Facebook, casual "stalking" of friends and acquaintances is typical, if not implicitly encouraged. But just because people know intimate details about acquaintances' lives does not necessarily make it OK to mention it when they see each other in person. Users are expected to abide by an unwritten code of conduct that applies both online and offline. Problem is, these rules of etiquette are, well, unwritten.

With so much personal information online, it can be hard to separate what you've assimilated through face-to-face interaction from what you've gleaned online. The secret lies in not slipping up when you see real people. Reus says the formula is simple: With close friends, it is always OK to comment on their profiles; they expect it and might even be upset if you don't. With distant acquaintances, it is almost never OK. It's those in the middle that are tricky; it's OK to bring up their profiles only if there is a reasonable explanation for why you were looking at it in the first place. Mutual friends are a good excuse; it is perfectly plausible that you were looking at your friend's pictures—which this other person just happened to be in and which link to his or her profile. In any case, it's always possible to extricate yourself from an awkward situation by joking about how creepy Facebook stalking really is.

Byron Dubow, *USA Today*

Be Mindful of Bystanders   If you spend even a little time in most public spaces, you're likely to encounter communicators whose use of technology interferes with others: Restaurant patrons whose phone voices intrude on your conversation, pedestrians who are more focused on their handheld device than on avoiding others, or people in line who are trying to pay the cashier and talk on their cell phone at the same time. If you aren't bothered by this sort of behavior, it can be hard to feel sympathetic with others who are offended by it. Nonetheless, this is another situation where the "platinum rule" applies: Consider treating others the way *they* would like to be treated.

Balance Mediated and Face Time   It's easy to make a case that many relationships are better because of social media. And as you've already read in this chapter, research supports this position. With all the benefits of communication technology, it's worth asking whether there is such a thing as *too much* mediated socializing.

Indeed, there is a link between heavy reliance on mediated communication and conditions including depression, loneliness, and social anxiety.[66] People who spend excessive time on the Internet may begin to experience problems at school or work and withdraw further from their offline relationships.[67] Many people who pursue exclusively online social contacts do so because they have social anxiety or low social skills to begin with. For these people, retreating further from offline relationships may diminish their already low social skills.

Researchers have been especially interested in determining when cyber communication crosses the bridge from normal to excessive. Danger signs of excessive Internet use include

- Failure to resist the urge to use the Internet
- Increase in time needed online to achieve satisfaction
- Time of Internet use exceeds the amount anticipated or intended
- Failure in attempts to reduce Internet use

- Internet use results in failure to fulfill responsibilities at work, home, or school
- Important social or recreational activities are given up or reduced[68]

Although experts disagree about whether Internet Addiction Disorder (IAD) is a certifiable addiction or just a symptom of another issue, they suggest several strategies for reining in excessive Internet use. Unlike other addictions, such as those to drugs and alcohol, treatment for Internet addiction focuses on moderation and controlled use of the Internet rather than abstinence.[69] If you are worried about your Internet use:

- Keep track of the amount of time you spend online so you can accurately assess whether it is too much.
- Insert planned Internet time into your daily schedule and see if you can stick to it.
- Make a list of problems in your life that may have occurred because of your time spent online.
- If you do not feel able to change your behavior on your own, seek the help of a counselor or therapist.

Be Safe   As more and more people spend time online, safety has become a major issue in cyberspace. Predators used to be people who burglarized your home or approached you in a dark alley. Now, thieves and con artists don't have to find us, because we find them. Many people fail to realize the hazards of posting certain information in public forums, and other people don't even realize that what they are posting is public. You may post your "on vacation" status in Facebook, assuming that only your friends can see your message. But if a friend uses a public computer or lets another friend see your page, unintended recipients are viewing your information.[70]

As a rule, don't disclose information in a public-access medium that you would not tell a stranger on the street. Even personal e-mails present a problem: They can be forwarded, and accounts can even be hacked. The safest bet is to assume that mediated messages can be seen by unintended recipients, some of whom you may not know or trust.

Careless use of social media can damage more than your reputation. Talking on a cell phone while driving is just as dangerous as driving under the influence of alcohol or drugs. Cell phone use while driving (handheld or hands-free) lengthens a driver's reaction as much as having a blood alcohol concentration at the legal limit of .08 percent.[71] In the United States alone, drivers distracted by cell phones cause 2,600 deaths and 330,000 injuries every year.[72] Even a hands-free device doesn't eliminate the risks. Drivers carrying on a phone conversation are 18 percent slower to react to brake lights. They also take 17 percent longer to regain the speed they lost when they braked.[73]

Text messaging poses even a greater hazard on the road than conversing. In 2007, before a large-scale campaign to discourage the practice, one-fifth of experienced adult drivers in the United States sent text messages while driving.[74] Studies have found that texting while driving causes a 400 percent increase in time spent with eyes off the road. Drivers who are sending or reading a text message spend about five seconds looking at their devices before a crash or near crash, allowing them to travel more than one hundred yards at typical highway speeds with their eyes off the road.[75]

Summary

The nature of human communication has changed more rapidly in the last century than at any time in history. These transformations come from two sources: changing demographics and new technologies. Over the past century, the academic discipline of communication has evolved to reflect those changes.

Increased travel, immigration, and new communication technologies have made encounters with others from different backgrounds more common. This chapter emphasized that success in today's changing world calls for competence in intercultural and cocultural communication. This competence requires both flexible attitudes and skills.

New communication technologies have expanded the options for how to communicate. Because every communication channel possesses unique characteristics, the increased number of methods for communicating present both opportunities and challenges. This chapter described the characteristics of various communication media, described how they are used in contemporary society, and offered guidelines for using social media competently.

Key Terms

asynchronous communication Communication that occurs when there's a time gap between when a message is sent and when it is received. *p. 46*

coculture The perception of membership in a group that is part of an encompassing culture. *p. 34*

collectivistic culture A culture where members focus on the welfare of the group as a whole, rather than a concern by individuals for their own success. See also *Individualistic orientation. p. 38*

culture The language, values, beliefs, traditions, and customs people share and learn. *p. 34*

disinhibition The tendency to transmit messages without considering their consequences. See also *Flaming. p. 51*

ethnocentrism The attitude that one's own culture is superior to others'. See also *Disinhibition. p. 42*

flaming Sending angry and/or insulting e-mails, text messages, and website postings. *p. 51*

high-context culture A culture that relies heavily on subtle, often nonverbal cues to maintain social harmony. *p. 37*

in-groups Groups with which we identify. See also *Out-groups. p. 36*

individualistic culture A culture where members focus on the value and welfare of individual members, as opposed to a concern for the group as a whole. *p. 38*

intergroup communication The interaction between members of different cocultures. *p. 35*

low-context culture A culture that uses language primarily to express thoughts, feelings, and ideas as directly as possible. *p. 37*

out-groups Groups of people that we view as different from us. See also *In-groups. p. 36*

power distance The degree to which members of a group are willing to accept a difference in power and status. *p. 38*

prejudice An unfairly biased and intolerant attitude toward others who belong to an out-group. *p. 43*

richness A term used to describe the abundance of nonverbal cues that add clarity to a verbal message. *p. 45*

salience How much weight we attach to a particular person or phenomenon. *p. 35*

social media Digital communication channels used primarily for personal reasons, often to reach small groups of receivers. *p. 43*

stereotyping The perceptual process of applying exaggerated beliefs associated with a categorizing system. *p. 43*

synchronous communication Communication that occurs in real time. *p. 46*

uncertainty avoidance The cultural tendency to seek stability and honor tradition instead of welcoming risk, uncertainty, and change. *p. 39*

Web 2.0 A term used to describe how the Internet has evolved from a one-way medium into a "masspersonal" phenomenon. *p. 43*

Case Study Questions

Instructions: Reread the case study on pages xx–1 to answer the following questions in light of what you have learned in this chapter.

1. Interview an American who came of age in the second half of the twentieth century. Use the information you glean from that conversation to explain how communication technology has changed the nature of communication and relationships in the USA.

2. Describe an element of communication that you believe is characteristically American, contrasting it to practices of at least one other culture. Explain to visitors from abroad how that principle operates in the USA.

3. Describe two interesting cases when cocultural differences in communication have led to problems. Based on your studies, explain how the problematic communication might have been prevented or overcome.

Activities

1. **Coculture Tree** Using the model format below, create a diagram resembling a family tree that shows your various cultural and cocultural identities. Describe how your communication with others is shaped by various dimensions of your identity.

2. **Medium and Message Effectiveness** Send the same message to four friends, but use a different medium for each person. For example, ask the question "How's it going?" Use the following media:

   - e-mail
   - instant message
   - text message
   - telephone

   Notice how each response differs and what that may say about the nature of the medium.

3. **Social Media Analysis** Construct a diary of the ways you use social media in a three-day period. For each instance when you use social media (e-mail, social networking website, phone, Twitter, etc.), describe

   a. The kind(s) of social media you use

   b. The nature of the communication (e.g., "Wrote on friend's Facebook wall," "Reminded roommate to pick up dinner on the way home")

   c. The type of need you are trying to satisfy (information, relational, identity, entertainment)

   Based on your observations, describe the types of media you use most often and the importance of social media in satisfying your communication needs.

4. **Media Fast** Gain insight about the role of mediated communication in your life by going on a "media fast." For a twenty-four-hour period, restrict your communication to only face-to face interaction. Avoid all print and electronic channels: telephone, TV and radio, the Internet. Then explore the impact of mediated communication by describing both the negative and positive effects of life without media. Consider how you could modify your everyday life to enhance its quality by modifying the ways you use media.

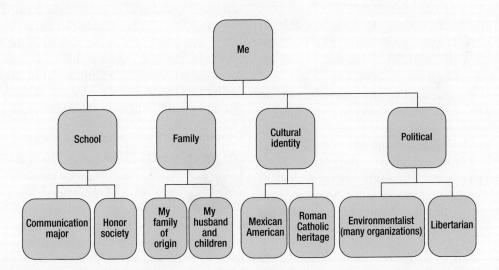

For Further Exploration

For more resources about the nature of communication, see the *Understanding Human Communication* website at www.oup.com/us/uhc11. There you will find a variety of resources: a list of books and articles, links to descriptions of feature films and television shows at the *Now Playing* website, study aids, and a self-test to check your understanding of the material in this chapter.

MEDIA ROOM

For more resources about communication in film and television, see *Now Playing* on the *Understanding Human Communication* website at www.oup.com/us/uhc11.

When Cocultures Collide

Crash (2004, Rated R)

Over thirty-six hours in Los Angeles, the lives of several strangers collide. Because they come from such different backgrounds, this diverse group of people rely on stereotypes to form snap judgments of each other. Unfortunately, their judgments are almost always wrong.

Again and again, the characters' assumptions keep them from understanding the human beings they are encountering. Matt Dillon plays an angry cop who goes out of his way to humiliate a black citizen. An upper-class housewife (Sandra Bullock) believes a Mexican American locksmith (Michael Peña) is a gangbanger who plans to burgle her home, even though he actually is a gentle man struggling to build a safe life for his family. An Iranian businessman (Shaun Toub) keeps being misidentified as an Arab. Two clean-cut young black men (Larenz Tate and Ludacris) bemoan the fact that they are regarded with fear by whites in an upscale neighborhood. Since childhood, most of us have been reminded not to judge a book by its cover. *Crash* provides a dramatic example of the problems that can result from ignoring this maxim.

Spanglish (2004, Rated PG-13)

As its name implies, *Spanglish* explores communication at the intersection of two cultures. Flor (Paz Vega) is an undocumented Latina immigrant, hired by wealthy Californians Deborah and John Clasky (Téa Leoni and Adam Sandler) to take care of their children and the family's upscale homes. After Flor's daughter Cristina (Shelbie Bruce) moves in with the family, Deborah uses all the tools of charm and privilege at her disposal to win the young Latina's affection. (When Deborah takes Cristina shopping, the teen declares that Deborah is "the most amazing white woman" she has ever known.) John intervenes in the growing conflict between the two mothers, showing emotion and compassion that surprises Cristina, who says "To someone with firsthand knowledge of Latin machismo, he seemed to have the emotions of a Mexican . . . woman." *Spanglish* illustrates how cultural background intersects with personality to create a blend of factors that make communication both fascinating (to observers) and challenging (to those living the story).

Cultural Values and Family Relations

Whale Rider (2002, Rated PG-13)

In current-day New Zealand, twelve-year-old Pai (Keisha Castle-Hughes) is coming of age in an all-Maori community led by her loving grandfather Koro (Rawiri Paratene). It's Maori tradition that chiefs are always males, but Pai is convinced that she could become the next leader. Despite his love for his granddaughter, Koro fiercely resists her ambition. His disapproving messages cause Pai great pain.

Anyone who appreciates the value of individualism will root for Pai. But from a collectivist perspective, it's easy to sympathize with her grandfather's expectation that his family should act in the best interests of the Maori community by honoring ancient traditions. Despite its focus on Maori culture, *Whale Rider* illustrates a broader theme—the challenge of creating a unique identity in the face of a community with different ideas about who we should be.

Competence in Cocultural Communication

World's Fastest Indian (2006, Rated PG-13)

Burt Munro (Anthony Hopkins) meets a diverse array of characters while pursuing his dream to race at Utah's Bonneville Salt Flats. Those characters include a motorcycle gang, a transvestite hotel clerk, a Latino car salesman, a desert-dwelling Native American, and a U.S. Air Force officer on leave from dropping napalm in Vietnam. In all these encounters, Burt shows how open-mindedness and tolerance for ambiguity can turn potential adversaries into friends.

CULTURAL IDIOM

judge a book by its cover:
rely on appearances to form an impression

Changes in Communication Technology

American Teen (2008, Rated PG-13) and *American Graffiti* (1973, Rated PG)

Set in 1962, *American Graffiti* follows four teens on their last summer night before college. (Movie fans will enjoy seeing young Harrison Ford and Ron Howard.) The documentary *American Teen* profiles the triumphs and struggles of five high school seniors in 2006.

The character types and personal dramas in both films are similar, but the technologies in each reflect the pace of change in just two generations. Communication in the 1960s centered on face-to-face interaction. Most homes only had one landline telephone, and neither the Internet nor cell phones existed. By contrast, the twenty-first-century characters in *American Teen* rely on a host of technologies to keep in touch. (One poignant scene captures a high school jock breaking up with his girlfriend via text message.)

Taken together, these films capture the enduring theme of relational communication and show how technology affects the way events play out.

Mediated Versus Face-to-Face Relationships

You've Got Mail (1999, Rated PG)

Joe Fox (Tom Hanks) and Kathleen Kelly (Meg Ryan) detest each other—at least in person. Kathleen despises Joe's arrogant, self-absorbed style of communicating. She also views him as heartless because his discount bookstore chain threatens to bankrupt Kathleen's family-owned bookshop. But unknown to both Joe and Kathleen, they have been communicating anonymously for months after meeting in an online chat room, using the names "NY152" and "Shopgirl." In cyberspace, Joe seems like a different person. The e-mail messages he sends Kathleen are tender and self-disclosing. She falls for NY152 without knowing that the same man she can't stand in person writes the enchanting messages. For students of communication, this romance demonstrates that each of us has many identities and that the way we present ourselves can shape the fate of our relationships.

The Influence of Social Media on Communication

Second Skin (2008, Rated R)

By following three sets of online gamers, this documentary explores how social media are expanding and changing the nature of human connection. The film treats the pros and cons of mediated relationships evenhandedly, depicting both the benefits and drawbacks of life in cyberspace. It presents research findings on both obvious and subtle effects of mediated human interaction, especially in the world of gaming and virtual reality.

The Self, Perception, and Communication

Chapter Outline

After studying the material in this chapter . . .

YOU SHOULD UNDERSTAND:

1. The communicative influences that shape the self-concept.
2. How self-fulfilling prophecies influence behavior.
3. How perceptual tendencies and situational factors influence perception.
4. The influence of culture on perception and the self-concept.
5. The importance of empathy in communication.
6. How the process of identity management can result in presentation of multiple selves.
7. The reasons for and the ethical dimensions of identity management.

YOU SHOULD BE ABLE TO:

1. Identify the ways you influence the self-concepts of others and the ways significant others influence your self-concept.
2. Identify the communication-related self-fulfilling prophecies that you have imposed on yourself, that others have imposed on you, and that you have imposed on others.
3. Identify how the perceptual tendencies described in this chapter have led you to develop distorted perceptions of yourself and others.
4. Use perception checking and empathy to be more accurate in your perceptions of others' behavior.
5. Describe the various identities you attempt to create and the ethical merit of your identity management strategies.

- In biology class, a shy but earnest student mistakenly uses the term *orgasm* instead of *organism* when answering the professor's question. The entire class breaks into raucous laughter. The student remains quiet for the remainder of the semester.

- After a month of encouraging correspondence online, members of an Internet dating service meet face-to-face. Both are surprised to discover that the person they found so attractive online isn't at all the way they seemed.

- Two classmates, one black and the other white, are discussing their latest reading assignment in an American history class. "Malcolm X was quite a guy," the white student says sincerely to the black one. "You must be very proud of him." The black student is offended at what sounds like a condescending remark.

- A student is practicing his first speech for a public address class with several friends. "This is a stupid topic," he laments. The others assure him that the topic is interesting and that the speech sounds good. Later in class he becomes flustered because he believes that his speech is awful—and that belief affects his performance. As a result of his unenthusiastic delivery, the student receives a low grade on the assignment.

Stories like these probably sound familiar. Yet behind this familiarity lie principles that affect our communication more than almost any others discussed in this book.

- The messages we send can shape others' self-concepts and thus influence their communication.
- The image we present to the world in person and via mediated channels varies from one situation to another.
- Two or more people often perceive the world in radically different ways, which presents major challenges for successful communicating.
- The beliefs each of us hold about ourselves—our self-concept—have a powerful effect on our own communication behavior.

These simple truths play a role in virtually all the important messages we send and receive. The goal of this chapter is to demonstrate the significance of these truths by describing how the ways in which we perceive ourselves and others shape our communication.

Communication and the Self

Nothing is more fundamental to understanding how we communicate than our sense of self. For that reason, the following pages introduce the notion of self-concept and explain how the way we view ourselves shapes our interaction with others.

Self-Concept Defined

The **self-concept** is a set of relatively stable perceptions that each of us holds about ourselves. The self-concept includes our conception of what is unique about us and what makes us both similar to and different from others. To put it differently, the self-concept is rather like a mental mirror that reflects how we view ourselves: not only physical features, but also emotional states, talents, likes and dislikes, values, and roles.

We will have more to say about the nature of the self-concept shortly, but first you will find it valuable to gain a personal understanding of how this theoretical construct applies to you. You can do so by answering a simple question: "Who are you?"

A man or woman? What is your age? Your religion? Occupation?

There are many ways of identifying yourself. Take a few more minutes and list as many ways as you can to identify who you are. You'll need this list later in this chapter, so be sure to complete it now. Try to include all the characteristics that describe you, including:

- Your moods or feelings
- Your appearance and physical condition
- Your social traits
- Talents you possess or lack
- Your intellectual capacity
- Your belief systems (religion, philosophy)
- Your strong beliefs
- Your social roles

Even a list of twenty or thirty terms would be only a partial description. To make this written self-portrait complete, your list would have to be hundreds—or even thousands—of words long.

Of course, not all items on such a list would be equally important. For example, the most significant part of one person's self-concept might consist of social roles, whereas for another it might consist of physical appearance, health, friendships, accomplishments, or skills.

An important element of the self-concept is **self-esteem**: our evaluations of self-worth. One person's self-concept might include being religious, tall, or athletic. That person's self-esteem would be shaped by how he or she felt about these qualities: "I'm glad that I am athletic," or "I am embarrassed about being so tall," for example.

Self-esteem has a powerful effect on the way we communicate.[1] People with high self-esteem are more willing to communicate than people with low self-esteem. They are more likely to think highly of others and expect to be accepted by others. They aren't afraid of others' reactions and perform well when others are watching them. They work harder for people who demand high standards of performance, and they are comfortable with others whom they view as superior in some way. When confronted with critical comments, they are comfortable defending themselves. By contrast, people with low self-esteem are likely to be critical of others and expect rejection from them. They are also critical of their own performances. They are sensitive to possible disapproval of others and perform poorly when being watched. They work harder for undemanding, less critical people. They feel threatened by people they view as superior in some way and have difficulty defending themselves against others' negative comments.

> Self-esteem has a powerful effect on the way we communicate.

Despite its obvious benefits, self-esteem doesn't guarantee success in personal and professional relationships.[2] People with exaggerated sense of self-worth may *think* they make better impressions on others, but neither impartial observers nor objective tests verify these beliefs. It's easy to see how people with an inflated sense of self-worth could irritate others by coming across as condescending know-it-alls, especially when their self-worth is challenged.[3]

Communication and Development of the Self

So far we've talked about what the self-concept is, but at this point you may be asking what it has to do with the study of human communication. We can begin to answer this question by looking at how you came to possess your own self-concept.

Our identity comes almost exclusively from communication with others. As psychologists Arthur Combs and Donald Snygg put it:

> The self is essentially a social product arising out of experience with people. . . . We learn the most significant and fundamental facts about ourselves from . . . "reflected appraisals," inferences about ourselves made as a consequence of the ways we perceive others behaving toward us.[4]

The term **reflected appraisal** metaphorically describes how we develop an image of ourselves from the way we think others view us. As we learn to speak and understand language, verbal messages—both positive and negative—contribute to the developing self-concept. These messages continue later in life, especially when they come from what social scientists term **significant others**—people whose opinions we especially value. A teacher from long ago, a special friend or relative, or perhaps a barely known acquaintance whom you respected can all leave an imprint on how you view yourself. To see the importance of significant others, ask yourself how you arrived at your opinion of you as a student, as a potential romantic partner, as a competent worker, and so on, and you will see that these self-evaluations were probably influenced by the way others regarded you.

As we grow older, the influence of significant others is less powerful.[5] The evaluations of others still influence beliefs about the self in some areas, such as physical attractiveness and popularity. For example, TV makeover shows, with their underlying message of "you must improve your appearance," can lead viewers to feel worse about themselves.[6] In other areas, however, the looking glass of the self-concept has become distorted, so that it shapes the input of others to make it conform with our existing beliefs. For example, if your self-concept includes the element "poor student," you might respond to a high grade by thinking "I was just lucky" or "The professor must be an easy grader."

You might argue that not every part of one's self-concept is shaped by others, insisting there are certain objective facts that are recognizable by self-observation. After all, nobody needs to tell you that you are taller than others, speak with an accent, can run quickly, and so on. These facts are obvious.

Though it's true that some features of the self are immediately apparent, the *significance* we attach to them—the rank we assign them in the hierarchy of our list and the interpretation we give them—depends greatly on the social environment. The interpretation of characteristics such as weight depends on the way people important to us regard them. Being anything less than trim and muscular is generally regarded as undesirable because others tell us that slenderness is an ideal. In one study, young women's perceptions of their bodies changed for the worse after watching just thirty minutes of televised images of the "ideal" female form.[7] In cultures and societies where greater weight is considered beautiful, a Western supermodel would be considered unattractive. In the same way, the fact that one is single or married, solitary or sociable, aggressive or passive takes on meaning depending on the interpretation that society attaches to those traits. Thus, the importance of a given characteristic in your self-concept has as much to do with the significance that you and others attach to it as with the existence of the characteristic.

By now it should be clear that each of us has the power to influence others' self-concepts. Even with the best of intentions, there are cases when an honest message is likely to reduce another person's self-esteem. Consider a few examples:

- Your friend, an aspiring artist, asks, "What do you think of my latest painting?" You think it's terrible.
- After a long, hard week you are looking forward to spending the evening at home. A somewhat insecure friend who just broke off a long romantic relationship calls to ask if you want to get together. You don't.
- A good friend asks to use your name as a reference for a potential employer. You can't honestly tell the employer that your friend is qualified for the job.

In situations like these, how do you reconcile the desire to avoid diminishing another person's self-esteem with the need to be honest? Based on your conclusions, is it possible to always be both honest and supportive?

Ethical Challenge

Is Honesty the Best Policy?

The power of culture
is far more basic and
powerful than most
people realize.

Culture and the Self-Concept

The challenges and opportunities that come from cultural diversity are becoming more apparent with every passing year. But the power of culture is far more basic and powerful than most people realize. Although we seldom recognize the fact, our whole notion of the self is shaped by the culture in which we have been reared.[8]

The most obvious feature of a culture is the language its members use. If you live in an environment where everyone speaks the same tongue, then language will have little noticeable impact. But when your primary language is not the majority one, or when it is not prestigious, the sense of being a member of what social scientists call the "out-group" is strong. At this point the speaker of a nondominant language can react in one of two ways: either to feel pressured to assimilate by speaking the "better" language, or to refuse to accede to the majority language and maintain loyalty to the ethnic language.[9] In either case, the impact of language on the self-concept is powerful. On one hand, the feeling is likely to be "I'm not as good as speakers of the native language," and on the other, the belief is "there's something unique and worth preserving in my language." A case study of Hispanic managers illustrates the dilemma of speaking a nondominant language.[10] The managers—employees in a predominantly Anglo organization—felt their "Mexican" identity threatened when they found that the road to advancement would be smoother if they deemphasized their Spanish and adopted a more colloquial English style of speaking.

Cultures affect the self-concept in more subtle ways, too. As you read in Chapter 2, most Western cultures are highly individualistic, whereas other cultures—most Asian ones, for example—are traditionally much more collective.[11] When asked to identify themselves, Americans, Canadians, Australians, and Europeans would probably respond by giving their first name, surname, street, town, and country. Many Asians do it the other way around.[12] If you ask Hindus for their identity, they will give you their caste and village as well as their name. The Sanskrit formula for identifying oneself begins with lineage and goes on to family and house and ends with one's personal name.[13]

These conventions for naming aren't just cultural curiosities: They reflect a very different way of viewing oneself.[14] In collective cultures a person gains identity by belonging to a group. This means that the degree of interdependence among members of the society and its subgroups is much higher. Feelings of pride and self-worth are likely to be shaped not only by what the individual does but also by the behavior of other members of the community. This linkage to others explains the traditional Asian denial of self-importance—a strong contrast to the self-promotion that is common in individualistic Western cultures. In Chinese written language, for example, the pronoun "I" looks very similar to the word for "selfish."[15]

This sort of cultural difference affects the level of comfort or anxiety that people feel when communicating. In societies where the need to conform is great, there is a higher degree of communication apprehension. For example, as a group, residents of China, Korea, and Japan exhibit significantly more anxiety about speaking out than do members of individualistic cultures such as the United States and Australia.[16] It's important to realize that different levels of communication apprehension don't mean that shyness is a "problem" in some cultures. In fact, just the opposite is true: In these cultures, reticence is valued. When the goal is to avoid being the nail that sticks out, it's logical to feel nervous when you make yourself appear different by calling attention to yourself. A self-concept that includes "assertive" might make a Westerner feel proud, but in much of Asia it would more likely be cause for shame.

The difference between individualism and collectivism shows up in everyday interaction. Communication researcher Stella Ting-Toomey has developed a theory that explains cultural differences in important norms, such as honesty and directness.[17] She suggests that in individualistic Western cultures where there is a strong "I" orientation, the low-context norm of speaking directly is honored, whereas in collectivistic cultures where the main desire is to build connections between the self and others, high-context, indirect approaches that maintain harmony are considered more desirable. "I gotta be me" could be the motto of a Westerner, but "If I hurt you, I hurt myself" is closer to the Asian way of thinking.

The Self-Concept and Communication with Others

So far we've focused on how the self-concept has been shaped by our interpretations of messages from our cultural environment and influential others. Now we will explore how the self-concept shapes the way we communicate *with* other people.

Figure 3-1 pictures the relationship between the self-concept and behavior. It illustrates how the self-concept both shapes much of our communication behavior and is shaped by it. We can begin to examine the process by considering the self-concept you bring to an event. Suppose, for example, that one element of your self-concept is "nervous with authority figures." That image probably comes from the evaluations of significant others in the past—perhaps teachers or former employers. If you view yourself as nervous with authority figures like these, you will probably behave in nervous ways when you encounter them in the future—in a teacher-student conference or a job interview. That nervous behavior is likely to influence how others view your personality, which in turn will shape how they respond to you—probably in ways that reinforce the self-concept you brought to the event. Finally, the responses of others will affect

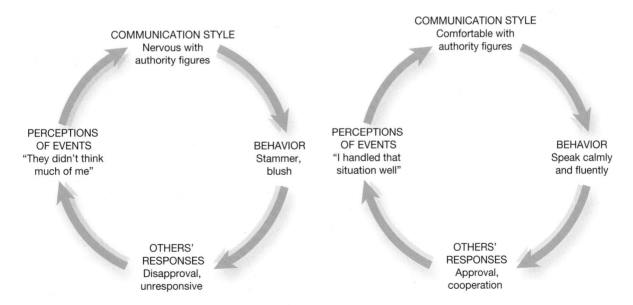

FIGURE 3-1 The Relationship Between the Self-Concept and Behavior

the way you interpret future events: other job interviews, meetings with professors, and so on. This cycle illustrates how the chicken-and-egg nature of the self-concept, which is shaped by significant others in the past, helps to govern your present behavior, and influences the way others view you.

Not all communication behavior is driven by the self-concept. Some of our communication style is a function of our innate *personality*—a relatively consistent set of traits each of us exhibits across a variety of situations.[18] We use the notion of personality to characterize others as friendly or aloof, energetic or lazy, smart or stupid, and in literally thousands of other ways. In fact, one survey revealed almost eighteen thousand trait words in the English language that can be used to describe a personality.[19] People do seem to possess some innate personality traits. Researchers have found that 10 percent of all children seem to be born with a biological disposition toward shyness.[20] Babies who stop playing when a stranger enters the room, for example, are more likely than others to be reticent and introverted as adolescents. Likewise, another 10 percent of children seem to be born with especially sociable dispositions. Research with twins also suggests that personality may be at least partially a matter of physical destiny.[21] Biologically identical twins are much more similar in sociability than are fraternal twins. These similarities are apparent not only in infancy but also when the twins have grown to adulthood, and are noticeable even when the twins have had different experiences.

> One survey revealed almost 18,000 trait words in the English language that can be used to describe a personality.

The Self-Fulfilling Prophecy and Communication

The self-concept is such a powerful force on the personality that it not only determines how we communicate in the present but also can actually influence our behavior and that of others in the future. Such occurrences come about through a phenomenon called the self-fulfilling prophecy.

A **self-fulfilling prophecy** occurs when a person's expectation of an outcome, and subsequent behavior, makes the outcome more likely to occur than would otherwise have been true. Self-fulfilling prophecies occur all the time although you might never have given them that label. For example, think of some instances you may have known:

- You expected to become nervous during a job interview, and your anxiety caused you to botch the session.

- You anticipated having a good (or terrible) time at a social affair, and your expectations led you to act in ways that shaped the outcome to fit your prediction.

- A teacher or boss explained a new task to you, saying that you probably wouldn't do well at first. You took these comments to heart, and as a result you didn't do well.

- A friend described someone you were about to meet, saying that you wouldn't like the person. Due in part to the prediction, you looked for—and found—reasons to dislike the new acquaintance.

In each of these cases, the outcome happened at least in part because it was predicted to occur. You needn't have botched the interview, the party might have been boring only because you helped make it so, you might have done better on the new task if your boss hadn't spoken up, and you might have liked the new acquaintance if your friend hadn't given you preconceptions. In other words, what helped make each outcome occur was the expectation that it would happen.

CULTURAL IDIOM
botched:
destroyed, ruined

There are two types of self-fulfilling prophecies. The first type occurs when your own expectations influence your own behavior. Like the job interview and the party described earlier, there are many times when an outcome that needn't have occurred does occur because you expect it to. In sports you have probably psyched yourself into playing either better or worse than usual, so that the only explanation for your unusual performance was your attitude that you would behave differently. The same principle operates for nervous public speakers: Communicators who feel anxious about facing an audience often create self-fulfilling prophecies about doing poorly that cause them to perform less effectively.[22] (Chapter 11 offers advice on overcoming this kind of communication apprehension.)

Research has demonstrated the power of self-fulfilling prophecies. In one study, communicators who believed they were incompetent proved less likely than others to pursue rewarding relationships and more likely to sabotage their existing relationships than did people who were less critical of themselves.[23] On the other hand, students who perceived themselves as capable achieved more academically.[24] In another study, subjects who were sensitive to social rejection tended to expect rejection, perceive it where it might not have existed, and overreact to their exaggerated perceptions in ways that jeopardized the quality of their relationships.[25] The self-fulfilling prophecy also operates on the job. For example, salespeople who perceive themselves as being effective communicators are more successful than those who perceive themselves as less effective, despite the fact that there was no difference in the approach that members of each group used with customers. In other words, the apparent reason why some salespeople are successful is because they expect to succeed. As the nearby cartoon suggests, self-fulfilling prophecies can be physiologically induced: Researchers have found that putting a smile on your face, even if you're not in a good mood, can lead to a more positive disposition.[26]

A second category of self-fulfilling prophecies occurs when one person's expectations govern another's actions.[27] This principle was demonstrated in a classic experiment.[28] Researchers told teachers that 20 percent of the children in a certain elementary school showed unusual potential for intellectual growth. The names of the 20 percent were drawn by means of a table of random numbers—much as if they were drawn out of a hat. Eight months later these unusual or "magic" children showed significantly greater gains in IQ than did the remaining children, who had not been singled out for the teachers' attention. The change in the teachers' behavior toward these allegedly "special" children led to changes in the intellectual performance of these randomly selected children. Among other things, the teachers gave the "smart" students more time to answer questions and provided more feedback to them. These children did better, not because they were any more intelligent than their classmates, but because their teachers—significant others—communicated the expectation that they could. In other words, it wasn't just what the teachers believed that made a difference; it was how these beliefs were conveyed by the teachers' behavior.

To put this phenomenon in context with the self-concept, we can say that when a teacher communicates to students the message "I think you're bright," they accept that

"I don't sing because I am happy. I am happy because I sing."

Source: © The New Yorker Collection 1991 Ed Frascino from cartoonbank.com. All Rights Reserved.

CULTURAL IDIOM
psyched yourself:
boosted confidence by thinking positively

evaluation and change their self-concepts to include that evaluation. Unfortunately, we can assume that the same principle holds for those students whose teachers send the message "I think you're stupid."

This type of self-fulfilling prophecy has been shown to be a powerful force for shaping the self-concept and thus the behavior of people in a wide range of settings outside of the schools. In medicine, patients who unknowingly receive placebos—substances such as injections of sterile water or doses of sugar pills that have no curative value—often respond just as favorably to treatment as do people who actually receive a drug. The patients believe they have taken a substance that will help them feel better, and this belief actually brings about a "cure." In psychotherapy, Rosenthal and Jacobson describe several studies that suggest that patients who believe they will benefit from treatment do so, regardless of the type of treatment they receive. In the same vein, when a doctor believes a patient will improve, the patient may do so precisely because of this expectation, whereas another person for whom the doctor has little hope often fails to recover. Apparently the patient's self-concept as sick or well—as shaped by the doctor—plays an important role in determining the actual state of health.

> The self-fulfilling prophecy is an important force in communication, but it doesn't explain all behavior.

The self-fulfilling prophecy operates in families as well. If parents tell their children long enough that they can't do anything right, the children's self-concepts will soon incorporate this idea, and they will fail at many or most of the tasks they attempt. On the other hand, if children are told they are capable or lovable or kind persons, there is a much greater chance of their behaving accordingly.[29]

The self-fulfilling prophecy is an important force in communication, but it doesn't explain all behavior. There are certainly times when the expectation of an event's outcome won't bring about that outcome. Your hope of drawing an ace in a card game won't in any way affect the chance of that card turning up in an already shuffled deck, and your belief that good weather is coming won't stop the rain from falling. In the same way, believing you'll do well in a job interview when you're clearly not qualified for the position is unrealistic. Similarly, there will probably be people you don't like and occasions you won't enjoy, no matter what your attitude. To connect the self-fulfilling prophecy with the "power of positive thinking" is an oversimplification.

In other cases, your expectations will be borne out because you are a good predictor and not because of the self-fulfilling prophecy. For example, children are not equally well equipped to do well in school, and in such cases it would be wrong to say that a child's performance was shaped by a parent or teacher even though the behavior did match what was expected. In the same way, some workers excel and others fail, some patients recover and others don't—all according to our predictions but not because of them.

As we keep these qualifications in mind, it's important to recognize the tremendous influence that self-fulfilling prophecies play in our lives. To a great extent we are what we believe we are. In this sense we and those around us constantly create our self-concepts and thus ourselves.

Perceiving Others

The first part of this chapter explored how our self-perceptions affect the way we communicate. The following pages examine how the ways we perceive others shape our interaction with them.

Steps in the Perception Process

In 1890 the psychologist William James described an infant's world as "one great blooming, buzzing confusion."[30] Babies—all humans, in fact—need some mechanisms to sort out the avalanche of stimuli that bombard us every moment. As you will read in the following pages, many of these stimuli involve others' behavior, and how we deal with those stimuli shapes our communication.

We sort out and make sense of others' behavior in three steps: selection, organization, and interpretation.

Selection   Since we're exposed to more input than we can possibly manage, the first step in perception is the **selection** of which data we will attend to.

Some external factors help shape what we notice about others. For example, stimuli that are *intense* often attract our attention. Something that is louder, larger, or brighter stands out. This explains why—other things being equal—we're more likely to remember extremely tall or short people and why someone who laughs or talks loudly at a party attracts more attention (not always favorable) than do more quiet guests.

We also pay attention to *contrast* or *change* in stimulation. Put differently, unchanging people or things become less noticeable. This principle offers an explanation (excuse?) for why we take consistently wonderful people for granted when we interact with them frequently. It's only when they stop being so wonderful or go away that we appreciate them.

Along with external factors like intensity and contrast, *internal factors* shape how we make sense of others. For example, our *motives* often determine how we perceive people. Someone on the lookout for a romantic adventure will be especially aware of attractive potential partners, whereas the same person in an emergency might be oblivious to anyone but police or medical personnel.

Our *emotional state* also shapes what we select. For example, one study revealed that people in a happy mood were quick to notice when happy-appearing characters in a film appeared sadder, while unhappy subjects were quicker at noticing when sad characters appeared more happy.[31]

Organization   After selecting information from the environment, we must arrange it in some meaningful way in order to make sense of the world. We call this stage **organization**.

The raw sense data we perceive can be organized in more than one way. The cube in Figure 3-2 illustrates this principle. If you look at the drawing long enough, you'll find that the faces of the cube change places. From one perspective you are looking down on the figure from above, but if you shift your point of view you will see it from beneath.

We organize our perceptions of other people using *perceptual schema,* cognitive frameworks that allow us to give order to the information we have selected.[32] Four types of schema help us classify others:

Physical constructs classify people according to their appearance: beautiful or ugly, fat or thin, young or old, etc.

Role constructs use social position: student, attorney, wife, etc.

Interaction constructs focus on social behavior: friendly, helpful, aloof, sarcastic, etc.

Psychological constructs refer to internal states of mind and dispositions: confident, insecure, happy, neurotic, etc.

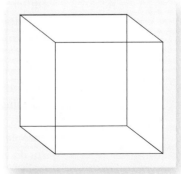

FIGURE 3-2 Shape-shifting Cube

The kinds of constructs we use strongly affect the way we relate to others. For example, boys between eight and eleven years old tend to categorize peers according to their achievements, what they like and dislike, and personality, whereas girls in the same age range tend to perceive them according to their background and family.[33]

In cyberspace, where few nonverbal cues exist, it's harder to categorize people we haven't met in person. In text-based situations, strangers often rely on text-based cues to form impressions of others. In one study, for example, students relied on screen names to form impressions of strangers.[34] Experimenters asked college students to form impressions of fictional characters with names like "packer-fan4" and "stinkybug." Using just the screen names, most of the respondents assigned attributes including biological sex, ethnicity, and age to the supposed owners of these names.

> What constructs do you use to classify the people you encounter in your life?

What constructs do you use to classify the people you encounter in your life? Consider how your relationships might change if you used different schema.

Once we have an organizing scheme to classify people, we use that scheme to make generalizations about members of the groups who fit our categories. For example, if you are especially aware of a person's sex, you might be alert to the differences between the way men and women behave or the way they are treated. If religion plays an important part in your life, you might think of members of your faith differently than you do others. If ethnicity is an important issue for you, you probably tune in to the differences between members of various ethnic groups. There's nothing wrong with generalizations about groups as long as they are accurate. In fact, it would be impossible to get through life without them. But faulty overgeneralizations can lead to problems of stereotyping, which you'll read a few pages later.

Interpretation   Once we have selected and organized our perceptions, we interpret them in a way that makes some sort of sense. **Interpretation** plays a role in virtually every type of communication. Is the person who smiles at you across a crowded room interested in romance or simply being polite? Is a friend's kidding a sign of affection or irritation? Should you take an invitation to "drop by any time" literally or not?

There are several factors that cause us to interpret a person's behavior in one way or another. The first is our *degree of involvement* with the person. For example, research suggests that we tend to view people with whom we have or seek a relationship more favorably than those whom we observe from a detached perspective.[35]

Relational satisfaction is a second factor that influences our interpretation. The behavior that seems positive when you are happy with a partner might seem completely different when the relationship isn't satisfying. For example, couples in unsatisfying relationships are more likely than satisfied partners to blame one another when things go wrong.[36]

A third factor that influences interpretations is *personal experience*. What meanings have similar events held? For instance, if you've been gouged by landlords in the past, you might be skeptical about an apartment manager's assurances that careful housekeeping will ensure the refund of your cleaning deposit.

Assumptions about human behavior also influence interpretations. Do you assume people are lazy, dislike work, avoid responsibility, and must be coerced to do things, or do you believe people exercise self-direction and self-control, possess creativity, and seek responsibility? Imagine the differences in a boss who assumes workers fit the first description versus one who assumes they fit the second.

Expectations are another factor that shape our interpretations. When we anticipate people will behave in certain ways, our expectations color the way we interpret their

CULTURAL IDIOM
gouged by:
charged an excessive amount

behavior. For instance, if you go into a conversation expecting a hostile attitude, you're likely to hear a negative tone in the other person's voice—even if that tone isn't there. We'll talk more about how expectations affect perception later in this chapter.

Knowledge of others affects the way we interpret their actions. For instance, if you know a friend has just been jilted by a lover or fired from a job, you'll interpret his or her aloof behavior differently than if you were unaware of what happened. If you know an instructor is rude to all students, then you won't be likely to take his or her remarks personally.

Although we have talked about selection, organization, and interpretation separately, the three phases of perception can occur in differing sequences. For example, a parent's or babysitter's past interpretation (such as "Jason is a troublemaker") can influence future selections (his behavior becomes especially noticeable) and the organization of events (when there's a fight, the assumption is that Jason started it). As with all communication, perception is an ongoing process in which it is hard to pin down beginnings and endings.

Narratives, Perception, and Communication

We all have our own story of the world, and often our story is quite different from those of others. A family member or roommate might think your sense of humor is inappropriate, whereas you think you're quite clever. You might blame an unsatisfying class on the professor, who you think is a long-winded bore. On the other hand, the professor might characterize the students as superficial and lazy and blame the class environment on them. (The discussion of emotive language in Chapter 4 will talk about the sort of name-calling embedded in the previous sentences.)

Social scientists call the personal stories that we and others create to make sense of our personal world **narratives**.[37] In a few pages we will look at how a tool called "perception checking" can help bridge the gap between different narratives. For now, though, the important point is that differing narratives can lead to problematic communication.

After they take hold, narratives offer a framework for explaining behavior and shaping future communication. One study of sense making in organizations illustrates how the process operates on the job.[38] Researchers located employees who had participated in office discussions about cases where a fellow worker had received "differential treatment" from management about matters such as time off, pay, or work assignments. The researchers then analyzed the conversations that employees held with fellow workers about the differential treatment. The analysis revealed that these conversations were the occasion in which workers created and reinforced the meaning of the employee's behavior and management's response. For example, consider the way workers made sense of Jane Doe's habit of taking late lunches. As Jane's coworkers discuss her behaviors, they might decide

CULTURAL IDIOM
jilted:
rejected
long-winded:
speaking for a long time

We all have our own story of the world, and often our story is quite different from those of others.

"I know what you're thinking, but let me offer a competing narratve."

Source: © The New Yorker Collection 2004 Harry Bliss from cartoonbank.com. All Rights Reserved.

that her late lunches aren't fair—or they might agree that late lunches aren't a big deal. Either way, the coworker's narrative of office events *defines* those events. Once they are defined, coworkers tend to seek reinforcement for their perceptions by keeping a mental scorecard rating their fellow employees and management. ("Did you notice that Bob came in late again today?" "Did you notice that the boss chose Jane to go on that trip to New York?") Although most of us like to think we make judgments about others on our own, this research suggests that sense making is an *interactive* process. In other words, reality in the workplace and elsewhere isn't "out there"; rather, we create it with others through communication.

Research on long-term happy marriages demonstrates that shared narratives don't have to be accurate to be powerful.[39] Couples who report being happily married after fifty or more years seem to collude in a relational narrative that doesn't always jibe with the facts. They agree that they rarely have conflict, although objective analysis reveals that they have had their share of disagreements and challenges. Without overtly agreeing to do so, they choose to blame outside forces or unusual circumstances for problems instead of attributing responsibility to one another. They offer the most charitable interpretations of one another's behavior, believing that the spouse acts with good intentions when things don't go well. They seem willing to forgive, or even forget, transgressions. Examining this research, one scholar concludes:

> Should we conclude that happy couples have a poor grip on reality? Perhaps they do, but is the reality of one's marriage better known by outside onlookers than by the players themselves? The conclusion is evident. One key to a long happy marriage is to tell yourself and others that you have one and then to behave as though you do![40]

Common Perceptual Tendencies

Shared narratives may be desirable, but they can be hard to achieve. Some of the biggest problems that interfere with understanding and agreement arise from errors in what psychologists call **attribution**—the process of attaching meaning to behavior. We attribute meaning to both our own actions and the actions of others, but we often use different yardsticks. Research has uncovered several perceptual errors that can lead to inaccurate attributions—and to troublesome communication.[41] By becoming aware of these errors, we can guard against them and avoid unnecessary conflicts.

We Make Snap Judgments   Our ancestors often had to make quick judgments about whether strangers were likely to be dangerous, and there are still times when this ability can be a survival skill.[42] But there are many cases when judging others without enough knowledge or information can get us into trouble. If you've ever been written off by a potential employer in the first few minutes of an interview, or have been unfairly rebuffed by someone you just met, then you know the feeling. Snap judgments become particularly problematic when they are based on **stereotyping**—exaggerated beliefs associated with a categorizing system. Stereotypes based on "primitive categories" like race, sex, and age may be founded on a kernel of truth, but they go beyond the facts at hand and make claims that usually have no valid basis.[43]

Three characteristics distinguish stereotypes from reasonable generalizations:

- *Categorizing others on the basis of easily recognized but not necessarily significant characteristics.* For example, perhaps the first thing you notice about a person is his or her skin color—but that may not be nearly as significant as the person's intelligence or achievements.

- *Ascribing a set of characteristics to most or all members of a group.* For example, you might unfairly assume that all older people are doddering or that all men are insensitive to women's concerns.

- *Applying the generalization to a particular person.* Once you believe all old people are geezers and all men are jerks, it's a short step to considering a particular senior citizen as senile, or a particular man as a chauvinist pig.

By adulthood, we tend to engage in stereotyping frequently, effortlessly, and often unconsciously.[44] Once we create and hold stereotypes, we seek out isolated behaviors that support our inaccurate beliefs. For example, men and women in conflict with each other often remember only behaviors of the opposite sex that fit their stereotypes.[45] They then point to these behaviors—which might not be representative of how the other person typically behaves—as "evidence" to suit their stereotypical and inaccurate claims: "Look! There you go criticizing me again. Typical for a woman!"

> Once we create and hold stereotypes, we seek out isolated behaviors that support our inaccurate beliefs.

Stereotypes can plague interracial communication.[46] For example, surveys of college-student attitudes show that many blacks characterize whites as "demanding" and "manipulative," while many whites describe blacks as "loud" and "ostentatious." Many African American women report having been raised with stereotypical characterizations of whites (e.g., "Most whites cannot be trusted").

One way to avoid the kinds of communication problems that come from excessive stereotyping is to "decategorize" others, giving yourself a chance to treat people as individuals instead of assuming that they possess the same characteristics as every other member of the group to which you assign them.

We Often Judge Ourselves More Charitably Than We Judge Others   In an attempt to convince ourselves and others that the positive face we show to the world is true, we tend to judge ourselves in the most generous terms possible. Social scientists have labeled this tendency the **self-serving bias**.[47] When others suffer, we often blame the problem on their personal qualities. On the other hand, when we suffer, we find explanations outside ourselves. Consider a few examples:

- When they botch a job, we might think they weren't listening well or trying hard enough; when we botch a job, the problem was unclear directions or not enough time.

- When he lashes out angrily, we say he's being moody or too sensitive; when we blow off steam, it's because of the pressure we've been under.

- When she gets caught speeding, we say she should have been more careful; when we get caught, we deny we were driving too fast or we say, "Everybody does it."

The egocentric tendency to rate ourselves more favorably than others see us has been demonstrated experimentally.[48] In one study, members of a random sample of men were asked to rank themselves on their ability to get along with others.[49] Defying mathematical laws, all subjects—every last one—put themselves in the top half of the population. Sixty percent rated themselves in the top 10 percent of the population, and an amazing 25 percent believed they were in the top 1 percent. In the same study, 70 percent of the men ranked their leadership in the top 25 percent of the population, whereas only 2 percent thought they were below average. Sixty percent said they were

CULTURAL IDIOM

lashes out:
attacks verbally

blow off steam:
release excess energy or anger

in the top 25 percent in athletic abilities, whereas only 6 percent viewed themselves as below average.

Evidence like this suggests how uncharitable attitudes toward others can affect communication. Your harsh opinions of others can lead to judgmental messages, and self-serving defenses of your own actions can result in a defensive response when others question your behavior.

We Pay More Attention to Negative Impressions Than Positive Ones What do you think about Harvey? He's handsome, hardworking, intelligent, and honest. He's also very conceited.

Did the last quality mentioned make a difference in your evaluation? If it did, you're not alone. Research shows that when people are aware of both the positive and negative traits of another, they tend to be more influenced by the negative traits. In one study, for example, researchers found that job interviewers were likely to reject candidates who revealed negative information even when the total amount of information was highly positive.[50]

Sometimes this attitude makes sense. If the negative quality clearly outweighs any positive ones, you'd be foolish to ignore it. A surgeon with shaky hands and a teacher who hates children, for example, would be unsuitable for their jobs whatever their other virtues. But much of the time it's a bad idea to pay excessive attention to negative qualities and overlook positive ones. This is the mistake some people make when screening potential friends or dates. They find some who are too outgoing or too reserved, others who aren't intelligent enough, and still others who have the wrong sense of humor. Of course, it's important to find people you truly enjoy, but expecting perfection can lead to much unnecessary loneliness.

We Are Influenced by What Is Most Obvious Every time we encounter another person, we are bombarded with more information than we can possibly manage. You can appreciate this by spending two or three minutes just reporting on what you can observe about another person through your five senses. ("Now I see you blinking your eyes . . . Now I notice you smiling . . . Now I hear you laugh and then sigh . . . Now I notice you're wearing a red shirt . . .") You will find that the list seems almost endless and that every time you seem to near the end, a new observation presents itself.

Faced with this tidal wave of sense data, we need to whittle down the amount of information we will use to make sense of others. There are three factors that cause us to notice some messages and ignore others. For example, we pay attention to stimuli that are *intense* (loud music, brightly dressed people), *repetitious* (dripping faucets, persistent people), or *contrastive* (a normally happy person who acts grumpy or vice versa). *Motives* also determine what information we select from our environment. If you're anxious about being late for a date, you'll notice whatever clocks may be around you; if you're hungry, you'll become aware of any restaurants, markets, and billboards advertising food in your path. Motives also determine how we perceive people.

If intense, repetitious, or contrastive information were the most important thing to know about others, there would be no problem. But the most noticeable behavior of others isn't always the most important. For example:

- When two children (or adults, for that matter) fight, it may be a mistake to blame the one who lashes out first. Perhaps the other one was at least equally responsible, by teasing or refusing to cooperate.

■ You might complain about an acquaintance whose malicious gossiping or arguing has become a bother, forgetting that, by previously tolerating that kind of behavior, you have been at least partially responsible.

■ You might blame an unhappy working situation on the boss, overlooking other factors beyond her control such as a change in the economy, the policy of higher management, or demands of customers or other workers.

We Cling to First Impressions, Even If Wrong   Labeling people according to our first impressions is an inevitable part of the perception process. These labels are a way of making interpretations. "She seems cheerful." "He seems sincere." "They sound awfully conceited."

If they're accurate, impressions like these can be useful ways of deciding how to respond best to people in the future. Problems arise, however, when the labels we attach are inaccurate, because after we form an opinion of someone, we tend to hang on to it and make any conflicting information fit our image.

Suppose, for instance, you mention the name of your new neighbor to a friend. "Oh, I know him," your friend replies. "He seems nice at first, but it's all an act." Perhaps this appraisal is off-base. The neighbor may have changed since your friend knew him, or perhaps your friend's judgment is simply unfair. Whether the judgment is accurate or not, after you accept your friend's evaluation, it will probably influence the way you respond to the neighbor. You'll look for examples of the insincerity you've heard about—and you'll probably find them. Even if the neighbor were a saint, you would be likely to interpret his behavior in ways that fit your expectations. "Sure he *seems* nice," you might think, "but it's probably just a front." As you read earlier in this chapter, this sort of suspicion can create a self-fulfilling prophecy, transforming a genuinely nice person into someone who truly becomes an undesirable neighbor as he reacts to your suspicious behavior.

The power of first impressions is important in personal relationships. A study of college roommates found that those who had positive initial impressions of each other were likely to have positive subsequent interactions, manage their conflicts constructively, and continue living together.[51] The converse was also true: Roommates who got off to a bad start tended to spiral negatively. This reinforces the wisdom and importance of the old adage, "You never get a second chance to make a first impression."

Given the almost unavoidable tendency to form first impressions, the best advice we can offer is to keep an open mind and be willing to change your opinion as events prove that the first impressions were mistaken.

We Tend to Assume That Others Are Similar to Us   People commonly imagine that others possess the same attitudes and motives that they do. For example, research shows that people with low self-esteem imagine that others view them unfavorably, whereas people who like themselves imagine that others like them, too.[52] The frequently mistaken assumption that others' views are similar to our own applies in a wide range of situations. For example:

■ You've heard a raunchy joke that you found funny. You might assume that it won't offend a somewhat conservative friend. It does.

■ You've been bothered by an instructor's tendency to get off the subject during lectures. If you were a professor, you'd want to know if anything you were doing was creating problems for your students, so you decide that your instructor will probably be grateful for some constructive criticism. Unfortunately, you're wrong.

■ You lost your temper with a friend a week ago and said some things you regret. In fact, if someone said those things to you, you would consider the relationship finished. Imagining that your friend feels the same way, you avoid making contact. In fact, your friend feels that he was partly responsible and has avoided you because he thinks you're the one who wants to end things.

Examples like these show that others don't always think or feel the way we do and that assuming that similarities exist can lead to problems. For example, one study revealed that men evaluate women who initiate first dates as being more interested in sex than do the women who initiated the dates.[53]

How can you find out the other person's real position? Sometimes by asking directly, sometimes by checking with others, and sometimes by making an educated guess after you've thought the matter out. All these alternatives are better than simply assuming that everyone would react the way you do.

Don't misunderstand: We don't always commit the kind of perceptual errors described in this section. Sometimes, for instance, people are responsible for their misfortunes, and sometimes our problems are not our fault.

Likewise, the most obvious interpretation of a situation may be the correct one. Nonetheless, a large amount of research has proved again and again that our perceptions of others are often distorted in the ways listed here. The moral, then, is clear: Don't assume that your first judgment of a person is accurate.

> Don't assume that your first judgment of a person is accurate.

Perception in Mediated Communication

As the cartoon on this page suggests, mediated communication offers fewer cues about others than you get in face-to-face interaction. As you read in Chapter 2, the ability to edit a message before posting makes it easy to craft an identity that doesn't match what you would encounter in person.

Despite the apparent barriers to accurate perception in mediated channels, people can form accurate impressions of one another over mediated channels—though not in the same ways as when they communicate in person.[54] Whereas first impressions dominate perception in person, the process takes longer online due to fewer cues and the asynchronous nature of interaction.[55]

In text-based channels, receivers depend more heavily on the writing style[56] and symbols (e.g., smiley-faced emoticons)[57] to get a sense of the sender. Once you know how to spot them, other cues abound. For example, spelling errors create impressions about the writer.[58] The time it takes to get a response to your message also shapes perceptions.[59] A quick reply to your invitation suggests different things than does a long delay.

"On the Internet, nobody knows you're a dog."

Perception and Culture

Perceptual differences make communication challenging enough between members of the same culture. But when communicators come from different cultures, the potential for misunderstandings is even greater.

Culture provides a perceptual filter that influences the way we interpret even the simplest events. This fact was demonstrated in studies exploring the domination of vision in one eye over the other.[60] Researchers used a binocularlike device that projects different images to each eye. The subjects were twelve Americans and twelve Mexicans. Each was presented with ten pairs of photographs, each pair containing one picture from U.S. culture (e.g., a baseball game) and one from Mexican culture (e.g., a bullfight). After viewing each pair of images, the subjects reported what they saw. The results clearly indicated the power of culture to influence perceptions: Subjects had a strong tendency to see the image from their own background.

The same principle causes people from different cultures to interpret similar events in different ways. Blinking while another person talks may be hardly noticeable to North Americans, but the same behavior is considered impolite in Taiwan. The beckoning finger motion that is familiar to Americans is an insulting gesture in most Middle and Far Eastern countries.

Even beliefs about the very value of talk differ from one culture to another.[61] North American culture views talk as desirable and uses it to achieve social purposes as well as to perform tasks. Silence in conversational situations has a negative value. It is likely to be interpreted as lack of interest, unwillingness to communicate, hostility, anxiety, shyness, or a sign of interpersonal incompatibility. Furthermore, the kind of talk that Westerners admire is characterized by straightforwardness and honesty. Being indirect or vague—"beating around the bush," it might be labeled—has a negative connotation.

On the other hand, most Asian cultures discourage the expression of thoughts and feelings. Silence is valued, as Taoist sayings indicate: "In much talk there is great weariness," or "One who speaks does not know; one who knows does not speak." Unlike Westerners, who are uncomfortable with silence, Japanese and Chinese believe that remaining quiet is the proper state when there is nothing to be said. To Easterners, a talkative person is often considered a show-off or insincere. And when an Asian does speak up on social matters, the message is likely to be phrased indirectly to "save face" for the recipient.

It is easy to see how these different views of speech and silence can lead to communication problems when people from different cultures meet. Both the talkative Westerner and the silent Easterner are behaving in ways they believe are proper, yet each views the other with disapproval and mistrust. This may require them to recognize and deal with their **ethnocentrism**—the attitude that one's own culture is superior to others. An ethnocentric person thinks—either privately or openly—that anyone who does not belong to his or her in-group is somehow strange, wrong, or even inferior. Only when people recognize the different standards of behavior can they adapt to one another, or at least understand and respect their differences.

> Different views of speech and silence can lead to communication problems when people from different cultures meet.

Perceptual differences are just as important right at home when members of different cocultures interact. Failure to recognize cocultural differences can lead to unfortunate and unnecessary misunderstandings. For example, an uninformed white teacher or police officer might interpret the downcast eyes of a Latino female as a sign of avoidance, or even dishonesty, when in fact this is the proper behavior in her culture for a female being addressed by an older man. To make direct eye contact in such a case would be considered undue brashness or even a sexual come-on.

Cross-cultural differences can be quite subtle. For example, one study revealed that, when meeting with academic counselors, Latinos preferred to be respected as members of their own culture as well as individuals. On the other hand, blacks preferred to be acknowledged as individuals rather than being identified as members of an ethnic group.[62]

CULTURAL IDIOM

save face:
protect one's dignity, presenting self

come-on:
sexual advance

Along with ethnicity, geography also can influence perception. A fascinating series of studies revealed that climate and geographic latitude were remarkably accurate predictors of communication predispositions.[63] People living in southern latitudes of the United States are more socially isolated, less tolerant of ambiguity, higher in self-esteem, more likely to touch others, and more likely to verbalize their thoughts and feelings. This sort of finding helps explain why communicators who travel from one part of a country to another find that their old patterns of communicating don't work as well in their new location. A southerner whose relatively talkative, high-touch style seemed completely normal at home might be viewed as pushy and aggressive in a new northern home.

Empathy, Perception, and Communication

By now it's clear that differing perceptions present a major challenge to communicators. One solution is to increase the ability to empathize. **Empathy** is the ability to re-create another person's perspective, to experience the world from the other's point of view.

Dimensions of Empathy   As we'll use the term here, *empathy* has three dimensions.[64] On one level, empathy involves *perspective taking*—the ability to take on the viewpoint of another person. This understanding requires a suspension of judgment, so that for the moment you set aside your own opinions and take on those of the other person. Besides cognitive understanding, empathy also has an *emotional* dimension that allows us to experience the feelings that others have. We know their fear, joy, sadness, and so on. When we combine the perspective-taking and emotional dimensions, we see that empathizing allows us to experience the other's perception—in effect, to become that person temporarily. A third dimension of empathy is a genuine *concern* for the welfare of the other person. When we empathize we go beyond just thinking and feeling as others do and genuinely care about their well-being.

> When you sympathize, it is the other's confusion, joy, or pain. When you empathize, the experience becomes your own, at least for the moment.

It is easy to confuse empathy with **sympathy**, but the concepts are different in two important ways. First, sympathy means you feel compassion for another person's predicament, whereas empathy means you have a personal sense of what that predicament is like. Consider the difference between sympathizing with an unwed mother or a homeless person and empathizing with them—imagining what it would be like to be in their position. Despite your concern, sympathy lacks the degree of identification that empathy entails. When you sympathize, it is the other's confusion, joy, or pain. When you empathize, the experience becomes your own, at least for the moment. Both perspectives are important ones, but empathy is clearly the more complete of the two.

Empathy is different from sympathy in a second way. We only sympathize when we accept the reasons for another's pain as valid, whereas it's possible to empathize without feeling sympathy. You can empathize with a difficult relative, a rude stranger, or even a criminal without feeling much sympathy for that person. Empathizing allows you to understand another person's motives without

"How would you feel if the mouse did that to you?"

requiring you to agree with them. After empathizing, you will almost certainly understand a person better, but sympathy won't always follow.

The ability to empathize seems to exist in a rudimentary form in even the youngest children.[65] Virtually from birth, infants become visibly upset when they hear another infant crying, and children who are a few months old cry when they observe another child crying. Young children have trouble distinguishing others' distress from their own. If, for example, one child hurts his finger, another child might put her own finger in her mouth as if she were feeling pain. Researchers report cases in which children who see their parents crying wipe their own eyes, even though they are not crying.

Although infants and toddlers may have a basic capacity to empathize, studies with twins suggest that the degree to which we are born with the ability to sense how others are feeling varies according to genetic factors. Although some people may have an inborn edge, environmental experiences are the key to developing the ability to understand others. Specifically, the way in which parents communicate with their children seems to affect their ability to understand others' emotional states. When parents point out to children the distress that others feel from their misbehavior ("Look how sad Jessica is because you took her toy. Wouldn't you be sad if someone took away your toys?"), those children gain a greater appreciation that their acts have emotional consequences than they do when parents simply label behavior as inappropriate ("That was a mean thing to do!").

There is no consistent evidence that suggests that the ability to empathize is greater for one sex or the other.[66] Some people, however, seem to have a hereditary capacity for greater empathizing than do others.[67] Studies of identical and fraternal twins indicate that identical female twins are more similar to one another in their ability to empathize than are fraternal twins. Interestingly, there seems to be no difference between males. Although empathy may have a biological basis, environment can still play an important role. For example, parents who are sensitive to their children's feelings tend to have children who reach out to others.[68]

Total empathy is impossible to achieve. Completely understanding another person's point of view is simply too difficult a task for humans with different backgrounds and limited communication skills. Nonetheless, it is possible to get a strong sense of what the world looks like through another person's eyes.

A willingness to empathize can make a difference in everyday disputes. For example, communication researchers have spelled out how understanding opposing views can increase understanding and constructive problem solving in conflicts between environmentalists who want to preserve native species and landowners who want to earn a profit. After the parties begin to see one another's point of view, they can discover ways of protecting native species *and* allow landowners to carry on their enterprises.[69]

> A willingness to empathize can make a difference in everyday disputes.

Perception Checking   Good intentions and a strong effort to empathize are one way to understand others. Along with a positive attitude, however, there is a simple tool that can help you interpret the behavior of others more accurately. To see how this tool operates, consider how often others jump to mistaken conclusions about your thoughts, feelings, and motives:

"Why are you mad at me?" (Who said you were?)

"What's the matter with you?" (Who said anything was the matter?)

"Come on now. Tell the truth." (Who said you were lying?)

Cathy

As you'll learn in Chapter 7, even if your interpretation is correct, a dogmatic, mind-reading statement is likely to generate defensiveness. The skill of **perception checking** provides a better way to handle your interpretations. A complete perception check has three parts:

- A description of the behavior you noticed;
- At least two possible interpretations of the behavior;
- A request for clarification about how to interpret the behavior.

Perception checks for the preceding three examples would look like this:

"When you stomped out of the room and slammed the door *[behavior]*, I wasn't sure whether you were mad at me *[first interpretation]* or just in a hurry *[second interpretation]*. How did you feel *[request for clarification]*?"

"You haven't laughed much in the last couple of days *[behavior]*. I wonder whether something's bothering you *[first interpretation]* or whether you're just feeling quiet *[second interpretation]*. What's up *[request for clarification]*?"

"You said you really liked the job I did *[behavior]*, but there was something about your voice that made me think you may not like it *[first interpretation]*. Maybe it's just my imagination, though *[second interpretation]*. How do you really feel *[request for clarification]*?"

Perception checking is a tool for helping us understand others accurately instead of assuming that our first interpretation is correct. Because its goal is mutual understanding, perception checking is a cooperative approach to communication. Besides leading to more accurate perceptions, it minimizes defensiveness by preserving the other person's face. Instead of saying in effect "I know what you're thinking . . ." a perception check takes the more respectful approach that states or implies "I know I'm not qualified to judge you without some help."

Sometimes a perception check won't need all of the parts listed earlier to be effective:

"You haven't dropped by lately. Is anything the matter *[single interpretation combined with request for clarification]*?"

"I can't tell whether you're kidding me about being cheap or if you're serious *[behavior combined with interpretations]*. Are you mad at me?"

"Are you sure you don't mind driving? I can use a ride if it's no trouble, but I don't want to take you out of your way *[no need to describe behavior]*."

Of course, a perception check can succeed only if your nonverbal behavior reflects the open-mindedness of your words. An accusing tone of voice or a hostile glare will contradict the sincerely worded request for clarification, suggesting that you have already made up your mind about the other person's intentions.

Communication and Identity Management

So far we have described how communication shapes the way communicators view themselves and others. In the remainder of this chapter we turn the tables and focus on **identity management**—the communication strategies people use to influence how others view them. In the following pages you will see that many of our messages aim at creating desired impressions.

Public and Private Selves

To understand why identity management exists, we have to discuss the notion of self in more detail. So far we have referred to the "self" as if each of us had only one identity. In truth, each of us possesses several selves, some private and others public. Often these selves are quite different.

The **perceived self** is a reflection of the self-concept. Your perceived self is the person you believe yourself to be in moments of honest self-examination. We can call the perceived self "private" because you are unlikely to reveal all of it to another person. You can verify the private nature of the perceived self by reviewing the self-concept list you developed while reading pages 61–62. You'll probably find some elements of yourself there that you would not disclose to many people, and some that you would not share with anyone. You might, for example, be reluctant to share some feelings about your appearance ("I think I'm rather unattractive"), your intelligence ("I'm not as smart as I wish I were"), your goals ("the most important thing to me is becoming rich"), or your motives ("I care more about myself than about others").

"Hah! This is the Old King Cole nobody ever sees."

TABLE 3-1   Self-Selected Adjectives Describing Perceived and Presenting Selves of College Students

| PERCEIVED SELF | | PRESENTING SELF | |
MEN	WOMEN	MEN	WOMEN
1. Friendly	1. Friendly	1. Wild	1. Active
2. Active	2. Responsible	2. Able	2. Responsible
3. Responsible	3. Independent	3. Active	3. Able
4. Independent	4. Capable	4. Strong	4. Bright
5. Capable	5. Sensible	5. Proud	5. Warm
6. Polite	6. Active	6. Smart	6. Funny
7. Attractive	7. Happy	7. Brave	7. Independent
8. Smart	8. Curious	8. Capable	8. Proud
9. Happy	9. Faithful	9. Responsible	9. Sensible
10. Funny	10. Attractive	10. Rough	10. Smart

Adapted from C. M. Shaw and R. Edwards, "Self-Concepts and Self-Presentations of Males and Females: Similarities and Differences," *Communication Reports* 10 (1997): 55–62.

In contrast to the perceived self, the **presenting self** is a public image—the way we want to appear to others.

In most cases the presenting self we seek to create is a socially approved image: diligent student, loving partner, conscientious worker, loyal friend, and so on. Social norms often create a gap between the perceived and presenting selves. For instance, Table 3-1 shows that the self-concepts of the members of one group of male and female college students were quite similar, but that their public selves were different in several respects from both their private selves and the public selves of the opposite sex.[70]

Sociologist Erving Goffman used the word **face** to describe the presenting self, and he coined the term **facework** to describe the verbal and nonverbal ways we act to maintain our own presenting image and the images of others.[71] He argued that each of us can be viewed as a kind of playwright, who creates roles that we want others to believe, as well as the performer who acts out those roles.

Facework involves two tasks: Managing our own identity and communicating in ways that reinforce the identities that others are trying to present.[72] You can see how these two goals operate by recalling a time when you've used self-deprecating humor to defuse a potentially unpleasant situation. Suppose, for example, that a friend gave you confusing directions to a party that caused you to be late. "Sorry I got lost," you might have said. "I'm a terrible navigator." This sort of mild self-putdown accomplishes two things at once: It preserves the other person's face by implicitly saying "It's not your fault." At the same time, your mild self-debasement shows that you're a nice person who doesn't find faults in others or make a big issue out of small problems.[73]

Characteristics of Identity Management

Now that you have a sense of what identity management is, we can look at some characteristics of this process.

We Have Multiple Identities   In the course of even a single day, most people play a variety of roles: respectful student, joking friend, friendly neighbor, and helpful worker, to suggest just a few. We even play a variety of roles with the same person. As you grew up you almost certainly changed characters as you interacted with your parents. In one context you acted as the responsible adult ("You can trust me with the car!"), and in another context you were the helpless child ("I can't find my socks!"). At some times—perhaps on birthdays or holidays—you were a dedicated family member, and at other times you may have played the role of rebel. Likewise, in romantic relationships we switch among many ways of behaving, depending on the context: friend, lover, business partner, scolding critic, apologetic child, and so on.

The ability to construct multiple identities is one element of communication competence. For example, the style of speaking or even the language itself can reflect a choice about how to construct one's identity. We recall an African American colleague who was also minister of a Southern Baptist congregation consisting mostly of black members. On campus his manner of speaking was typically professorial, but a visit to hear him preach one Sunday revealed a speaker whose style was much more animated and theatrical, reflecting his identity in that context. Likewise, one scholar pointed out that bilingual Latinos in the United States often choose whether to use English or Spanish depending on the kind of identity they are seeking in a given conversation.[74]

Identity Management Is Collaborative   As we perform like actors trying to create a front, our "audience" is made up of other actors who are trying to create their own characters. Identity-related communication is a kind of process theater in which we collaborate with other actors to improvise scenes in which our characters mesh.

You can appreciate the collaborative nature of identity management by thinking about how you might handle a gripe with a friend or family member who has failed to pass along a phone message that arrived while you were away from home. Suppose that you decide to raise the issue tactfully in an effort to avoid seeming like a nag (desired role for yourself: "nice person") and also to save the other person from the embarrassment of being confronted (hoping to avoid suggesting that the other person's role is "screw-up"). If your tactful bid is accepted, the dialogue might sound like this:

You: ". . . By the way, Jenny told me she called yesterday. If you wrote a note, I guess I missed seeing it."

Other: "Oh . . . sorry. I meant to write a note, but as soon as I hung up, the doorbell rang, and then I had to run off to class."

You: *(in friendly tone of voice)* "That's okay. I sure would appreciate from now on if you'd leave me a note."

Other: "No problem."

In this upbeat conversation, both you and the other person accepted one another's bids for identity as basically thoughtful people. As a result, the conversation ran smoothly. Imagine, though, how different the outcome would be if the other person didn't accept your role as "nice person":

You: ". . . By the way, Jenny told me she called yesterday. If you wrote a note, I guess I missed seeing it."

Other: *(defensively)* "Okay, so I forgot. It's not that big a deal. You're not perfect yourself, you know!"

Understanding Diversity

Managing Identity and Coming Out

I grew up in a mid-size town in Mexico. My siblings and I were taught to never do anything to "dishonor" the name of our family.

From a very early age I sensed I was not a boy who liked girls. My father was very involved in Mexican rodeo, and he expected me to ride a horse, rope, and deal with cattle. I quit when I was twelve. My dad never understood why.

Middle school was hard. I coped with bullies by being funny and making fun of others before they could make fun of me. I had a girlfriend for a year. It was all pretend but it helped ease the harassment. By high school I knew was gay and wanted to live openly. But my religious upbringing, peer group, and family's reputation were all in the way of me coming out.

I started living a double life during college. Guilt became the main emotion I felt. I became very cold and distant with everyone in my family. To cover up my identity, I had a girlfriend for three years. After college I met the first openly gay men who were comfortable

and happy. I fell in love with one of them and he helped me understand that I needed to have the courage to accept who I am and to stop hiding this from my family.

It took three more years for me to come out to my siblings. Those were the hardest conversations I have ever endured. My siblings urged me to not tell my parents, who they said would be upset and saddened. Unfortunately I followed their suggestion and my mom passed without me ever sharing this part of myself. Still, I am sure she knew the truth. I have never told my dad directly that I am gay. When we talk, he always asks me how I am doing and how John (my partner) is doing. That is his way of letting me know he knows.

I can sleep much better at night since I came out sixteen years ago. Since then, I have stopped worrying what others think about me. There is no guilt and I feel complete. I know I am happy.

J. C. Rivas

Your first bid as "nice, face-saving person" was rejected. At this point you have the choice of persisting in trying to play the original role: "Hey, I'm not mad at you, and I know I'm not perfect!" Or, you might switch to the new role of "unjustly accused person," responding with aggravation "I never said I was perfect. But we're not talking about me here . . ."

As this example illustrates, *collaboration* doesn't mean the same thing as *agreement*.[75] The small issue of the phone message might mushroom into a fight in which you and the other person both adopt the role of combatants. The point here is that virtually all conversations provide an arena in which communicators construct their identities in response to the behavior of others. As you read in Chapter 1, communication isn't made up of discrete events that can be separated from one another. Instead, what happens at one moment is influenced by what each party brings to the interaction and by what happened in their relationship up to that point.

> Virtually all conversations provide an arena in which communicators construct their identities.

Identity Management Can Be Conscious or Unconscious   At this point you might object to the notion of strategic identity management, claiming that most of your communication is spontaneous and not a deliberate attempt to present yourself in a certain way. However, you might acknowledge that some of your communication involves a conscious attempt to manage impressions.

There's no doubt that sometimes we are highly aware of managing our identities. Most job interviews and first dates are clear examples of conscious identity management. But in other cases we unconsciously act in ways that are really small public performances.[76] For example, experimental subjects expressed facial disgust in reaction to eating sandwiches laced with a supersaturated saltwater solution only when there was

CULTURAL IDIOM

"face-saving person":
person who preserves the self-image of another

might mushroom:
might escalate

another person present: When they were alone, they made no faces when eating the same sandwiches.[77] Another study showed that communicators engage in facial mimicry (such as smiling or looking sympathetic in response to another's message) in face-to-face settings only when their expressions can be seen by the other person. When they are speaking over the phone and their reactions cannot be seen, they do not make the same expressions.[78] Studies like these suggest that most of our behavior is aimed at sending messages to others—in other words, identity management.

The experimental subjects described in the last paragraph didn't consciously think, "Somebody is watching me eat this salty sandwich, so I'll make a face," or, "Since I'm in a face-to-face conversation I'll show I'm sympathetic by mimicking the facial expressions of my conversational partner." Reactions like these are often instantaneous and outside of our conscious awareness.

In the same way, many of our choices about how to act in the array of daily interactions aren't deliberate, strategic decisions. Rather, they rely on "scripts" that we have developed over time. You probably have a variety of roles for managing your identity from which to choose in familiar situations such as dealing with strangers, treating customers at work, interacting with family members, and so on. When you find yourself in familiar situations like these, you probably slip into these roles quite often. Only when those roles don't seem quite right do you deliberately construct an approach that reflects how you want the scene to play out.

Despite the claims of some theorists, it seems like an exaggeration to suggest that all behavior is aimed at managing identities. Young children certainly aren't strategic communicators. A baby spontaneously laughs when pleased, and cries when sad or uncomfortable, without any notion of creating an impression in others. Likewise, there are almost certainly times when we, as adults, act spontaneously. But when a significant other questions the self we try to present, the likelihood of acting to prop it up increases. This process isn't always conscious: At a nonconscious level of awareness we monitor others' reactions and swing into action when our face is threatened—especially by significant others.[79]

People Differ in Their Degree of Identity Management   Some people are much more aware of their identity management behavior than others. These high self-monitors have the ability to pay attention to their own behavior and others' reactions, adjusting their communication to create the desired impression. By contrast, low self-monitors express what they are thinking and feeling without much attention to the impression their behavior creates.[84]

There are certainly advantages to being a high self-monitor.[85] People who pay attention to themselves are generally good actors who can create the impression they want, acting interested when bored, or friendly when they really feel quite the opposite. This allows them to handle social situations smoothly, often putting others at ease. They are also good "people-readers" who can adjust their behavior to get the desired reaction from others. Along with these advantages, there are some potential disadvantages to being an extremely high self-monitor. The analytical nature of high self-monitors may prevent them from experiencing events completely, because a portion of their attention will always be viewing the situation from a detached position. High self-monitors' ability to act means that it is difficult to tell how they are really feeling. In fact, because high self-monitors change roles often, they may have a hard time knowing themselves how they really feel.

CULTURAL IDIOM

"scripts":
reflexive responses

play out:
proceed to a conclusion

People who score low on the self-monitoring scale live life quite differently from their more self-conscious counterparts. They have a simpler, more focused idea of who they are and who they want to be. Low self-monitors are likely to have a narrower repertoire of behaviors, so that they can be expected to act in more or less the same way regardless of the situation. This means that low self-monitors are easy to read. "What you see is what you get" might be their motto. Although this lack of flexibility may make their social interaction less smooth in many situations, low self-monitors can be counted on to be straightforward communicators.

> Neither extremely high nor low self-monitoring is the ideal.

By now it should be clear that neither extremely high nor low self-monitoring is the ideal. There are some situations when paying attention to yourself and adapting your behavior can be useful, but there are other situations when reacting without considering the effect on others is a better approach. This need for a range of behaviors demonstrates again the notion of communicative competence outlined in Chapter 1: Flexibility is the key to successful relationships.

Why Manage Identities?

Why bother trying to shape others' opinions? Sometimes we create and maintain a front to follow social rules. As children we learn to act polite, even when bored. Likewise, part of growing up consists of developing a set of manners for various occasions: meeting strangers, attending school, going to religious services, and so on. Young children who haven't learned all the do's and don'ts of polite society often embarrass their parents by behaving inappropriately ("Mommy, why is that man so fat?"), but by the time they enter school, behavior that might have been excusable or even amusing just isn't acceptable. Good manners are often aimed at making others more comfortable. For

CULTURAL IDIOM
front:
a pretense

@Work

Identity Management in the Workplace

Some advisors encourage workers to "Just be yourself" on the job. But there are times when disclosing certain information about your personal life can damage your chances for success.[80] This is especially true for people with "invisible stigmas"—traits that run the risk of being viewed unfavorably.[81]

Many parts of a worker's identity have the potential to be invisible stigmas: religion (evangelical Christian, Muslim), sexual orientation (gay, lesbian, bisexual), health (bipolar, HIV positive). What counts as a stigma to some people (politically progressive, conservative) might be favored in another organization.[82]

As you consider how to manage your identity at work, consider the following:

■ *Proceed with caution.*

In an ideal world, everyone would be free to reveal themselves without hesitation. But in real life, total candor can have consequences, so it can be best to move slowly.

■ *Assess the organization's culture.*

If your workplace seems supportive of differences—and especially if it appears to welcome people like you—then revealing more of yourself may be safe.

■ *Consider the consequences of not opening up.*

Keeping an important part of your identity secret can also take an emotional toll.[83] If keeping quiet is truly necessary, you may be better off finding a more welcoming place to work.

■ *Test the waters.*

If you have a trusted colleague or manager, think about revealing yourself to that person and asking advice about whether and how to go further. But realize that even close secrets can leak, so be sure the person you approach can keep confidences.

example, able-bodied people often mask their discomfort upon encountering someone who is disabled by acting nonchalant or stressing similarities between themselves and the disabled person.[86]

Social rules govern our behavior in a variety of settings. It would be impossible to keep a job, for example, without meeting certain expectations. Salespeople are obliged to treat customers with courtesy. Employees need to appear reasonably respectful when talking to the boss. Some forms of clothing would be considered outrageous at work. By agreeing to take on a job, you are signing an unwritten contract that you will present a certain face at work, whether or not that face reflects the way you might be feeling at a particular moment.

> Social rules govern our behavior in a variety of settings.

Even when social roles don't dictate the proper way to behave, we often manage identities for a second reason: to accomplish personal goals. You might, for example, dress up for a visit to traffic court in the hope that your front (responsible citizen) will convince the judge to treat you sympathetically. You might act sociable to your neighbors so they will agree to your request that they keep their dog off your lawn. We also try to create a desired impression to achieve one or more of the social needs described in Chapter 1: affection, inclusion, control, and so on. For instance, you might act more friendly and lively than you feel upon meeting a new person, so that you will appear likable. You could sigh and roll your eyes when arguing politics with a classmate to gain an advantage in an argument. You might smile and preen to show the attractive stranger at a party that you would like to get better acquainted. In situations like these you aren't being deceptive as much as putting "your best foot forward."

All these examples show that it is difficult—even impossible—not to create impressions. After all, you have to send some sort of message. If you don't act friendly when meeting a stranger, you have to act aloof, indifferent, hostile, or in some other manner. If you don't act businesslike, you have to behave in an alternative way: casual, goofy, or whatever. Often the question isn't whether or not to present a face to others; the question is only which face to present.

Identity Management in Mediated Communication

At first glance, computer-mediated communication (CMC) seems to have limited potential for identity management. As you read in Chapter 2, text-based messages lack the "richness" of other channels. They don't convey the postures, gestures, or facial expressions that are an important part of face-to-face communication. They even lack the vocal information available in telephone messages. These limitations might seem to make it harder to create and manage an identity when communicating via computer.

Recently, though, communication scholars have begun to recognize that what is missing in CMC can actually be an advantage for communicators who want to manage the impressions they make.[87] E-mail authors can edit their messages until they create just the desired impression.[88] They can choose the desired level of clarity or ambiguity, seriousness or humor, logic or emotion. Unlike face-to-face communication, electronic correspondence allows

CULTURAL IDIOM

putting "your best foot forward":
making the best appearance possible

"richness":
completeness

a sender to say difficult things without forcing the receiver to respond immediately, and it permits the receiver to ignore a message rather than give an unpleasant response. Options like these show that CMC can serve as a tool for impression management at least as well as face-to-face communication.

CMC generally gives us more control over managing identities than we have in face-to-face communication. Asynchronous forms of CMC like e-mail, blogs, and web pages allow you to edit your messages until you convey the right impression. With e-mail (and, to a lesser degree, with texting and instant messaging) you can compose difficult messages without forcing the receiver to respond immediately, and ignore others' messages rather than give an unpleasant response. Perhaps most important, with CMC you don't have to worry about stammering or blushing, apparel or appearance, or any other unseen factor that might detract from the impression you want to create.

CMC allows strangers to change their age, history, personality, appearance, and other matters that would be impossible to hide in person.[89] A quarter of teens have pretended to be a different person online, and a third confess to having given false information about themselves while e-mailing and instant messaging. A survey of one online dating site's participants found that 86 percent felt others misrepresented their physical appearance in their posted descriptions.[90]

Like the one-to-one and small group channels of e-mail and instant messaging, "broadcasting" on the media is also a tool for managing one's identity. Blogs, personal web pages, and profiles on social networking websites all provide opportunities for communicators to construct an identity.[91]

Ethical Challenge

Honesty and Multiple Identities

Your text argues that presenting different identities to the world isn't inherently dishonest. Nonetheless, there are certainly cases when it is deceitful to construct an identity that doesn't match your private self. You can explore the ethics of multiple identities by identifying two situations from your life:

1. A time when you presented a public identity that didn't match your private self in a manner that wasn't unethical.

2. A situation (real or hypothetical) in which you have presented or could present a dishonest identity.

Based on the situations you and your classmates present, develop a code of ethics that identifies the boundary between ethical and unethical identity management.

Identity Management and Honesty

After reading this far, you might think that identity management sounds like an academic label for manipulation or phoniness. If the perceived self is the "real" you, it might seem that any behavior that contradicts it would be dishonest.

There certainly are situations where identity management is dishonest. A manipulative date who pretends to be affectionate in order to gain sexual favors is clearly unethical and deceitful. So are job applicants who lie about academic records to get hired or salespeople who pretend to be dedicated to customer service when their real goal is to make a quick buck. But managing identities doesn't necessarily make you a liar. In fact, it is almost impossible to imagine how we could communicate effectively without making decisions about which front to present in one situation or another. It would be

CULTURAL IDIOM

to make a quick buck:
to earn money with little effort

ludicrous for you to act the same way with strangers as you do with close friends, and nobody would show the same face to a two-year-old as to an adult.

Each of us has a repertoire of faces—a cast of characters—and part of being a competent communicator is choosing the best role for the situation. Consider a few examples:

- You have been communicating online for several weeks with someone you just met, and the relationship is starting to turn romantic. You have a physical trait that you haven't mentioned yet.

- You offer to teach a friend a new skill: playing the guitar, operating a computer program, or sharpening a tennis backhand. Your friend is making slow progress with the skill, and you find yourself growing impatient.

- At a party with a companion, you meet someone you find very attractive, and you are pretty sure that the feeling is mutual. You feel an obligation to spend most of your time with the person with whom you came, but the opportunity here is very appealing.

- At work you face a belligerent customer. You don't believe that anyone has the right to treat you this way.

- A friend or family member makes a joke about your appearance that hurts your feelings. You aren't sure whether to make an issue of the remark or pretend that it doesn't bother you.

In each of these situations—and in countless others every day—you have a choice about how to act. It is an oversimplification to say that there is only one honest way to behave in each circumstance and that every other response would be insincere and dishonest. Instead, impression management involves deciding which face—which part of yourself—to reveal. For example, when teaching a new skill you can choose to display the patient instead of the impatient side of yourself. In the same way, at work you have the option of acting hostile or nondefensive in difficult situations. With strangers, friends, or family you can choose whether or not to disclose your feelings. Which face to show to others is an important decision, but in any case you are sharing a real part of yourself. You may not be revealing everything—but, as you will learn in Chapter 7, complete self-disclosure is rarely appropriate.

It's also worth noting that not all misrepresentations are intentional. Researchers have used the term "foggy mirror" to describe the gap between participants' self-perceptions and a more objective assessment. An online dater who describes himself or herself as being "average" in weight might be engaging in wishful thinking rather than telling an outright lie.[92]

> Which face to show to others is an important decision, but in any case you are sharing a real part of yourself.

Summary

Perceptions of others are always selective and are often distorted. The chapter began by describing how personal narratives shape our perceptions. It then outlined several perceptual errors that can affect the way we view and communicate with others. Along with universal psychological influences, cultural factors affect perceptions. Increased empathy is a valuable tool for increasing understanding of others and hence communicating more effectively with them. Perception checking is one tool for increasing the accuracy of perceptions and for increasing empathy.

Perceptions of oneself are just as subjective as perceptions of others, and they influence communication at least as much. Although individuals are born with some innate personality characteristics, the self-concept is shaped dramatically by communication with others, as well as by cultural factors. Once established, the self-concept can lead us to create self-fulfilling prophecies that determine how we behave and how others respond to us.

Identity management consists of strategic communication designed to influence others' perceptions of an individual. Identity management operates when we seek, consciously or unconsciously, to present one or more public faces to others. These faces may be different from the private, spontaneous behavior that occurs outside of others' presence. Identity management is usually collaborative: Communication goes most smoothly when we communicate in ways that support others' faces, and they support ours. Some communicators are high self-monitors who are intensely conscious of their own behavior, whereas others are low self-monitors who are less aware of how their words and actions affect others.

Identity management occurs for two reasons. In many cases it aims at following social rules and conventions. In other cases it aims at achieving a variety of content and relational goals. In either case, communicators engage in creating impressions by managing their manner, appearance, and the settings in which they interact with others. Although identity management might seem manipulative, it can be an authentic form of communication. Because each person has a variety of faces that he or she can present, choosing which one to present need not be dishonest.

Key Terms

attribution The process of attaching meaning. *p. 72*

empathy The ability to project oneself into another person's point of view, so as to experience the other's thoughts and feelings. *p. 78*

ethnocentrism The attitude that one's own culture is superior to others. *p. 77*

face The socially approved identity that a communicator tries to present. *p. 82*

facework Verbal and nonverbal behavior designed to create and maintain a communicator's face and the face of others. *p. 82*

identity management Strategies used by communicators to influence the way others view them. *p. 81*

interpretation The perceptual process of attaching meaning to stimuli that have previously been selected and organized. *p. 70*

narrative The stories people create and use to make sense of their personal worlds. *p. 71*

organization The perceptual process of organizing stimuli into patterns. *p. 69*

perceived self The person we believe ourselves to be in moments of candor. It may be identical with or different from the presenting and ideal selves. *p. 81*

perception checking A three-part method for verifying the accuracy of interpretations, including a description of the sense data, two possible interpretations, and a request for confirmation of the interpretations. *p. 80*

presenting self The image a person presents to others. It may be identical to or different from the perceived and ideal selves. See also *Face. p. 82*

reflected appraisal The influence of others on one's self-concept. *p. 62*

selection The perceptual act of attending to some stimuli in the environment and ignoring others. *p. 69*

self-concept The relatively stable set of perceptions each individual holds of himself or herself. *p. 61*

self-esteem The part of the self-concept that involves evaluations of self-worth. *p. 62*

self-fulfilling prophecy A prediction or expectation of an event that makes the outcome more likely to occur than would otherwise have been the case. *p. 66*

self-serving bias The tendency to interpret and explain information in a way that casts the perceiver in the most favorable manner. *p. 73*

significant other A person whose opinion is important enough to affect one's self-concept strongly. *p. 62*

stereotyping The perceptual process of applying exaggerated beliefs associated with a categorizing system. *p. 72*

sympathy Compassion for another's situation. See also *Empathy. p. 78*

Case Study Questions

Instructions: Reread the case study on pages xx–1 to answer the following questions in light of what you have learned in this chapter.

1. Describe a case where an American and someone from another country might have incompatible narratives.

2. Discuss how common perceptual tendencies (pages 72–76) led to friction. How might greater empathy have helped the people involved communicate more smoothly?

3. Explain some of the factors (personal and cultural) that have helped shape your self-concept.

4. Using yourself or someone you know as an example, describe how the process of identity management operates during an average day. Discuss the ethics of presenting multiple identities.

Activities

1. **Exploring Narratives** Think about a situation where relational harmony is due to you and the other people involved sharing the same narrative. Then think about another situation where you and the other person use different narratives to describe the same situation. What are the consequences of having different narratives in this situation?

2. **Experiencing Another Culture** Spend at least an hour in a culture that is unfamiliar to you and where you are a minority. Visit an area where another cultural, age, or ethnic group is the majority. Attend a meeting or patronize an establishment where you are in the minority. Observe how communication practices differ from those of your own culture. Based on your experience, discuss what you can do to facilitate communication with people from other cultural backgrounds whom you may encounter in your everyday life. (As you develop a list of ideas, realize that what

you might consider helpful behavior could make communicators from different cultures even more uncomfortable.)

3. **Empathy Exercise** Choose a disagreement you presently have with another person or group. The disagreement might be a personal one—such as an argument about how to settle a financial problem or who is to blame for a present state of affairs—or it might be a dispute over a contemporary public issue, such as the right of women to obtain abortions on demand or the value of capital punishment.

   1. In three hundred words or so, describe your side of the issue. State why you believe as you do, just as if you were presenting your position to an important jury.

   2. Now take three hundred words or so to describe in the first-person singular the other person's perspective on the same issue. For instance, if you are a religious person, write this section as if you were an atheist: For a short while get in touch with how the other person feels and thinks.

   3. Now show the description you wrote to your "opponent," the person whose beliefs are different from yours. Have that person read your account and correct any statements that don't reflect his or her position accurately. Remember: You're doing this so that you can more clearly understand how the issue looks to the other person.

   4. Make any necessary corrections in the account you wrote, and again show it to your partner. When your partner agrees that you understand his or her position, have your partner sign your paper to indicate this.

   5. Now record your conclusions to this experiment. Has this perceptual shift made any difference in how you view the issue or how you feel about your partner?

4. **Perception-Checking Practice** Practice your perception-checking ability by developing three-part verifications for the following situations:

   1. You made what you thought was an excellent suggestion to an instructor. The instructor looked uninterested but said she would check on the matter right away. Three weeks have passed, and nothing has changed.

   2. A neighbor and good friend has not responded to your "Good morning" for three days in a row. This person is usually friendly.

3. You haven't received the usual weekly phone call from the folks back home in over a month. The last time you spoke, you had an argument about where to spend the holidays.

4. An old friend with whom you have shared the problems of your love life for years has recently changed when around you: The formerly casual hugs and kisses have become longer and stronger, and the occasions where you "accidentally" brush up against one another have become more frequent.

5. **Identifying Your Identities** Keep a one-day log listing the identities you create in different situations: at school, at work, and with strangers, various family members, and different friends. For each identity,

1. Describe the persona you are trying to project (e.g., "responsible son or daughter," "laid-back friend," "attentive student").

2. Explain how you communicate to promote this identity. What kinds of things do you say (or not say)? How do you act?

For Further Exploration

For more resources about the self and perception, see the *Understanding Human Communication* website at www.oup.com/us/uhc11. There you will find a variety of resources: a list of books and articles, links to descriptions of feature films and television shows at the *Now Playing* website, study aids, and a self-test to check your understanding of the material in this chapter.

MEDIA ROOM

For more resources about communication in film and television, see *Now Playing* at the *Understanding Human Communication* website at www.oup.com/us/uhc11.

Development of the Self Through Communication

Precious (2009, Rated R)
Claireece "Precious" Jones (Gabourey Sidibe) believes she is what the abusive people in her life have said she is: stupid, fat, ugly, and unworthy of love. Illiterate and faced with expulsion, Precious transfers to an alternative school. It's here that her life turns around thanks to the appraisals of teacher Ms. Rain (Paula Patton) and social worker Ms. Weiss (Mariah Carey). Through her contact with these new significant others, Precious finally gains enough strength to leave her abusive household and start a new life.

The Challenges of Identity Management

Shark Tale (2004, Rated PG)
This animated film is an amusing illustration of characters who reap the benefits and suffer the consequences of presenting false identities. Oscar (Will Smith) is a fast-talking small fish who changes from nobody to celebrity when he is mistaken for a brazen "shark slayer." Given his newfound fame and happiness, it's not surprising that Oscar is willing to live a lie. Lenny (Jack Black) is a great white shark with a sensitive side and a secret about his identity: He's a vegetarian. When Lenny's secret is revealed, he becomes the object of scorn and ridicule. Both characters find themselves exhausted from managing their false identities and ultimately return to their true nature, which they learn is also preferred by those who love them most.

Brokeback Mountain (2005, Rated R)
Brokeback Mountain is a disturbing account of the dilemmas that can come from both disclosing and hiding our true identities. In 1963, Ennis Del Mar (Heath Ledger) and Jack Twist (Jake Gyllenhaal) are hired to tend sheep on Montana's Brokeback. In their remote campsite, the two men surprise themselves by becoming lovers. After the summer ends, they return to their separate lives. Both marry and have children, managing to ignore their feelings for one another until they meet again. At that point the consequences of both honesty and deception become apparent, showing that in real life there often is no easy answer to the question of whether or not to reveal one's true identity.

PART TWO

Communication Elements

Consulting Report

C ommunication consulting firms provide insight and advice to corporate, government, and individual clients. The best consultants combine research findings and theory with real world experience, giving their clients tools for accomplishing their mission more effectively.

Imagine that you have been invited to intern with the marketing department of a respected consulting organization. Your job is to provide information that will become part of a promotional piece aimed demonstrating the need for improving organizational and personal communication to potential clients.

For the marketing piece, your job is to provide information on the frequency and consequences of misunderstandings, and to suggest how communication training can minimize these sorts of problems. A quick look at Chapters 4, 5, and 6 in this unit convinced you that the information there can give you a framework for identifying examples of miscommunication and suggesting remedies.

You can find specific questions and activities involving this case study on page 127 (Chapter 4), page 161 (Chapter 5), and page 188 (Chapter 6).

Most of us don't have the luxury of hiring a consultant to provide tips on how to communicate better. Once you've studied the chapters in this unit, though, you'll be on the way to becoming your own consultant. The information in this section provides a framework for understanding the fundamental elements of any communication transaction.

After studying the material in Chapters 4, 5, and 6, you will understand better

- Why misunderstandings occur so often among people who speak the same language.
- The unspoken dimensions of nonverbal behavior, both yours and others'.
- The challenges of receiving and processing messages, and how to deal with those challenges.

Language

Chapter Outline

The Nature of Language
- Language Is Symbolic
- Meanings Are in People, Not Words
- Language Is Rule Governed

The Power of Language
- Language Shapes Attitudes
- Language Reflects Attitudes

Troublesome Language
- The Language of Misunderstandings
- Disruptive Language
- Evasive Language

Gender and Language
- Content
- Reasons for Communicating
- Conversational Style
- Nongender Variables

Culture and Language
- Verbal Communication Styles
- Language and Worldview

Features
- **INVITATION TO INSIGHT** What the *@#$!?
- **@WORK** What's in a Name?
- **UNDERSTANDING DIVERSITY** Lost in Translation

YOU SHOULD UNDERSTAND:

1. The symbolic, person-centered nature of language.
2. Phonological, semantic, syntactic, and pragmatic rules that govern language.
3. The ways in which language shapes and reflects attitudes.
4. The types of troublesome language and the skills to deal with each.
5. The gender and nongender factors that affect speech style.
6. The verbal styles that distinguish various cultures, and the effect that language can have on worldview.

YOU SHOULD BE ABLE TO:

1. Discuss how you and others use syntactic, semantic, phonological, and pragmatic rules and how their use affects a message's comprehension.
2. Identify at least two ways in which language has shaped your attitudes.
3. Identify at least two ways in which language reflects your attitudes.
4. Recognize and suggest alternatives for equivocal language, slang and jargon, relative terms, and overly abstract language.
5. Identify and suggest alternatives for fact-inference and fact-opinion confusion and for emotive statements.
6. Suggest appropriate alternatives for unnecessary or misleading euphemisms and equivocal statements.
7. Identify the degree to which your speech reflects gender stereotypes.
8. Identify your cultural speech patterns and reflect on how they may be interpreted by members of other cultures.

At one time or another, every one of us has suffered the limits and traps of language. Even though we are using familiar words, it's clear that we often don't use them in ways that allow us to communicate smoothly with one another.

In the following pages we will explore the nature of linguistic communication. By the time you have finished reading this chapter, you will better appreciate the complexity of language, its power to shape our perceptions of people and events, and its potential for incomplete and inaccurate communication. Perhaps more importantly, you will be better equipped to use the tool of language more skillfully to improve your everyday interaction.

The Nature of Language

Humans speak about ten thousand dialects.[1] Although most of these sound different from one another, all possess the same characteristics of **language**: a collection of symbols governed by rules and used to convey messages between individuals. A closer look at this definition can explain how language operates and suggest how we can use it more effectively.

"What part of oil lamp next to double squiggle over ox don't you understand?"

Language Is Symbolic

There's nothing natural about calling your loyal four-footed companion a "dog" or the object you're reading right now a "book." These words, like virtually all language, are **symbols**—arbitrary constructions that represent a communicator's thoughts. Not all linguistic symbols are spoken or written words. Sign language, as "spoken" by most deaf people, is symbolic in nature and not the pantomime it might seem to nonsigners. There are literally hundreds of different sign languages spoken around the world that represent the same ideas differently.[2] These distinct languages include American Sign Language, British Sign Language, French Sign Language, Danish Sign Language, Chinese Sign Language—even Australian Aboriginal and Mayan sign languages.

> Symbols are more than just labels: They are the way we experience the world.

Symbols are more than just labels: They are the way we experience the world. You can prove this by trying a simple experiment.[3] Work up some saliva in your mouth, and then spit it into a glass. Take a good look, and then drink it up. Most people find this process mildly disgusting. But ask yourself why this is so. After all, we swallow our own saliva all the time. The answer arises out of the symbolic labels we use. After the saliva is in the glass, we call it *spit* and think of it in a different way. In other words, our reaction is to the name, not the thing.

The naming process operates in virtually every situation. How you react to a stranger will depend on the symbols you use to categorize him or her: gay (or straight), religious (or not), attractive (or unattractive), and so on.

Meanings Are in People, Not Words

Ask a dozen people what the same symbol means, and you are likely to get twelve different answers. Does an American flag bring up associations of patriots giving their lives for their country? Fourth of July parades? Cultural imperialism? How about a cross:

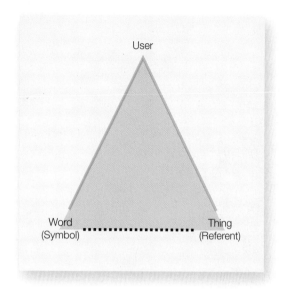

User

Word
(Symbol)   Thing
(Referent)

FIGURE 4-1 Ogden and Richards's Triangle of Meaning

What does it represent? The message of Jesus Christ? Firelit rallies of Ku Klux Klansmen? Your childhood Sunday school? The necklace your sister always wears?

As with physical symbols, the place to look for meaning in language isn't in the words themselves but rather in the way people make sense of them. One unfortunate example of this fact occurred in Washington DC, when the newly appointed city ombudsman used the word "niggardly" to describe an approach to budgeting.[4] Some African American critics accused him of uttering an unforgivable racial slur. His defenders pointed out that the word, which means "miserly," is derived from Scandinavian languages and that it has no link to the racial slur it resembles. Even though the criticisms eventually died away, they illustrate that, correct or not, the meanings people associate with words have far more significance than do their dictionary definitions.

Linguistic theorists C. K. Ogden and I. A. Richards illustrated the fact that meanings are social constructions in their well-known "triangle of meaning" (Figure 4-1).[5] This model shows that there is only an indirect relationship—indicated by a broken line—between a word and the thing it claims to represent. Some of these "things" or referents do not exist in the physical world. For instance, some referents are mythical (such as unicorns), some are no longer tangible (such as Elvis, if he really is dead), and others are abstract ideas (such as "love").

Problems arise when people mistakenly assume that others use words in the same way they do. It's possible to have an argument about *feminism* without ever realizing that you and the other person are using the word to represent entirely different things. The same goes for *environmentalism*, *Republicans*, *rock music*, and thousands upon thousands of other symbols. Words don't mean; people do—and often in widely different ways.

> Problems arise when people mistakenly assume that others use words in the same way they do.

Despite the potential for linguistic problems, the situation isn't hopeless. We do, after all, communicate with one another reasonably well most of the time. And with enough effort, we can clear up most of the misunderstandings that do occur. The key to more accurate use of language is to avoid assuming that others interpret words the same way we do. In truth, successful communication occurs when we negotiate the meaning of a statement.[6] As one French proverb puts it: The spoken word belongs half to the one who speaks it and half to the one who hears.

Language Is Rule Governed

Languages contain several types of rules. **Phonological rules** govern how words sound when pronounced. For instance, the words *champagne*, *double*, and *occasion* are spelled identically in French and English, but all are pronounced differently. Nonnative speakers learning English are plagued by inconsistent phonological rules, as a few examples illustrate:

He could lead if he would get the lead out.

A farm can produce produce.

The dump was so full it had to refuse refuse.

The present is a good time to present the present.

I did not object to the object.

The bandage was wound around the wound.

I shed a tear when I saw the tear in my clothes.

Phonological rules aren't the only ones that govern the way we use language to communicate. Syntactic rules govern the structure of language—the way symbols can be arranged. For example, correct English syntax requires that every word contain at least one vowel and prohibits sentences such as "Have you the cookies brought?", which is a perfectly acceptable word order in German. Although most of us aren't able to describe the syntactic rules that govern our language, it's easy to recognize their existence by noting how odd a statement that violates them appears.

Technology has spawned subversions of English with their own syntactic rules.[7] For example, users of instant messaging on the Internet have devised a streamlined version of English that speeds up typing in real-time communication (although it probably makes teachers of composition grind their teeth in anguish):

A: Hey

B: r u @ home?

A: ys

B: k I'm getting offline now

A: y

B: cuz i need to study for finals u can call me tho bye

A: TTYL

Semantic rules deal with the meaning of specific words. Semantic rules are what make it possible for us to agree that "bikes" are for riding and "books" are for reading; they also help us to know whom we will and won't encounter when we open doors marked "men" or "women." Without semantic rules, communication would be impossible, because each of us would use symbols in unique ways, unintelligible to one another.

> Without semantic rules, communication would be impossible.

Semantic misunderstandings occur when words can be interpreted in more than one way, as the following humorous notices prove:

The peacemaking meeting scheduled for today has been canceled due to a conflict.

For those of you who have children and don't know it, we have a nursery downstairs.

The ladies of the Church have cast off clothing of every kind. They may be seen in the basement on Friday afternoon.

Sunday's sermon topic will be "What Is Hell?" Come early and listen to our choir practice.

Pragmatic rules govern how people use language in everyday interaction, which communication theorists have characterized as a series of *speech acts*.[8] Consider the example of a male boss saying "You look very pretty today" to a female employee. It's easy to imagine how the subordinate might be offended by a comment that her boss considered an innocent remark. Scholars of language have pointed out several levels at which the rules each person uses can differ. You can understand these levels by imagining how they would operate in our example:

Each person's self-concept
Boss: Views himself as a nice guy.
Subordinate: Determined to succeed on her own merits, and not her appearance.

Invitation to Insight

What the *@#$!?

How do you react when someone unexpectedly uses profanity during normal conversation? Are you offended? Surprised? Intrigued? Like all verbal messages, swearwords speak volumes beyond their literal meaning.

A semantic analysis doesn't reveal much about the meaning of swearwords and phrases like "Damn it" or "S—t." A closer look at when and how people curse reveals that the use and interpretation of profanity are governed by pragmatic rules. People who swear are more likely to do so in the company of others they know and trust, because doing so often indicates a level of comfort and acceptance of the other: "It's great to see you, you old S.O.B.!" Cursing can also define relational boundaries, showing who is a member of one's in-group. For example, some African Americans use the "n" word to describe close in-group members, while the same word would be unacceptable from an out-group member. Swearing can also be a way to enhance solidarity between people. For example, research suggests that the swearing patterns of bosses and coworkers can help people feel connected on the job. Looking at the pragmatic rules governing profanity helps explain why some people are offended by language that others consider benign.

Although profanity isn't for everyone, it's a part of our culture, and it appears that it's here to stay. Whether you like it or not, keep in mind that profanity is used for much more than shock value: It can contain deeper meaning about the goals, intentions, and relationship expectations of the speaker.

The episode in which the comment occurs
Boss: Casual remark at the start of the workday.
Employee: A possible come-on?

Perceived relationship
Boss: Views employees like members of the family.
Employee: Depends on boss's goodwill for advancement.

Cultural background
Boss: Member of generation in which comments about appearance were common.
Employee: Member of generation sensitive to sexual harassment.

As this example shows, pragmatic rules don't involve semantic issues, since the words themselves are usually understood well by almost everybody. Instead, they involve how those words are understood and used.

The Power of Language

On the most obvious level, language allows us to satisfy basic functions such as describing ideas, making requests, and solving problems. But beyond these functions, the way we use language also influences others and reflects our attitudes in more subtle ways, which we will examine now.

Language Shapes Attitudes

The power of language to shape ideas has been recognized throughout history. The first chapters of the Bible report that Adam's dominion over animals was demonstrated by his being given the power to give them names.[9] As we will now see, our speech—sometimes consciously and sometimes not—shapes others' values, attitudes, and beliefs in a variety of ways.

Naming   "What's in a name?" Juliet asked rhetorically. If Romeo had been a social scientist, he would have answered, "A great deal." Research has demonstrated that names are more than just a simple means of identification: They shape the way others think of us, the way we view ourselves, and the way we act.

At the most fundamental level, some research suggests that even the phonetic sound of a person's name affects the way we regard him or her, at least when we don't have other information available. One study revealed that reasonably accurate predictions about who will win an election can be made on the basis of some phonetic features of the candidates' surnames.[13] Names that were simple, easily pronounced, and rhythmic were judged more favorably than ones that lack these qualities. For example, in one series of local elections, the winning candidates had names that resonated with voters: Sanders beat Pekelis, Rielly defeated Dellwo, Grady outpolled Schumacher, Combs trounced Bernsdorf, and Golden prevailed over Nuffer. Names don't guarantee victory, but in seventy-eight elections, forty-eight outcomes supported the value of having an appealing name.

"Look, I'd rather be free, too, but at least we're not in a zoo anymore."

Source: © The New Yorker Collection 1993 Robert Mankoff from cartoonbank.com. All Rights Reserved.

@Work

What's in a Name?

When it comes to career success, names matter more than you might imagine.

Research suggests that many people pass judgment on prospective workers simply on the basis of their first name. In one study, prospective employers rated applicants with common first names more highly than those with unique or unusual ones.[10] This bias presents challenges for people with unique names, and for those from cultures with different naming practices.

Sometimes naming biases reflect stereotypes about gender. People predict career success based on how closely a person's name matches the gender associated with his or her job.[11] When college students were asked how people with various names were likely to do in their careers, they predicted that women with feminine names like Emma or Marta were more likely to be successful in traditionally female occupations like nursing. By contrast, they estimated that men with masculine names like Hank or Bruno would do better in traditionally male jobs like plumbing.

Findings like this are worth noting if you hope to succeed in a field where your identity doesn't match traditional expectations. For example, if you are a woman thinking about the field of law, research suggests that your chances of success are greatest if your parents had the foresight to give you a traditionally male name. Researchers examined the relationship between the perceived masculinity of a person's name and his or her success in the field of law.[12] They found that a woman named "Cameron" is roughly three times more likely to become a judge than one named "Sue." A female "Bruce" is five times more likely.

Most people aren't willing to change their name to further career goals. But it is possible to choose variants on a name that have a professional advantage. For example, Marie Celeste Smith might consider identifying herself on job application documents as M. C. Smith, and Christina Jones might encourage people to use her nickname, Chris. Someone with a hard-to-pronounce name might choose a nickname for work purposes. For example, it's a custom in China for businesspeople and students of English to choose a Western name that complements the one they were born with: Guanghiui goes by Arthur and Junyuan is called Joanna. In a competitive job market, little differences can mean a great deal.

Names are one way to shape and reinforce a child's personal identity. Naming a baby after a family member (e.g., "Junior" or "Trey") can create a connection between the youngster and his or her namesake. Name choice can also be a powerful way to make a statement about cultural identity. For example, in recent decades a large percentage of names given to African American babies have been distinctively black.[14] In California, over 40 percent of black girls born in a single year had names that not a single white baby born in the entire state was given. Researchers suggest that distinctive names like these are a symbol of solidarity with the African American community. Conversely, choosing a less distinctive name can be a way of integrating the baby into the majority culture. Whether common or unusual, the impact of names recedes after communicators become more familiar with one another.[15]

Choosing a newborn's name can be especially challenging for people from nondominant cultures with different languages. One writer from India describes the problem he and his wife faced when considering names for their first child:

> How will the child's foreign name sound to American ears? (That test ruled out Shiva, my family deity; a Jewish friend put her foot down.) Will it provoke bullies to beat him up on the school playground? (That was the end of Karan, the name of a warrior from the Mahabharata, the Hindu epic. A boy called "Karen" wouldn't stand a chance.) Will it be as euphonic in New York as it is in New Delhi? (That was how Sameer failed to get off the ground. "Like a bagel with a schmear!" said one ruthless well-wisher.)[16]

First names aren't the only linguistic elements that may shape attitudes about men and women.

Credibility   Scholarly speaking is a good example of how speech style influences perception. We refer to what has been called the Dr. Fox hypothesis.[17] "An apparently legitimate speaker who utters an unintelligible message will be judged competent by an audience in the speaker's area of apparent expertise." The Dr. Fox hypothesis got its name from one Dr. Myron L. Fox, who delivered a talk followed by a half-hour discussion on "Mathematical Game Theory as Applied to Physical Education." The audience included psychiatrists, psychologists, social workers, and educators. Questionnaires collected after the session revealed that these educated listeners found the lecture clear and stimulating.

> "An apparently legitimate speaker who utters an unintelligible message will be judged competent by an audience in the speaker's area of apparent expertise."

Despite his warm reception by this learned audience, Fox was a complete fraud. He was a professional actor whom researchers had coached to deliver a lecture of double-talk—a patchwork of information from a *Scientific American* article mixed with jokes, non sequiturs, contradictory statements, and meaningless references to unrelated topics. When wrapped in a linguistic package of high-level professional jargon, however, the meaningless gobbledygook was judged as important information. In other words, Fox's audience reaction was based more on the credibility that arose from his use of impressive-sounding language than from the ideas he expressed.

The same principle seems to hold for academic writing.[18] A group of thirty-two management professors rated material according to its complexity rather than its content. When a message about consumer behavior was loaded with unnecessary words and long, complex sentences, the professors rated it highly. When the same message was translated into more readable English, with shorter words and clearer sentences, the professors judged the same research as less competent.

Status   In the classic musical *My Fair Lady*, Professor Henry Higgins transformed Eliza Doolittle from a lowly flower girl into a high-society woman by replacing her cockney accent with an upper-crust speaking style. Decades of research have demonstrated that the power of speech to influence status is a fact.[19] Several factors combine to create positive or negative impressions: accent, choice of words, speech rate, and even the apparent age of a speaker. In most cases, speakers of standard dialect are rated higher than nonstandard speakers in a variety of ways: They are viewed as more competent and more self-confident, and the content of their messages is rated more favorably. The unwillingness or inability of a communicator to use the standard dialect fluently can have serious consequences. For instance, speakers of Black English, a distinctive dialect with its own accent, grammar, syntax, and semantic rules, are rated as less intelligent, professional, capable, socially acceptable, and employable by speakers of standard English.[20]

> Several factors combine to create positive or negative impressions: accent, choice of words, speech rate, and even the apparent age of a speaker.

Sexism and Racism   By now it should be clear that the power of language to shape attitudes goes beyond individual cases and influences how we perceive entire groups of people. For example, Casey Miller and Kate Swift argue that incorrect use of the pronoun *he* to refer to both men and women can have damaging results.

> On the television screen, a teacher of first-graders who has just won a national award is describing her way of teaching. "You take each child where you find him," she says. "You watch to see what he's interested in, and then you build on his interests."
>
> A five-year-old looking at the program asks her mother, "Do only boys go to that school?"
>
> "No," her mother begins, "she's talking about girls too, but—"
>
> But what? The teacher being interviewed on television is speaking correct English. What can the mother tell her daughter about why a child, in any generalization, is always he rather than she? How does a five-year-old comprehend the generic personal pronoun?[21]

It's usually easy to use nonsexist language. For example, the term *mankind* may be replaced by *humanity, human beings, human race,* or *people; man-made* may be replaced by *artificial, manufactured,* and *synthetic; manpower* may be replaced by *human power, workers,* and *workforce;* and *manhood* may be replaced by *adulthood.*

The use of labels for racist purposes has a long and ugly past. Names have been used throughout history to stigmatize groups that other groups have disapproved of.[22] By using derogatory terms to label some people, the out-group is set apart and pictured in an unfavorable light. Diane Mader provides several examples of this:

> We can see the process of stigmatization in Nazi Germany when Jewish people became vermin, in the United States when African Americans became "niggers" and chattel, in the military when the Vietnam-era enemy became "gooks."[23]

The power of racist language to shape attitudes is difficult to avoid, even when it is obviously offensive. In one study, experimental subjects who heard a derogatory label used against a member of a minority group expressed annoyance at this sort of slur, but despite their disapproval, the negative emotional terms did have an impact.[24] Not only did the unwitting subjects rate the minority individual's competence lower when that person performed poorly, but also they found fault with others who associated socially with the minority person—even members of the subject's own ethnic group.

One of the most treasured civil liberties is freedom of speech. At the same time, most people would agree that some forms of racist and sexist speech are hateful and demeaning to their targets. As you have read in these pages, language shapes the attitudes of those who hear it.

How do you reconcile the principle of free speech and the need to minimize hateful and discriminatory messages? Do you think laws and policies can and should be made that limit certain types of communication? If so, how should those limits be drafted to protect civil liberties? If not, can you justify the necessary protection of even sexist and racist language?

Language Reflects Attitudes

Besides shaping the way we view ourselves and others, language reflects our attitudes. Feelings of control, attraction, commitment, responsibility—all these and more are reflected in the way we use language.

Power Communication researchers have identified a number of language patterns that add to, or detract from, a speaker's ability to influence others, as well as reflecting how a speaker feels about his or her degree of control over a situation.[25] Table 4-1 summarizes some of these findings by listing several types of "powerless" language.

You can see the difference between powerful language and powerless language by comparing the following statements:

> "Excuse me, sir, I hate to say this, but I . . . uh . . . I guess I won't be able to turn in the assignment on time. I had a personal emergency and . . . well . . . it was just impossible to finish it by today. I'll have it in your mailbox on Monday, okay?"

> "I won't be able to turn in the assignment on time. I had a personal emergency, and it was impossible to finish it by today. I'll have it in your mailbox on Monday."

Even a single type of powerless speech mannerism, such as hedges, appears to make a person appear less authoritative or socially attractive.[26] By contrast, speakers whose

TABLE 4-1 Powerless Language

TYPE OF USAGE	EXAMPLE
Hedges	"I'm kinda disappointed . . ." "I think we should . . ." "I guess I'd like to . . ."
Hesitations	"Uh, can I have a minute of your time?" "Well, we could try this idea . . ." "I wish you would—er—try to be on time."
Intensifiers	"So that's how I feel . . ." "I'm not very hungry."
Polite forms	"Excuse me, sir . . ."
Tag questions	"It's about time we got started, isn't it?" "Don't you think we should give it another try?"
Disclaimers	"I probably shouldn't say this, but . . ." "I'm not really sure, but . . ."

talk is free of powerless mannerisms are rated as more competent, dynamic, and attractive than speakers who sound powerless.[27] In employment interviews, powerful speech results in more positive attributions of competence and employability than powerless speech.[28]

Despite the potential drawbacks of powerless speech, don't assume that the best goal is always to sound as powerful as you can. Along with gaining compliance, another conversational goal is often building a supportive, friendly relationship, and sharing power with the other person can help you in this regard. For this reason, many everyday statements will contain a mixture of powerful speech and powerless speech.[29] Our student-teacher example illustrates how this combination of powerless mannerisms and powerful mannerisms can help the student get what she wants while staying on good terms with the professor:

> "Excuse me, Professor Rodman. I want you to know that I won't be able to turn in the assignment on time. I had a personal emergency, and it was impossible to finish it by today. I'll definitely have it in your mailbox on Monday."

Whether or not the professor finds the excuse acceptable, it's clear that this last statement combines the best features of powerful speech and powerless speech: a combination of self-assurance and goodwill.

Simply counting the number of powerful or powerless statements won't always reveal who has the most control in a relationship. Social rules often mask the real distribution of power. Sociolinguist Deborah Tannen describes how politeness can be a face-saving way of delivering an order:

> I hear myself giving instructions to my assistants without actually issuing orders: "Maybe it would be a good idea to . . .;" "It would be great if you could . . ." all the while knowing that I expect them to do what I've asked right away . . . This rarely creates problems, though, because the people who work for me know that there is only one reason I mention tasks—because I want them done. I *like* giving instructions in this way; it appeals to my sense of what it means to be a good person . . . taking others' feelings into account.[30]

As this quote suggests, high-status speakers often realize that politeness is an effective way to get their needs met while protecting the face of the less powerful person. The importance of achieving both content goals and relational goals helps explain why a mixture of powerful speech and polite speech is usually most effective.[31] Of course, if the other person misinterprets politeness for weakness, it may be necessary to shift to a more powerful speaking style.

Powerful speech that gets the desired results in mainstream North American and European culture doesn't succeed everywhere with everyone.[32] In Japan, saving face for others is an important goal, so communicators there tend to speak in ambiguous terms and use hedge words and qualifiers. In most Japanese sentences the verb comes at the end of the sentence so the "action" part of the statement can be postponed. Traditional Mexican culture, with its strong emphasis on cooperation, makes a priority of using language to create harmony in interpersonal relationships, rather than taking a firm or oppositional stance, in order to make others feel more at ease. Korean culture represents yet another group of people that prefers "indirect" (for example, "perhaps," "could be") to "direct" speech.

CULTURAL IDIOM
saving face:
protecting one's dignity

Affiliation   Power isn't the only way language reflects the status of relationships. Language can also be a way of building and demonstrating solidarity with others. An impressive body of research has demonstrated that communicators who want to show affiliation with one another adapt their speech in a variety of ways, including their choice of vocabulary, rate of talking, number and placement of pauses, and level of politeness.[33] On an individual level, close friends and lovers often develop special terms that serve as a way of signifying their relationship.[34] Using the same vocabulary sets these people apart from others, reminding themselves and the rest of the world of their relationship. The same process works among members of larger groups, ranging from street gangs to military personnel. Communication researchers call this linguistic accommodation **convergence**.

> Language can also be a way of building and demonstrating solidarity with others.

Communicators can experience convergence in cyberspace as well as in face-to-face interactions. Members of online communities often develop a shared language and conversational style, and their affiliation with each other can be seen in increased uses of the pronoun "we."[35] On a larger scale, IM and e-mail users create and use shortcuts that mark them as Internet-savvy. If you know what ROTF, IMHO, and JK mean, you're probably part of that group. (For the uninitiated, those acronyms mean "Rolling on the floor laughing," "In my humble opinion," and "Just kidding.") Interestingly, instant-messagers may find that their cyberlanguage creeps into everyday conversations.[36] (Have you ever said "LOL" instead of the words "laughing out loud"—or instead of actually laughing out loud?)

When two or more people feel equally positive about one another, their linguistic convergence will be mutual. But when communicators want or need the approval of others they often adapt their speech to suit the others' style, trying to say the "right thing" or speak in a way that will help them fit in. We see this process when immigrants who want to gain the rewards of material success in a new culture strive to master the prevalent language. Likewise, employees who seek advancement tend to speak more like their superiors: Supervisors adopt the speech style of managers, and managers converge toward their bosses.

The principle of speech accommodation works in reverse, too. Communicators who want to set themselves apart from others adopt the strategy of **divergence**, speaking in a way that emphasizes their difference from others. For example, members of an ethnic group, even though fluent in the dominant language, might use their own dialect as a way of showing solidarity with one another—a sort of "us against them" strategy. Divergence also operates in other settings. A physician or attorney, for example, who wants to establish credibility with his or her client might speak formally and use professional jargon to create a sense of distance. The implicit message here is "I'm different (and more knowledgeable) than you."

Convergence and divergence aren't the only ways to express affiliation. **Linguistic intergroup bias** reflects whether or not we regard others as part of our in-group. Researchers have discovered a tendency to describe the *positive* behaviors of others with whom we identify as personality traits.[37] A positive bias leads us to describe in-group members in favorable terms and out-group members negatively. For example, if an in-group member gives money to a homeless person, we are likely to describe her behavior as a positive personality trait: "Sue is a generous person." If an out-group member (someone with whom we don't identify) gives the same homeless person some money, we are likely to describe her behavior as a discrete behavior: "Sue gave away money."

The same in-group preferences are revealed when we describe undesirable behaviors. If an in-group member behaves poorly, we are likely to describe the behavior using a concrete descriptive action verb, such as "John cheated in the game." In contrast, if the person we are describing is an out-group member, we are more likely to use general disposition adjectives such as "John is a cheater." These selective language choices are so subtle and subconscious that when asked, people being studied report that there were no differences in the way they described in-group versus out-group members' behavior. We tend to believe we are less biased than we are, but our language reveals the truth about our preferences.

CULTURAL IDIOM
a clod:
a dull or stupid person

Attraction and Interest   Social customs discourage us from expressing like or dislike in many situations. Only a clod would respond to the question "What do you think of the cake I baked for you?" by saying, "It's terrible." Bashful or cautious suitors might not admit their attraction to a potential partner. Even when people are reluctant to speak candidly, the language they use can suggest their degree of interest and attraction toward a person, object, or idea. Morton Weiner and Albert Mehrabian outline a number of linguistic clues that reveal these attitudes.[38]

> We tend to believe we are less biased than we are, but our language reveals the truth about our preferences.

- **Demonstrative pronoun choice.** *These* people want our help (positive) versus *Those* people want our help (less positive).

- **Negation.** It's *good* (positive) versus It's *not bad* (less positive).

- **Sequential placement.** Dick and Jane (Dick is more important) versus Jane and Dick (Jane is more important). However, sequential placement isn't always significant. You may put "toilet bowl cleaner" at the top of your shopping list simply because it's closer to the market door than is champagne.

Responsibility   In addition to suggesting liking and importance, language can reveal the speaker's willingness to accept responsibility for a message.

- **"It" versus "I" statements.** *It's* not finished (less responsible) versus *I* didn't finish it (more responsible).

- **"You" versus "I" statements.** Sometimes *you* make me angry (less responsible) versus Sometimes *I* get angry when you do that (more responsible). "I" statements are more likely to generate positive reactions from others as compared to accusatory ones.[39]

- **"But" statements.** It's a good idea, *but* it won't work. You're really terrific, *but* I think we ought to spend less time together. (*But* cancels everything that went before the word.)

- **Questions versus statements.** Do you think we ought to do that? (less responsible) versus I don't think we ought to do that (more responsible).

Troublesome Language

Besides being a blessing that enables us to live together, language can be something of a curse. We have all known the frustration of being misunderstood, and most of us have been baffled by another person's overreaction to an innocent comment. In the following pages we will look at several kinds of troublesome language, with the goal of helping you communicate in a way that makes matters better instead of worse.

The Language of Misunderstandings

The most obvious kind of language problems are semantic: We simply don't understand others completely or accurately. Most misunderstandings arise from some common problems that are easily remedied—after you recognize them.

Equivocal Language   **Equivocal words** have more than one correct dictionary definition. Some equivocal misunderstandings are simple, at least after they are exposed. A nurse once told her patient that he "wouldn't be needing" the materials he requested from home. He interpreted the statement to mean he was near death when the nurse meant he would be going home soon. A colleague of ours mistakenly sent some confidential materials to the wrong person after his boss told him to "send them to Richard," without specifying which Richard. Some equivocal misunderstandings can be embarrassing, as one woman recalls:

> In the fourth grade the teacher asked the class what a period was. I raised my hand and shared everything I had learned about girls' getting their period. But he was talking about the dot at the end of a sentence. Oops![40]

Equivocal misunderstandings can have serious consequences. Equivocation at least partially explains why men may sometimes persist in attempts to become physically intimate when women have expressed unwillingness to do so.[41] Interviews and focus groups with college students revealed that women often use ambiguous phrases to say "no" to a man's sexual advances: "I'm confused about this." "I'm not sure that we're ready for this yet." "Are you sure you want to do this?" "Let's be friends" and even "That tickles." (The researchers found that women were most likely to use less direct phrases when they hoped to see or date the man again. When they wanted to cut off the relationship, they were more likely to give a direct response.) Whereas women viewed indirect statements as equivalent to saying "no," men were more likely to interpret them as less clear-cut requests to stop. As the researchers put it, "male/female misunderstandings are not so much a matter of males hearing resistance messages as 'go,' but rather their not hearing them as 'stop.'" Under the law, "no" means precisely that, and anyone who argues otherwise can be in for serious legal problems.

Relative Words   **Relative words** gain their meaning by comparison. For example, is the school you attend large or small? This depends on what you compare it to: Alongside a campus like UCLA, with an enrollment of over thirty thousand students, it probably looks small, but compared to a smaller institution, it might seem quite large. In the same way, relative words like *fast* and *slow*, *smart* and *stupid*, *short* and *long* depend for their meaning on what they're compared to. (The "large" size can of olives is the smallest you can buy; the larger ones are "giant," "colossal," and "supercolossal.")

Some relative words are so common that we mistakenly assume that they have a clear meaning. For instance, if a new acquaintance says "I'll call you soon," when can you expect to hear from him or her? In one study, graduate students were asked to assign numerical values to terms such as *doubtful*, *toss-up*, *likely*, *probable*, *good chance*, and *unlikely*.[42] There was a tremendous variation in the meaning of most of these terms. For example, the responses for *possible* ranged from 0 to 99 percent. *Good chance* meant between 35 and 90 percent, whereas *unlikely* fell between 0 and 40 percent.

CULTURAL IDIOM

a period:
occurrence of menstruation

Using relative words without explaining them can lead to communication problems. Have you ever responded to someone's question about the weather by saying it was warm, only to find out that what was warm to you was cold to the other person? Or have you followed a friend's advice and gone to a "cheap" restaurant, only to find that it was twice as expensive as you expected? Have you been disappointed to learn that classes you've heard were "easy" turned out to be hard, that journeys you were told would be "short" were long, that "unusual" ideas were really quite ordinary? The problem in each case came from failing to anchor the relative word used to a more precisely measurable word.

> Using relative words without explaining them can lead to communication problems.

Slang and Jargon   **Slang** is language used by a group of people whose members belong to a similar coculture or other group. Some slang is related to specialized interests and activities. For instance, cyclists who talk about "bonking" are referring to running out of energy. Rapsters know that "bling" refers to jewelry and a "whip" is a nice-looking car.

Other slang consists of *regionalisms*—terms that are understood by people who live in one geographic area but that are incomprehensible to outsiders. This sort of use illustrates how slang defines insiders and outsiders, creating a sense of identity and solidarity.[43] Residents of the fiftieth U.S. state know that when a fellow Alaskan says, "I'm going outside," he or she is leaving the state. In the East End of London, cockney dialect uses rhyming words as substitutes for everyday expressions: "bacon and eggs" for "legs," and "Barney Rubble" for "trouble." This sort of use also illustrates how slang can be used to identify insiders and outsiders: With enough shared rhyming, slang users could talk about outsiders without the clueless outsiders knowing that they were the subject of conversation ("Lovely set of bacons, eh?" "Stay away from him. He's Barney.").

Slang can also be age related. Most college students know that drinkers wearing "beer goggles" have consumed enough alcohol that they find almost everyone of the opposite—or sometimes the same—sex attractive. At some schools, a "monkey" is the "other" woman or man in a boyfriend's or girlfriend's life: "I've heard Mitch is cheating on me. When I find his monkey, I'm gonna do her up!"[44]

Almost everyone uses some sort of **jargon**: the specialized vocabulary that functions as a kind of shorthand for people with common backgrounds and experience. Skateboarders have their own language to describe maneuvers: "ollie," "grind," and "shove it." Some jargon consists of *acronyms*—initials of terms that are combined to form a word. Stock traders refer to the NASDAQ (pronounced "naz-dak") securities index, and military people label failure to serve at one's post as being AWOL (absent without leave). The digital age has spawned its own vocabulary of jargon. For instance, computer users know that "viruses" are malicious programs that migrate from one computer to another, wreaking havoc. Likewise, "cookies" are tiny files that remote observers can use to monitor a user's computer habits. Some jargon goes beyond being descriptive and conveys attitudes. For example, cynics in the high-tech world sometimes refer to being fired from a job as being "uninstalled." They talk dismissively about the nonvirtual world as the "carbon community" and of books and newspapers as "treeware." Some technical support staffers talk of "banana problems," meaning those that could be figured out by monkeys, as in "This is a two-banana problem at worst."[45]

Jargon can be a valuable kind of shorthand for people who understand its use. The trauma team in a hospital emergency room can save time, and possibly lives, by speaking in shorthand, referring to "GSWs" (gunshot wounds), "chem 7" lab tests, and so

CULTURAL IDIOM

techies:
computer experts

on, but the same specialized vocabulary that works so well among insiders can mystify and confuse family members of the patient, who don't understand the jargon. The same sort of misunderstandings can arise in less critical settings when insiders use their own language with people who don't share the same vocabulary. Jeffrey Katzman of the William Morris Agency's Hollywood office experienced this sort of problem when he met with members of a Silicon Valley computer firm to discuss a joint project.

> When he used the phrase "in development," he meant a project that was as yet merely an idea. When the techies used it, on the other hand, they meant designing a specific game or program. Ultimately, says Katzman, he had to bring in a blackboard and literally define his terms. "It was like when the Japanese first came to Hollywood," he recalls. "They had to use interpreters, and we did too."[46]

Overly Abstract Language   Most objects, events, and ideas can be described with varying degrees of specificity. Consider the material you are reading. You could call it:

A book
A textbook
A communication textbook

Understanding Human Communication
Chapter 4 of *Understanding Human Communication*
Page 112 of Chapter 4 of *Understanding Human Communication*

In each case your description would be more and more specific. Semanticist S. I. Hayakawa created an **abstraction ladder** to describe this process.[47] This ladder consists of a number of descriptions of the same thing. Lower items focus specifically on the person, object, or event, whereas higher terms are generalizations that include the subject as a member of a larger class. To talk about "college," for example, is more abstract than to talk about a particular school. Likewise, referring to "women" is more abstract than referring to "feminists," or more specifically naming feminist organizations or even specific members who belong to them.

Higher-level abstractions are a useful tool, because without them language would be too cumbersome to be useful. It's faster, easier, and more useful to talk about *Europe* than to list all of the countries on that continent. In the same way, using relatively abstract terms like *friendly* or *smart* can make it easier to describe people than listing their specific actions.

Abstract language—speech that refers to events or objects only vaguely—serves a second, less obvious function. At times it allows us to avoid confrontations by deliberately being unclear.[48] Suppose, for example, your boss is enthusiastic about a new approach to doing business that you think is a terrible idea. Telling the truth might seem too risky, but lying—saying "I think it's a great idea"—wouldn't feel right either. In situations like this an abstract answer can hint at your true belief without a direct confrontation: "I don't know . . . It's sure unusual . . . It *might* work." The same sort of abstract language can help you avoid embarrassing friends who ask for your opinion with questions like "What do you think of my new haircut?" An abstract response like "It's really different!" may be easier for you to deliver—and for your friend to receive—than the clear, brutal truth: "It's really ugly!" We will have more to say about this linguistic strategy of equivocation later in this chapter.

Although vagueness does have its uses, highly abstract language can cause several types of problems. The first is *stereotyping*. Consider claims like "All whites are bigots,"

"Men don't care about relationships," "The police are a bunch of goons," or "Professors around here care more about their research than they do about students." Each of these claims ignores the very important fact that abstract descriptions are almost always too general, that they say more than we really mean.

Besides creating stereotypical attitudes, abstract language can lead to the problem of *confusing others*. Imagine the lack of understanding that results from imprecise language in situations like this:

A: We never do anything that's fun anymore.

B: What do you mean?

A: We used to do lots of unusual things, but now it's the same old stuff, over and over.

B: But last week we went on that camping trip, and tomorrow we're going to that party where we'll meet all sorts of new people. Those are new things.

A: That's not what I mean. I'm talking about really unusual stuff.

B: *(becoming confused and a little impatient)* Like what? Taking hard drugs or going over Niagara Falls in a barrel?

A: Don't be stupid. All I'm saying is that we're in a rut. We should be living more exciting lives.

B: Well, I don't know what you want.

The best way to avoid this sort of overly abstract language is to use **behavioral descriptions** instead. (See Table 4-2.) Behavioral descriptions move down the abstraction ladder to identify the specific, observable phenomenon being discussed. A thorough description should answer three questions:

1. **Who Is Involved?** Are you speaking for just yourself or for others as well? Are you talking about a group of people ("the neighbors," "women") or specific individuals ("the people next door with the barking dog," "Lola and Lizzie")?

2. **In What Circumstances Does the Behavior Occur?** Where does it occur: everywhere or in specific places (at parties, at work, in public)? When does it occur: When you're tired or when a certain subject comes up? The behavior you are describing probably doesn't occur all the time. In order to be understood, you need to pin down what circumstances set this situation apart from other ones.

3. **What Behaviors Are Involved?** Though terms such as *more cooperative* and *helpful* might sound like concrete descriptions of behavior, they are usually too vague to do a clear job of explaining what's on your mind. Behaviors must be *observable*, ideally both to you and to others. For instance, moving down the abstraction ladder from the relatively vague term *helpful*, you might come to behaviors such as *does the dishes every other day*, *volunteers to help me with my studies*, or *fixes dinner once or twice a week without being asked*. It's easy to see that terms like these are easier for both you and others to understand than are more vague abstractions.

Behavioral descriptions can improve communication in a wide range of situations, as Table 4-2 illustrates. Research also supports the value of specific language. One study found that well-adjusted couples had just as many conflicts as poorly adjusted couples, but the way the well-adjusted couples handled their problems was significantly different. Instead of blaming one another, the well-adjusted couples expressed their complaints in behavioral terms.[49] For instance, instead of saying "You're a slob," an enlightened partner might say, "I wish you wouldn't leave your dishes in the sink."

TABLE 4-2   Abstract and Behavioral Descriptions

	ABSTRACT DESCRIPTION	BEHAVIORAL DESCRIPTION			
		WHO IS INVOLVED	IN WHAT CIRCUMSTANCES	SPECIFIC BEHAVIORS	REMARKS
PROBLEM	I talk too much.	People I find intimidating	When I want them to like me	I talk (mostly about myself) instead of giving them a chance to speak or asking about their lives.	Behavioral description more clearly identifies behaviors to change.
GOAL	I want to be more constructive.	My roommate	When we talk about household duties	Instead of finding fault with her ideas, suggest alternatives that might work.	Behavioral description clearly outlines how to act; abstract description doesn't.
APPRECIATION	"You've really been helpful lately."	(Deliver to fellow workers)	"When I've had to take time off work because of personal problems"	"You took my shifts without complaining."	Give both abstract and behavioral descriptions for best results.
REQUEST	"Clean up your act!"	(Deliver to target person)	"When we're around my family"	"Please don't tell jokes that involve sex."	Behavioral description specifies desired behavior.

Disruptive Language

Not all linguistic problems come from misunderstandings. Sometimes people understand one another perfectly and still end up in conflict. Of course, not all disagreements can, or should be, avoided. But eliminating three bad linguistic habits from your communication repertoire can minimize the kind of clashes that don't need to happen, allowing you to save your energy for the unavoidable and important struggles.

Confusing Facts and Opinions   **Factual statements** are claims that can be verified as true or false. By contrast, **opinion statements** are based on the speaker's beliefs. Unlike matters of fact, they can never be proved or disproved. Consider a few examples of the difference between factual statements and opinion statements:

FACT	OPINION
It rains more in Seattle than in Portland.	The climate in Portland is better than in Seattle.
Kareem Abdul Jabbar is the all-time leading scorer in the National Basketball Association.	Kareem is the greatest basketball player in the history of the game.
Per capita income in the United States is higher than in several other countries.	The United States is not the best model of economic success in the world.

When factual statements and opinion statements are set side by side like this, the difference between them is clear. In everyday conversation, we often present our opinions as if they were facts, and in doing so we invite an unnecessary argument. For example:

"That was a dumb thing to say!"

"Spending that much on [   ] is a waste of money!"

"You can't get a fair shake in this country unless you're a white male."

Notice how much less antagonistic each statement would be if it were prefaced by a qualifier like "In my opinion . . ." or "It seems to me. . . ."

Confusing Facts and Inferences   Labeling your opinions can go a long way toward relational harmony, but developing this habit won't solve all linguistic problems. Difficulties also arise when we confuse factual statements with **inferential statements**—conclusions arrived at from an interpretation of evidence. Consider a few examples:

FACT	INFERENCE
He hit a lamppost while driving down the street.	He was daydreaming when he hit the lamppost.
You interrupted me before I finished what I was saying.	You don't care about what I have to say.
You haven't paid your share of the rent on time for the past three months.	You're trying to weasel out of your responsibilities.
I haven't gotten a raise in almost a year.	The boss is exploiting me.

There's nothing wrong with making inferences as long as you identify them as such: "She stomped out and slammed the door. It looked to me as if she were furious." The danger comes when we confuse inferences with facts and make them sound like the absolute truth.

One way to avoid fact-inference confusion is to use the perception-checking skill described in Chapter 3 to test the accuracy of your inferences. Recall that a perception check has three parts: a description of the behavior being discussed, your interpretation of that behavior, and a request for verification. For instance, instead of saying "Why are you laughing at me?" you could say, "When you laugh like that *[description of behavior]*, I get the idea you think something I did was stupid *[interpretation]*. Are you laughing at me *[question]*?"

Emotive Language   **Emotive language** contains words that sound as if they're describing something when they are really announcing the speaker's attitude toward something. Do you like that old picture frame? If so, you would probably call it "an antique," but if you think it's ugly, you would likely describe it as "a piece of junk." Emotive words may sound like statements of fact but are always opinions.

Barbra Streisand pointed out how some people use emotive language to stigmatize behavior in women that they admire in men:

A man is commanding—a woman is demanding.

A man is forceful—a woman is pushy.

A man is uncompromising—a woman is a ball-breaker.

A man is a perfectionist—a woman's a pain in the ass.

CULTURAL IDIOM

a fair shake:
honest treatment

to weasel out of:
to get out of doing something

He's assertive—she's aggressive.

He strategizes—she manipulates.

He shows leadership—she's controlling.

He's committed—she's obsessed.

He's persevering—she's relentless.

He sticks to his guns—she's stubborn.

If a man wants to get it right, he's looked up to and respected.

If a woman wants to get it right, she's difficult and impossible.[50]

Problems occur when people use emotive words without labeling them as such. You might, for instance, have a long and bitter argument with a friend about whether a third person was "assertive" or "obnoxious," when a more accurate and peaceable way to handle the issue would be to acknowledge that one of you approves of the behavior and the other doesn't.

Critical Thinking Probe
Emotive Language

Test your ability to identify emotive language by playing the following word game.

1. Take an action, object, or characteristic and show how it can be viewed either favorably or unfavorably, according to the label it is given. For example:

   a. I'm casual.

      You're careless.

      He's a slob.

   b. I read adult love stories.

      You read erotic literature.

      She reads pornography.

2. Now create three-part descriptions of your own, using the following statements as a start:

   a. I'm tactful.

   b. She's a liar.

   c. I'm conservative.

   d. You have a high opinion of yourself.

   e. I'm quiet.

   f. You're pessimistic.

3. Now recall two situations in which you used emotive language as if it were a description of fact. How might the results have differed if you had used more objective language?

Evasive Language

None of the troublesome language habits we have described so far is a deliberate strategy to mislead or antagonize others. Now, however, we'll consider euphemisms and equivocations, two types of language that speakers use by design to avoid communicating clearly. Although both of these have some very legitimate uses, they also can lead to frustration and confusion.

Euphemisms   A **euphemism** (from the Greek word meaning "to use words of good omen") is a pleasant term substituted for a more direct but potentially less pleasant one. We are using euphemisms when we say "restroom" instead of "toilet" or "full-figured" instead of "overweight." There certainly are cases where the euphemistic pulling of linguistic punches can be face-saving. It's probably more constructive to question a possible "statistical misrepresentation" than to call someone a liar, for example. Likewise, it may be less disquieting to some to refer to people as "senior citizens" than "old."

Like many businesses, the airline industry uses euphemisms to avoid upsetting already nervous flyers.[51] For example, rather than saying "turbulence," pilots and flight attendants use the less frightening term "bumpy air." Likewise, they refer to thunderstorms as "rain showers," and fog as "mist" or "haze." And savvy flight personnel never use the words "your final destination."

"Be honest with me Roger. By 'mid-course correction' you mean divorce, don't you."

Source: © 2000 Lee Cullum from cartoonbank.com. All Rights Reserved.

Despite their occasional advantages, many euphemisms are not worth the effort it takes to create them. Some are pretentious and confusing, such as a middle school's labeling of hallways as "behavior transition corridors." Other euphemisms are downright deceptive, such as the U.S. Senate's labeling of a $23,200 pay raise as a "pay equalization concept."

Equivocation   It's 8:15 P.M., and you are already a half-hour late for your dinner reservation at the fanciest restaurant in town. Your partner has finally finished dressing and confronts you with the question "How do I look?" To tell the truth, you hate your partner's outfit. You don't want to lie, but on the other hand you don't want to be hurtful. Just as important, you don't want to lose your table by waiting around for your date to choose something else to wear. You think for a moment and then reply, "You look amazing. I've never seen an outfit like that before. Where did you get it?"

Your response in this situation was an **equivocation**—a deliberately vague statement that can be interpreted in more than one way. Earlier in this chapter we talked about how *unintentional* equivocation can lead to misunderstandings. But our discussion here focuses on *intentionally ambiguous speech* that is used to avoid lying on one hand and telling a painful truth on the other. Equivocations have several advantages.[52] They spare the receiver from the embarrassment that might come from a completely truthful answer, and it can be easier for the sender to equivocate than to suffer the discomfort of being honest.

CULTURAL IDIOM

"beating around the bush": approaching something in an indirect way

---

For most people, "telling it like it is" is usually considered a virtue and "beating around the bush" is a minor sin. You can test the function of indirect speech by following these directions:

1. Identify five examples of euphemisms and equivocations in everyday interaction.
2. Imagine how matters would have been different if the speakers or writers had used direct language in each situation.
3. Based on your observations, discuss whether equivocation and euphemisms have any place in face-to-face communication.

Ethical Challenge

Euphemisms and Equivocations

As with euphemisms, high-level abstractions, and many other types of communication, it's impossible to say that equivocation is always helpful or harmful. As you learned in Chapter 1, competent communication behavior is situational. Your success in relating to others will depend on your ability to analyze yourself, the other person, and the situation when deciding whether to be equivocal or direct.

Gender and Language

So far we have discussed language use as if it were identical for both sexes. Some theorists and researchers, though, have argued that there are significant differences between the way men and women speak, whereas others have argued that any differences are not significant.[53] What are the similarities and differences between male and female language use?

Content

The first research on the influence of gender on conversational topics was conducted over seventy years ago. Despite the changes in male and female roles since then, the results of more recent studies are remarkably similar.[54] In these studies, women and men ranging in age from seventeen to eighty described the range of topics each discussed with friends of the same sex. Certain topics were common to both sexes: Work, movies, and television proved to be frequent for both groups. Both men and women reserved discussions of sex and sexuality for members of the same gender.

> Both men and women use language to build and maintain social relationships. How they accomplish these goals is often different, though.

The differences between men and women were more striking than the similarities, however. Female friends spent much more time discussing personal and domestic subjects, relationship problems, family, health and reproductive matters, weight, food and clothing, men, and other women. Men, on the other hand, were more likely to discuss music, current events, sports, business, and other men. Both men and women were equally likely to discuss personal appearance, sex, and dating in same-sex conversations. True to one common stereotype, women were more likely to gossip about close friends and family. By contrast, men spent more time gossiping about sports figures and media personalities. Women's gossip was no more derogatory than men's.

These differences can lead to frustration when men and women try to converse with one another. Researchers report that *trivial* is the word often used by both sexes to describe topics discussed by the opposite sex.

Reasons for Communicating

Research shows that the notion that men and women communicate in dramatically different ways is exaggerated. Both men and women, at least in the dominant cultures of the United States and Canada, use language to build and maintain social relationships.[55] How men and women accomplish these goals is often different, though. Although most communicators try to make their interaction enjoyable, men are more likely than women to emphasize making conversation fun. Their discussions involve a greater amount of joking and good-natured teasing. By contrast, women's conversations focus more frequently on feelings, relationships, and personal problems. In fact, communication researcher Julia Wood flatly states that "for women, talk is the essence of relationships."[56] When a group of women was surveyed to find out what kinds of satisfaction they gained from talking with their friends, the most common theme mentioned was a feeling of empathy—"To know you're not alone," as some put it.[57] Whereas men commonly described same-sex conversations as something they liked, women characterized their woman-to-woman talks as a kind of contact they needed. The greater frequency of female conversations reflects their importance. Nearly 50 percent of the women surveyed said they called friends at least once a week just to talk, whereas less than half as many men did so. In fact, 40 percent of the men surveyed reported that they never called another man just to talk.

Because women use conversation to pursue social needs, female speech typically contains statements showing support for the other person, demonstrations of equality, and efforts to keep the conversation going. With these goals, it's not surprising that traditionally female speech often contains statements of sympathy and empathy: "I've felt just like that myself," "The same thing happened to me!" Women are also inclined to ask lots of questions that invite the other person to share information: "How did you feel about that?" "What did you do next?" The importance of nurturing a relationship also explains why female speech is often somewhat powerless and tentative. Saying, "This is just my opinion . . ." is less likely to put off a conversational partner than a more definite "Here's what I think. . . ."

Men's speech is often driven by quite different goals than women's. Men are more likely to use language to accomplish the job at hand than to nourish relationships. This explains why men are less likely than women to disclose their vulnerabilities, which would be a sign of weakness. When someone else is sharing a problem, instead of empathizing, men are prone to offer advice: "That's nothing to worry about . . ." or "Here's what you need to do. . . ." Besides taking care of business, men are more likely than women to use conversations to exert control, preserve their independence, and enhance their status. This explains why men are more prone to dominate conversations and one-up their partners. Men interrupt their conversational partners to assert their own experiences or point of view. (Women interrupt too, but they usually do so to offer support: quite a different goal.) Just because male talk is competitive doesn't mean it's not enjoyable. Men often regard talk as a kind of game: When researchers asked men what they liked best about their all-male talk, the most frequent answer was its ease.[58] Another common theme was appreciation of the practical value of conversation: new ways to solve problems. Men also mentioned enjoying the humor and rapid pace that characterized their all-male conversations.

Conversational Style

Some scholarship shows little difference between the ways men and women converse. For example, the popular myth that women are more talkative than men may not be accurate. Researchers found that men and women speak roughly the same number of words per day.[59]

CULTURAL IDIOM

one-up:
respond in order to maintain one's superiority

On the other hand, there are ways in which women do behave differently in conversations than do men.[60] For example, women ask more questions in mixed-sex conversations than do men—nearly three times as many, according to one study. Other research has revealed that in mixed-sex conversations, men interrupt women far more than the other way around. Some theorists have argued that differences like these result in women's speech that is less powerful and more emotional than men's. Research has supported these theories—at least in some cases. Even when clues about the speakers' sex were edited out, raters found clear differences between transcripts of male speech and female speech. In one study women's talk was judged more aesthetic, whereas men's talk was seen as more dynamic, aggressive, and strong. In another, male job applicants were rated more fluent, active, confident, and effective than female applicants.

Some gender differences also exist in mediated communication. For example, instant messages written by women tend to be more expressive than ones composed by men.[61] They are more likely to contain laughter ("hehe") emoticons (smiley faces), emphasis (italics, boldface, repeated letters), and adjectives. However, there are no significant gender differences in a number of other variables—such as questions, words per turn, and hedges.

> Instant messages written by women tend to be more expressive than ones composed by men.

Given these differences, it's easy to wonder how men and women manage to communicate with one another at all. One reason why cross-sex conversations do run smoothly is because women accommodate to the topics men raise. Both men and women regard topics introduced by women as tentative, whereas topics that men introduce are more likely to be pursued. Thus, women seem to grease the wheels of conversation by doing more work than men in maintaining conversations. A complementary difference between men and women also promotes cross-sex conversations: Men are more likely to talk about themselves with women than with other men, and because women are willing to adapt to this topic, conversations are likely to run smoothly, if one-sidedly.

An accommodating style isn't always a disadvantage for women. One study revealed that women who spoke tentatively were actually more influential with men than those who used more powerful speech.[62] On the other hand, this tentative style was less effective in persuading women. (Language use had no effect on men's persuasiveness.) This research suggests that women who are willing and able to be flexible in their approach can persuade both other women and men—as long as they are not dealing with a mixed-sex audience.

Nongender Variables

Despite the differences in the ways men and women speak, the link between gender and language use isn't as clear-cut as it might seem. Research reviews have found that the ways women and men communicate are much more similar than different. For example, one analysis of over twelve hundred research studies found that only 1 percent of variance in communication behavior resulted from sex difference.[63] There is no significant difference between male speech and female speech in areas such as use of profanity, use of qualifiers such as "I guess" or "This is just my opinion," tag questions, and vocal fluency.[64] Some on-the-job research shows that male and female supervisors in similar positions behave the same way and are equally effective. In light of the considerable similarities between the sexes and the relatively minor differences, some communication scholars suggest that the "men are from Mars, women are from Venus"

CULTURAL IDIOM

to grease the wheels:
to facilitate

claim should be replaced by the metaphor that "men are from North Dakota, women are from South Dakota."[65]

A growing body of research explains some of the apparent contradictions between the similarities and differences between male speech and female speech. They have revealed other factors that influence language use as much or more than does gender. For example, social philosophy plays a role. Feminist wives talk longer than their partners, whereas nonfeminist wives speak less than their husbands. Orientation toward problem solving also plays a role in conversational style. The cooperative or competitive orientations of speakers have more influence on how they interact than does their gender.

The speaker's occupation and social role also influence speaking style. For example, male day-care teachers' speech to their students resembles the language of female teachers more closely than it resembles the language of fathers at home. Overall, doctors interrupt their patients more often than the reverse, although male patients do interrupt female physicians more often than their male counterparts. At work, task differences exert more powerful effects on whether speakers use gender-inclusive language (such as "he or she" instead of just "he") than does biological sex.[66] A close study of trial transcripts showed that the speaker's experience on the witness stand and occupation had more to do with language use than did gender. If women generally use "powerless" language, this may possibly reflect their historical social role in society at large. As the balance of power grows more equal between men and women, we can expect many linguistic differences to shrink.

Another powerful force that influences the way individual men and women speak is their **sex role**—the social orientation that governs behavior—rather than their biological gender. Researchers have identified three sex roles: masculine, feminine, and androgynous. These sex roles don't always line up neatly with gender. There are "masculine" females, "feminine" males, and androgynous communicators who combine traditionally masculine and feminine characteristics.

Research shows that linguistic differences are often a function of these sex roles more than the speaker's biological sex. Masculine sex-role communicators—whether male or female—use more dominant language than either feminine or androgynous speakers. Feminine speakers have the most submissive speaking style, whereas androgynous speakers fall between these extremes. When two masculine communicators are in a conversation, they often engage in a one-up battle for dominance, responding to the other's bid for control with a counterattempt to dominate the relationship. Feminine sex-role speakers are less predictable. They use dominance, submission, and equivalent behavior in an almost random fashion. Androgynous individuals are more predictable: They most frequently meet another's bid for dominance with a symmetrical attempt at control, but then move quickly toward an equivalent relationship.

> Research suggests that neither a stereotypically male style nor female style is the best choice.

All this information suggests that, when it comes to communicating, "masculinity" and "femininity" are culturally recognized sex roles, not biological traits. Research suggests that neither a stereotypically male style nor female style is the best choice. For example, one study showed that a "mixed-gender strategy" that balanced the stereotypically male task-oriented approach with the stereotypically female relationship-oriented approach received the highest marks by both male and female respondents.[67] As opportunities for men and women become more equal, we can expect that the differences between male and female use of language will become smaller.

Understanding Diversity

Lost in Translation

Semantic confusion is common even between speakers of the same language. Translating from one language to another offers an even greater challenge. Here are a few examples of semantic blunders committed across the globe:

■ Kellogg had to rename its Bran Buds cereal in Sweden when it discovered that the name roughly translated to "burned farmer."

■ When PepsiCo advertised Pepsi in Taiwan with the ad "Come Alive with Pepsi," it had no idea that the slogan would be translated into Chinese as "Pepsi brings your ancestors back from the dead."

■ American medical containers were distributed in Great Britain and caused quite a stir. The instructions to "Take off top and push in bottom," innocuous to Americans, had very strong sexual connotations to the British.

■ Frank Perdue's chicken slogan, "It takes a strong man to make a tender chicken," was translated into Spanish as "It takes an aroused man to make a chicken affectionate."

CULTURAL IDIOM

bungled:
done something imperfectly

Culture and Language

Anyone who has tried to translate ideas from one language to another knows that communication across cultures can be a challenge.[68] As the "Lost in Translation" box on this page shows, the results of a bungled translation can sometimes be amusing.

Even choosing the right words during translation won't guarantee that nonnative speakers will use an unfamiliar language correctly. For example, Japanese insurance companies warn their policyholders who are visiting the United States to avoid their cultural tendency to say "excuse me" or "I'm sorry" if they are involved in a traffic accident.[69] In Japan, apologizing is a traditional way to express goodwill and maintain social harmony, even if the person offering the apology is not at fault. But in the United States, an apology can be taken as an admission of guilt and may result in Japanese tourists' being held accountable for accidents for which they may not be responsible.

Difficult as it may be, translation is only a small part of the communication challenges facing members of different cultures. Differences in the way language is used and the very worldview that a language creates make communicating across cultures a challenging task.

Verbal Communication Styles

Using language is more than just choosing a particular group of words to convey an idea. Each language has its own unique style that distinguishes it from others. And when a communicator tries to use the verbal style from one culture in a different one, problems are likely to arise.[70]

Direct–Indirect   As you read in Chapter 2, one way in which verbal styles vary is in their *directness*. You'll recall that **low-context cultures** use language primarily to express thoughts, feelings, and ideas as clearly and logically as possible. By contrast, **high-context cultures** value language as a way to maintain social harmony. Rather than upset others by speaking clearly, communicators in these cultures learn to discover meaning from the context in which a message is delivered: the nonverbal behaviors of the speaker, the history of the relationship, and the general social rules that govern interaction between people.

The clash between cultural norms of directness and indirectness can aggravate problems in cross-cultural situations such as encounters between straight-talking low-context Israelis, who value speaking directly, and Arabs, whose high-context culture stresses smooth interaction. It's easy to imagine how the clash of cultural styles could lead to misunderstandings and conflicts between Israelis and their Palestinian neighbors. Israelis could view their Arab counterparts as evasive, whereas the Palestinians could perceive the Israelis as insensitive and blunt.

Even within a single country, subcultures can have different notions about the value of direct speech. For example, Puerto Rican language style resembles high-context Japanese or Korean more than low-context English.[71] As a group, Puerto Ricans value social harmony and avoid confrontation, which leads them to systematically speak in an indirect way to avoid giving offense. Asian Americans are more offended by indirectly racist statements than are African Americans, Hispanics, and Anglo Americans.[72] Researchers Laura Leets and Howard Giles suggest that the traditional Asian tendency to favor high-context messages explains the difference: Adept at recognizing hints and nonverbal cues, high-context communicators are more sensitive to messages that are overlooked by people from cultural groups that rely more heavily on unambiguous, explicit low-context messages.

It's worth noting that even generally straight-talking residents of the United States raised in the low-context Euro-American tradition often rely on context to make their point. When you decline an unwanted invitation by saying "I can't make it," it's likely that both you and the other person know that the choice of attending isn't really beyond your control. If your goal was to be perfectly clear, you might say, "I don't want to get together."

Elaborate–Succinct   Another way in which language styles can vary across cultures is in terms of whether they are elaborate or succinct. Speakers of Arabic, for instance, commonly use language that is much more rich and expressive than most communicators who use English. Strong assertions and exaggerations that would sound ridiculous in English are a common feature of Arabic. This contrast in linguistic style can lead to misunderstandings between people from different backgrounds. As one observer put it,

> . . . [A]n Arab feels compelled to overassert in almost all types of communication because others expect him [or her] to. If an Arab says exactly what he [or she] means without the expected assertion, other Arabs may still think that he [or she] means the opposite. For example, a simple "no" to a host's requests to eat more or drink more will not suffice. To convey the meaning that he [or she] is actually full, the guest must keep repeating "no" several times, coupling it with an oath such as "By God" or "I swear to God."[73]

Succinctness is most extreme in cultures where silence is valued. In many American Indian cultures, for example, the favored way to handle ambiguous social situations is to remain quiet.[74] When you contrast this silent style to the talkativeness common in mainstream American cultures when people first meet, it's easy to imagine how the first encounter between an Apache or Navajo and a white person might feel uncomfortable to both people.

Formal–Informal   Along with differences such as directness-indirectness and elaborate-succinct styles, a third way languages differ from one culture to another involves *formality* and *informality*. The informal approach that characterizes relationships in countries like

CULTURAL IDIOM
tongue:
language

the United States, Canada, and Australia is quite different from the great concern for using proper speech in many parts of Asia and Africa. Formality isn't so much a matter of using correct grammar as of defining social position. In Korea, for example, the language reflects the Confucian system of relational hierarchies.[75] It has special vocabularies for different sexes, for different levels of social status, for different degrees of intimacy, and for different types of social occasions. For example, there are different degrees of formality for speaking with old friends, nonacquaintances whose background one knows, and complete strangers. One sign of being a learned person in Korea is the ability to use language that recognizes these relational distinctions. When you contrast these sorts of distinctions with the casual friendliness many North Americans use even when talking with complete strangers, it's easy to see how a Korean might view communicators in the United States as boorish and how an American might view Koreans as stiff and unfriendly.

Language and Worldview

Different linguistic styles are important, but there may be even more fundamental differences that separate speakers of various languages. For almost 150 years, some theorists have put forth the notion of **linguistic relativism**: the notion that the worldview of a culture is shaped and reflected by the language its members speak.[76] The best-known example of linguistic relativism is the notion that Eskimos have a large number of words (estimated from seventeen to one hundred) for what we simply call "snow." Different terms are used to describe conditions like a driving blizzard, crusty ice, and light powder. This example suggests how linguistic relativism operates. The need to survive in an Arctic environment led Eskimos to make distinctions that would be unimportant to residents of warmer environments, and after the language makes these distinctions, speakers are more likely to see the world in ways that match the broader vocabulary.

> Linguistic relativism is the notion that the worldview of a culture is shaped and reflected by the language its members speak.

Even though there is some doubt that Eskimos really do have one hundred words for snow,[77] other examples do seem to support the principle of linguistic relativism.[78] For instance, bilingual speakers seem to think differently when they change languages. In one study, French Americans were asked to interpret a series of pictures. When they spoke in French, their descriptions were far more romantic and emotional than when they used English to describe the same kind of pictures. Likewise, when students in Hong Kong were asked to complete a values test, they expressed more traditional Chinese values when they answered in Cantonese than when they answered in English. In Israel, both Arab and Jewish students saw bigger distinctions between their group and "outsiders" when using their native language than when they used English, a neutral tongue. Examples like these show the power of language to shape cultural identity—sometimes for better and sometimes for worse.

"The Eskimos have eighty-seven words for snow and not one for malpractice."

Source: © 1999 Leo Cullum from cartoonbank.com. All Rights Reserved.

Linguistic influences start early in life. English-speaking parents often label the mischievous pranks of their children as "bad," implying that there is something immoral about acting wild. "Be good!" they are inclined to say. On the other hand, French parents are more likely to say "Sois sage!"—"Be wise." The linguistic implication is that misbehaving is an act of foolishness. Swedes would correct the same action with the words "Var snall!"—"Be friendly, be kind." By contrast, German adults would use the command "Sei artig!"—literally, "Be of your own kind"—in other words, get back in step, conform to your role as a child.[79]

The best-known declaration of linguistic relativism is the **Sapir-Whorf hypothesis**, formulated by Benjamin Whorf, an amateur linguist, and anthropologist Edward Sapir.[80] Following Sapir's theoretical work, Whorf found that the language spoken by the Hopi represents a view of reality that is dramatically different from more familiar tongues. For example, the Hopi language makes no distinction between nouns and verbs. Therefore, the people who speak it describe the entire world as being constantly in process. Whereas we use nouns to characterize people or objects as being fixed or constant, the Hopi view them more as verbs, constantly changing. In this sense our language represents much of the world rather like a snapshot camera, whereas Hopi reflects a worldview more like video.

> Language is a powerful force for shaping our thoughts, and our relationship with others.

Although the Sapir-Whorf hypothesis originally focused on foreign languages, Neil Postman illustrates the principle with an example closer to home. He describes a hypothetical culture where physicians identify patients they treat as "doing" arthritis and other diseases instead of "having" them and where criminals are diagnosed as "having" cases of criminality instead of "being" criminals.[81]

The implications of such a linguistic difference are profound. We believe that characteristics people "have"—what they "are"—are beyond their control, whereas they are responsible for what they "do." If we changed our view of what people "have" and what they "do," our attitudes would most likely change as well. Postman illustrates the consequences of this linguistic difference as applied to education:

> In schools, for instance, we find that tests are given to determine how smart someone is or, more precisely, how much smartness someone "has." If one child scores a 138, and another a 106, the first is thought to "have" more smartness than the other. But this seems to me a strange conception—every bit as strange as "doing" arthritis or "having" criminality. I do not know anyone who *has* smartness. The people I know sometimes *do* smart things (as far as I can judge) and sometimes *do* stupid things—depending on what circumstances they are in, and how much they know about a situation, and how interested they are. "Smartness," so it seems to me, is a specific performance, done in a particular set of circumstances. It is not something you *are* or have in measurable quantities. . . . What I am driving at is this: All language is metaphorical, and often in the subtlest ways. In the simplest sentence, sometimes in the simplest word, we do more than merely express ourselves. We construct reality along certain lines. We make the world according to our own imagery.[82]

Subtle changes like this illustrate the theme of this chapter: that language is a powerful force for shaping our thoughts, and our relationship with others.

Summary

Language is both one of humanity's greatest assets and the source of many problems. This chapter highlighted the characteristics that distinguish language and suggested methods of using it more effectively.

Any language is a collection of symbols governed by a variety of rules and used to convey messages between people. Because of its symbolic nature, language is not a precise tool: Meanings rest in people, not in words themselves. In order for effective communication to occur, it is necessary to negotiate meanings for ambiguous statements.

Language not only describes people, ideas, processes, and events; it also shapes our perceptions of them in areas including status, credibility, and attitudes about gender and ethnicity. Along with influencing our attitudes, language reflects them. The words we use and our manner of speech reflect power, responsibility, affiliation, attraction, and interest.

Many types of language have the potential to create misunderstandings. Other types of language can result in unnecessary conflicts. In other cases, speech and writing can be evasive, avoiding expression of unwelcome messages.

The relationship between gender and language is complex. While there are differences in the ways men and women speak, not all differences in language use can be accounted for by the speaker's gender. Occupation, social philosophy, and orientation toward problem solving also influence the use of language, and psychological sex role can be more of an influence than biological sex.

Language operates on a broad level to shape the consciousness and communication of an entire society. Different languages often shape and reflect the views of a culture. Low-context cultures like that of the United States use language primarily to express feelings and ideas as clearly and unambiguously as possible, whereas high-context cultures avoid specificity to promote social harmony. Some cultures value brevity and the succinct use of language, whereas others value elaborate forms of speech. In some societies formality is important, whereas in others informality is important. Beyond these differences, there is evidence to support linguistic relativism—the notion that language exerts a strong influence on the worldview of the people who speak it.

Key Terms

abstract language Language that lacks specificity or does not refer to observable behavior or other sensory data. See also *Behavioral description. p. 112*

abstraction ladder A range of more- to less-abstract terms describing an event or object. *p. 112*

behavioral description An account that refers only to observable phenomena. *p. 113*

convergence Accommodating one's speaking style to another person, who usually is desirable or has higher status. *p. 108*

divergence A linguistic strategy in which speakers emphasize differences between their communicative style and others' in order to create distance. *p. 108*

emotive language Language that conveys the sender's attitude rather than simply offering an objective description. *p. 115*

equivocal language Language with more than one likely interpretation. *p. 110*

equivocal words Words that have more than one dictionary definition. *p. 110*

equivocation A vague statement that can be interpreted in more than one way. *p. 117*

euphemism A pleasant-sounding term used in place of a more direct but less pleasant one. *p. 117*

factual statement A statement that can be verified as being true or false. See also *Inferential statement; Opinion statement. p. 114*

high-context culture A culture that avoids direct use of language to express information, especially about relational matters. Instead, members of the culture rely on the context of a message to convey meaning. See also *Low-context culture. p. 122*

inferential statement Conclusion arrived at from an interpretation of evidence. See also *Factual statement. p. 115*

jargon The specialized vocabulary that is used as a kind of shorthand by people with common backgrounds and experience. *p. 111*

language A collection of symbols, governed by rules and used to convey messages between individuals. *p. 98*

linguistic intergroup bias The tendency to label people and behaviors in terms that reflect their in-group or out-group status. *p. 108*

linguistic relativism A moderate form of linguistic determinism that argues that language exerts a strong influence on the perceptions of the people who speak it. *p. 124*

low-context culture A culture that relies heavily on language to make messages, especially of a relational nature, explicit. See also *High-context culture. p. 122*

opinion statement A statement based on the speaker's beliefs. See also *Factual statement. p. 114*

phonological rules Linguistic rules governing how sounds are combined to form words. *p. 100*

pragmatic rules Rules that govern how people use language in everyday interaction. *p. 101*

relative words Words that gain their meaning by comparison. *p. 110*

Sapir-Whorf hypothesis Theory that the structure of a language shapes the worldview of its users. *p. 125*

semantic rules Rules that govern the meaning of language as opposed to its structure. See also *Syntactic rules. p. 101*

sex role The social orientation that governs behavior, in contrast to a person's biological gender. *p. 121*

slang Language used by a group of people whose members belong to a similar coculture or other group. *p. 111*

symbols Arbitrary constructions that represent a communicator's thoughts. *p. 99*

syntactic rules Rules that govern the ways in which symbols can be arranged as opposed to the meanings of those symbols. See also *Semantic rules. p. 101*

Case Study Questions

Instructions: Reread the case study on pages 94–95 to answer the following questions in light of what you have learned in this chapter.

1. Describe an incident illustrating how meanings reside in people, not words.

2. Recall incidents when (a) language shaped attitudes and (b) choice of words reflected a communicator's attitudes.

3. Explain how the types of troublesome language described on pages 109–118 have caused problems in a situation you experienced or observed.

4. Describe how gender and nongender variables described on pages 118–120 affect communication.

5. Give examples illustrating how the communication styles described on pages 122–124 operate.

Activities

1. **Powerful Speech and Polite Speech** Increase your ability to achieve an optimal balance between powerful speech and polite speech by rehearsing one of the following scenarios:

   - Describing your qualifications to a potential employer for a job that interests you.

   - Requesting an extension on a deadline from one of your professors.

   - Explaining to a merchant why you want a cash refund on an unsatisfactory piece of merchandise when the store's policy is to issue credit vouchers.

   - Asking your boss for three days off so you can attend a friend's out-of-town wedding.

   - Approaching your neighbors whose dog barks while they are away from home.

   Your statement should gain its power by avoiding the types of powerless language listed in Table 4-1. You should not become abusive or threatening, and your statement should be completely honest.

2. **Slang and Jargon** Find a classmate, neighbor, coworker, or other person whose background differs significantly from yours. In an interview, ask this person to identify the slang and jargon terms that you take for granted but that he or she has found confusing. Explore the following types of potentially confusing terms:

   1. regionalisms

   2. age-related terms

   3. technical jargon

   4. acronyms

3. **Low-Level Abstractions** You can develop your ability to use low-level abstractions by following these steps:

   1. Use your own experience to write each of the following:

      a. a complaint or gripe

      b. one way you would like someone with whom you interact to change

YOU SHOULD UNDERSTAND:

1. The most common misconceptions about listening.
2. The five components of the listening process.
3. The most common types of ineffective listening.
4. The challenges that make effective listening difficult.
5. The skills necessary to listen effectively in informational, critical, and empathic settings.

YOU SHOULD BE ABLE TO:

1. Identify situations where you listen ineffectively and explain the reasons for your lack of effectiveness.
2. Identify the consequences of your ineffective listening.
3. Follow the guidelines for informational listening.
4. Analyze an argument or claim by evaluating the credibility of its proponent, the quality of evidence offered, and the soundness of its reasoning.
5. Apply appropriate response styles in an empathic listening context.

In a world where almost everyone acknowledges the importance of better communication, the need for good listening is obvious. On the most basic level, listening is just as important as speaking. After all, it's impossible for communication to occur without someone receiving a message. (Imagine how ridiculous it would be to speak to an empty room or talk into a disconnected telephone.)

If frequency is a measure of importance, then listening easily qualifies as the most prominent kind of communication. We spend more time in listening to others than in any other type of communication. One study revealed that of their total communicating time, college students spent an average of 11 percent writing, 16 percent speaking, 17 percent reading, but more than 55 percent listening.[1] On the job, listening is by far the most common form of communication. On average, employees of major corporations in North America spend about 60 percent of each working day listening to others.[2] The *International Journal of Listening* devoted an entire issue to exploring various contexts in which listening skills are crucial, including education,[3] health care,[4] religion,[5] and the business world.[6]

> Employees of major corporations in North America spend about 60 percent of each working day listening to others.

In his best-selling book, Stephen Covey identifies listening—making understanding others a top priority—as one of the "seven habits of highly effective people."[7] An impressive body of evidence backs up this claim. For example, when a group of adults was asked to identify the most important on-the-job communication skills, listening ranked at the top of the list. A study examining the link between listening and career success revealed that better listeners rose to higher levels in their organizations.[8] A survey of personnel managers identified listening as the most critical skill for working effectively in teams.[9] In small groups, other members view people who listen well as leaders.[10] Dennis Hastert, former Speaker of the U.S. House of Representatives, emphasized the value of understanding others when describing how he spent most of his time in this leadership role: "They call me the Speaker, but they ought to call me the Listener."[11]

Listening is just as important in personal relationships. In one survey, marital counselors identified "failing to take the other's perspective when listening" as one of the most frequent communication problems in the couples with whom they work.[12] When another group of adults was asked which communication skills were most important in family and social settings, listening was ranked first.[13] In committed relationships, listening to personal information in everyday conversations is considered an important ingredient of satisfaction.[14] For this reason, some theorists have argued that effective listening is an essential ingredient in effective relational communication.[15]

Despite the importance of listening, experience shows that much of the listening we and others do is not at all effective. We misunderstand others and are misunderstood in return. We become bored and feign attention while our minds wander. We engage in a battle of interruptions where each person fights to speak without hearing the other's ideas.

Some of this poor listening is inevitable, perhaps even justified. But in other cases we can be better receivers by learning a few basic listening skills. This chapter will help you become a better listener by giving you some important information about the subject. We'll talk about some common misconceptions concerning listening and show you what really happens when listening takes place. We'll discuss some poor listening habits, explain why they occur, and suggest better alternatives.

Misconceptions About Listening

In spite of its importance, listening is misunderstood by most people. Because these misunderstandings so greatly affect our communication, we need to take a look at four common misconceptions that many communicators hold.

Listening and Hearing Are Not the Same Thing

Hearing is the process in which sound waves strike the eardrum and cause vibrations that are transmitted to the brain. **Listening** occurs when the brain reconstructs these electrochemical impulses into a representation of the original sound and then gives

Source: King Feature Syndicate.

them meaning. Barring illness, injury, or earplugs, hearing can't be stopped. Your ears will pick up sound waves and transmit them to your brain whether you want them to or not. Listening, however, isn't automatic. Many times we hear but do not listen. Sometimes we deliberately tune out unwanted signals: everything from a neighbor's power lawn mower or the roar of nearby traffic to a friend's boring remarks or a boss's unwanted criticism.

A closer look at listening—at least the successful variety—shows that it consists of several stages. After hearing, the next stage is **attending**—the act of paying attention to a signal. An individual's needs, wants, desires, and interests determine what is attended to, or selected, to use the term introduced in Chapter 3.

The next step in listening is **understanding**—the process of making sense of a message. Communication researchers use the term **listening fidelity** to describe the degree of congruence between what a listener understands and what the message sender was attempting to communicate.[16] Chapter 4 discussed many of the ingredients that combine to make understanding possible: a grasp of the syntax of the language being spoken, semantic decoding, and knowledge of the pragmatic rules that help you figure out a speaker's meaning from the context. In addition to these steps, understanding often depends on the ability to organize the information we hear into recognizable form. As early as 1948, Ralph Nichols related successful understanding to a large number of factors, most prominent among which were verbal ability, intelligence, and motivation.[17]

Responding to a message consists of giving observable feedback to the speaker. Offering feedback serves two important functions: It helps you clarify your understanding of a speaker's message, and it shows that you care about what that speaker is saying.

Listeners don't always respond visibly to a speaker—but research suggests that they should. In one study, children distinguished "good" from "bad" listeners in terms of eye contact and reacting with appropriate facial expressions.[18] Nonverbal responding is just as important in the business world. One study of 195 critical incidents in banking and medical settings showed that a major difference between effective listening and ineffective listening was the kind of feedback offered.[19] Good listeners showed that they were attentive by nonverbal behaviors such as keeping eye contact and reacting with appropriate facial expressions. Their verbal behavior—answering questions and exchanging ideas, for example—also demonstrated their attention. It's easy to imagine how other responses would signal less effective listening. A slumped posture, bored expression, and yawning send a clear message that you are not tuned in to the speaker.

> Listeners don't always respond visibly to a speaker—but research suggests that they should.

Adding responsiveness to our listening model demonstrates the fact, discussed in Chapter 1, that communication is transactional in nature. Listening isn't just a passive activity. As listeners we are active participants in a communication transaction. At the same time that we receive messages we also send them.

The final step in the listening process is **remembering**.[20] Research has revealed that people remember only about half of what they hear *immediately after* hearing it.[21] This is true even if people work hard at listening. This situation would probably not be too bad if the half remembered right after were retained, but it isn't. Within two months half of the half is forgotten, bringing what we remember down to about 25 percent of the original message. This loss, however, doesn't take two months: People start forgetting immediately (within eight hours the 50 percent remembered drops to about 35 percent). Of course, these amounts vary from person to person and depend on the importance of the information being recalled.[22] Given the amount of information we process every

TABLE 5-1   Comparison of Communication Activities

	LISTENING	SPEAKING	READING	WRITING
LEARNED	First	Second	Third	Fourth
USED	Most	Next to most	Next to least	Least
TAUGHT	Least	Next to least	Next to most	Most

day—from instructors, friends, the radio, TV, and other sources—the **residual message** (what we remember) is a small fraction of what we hear.

Listening Is Not a Natural Process

Another common myth is that listening is like breathing: a natural activity that people do well. The truth is that listening is a skill much like speaking: Everybody does it, though few people do it well. One study illustrates this point: 144 managers in a study were asked to rate their listening skills. Astonishingly, not one of the managers described himself or herself as a "poor" or "very poor" listener, whereas 94 percent rated themselves as "good" or "very good."[23] The favorable self-ratings contrasted sharply with the perceptions of the managers' subordinates, many of whom said their boss's listening skills were weak. As we have already discussed, some poor listening is inevitable. The good news is that listening can be improved through instruction and training.[24] Despite this fact, the amount of time devoted to teaching listening is far less than that devoted to other types of communication. Table 5-1 reflects this upside-down arrangement.

All Listeners Do Not Receive the Same Message

When two or more people are listening to a speaker, we tend to assume that they all are hearing and understanding the same message. In fact, such uniform comprehension isn't the case. Recall the discussion of perception in Chapter 3, where we pointed out the many factors that cause each of us to perceive an event differently. Physiological factors, social roles, cultural background, personal interests, and needs all shape and distort the raw data we hear into uniquely different messages.

Overcoming Challenges to Effective Listening

Despite the importance of good listening, people seem to get worse at the skill as they grow older.[25] Teachers at various grade levels were asked to stop their lectures periodically and ask students what they were talking about. Ninety percent of first-grade children could repeat what the teacher had been saying, and 80 percent of the second-graders could do so, but when the experiment was repeated with teenagers, the results were much less impressive. Only 44 percent of junior high school students and 28 percent of senior high school students could repeat their teachers' remarks.

Research suggests that adults listen even more poorly—at least in some important relationships. One experiment found that people listened more attentively and courteously to strangers than to their spouses. When faced with decision-making tasks, couples interrupted one another more frequently and were generally less polite than they were to strangers.[26]

What kinds of poor listening habits plague communication? To find out, read on.

Mindful Listening Requires Effort

Most people assume that listening is fundamentally a passive activity in which the receiver absorbs a speaker's ideas, rather the way a sponge absorbs water. It's true that some listening is basically passive. Social scientists use the term **mindless listening** to describe this sort of activity.[27] The term "mindless" may sound negative, but given the number of messages to which we're exposed, it's impractical to listen carefully and thoughtfully 100 percent of the time. Furthermore, this sort of low-level information processing can free us to focus on messages that do require more careful attention.[28] By contrast, **mindful listening** is hard work. The physical changes that occur during careful listening show the effort it takes: Heart rate quickens, respiration increases, and body temperature rises.[29] Notice that these changes are similar to the body's reaction to physical effort. This is no coincidence, because mindful listening can be just as taxing as more obvious efforts.

> It's impractical to listen carefully and thoughtfully 100 percent of the time.

Faulty Listening Behaviors

Although we can't listen effectively all the time, most people possess one or more habits that keep them from understanding truly important messages.

Pseudolistening   Pseudolistening is an imitation of the real thing. Pseudolisteners give the appearance of being attentive: They look you in the eye, nod and smile at the right times, and even may answer you occasionally. That appearance of interest, however, is a polite facade to mask thoughts that have nothing to do with what the speaker is saying.

Selective Listening   Selective listeners respond only to the parts of a speaker's remarks that interest them. All of us are selective listeners from time to time, as, for instance, when we screen out media commercials and music while keeping an ear cocked for a weather report or an announcement of time. In other cases, selective listening occurs in conversations with people who expect a thorough hearing but get their partner's attention only when the conversation turns to the partner's favorite topic.

Defensive Listening   Defensive listeners take innocent comments as personal attacks. Teenagers who perceive parental questions about friends and activities as distrustful snooping are defensive listeners, as are insecure breadwinners who explode when their mates mention money and touchy parents who view any questioning by their children as a threat to their authority and parental wisdom. Many defensive listeners are suffering from shaky public images and avoid admitting this by projecting their insecurities onto others.

CULTURAL IDIOM

keeping an ear cocked:
listening alertly

breadwinners:
those who support their families with their earnings

Source: © Scott Adams/Dist. By United Feature Syndicate, Inc.

Ambushing   Ambushers listen carefully, but only because they are collecting information to attack what you have to say. The cross-examining prosecution attorney is a good example of an ambusher. Using this kind of strategy will justifiably initiate defensiveness on the other's part.

Insulated Listening   Insulated listeners are almost the opposite of their selective-listening cousins. Instead of looking for something specific, these people avoid certain topics. Whenever a subject arises they'd rather not deal with, insulated listeners simply fail to hear it or, rather, to acknowledge it.

Insensitive Listening   Insensitive listeners are the final example of people who don't receive another person's messages clearly. People often don't express their thoughts or feelings openly but instead communicate them through subtle and unconscious choice of words or nonverbal clues or both. Insensitive listeners aren't able to look beyond the words and behavior to understand their hidden meanings. Instead, they take a speaker's remarks at face value.

Stage Hogging   Stage hogs (sometimes called "conversational narcissists") try to turn the topic of conversations to themselves instead of showing interest in the speaker.[30] Interruptions are a hallmark of stage hogging. Besides preventing the listener from learning potentially valuable information, stage hogging can damage the relationship between the interrupter and the speaker. For example, applicants who interrupt the questions of an employment interviewer are likely to be rated less favorably than job seekers who wait until the interviewer has finished speaking before they respond.[31]

Reasons for Poor Listening

What causes people to listen poorly? There are several reasons, some of which can be avoided and others that are sad but inescapable facts of life.

Message Overload   The amount of speech most of us encounter every day makes careful listening to everything we hear impossible. Along with the deluge of face-to-face messages, we are bombarded by phone calls, e-mails, tweets, texts, and instant messages. Besides those personal messages, we're awash in

> Along with the deluge of face-to-face messages, we are bombarded by phone calls, e-mails, tweets, texts, and instant messages.

@Work

Multitasking: A Recipe for Inattention

Multitasking may be a fact of life on the job, but research suggests that dividing your attention has its costs. In one widely reported study, volunteers tried to carry out various problem-solving tasks while being deluged with phone calls and e-mails.[32] Even though experimenters told the subjects to ignore these distractions, the average performance drop was equivalent to a ten-point decline in IQ. In other words, trying to work on one task while listening to messages about a different matter can make you more stupid.

You might expect that greater exposure to multiple messages would improve multitasking performance, but just the opposite seems to be the case. Heavy media multitaskers perform worse on task switching than light media multitaskers.[33] While chronic multitaskers believe they are competent at processing information, in fact they're worse than those who focus more on a single medium.[34]

You may not be able to escape multiple demands at work, but don't hold any illusions about the cost of information overload. When the matter at hand is truly important, the most effective approach may be to turn off the phone and computer, and devote your attention to the single task before you.

CULTURAL IDIOM

charade:
pretense

programming from the mass media. This deluge of communication has made the challenge of attending tougher than at any time in human history.[35] The "@Work" box on page 137 highlights the dangers of multitasking and argues that managing information overload can lead to better results.

Rapid Thought   Listening carefully is also difficult for a physiological reason. Although we are capable of understanding speech at rates up to 600 words per minute, the average person speaks between 100 and 140 words per minute.[36] Thus, we have a great deal of mental "spare time" to spend while someone is talking. And the temptation is to use this time in ways that don't relate to the speaker's ideas, such as thinking about personal interests, daydreaming, planning a rebuttal, and so on. The trick is to use this spare time to understand the speaker's ideas better rather than to let your attention wander. Try to rephrase the speaker's ideas in your own words. Ask yourself how the ideas might be useful to you. Consider other angles that the speaker might not have mentioned.

Psychological Noise   Another reason why we don't always listen carefully is that we're often wrapped up in personal concerns that are of more immediate importance to us than the messages others are sending. It's hard to pay attention to someone else when you're anticipating an upcoming test or thinking about the wonderful time you had last night with good friends. Yet, we still feel we have to "listen" politely to others, and so we continue with our charade. It usually takes a conscious effort to set aside your personal concerns if you expect to give others' messages the attention they deserve.

Figure 5-1 illustrates four ways in which preoccupied listeners lose focus when distracted by psychological noise. Everyone's mind wanders at one time or another, but excessive preoccupation is both a reason for and a sign of poor listening.

Physical Noise   The world in which we live often presents distractions that make it hard to pay attention to others. The sound of traffic, music, others' speech, and the like interfere with our ability to hear well. Also, fatigue or other forms of discomfort can distract us from paying attention to a speaker's remarks. Consider, for example, how the efficiency of your listening decreases when you are seated in a crowded, hot, stuffy room that is surrounded by traffic and other noises. In such circumstances even the best intentions aren't enough to ensure clear understanding. You can often listen better by insulating yourself from outside distractions. This may involve removing the sources of noise: turning off the television, shutting the book you were reading, closing the window, and so on. In some cases, you and the speaker may need to find a more hospitable place to speak in order to make listening work.

Hearing Problems   Sometimes a person's listening ability suffers from a hearing problem—the most obvious sort of physiological noise, as defined in Chapter 1. One survey explored the feelings of adults who have spouses with hearing loss. Nearly two-thirds of the respondents said they feel annoyed when their partner can't hear them clearly. Almost a quarter said that beyond just being annoyed, they felt ignored, hurt, or sad. Many of the respondents believe their spouses are in denial about their condition, which makes the problem even more frustrating.[37]

After a hearing problem has been diagnosed, it's often possible to treat it. The real tragedy occurs when a hearing loss goes undetected. In such cases, both the person with the defect and others can become frustrated and annoyed at the ineffective communication that results. If you suspect that you or someone you know suffers from a hearing loss, it's wise to have a physician or audiologist perform an examination.

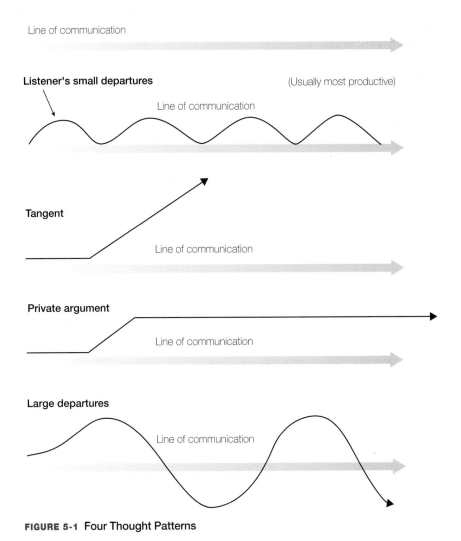

FIGURE 5-1 Four Thought Patterns

Faulty Assumptions   We often give others a mental brush-off because we assume their remarks don't have much value. When one business consultant asked some of her clients why they interrupted colleagues, she received the following responses:

My idea is better than theirs.

If I don't interrupt them, I'll never get to say my idea.

I know what they are about to say.

They don't need to finish their thoughts since mine are better.

Nothing about their idea will improve with further development.

It is more important for me to get recognized than it is to hear their idea.

I'm more important than they are.[38]

The egotism behind these comments is stunning. Dismissing others' ideas before considering them may be justified sometimes, but it's obviously a mistake to rule out so much of what others say . . . especially when you consider how you would feel if other people dismissed your comments without hearing you out.

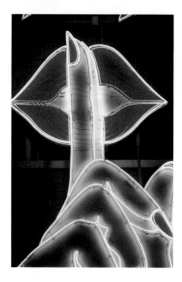

Talking Has More Apparent Advantages   It often appears that we have more to gain by speaking than by listening. Whatever the goal—to have a prospective boss hire you, to convince others to vote for the candidate of your choice, or to describe the way you want your hair cut—the key to success seems to be the ability to speak well. Another apparent advantage of speaking is the chance it provides to gain the admiration, respect, or liking of others—or so you may think. Tell jokes, and everyone may think you're a real wit. Offer advice, and they might be grateful for your help. Tell them all you know, and they could be impressed by your wisdom.

Although speaking at the right time can lead people to appreciate you, talking too much can result in the kind of stage hogging described on page 137. Not all interruptions are attempts at stage hogging. One study revealed a difference between male and female interrupters.[39] Men typically interrupted conversations far more than women. Their goal was usually to control the discussion. Women interrupted for very different reasons: to communicate agreement, to elaborate on the speaker's idea, or to participate in the topic of conversation. These sorts of responses are more likely to be welcomed as a contribution to the conversation and not as attempts to grab the stage.

If you find yourself hogging the conversation, try a simple experiment. Limit the frequency and length of your responses to a fraction of their usual amount. If you were speaking 50 percent of the time, cut back to 25 percent—or even less. If you interrupt the speaker every fifteen seconds, try to let him or her talk for closer to a minute. You are likely to discover that you're learning more—and probably gaining the appreciation of the other person.

Cultural Differences   The way members of different cultures communicate can affect listening.[40] For instance, one study of young adults in various countries showed marked differences in listening preferences. Young Germans favored an action-oriented approach: They engaged speakers directly and were highly inquisitive. This style contrasts with the indirect approach of high-context Japanese listeners. Young Israelis were also less vocal than Germans and focused on careful analysis of others' statements. By contrast, young Americans emphasized the social dimension of a conversation and were more focused on how much time a conversation was taking.

Media Influences   A final challenge to serious listening is the influence of contemporary mass media, especially television and radio. A growing amount of programming consists of short segments: news items, commercials, music videos, and so on. (Think of *Sesame Street* and MTV.) In the same vein, news stories (for example, *USA Today* and the television news) consist of brief stories with a declining portion of text and a growing amount of graphical information. These trends discourage the kind of focused attention that is necessary for careful listening, especially to complicated ideas and feelings.

CULTURAL IDIOM

wit:
a clever conversationalist

grab the stage:
gain attention

Ethical Challenge

How Carefully Should You Listen?

What responsibility do communicators have to listen as carefully and thoughtfully as possible? Are there ever cases where we are justified in pseudolistening? Stage hogging? Defensive listening? Selective attention? Responding defensively? Ambushing? Insensitivity?

Is it dishonest to fake careful listening when you are not doing so, or do communicators have an obligation to confess that they are not listening? How would you feel if you knew others weren't listening to you?

Invitation to Insight

What Good Is Free Speech if No One Listens?

It is the law in this country, as in no other, that the individual has an extraordinary right to personal expression. The First Amendment to the Constitution protects the right to speak and to publish; these rights and the degree to which they are safeguarded are the distinguishing characteristics of American society.

For that we have only the courts to thank. Americans seem to be almost completely uninterested in any point of view other than their individual one. We are absolutely up to our necks in groups and blocs and religious and economic interests certain beyond all reason that they are correct and actively interested in imposing their rules and values and self-selected morals on the rest of us. They prattle about democracy, and use it when it suits them without the slightest regard or respect for what it means and costs and requires. These people are—please believe me—dangerous.

The right to speak is meaningless if no one will listen, and the right to publish is not worth having if no one will read. It is simply not enough that we reject censorship and will not countenance suppression; we have an affirmative responsibility to hear the argument before we disagree with it.

I think that you think that you agree with me, that you are fair and open-minded and good citizens. But if we put it to the test—if I make up some speeches about gun control, abortion, gay rights,

racial and ethnic characteristics, political terrorism and genocide—I believe that I can make you boo and jeer or at least walk out in protest.

We cannot operate that way. It's not difficult to listen to the philosophy you agree with or don't care about. It's the one that galls that must be heard. No idea is so repugnant that it must not be advocated. If we are not free to speak heresy and utter awful thoughts, we are not free at all. And if we are unwilling to hear that with which we most violently disagree, we are no longer citizens but have become part of the mob.

Nowhere is the willingness to listen more important than at a university, and nowhere is our failure more apparent than at the university whose faculty members or students think that it's legitimate to parade their own moral or political purity by shouting down the unpopular view of the day.

It will not be a week, and certainly not a month, before you will become aware that someone in your own circle of influence is saying something or thinking something very wrong. I think you have to do something about that. I think you have to help them be heard. I think you are required to listen.

Kurt Luedtke

Personal Listening Styles

Not everyone listens the same way. Communication researchers have identified four styles, each of which has both strengths and weaknesses.[41]

Content-Oriented

As the label that characterizes them suggests, **content-oriented listeners** are most interested in the quality of messages they hear. They want to seek details and are good at analyzing an issue from several perspectives. They give weight to the messages of experts and other credible sources of information. Content-oriented listeners often enjoy ideas for their own sake and are willing to spend time exploring them in thorough exchanges of ideas.

A content-oriented approach is valuable when the goal is to evaluate the quality of ideas and when there is value in looking at issues from a wide range of perspectives. It is especially valuable when the topic is a complicated one. On the other hand, a content-oriented approach risks annoying people who don't have the same sort of analytical orientation. A content-oriented approach can take more time than others may be willing to give, and the challenging of ideas that comes with it can be perceived as overly critical or even hostile.

CULTURAL IDIOM

give weight to:
give priority to

CULTURAL IDIOM

tuned in:
focused, paying attention

put off:
displease

People-Oriented

People-oriented listeners are especially concerned with creating and maintaining positive relationships. They tune in to others' moods, and they respond to speakers' feelings as well as their ideas. People-oriented listeners are typically less judgmental about what others have to say than are content-oriented types: They are more interested in understanding and supporting people than in evaluating them.[42]

A people orientation has obvious strengths. But a strong concern for relationships has some less obvious drawbacks. It is easy to become overly involved with others' feelings. People-oriented listeners may lose their detachment and ability to assess the quality of information others are giving in an effort to be congenial and supportive. Less personally oriented communicators can view them as overly expressive and even intrusive.

Action-Oriented

Unlike people-oriented listeners, who focus on relationships, and content-oriented listeners, who are fascinated with ideas for their own sake, **action-oriented listeners** are most concerned with the task at hand. Their main concern is to figure out what sort of response is required by a message. They want to get to the heart of the matter quickly, and so they appreciate clear, concise messages and often translate others' remarks into well-organized mental outlines.

Action-oriented listening is most appropriate when taking care of business is the primary concern: Such listeners keep a focus on the job at hand and encourage others to be organized and concise. But their no-nonsense approach isn't always appreciated by speakers who lack the skill or inclination to be clear and direct. Action-oriented listeners seem to minimize emotional issues and concerns, which may be an important part of business and personal transactions.

Time-Oriented

Time-oriented listeners are most concerned with efficiency. They view time as a scarce and valuable commodity. They grow impatient when they view others as wasting it. A time orientation can be an asset when deadlines and other pressures demand fast action. On the other hand, a time orientation can put off others when it seems to disregard their feelings. Also, an excessive focus on time can hamper the kind of thoughtful deliberation that some jobs require.

> Whichever styles you use, it is important to recognize that you can control the way you listen and to use the styles that best suit the situation at hand.

As you read the preceding descriptions, you may have found that you use more than one of the listening styles. If so, you aren't alone: 40 percent of the populations measured indicate at least two strong listening preferences.[43] Whichever styles you use, it is important to recognize that you can control the way you listen and to use the styles that best suit the situation at hand. When your relationship with the speaker needs attention, adopt a people-oriented approach. When clarity is the issue, be an action-oriented listener. If analysis is called for, put on your content-oriented persona. And when the clock is what matters most, become a model of time orientation. You can also boost your effectiveness by assessing the listening preferences of your conversational partners and adapting your style to them.

Informational Listening

Informational listening is the approach to take when you want to understand another person. When you are an informational listener, your goal is to make sure you are receiving the same thoughts the other person is trying to convey—not always an easy feat when you consider the forces listed on pages 137–140 that interfere with understanding.

The situations that call for informational listening are endless and varied: following an instructor's comments in class, listening to a friend's account of a night on the town, hearing a description of a new piece of equipment that you're thinking about buying, learning about your family history from a relative's tales, swapping ideas in a discussion about religion or politics—the list goes on and on. You can become more effective as an informational listener by approaching others with a constructive attitude and by using some simple but effective skills.

Don't Argue or Judge Prematurely

Ever since ancient Greece and later Rome, Western civilization has admired the ability to persuade others.[44] This tradition has led us to measure the success of much communication in terms of whether it changes the way others think and act. Recall, for example, what often happens when people encounter someone with differing opinions. Rather than try to understand one another, their conversation often turns into an argument or

---

Understanding Diversity

Council: Reviving the Art of Listening

Not too long ago, before our ears became accustomed to an increasing barrage of stimulation, many people knew how to listen attentively, while tracking an animal or hearing the approach of rain—or sitting in council with a group of their peers.

We know of no more effective way to invoke this state of listening than in what we have come to call the "council process." The origin of this process can be traced to the League of the Iroquois (which had a powerful influence on the beginnings of our present governmental system) and the peoples of the plains and of the Southwestern pueblos. More recently, the traditional practice of council has emerged in contemporary form through the Native American Church. The roots of council also can be found in Homer's *Iliad*, where a talking wand was used by a gathering of men to resolve the bitter dispute between Achilles and Agamemnon.

As we have practiced it, the basic form of council is simple. In order to empower each person to speak in turn, a "talking" object or "stick" is chosen to be passed around the circle—traditionally clockwise, in the "sun direction." The talking stick can be as innocent as a flower just picked for the occasion or as venerable as a traditional hand-crafted artifact familiar to the group. Many councils that meet regularly use the same object over a period of months or even years, so that it becomes a symbol of the group's integrity and its capability for spirited communication.

We often set three simple rules for council: Speak honestly, be brief, and listen from the heart. One of the great challenges is to not be thinking about what you're going to say until it's your turn to speak. Preparing your contribution before you receive the talking stick obviously diminishes its spontaneity and its responsiveness to what others have said. A good practice is to wait until the talking stick is in your hands and then pause to see what springs to mind. Often we are surprised at the humor, tears, wisdom, or vision that comes forth.

We share the concern many people have today about the superficial "playing Indian"—that is, the appropriation of another culture's traditions. We want to acknowledge how much we have learned from the teachings of Native American peoples and our own ancestors. Council for us is a spiritual practice growing out of all our history, and a practice in which we seek to express these roots in a contemporary context.

Jack Zimmerman and Virginia Coyle
The Way of Council

Calvin and Hobbes

by Bill Watterson

Source: CALVIN and HOBBES © 1995 Watterson. Reprinted with permission of UNIVERSAL PRESS SYNDICATE. All Rights Reserved.

debate (sometimes friendly, sometimes not) in which the participants try to change one another's minds.

Persuasion is certainly one important goal of communication, but it isn't the only one. Most people would agree with the principle that it's essential to understand a speaker's ideas before judging them. Despite this common-sense fact, all of us are guilty of forming snap judgments, evaluating others before hearing them out. This tendency is greatest when the speaker's ideas conflict with our own.

Not all premature judgments are negative. It's also possible to jump to overly favorable conclusions about the quality of a speaker's remarks when we like that person or agree with the ideas being expressed. The lesson contained in these examples is clear: Listen first. Make sure you understand. Then evaluate or argue, if you choose.

> Listen first. Make sure you understand. Then evaluate or argue, if you choose.

Separate the Message from the Speaker

The first recorded cases of blaming the messenger for an unpleasant message occurred in ancient Greece. When messengers would arrive reporting losses in battles, their generals were known to respond to the bad news by having the messengers put to death. This sort of irrational reaction is still common (though fortunately less violent) today. Consider a few situations in which there is a tendency to get angry with a communicator bearing unpleasant news: An instructor tries to explain why you did poorly on a major paper; a friend explains what you did to make a fool of yourself at the party last Saturday night; the boss points out how you could do your job better. At times like this, becoming irritated with the bearer of unpleasant information not only can cause you to miss important information but also can harm your relationships.

There's a second way that confusing the message and the messenger can prevent you from understanding important ideas. At times you may mistakenly discount the value of a message because of the person who is presenting it. Even the most boring instructors, the most idiotic relatives, and the most demanding bosses occasionally make good points. If you write off everything a person says before you consider it, you may be cheating yourself out of some valuable information.

Search for Value

CULTURAL IDIOM

write off:
dismiss as worthless or unimportant

Even if you listen with an open mind, sooner or later you will end up hearing information that is either so unimportant or so badly delivered that you're tempted to tune out. Although making a quick escape from such tedious situations is often the best thing to do, there are times when you can profit from paying close attention to apparently worthless communication. This is especially true when you're trapped in a situation where the only alternatives to attentiveness are pseudolistening or downright rudeness.

Once you try, you probably can find some value in even the worst situations. Consider how you might listen opportunistically when you find yourself locked in a boring conversation with someone whose ideas are worthless. Rather than torture yourself until escape is possible, you could keep yourself amused—and perhaps learn something useful—by listening carefully until you can answer the following (unspoken) questions:

"Is there anything useful in what this person is saying?"

"What led the speaker to come up with ideas like these?"

"What lessons can I learn from this person that will keep me from sounding the same way in other situations?"

Listening with a constructive attitude is important, but even the best intentions won't always help you understand others. The following skills can help you figure out messages that otherwise might be confusing, as well as help you see how those messages can make a difference in your life.

Look for Key Ideas

It's easy to lose patience with long-winded speakers who never seem to get to the point— or have a point, for that matter. Nonetheless, most people do have a central idea, or what we will call a "thesis" in Chapter 11. By using your ability to think more quickly than the speaker can talk, you may be able to extract the thesis from the surrounding mass of words you're hearing. If you can't figure out what the speaker is driving at, you can always ask in a tactful way by using the skills of questioning and paraphrasing, which we examine now.

Ask Questions

Questioning involves asking for additional information to clarify your idea of the sender's message. If you ask directions to a friend's house, typical questions might be "Is your place an apartment?" or "How long does it take to get there from here?" In more serious situations, questions could include "Why does that bother you so much?" or "You sound upset—is there something wrong?" Notice that one key element of these questions is that they request the speaker to elaborate on information already given.

Despite their apparent benefits, not all questions are equally helpful. Whereas **sincere questions** are aimed at understanding others, **counterfeit questions** are really disguised attempts to send a message, not receive one.

Counterfeit questions come in several varieties:

- *Questions that make statements.* "Are you finally ready to go now?" "You can't be serious about that, right?" Comments like these are certainly not genuine requests for information. Emphasizing certain words can also turn a question into a statement: "You lent money to *Tony?*" We also use questions to offer advice. The person who responds with "Are you going to stand up to him and give him what he deserves?" clearly has stated an opinion about what should be done.

Not all questions are equally helpful.

CULTURAL IDIOM
long-winded:
speaking for a long time
to stand up to:
to confront courageously

FIGURE 5-2 Asking Questions Doesn't Guarantee Understanding

■ *Questions that carry hidden agendas.* "Are you busy Friday night?" is a dangerous question to answer. If you say, "No," thinking the person has something fun in mind, you won't like hearing, "Good, because I need some help moving my piano."

■ *Questions that seek "correct" answers.* Most of us have been victims of question-askers who want to hear only a particular response. "Which shoes do you think I should wear?" can be a sincere question—unless the asker has a predetermined preference. When this happens, the asker isn't interested in listening to contrary opinions, and "incorrect" responses get shot down. Some of these questions may venture into delicate territory. "Honey, do you think I look ugly?" can be a request for a "correct" answer.

■ *Questions that are based on unchecked assumptions.* "Why aren't you listening to me?" assumes the other person isn't paying attention. "What's the matter?" assumes that something is wrong. As Chapter 3 explains, perception checking is a much better way of checking out assumptions: "When you kept looking over at the TV, I thought you weren't listening to me, but maybe I was wrong. *Were* you paying attention?"

Unlike counterfeit questions, sincere questions are genuine requests for new information that clarifies a speaker's thoughts or feelings. Although the value of sincere questioning might seem obvious, people don't use this information-seeking approach enough. Communicators are often reluctant to show their ignorance by asking for explanation of what seems like an obvious point. At times like this it's a good idea to recall a quote attributed to Confucius: "He who asks a question is a fool for five minutes. He who does not ask is a fool for life."

Paraphrase

Questioning is often a valuable tool for increasing understanding. Sometimes, however, questions won't help you understand a speaker's ideas any more clearly. As the humorous drawing on this page shows, questions can even lead to greater misunderstandings. Now consider another type of feedback—one that would tell you whether you understood what had already been said before you asked additional questions. This sort of feedback, termed **paraphrasing**, involves restating in your own words the message you thought the speaker had just sent, without adding anything new.

> *(To a direction giver)* "You're telling me to drive down to the traffic light by the high school and turn toward the mountains, is that it?"
>
> *(To the boss)* "So you need me both this Saturday *and* next Saturday—right?"
>
> *(To a professor)* "When you said, 'Don't worry about the low grade on the quiz,' did you mean it won't count against my grade?"

In other cases, a paraphrase will reflect your understanding of the speaker's *feelings*:

> "You said 'I've had it with this relationship!' Are you angry or relieved that it's over?"

"You said you've got a minute to talk, but I'm not sure whether it's a good time for you."

"You said 'Forget it,' but it sounds like you're mad. Are you?"

Whether your paraphrasing reflects a speaker's thoughts or feelings, and whether it focuses on a specific comment or a general theme, the key to success is to restate the other person's comments in your own words as a way of cross-checking the information. If you simply repeat the speaker's comments verbatim, you will sound foolish—and you still might well be misunderstanding what has been said. Notice the difference between simply parroting a statement and really paraphrasing:

Speaker:	"I'd like to go, but I can't afford it."
Parroting:	"You'd like to go, but you can't afford it."
Paraphrasing:	"So if we could find a way to pay for you, you'd be willing to come. Is that right?"
Speaker:	"What's the matter with you?"
Parroting:	"You think there's something wrong with me?"
Paraphrasing:	"You think I'm mad at you?"

As these examples suggest, effective paraphrasing is a skill that takes time to develop. You can make your paraphrasing sound more natural by taking any of three approaches, depending on the situation:

1. **Change the speaker's wording.**

Speaker:	"Bilingual education is just another failed idea of bleeding-heart liberals."
Paraphrase:	"Let me see if I've got this right. You're mad because you think bilingual ed sounds good, but it doesn't work?" *(Reflects both the speaker's feeling and the reason for it.)*

2. **Offer an example of what you think the speaker is talking about.** When the speaker makes an abstract statement, you may suggest a specific example or two to see if your understanding is accurate.

Speaker:	"Lee is such a jerk. I can't believe the way he acted last night."
Paraphrase:	"You think those jokes were pretty offensive, huh?" *(Reflects the listener's guess about speaker's reason for objecting to the behavior.)*

3. **Reflect the underlying theme of the speaker's remarks.** When you want to summarize the theme that seems to have run through another person's conversation, a complete or partial perception check is appropriate:

Paraphrase:	"You keep reminding me to be careful. Sounds like you're worried that something might happen to me. Am I right?" *(Reflects both the speaker's thoughts and feelings and explicitly seeks clarification.)*

Learning to paraphrase isn't easy, but it can be worth the effort, because it offers two very real advantages. First, it boosts the odds that you'll accurately and fully understand what others are saying. We've already seen that using one-way listening or even asking questions may lead you to think that you've understood a speaker when, in fact, you haven't. Paraphrasing, on the other hand, serves as a way of double-checking your interpretation for accuracy. Second, paraphrasing guides you toward sincerely trying to understand another person instead of using nonlistening styles such as stage hogging,

CULTURAL IDIOM

shot down:
rejected or defeated

parroting:
repeating without understanding

bleeding-heart liberals:
persons motivated by sympathy rather than practicality

boosts the odds:
increases the chances of success

selective listening, and so on. If you force yourself to reflect the other person's ideas in your own words, you'll spend your mental energy trying to understand that speaker instead of using less constructive listening styles. For this reason, some communication experts suggest that the ratio of questioning and paraphrasing to confronting should be at least 5:1, if not more.[45]

Take Notes

Understanding others is crucial, of course, but comprehending their ideas doesn't guarantee that you will remember them. As you read earlier in this chapter, listeners usually forget almost two-thirds of what they hear.

Sometimes recall isn't especially important. You don't need to retain many details of the vacation adventures recounted by a neighbor or the childhood stories told by a relative. At other times, though, remembering a message—even minute details—is important. The lectures you hear in class are an obvious example. Likewise, it can be important to remember the details of plans that involve you: the time of a future appointment, the name of a phone caller whose message you took for someone else, or the orders given by your boss at work.

At times like these it's smart to take notes instead of relying on your memory. Sometimes these notes may be simple and brief: a phone number jotted on a scrap of paper or a list of things to pick up at the market. In other cases—a lecture, for example—your notes need to be much longer. When detailed notes are necessary, a few simple points will help make them effective:

1. *Don't wait too long before beginning to jot down ideas.* If you don't realize that you need to take notes until five minutes into a conversation, you're likely to forget much of what has been said and miss out on other information as you scramble to catch up.

2. *Record only key ideas.* Don't try to capture every word of long messages. If you can pin down the most important points, your notes will be easier to follow and much more useful.

3. *Develop a note-taking format.* The exact form you choose isn't important. Some people use a formal outlining scheme with headings designated by roman numerals, letters, and numbers, whereas others use simple lists. You might come up with useful symbols: boxes around key names and numbers or asterisks next to especially important information. After you develop a consistent format, your notes will not only help you remember information but also help you whip others' ideas into a shape that's useful to you.

Critical Listening

Whereas the goal of informational listening is to understand a speaker, the goal of **critical listening** (also called "evaluative listening") is to judge the quality of a message in order to decide whether to accept or reject it. At first the words *critical* and *evaluative* may put you off, because both words carry the negative connotations of carping and fault finding. But critical listeners needn't be hostile. Critical listening—at least in the sense we're discussing here—involves evaluating an idea to test its merit. In this sense, we could say that noncritical listeners are unquestioning, or even naive and gullible. Critical listening is appropriate when someone is trying to persuade you to buy a product, to act in a certain way, or to accept a belief—to cite a few examples. You will be most effective as a critical listener if you follow several guidelines:

Listen for Information Before Evaluating

The principle of listening for information before evaluating seems almost too obvious to mention, yet all of us are guilty of judging a speaker's ideas before we completely understand them. The tendency to make premature judgments is especially strong when the idea you are hearing conflicts with your own beliefs.

You can avoid the tendency to judge before understanding by following the simple rule of paraphrasing a speaker's ideas before responding to them. The effort required to translate the other person's ideas into your own words will keep you from arguing, and if your interpretation is mistaken, you'll know immediately.

> You can avoid the tendency to judge before understanding by following the simple rule of paraphrasing.

Evaluate the Speaker's Credibility

The acceptability of an idea often depends on its source. If your longtime family friend, the self-made millionaire, invited you to invest your life savings in jojoba fruit futures, you might be grateful for the tip. If your deadbeat brother-in-law made the same offer, you would probably laugh off the suggestion.

Chapter 14 discusses credibility in detail, but two questions provide a quick guideline for deciding whether or not to accept a speaker as an authority:

1. *Is the speaker competent?* Does the speaker have the experience or the expertise to qualify as an authority on this subject? Note that someone who is knowledgeable in one area may not be as well qualified to comment in another area. For instance, your friend who can answer any question about computer programming might be a terrible advisor when the subject turns to romance.

2. *Is the speaker impartial?* Knowledge alone isn't enough to certify a speaker's ideas as acceptable. People who have a personal stake in the outcome of a topic are more likely to be biased. The unqualified praise a commission-earning salesperson gives a product may be more suspect than the mixed review you get from a user. This doesn't mean you should disregard any comments you hear from an involved party—only that you should consider the possibility of intentional or unintentional bias.

Examine the Speaker's Evidence and Reasoning

Speakers usually offer some kind of support to back up their statements. A car dealer who argues that domestic cars are just as reliable as imports might cite frequency-of-repair statistics from *Consumer Reports* or refer you to satisfied customers, for example; and a professor arguing that students don't work as hard as they used to might tell stories about then and now to back up the thesis.

Chapter 12 describes several types of supporting material that can be used to prove a point: definitions, descriptions, analogies, statistics, and so on. Whatever form the support takes, you can ask several questions to determine the quality of a speaker's evidence and reasoning:[46]

1. *Is the evidence recent enough?* In many cases, ranging from trivial to important, old evidence is worthless. If the honors were earned several years ago, the cuisine from an "award-winning" restaurant may be barely edible today. The claim "Tony is a jerk" may have been true in the past, but people do change. Before you accept even the most credible evidence, be sure it isn't obsolete.

2. *Is enough evidence presented?* One or two pieces of support may be exceptions and not conclusive evidence. You might have heard this example of generalizing from limited

CULTURAL IDIOM

deadbeat:
one who does not regularly pay bills

laugh off:
dismiss with a laugh

evidence: "I never wear seat belts. I knew somebody who wasn't wearing them in an accident, and his life was saved because he was thrown clear from the car." Although not wearing seat belts might have been safer in this instance, on the average, experts agree when you consider all vehicle accidents, the chances of avoiding serious injury are much greater if you wear seat belts.

3. *Is the evidence from a reliable source?* Even a large amount of recent evidence may be worthless if the source is weak. Your cousin, the health-food fanatic, might not have the qualifications to talk about the poisonous effects of commercially farmed vegetables. On the other hand, the opinion of an impartial physician, nutritionist, or toxologist would carry more weight.

4. *Can the evidence be interpreted in more than one way?* A piece of evidence that supports one claim might also support others. For example, you might hear someone argue that statistics showing women are underrepresented in the management of a company are part of a conspiracy to exclude them from positions of power. The same statistics, though, could have other explanations: Perhaps fewer women have been with the company long enough to be promoted, or perhaps this is a field that has not attracted large numbers of women. Alternative explanations don't necessarily mean that the one being argued is wrong, but they do raise questions that need to be answered before you accept an argument.

Besides taking a close look at the evidence a speaker presents, a critical listener will also look at how that evidence is put together to prove a point. Logicians have identified a number of logical fallacies—errors in reasoning that can lead to false conclusions. In fact, logicians have identified over one hundred fallacies.[47] Chapter 14 identifies some of the most common ones.

Examine Emotional Appeals

Sometimes emotion alone may be enough reason to persuade you. You might lend your friend $20 just for old times' sake even though you don't expect to see the money again soon. In other cases, it's a mistake to let yourself be swayed by emotion when the logic of a point isn't sound. The excitement or fun in an ad or the lure of low monthly payments probably isn't good enough reason to buy a product you can't afford. Again, the fallacies described in Chapter 14 will help you recognize flaws in emotional appeals.

Critical Thinking Probe

Understanding and Evaluating

Think of three recent incidents when trying to understand the other person would have been the most appropriate listening style. Then think of three different situations when an evaluative approach would have been the most appropriate way to listen.

Based on your conclusions (and perhaps those of your classmates), develop a set of guidelines describing when it's best to listen purely for information, suspending judgment and attempting to uncritically understand another person's point of view. Next, describe the circumstances when it is more appropriate to listen evaluatively.

Listening as Social Support

We listen both informationally and critically out of self-interest. In **supportive listening**, however, the goal is to build a relationship or help the speaker solve a problem.[48] Supportive listening is the approach to use when others seek help for personal dilemmas. Sometimes the problem is a big one: "I'm not sure this marriage is going to work."

At other times the problem is more modest. A friend might be trying to decide what birthday gift to buy or where to spend a vacation. Supportive listening is also a good approach to take when you simply want to become better acquainted with others and to show them that their opinions and feelings matter to you.

There's no question about the value of receiving support when faced with personal problems. Social support has been shown to be among the most important communication skills a friend—or a teacher or a parent—can have.[49]

Social Support and Mediated Communication

Until recently most social support came from personal acquaintances: friends, family, coworkers, neighbors, and so on. In the last fifteen years, though, there has been an explosion of "virtual communities" in which strangers meet online to share interests and concerns, and to gain support from one another on nearly every problem. The most popular support topics include medical conditions, eating disorders, sexual orientation, divorce, shyness, addictions, and loneliness.[50]

In some aspects, online help is similar to the face-to-face variety. The goals are to gain information and emotional support. In other ways, online support differs from the kind people seek in person.[51] The most obvious difference is *anonymity:* Most members of online communities are strangers who usually have not met in person, and may not even know each other's real names. Also, online groups often focus specifically on a single issue, while traditional relationships cover a wide range of topics. Another difference involves the rate and amount of self-disclosure: In traditional relationships, people usually reveal personal information slowly and carefully, but with the anonymity of online support groups, they typically open up almost immediately.

It's unlikely that online support groups will ever replace face-to-face relationships, but for hundreds of thousands of people, they provide another valuable tool for getting the help they often desperately need.

Gender and Social Support

Researchers have found some important ways that men and women respond differently to others' problems.[52] As a group, women are more likely than men to give supportive responses when presented with another person's problem. They are also more skillful at composing supportive messages. By contrast, men tend to respond to others' problems by offering advice, or by diverting the topic. In a study of helping styles in sororities and fraternities, researchers found that sorority women frequently respond with emotional support when asked to help; also, they rated their sisters as being better at listening nonjudgmentally, and on comforting and showing concern for them. Fraternity men, on the other hand, fit the stereotypical pattern of offering help by challenging their brothers to evaluate their attitudes and values.

> Men are as likely as women to respond supportively when they perceive that the other person is feeling a high degree of emotional stress.

These differences are real, but they aren't as dramatic as they might seem. For example, men are as likely as women to respond supportively when they perceive that the other person is feeling a high degree of emotional stress. Women, on the other hand, are more likely to respond supportively even when others are only moderately stressed.

A number of factors interact with gender to shape how people provide social support, including cultural background, personal goals, expressive style, and cognitive complexity. Based on these findings, it's important to respond in a way that fits with your personal style and is likely to be appreciated by the other person.

CULTURAL IDIOM

pin the blame on:
claim the fault lies with

respecting the face needs:
protecting one's dignity

face-saving:
protecting one's dignity

Types of Supportive Responses

Whatever the relationship and topic, there are several styles by which you can respond supportively to another person's remarks.[53] Each of these styles has its advantages and disadvantages. As you read them, you can aim to choose the best style for the situation at hand.

Advising   When approached with another's problem, the most common tendency is an **advising response**: to help by offering a solution.[54] Although such a response is sometimes valuable, often it isn't as helpful as you might think.[55] In fact, researchers have discovered that advice is actually unhelpful at least as often as it is helpful.[56]

There are several reasons why advice doesn't work especially well. First, it can be hard to tell when the other person wants to hear the helper's idea of a solution.[57] Sometimes the request is clear: "What do you think I should do?" At other times, though, it isn't clear whether certain statements are requests for direct advice. Ambiguous statements include requests for opinions ("What do you think of Jeff?"), soliciting information ("Would that be an example of sexual harassment?"), and announcement of a problem ("I'm really confused . . .").

Even when someone with a problem asks for advice, offering it may not be helpful. Your suggestion may not offer the best course to follow, in which case it can even be harmful. There's often a temptation to tell others how we would behave in their place, but it's important to realize that what's right for one person may not be right for another.[58] A related consequence of advising is that it often allows others to avoid responsibility for their decisions. A partner who follows a suggestion of yours that doesn't work out can always pin the blame on you. Finally, often people simply don't want advice: They may not be ready to accept it, needing instead simply to talk out their thoughts and feelings.

Advice is most welcome under two conditions: when it has been requested and when the advisor seems concerned with respecting the face needs of the recipient.[59]

Before offering advice, you need to be sure that four conditions are present:[60]

1. *Be confident that the advice is correct.* You may be certain about some matters of fact, such as the proper way to solve a school problem or the cost of a piece of merchandise, but resist the temptation to act like an authority on matters you know little about. Furthermore, it is both unfair and risky to make suggestions when you aren't positive that they are the best choice. Realize that just because a course of action worked for you doesn't guarantee that it will work for everybody.

2. *Ask yourself whether the person seeking your advice seems willing to accept it.* In this way you can avoid the frustration of making good suggestions, only to find that the person with the problem had another solution in mind all the time.

3. *Be certain that the receiver won't blame you if the advice doesn't work out.* You may be offering the suggestions, but the choice and responsibility for accepting them are up to the recipient of your advice.

4. *Deliver your advice supportively, in a face-saving manner.* Advice that is perceived as being offered constructively, in the context of a solid relationship, is much better than critical comments offered in a way that signals a lack of respect for the receiver.[61]

Judging   A **judging response** evaluates the sender's thoughts or behaviors in some way. The judgment may be favorable—"That's a good idea" or "You're on the right track now"—or unfavorable—"An attitude like that won't get you anywhere." But in either case it implies that the person doing the judging is in some way qualified to pass judgment on the speaker's thoughts or behaviors.

Sometimes negative judgments are purely critical. How many times have you heard such responses as "Well, you asked for it!" or "I told you so!" or "You're just feeling sorry for yourself"? Although comments like these can sometimes serve as a verbal wake-up call, they usually make matters worse.

At other times negative judgments are less critical. These involve what we usually call *constructive criticism*, which is intended to help the problem-holder improve in the future. This is the sort of response given by friends about everything from the choice of clothing to jobs to friends. Another common setting for constructive criticism occurs in school, where instructors evaluate students' work to help them master concepts and skills. But whether it's justified or not, even constructive criticism runs the risk of arousing defensiveness because it may threaten the self-concept of the person at whom it is directed.

Judgments have the best chance of being received when two conditions exist:

CULTURAL IDIOM

wake-up call:
a warning or caution to pay attention

a put-down:
an insult, degrading remark

> How many times have you heard such responses as "Well, you asked for it!" or "I told you so!"

1. *The person with the problem should have requested an evaluation from you.* Occasionally an unsolicited judgment may bring someone to his or her senses, but more often this sort of uninvited evaluation will trigger a defensive response.

2. *Your judgment is genuinely constructive and not designed as a put-down.* If you are tempted to use judgments as a weapon, don't fool yourself into thinking that you are being helpful. Often the statement "I'm telling you this for your own good" simply isn't true.

If you can remember to follow these two guidelines, your judgments will probably be less frequent and better received.

Analyzing   In an **analyzing statement**, the listener offers an interpretation of a speaker's message. Analyses like these are probably familiar to you:

"I think what's really bothering you is . . ."

"She's doing it because . . ."

"I don't think you really meant that."

"Maybe the problem started when she . . ."

Interpretations are often effective ways to help people with problems to consider alternative meanings—meanings they would have never thought of without your help. Sometimes a clear analysis will make a confusing problem suddenly clear, either suggesting a solution or at least providing an understanding of what is occurring.

At other times, an analysis can create more problems than it solves. There are two problems with analyzing. First, your interpretation may not be correct, in which case the speaker may become even more confused by accepting it. Second, even if your interpretation is correct, telling it to the problem-holder might not be useful. There's a chance that it will arouse defensiveness (because analysis implies

© 1997 Ted Goff www.tedgoff.com.

CULTURAL IDIOM

wipe out:
deplete

coming on to:
making a sexual advance to

helpful than trying to reassure grief-stricken family members who had lost loved ones in the tragedy:

> Listen. Don't say anything. Saying "it'll be okay," or "I know how you feel" can backfire. Right now that's not what a victim wants to hear. They want to know people are there and care about them. Be there, be present, listen. The clergy refer to it as a "ministry of presence." You don't need to do anything, just be there or have them know you're available.[65]

Prompting   Advising, judging, analyzing, questioning, and comforting are all active approaches to helping that call for a great deal of input from the respondent. Another approach to problem solving is more passive. **Prompting** involves using silences and brief statements of encouragement to draw others out, and in so doing to help them solve their own problems. Consider this example:

Pablo: Julie's dad is selling a complete computer system for only $1,200, but if I want it I have to buy it now. He's got another interested buyer. It's a great deal. But buying it would wipe out my savings. At the rate I spend money, it would take me a year to save up this much again.

Tim: Uh huh.

Pablo: I wouldn't be able to take that ski trip over winter break . . . but I sure could save time with my schoolwork . . . and do a better job, too.

Tim: That's for sure.

Pablo: Do you think I should buy it?

Tim: I don't know. What do you think?

Pablo: I just can't decide.

Tim: *(silence)*

Pablo: I'm going to do it. I'll never get a deal like this again.

Prompting works especially well when you can't help others make a decision. At times like this your presence can act like a catalyst to help others find their own answers. Prompting will work best when it's done sincerely. Your nonverbal behaviors—eye contact, posture, facial expression, tone of voice—have to show that you are concerned with the other person's problem. Mechanical prompting is likely to irritate instead of help.

Reflecting   A few pages ago you read about the value of paraphrasing to understand others. The same approach can be used as a helping tool. We will use the term **reflecting** to describe it here, to emphasize that the goal here is not as much to clarify your understanding as to help the other person hear and think about the words he or she has just spoken. When you use this approach, be sure to reflect both the *thoughts* and the *feelings* you hear being expressed. This conversation between two friends shows how reflecting can offer support and help a person find the answer to her own problem:

Jill: I've had the strangest feeling about my boss lately.

Mark: What's that? *(A simple question invites Jill to go on.)*

Jill: I'm starting to think maybe he has this thing about women—or maybe it's just about me.

Mark: You mean he's coming on to you? *(Mark paraphrases what he thinks Jill has said.)*

Jill: Oh no, not at all! But it seems like he doesn't take women—or at least me—seriously. *(Jill corrects Mark's misunderstanding and explains herself.)*

Mark: What do you mean? *(Mark asks another simple question to get more information.)*

Jill: Well, whenever we're in a meeting or just talking around the office and he asks for ideas, he always seems to pick men. He gives orders to women—men, too—but he never asks the women to say what they think.

Mark: So you think maybe he doesn't take women seriously, is that it? *(Mark paraphrases Jill's last statement.)*

Jill: Yeah. Well, he sure doesn't seem interested in their ideas. But that doesn't mean he's a total woman-hater or a male chauvinist pig. I know he counts on some women in the office. Our accountant Teresa has been there forever, and he's always saying he couldn't live without her. And when Brenda got the new computer system up and running last month, I know he appreciated that. He gave her a day off and told everybody how she saved our lives.

Mark: Now you sound confused. *(Reflects her apparent feeling.)*

Jill: I am confused. I don't think it's just my imagination. I mean I'm a good producer, but he has never—not once—asked me for my ideas about how to improve sales or anything. And I can't remember a time when he's asked any other women. But maybe I'm overreacting.

Mark: You're not positive whether you're right, but I can tell that this has you concerned. *(Mark paraphrases both Jill's central theme and her feeling.)*

Jill: Yes. But I don't know what to do about it.

Mark: Maybe you should . . . *(Starts to offer advice but catches himself and decides to ask a sincere question instead.)* So what are your choices?

Jill: Well, I could just ask him if he's aware that he never asks women's opinions. But that might sound too aggressive and angry.

Mark: And you're not angry? *(Tries to clarify how Jill is feeling.)*

Jill: Not really. I don't know whether I should be angry because he's not taking ideas seriously, or whether he just doesn't take my ideas seriously, or whether it's nothing at all.

Mark: So you're mostly confused. *(Reflects Jill's apparent feeling again.)*

Jill: Yes! I don't know where I stand with my boss, and not being sure is starting to get to me. I wish I knew what he thinks of me. Maybe I could just tell him I'm confused about what is going on here and ask him to clear it up. But what if it's nothing? Then I'll look insecure.

Mark: *(Mark thinks Jill should confront her boss, but he isn't positive that this is the best approach, so he paraphrases what Jill seems to be saying.)* And that would make you look bad.

Jill: I'm afraid maybe it would. I wonder if I could talk it over with anybody else in the office and get their ideas . . .

Mark: . . . see what they think . . .

Jill: Yeah. Maybe I could ask Brenda. She's easy to talk to, and I do respect her judgment. Maybe she could give me some ideas about how to handle this.

Mark: Sounds like you're comfortable with talking to Brenda first.

Jill: *(Warming to the idea.)* Yes! Then if it's nothing, I can calm down. But if I do need to talk to the boss, I'll know I'm doing the right thing.

Mark: Great. Let me know how it goes.

CULTURAL IDIOM

a male chauvinist pig:
a male who believes that men are superior to women

where I stand with:
how I am perceived by

over the
person.
helping
two styl
You
tion by

1. Th
    er
    ti
    se
    fir

2. Th
    wl
    co
    ju
    cl

3. Yo
    pr
    tru
    sty
    wl

In m
a way th
style.[74]

After studying the material in this chapter . . .

YOU SHOULD UNDERSTAND:

1. The characteristics of nonverbal communication.
2. The differences between verbal and nonverbal communication.
3. How culture and gender influence nonverbal communication.
4. The functions that nonverbal communication can serve.
5. How each type of nonverbal communication operates.

YOU SHOULD BE ABLE TO:

1. Identify and describe your own and others' nonverbal behavior across various contexts.
2. Identify when nonverbal behaviors repeat, substitute for, complement, accent, regulate, and contradict verbal messages.
3. Recognize the emotional and relational dimensions of your own nonverbal behavior.
4. Share your interpretation of another person's nonverbal behavior when such sharing is appropriate.

There is often a big gap between what people say and what they feel. An acquaintance says, "I'd like to get together again" in a way that leaves you suspecting the opposite. (But how do you know?) A speaker tries to appear confident but acts in a way that almost screams out, "I'm nervous!" (What tells you this?) You ask a friend what's wrong, and the "nothing" you get in response rings hollow. (Why does it sound untrue?)

Then, of course, there are times when another's message comes through even though there are no words at all. A look of irritation, a smile, a sigh—signs like these can say more than a torrent of words.

All situations like these have one element in common—the message was sent nonverbally. The goal of this chapter is to introduce you to this world of nonverbal communication. Although you have certainly recognized nonverbal messages before, the following pages should introduce you to a richness of information you have never noticed. And though your experience won't transform you into a mind reader, it will make you a far more accurate observer of others—and yourself.

We need to begin our study of *nonverbal communication* by defining this term. At first this might seem like a simple task. If *non* means "not" and *verbal* means "words," then *nonverbal communication* appears to mean "communication without words." This is a good starting point after we distinguish between vocal communication (by mouth) and verbal communication (with words). After this distinction is made, it becomes clear that some nonverbal messages are vocal, and some are not. Likewise, although many verbal messages are vocal, some aren't. Table 6-1 illustrates these differences.

What about languages that don't involve spoken words? For example, is American Sign Language considered verbal or nonverbal communication? Most scholars would

---

CULTURAL IDIOM

rings hollow:
sounds insincere

TABLE 6-1 Types of Communication

	VOCAL COMMUNICATION	NONVOCAL COMMUNICATION
VERBAL COMMUNICATION	Spoken words	Written words
NONVERBAL COMMUNICATION	Tone of voice, sighs, screams, vocal qualities (loudness, pitch, and so on)	Gestures, movement, appearance, facial expression, and so on

Adapted from John Stewart and Gary D'Angelo, *Together: Communicating Interpersonally*, 2nd ed. (Reading, MA: Addison-Wesley, 1980), p. 22. Copyright © 1993 by McGraw-Hill. Reprinted/adapted by permission.

say sign language is verbal,[1] which helps to narrow our working definition of **nonverbal communication**: "messages expressed through nonlinguistic means." This rules out not only sign languages but also written words, but it includes messages transmitted by vocal means that don't involve language—sighs, laughs, and other utterances we will discuss soon.

Characteristics of Nonverbal Communication

Our brief definition only hints at the richness of nonverbal messages. You can begin to understand their prevalence by trying a simple experiment. Spend an hour or so around a group of people who are speaking a language you don't understand. (You might find such a group in the foreign students' lounge on campus, in an advanced language class, or in an ethnic neighborhood.) Your goal is to see how much information you can learn about the people you're observing from means other than the verbal messages they transmit. This experiment will reveal several characteristics of nonverbal communication.

Nonverbal Behavior Has Communicative Value

It's virtually impossible to not communicate nonverbally.[2] Suppose you were instructed to avoid communicating any messages at all. What would you do? Close your eyes? Withdraw into a ball? Leave the room? As the photo on this page illustrates, the meaning of some nonverbal behavior can be ambiguous. You may not be able to tell exactly what is going on, but the nonverbal cues certainly have communicative value.

> It's virtually impossible to not communicate nonverbally.

Of course, we don't always intend to send nonverbal messages. Unintentional nonverbal behaviors differ from intentional ones.[3] For example, we often stammer, blush, frown, and sweat without meaning to do so. Some theorists argue that unintentional behavior may provide information, but it shouldn't count as communication. Others draw the boundaries of nonverbal communication more broadly, suggesting that even unconscious and unintentional behavior conveys messages and thus is worth studying as communication.[4] We take the broad view here because, whether or not nonverbal behavior is intentional, we use it to form impressions about one another.

Although nonverbal behavior reveals information, we aren't always conscious of what we are communicating

nonverbally. In one study, less than a quarter of experimental subjects who had been instructed to show increased or decreased liking of a partner could describe the nonverbal behaviors they used.[5] Furthermore, just because communicators are nonverbally expressive doesn't mean that others will tune in to the abundance of unspoken messages that are available. One study comparing the richness of e-mail to in-person communication confirmed the greater amount of information available in face-to-face conversations, but it also showed that some communicators (primarily men) failed to recognize these messages.[6]

The fact that you and everyone around you are constantly sending nonverbal clues is important because it means that you have a constant source of information available about yourself and others. If you can tune in to these signals, you will be more aware of how those around you are feeling and thinking, and you will be better able to respond to their behavior.

Nonverbal Communication Is Primarily Relational

Some nonverbal messages serve utilitarian functions. For example, a police officer uses gestures to direct the flow of traffic, and a conductor leads members of a symphony. But nonverbal communication also serves a far more common (and more interesting) series of social functions.[7]

One important social function of nonverbal communication involves identity management. Chapter 3 discussed how we strive to create an image of ourselves as we want others to view us. Nonverbal communication plays an important role in this process—in many cases more important than verbal communication. Consider, for example, what happens when you attend a party where you are likely to meet strangers you would like to get to know better. Instead of projecting your image verbally ("Hi! I'm attractive, friendly, and easygoing"), you behave in ways that will present this identity. You might smile a lot, and perhaps try to strike a relaxed pose. It's also likely that you dress carefully—even if the image involves looking as if you hadn't given a lot of attention to your appearance.

Along with identity management, nonverbal communication allows us to define the kind of relationships we want to have with others. You can appreciate this fact by thinking about the wide range of ways you could behave when greeting another person. You could wave, shake hands, nod, smile, pat the other person on the back, give a hug, or avoid all contact. Each one of these decisions would send a message about the nature of your relationship with the other person.

Nonverbal communication performs a third valuable social function: conveying emotions that we may be unwilling or unable to express—or ones we may not even be aware of. In fact, nonverbal communication is much better suited to expressing attitudes and feelings than ideas.[8] You can prove this for yourself by imagining how you could express each item on the following list nonverbally:

- You're bored.
- You are opposed to capital punishment.

CULTURAL IDIOM

tune in to:
pay attention to

- You are attracted to another person in the group.
- You want to know if you will be tested on this material.
- You are nervous about trying this experiment.

The first, third, and fifth items in this list all involve attitudes; you could probably imagine how each could be expressed nonverbally. By contrast, the second and fourth items involve ideas, and they would be quite difficult to convey without using words. The same principle holds in everyday life: Nonverbal behavior offers many cues about the way people feel—often more than we get from their words alone.

Nonverbal Communication Is Ambiguous

Before you get the idea that this chapter will turn you into a mind reader, it is important to realize that nonverbal communication is often difficult to interpret accurately. To appreciate the ambiguous nature of nonverbal communication, study the photo on page 168. What emotions do you imagine the couple are feeling: Grief? Anguish? Agony? In fact, none of these is even close. The couple just learned that they won $1 million in the New Jersey state lottery!

Nonverbal communication can be just as ambiguous in everyday life. For example, relying on nonverbal cues in romantic situations can lead to inaccurate guesses about a partner's interest in a sexual relationship.[9] Workers of the Safeway supermarket chain discovered firsthand the problems with nonverbal ambiguity when they tried to follow the company's new "superior customer service" policy that required them to smile and make eye contact with customers. Twelve employees filed grievances over the policy, reporting that several customers had propositioned them, misinterpreting their actions as come-ons.[10]

> Nonverbal behavior offers many cues about the way people feel—often more than we get from their words alone.

Although all nonverbal behavior is ambiguous, some emotions are easier to decode accurately than others. In laboratory experiments, subjects are better at identifying positive facial expressions such as happiness, love, surprise, and interest than negative ones such as fear, sadness, anger, and disgust.[11] In real life, however, spontaneous nonverbal expressions are so ambiguous that observers are able to identify the emotions they convey no more accurately than by blind guessing.[12]

Some people are more skillful than others at accurately decoding nonverbal behavior.[13] For example, those who are better senders of nonverbal messages also are better receivers. Decoding ability also increases with age and training, although there are still differences in ability owing to personality and occupation. For instance, extroverts are relatively accurate judges of nonverbal behavior, whereas dogmatists are not. Interestingly, women seem to be better than men at decoding nonverbal messages. Over 95 percent of the studies examined in one analysis showed that women are more accurate at interpreting nonverbal signals.[14] Despite these differences, even the best nonverbal decoders do not approach 100 percent accuracy.

When you do try to make sense out of ambiguous nonverbal behavior, you need to consider several factors: the context in which they occur (e.g., smiling at a joke suggests a different feeling from what is suggested by smiling at another's misfortune); the history of your relationship with the sender (friendly, hostile, etc.); the other's mood at the time; and your feelings (when you're feeling insecure, almost anything can seem like a threat). The important idea is that when you become aware of nonverbal messages, you should think of them not as facts but rather as clues that need to be checked out.

CULTURAL IDIOM

come-ons:
sexual advances

blind guessing:
coming to a conclusion without any factual basis for judgment

TABLE 6-2   Some Differences Between Verbal and Nonverbal Communication

	VERBAL COMMUNICATION	NONVERBAL COMMUNICATION
COMPLEXITY	One dimension (words only)	Multiple dimensions (voice, posture, gestures, distance, etc.)
FLOW	Intermittent (speaking and silence alternate)	Continuous (it's impossible not to communicate nonverbally)
CLARITY	Less subject to misinterpretation	More ambiguous
IMPACT	Has less impact when verbal and nonverbal cues are contradictory	Has stronger impact when verbal and nonverbal cues are contradictory
INTENTIONALITY	Usually deliberate	Often unintentional

Nonverbal Communication Is Different from Verbal Communication

As Table 6-2 shows, nonverbal communication differs in several important ways from spoken and written language. These differences suggest some reasons why it is so valuable to focus on nonverbal behavior. For example, while verbal messages are almost always intentional, nonverbal cues are often unintended, and sometimes unconscious.

Nonverbal Skills Are Important

It's hard to overemphasize the importance of effective nonverbal expression and the ability to read and respond to others' nonverbal behavior. Nonverbal encoding and decoding skills are a strong predictor of popularity, attractiveness, and socio-emotional well-being.[15] Good nonverbal communicators are more persuasive than people who are less skilled, and they have a greater chance of success in settings ranging from careers to poker to romance. Nonverbal sensitivity is a major part of what some social scientists have called "emotional intelligence," and researchers have come to recognize that it is impossible to study spoken language without paying attention to its nonverbal dimensions.[16]

> Nonverbal sensitivity is a major part of what some social scientists have called "emotional intelligence."

Influences on Nonverbal Communication

Much nonverbal communication is universal. For example, researchers have found at least six facial expressions that all humans everywhere use and understand: happiness, sadness, fear, anger, disgust, and surprise.[17] Even children who have been blind since birth reveal their feelings using these expressions. Despite these similarities, there are some important differences in the way people use and understand nonverbal behavior. We'll look at some of these differences now.

Culture

Cultures have different nonverbal languages as well as verbal ones. Fiorello LaGuardia, legendary mayor of New York from 1933 to 1945, was fluent in English, Italian, and Yiddish. Researchers who watched films of his campaign speeches with the sound turned off found that they could tell which language he was speaking by the changes in his nonverbal behavior.[18]

Source: DILBERT © Scott Adams/Dist. by United Feature Syndicate, Inc.

The meaning of some gestures varies from one culture to another. The "okay" gesture made by joining thumb and forefinger to form a circle is a cheery affirmation to most Americans, but it has less positive meanings in other parts of the world.[19] In France and Belgium it means "You're worth zero." In Greece and Turkey it is a vulgar sexual invitation, usually meant as an insult. Given this sort of cross-cultural ambiguity, it's easy to imagine how an innocent tourist might wind up in serious trouble.

CULTURAL IDIOM
wind up in:
end up being in

Less obvious cross-cultural differences can damage relationships without the parties ever recognizing exactly what has gone wrong. Edward Hall points out that whereas Americans are comfortable conducting business at a distance of roughly four feet, people from the Middle East stand much closer.[20]

It is easy to visualize the awkward advance and retreat pattern that might occur when two diplomats or businesspeople from these cultures meet. The Middle Easterner would probably keep moving forward to close the gap that feels so wide, whereas the American would continually back away. Both would feel uncomfortable, probably without knowing why.

Like distance, patterns of eye contact vary around the world.[21] A direct gaze is considered appropriate for speakers in Latin America, the Arab world, and southern Europe. On the other hand, Asians, Indians, Pakistanis, and northern Europeans gaze at a listener peripherally or not at all. In either case, deviations from the norm are likely to make a listener uncomfortable.

Even within a culture, various groups can have different nonverbal rules. For example, many white teachers in the United States use quasi-questions that hint at the information they are seeking. An elementary teacher might encourage the class to speak up by making an incorrect statement that demands refutation: "So twelve divided by four is six, right?" Most white students would recognize this behavior as a way of testing their understanding. But this style of questioning is unfamiliar to many students raised in traditional black cultures, who aren't likely to respond until they are directly questioned by the teacher.[22] Given this difference, it is easy to imagine how some teachers might view minority children as unresponsive or slow, when in fact they are simply playing by a different set of rules.

Communicators become more tolerant of others after they understand that many unusual nonverbal behaviors that seem unusual are the result of cultural differences. In one study, American adults were presented with videotaped scenes of speakers from the United States, France, and Germany.[23] When the sound was cut off, viewers judged

> Nonverbal behaviors that seem unusual are the result of cultural differences.

Understanding Diversity

Nonverbal Learning Disorder

A syndrome called nonverbal learning disorder (NVLD) makes reading facial expression, tone of voice, and other cues dramatically more difficult.[27] Due to a processing deficit in the right hemisphere of the brain, someone with NVLD has trouble making sense of many nonverbal cues. People with NVLD—especially children—often misinterpret humorous or sarcastic messages literally, since those cues are based heavily on nonverbal signals.

People with NVLD also have trouble figuring out how to behave appropriately in new social situations, so they rely on rote formulas that often don't work. For example, a child who has learned the formal way of meeting an adult for the first time by shaking hands and saying "Pleased to meet you" might try this approach with a group of peers. The result, of course, is to be regarded as odd or nerdy. And their disability leads them to miss nonverbal cues sent by other children that this isn't the right approach.[28]

Even for those of us who don't suffer from NVLD, the nuances of nonverbal behavior can be confusing. It's worth considering that there may be a physiological explanation for clueless people who seem socially inept.

foreigners more negatively than their fellow citizens. But when the speakers' voices were added (allowing viewers to recognize that they were from a different country), the critical ratings dropped.

Despite differences like these, many nonverbal behaviors have the same meanings around the world. Smiles and laughter are a universal signal of positive emotions, for example, whereas the same sour expressions convey displeasure in every culture.[24] Charles Darwin believed that expressions like these are the result of evolution, functioning as survival mechanisms that allowed early humans to convey emotional states before the development of language.

Although nonverbal expressions like these may be universal, the way they are used varies widely around the world. In some cultures display rules discourage the overt demonstration of feelings like happiness or anger. In other cultures the same feelings are perfectly appropriate. Thus, a person from Japan might appear much more controlled and placid than an Arab when in fact their feelings might be identical.[25]

The same principle operates closer to home among co-cultures. For example, observations have shown that black women in all-black groups are nonverbally more expressive and interrupt one another more than do white women in all-white groups.[26] This doesn't mean that black women always feel more intensely than their white counterparts. A more likely explanation is that the two groups follow different cultural rules. The researchers found that in racially mixed groups both black and white women moved closer to the others' style. This nonverbal convergence shows that skilled communicators can adapt their behavior when interacting with members of other cultures or co-cultures in order to make the exchange more smooth and effective.

Gender

It's easy to identify stereotypical differences in masculine and feminine styles of nonverbal communication. Just think about exaggerated caricatures of macho men and delicate women that appear in animated films such as *Tarzan* and *The Little Mermaid*. Many humorous films and plays have been created around the results that arise when characters try to act like members of the opposite sex. (For some examples, see the Media Room feature at the end of the chapter.)

Although few of us behave like stereotypically masculine or feminine movie characters, there are recognizable differences in the way men and women look and act. Some of the most obvious differences are physiological: height, depth and volume of the voice, and so on. Other differences are social. For example, females are usually more nonverbally expressive, and they are better at recognizing others' nonverbal behavior.[29]

Most communication scholars agree that social factors have more influence than biology does in shaping how men and women behave. For example, the ability to read nonverbal cues may have more to do with women's historically less powerful social status: People in subordinate work positions also have better decoding skills.[30] As women continue to gain equal status in the workplace and home, a paradoxical result may be less sensitivity at reading nonverbal cues.

Cultural norms in the Western world distinguish male from female behaviors.[31] For example, women make more eye contact than do men with conversational partners. They are more vocally expressive than men. Women interact at closer distances, both with men and with other women, than do men in same-sex conversations. Men are more likely to lean forward in conversations than women. They require and are given more personal space. Women are more likely to face conversational partners head-on, whereas men more typically stand at an angle. Women express more emotions via facial expressions than men. Most noticeably, women smile considerably more than men. Women gesture more, whereas men use more expansive gestures.

After looking at differences like these, it might seem as if men and women communicate in radically different ways. In fact, men's and women's nonverbal communication is more similar than different in many respects.[32] Differences like the ones described in the preceding paragraph are noticeable, but they are outweighed by the similar rules we follow in areas such as making eye contact, posture, and gestures. You can prove this by imagining what it would be like to use radically different nonverbal rules: standing only an inch away from others, sniffing strangers, or tapping the forehead of someone when you want his or her attention. While biological sex and cultural norms certainly have an influence on nonverbal style, they aren't as dramatic as the "men are from Mars, women are from Venus" thesis suggests.

> Men's and women's nonverbal communication is more similar than different in many respects.

The awareness of the communicative power of nonverbal behavior can often give you an edge in understanding and influencing it. Suppose that your skill at controlling your own nonverbal behavior became great enough that you were able to present yourself to others in precisely the way you desire (even if that image wasn't completely accurate), and your ability to analyze others' nonverbal behavior gave you a high degree of accuracy in interpreting others' unexpressed feelings.

What ethical obligations would come with your increased nonverbal skill? Would you be obliged to disclose your ability to others? To reveal your motives when trying to influence them? To share your analysis of their behavior?

Functions of Nonverbal Communication

Although verbal and nonverbal messages differ in many ways, the two forms of communication operate together on most occasions. The following discussion explains the many functions of nonverbal communication and shows how nonverbal messages relate to verbal ones.

Understanding Communication Technology

Expressiveness in Online Communication

Communication scholars have characterized face-to-face interaction as "rich" in nonverbal cues that convey feelings and attitudes. Even telephone conversations carry a fair amount of emotional information via the speakers' vocal qualities. By comparison, most text-based communication on the Internet, such as e-mail and instant messaging, is relatively lean in relational information. With only words, subtlety is lost. This is why hints and jokes that might work well in person or on the phone often fail when communicated online.

Ever since the early days of e-mail, Internet correspondents have devised a series of "emoticons" using typed characters to convey feelings. The most common of these is the symbol :) , which, of course, represents humorous intent. Less commonly used emoticons convey other emotions. A frown is :-(and surprise is :-0, for example.

Even though you can't make your voice louder or softer or change its tone in type, you can use regular keyboard characters to convey a surprisingly large range of feelings.

Asterisks   Not all e-mail and instant messaging systems allow the use of italics, which are useful for emphasizing a point. Enclosing a statement in asterisks can add the same sort of light emphasis. Instead of saying

```
I really want to hear from you, you can say
I *really* want to hear from you.
```

Notice how changing the placement of asterisks produces a different message:

```
I really want to hear from *you.*
```

Capitalization   Capitalizing a word or phrase can also emphasize the point:

```
I hate to be a pest, but I need the $20 you
owe me TODAY.
```

Overuse of capitals can be offensive. Be sure to avoid typing messages in all uppercase letters, which creates the impression of shouting:

```
HOW ARE YOU DOING? WE ARE HAVING A GREAT TIME
HERE. BE SURE TO COME SEE US SOON.
```

Multiple Methods of Emphasis   When you want to emphasize a point, you can use multiple methods:

```
I can't believe you told the boss that I sleep
with a teddy bear! I wanted to *die* of em-
barrassment. Please don't *EVER* **EVER** do
that kind of thing again.
```

Use this type of emphasis sparingly, and only where you want to make your point very strongly.

Repeating

If someone asked you for directions to the nearest drugstore, you could say, "North of here about two blocks," repeating your instructions nonverbally by pointing north. This sort of repetition isn't just decorative: People remember comments accompanied by gestures more than those made with words alone.[33]

Substituting

When a friend asks you what's new, you might shrug your shoulders instead of answering in words. Social scientists use the term **emblems** to describe deliberate nonverbal behaviors that have precise meanings known to everyone within a cultural group. For example, we all know that a head nod means "yes," a head shake means "no," a wave means "hello" or "good-bye," and a hand to the ear means "I can't hear you."

Not all substituting consists of emblems, however. Sometimes substituting responses are more ambiguous and less intentional. A sigh, smile, or frown may substitute for a verbal answer to your question "How's it going?" As this example suggests, nonverbal substituting is especially important when people are reluctant to express their feelings in words.

Complementing

Sometimes nonverbal behaviors match the content of a verbal message. Consider, for example, a friend apologizing for forgetting an appointment with you. Your friend's sincerity would be reinforced if the verbal apology were accompanied by the appropriate nonverbal behaviors: the right tone of voice, facial expression, and so on. We often recognize the significance of complementary nonverbal behavior when it is missing. If your friend's apology were delivered with a shrug, a smirk, and a light tone of voice, you probably would doubt its sincerity, no matter how profuse the verbal explanation was.

Much complementing behavior consists of **illustrators**—nonverbal behaviors that accompany and support spoken words. Scratching the head when searching for an idea and snapping your fingers when it occurs are examples of illustrators that complement verbal messages. Research shows that North Americans use illustrators more often when they are emotionally aroused—trying to explain ideas that are difficult to put into words—when they are furious, horrified, very agitated, distressed, or excited.[34]

Accenting

Just as we use italics to emphasize an idea in print, we use nonverbal devices to emphasize oral messages. Pointing an accusing finger adds emphasis to criticism (as well as probably creating defensiveness in the receiver). Stressing certain words with the voice ("It was *your* idea!") is another way to add nonverbal accents.

Regulating

Nonverbal behaviors can control the flow of verbal communication. For example, parties in a conversation often unconsciously send and receive turn-taking cues.[35] When you are ready to yield the floor, the unstated rule is: Create a rising vocal intonation pattern, then use a falling intonation pattern, or draw out the final syllable of the clause at the end of your statement. Finally, stop speaking. If you want to maintain your turn when another speaker seems ready to cut you off, you can suppress the attempt by taking an audible breath, using a sustained intonation pattern (because rising and falling patterns suggest the end of a statement), and avoiding any pauses in your speech. Other nonverbal cues exist for gaining the floor and for signaling that you do not want to speak.

Contradicting

People often simultaneously express different and even contradictory messages in their verbal and nonverbal behaviors. A common example of this sort of mixed message is the experience we've all had of hearing someone with a red face and bulging veins yelling, "Angry? No, I'm not angry!"

Even though some of the ways in which people contradict themselves are subtle, mixed messages have a strong impact. Studies suggest that when a receiver perceives an inconsistency between verbal and nonverbal messages, the nonverbal one carries more weight—more than 12.5 percent more, according to some research.[36]

Deliberately sending mixed messages might sound foolish at first, but there are times when we do just this. One deliberate use of mixed messages is to send a message politely but clearly that might be difficult to handle if it were expressed in words. For instance, think of a time when you became bored with a conversation while your companion kept rambling on. At such a time the most straightforward

When a receiver perceives an inconsistency between verbal and nonverbal messages, the nonverbal one carries more weight.

Source: DILBERT © Scott Adams/Dist. by United Feature Syndicate, Inc.

CULTURAL IDIOM

surefire:
certain to succeed

statement would be "I'm tired of talking to you and want to go meet someone else." Although it might feel good to be so direct, this kind of honesty is impolite for anyone over five years of age. Instead of being blunt in situations like this, a face-saving alternative is to express your interest nonverbally. While nodding politely and murmuring "uh-huh" and "no kidding?" at the appropriate times, you can signal a desire to leave by looking around the room, turning slightly away from the speaker, or even making a point of yawning. In most cases such clues are enough to end the conversation without the awkwardness of expressing outright what's going on.

Deceiving

Some people are better at hiding deceit than others. For example, most people become more successful liars as they grow older. Research shows that this is especially true for women.[37] High self-monitors are usually better at hiding their deception than communicators who are less self-aware, and raters judge highly expressive liars as more honest than those who are more subdued.[38] Not surprisingly, people whose jobs require them to act differently than they feel, such as actors, lawyers, diplomats, and salespeople, are more successful at deception than the general population.[39]

Decades of research have revealed that there are no surefire nonverbal cues that indicate deception.[40] This fact helps explain why most people have only a coin flip's

> No matter how skillful or inept we may be at interpreting nonverbal behavior, training can make us better.

chance—50 percent—of accurately identifying a liar.[41] We seem to be worse at catching deceivers when we participate actively in conversations than when we observe from the sidelines.[42] It's easiest to catch liars when they haven't had a chance to rehearse, when they feel strongly about the information being hidden, or when they feel anxious or guilty about their lies.[43] Trust (or lack of it) also plays a role in which deceptive messages are successful: People who are suspicious that a speaker may be lying pay closer attention to the speaker's nonverbal behavior (e.g., talking faster than normal, shifted posture) than do people who are not suspicious.[44] Table 6-3 lists situations in which deceptive messages are most likely to be obvious.

Some people are better than others at uncovering deception. For example, women are consistently more accurate than men at detecting lying and what the underlying truth is.[45] The same research showed that, as people become more intimate, their accuracy in detecting lies actually declines. This is a surprising fact: Intuition suggests that we ought to be better at judging honesty as we become more familiar with others.

TABLE 6-3 Leakage of Nonverbal Clues to Deception

DECEPTION CLUES ARE MOST LIKELY WHEN THE DECEIVER	DECEPTION CLUES ARE LEAST LIKELY WHEN THE DECEIVER
Wants to hide emotions being experienced at the moment.	Wants to hide information unrelated to his or her emotions.
Feels strongly about the information being hidden.	Has no strong feelings about the information being hidden.
Feels apprehensive about the deception.	Feels confident about the deception.
Feels guilty about being deceptive.	Experiences little guilt about the deception.
Gets little enjoyment from being deceptive.	Enjoys the deception.
Needs to construct the message carefully while delivering it.	Knows the deceptive message well and has rehearsed it.

Based on material from "Mistakes When Deceiving" by Paul Ekman, in Thomas A. Sebok and Robert Rosenthal, eds., *The Clever Hans Phenomenon: Communication with Horses, Whales, Apes and People* (New York: New York Academy of Sciences, 1981), pp. 269–278.

Perhaps an element of wishful thinking interferes with our accurate decoding of these messages. After all, we would hate to think that a lover would lie to us. When intimates *do* become suspicious, however, their ability to recognize deception increases.[46] Despite their overall accuracy at detecting lies, women are more inclined to fall for the deception of intimate partners than are men. No matter how skillful or inept we may be at interpreting nonverbal behavior, training can make us better.[47]

There are some cues that are worth paying attention to when trying to decode deception. Research suggests that liars blink less often than normal when lying and more often than normal immediately after they have told the lie.[48] Picking up on this clue depends on your knowledge of what is "normal" for the person you suspect is lying, otherwise known as "baseline" behavior. Another way to recognize deception is to tune in to **microexpressions**—fleeting facial expressions that reflect emotional states.[49] Because most microexpressions only last for a fraction of a second, they are easy to miss, especially without training.[50]

Before we finish considering how nonverbal behaviors can deceive, it's important to realize that not all deceptive communication is aimed at taking advantage of the recipient. Sometimes we use nonverbal messages as a polite way to express an idea that would be difficult to handle if expressed in words. In this sense, the ability to deliberately send nonverbal messages that contradict your words can be a kind of communication competence.

Types of Nonverbal Communication

Now that you understand how nonverbal messages operate as a form of communication, we can look at the various forms of nonverbal behavior. The following pages explain how our bodies, artifacts, environments, and the way we use time all send messages.

Body Movements

For many people, the most noticeable elements of nonverbal communication involve visible body movements. In the following pages, we will examine some of the ways both the body and face can convey meanings.

CULTURAL IDIOM

let their guard down:
act or speak naturally without
worrying how others will react

Posture and Gesture   Stop reading for a moment and notice how you are sitting. What does your position say nonverbally about how you feel? Are there other people near you now? What messages do you get from their posture and movements? Tune your television to any program, and without turning up the sound, see what messages are communicated by the movements and body position of the people on the screen. These simple experiments illustrate the communicative power of **kinesics**, the study of body movement, gesture, and posture.

Posture is a rich channel for conveying nonverbal information. From time to time postural messages are obvious. If you see a person drag through the door or slump over while sitting in a chair, it's apparent that something significant is going on. But most postural cues are more subtle. For instance, the act of mirroring the posture of another person can have positive consequences. One experiment showed that career counselors who used "posture echoes" to copy the postures of clients were rated as more empathic than those who did not reflect the clients' postures.[51] Researchers have also found that partners in romantic relationships mirror one another's behaviors.[52]

Posture can communicate vulnerability in situations far more serious than mere social or business settings. One study revealed that rapists sometimes use postural clues to select victims that they believe will be easy to intimidate.[53] Easy targets are more likely to walk slowly and tentatively, stare at the ground, and move their arms and legs in short, jerky motions.

Gestures are a fundamental element of communication—so fundamental, in fact, that people who have been blind from birth use them.[54] One group of ambiguous gestures consists of what we usually call fidgeting—movements in which one part of the body grooms, massages, rubs, holds, fidgets, pinches, picks, or otherwise manipulates another body part. Social scientists call these behaviors **manipulators**.[55] Social rules may discourage us from performing most manipulators in public, but people still do so without noticing. For example, one study revealed that deceivers bob their heads more often than truth-tellers.[56] Research confirms what common sense suggests—that increased use of manipulators is often a sign of discomfort.[57] But not all fidgeting signals uneasiness. People also are likely to use manipulators when relaxed. When they let their guard down (either alone or with friends), they will be more likely to fiddle with an earlobe, twirl a strand of hair, or clean their fingernails. Whether or not the fidgeter is hiding something, observers are likely to interpret manipulators as a signal of dishonesty. Because not all fidgeters are liars, it's important not to jump to conclusions about the meaning of manipulators.

> Because not all fidgeters are liars, it's important not to jump to conclusions about the meaning of manipulators.

Face and Eyes   The face and eyes are probably the most noticed parts of the body, and their impact is powerful. For example, smiling cocktail waitresses earn larger tips than unsmiling ones, and smiling nuns collect larger donations than ones with glum expressions.[58] The influence of facial expressions and eye contact doesn't mean that their nonverbal messages are always easy to read. The face is a tremendously complicated channel of expression for several reasons. One reason is the number of expressions people can produce. Another is the speed with which they can change. For example, slow-motion films have been taken that show expressions fleeting across a subject's face in as short a time as a fifth of a second. Finally, it seems that different emotions show most clearly in different parts of the face: happiness and surprise in the eyes and lower face, anger in the lower face and brows and forehead, fear and sadness in the eyes, and disgust in the lower face.

Expressions reflecting many emotions seem to be recognizable in and between members of all cultures.[59] Of course, **affect blends**—the combination of two or more expressions showing different emotions—are possible. For instance, it's easy to imagine how someone would look who is fearful and surprised or disgusted and angry.

Research indicates that people are quite accurate at judging facial expressions of these emotions.[60] Accuracy increases when judges know the "target" or have knowledge of the context in which the expression occurs or when they have seen several samples of the target's expressions.

In mainstream Euro-American culture, meeting someone's glance with your eyes is usually a sign of involvement or interest, whereas looking away signals a desire to avoid contact. Prolonged eye contact has been identified by researchers as one of the main ways people indicate attraction.[61]

Solicitors on the street—panhandlers, salespeople, petitioners—try to catch our eye because after they've managed to establish contact with a glance, it becomes harder for the approached person to draw away.

Voice

The voice is another form of nonverbal communication. Social scientists use the term **paralanguage** to describe nonverbal, vocal messages. You can begin to understand the power of vocal cues by considering how the meaning of a simple sentence can change just by shifting the emphasis from word to word:

- *This* is a fantastic communication book.
  (Not just any book, but this one in particular.)

- This is a *fantastic* communication book.
  (This book is superior, exciting.)

- This is a fantastic *communication* book.
  (The book is good as far as communication goes; it may not be so good as literature or drama.)

- This is a fantastic communication *book*.
  (It's not a play or a compact disc; it's a book.)

The impact of paralinguistic cues is strong. In fact, research shows that listeners pay more attention to the vocal messages than to the words that are spoken when asked to determine a speaker's attitudes.[62] Furthermore, when vocal factors contradict a verbal message, listeners judge the speaker's intention from the paralanguage, not from the words themselves.[63]

There are many other ways the voice communicates—through its tone, speed, pitch, volume, number and length of pauses, and **disfluencies** (such as stammering, use of "uh," "um," "er," and so on). All these factors can do a great deal to reinforce or contradict the message our words convey.

Sarcasm is one instance in which both emphasis and tone of voice help change a statement's meaning to the opposite of its verbal message. Experience this yourself with the following three statements. The first time through, say them literally, and then say them sarcastically.

- Thanks for waking me up.
- I really had a wonderful time on my blind date.
- There's nothing I like better than waking up before sunrise.

MEXICAN IDEAL SPEAKER'S VOICE

Medium in pitch
Medium in rate
Loud in volume

Clear enunciation
Well-modulated
Without regional accent
Cheerful

Firm
Low in pitch
Somewhat slow with pauses

U.S. IDEAL SPEAKER'S VOICE

FIGURE 6-1 Ideal Speaker's Voice Types in Mexico and the United States

Researchers have identified the communicative value of paralanguage through the use of content-free speech—ordinary speech that has been electronically manipulated so that the words are unintelligible, but the paralanguage remains unaffected. (Hearing a foreign language that you do not understand has the same effect.) Subjects who hear content-free speech can consistently recognize the emotion being expressed, as well as identifying its strength.[64]

Paralanguage can affect behavior in many ways, some of which are rather surprising. Researchers have discovered that communicators were most likely to comply with requests delivered by speakers whose rate was similar to their own.[65] Besides complying with same-rate speakers, listeners also feel more positively about people who seem to talk at their own rate.

Some vocal factors influence the way a speaker is perceived by others. For example, communicators who speak loudly and without hesitations are viewed as more confident than those who pause and speak quietly.[66] People who speak more slowly are judged as having greater conversational control than fast talkers.[67] Research has also demonstrated that people with more attractive voices are rated more highly than those whose voice sounds less attractive.[68] Just what makes a voice attractive can vary. As Figure 6-1 shows, culture can make a difference. Surveys show that there are both similarities and differences between what Mexicans and Americans view as the "ideal" voice.

Along with vocal qualities, accent can shape perceptions. For example, the accents of some nonnative English-speaking job seekers (e.g., those with a pronounced French accent) created favorable impressions with employers, while other strong accents (e.g., Japanese) had the opposite effect.[69]

Appearance

How we appear can be just as revealing as how we sound and move. For that reason, we need to explore the communicative power of physical attractiveness and clothing.

Physical Attractiveness   Most people claim that looks aren't the best measure of desirability or character, but they typically prefer others who they find attractive.[70] For example, women who are perceived as attractive have more dates, receive higher grades in college, persuade males with greater ease, and receive lighter court sentences. Both men and women whom others view as attractive are rated as being more sensitive, kind, strong, sociable, and interesting than their less-fortunate brothers and sisters. Who is most likely to succeed in business? Place your bet on the attractive job applicant. For example, shorter men have more difficulty finding jobs in the first place, and men over six-foot-two receive starting salaries that average 12.4 percent higher than comparable applicants under six feet.[71] Tall presidential candidates are historically more likely to win than short ones. If you happen to be on the shorter side, you may find hope in new research conducted at Stanford University's Virtual Human Interaction Laboratory.[72] They reveal that people who create a tall avatar are more persuasive in virtual reality interactions, even if they are short in real life. Furthermore, once two communicators enter back into the "real" world, the person who had the taller avatar continues to be more persuasive, regardless of real-life height.

> People who create a tall avatar are more persuasive in virtual reality interactions, even if they are short in real life.

CULTURAL IDIOM

lighter:
lesser in duration

place your bet on:
predict with confidence

The influence of attractiveness begins early in life. Preschoolers were shown photographs of children their own age and asked to choose potential friends and enemies. The researchers found that children as young as three agreed as to who was attractive ("cute") and unattractive ("homely"). Furthermore, they valued their attractive counterparts—both of the same and the opposite sex—more highly. Also, preschool children rated by their peers as pretty were most liked, and those identified as least pretty were least liked. Children who were interviewed rated good-looking children as having positive social characteristics ("He's friendly to other children") and unattractive children as having negative ones ("He hits other children without reason").

Teachers also are affected by students' attractiveness. Physically attractive students are usually judged more favorably—more intelligent, friendly, and popular—than their less attractive counterparts.[73] Fortunately, attractiveness is something we can control without having to call a plastic surgeon. If you aren't totally gorgeous or handsome, don't despair: Evidence suggests that, as we get to know more about people and like them, we start to regard them as better looking.[74] Moreover, we view others as beautiful or ugly not just on the basis of their "original equipment" but also on how they use that equipment. Posture, gestures, facial expressions, and other behaviors can increase the attractiveness of an otherwise unremarkable person. Exercise can improve the way each of us looks. Finally, the way we dress can make a significant difference in the way others perceive us, as you'll now see.

> We are more likely to obey people dressed in a high-status manner.

Clothing Besides protecting us from the elements, clothing is a means of nonverbal communication, providing a relatively straightforward (if sometimes expensive) method of impression management. Clothing can be used to convey economic status, educational level, social status, moral standards, athletic ability and/or interests, belief system (political, philosophical, religious), and level of sophistication.

Research shows that we do make assumptions about people based on their clothing. Communicators who wear special clothing often gain persuasiveness. For example, experimenters dressed in uniforms resembling police officers were more successful than those dressed in civilian clothing in requesting pedestrians to pick up litter and in persuading them to lend a dime for a parking meter to a motorist.[75] Likewise, solicitors wearing sheriff's and nurse's uniforms increased the level of contributions to law enforcement and health-care campaigns.[76] We are more likely to obey people dressed in a high-status manner. Pedestrians were more likely to return lost coins to well-dressed people than to those dressed in low-status clothing.[77] Women who are wearing a jacket are rated as being more powerful than those wearing only a dress or skirt and blouse.[78]

As we get to know others better, the importance of clothing shrinks.[79] This fact suggests that clothing is especially important in the early stages of a relationship, when making a positive first impression is necessary in order to encourage others to get to know us better. This advice is equally important in personal situations and in employment interviews. In both cases, your style of dress (and personal grooming) can make all the difference between the chance to progress further and outright rejection.

"Tell me about yourself, Kugelman— your hopes, dreams, career path, and what that damn earring means."

Source: From the Wall Street Journal—Permission, Cartoon Features Syndicate.

Ethical Challenge

Clothing and Impression Management

Using clothing as a method of creating impressions is a fact of life. Discover for yourself how dressing can be a type of deception.

1. Identify three examples from your experience when someone dressed in a manner that disguised or misrepresented his or her true status or personal attributes. What were the consequences of this misrepresentation for you or others?

2. Now identify three occasions in which you successfully used clothing to create a favorable but inaccurate impression. What were the consequences of this deception for others?

3. Based on your conclusions, define any situations when clothing may be used as an unethical means of impression management. List both "misdemeanors," in which the consequences are not likely to cause serious harm, and "felonies," in which the deception has the potential to cause serious harm.

Touch

Physical touch can "speak" volumes. A supportive pat on the back, a high five, or even an inappropriate graze can be more powerful than words, eliciting a strong emotional reaction in the receiver. Social scientists use the term **haptics** when they refer to the study of touch in human behavior.

Experts argue that one reason actions speak louder than words is because touch is the first language we learn as infants.[80] Besides being the earliest means we have of making contact with others, touching is essential to healthy development. During the nineteenth and early twentieth centuries many babies died from a disease then called *marasmus*, which, translated from Greek, means "wasting away." In some orphanages the mortality rate was quite high, but even children in "progressive" homes, hospitals, and other institutions died regularly from the ailment. When researchers finally tracked down the causes of this disease, they found that many infants suffered from lack of physical contact with parents or nurses rather than poor nutrition, medical care, or other factors. They hadn't been touched enough, and as a result they died. From this knowledge came the practice of "mothering" children in institutions—picking babies up, carrying them around, and handling them several times each day. At one hospital that began this practice, the death rate for infants fell from between 30 and 35 percent to below 10 percent.[81]

> One study showed that fleeting touches on the hand and shoulder resulted in larger tips for restaurant waiters.

Touch seems to increase a child's mental functioning as well as physical health. Babies who have been given plenty of physical stimulation by their mothers develop significantly higher IQs than those receiving less contact.[82] By contrast, insufficient physical contact correlates with social problems including communication apprehension and low self-disclosure.[83]

Touch also increases compliance.[84] In one study, subjects were approached by a female confederate who requested that they return a dime left in the phone booth from which they had just emerged. When the request was accompanied by a light touch on the subject's arm, the probability that the subject would return the dime increased significantly.[85] In a similar experiment, subjects were asked by a male or female confederate to sign a petition or complete a rating scale. Again, subjects were more likely to cooperate when they were touched lightly on the arm. In the rating-scale variation of the study, the results were especially dramatic: 70 percent of those who were touched complied, whereas only 40 percent of the untouched subjects complied.[86] An additional power of touch is its on-the-job utility. One study showed that fleeting touches on the hand and shoulder resulted in larger tips for restaurant waiters.[87]

@Work

Touch and Career Success

The old phrase "keeping in touch" takes on new meaning once you understand the relationship between haptics and career effectiveness.

Some of the most pronounced benefits of touching occur in medicine and the health and helping professions. For example, patients are more likely to take their medicines when physicians give a slight touch while prescribing.[88] In counseling, touch increases self-disclosure and verbalization of psychiatric patients.[89]

Touch can also enhance success in sales and marketing. Touching customers in a store increases their shopping time, their evaluation of the store, and also the amount of shopping.[90] When an offer to try samples of a product is accompanied by a touch, customers are more likely to try the sample and buy the product.[91]

Touch also has an impact in school. Students are twice as likely to volunteer and speak up in class if they have received a supportive touch on the back or arm from their teacher.[92]

Even athletes benefit from touch. One study of the National Basketball Association revealed that the touchiest teams had the most successful records while the lowest scoring teams touched each other the least.[93]

Of course, touch has to be culturally appropriate. Furthermore, touching by itself is no guarantee of success, and too much contact can be bothersome, annoying, or even downright creepy. But research confirms that appropriate contact can enhance your success.

Space

There are two ways that the use of space can create nonverbal messages: the distance we put between ourselves and the territory we consider our own. We'll now look at each of these dimensions.

Distance The study of the way people and animals use space has been termed **proxemics**. Preferred spaces are largely a matter of cultural norms. For example, people living in hyperdense Hong Kong manage to live in crowded residential quarters that most North Americans would find intolerable.[94] Anthropologist Edward T. Hall has defined four distances used in mainstream North American culture.[95] He says that we choose a particular distance depending on how we feel toward the other person at a given time, the context of the conversation, and our personal goals.

> We choose a particular distance depending on how we feel toward the other person at a given time, the context of the conversation, and our personal goals.

Intimate distance begins with skin contact and ranges out to about eighteen inches. The most obvious context for intimate distance involves interaction with people to whom we're emotionally close—and then mostly in private situations. Intimate distance between individuals also occurs in less intimate circumstances: visiting the doctor or dentist, at the hairdresser's, and during some athletic contests. Allowing someone to move into the intimate zone usually is a sign of trust.

Personal distance ranges from eighteen inches at its closest point to four feet at its farthest. Its closer range is the distance at which most relational partners stand in public. We are uncomfortable if someone else "moves in" to this area without invitation. The far range of personal distance runs from about two-and-one-half to four feet. This is the zone just beyond the other person's reach—the distance at which we can keep someone "at arm's length." This term suggests the type of communication that goes on at this range: Interaction is still reasonably personal, but less so than communication that occurs a foot or so closer.

Social distance ranges from four to about twelve feet. Within it are the kinds of communication that usually occur in business situations. Its closer range, from four to seven feet, is the distance at which conversations usually occur between salespeople and customers and between people who work together. We use the far range of social distance—seven to twelve feet—for more formal and impersonal situations. This is the range at which we generally sit from the boss.

Public distance is Hall's term for the farthest zone, running outward from twelve feet. The closer range of public distance is the one most teachers use in the classroom. In the farther range of public space—twenty-five feet and beyond—two-way communication becomes difficult. In some cases it's necessary for speakers to use public distance owing to the size of their audience, but we can assume that anyone who voluntarily chooses to use it when he or she could be closer is not interested in having a dialogue.

Choosing the optimal distance can have a powerful effect on how we regard others and how we respond to them. For example, students are more satisfied with teachers who reduce the distance between themselves and their classes. They also are more satisfied with the course itself, and they are more likely to follow the teacher's instructions.[96] Likewise, medical patients are more satisfied with physicians who don't "keep their distance."[97]

Territoriality   Whereas personal space is the invisible bubble we carry around as an extension of our physical being, **territory** is fixed space. Any area, such as a room, house, neighborhood, or country, to which we assume some kind of "rights" is our territory. Not all territory is permanent. We often stake out space for ourselves in the library, at the beach, and so on by using markers such as books, clothing, or other personal possessions.

The way people use space can communicate a good deal about power and status relationships. Generally, we grant people with higher status more personal territory and greater privacy.[98] We knock before entering the boss's office, whereas a boss can usually walk into our work area without hesitating. In traditional schools, professors have offices, dining rooms, and even toilets that are private, whereas the students, who are presumably less important, have no such sanctuaries. In the military, greater space and privacy usually come with rank: Privates sleep forty to a barracks, sergeants have their own private rooms, and generals have government-provided houses.

Environment

The physical environment people create can both reflect and shape interaction. This principle is illustrated right at home. Researchers showed ninety-nine students slides of the insides or outsides of twelve upper-middle-class homes and then asked them to infer the personality of the owners from their impressions.[99] The students were especially accurate after glancing at interior photos. The decorating schemes communicated accurate information about the homeowners' intellectualism, politeness, maturity, optimism, tenseness, willingness to take adventures, family orientations, and reservedness. The home exteriors also gave viewers accurate perceptions of the owners' artistic interests, graciousness, privacy, and quietness.

Besides communicating information about the designer, an environment can shape the kind of interaction that takes place in it. In one experiment, researchers found that the attractiveness of a room influenced the happiness and energy of the people working in it.[100] The experimenters set up three rooms: an "ugly" one, which resembled a janitor's closet in the basement of a campus building; an "average" room, which was a professor's office; and a "beautiful" room, which was furnished with carpeting, drapes, and comfortable furniture. The subjects in the experiment were asked to rate a series of pictures as a way of measuring their energy and feelings of well-being while at work. Results of the experiment showed that while in the ugly room the subjects became tired and bored more quickly and took longer to complete their task. When they moved to the beautiful room, however, they rated the faces they were judging higher, showed a greater desire to work, and expressed feelings of importance, comfort, and enjoyment. The results teach a lesson that isn't surprising: Workers generally feel better and do a better job when they're in an attractive environment.

The design of an entire building can shape communication among its users. Architects have learned that the way housing projects are designed controls to a great extent the contact neighbors have with each other. People who live in apartments near stairways and mailboxes have many more neighbor contacts than do those living in less heavily traveled parts of the building, and tenants generally have more contacts with immediate neighbors than with people even a few doors away.[101]

> The design of an entire building can shape communication among its users.

So far we have talked about how designing an environment can shape communication, but there is another side to consider. Watching how people use an already existing environment can be a way of telling what kind of relationships they want. For example, Sommer watched students in a college library and found that there's a definite pattern for people who want to study alone. While the library was uncrowded, students almost always chose corner seats at one of the empty rectangular tables.[102] Finally, each table was occupied by one reader. New readers would then choose a seat on the opposite side and far end of an occupied table, thus keeping the maximum distance between themselves and the other readers. One of Sommer's associates tried violating these "rules" by sitting next to, and across from, other female readers when more distant seats were available. She found that the approached women reacted defensively, either by signaling their discomfort through shifts in posture or gesturing or by eventually moving away.

Understanding Diversity

Doing Business Across Cultures

In a world where international business is becoming increasingly common, communicators who don't understand and adapt to cultural differences are likely to encounter problems that can disrupt their relationships. In this scenario, two businesspeople from different backgrounds fail to recognize and appreciate each other's cultural norms. Mike is from the United States and is used to a "time is money," task-oriented approach. Miguel is from Latin America, where personal understanding and trust must develop before business takes place.

If Mike and Miguel understood each other's cultural communication styles, they would have been more able to adapt to them and less upset by what seemed to each to be inappropriate behavior.

Mike

(To himself) Why aren't we getting on with it?

(To himself) It's a quarter to twelve. I've been here with Miguel for forty-five minutes already, and I haven't even begun to talk business. I know that both me and this proposal are new to Miguel, but how can I count on this guy when all he does is ask me questions about myself, my background, my interests, my family, and my "philosophy"! Why does he have to be so nosy? I don't know him well enough yet to get into that personal stuff. I know he's just invited me to have lunch with him, but it's a thirty-minute drive to the one o'clock appointment I scheduled, and I have to be on time. All I wanted to do was run through this proposal quickly the first time, see if he had any interest, and if he did, come back again to see about doing business. Sometimes I think that all these Hispanics want to do is talk about anything but business.

(To himself) Oh, well, I've never had any luck doing business with Hispanics before. Why should it be any different this time?

Thanks for the invitation to have lunch with you, Miguel, but I've got to get along to my next appointment. Here's my card. Maybe we can do business next time.

Miguel

(To himself) Why aren't we getting on with it?

(To himself) It's a quarter to twelve. I've been here with Mike for forty-five minutes already, and I haven't even begun to talk business. How can I know if I want to do business with him unless I know something about him and the kind of man he is? But I feel like a dentist pulling teeth. And he doesn't want to know anything about me! Where I come from, we don't like to do business with strangers. We like to know something about the other person and feel we can at least begin to trust them before we start to talk business seriously. It's too bad he turned me down for lunch. I think I can trust him and really am interested in his product line. With a little more time, I think we could do business. But first I've got to feel at least a little sure about who I'm doing business with. Sometimes I think that all these Anglos want to talk about is business.

(To himself) Oh, well, I've never had any luck doing business with gringos before. Why should it be any different this time?

Oh, that's all right, Mike. We'll have lunch another time. Come back again. I'd like to get to know you better. Maybe we can do business next time.

Adapted from John F. Kikoski and Catherine Kano Kikoski, *Reflexive Communication in the Culturally Diverse Workplace* (Westport, CT: Quorum, 1996), pp. 2–3.

Time

Social scientists use the term **chronemics** for the study of how human beings use and structure time. The way we handle time can express both intentional and unintentional messages.[103] Social psychologist Robert Levine describes several ways that time can communicate.[104] For instance, in a culture that values time highly, like the United States, waiting can be an indicator of status. "Important" people (whose time is supposedly more valuable than that of others) may be seen by appointment only, whereas it is acceptable to intrude without notice on lesser beings. To see how this rule operates, consider how natural it is for a boss to drop in to a subordinate's office unannounced, whereas some employees would never intrude into the boss's office without an appointment. A related rule is that low-status people must never make more important people wait. It would be a serious mistake to show up late for a job interview, although the interviewer might keep you cooling your heels in the lobby. Important people are often whisked to the head of a restaurant or airport line, whereas the presumably less exalted are forced to wait their turn.

The use of time depends greatly on culture.[105] Some cultures (e.g., North American, German, and Swiss) tend to be **monochronic**, emphasizing punctuality, schedules, and completing one task at a time. Other cultures (e.g., South American, Mediterranean, and Arab) are more **polychronic**, with flexible schedules in which multiple tasks are pursued at the same time. One psychologist discovered the difference between North and South American attitudes when teaching at a university in Brazil.[106] He found that some students arrived halfway through a two-hour class and that most of them stayed put and kept asking questions when the class was scheduled to end. A half hour after the official end of the class, the professor finally closed off discussion, because there was no indication that the students intended to leave. This flexibility of time is quite different from what is common in most North American colleges!

Even within a culture, rules of time vary. Sometimes the differences are geographic. In New York City, the party invitation may say "9 P.M.," but nobody would think of showing up before 9:30. In Salt Lake City, guests are expected to show up on time, or perhaps even a bit early.[107] Even within the same geographic area, different groups establish their own rules about the use of time. Consider your own experience. In school, some instructors begin and end class punctually, whereas others are more casual. With some people you feel comfortable talking for hours in person or on the phone, whereas with others time seems to be precious and not meant to be "wasted."

CULTURAL IDIOM

cooling your heels:
waiting impatiently

stayed put:
remained in space

Summary

Nonverbal communication consists of messages expressed by nonlinguistic means.

Nonverbal behavior is an integral part of virtually all communication, and nonverbal skill is a positive predictor of relational success. There are several important characteristics of nonverbal communication. First is the simple fact that it is impossible not to communicate nonverbally; humans constantly send messages about themselves that are available for others to receive. The second characteristic is that nonverbal communication is ambiguous; there are many possible interpretations for any behavior. This ambiguity makes it important for the receiver to verify any interpretation before jumping to conclusions about the meaning of a nonverbal message. Finally, nonverbal communication is different from verbal communication in complexity, flow, clarity, impact, and intentionality.

Some nonverbal communication is influenced by culture and gender. While there are some universal expressions, even the manner in which these expressions are used reflects the communicator's culture and gender. And behaviors that have special meanings in one culture may express different messages in another. We stated that nonverbal communication serves many functions: repeating, substituting, complementing, accenting, regulating, and contradicting verbal behavior, as well as deceiving.

The remainder of this chapter introduced the many ways in which humans communicate nonverbally: through posture, gesture, use of the face and eyes, voice, physical attractiveness and clothing, touch, distance and territoriality, environment, and time.

Key Terms

affect blend The combination of two or more expressions, each showing a different emotion. *p. 179*

chronemics The study of how humans use and structure time. *p. 185*

disfluency A nonlinguistic verbalization. For example, *um, er, ah. p. 179*

emblems Deliberate nonverbal behaviors with precise meanings, known to virtually all members of a cultural group. *p. 174*

haptics The study of touch. *p. 182*

illustrators Nonverbal behaviors that accompany and support verbal messages. *p. 175*

intimate distance One of Hall's four distance zones, ranging from skin contact to eighteen inches. *p. 183*

kinesics The study of body movement, gesture, and posture. *p. 178*

manipulators Movements in which one part of the body grooms, massages, rubs, holds, fidgets, pinches, picks, or otherwise manipulates another part. *p. 178*

microexpressions Momentary expressions that reflect an emotional state. *p. 177*

monochronic The use of time that emphasizes punctuality, schedules, and completing one task at a time. *p. 186*

nonverbal communication Messages expressed by other than linguistic means. *p. 167*

paralanguage Nonlinguistic means of vocal expression: rate, pitch, tone, and so on. *p. 179*

personal distance One of Hall's four distance zones, ranging from eighteen inches to four feet. *p. 183*

polychronic The use of time that emphasizes flexible schedules in which multiple tasks are pursued at the same time. *p. 186*

proxemics The study of how people and animals use space. *p. 183*

public distance One of Hall's four distance zones, extending outward from twelve feet. *p. 184*

social distance One of Hall's distance zones, ranging from four to twelve feet. *p. 183*

territory Fixed space that an individual assumes some right to occupy. *p. 184*

Case Study Question

Review the case study on pages 94–95. Use the information in this chapter to write a set of guidelines on how nonverbal communication can affect career success. Pay special attention to unspoken rules governing various types of nonverbal communication: touch, voice, time, etc.

Activities

1. **Observing and Reporting Nonverbal Behavior** This exercise will give you a clear idea of the many nonverbal behaviors that are available to you whenever you encounter another person. It will also help prevent you from jumping to conclusions about the meaning of those behaviors without checking out your interpretations. You can try the exercise either in or outside of class, and the period of time over which you do it is flexible, from a single class period to several days. In any case, begin by choosing a partner, and then follow these directions:

   1. For the first period of time (however long you decide to make it), observe the way your partner behaves. Notice how he or she moves; his or her mannerisms, postures, way of speaking; how he or she dresses; and so on. To remember your observations, jot them down. If you're doing this exercise out of class over an extended period of time, there's no need to let your observations interfere with whatever you'd normally be doing: Your only job here is to compile a list of your partner's behaviors. In this step, you should be careful not to interpret your partner's actions; just record what you see.

   2. At the end of the time period, share what you've seen with your partner. He or she will do the same with you.

   3. For the next period of time, your job is not only to observe your partner's behavior but also to interpret it. This time in your conference you should tell your partner what you thought his or her actions revealed. For example, if your partner dressed carelessly, did you think this meant that he or she overslept, that he or she is losing interest in his or her appearance, or that he or she was trying to be more comfortable? If you noticed him or her yawning frequently, did you think this meant that he or she

was bored, tired from a late night, or sleepy after a big meal? Don't feel bad if your guesses weren't all correct. Remember that nonverbal clues tend to be ambiguous. You may be surprised how checking out the nonverbal clues you observe can help build a relationship with another person.

2. **Culture and Nonverbal Communication**

   1. Identify at least three significant differences between nonverbal practices in two cultures or co-cultures (e.g., ethnic, age, or socioeconomic groups) within your own society.

   2. Describe the potential difficulties that could arise out of the differing nonverbal practices when members from the cultural groups interact. Are there any ways of avoiding these difficulties?

   3. Now describe the advantages that might come from differing cultural nonverbal practices. How might people from diverse backgrounds profit by encountering one another's customs and norms?

3. **Kinesics in Action** You can appreciate the many ways kinesic cues operate by identifying examples from your own experience when body movement served each of the following nonverbal functions:

   - Repeating
   - Substituting
   - Complementing
   - Accenting
   - Regulating
   - Contradicting

4. **The Eyes Have It** Prove for yourself the role eye contact plays in social influence by trying a simple experiment.

   1. Choose a situation where you can make simple requests from a series of strangers. You might, for example, ask to cut in line to use a photocopying machine.

   2. Make such a request to at least twenty people. Use the same words for each request but alternate your nonverbal behavior. Half the time make direct eye contact, and the other half of the time avoid looking directly at the other person when you make your request.

   3. Record your results, and see if your eye behavior played any role in generating compliance to your request.

   4. If eye contact does make a difference, describe how you could apply your findings to real-life situations.

5. **Building Vocal Fluency** You can become more adept at both conveying and interpreting vocal messages by following these directions.

   1. Join with a partner and designate one person A and the other B.

   2. Partner A should choose a passage of twenty-five to fifty items from the telephone directory, using his or her voice to convey one of the following attitudes:

      a. Egotism
      b. Friendliness
      c. Insecurity
      d. Irritation
      e. Confidence

   3. Partner B should try to detect the emotion being conveyed.

   4. Switch roles and repeat the process. Continue alternating roles until each of you has both conveyed and tried to interpret at least four emotions.

   5. After completing the preceding steps, discuss the following questions:

      a. What vocal cues did you use to make your guesses?

      b. Were some emotions easier to guess than others?

      c. Given the accuracy of your guesses, how would you assess your ability to interpret vocal cues?

   6. How can you use your increased sensitivity to vocal cues to improve your everyday communication competence?

6. **The Rules of Touch** Like most types of nonverbal behavior, touching is governed by cultural and social rules. Imagine you are writing a guidebook for visitors from another culture. Describe the rules that govern touching in the following relationships. In each case,

PART THREE

Interpersonal Communication

A Challenging Business Friendship

Last year you met Hideki in a business class. Like you, he was genuinely interested in the subject, and after a few weeks of conversations in class and over coffee, you decided to become study partners. Working together helped both your grades, and you enjoyed one another's company as well. You had never known anyone from Japan before, and learning about that country and its culture was really interesting. You began spending time together socially, and after a couple of months you considered him a friend as well as a fellow student.

Toward the end of the semester you worked together on a term project, which was to develop a business plan for a start-up enterprise. Your idea was a textbook co-op—a service by which students could buy, sell, and trade course books without paying the college bookstore.

The plan earned an A grade, but more importantly you were convinced that it had real potential for success. Over the summer you and Hideki spent an increasing amount of time together working on the co-op idea. You met his family when they visited town, and the two of you went on out-of-town vacations with other friends. By the end of the summer, you decided to file for a business license and open a bank account for the co-op.

For the most part, you are glad to have Hideki as a partner. But you are beginning to have a few concerns. For one thing, his personal style is a bit hard to take. His politeness sometimes crosses the line and feels aloof. He is usually right about business matters, but getting him to critique your ideas is very hard. For example, it took you a week to get Hideki to confess that he didn't like the name you had suggested for the business. "Why didn't you just tell me?" you asked. "Perhaps I was wrong and overreacting," he replied. You would feel much better if he just told you what was on his mind.

On the personal side, you are starting to feel a little cramped by Hideki's friendship. Given the choice, he would spend almost all his free time socializing with you and your friends. You do enjoy his company, but a little time apart would be good too. But knowing how kind and diplomatic Hideki is, you are afraid that bringing up this matter would hurt his feelings. Although you value Hideki's commitment to the co-op and his hard work, you are beginning to feel bored by the day-to-day routine of working on the job.

You don't want to jeopardize your friendship or the business partnership, but you need to do something so you don't start holding grudges against Hideki. Use the information in Part Three of this textbook to explore what you might do to improve matters.

You can find the questions and activities involving this case study on page 230 (Chapter 7) and page 261 (Chapter 8).

It may be impossible to live without others, but it can be sometimes infuriatingly difficult to communicate *with* them. The chapters in this unit will help you recognize the nature of communication in close relationships.

After studying Chapters 7 and 8, you will understand better

- The kinds of communication that distinguish truly interpersonal relationships from more superficial ones.
- The dynamics that shape communication in close relationships, including self-disclosure and its alternatives.
- How culture, gender, and other factors affect communication in interpersonal relationships.
- Ways of communicating when conflicts arise that can damage relationships, and more constructive alternatives.

CHAPTER 7

Understanding Interpersonal Relationships

Chapter Outline

YOU SHOULD UNDERSTAND:

1. The factors that shape interpersonal attraction.
2. Knapp's model of relational development.
3. Dialectical tensions in interpersonal relationships.
4. The characteristics that distinguish interpersonal relationships from impersonal ones.
5. The content and relational dimensions of messages.
6. The role of metacommunication in relational messages.
7. Dimensions and influences of intimacy in relationships.
8. Reasons for self-disclosure and the Johari Window model of self-disclosure.
9. Characteristics of effective and appropriate self-disclosure.
10. The functions served by lies, equivocation, and hints.

YOU SHOULD BE ABLE TO:

1. Describe the factors that cause you to be attracted to certain other individuals.
2. Identify the developmental stages of a given relationship and its dialectical tensions.
3. Identify interpersonal and impersonal communication.
4. Identify the content and relational dimensions of a message.
5. Distinguish among types of intimacy and influences on intimacy.
6. Identify the degree of self-disclosure in your relationships and the functions this serves.
7. Compose effective and appropriate disclosing messages.
8. Identify the types, functions, and ethical validity of nondisclosing messages you use.

Your own experience will show that some interpersonal relationships can be a source of tremendous satisfaction. Unfortunately, you probably know that other relationships can cause great pain. In this chapter we'll take a first look at the vitally important topic of interpersonal relationships. We will begin by exploring the reasons we form relationships with others. We will go on to explore two approaches that characterize how communication operates throughout the lifetime of relationships. Next, we'll explore what kinds of communication make some relationships much more personal than others. We will also look at some ways—both subtle and obvious—that we show others how we regard them and what kind of relationship we are seeking with them. Finally, we will look at the role of self-disclosure in interpersonal communication.

Why We Form Relationships

Sometimes we don't have a choice about our relationships: Children can't select their parents, and most workers aren't able to choose their bosses or colleagues. In many other cases, though, we seek out some people and actively avoid others. Social scientists have collected an impressive body of research on interpersonal attraction.[1] The following are some of the factors they have identified that influence our choice of relational partners.

Appearance

Most people claim that we should judge others on the basis of character, not appearance. The reality, however, is quite the opposite—at least in the early stages of a relationship.[2] In one study, a group of over seven hundred men and women were matched as blind dates. After the party was over, they were asked whether or not they would like to date their partners again. The result? The more physically attractive the person (as judged in advance by independent raters), the more likely he or she was seen as desirable. Other factors—social skills and intelligence, for example—didn't seem to affect the decision.[3]

> Physical factors become less important as a relationship progresses.

Even if your appearance isn't beautiful by societal standards, consider these encouraging facts: After initial impressions have passed, ordinary-looking people with pleasing personalities are likely to be judged as attractive.[4] Furthermore, physical factors become less important as a relationship progresses.[5] As one social scientist put it, "Attractive features may open doors, but apparently, it takes more than physical beauty to keep them open."[6]

Similarity

A large body of research confirms the fact that, in most cases, we like people who are similar to us.[7] For example, the more similar a married couple's personalities are, the more likely they are to report being happy and satisfied in their marriage.[8] Friends in middle and high school report being similar to one another in many ways, including having mutual friends, enjoying the same sports, liking the same social activities, and using (or not using) alcohol and cigarettes to the same degree.[9] For adults, similarity is more important to relational happiness than even communication ability: Friends who have equally low levels of communication skills are just as satisfied with their relationships as are friends having high levels of communication skills.[10]

Attraction is greatest when we are similar to others in a high percentage of important areas. For example, two people who support each other's career goals, enjoy the same friends, and have similar beliefs about human rights can endure trivial disagreements about the merits of sushi or hip-hop music.

Complementarity

The folk wisdom that "opposites attract" seems to contradict the similarity principle just described. In truth, both are valid. Differences strengthen a relationship when they are *complementary*—when each partner's characteristics satisfy the other's needs. Individuals, for instance, are often

likely to be attracted to each other when one partner is dominant and the other passive.[11] Relationships also work well when the partners agree that one will exercise control in certain areas ("You make the final decisions about money") and the other will exercise control in different areas ("I'll decide how we ought to decorate the place"). Strains occur when control issues are disputed.

Successful couples find ways to keep a balance between their similarities and differences.

When successful and unsuccessful couples are compared over a twenty-year period, it becomes clear that partners in successful marriages are similar enough to satisfy each other physically and mentally but different enough to meet each other's needs and keep the relationship interesting. Successful couples find ways to keep a balance between their similarities and differences, adjusting to the changes that occur over the years. We'll have more to say about balancing similarities and differences later in this chapter.

Reciprocal Attraction

We are attracted to people who like us—usually.[12] The power of reciprocal attraction is especially strong in the early stages of a relationship. Conversely, we will probably not care for people who clearly dislike or seem indifferent toward us.

It's no mystery why reciprocal liking builds attractiveness. People who approve of us bolster our feelings of self-esteem. This approval is rewarding in its own right, and it can also confirm the part of our self-concept that says, "I'm a likable person."

Of course, we aren't drawn toward everyone who seems to like us. If we don't find the other person's attributes attractive, their interest can be a turn-off. Attraction has to be mutual to spark and maintain a relationship.

Competence

We like to be around talented people, probably because we hope their skills and abilities will rub off on us. On the other hand, we are uncomfortable around those who are *too* competent—probably because we look bad by comparison. Given these contrasting attitudes, it's no surprise that people are generally attracted to those who are talented but who have visible flaws that show that they are human, just like us.[13]

There are some qualifications to this principle. People with especially high or low self-esteem find "perfect" people more attractive than those who are competent but flawed, and some studies suggest that women tend to be more impressed by uniformly superior people of both sexes, whereas men tend to be more impressed by desirable but "human" others. On the whole, though, the principle stands: The best way to gain the liking of others is to be good at what you do but to admit your mistakes and flaws.

Disclosure

Revealing important information about yourself through self-disclosure can help build liking.[14] Sometimes the basis of this liking comes from learning about how we are similar, either in experiences ("I broke off an engagement myself") or in attitudes ("I feel nervous with strangers, too"). Self-disclosure also builds liking because it is a sign of regard. When people share private information with you, it suggests that they respect and trust you—a kind of liking that we've already seen increases attractiveness. Disclosure plays an even more important role as relationships develop beyond their earliest stages.

Not all disclosure leads to liking. The information you reveal ought to be appropriate for the setting and stage of the relationship. You'll read more about self-disclosure later in this chapter.

Proximity

In many cases, proximity leads to liking.[15] For instance, we're more likely to develop friendships with close neighbors than with distant ones, and chances are good that we'll choose a mate with whom we cross paths often. Facts like these are understandable when we consider that proximity allows us to get more information about other people and benefit from a relationship with them. Also, people in close proximity may be more similar to us than those not close— for example, if we live in the same neighborhood, odds are we share the same socioeconomic status. The Internet provides a new means for creating closeness, as users are able to experience "virtual proximity" in cyberspace.[16]

> You are likely to develop strong feelings regarding others you encounter frequently, whether these feelings are positive or negative.

Familiarity, on the other hand, can also breed contempt. Spousal and child abuse are distressingly common. Most aggravated assaults occur within the family or among close neighbors. You are likely to develop strong feelings regarding others you encounter frequently, whether these feelings are positive or negative.

Rewards

Some social scientists argue that all relationships—both impersonal and personal—are based on a semieconomic model called *social exchange theory*.[17] This model suggests that we often seek out people who can give us rewards that are greater than or equal to the costs we encounter in dealing with them. Rewards may be tangible (a nice place to live, a high-paying job) or intangible (prestige, emotional support, companionship). Costs are undesirable outcomes: unpleasant work, emotional pain, and so on. A simple formula captures the social exchange theory of why we form and maintain relationships:

$$\text{Rewards} - \text{Costs} = \text{Outcome}$$

According to social exchange theorists, we use this formula (usually unconsciously) to decide whether dealing with another person is a "good deal" or "not worth the effort," based on whether the outcome is positive or negative.

At its most blatant level, an exchange approach seems cold and calculating, but in some types of relationships it seems quite appropriate. A healthy business relationship is based on how well the parties help one another, and some friendships are based on an informal kind of barter: "I don't mind listening to the ups and downs of your love life because you rescue me when the house needs repairs." Even close relationships have an element of exchange. Friends and lovers often tolerate each other's quirks because the comfort and enjoyment they get make the less-than-pleasant times worth accepting. In more serious cases, social exchange explains why some people stay in abusive relationships. Sadly, these people often report that they would rather be in a bad relationship than have no relationship at all.

"I'd like to buy everyone a drink. All I ask in return is that you listen patiently to my shallow and simplistic views on a broad range of social and political issues."

Source: © Cartoonbank.com

Characteristics of Interpersonal Communication

What is interpersonal communication? How does it differ from other types of interaction? When and how are interpersonal messages communicated? Read on and see.

What Makes Communication Interpersonal?

The most obvious way to define *interpersonal communication* is by looking at the number of people involved. In this sense we could consider all dyadic interaction as **contextually interpersonal communication**.

Although looking at communication by context is useful, this approach raises some problems. Consider, for example, a routine transaction between a sales clerk and customer, or the rushed exchange when you ask a stranger on the street for directions. Communication of this sort hardly seems interpersonal—or personal in any sense of the word. In fact, after transactions like this we commonly remark, "I might as well have been talking to a machine."

The impersonal nature of some two-person exchanges has led some scholars to say that *quality*, not quantity, is what distinguishes interpersonal communication. **Qualitatively interpersonal communication** occurs when people treat one another as unique individuals, regardless of the context in which the interaction occurs or the number of people involved.[18] When quality of interaction is the criterion, the opposite of interpersonal communication is *impersonal* interaction, not group, public, or mass communication.

The majority of our communication, even in dyadic contexts, is relatively impersonal. We chat pleasantly with shopkeepers or fellow passengers on the bus or plane; we discuss the weather or current events with most classmates and neighbors; we deal with coworkers in a polite way. Considering the number of people we communicate with, qualitatively interpersonal interaction is rather scarce. This scarcity isn't necessarily unfortunate: Most of us don't have the time or energy to create personal relationships with everyone we encounter—or even to act in a personal way all the time with the people we know and love best. In fact, the scarcity of qualitatively interpersonal communication contributes to its value. Like precious jewels and one-of-a-kind artwork, qualitatively interpersonal relationships are special because of their scarcity. You can get a sense of how interpersonal your relationships are by trying Activity number 1 at the end of the chapter.

Interpersonal Communication in Mediated Relationships

There's no question that mediated relationships pass the test of being contextually interpersonal. You can stay in touch via text messaging, IM, tweets, e-mail, and social networking websites more efficiently than in person. But what about the *quality* of mediated interaction? Is online communication a poor substitute for face-to-face contact, or is it a rich medium for developing close personal relationships?

Some observers have argued that mediated communication reduces the frequency and quality of face-to-face interaction.[19] As one critic put it, "[electronic] devices seem to wall us off from one another in some ways while both intensifying and yet perhaps also trivializing interpersonal contact in other ways."[20] Some evidence does suggest that mediated relationships can squeeze out face-to-face contacts. One survey revealed that people who relied heavily on the Internet to meet their communication needs grew to rely less and less on their face-to-face networks. More significantly, they tended to feel more lonely and depressed as their online communication increased.[21] Some critics argue that communicators who strive to acquire a large number of "friends" on social networking websites like Facebook and Twitter are engaging in superficial, impersonal relationships. As one critic put it:

> The idea . . . is to attain as many of these not-really-friends as possible. . . . Like cheap wine, "friends" provide a high that can only be sustained by acquiring more and more of them. Quantity trumps quality.[22]

Despite criticism like this, a growing body of research disputes the notion that mediated communication lacks quality.[23] Writing (online, of course) in *CMC Magazine*, Brittney G. Chenault summarized research concluding that e-mail, chat rooms, Internet newsgroups, and computer conferences can and do allow electronic correspondents to develop a degree of closeness similar to what can be achieved in person.[24]

Research confirms the claim that mediated communication can *enhance*, not diminish, the quantity and quality of interpersonal communication. Over half of the respondents in one survey reported that the number of their personal relationships had grown since they started to use the Internet. In another survey of over three thousand adults in the United States (again, both Internet users and nonusers), 72 percent of the Internet users had communicated with a relative or a friend within the past day, compared with 61 percent for nonusers.[25] Surprisingly, the Internet users were also more likely to have phoned friends and relatives. Research like this suggests that the difference between face-to-face and virtual relationships is eroding.[26]

Even more significant than the amount of communication that occurs online is its quality: 55 percent of Internet users said that e-mail had improved communications with family, and 66 percent said that their contact with friends had increased because of e-mail. Among women, the rate of satisfaction was even higher: 60 percent reported better contact with family and 71 percent with friends. Families that use mediated communication—particularly cell phones—stay in touch more regularly.[27] Over three-quarters of the Internet users polled said they never felt ignored by another household member's spending time online.[28] The majority of the Internet users said that e-mail, websites, and chat rooms had a "modestly positive impact" on their ability to communicate more with family members and make new friends. Among women, the rate of satisfaction was even higher: 60 percent reported better contact with family and 61 percent with friends.

For some people, mediated channels make it easier to build close relationships. Sociolinguist Deborah Tannen describes a situation where e-mail enhanced a relationship that wouldn't have developed to the same degree in person:

> E-mail deepened my friendship with Ralph. Though his office was next to mine, we rarely had extended conversations because he is shy. Face to face he mumbled so I could barely tell he was speaking. But when we both got on e-mail, I started receiving long, self-revealing messages; we poured our hearts out to each other. A friend discovered that e-mail opened up that kind of communication with her father. He would never talk much on the phone (as her mother would), but they have become close since they both got on line.[29]

> 55 percent of Internet users said that e-mail had improved communications with family, and 66 percent said that their contact with friends had increased because of e-mail.

CULTURAL IDIOM

poured our hearts out:
revealed our innermost thoughts and feelings

This story illustrates how CMC can provide rich opportunities for establishing depth and maintaining relationships. An Internet connection makes it possible to send and receive messages at any time of the day or night from people around the world. In cases where face-to-face contact is impossible and telephone conversations difficult due to cost or time differences, computer-mediated messages are cheap, quick, and easy.

Researchers have found differences between mediated relationships that started online and those in which people rely on both mediated and face-to-face channels. Exclusively online relationships can develop rapidly because of the nature of the communication. While face-to-face relationships often rely on shared activities and spending time together, online relationships rely entirely on communication. The focus on self-expression, combined with the somewhat anonymous nature of online interactions, tends to result in greater self-disclosure than that which takes place in budding face-to-face relationships.[30] On the other hand, without personal contact communicators tend to idealize one another, creating the potential for disappointment once they actually meet in person. In one study, 68 percent of respondents reported that their online relationship terminated due to their first face-to-face interaction going poorly.[31]

Content and Relational Messages

Virtually every verbal statement contains two kinds of messages. **Content messages**, which focus on the subject being discussed, are the most obvious. The content of such statements as "It's your turn to do the dishes" or "I'm busy Saturday night" is obvious.

Content messages aren't the only kind that are exchanged when two people interact. In addition, virtually all communication—both verbal and nonverbal—contains **relational messages**, which make statements about how the parties feel toward one another.[32] These relational messages express communicators' feelings and attitudes involving one or more dimensions:

Affinity   One dimension of relational communication is **affinity**: the degree to which people like or appreciate one another.

Respect   **Respect** is the degree to which we admire others and hold them in esteem. Respect and affinity might seem identical, but they are actually different dimensions of a relationship.[33] For example, you might like a three-year-old child tremendously without respecting her. Likewise, you could respect a boss or teacher's talents without liking him or her. Respect is a tremendously important and often overlooked ingredient in satisfying relationships. It is a better predictor of relational satisfaction than liking, or even loving.[34]

Immediacy   Communication scholars use the term **immediacy** to describe the degree of interest and attraction we feel toward and communicate to others. Immediacy is different than affinity. You can like someone (high affinity) but not demonstrate that feeling (low immediacy). Likewise, it's easy to imagine high affinity/high immediacy and low affinity/low immediacy, as well as low affinity and high immediacy. Which of these conditions do you think exists in the photo on this page?

Control   In every conversation and every relationship there is some distribution of **control**: the amount of influence communicators seek. Control can be distributed evenly among relational partners, or one person can have more and the other(s) less. An uneven distribution of control won't cause problems as long as everyone involved accepts that arrangement. Struggles arise, though, when people disagree on how control should be distributed in their relationship.

You can get a feeling for how relational messages operate in everyday life by recalling the statements at the beginning of this section. Imagine two ways of saying "It's your turn to do the dishes": one that is demanding and another that is matter-of-fact. Notice how the different nonverbal messages make statements about how the sender views control in this part of the relationship. The demanding tone says, in effect, "I have a right to tell you what to do around the house," whereas the matter-of-fact one suggests, "I'm just reminding you of something you might have overlooked." Likewise, you can easily visualize two ways to deliver the statement "I'm busy Saturday night": one with little affection and the other with much liking.

Notice that in each of these examples the relational dimension of the message was never discussed. In fact, most of the time we aren't conscious of the relational messages that bombard us every day. Sometimes we are unaware of relational messages because they match our belief about the amount of respect, immediacy, control, and affinity that is appropriate. For example, you probably won't be offended if your boss tells you to do a certain job, because you agree that supervisors have the right to direct employees. In other cases, however, conflicts arise over relational messages even though content is not disputed. If your boss delivers the order in a condescending, sarcastic, or abusive tone of voice, you probably will be offended. Your complaint wouldn't be with the order itself but rather with the way it was delivered. "I may work for this company," you might think, "but I'm not a slave or an idiot. I deserve to be treated like a human being."

How are relational messages communicated? As the boss-employee example suggests, they are usually expressed nonverbally. To test this fact for yourself, imagine how you could act while saying "Can you help me for a minute?" in a way that communicates each of the following attitudes:

superiority   aloofness   friendliness

helplessness   sexual desire   irritation

Although nonverbal behaviors are a good source of relational messages, remember that they are ambiguous. The sharp tone you take as a personal insult might be due to fatigue, and the interruption you take as an attempt to ignore your ideas might be a sign of pressure that has nothing to do with you. Before you jump to conclusions about relational clues, it's a good idea to practice the skill of perception checking that you learned in Chapter 3: "When you use that tone of voice to tell me it's my turn to do the dishes, I get the idea you're mad at me. Is that right?" If your interpretation was indeed correct, you can talk about the problem. On the other hand, if you were overreacting, the perception check can prevent a needless fight.

Metacommunication

As the preceding example of perception checking shows, not all relational messages are nonverbal. Social scientists use the term **metacommunication** to describe messages that refer to other messages.[35] In other words, metacommunication is communication about communication. Whenever we discuss a relationship with others, we are metacommunicating: "It sounds like you're angry at me" or "I appreciate how honest you've been." As the cartoon on page 204 shows, even text messages can contain metacommunicative dimensions. An e-mail or instant message that calls you an "idiot" might be a joking token of affection, or something quite the opposite. Given the fact that nonverbal cues are limited in computer-mediated communication, it's often important to supplement them with metacommunication (such as "just kidding").

"She's texting me, but I think she's also subtexting me."

Source: © Cartoonbank.com

Metacommunication is an important method of solving conflicts in a constructive manner. It provides a way to shift discussion from the content level to relational questions, where the problem often lies. For example, consider a couple bickering because one partner wants to watch television, whereas the other wants to talk. Imagine how much better the chances of a positive outcome would be if they used metacommunication to examine the relational problems that were behind their quarrel: "Look, it's not the TV watching itself that bothers me. It's that I imagine you watch so much because you're mad at me or bored. Are you feeling bad about us?"

Metacommunication isn't just a tool for handling problems. It is also a way to reinforce the good aspects of a relationship: "I really appreciate it when you compliment me about my work in front of the boss." Comments like this serve two functions: First, they let others know that you value their behavior. Second, they boost the odds that the other people will continue the behavior in the future.

Despite the benefits of metacommunication, bringing relational issues out in the open does have its risks. Discussing problems can be interpreted in two ways. On the one hand, the other person might see it in a positive light—"Our relationship is working because we can still talk things out." On the other hand, your desire to focus on the relationship might look like a bad omen—"Our relationship isn't working if we have to keep talking it over." Furthermore, metacommunication does involve a certain degree of analysis ("It seems like you're angry at me"), and some people resent being analyzed. These cautions don't mean verbal metacommunication is a bad idea. They do suggest, though, that it's a tool that needs to be used carefully.

Communication over the Relational Life Span

Qualitatively interpersonal relationships aren't stable. Instead, they are constantly changing. Communication scholars have described the way relationships develop and shift in two ways. We will examine each of them now.

A Developmental Perspective

One of the best-known explanations of how communication operates in relationships was created by Mark Knapp, whose **developmental model** broke down the rise and fall of relationships into ten stages, contained in the two broad phases of "coming together" and "coming apart."[36] Other researchers have suggested that any model of relational communication ought to contain a third part of the relational process—a stage where communication is aimed at keeping stable relationships operating smoothly and satisfactorily.[37] Figure 7-1 shows how Knapp's ten stages fit into this three-part view of relational communication.

The following stages are especially descriptive of intimate, romantic relationships and close friendships. The pattern for other intimate relationships, such as families, would follow different paths.

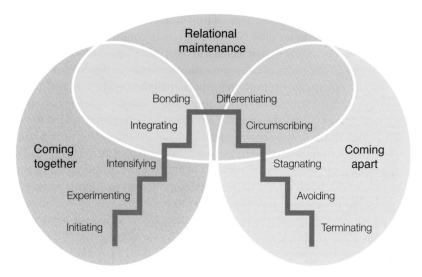

FIGURE 7-1 Stages of Relational Development

Initiating   The stage of initiation involves the initial making of contact with another person. Knapp restricts this stage to conversation openers, both in initial contacts and in contacts with acquaintances: "Nice to meet you," "How's it going?" and so on.

Whatever your preference for opening remarks, this stage is important because you are formulating your first impressions and presenting yourself as interested in the other person.

Initiating relationships can be particularly hard for people who are shy. Making contact via the Internet can be helpful for people who have a hard time conversing in person. One study of an online dating service found that participants who identified themselves as shy expressed a greater appreciation for the system's anonymous, non-threatening environment than did nonshy users.[38] The researchers found that many shy users employed the online service specifically to help overcome their inhibitions about initiating relationships in face-to-face settings.

Experimenting   In the stage of experimenting, conversation develops as people get acquainted by making "small talk." We ask: "Where are you from?" or "What do you do?" or "Do you know Josephine Mandoza? She lives in San Francisco, too."

Though small talk might seem meaningless, Knapp points out that it serves four purposes:

- It is a useful process for uncovering integrating topics and openings for more penetrating conversation.
- It can be an audition for a future friendship or a way of increasing the scope of a current relationship.
- It provides a safe procedure for indicating who we are and how another can come to know us better (reduction of uncertainty).
- It allows us to maintain a sense of community with our fellow human beings.

The relationship during this stage is generally pleasant and uncritical, and the commitments are minimal.

CULTURAL IDIOM
small talk:
unimportant or trivial conversation

Intensifying   At the next stage, the kind of truly interpersonal relationship defined earlier in this chapter begins to develop. Several changes in communication patterns occur during intensifying. The expression of feelings toward the other becomes more common. Dating couples use a wide range of communication strategies to describe their feelings of attraction.[39] About a quarter of the time they express their feelings directly, using metacommunication to discuss the state of the relationship. More often they use less-direct methods of communication: spending an increasing amount of time together, asking for support from one another, doing favors for the partner, giving tokens of affection, hinting and flirting, expressing feelings nonverbally, getting to know the partner's friends and family, and trying to look more physically attractive. Touching is more common during this stage than in either earlier or later ones.[40] Other changes mark the intensifying stage. Forms of address become more familiar. The parties begin to see themselves as "we" instead of as separate individuals. It is during the intensifying stage that individuals begin to directly express feelings of commitment to one another: "I'm sure glad we met." "You're the best thing that's happened to me in a long time."

Integrating   As the relationship strengthens, the parties begin to take on an identity as a social unit. Invitations begin to come addressed to the couple. Social circles merge. The partners begin to take on each other's commitments: "Sure, we'll spend Thanksgiving with your family." Common property may begin to be designated—our apartment, our car, our song.[41] Partners develop their own rituals for everything from expressing intimacy to handling daily routines.[42] They even begin to speak alike, using common words and sentence patterns.[43] In this sense, the integration stage is a time when we give up some characteristics of our old selves and become different people.

> The integration stage is a time when we give up some characteristics of our old selves and become different people.

As we become more integrated with others, our sense of obligation to them grows.[44] We feel obliged to provide a variety of resources such as class notes and money, whether or not the other person asks for them. When intimates do make requests of one another, they are relatively straightforward. Gone are the elaborate explanations, inducements, and apologies. In short, partners in an integrated relationship expect more from one another than they do in less-intimate associations.

Bonding   During the bonding stage, the parties make symbolic public gestures to show the world that their relationship exists. The most common form of bonding in romantic relationships is a wedding ceremony or civil union. Bonding generates social support for the relationship. Both custom and law impose certain obligations on partners who have officially bonded.

Bonding marks a turning point in a relationship. Up to now the relationship may have developed at a steady pace: Experimenting gradually moved into intensifying and then into integrating. Now, however, there is a spurt of commitment. The public display and declaration of exclusivity make this a critical period in the relationship.

Relationships don't have to be romantic to have a bonding stage. Business contracts form a bond, as does being initiated into a fraternity or sorority. Acts like these "officialize" a relationship and involve a measure of public commitment.

Differentiating   Now that the two people have formed this commonality, they need to reestablish individual identities. This is the point where the "hold me tight" orientation that has existed shifts, and "put me down" messages begin to occur. Partners use a variety of strategies to gain privacy from one another.[45] Sometimes they confront the other party directly, explaining that they don't want to continue a discussion. At other times they are less direct, offering nonverbal cues, changing the topic, or leaving the room.

Differentiation is likely to occur when a relationship begins to experience the first, inevitable stress. This desire for autonomy needn't be a negative experience, however. People need to be individuals as well as parts of a relationship, and differentiation is a necessary step toward autonomy. As you'll read later in this chapter, the key to successful differentiation is maintaining a commitment to the relationship while creating the space for being an individual as well.

> People need to be individuals as well as parts of a relationship.

Circumscribing   In the circumscribing stage, communication between members decreases in quantity and quality. Restrictions and restraints characterize this stage, and dynamic communication becomes static. Rather than discuss a disagreement (which requires some degree of energy on both parts), members opt for withdrawal: either mental (silence or daydreaming and fantasizing) or physical (where people spend less time together). Circumscribing doesn't involve total avoidance, which comes later. Rather, it entails a certain shrinking of interest and commitment.

Stagnating   If circumscribing continues, the relationship begins to stagnate. Members behave toward each other in old, familiar ways without much feeling. No growth occurs. The relationship is a shadow of its former self. We see stagnation in many workers who have lost enthusiasm for their job yet continue to go through the motions for years. The same sad event occurs for some couples who unenthusiastically have the same conversations, see the same people, and follow the same routines without any sense of joy or novelty.

Avoiding   When stagnation becomes too unpleasant, parties in a relationship begin to create distance between each other. Sometimes this is done under the guise of excuses ("I've been sick lately and can't see you"), and sometimes it is done directly ("Please don't call me; I don't want to see you now"). In either case, by this point the handwriting about the relationship's future is clearly on the wall.

CULTURAL IDIOM

handwriting . . . is clearly on the wall:
an indication or foretelling of an unfortunate message

bitter jabs:
unkind comments

Terminating   Characteristics of this final stage include summary dialogues about where the relationship has gone and the desire to dissociate. The relationship may end with a cordial dinner, a note left on the kitchen table, a phone call, or a legal document stating the dissolution. Depending on each person's feelings, this stage can be quite short, or it may be drawn out over time, with bitter jabs at one another.

The deterioration of a relationship from bonding to circumscribing, stagnating, and avoiding isn't inevitable. One of the key differences between marriages that end in separation and those that are restored to their former intimacy is the communication that occurs when the partners are unsatisfied.[46] Unsuccessful couples deal with their problems by avoidance, indirectness, and less involvement with one another. By contrast, couples who "repair" their relationship communicate much more directly. They air their concerns and spend time and effort negotiating solutions to their problems.

Relationships don't always move toward termination in a straight line. Rather, they take a back-and-forth pattern, where the trend is toward dissolution.[47]

While the communication surrounding relational termination can sometimes be cruel and painful, it doesn't have to be totally negative. Understanding each other's investment in the relationship and need for personal growth may dilute the hard feelings. In fact, many relationships aren't so much terminated as redefined. A divorced couple, for example, may find new, less intimate ways to relate to each other.

Knapp's model of relational development and decline offers a good description of communication stages in traditional romantic relationships. Some critics have argued that it doesn't characterize other sorts of relationships so well. Identify your position in this debate by following these steps:

1. Explain how well (or poorly) the model describes one other type of relationship: among coworkers, friends (either close or more distant), parent and child, or another relational context of your choosing.

2. Construct a model describing communication stages in the relationship type you just identified. How does this model differ from Knapp's?

Understanding Communication Technology

To End a Romance, Just Press "Send": Instant Messaging Altering the Way We Love

It was the middle of a workday two weeks ago, and Larry was deep into a meeting when a text-message began scrolling across his cell phone screen. He glanced at it and thought: "You can't be serious."

It was no joke. His girlfriend was breaking up with him . . . again. And she was doing it by e-mail . . . again.

For the sixth time in eight months, she had ended their relationship electronically rather than face-to-face. He had sensed trouble—he had been opening his e-mail with trepidation for weeks—so the previous day he had suggested that they meet in person to talk things over. But she nixed that, instead choosing to send the latest in what Larry had begun to consider part of a virtual genre: "the goodbye e-mail."

Understandably, he'd like to say his own goodbye to that genre. "E-mail is horrible," says Larry, 36, an Air Force sergeant from New Hampshire who asked that his last name not be used. "You just get to the point where you hate it. You can't have dialogue. You don't have that person in front of you. You just have that black-and-white text. It's a very cold way of communicating."

Cold, maybe. Popular, for sure. The use of e-mail and instant-messaging to end intimate relationships is gaining popularity because instantaneous communication makes it easy—some say too easy—to just call the whole thing off. Want to avoid one of those squirmy, awkward breakup scenes? Want to control the dialogue while removing facial expressions, vocal inflections, and body language from the equation? A solution is as near as your keyboard or cell phone.

Sometimes there is a legitimate reason for wanting to avoid personal contact. Tara, a 32-year-old woman who lives near Boston, says her ex-husband was intimidating and emotionally abusive during their marriage.

So when she wanted to end the marriage several years ago, she felt more comfortable doing so by sending a text message.

Tara says that since then she has ended several other relationships by e-mail. "I'm a softie, and I hate hurting people's feelings," she says. Recently she laid the groundwork for breaking her engagement with a series of e-mails to her fiancé. After ending the engagement last week, she reached a moment of truth, she says, and has decided that from now on, if she wants to call it quits, "The e-mail option is out."

This sort of back-and-forth might reflect what Lee Rainey, director of the Pew Internet & American Life Project, sees as a blurring of the boundaries in modern romance between the real and virtual realms.

"People are living, in many respects, with a foot in both worlds," Rainey says. "They've got virtual stuff sitting next to real-world stuff. But we haven't worked out the social norms yet. For some people, this will feel really callous. Others feel that, 'This is how I communicate these days, and why shouldn't I break up with someone by e-mail?'"

Don Aucoin
The Boston Globe

A Dialectical Perspective

Developmental models like the one described in the preceding pages suggest that communication differs in important ways at various points in the life of a relationship. According to these stage-related models, the kinds of interaction that happen during initiating, experimenting, or intensifying are different from the interaction that occurs during differentiating, circumscribing, or avoiding.

Despite its value, a stage-related model isn't the only way to explain interaction in relationships. Some scholars suggest that communicators grapple with the same kinds of challenges whether a relationship is brand-new or has lasted decades. They argue that communicators seek important but inherently incompatible goals throughout virtually all of their relationships. This **dialectical model** suggests that struggling to achieve these goals creates **dialectical tensions**: conflicts that arise when two opposing or incompatible forces exist simultaneously. In recent years, communication scholars have identified the dialectical tensions that make successful communication challenging.[48] They suggest that the struggle to manage these dialectical tensions creates the most powerful dynamics in relational communication. In the following pages we will discuss three powerful dialectical tensions.

Connection Versus Autonomy   No one is an island. Recognizing this fact, we seek out involvement with others. But, at the same time, we are unwilling to sacrifice our entire identity to even the most satisfying relationship. The conflicting desires for connection and independence are embodied in the *connection-autonomy dialectic*. Research on relational breakups demonstrates the consequences for relational partners who can't find a way to manage these very different personal needs.[49] Some of the most common reasons for relational breakups involve failure of partners to satisfy one another's needs for connection: "We barely spent any time together"; "He wasn't committed to the relationship"; "We had different needs." But other relational complaints involve excessive demands for connection: "I was feeling trapped"; "I needed freedom."

The levels of connection and autonomy that we seek can change over time. In his book *Intimate Behavior*, Desmond Morris suggests that each of us repeatedly goes through three stages: "Hold me tight," "Put me down," and "Leave me alone."[50] This cycle becomes apparent in the first years of life when children move from the "Hold me tight" stage that characterizes infancy into a new "Put me down" stage of exploring the world by crawling, walking, touching, and tasting. This move for independence isn't all in one direction: The same three-year-old who insists "I can do it myself" in August may cling to parents on the first day of preschool in September. As children grow into adolescents, the "Leave me alone" orientation becomes apparent. Teenagers who used to happily spend time with their parents now may groan at the thought of a family vacation or even the notion of sitting down at the dinner table each evening. More time is spent with friends or alone. Although this time can be painful for parents, most developmental experts recognize it as a necessary stage in moving from childhood to adulthood.

As the need for independence from family grows, adolescents take care of their "hold me tight" needs by associating with their peers. Friendships during the teenage years are vital, and the level of closeness with contemporaries can be a barometer of happiness. This is the time when physical intimacy becomes an option, and sexual exploration may provide a new way of achieving closeness.

In adult relationships, the same cycle of intimacy and distance repeats itself. In marriages, for example, the "Hold me tight" bonds of the first year are often followed

Source: Reprinted by special permission of King Features Syndicate.

by a desire for independence. This need for autonomy can manifest itself in a number of ways, such as the desire to make friends or engage in activities that don't include the spouse, or the need to make a career move that might disrupt the relationship. As the discussion of relational stages later in this chapter will explain, this movement from closeness to autonomy may lead to the breakup of relationships, but it can also be part of a cycle that redefines the relationship in a new form that can recapture or even surpass the intimacy that existed in the past.

Predictability Versus Novelty   Stability is an important need in relationships, but too much of it can lead to feelings of staleness. The *predictability-novelty dialectic* reflects this tension. Humorist Dave Barry exaggerates only slightly when he talks about the boredom that can come when husbands and wives know each other too well:

> After a decade or so of marriage, you know *everything* about your spouse, every habit and opinion and twitch and tic and minor skin growth. You could write a seventeen-pound book solely about the way your spouse *eats*. This kind of intimate knowledge can be very handy in certain situations—such as when you're on a TV quiz show where the object is to identify your spouse from the sound of his or her chewing—but it tends to lower the passion level of a relationship.[51]

> The challenge for communicators is to juggle the desire for predictability with the need for novelty that keeps the relationship fresh and interesting.

Although too much familiarity can lead to the risk of boredom and stagnation, nobody wants a completely unpredictable relational partner. Too many surprises can threaten the foundations upon which the relationship is based ("You're not the person I married!").

The challenge for communicators is to juggle the desire for predictability with the need for novelty that keeps the relationship fresh and interesting. People differ in their need and desire for stability and surprises, so there is no optimal mixture of the two. As you will read shortly, there are a number of strategies people can use to manage these contradictory drives.

Openness Versus Privacy   As Chapter 1 explained, disclosure is one characteristic of interpersonal relationships. Yet, along with the need for intimacy, we have an equally important need to maintain some space between ourselves and others. These sometimes conflicting drives create the *openness-privacy dialectic*.

Even the strongest interpersonal relationships require some distance. On a short-term basis, the desire for closeness waxes and wanes. Lovers may go through periods

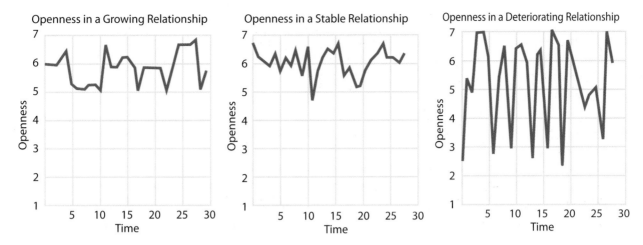

FIGURE 7-2 Cyclical Phases of Openness and Withdrawal in Relationships

of much sharing and times of relative withdrawal. Likewise, they experience periods of passion and then periods of little physical contact. Friends have times of high disclosure where they share almost every feeling and idea and then disengage for days, months, or even longer. Figure 7-2 illustrates some patterns of variation in openness uncovered in a study of college students' communication patterns.[52] The students reported the degree of openness in one of their important relationships—a friendship, romantic relationship, or marriage—over a range of thirty conversations. The graphs show a definite pattern of fluctuation between disclosure and privacy in every stage of the relationships.

Strategies for Managing Dialectical Tensions   Managing the dialectical tensions outlined in these pages presents communication challenges. There are a number of strategies by which these challenges can be managed.[53] One of the least functional is *denial* that tensions exist. People in denial insist that "everything is fine," that the inevitable tugs of dialectical tensions really aren't a problem. For example, coworkers who claim that they're *always* happy to be members of the team and *never* see conflicts between their personal goals and the organization's are probably operating in a state of denial.

Disorientation is another response to dialectical tensions. In this response, communicators feel so overwhelmed and helpless that they are unable to confront their problems. In the face of dialectical tensions they might fight, freeze, or even leave the relationship. A couple who discover soon after the honeymoon that living a "happily ever after" conflict-free life is impossible might become so terrified that they would come to view their marriage as a mistake.

In the strategy of *selection*, communicators respond to one end of the dialectical spectrum and ignore the other. For example, a couple caught between the conflicting desires for stability and novelty might find their struggle to change too difficult to manage and choose to stick with predictable, if unexciting, patterns of relating to one another.

Communicators choose the strategy of *alternation* to alternate between one end of the dialectical spectrum at some times and the other end at other times. Friends, for example, might manage the autonomy-connection dialectic by alternating between times when they spend a large amount of time together and other times when they live independent lives.

A fifth strategy is *segmentation*, a tactic in which partners compartmentalize different areas of their relationship. For example, a couple might manage the openness-closedness dialectic by sharing almost all their feelings about mutual friends with one another but keeping certain parts of their past romantic histories private.

Moderation is a sixth strategy. This strategy is characterized by compromises, in which communicators choose to back off from expressing either end of the dialectical spectrum. Adult children, for example, might manage the revelation-concealment dialectic with their inquisitive parents by answering some (though not all) unwelcome parental questions.

Communicators can also respond to dialectical challenges by *reframing* them in terms that redefine the situation so that the apparent contradiction disappears. Consider a couple who wince when their friends characterize them as a "perfect couple." On one hand, they want to escape from the "perfect couple" label that feels confining, but on the other hand, they enjoy the admiration that comes with this identity. By pointing out to their friends that "ideal couples" aren't always blissfully happy, they can both be themselves and keep the admiration of their friends.

A final strategy for handling dialectical tensions is *reaffirmation*—acknowledging that dialectical tensions will never disappear, accepting or even embracing the challenges they present. The metaphorical view of relational life as a kind of roller coaster reflects this orientation, and communicators who use reaffirmation view dialectical tensions as part of the ride.

> Even though a relationship may move back to a stage it has experienced before, it will never be the same.

Even though a relationship may move back to a stage it has experienced before, it will never be the same. For example, most healthy long-term relationships will go through several phases of experimenting, when the partners try out new ways of behaving with one another. Though each phase is characterized by the same general features, the specifics will feel different each time. As you learned in Chapter 1, communication is irreversible. Partners can never go back to "the way things were." Sometimes this fact may lead to regrets: It's impossible to take back a cruel comment or forget a crisis. On the other hand, the irreversibility of communication can make relationships exciting, because it lessens the chance for boredom.

Intimacy in Interpersonal Relationships

Even the closest relationships involve a mixture of personal and interpersonal communication. We alternate between a "we" and a "me" orientation, sometimes focusing on connecting with others and at other times focusing on our own needs and interests. In the next few pages we will examine how our communication is affected by these apparently conflicting drives for intimacy and distance.

Dimensions of Intimacy

The dictionary defines **intimacy** as arising from "close union, contact, association, or acquaintance." This definition suggests that the key element of intimacy is closeness, one element that "ordinary people" have reported as characterizing their intimate relationships.[54] However, it doesn't explain what *kinds* of closeness can create a state of intimacy. In truth, intimacy can have several qualities. The first is *physical*. Even before birth, the developing fetus experiences a kind of physical closeness with its mother that will never happen again, "floating in a warm fluid, curling inside a total embrace, swaying to the undulations of the moving body and hearing the beat of the pulsing heart."[55] As they grow up, fortunate children are continually nourished by physical intimacy: being rocked, fed, hugged, and held. As we grow older, the opportunities for physical intimacy are less regular, but still possible and important. Some, but by no means all, physical intimacy is sexual. In one survey, only one-quarter of the respondents (who were college students) stated that intimacy necessarily contained a romantic or sexual dimension.[56] Other forms of physical intimacy include affectionate hugs, kisses, and even struggles. Companions who have endured physical challenges together—in athletics or emergencies, for example—form a bond that can last a lifetime.

In other cases, intimacy comes from *intellectual* sharing. Not every exchange of ideas counts as intimacy, of course. Talking about next week's midterm with your professor or classmates isn't likely to forge strong relational bonds. But when you engage another person in an exchange of important ideas, a kind of closeness develops that can be powerful and exciting.

A third quality of intimacy is *emotion*: exchanging important feelings. This chapter will offer several guidelines for disclosing your thoughts and feelings to others. If you follow those guidelines, you will probably recognize a qualitative change in your relationships.

If we define *intimacy* as being close to another person, then *shared activities* can provide another way to achieve this state. Shared activities can include everything from working side by side at a job to meeting regularly for exercise workouts. Although shared activities are no guarantee of intimacy, people who spend time together can develop unique ways of relating that transform the relationship from an impersonal one that could be done with anybody to one with interpersonal qualities. For example, both friendships and romantic relationships are often characterized by several forms of play. Partners invent private codes, fool around by acting like other people, tease one another, and play games—everything from having punning contests to arm wrestling.[57]

Some intimate relationships exhibit all four qualities: physical intimacy, intellectual exchanges, emotional disclosure, and shared activities. Other intimate relationships exhibit only one or two. Some relationships, of course, aren't intimate in any way. Acquaintances, roommates, and coworkers may never become intimate. In some cases even family members develop smooth but relatively impersonal relationships.

Not even the closest relationships always operate at the highest level of intimacy. At some times you might share all of your thoughts or feelings with a friend, family member, or lover, and at other times you might withdraw. You might freely share your feelings about one topic and stay more aloof in another one. The same principle holds for physical intimacy, which waxes and wanes in most relationships. The dialectical view of relational maintenance described later in this chapter explains how intimacy can wax and wane, even in the closest relationships.

> Intimacy can wax and wane, even in the closest relationships.

Male and Female Intimacy Styles

Until recently most social scientists believed that women are better at developing and maintaining intimate relationships than men.[58] This belief grew from the assumption that the disclosure of personal information is the most important ingredient of intimacy. Most research *does* show that women (taken as a group, of course) are more willing than men to share their thoughts and feelings.[59] In terms of the amount and depth of information exchanged, female-female relationships are at the top of the disclosure list. Male-female relationships come in second, whereas relationships between men

CULTURAL IDIOM
fool around:
spend time joking

Sally Forth

Source: Reprinted by special permission of King Features Syndicate.

have less disclosure than any other type. At every age, women disclose more than men, and the information they disclose is more personal and more likely to involve feelings. Although both sexes are equally likely to reveal negative information, men are less likely to share positive feelings.[60]

Through the mid-1980s many social scientists interpreted the relative lack of male self-disclosure as a sign that men are unwilling or even unable to develop close relationships. Some argued that the female trait of disclosing personal information and feelings makes them more "emotionally mature" and "interpersonally competent" than men. Personal growth programs and self-help books urged men to achieve closeness by learning to open up and share their feelings.

Scholarship conducted in roughly the last two decades has begun to show that male-female differences aren't as great as they seem,[61] and emotional expression isn't the *only* way to develop close relationships. Unlike women, who value personal talk, men grow close to one another by doing things together. In one study more than 75 percent of the men surveyed said that their most meaningful experiences with friends came from activities other than talking.[62] They reported that through shared activities they "grew on one another," developed feelings of interdependence, showed appreciation for one another, and demonstrated mutual liking. Likewise, men regarded practical help from other men as a measure of caring. Research like this shows that, for many men, closeness grows from activities that don't depend heavily on disclosure: A friend is a person who does things *for* you and *with* you.

The difference between male and female measures of intimacy helps explain some of the stresses and misunderstandings that can arise between the sexes. For example, a woman who looks for emotional disclosure as a measure of affection may overlook an "inexpressive" man's efforts to show he cares by doing favors or spending time together. Fixing a leaky faucet or taking a hike may look like ways to avoid getting close, but to the man who proposes them they may be measures of affection and bids for intimacy. Likewise, differing ideas about the timing and meaning of sex can lead to misunderstandings. Whereas many women think of sex as a way to express intimacy that has already developed, men are more likely to see it as a way to *create* that intimacy.[63] In this sense, the man who encourages sex early in a relationship or after a fight may not just be a testosterone-crazed lecher: He may view the shared activity as a way to build closeness. By contrast, the woman who views personal talk as the pathway to intimacy may resist the idea of physical closeness before the emotional side of the relationship has been discussed.

CULTURAL IDIOM

to open up:
talk about subjects that otherwise might be withheld

Cultural Influences on Intimacy

The notion of how much intimacy is desirable and how to express it varies from one culture to another.[64] In one study, researchers asked residents of Great Britain, Japan, Hong Kong, and Italy to describe their use of thirty-three rules that governed interaction in a wide range of communication behaviors: everything from the use of humor to hand shaking to the management of money.[65] The results showed that the greatest differences between Asian and European cultures focused on the rules for dealing with intimacy: showing emotions, expressing affection in public, engaging in sexual activity, respecting privacy, and so on. Culture also plays a role in shaping how much intimacy we seek in different types of relationships. For instance, the Japanese seem to expect more intimacy in friendships, whereas Americans look for more intimacy in romantic relationships with a boy- or girlfriend, fiancée, or spouse.[66]

In some collectivist cultures such as Taiwan and Japan there is an especially great difference in the way members communicate with members of their "in-groups" (such as family and close friends) and with those they view as outsiders.[67] They generally do not reach out to strangers, often waiting until they are properly introduced before entering into a conversation. Once introduced, they address outsiders with a degree of formality. They go to extremes to hide unfavorable information about in-group members from outsiders, on the principle that one doesn't wash dirty laundry in public. By contrast, members of more individualistic cultures like the United States and Australia make less of a distinction between personal relationships and casual ones. They act more familiar with strangers and disclose more personal information, making them excellent "cocktail party conversationalists."

Within American culture, intimacy varies from one group to another. For example, working-class black men are much more disclosing than their white counterparts.[68] By contrast, upwardly mobile black men communicate more like white men with the same social agenda, disclosing less with their male friends.

> Members of more individualistic cultures like the United States and Australia make less of a distinction between personal relationships and casual ones.

Self-Disclosure in Interpersonal Relationships

"We don't have any secrets," some people proudly claim. Opening up certainly is important. Earlier in this chapter you learned that one ingredient in qualitatively interpersonal relationships is disclosure. You've also read that we find others more attractive when they share certain private information with us. Given the obvious importance of self-disclosure, we need to take a closer look at the subject. Just what is it? When is it desirable? How can it best be done?

The best place to begin is with a definition. **Self-disclosure** is the process of deliberately revealing information about oneself that is significant and that would not normally be known by others. Let's take a closer look at some parts of this definition. Self-disclosure must be *deliberate*. If you accidentally mentioned to a friend that you were thinking about quitting a job or proposing marriage,

"There's something you need to know about me, Donna. I don't like people knowing things about me."

Source: The New Yorker Collection 2003 Leo Cullum from cartoonbank.com. All Rights Reserved.

TABLE 7-1   Reasons for Self-Disclosure

Self-disclosure has the potential to improve and expand interpersonal relationships, but it serves other functions as well. As you read each of the following reasons why people reveal themselves, see which apply to you.

REASON	EXAMPLE/EXPLANATION
Catharsis	"I need to get this off my chest . . ."
Self-clarification	"I'm really confused about something I did last night. If I tell you, maybe I can figure out why I did it . . ."
Self-validation	"I think I did the right thing. Let me tell you why I did it . . ."
Reciprocity	"I really like you . . ." (Hoping for a similar disclosure by other person.)
Impression management	Salesperson to customer: "My boss would kill me for giving you this discount . . ." (Hoping disclosure will build trust.)
Relationship maintenance and enhancement	"I'm worried about the way things are going between us. Let's talk." or "I sure am glad we're together!"
Control	(Employee to boss, hoping to get raise) "I got a job offer yesterday from our biggest competitor."

Adapted from V. J. Derlega and J. Grezlak, "Appropriateness of Self-Disclosure," in G. J. Chelune, ed., *Self-Disclosure* (San Francisco, CA: Jossey-Bass, 1979).

that information would not fit into the category we are examining here. Self-disclosure must also be *significant*. Revealing relatively trivial information—the fact that you like fudge, for example—does not qualify as self-disclosure. The third requirement is that the information being revealed would *not be known by others*. There's nothing noteworthy about telling others that you are depressed or elated if they already know how you're feeling.

As Table 7-1 shows, people self-disclose for a variety of reasons. Some involve developing and maintaining relationships, but other reasons often drive revealing personal information. The reasons for disclosing vary from one situation to another, depending on several factors. The first important factor in whether we disclose seems to be how well we know the other person.[69] When the target of disclosure is a friend, the most frequent reason people give for volunteering personal information is relationship maintenance and enhancement. The second important reason is self-clarification—to sort out confusion, to understand ourselves better.

> The reasons for disclosing vary from one situation to another, depending on several factors.

With strangers, reciprocity becomes the most common reason for disclosing. We offer information about ourselves to strangers to learn more about them, so we can decide whether and how to continue the relationship. The second most common reason is impression formation. We often reveal information about ourselves to strangers to make ourselves look good. This information, of course, is usually positive—at least in the early stages of a friendship.

Models of Self-Disclosure

Over several decades, social scientists have created various models to represent and understand how self-disclosure operates in relationships. In the next few pages we will look at two of the best-known models.

Breadth and Depth: Social Penetration Social psychologists Irwin Altman and Dalmas Taylor describe two ways in which communication can be more or less disclosing.[70] Their **social penetration model** is pictured in Figure 7-3. The first dimension of self-disclosure in this model involves the **breadth** of information volunteered—the range of subjects being discussed. For example, the breadth of disclosure in your relationship with a fellow worker will expand as you begin revealing information about your life away from the job, as well as on-the-job details. The second dimension of disclosure is the **depth** of the information being volunteered, the shift from relatively nonrevealing messages to more personal ones.

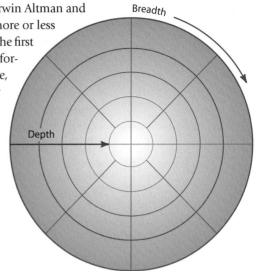

FIGURE 7-3 Social Penetration Model

Depending on the breadth and depth of information shared, a relationship can be defined as casual or intimate. In a casual relationship, the breadth may be great, but not the depth. A more intimate relationship is likely to have high depth in at least one area. The most intimate relationships are those in which disclosure is great in both breadth and depth. Altman and Taylor see the development of a relationship as a progression from the periphery of their model to its center, a process that typically occurs over time. Each of your personal relationships probably has a different combination of breadth of subjects and depth of disclosure. Figure 7-4 pictures a student's self-disclosure in one relationship.

What makes the disclosure in some messages deeper than others? One way to measure depth is by how far it goes on two of the dimensions that define self-disclosure. Some revelations are certainly more *significant* than others. Consider the difference between saying "I love my family" and "I love you." Other statements qualify as deep disclosure because they are *private*. Sharing a secret you've told to only a few close friends is certainly an act of self-disclosure, but it's even more revealing to divulge information that you've never told anyone.

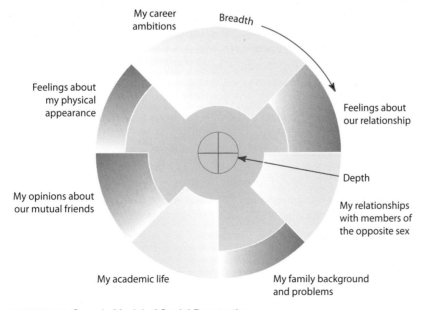

FIGURE 7-4 Sample Model of Social Penetration

Self-Disclosure, Self-Awareness, and Relational Quality   Another model that helps represent how self-disclosure operates is the **Johari Window**.[71] (The window takes its name from the first names of its creators, Joseph Luft and Harry Ingham.) Imagine a frame inside which is everything there is to know about you: your likes and dislikes, your goals, your secrets, your needs—everything. (See Figure 7-5.)

Of course, you aren't aware of everything about yourself. Like most people, you're probably discovering new things about yourself all the time. To represent this, we can divide the frame containing everything about you into two parts: the part you know about and the part you don't know about, as in Figure 7-6.

We can also divide this frame containing everything about you in another way. In this division the first part contains the things about you that others know, and the second part contains the things about you that you keep to yourself. Figure 7-7 represents this view.

When we impose these two divided frames one atop the other, we have a Johari Window. By looking at Figure 7-8 you can see the *everything about you* window divided into four parts.

Part 1 represents the information of which both you and the other person are aware. This part is your *open area*. Part 2 represents the *blind area*: information of which you are unaware but that the other person knows. You learn about information in the blind area primarily through feedback. Part 3 represents your *hidden area*: information that you know but aren't willing to reveal to others. Items in this hidden area become public primarily through self-disclosure, which is the focus of this chapter. Part 4 represents information that is *unknown* to both you and others. At first, the unknown area seems impossible to verify. After all, if neither you nor others know what it contains, how can you be sure it exists? We can deduce its existence because we are constantly discovering new things about ourselves. It is not unusual to discover, for example, that you have an unrecognized talent, strength, or weakness. Items move from the unknown area into the open area either directly when you disclose your insight or through one of the other areas first.

Interpersonal relationships of any depth are virtually impossible if the individuals involved have little open area. Going a step further, you can see that a relationship is limited by the individual who is less open, that is, who possesses the smaller open area. Figure 7-9 illustrates this situation with Johari Windows. A's window is set up in reverse

> Like most people, you're probably discovering new things about yourself all the time.

FIGURE 7-5 The Johari Window: Everything about You

FIGURE 7-6 The Johari Window: Known to Self; Not Known to Self

FIGURE 7-7 The Johari Window: Known to Others; Not Known to Others

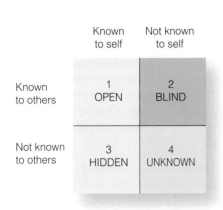

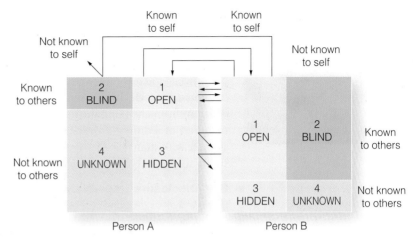

FIGURE 7-8 The Johari Window: Open; Blind; Hidden; Unknown

FIGURE 7-9 The Johari Window: Self-Disclosure Levels in Two-Way Communication

so that A's and B's open areas are adjacent. Notice that the amount of communication (represented by the arrows connecting the two open areas) is dictated by the size of the smaller open area of A. The arrows originating from B's open area and being turned aside by A's hidden and blind areas represent unsuccessful attempts to communicate.

You have probably found yourself in situations that resemble Figure 7-9. Perhaps you have felt the frustration of not being able to get to know someone who was too reserved. Perhaps you have blocked another person's attempts to build a relationship with you in the same way. Whether you picture yourself more like Person A or Person B, the fact is that self-disclosure on both sides is necessary for the development of any interpersonal relationship. This chapter will describe just how much self-disclosure is optimal and of what type.

Characteristics of Effective Self-Disclosure

Self-disclosure can certainly be valuable, but using it effectively requires an understanding of how it operates. Here are some findings from researchers that will help you decide when and how disclosure works best.

Self-Disclosure Is Influenced by Culture   The level of self-disclosure that is appropriate in one culture may seem completely inappropriate in another one. Disclosure is especially high in mainstream North American society. In fact, natives of the United States are more disclosing than members of any other culture studied.[72] They are likely to disclose more about themselves to acquaintances and even strangers. By contrast, Germans tend to disclose little about themselves except in intimate relationships with a select few, and Japanese reveal very little about themselves in even their closest relationships.

Cultural differences like this mean that what counts as disclosing communication varies from one culture to another. If you were raised in the United States, you might view people from certain other cultures as undisclosing or even standoffish. But the amount of personal information that the nonnatives reveal might actually be quite personal and revealing according to the standards of their culture. The converse is also

What counts as disclosing communication varies from one culture to another.

CULTURAL IDIOM
standoffish:
unfriendly

true: To members of some other cultures, North Americans probably appear like exhibitionists who spew personal information to anyone within earshot.

When communicating with people from different cultures it's important to consider their standards for appropriate disclosure. Don't mistakenly judge them according to your own standards. Likewise, be sensitive about honoring their standards when talking about yourself. In this sense, choosing the proper level of self-disclosure isn't too different from choosing the appropriate way of dressing or eating when encountering members of a different culture: What seems familiar and correct at home may not be suitable with strangers. As you read on, realize that the characteristics and guidelines that suit mainstream North American culture may not apply in other contexts.

Self-Disclosure Usually Occurs in Dyads   Although it is possible for people to disclose a great deal about themselves in groups, such communication usually occurs in one-to-one settings. Because revealing significant information about yourself involves a certain amount of risk, limiting the disclosure to one person at a time minimizes the chance that your disclosure will lead to unhappy consequences.

Effective Self-Disclosure Is Usually Symmetrical   Note in Figure 7-9 that the amount of successful, two-way communication (represented by the arrows connecting the two open areas) is dictated by the size of the smaller open area of A. The arrows that are originating from B's open area and being turned aside by A's hidden and blind areas represent unsuccessful attempts to communicate. In situations such as this, it's easy to imagine how B would soon limit the amount of disclosure to match that of A. On the other hand, if A were willing to match the degree of disclosure given by B, the relationship would move to a new level of intimacy. In either case, we can expect that most often the degree of disclosure between partners will soon stabilize at a symmetrical level.

Effective Self-Disclosure Occurs Incrementally   Although instances occur in which partners start their relationship by telling everything about themselves to each other, such cases are rare. In most cases, the amount of disclosure increases over time. We begin relationships by revealing relatively little about ourselves; then if our first bits of self-disclosure are well received and bring on similar responses from the other person, we're willing to reveal more. This principle is important to remember. It would usually be a mistake to assume that the way to build a strong relationship would be to reveal the most private details about yourself when first making contact with another person. Unless the circumstances are unique, such baring of your soul would be likely to scare potential partners away rather than bring them closer.

Self-Disclosure Is Relatively Scarce   Most conversations—even among friends—focus on everyday mundane topics and disclose little or no personal information.[73] Even partners in intimate relationships rarely talk about personal information.[74] Whether or not we open up to others is based on several criteria, some of which are listed in Table 7-2.

What is the optimal amount of self-disclosure? You might suspect that the correct answer is "the more, the better," at least in personal relationships. Research has shown that the matter isn't this simple, however.[75] For example, there seems to be a curvilinear relationship between openness and satisfaction in marriage, so that a moderate amount of openness produces better results than either extreme disclosure or withholding. One good measure of happiness is how well the level of disclosure matches the expectations of communicators: If we get what we believe is a reasonable amount of candor from others, we are happy. If they tell us too little—or even too much—we become less satisfied.

CULTURAL IDIOM

earshot:
the distance at which one can hear something or someone

TABLE 7-2   Some Criteria Used to Reveal Family Secrets

INTIMATE EXCHANGE
Does the other person have a similar problem?
Would knowing the secret help the other person feel better?
Would knowing the secret help the other person manage his or her problem?

EXPOSURE
Will the other person find out this information, even if I don't tell him or her?
Is the other person asking me directly to reveal this information?

URGENCY
Is it very important that the other person know this information?
Will revealing this information make matters better?

ACCEPTANCE
Will the other person still accept me if I reveal this information?

CONVERSATIONAL APPROPRIATENESS
Will my disclosure fit into the conversation?
Has the topic of my disclosure come up in this conversation?

RELATIONAL SECURITY
Do I trust the other person with this information?
Do I feel close enough to this person to reveal the secret?

IMPORTANT REASON
Is there a pressing reason to reveal this information?

PERMISSION
Have other people involved in the secret given their permission for me to reveal it?
Would I feel okay telling the people involved that I have revealed the secret?

MEMBERSHIP
Is the person to whom I'm revealing the secret going to join this group (i.e., family)?

Adapted from A. L. Vangelisti, J. P. Caughlin, and L. Timmerman, "Criteria for Revealing Family Secrets." *Communication Monographs* 68 (2001): 1–27.

Guidelines for Appropriate Self-Disclosure

One fear we've had while writing this chapter is that a few overenthusiastic readers may throw down their books and begin to share every personal detail of their lives with whomever they can find. As you can imagine, this kind of behavior isn't an example of effective interpersonal communication.

No single style of self-disclosure is appropriate for every situation. Let's take a look at some guidelines that can help you recognize how to express yourself in a way that's rewarding for you and the others involved.[76]

Is the Other Person Important to You?   There are several ways in which someone might be important. Perhaps you have an ongoing relationship deep enough so that sharing significant parts of yourself justifies keeping your present level of togetherness intact. Or perhaps the person to whom you're considering disclosing is someone with whom you've previously related on a less personal level. But now you see a chance to grow closer, and disclosure may be the path toward developing that personal relationship.

Is the Risk of Disclosing Reasonable?   Take a realistic look at the potential risks of self-disclosure. Even if the probable benefits are great, opening yourself up to almost certain rejection may be asking for trouble. For instance, it might be foolhardy to share your important feelings with someone you know is likely to betray your confidences or ridicule them. On the other hand, knowing that your partner is trustworthy and supportive makes the prospect of speaking out more reasonable.

Revealing personal thoughts and feelings can be especially risky on the job.[77] The politics of the workplace sometimes requires communicators to keep feelings to themselves in order to accomplish both personal and organizational goals. You might, for example, find the opinions of a boss or customer personally offensive but decide to bite your tongue rather than risk your job or lose goodwill for the company.

Are the Amount and Type of Disclosure Appropriate?   A third point to realize is that there are degrees of self-disclosure. Telling others about yourself isn't an all-or-nothing decision you must make. It's possible to share some facts, opinions, or feelings with one person while reserving riskier ones for others. In the same vein, before sharing very important information with someone who does matter to you, you might consider testing reactions by disclosing less personal data.

Is the Disclosure Relevant to the Situation at Hand?   The kind of disclosure that is often a characteristic of highly personal relationships usually isn't appropriate in less personal settings. For instance, a study of classroom communication revealed that sharing all feelings—both positive and negative—and being completely honest resulted in less cohesiveness than having a "relatively" honest climate in which pleasant but superficial relationships were the norm.[78]

> Revealing personal thoughts and feelings can be especially risky on the job.

Even in personal relationships—with close friends, family members, and so on—constant disclosure isn't a useful goal. The level of sharing in successful relationships rises and falls in cycles. You may go through a period of great disclosure and then spend another period of relative nondisclosure. Even during a phase of high disclosure, sharing *everything* about yourself isn't necessarily constructive. Usually the subject of appropriate self-disclosure involves the relationship rather than personal information.

Is the Disclosure Reciprocated?   There's nothing quite as disconcerting as talking your heart out to someone only to discover that the other person has yet to say anything to you that is half as revealing as what you've been saying. Unequal self-disclosure creates an unbalanced relationship, one doomed to fall apart.

There are few times when one-way disclosure is acceptable. Most of them involve formal, therapeutic relationships in which a client approaches a trained professional with the goal of resolving a problem. For instance, you wouldn't necessarily expect to hear about a physician's personal ailments during a visit to a medical office. Nonetheless, it's interesting to note that one frequently noted characteristic of effective psychotherapists, counselors, and teachers is a willingness to share their feelings about a relationship with their clients.

Will the Effect Be Constructive?   Self-disclosure can be a vicious tool if it's not used carefully. Psychologist George Bach suggests that every person has a psychological "belt line." Below that belt line are areas about which the person is extremely sensitive. Bach says that jabbing at a "below-the-belt" area is a surefire way to disable another person, although usually at great cost to the relationship. It's important to consider the effects of your candor before opening up to others. Comments such as "I've always thought you were pretty unintelligent" or "Last year I made love to your best friend" *may* sometimes resolve old business and thus be constructive, but they also can be devastating—to the listener, to the relationship, and to your self-esteem.

Is the Self-Disclosure Clear and Understandable?   When you express yourself to others, it's important that you share yourself in a way that's intelligible. This means describing the *sources* of your message clearly. For instance, it's far better to describe another's behavior by saying "When you don't answer my phone calls or drop by to visit anymore . . ." than to complain vaguely, "When you avoid me . . . "

It's also vital to express your *thoughts* and *feelings* explicitly. "I feel worried because I'm afraid you don't care about me" is more understandable than "I don't like the way things have been going."

Alternatives to Self-Disclosure

At first glance, our moral heritage leads us to abhor anything less than the truth. Ethicists point out that the very existence of a society seems based on a foundation of truthfulness.[79] Although isolated cultures do exist where deceit is a norm, they are dysfunctional and on the verge of breakdown.

Although honesty is desirable in principle, it often has risky, potentially unpleasant consequences. This explains why communicators—even those with the best intentions—aren't always completely honest when they find themselves in situations when honesty would be uncomfortable.[80] Three common alternatives to self-disclosure are lies, equivocation, and hinting. We will take a closer look at each one.

Lies   To most people, lying appears to be a breach of ethics. Although lying to gain unfair advantage over an unknowing victim seems clearly wrong, another kind of untruth isn't so easy to dismiss as completely unethical. White lies, more appropriately called **altruistic lies**, are defined (at least by the people who tell them) as being harmless, or even helpful, to the person to whom they are told.[81] As Table 7-3 shows, at least some of the lies we tell are indeed intended to be helpful, or at least relatively benign.

TABLE 7-3   Some Reasons for Lying

REASON	EXAMPLE
Acquire resources	"Oh, please let me add this class. If I don't get in, I'll never graduate on time!"
Protect resources	"I'd like to lend you the money, but I'm short myself."
Initiate and continue interaction	"Excuse me, I'm lost. Do you live around here?"
Avoid conflict	"It's not a big deal. We can do it your way. Really."
Avoid interaction or take leave	"That sounds like fun, but I'm busy Saturday night." "Oh, look what time it is! I've got to run!"
Present a competent image	"Sure, I understand. No problem."
Increase social desirability	"Yeah, I've done a fair amount of skiing."

Adapted from categories originally presented in C. Camden, M. T. Motley, and A. Wilson, "White Lies in Interpersonal Communication: A Taxonomy and Preliminary Investigation of Social Motivations." *Western Journal of Speech Communication* 48 (1984): 315.

Is It Ever Right to Lie?

Is it ever right to lie? What about the example from freshman philosophy: The Nazis come to your door asking if you are hiding a Jewish family. You are. Should you say "No"? Or, on a mundane level, your spouse or lover walks in with an utterly silly new hairdo and asks, "Do you like it?" Does morality dictate that you ruin the evening? Or can you, in both cases, finesse the answer, not lying but not telling the truth, either, perhaps by avoiding an answer to the question?

The demand for honesty is contextual. It depends on what the truth concerns. The Bible tells us not to bear false witness against our neighbor. Perjury, we can agree, is wrong: The consequences can be awful. But it seems to me absolutely crucial to distinguish here between public and private life. Perjury, by its very nature, is public, as is politics. Sex, with a few obvious exceptions, is part of our private life. And just about everyone is less than forthright about sex.

Not all untruths are malicious. Telling the truth can complicate or destroy social relationships. It can undermine precious collective myths. Honesty can be cruel. Sometimes, deception is not a vice but a social virtue, and systematic deception is an essential part of the order of the (social) world.

In many countries—Japan and Western Samoa, for example—social harmony is valued far more than truthfulness as such. To tell another person what he or she wants to hear, rather than what one might actually feel or believe, is not only permitted but expected. Could we not begin to see our own enlightened emphasis on "seeking the truth at all costs" as one more ethnocentric peculiarity, another curious product of our strong sense of individualism, and a dangerously unsociable conception?

The obvious truth is that our simplest social relationships could not exist without the opaque medium of the lie. The best answer to the question "What are you thinking?" is often "Oh, nothing." Perhaps deception, not truth, is the cement of civilization—cement that does not so much hold us together as safely separate us and our thoughts. Some things are better left in the dark.

In contrast to Kant, for whom the rule against lying was a moral law, a "categorical imperative" never to be overridden, utilitarian philosophers insist that lying is wrong only because a lie does, in fact, cause more harm than good. There is no absolute prohibition here, rather perhaps a "rule of thumb," and there may well be many cases, such as the "white lies" described above, in which lying causes no harm and may even be commendable. The problem, as Nietzsche so wisely complains, is "not that you lied to me, but that I no longer believe you." It is not the breach of the principle against lying that is so troublesome, nor is it the consequences of the lie or the character of the liar. It is that lying compromises and corrupts our relationships.

In other words, the wrongness of lying does not have to do primarily with breaches of principle or miscalculations of harm and good. Lying is wrong because it constitutes a breach of trust, which is not a principle but a very particular and personal relationship between people.

What is wrong with lying, in other words, is not exactly what philosophers have often supposed. Lying undermines relationships by undermining trust. But trust may just as often be supported by mutual myths, by religious faith, by a clear understanding of what is private and personal and what is "the public's right to know." Trust is usually violated by lies, but trust can be more deeply damaged by a violation of personal boundaries, which in turn may invite lies and deception to protect what has been violated.

Robert C. Solomon

Whether or not they are innocent, altruistic lies are certainly common. In one study, 130 subjects were asked to keep track of the truthfulness of their everyday conversational statements.[82] Only 38.5 percent of these statements—slightly more than a third—proved to be totally honest. In another experiment, 147 people between the ages of 18 and 71 kept a log of all the lies they told over a one-week period. Both men and women reported being untruthful in approximately a fifth of their conversations that lasted over ten minutes.[83] Over the course of the week, the subjects reported lying to about 30 percent of the people with whom they had one-on-one conversations. The rate was much higher in some relationships. For example, dating couples lie to each other in about a third of their interactions, and college students told at least one lie to their mothers in fully 50 percent of their conversations. In yet another study, subjects recorded their conversations over a two-day period and later counted their own deceptions. The average lie rate: three fibs for every ten minutes of conversation.[84]

What are the consequences of discovering that you've been lied to? In an interpersonal relationship, the discovery can be traumatic. As we grow closer to others, our expectations about their honesty grow stronger. After all, discovering that you've been deceived requires you to redefine not only the lie you just uncovered but also many of the messages you previously took for granted. Was last week's compliment really sincere? Was your joke really funny, or was the other person's laughter a put-on? Does the other person care about you as much as he or she claimed?

Research has shown that deception does, in fact, threaten relationships.[85] Not all lies are equally devastating, however. Feelings like dismay and betrayal are greatest when the relationship is most intense, when the importance of the subject is high, and when there was previous suspicion that the other person wasn't being completely honest. Of these three factors, the importance of the information lied about proved to be the key factor in provoking a relational crisis. We may be able to cope with "misdemeanor" lying, but "felonies" are a grave threat. In fact, the discovery of major deception can lead to the end of the relationship. More than two-thirds of the subjects in one study reported that their relationship had ended since they discovered a lie. Furthermore, they attributed the breakup directly to the lie. If preserving a relationship is important, honesty—at least about important matters—really does appear to be the best policy.

Equivocation   Lying isn't the only alternative to self-disclosure. When faced with the choice between lying and telling an unpleasant truth, communicators can—and often do—equivocate. As Chapter 4 explained, **equivocal language** has two or more equally plausible meanings. Sometimes people send equivocal messages without meaning to, resulting in confusion. "I'll meet you at the apartment" could refer to more than one place. But other times we are deliberately vague. For instance, when a friend asks what you think of an awful outfit, you could say, "It's really unusual—one of a kind!" Likewise, if you are too angry to accept a friend's apology but don't want to appear petty, you might say, "Don't mention it."

The value of equivocation becomes clear when you consider the alternatives. Consider the dilemma of what to say when you've been given an unwanted present—an ugly painting, for example—and the giver asks what you think of it. How can you respond? On the one hand, you need to choose between telling the truth and lying. On the other hand, you have a choice of whether to make your response clear or vague. Figure 7-10

CULTURAL IDIOM

a put-on:
a false show of emotion

More than two-thirds of the subjects in one study reported that their relationship had ended since they discovered a lie.

Source: © Zits Partnership. Reprinted with special permission of King Features Syndicate.

FIGURE 7-10 Dimensions of Truthfulness and Equivocation

displays these choices. After considering the alternatives, it's clear that the first choice—an equivocal, true response—is far preferable to the other choices in several respects. First, it spares the receiver from embarrassment. For example, rather than flatly saying "no" to an unappealing invitation, it may be kinder to say "I have other plans"—even if those plans are to stay home and watch television.

Besides saving face for the recipient, honest equivocation can be less stressful for the sender than either telling the truth bluntly or lying. Because equivocation is often easier to take than the cold, hard truth, it spares the teller from feeling guilty. It's less taxing on the conscience to say "I've never tasted anything like this" than to say "this meal tastes terrible," even though the latter comment is more precise. Few people *want* to lie, and equivocation provides an alternative to deceit.[86]

A study by communication researcher Sandra Metts and her colleagues shows how equivocation can save face in difficult situations.[87] Several hundred college students were asked how they would turn down the unwanted sexual overtures from a person whose feelings were important to them: either a close friend, a prospective date, or a dating partner. The majority of students chose a diplomatic reaction ("I just don't think I'm ready for this right now") as being more face saving and comfortable than a direct statement like "I just don't feel sexually attracted to you." The diplomatic reaction seemed sufficiently clear to get the message across but not so blunt as to embarrass or even humiliate the other person. (Interestingly, men said they would be able to handle a direct rejection more comfortably than women. The researchers suggest that one reason for the difference is that men stereotypically initiate sexual offers and thus are more likely to expect rejection.)

Besides preventing embarrassment, equivocal language can also save the speaker from being caught lying. If a potential employer asks about your grades during a job interview, you would be safe saying, "I had a B average last semester," even though your overall grade average is closer to C. The statement isn't a complete answer, but it is honest as far as it goes. As one team of researchers put it, "Equivocation is neither a false message nor a clear truth, but rather an alternative used precisely when both of these are to be avoided."[88]

@Work

Social Capital: Personal Relationships and Career Advancement

The old saying "It isn't what you know, it's *who* you know" is at least partly true. **Social capital** refers to the potential benefits that come from belonging to one or more social networks. An impressive body of research confirms that robust personal networks can pay off in your career.[89]

People with high social capital are more likely to find good jobs more quickly and be promoted early. They receive more positive performance evaluations from their bosses and earn larger bonuses. Social capital doesn't just benefit individuals. Group members who have rich and diverse personal networks enhance the performance of their teams, helping them generate more creative solutions and reach their goals more rapidly.

Social capital doesn't come only from close personal connections. Along with what sociologists call *strong ties*, we're linked to other networks by *weak ties*—relationships that are infrequent, but which have surprising value when it comes to seeking resources.[90] Reaching out to a distant relative, former classmate, old neighbor, former coworker, or boss at the right time can get the information you need to succeed. Likewise, reaching out to casual contacts can prove beneficial—your seatmate on a recent flight, someone at the gym, or the person you met at a recent party.

Along with contacts that you make and maintain through face-to-face and phone contact, online social networks can be a powerful tool for building and using social capital. Business-oriented resources like LinkedIn can be helpful, as can "friends" on more general sites like Facebook.[91] Within large organizations, company "intranets" can provide a way for employees to keep in touch.[92]

Whatever their nature, social networks can go beyond their obvious value as sources of friendship, providing you with the resources that can make a critical difference in your career success.

Given these advantages, it's not surprising that most people will usually choose to equivocate rather than tell a lie. In a series of experiments, subjects chose between telling a face-saving lie, telling the truth, and equivocating. Only 6 percent chose the lie, and between 3 and 4 percent chose the hurtful truth. By contrast, over 90 percent chose the equivocal response.[93] People *say* they prefer truth-telling to equivocating,[94] but given the choice, they prefer to finesse the truth.

> Most people will usually choose to equivocate rather than tell a lie.

Hinting   Hints are more direct than equivocal statements. Whereas an equivocal message isn't necessarily aimed at changing others' behavior, a hint seeks to get the desired response from others. Some hints are designed to save the *receiver* from embarrassment:[95]

DIRECT STATEMENT	FACE-SAVING HINT
I'm bored. I want to get out of this conversation.	You must be busy. I'd better let you go.
You aren't qualified for that job.	I've heard they only hire insiders for jobs like that.

Other hints are strategies for saving the *sender* from embarrassment:

DIRECT STATEMENT	FACE-SAVING HINT
Your smoking bothers me.	I'm pretty sure that smoking isn't permitted here.
I'd like to invite you out for lunch, but I don't want to risk a "no" answer to my invitation.	Gee, it's almost lunchtime. Have you ever eaten at that new Italian restaurant around the corner?

The success of a hint depends on the other person's ability to pick up the unexpressed message. Your subtle remarks might go right over the head of an insensitive

CULTURAL IDIOM

to pick up:
to understand

go right over the head of:
fail to be understood by

Ethical Challenge

The Ethics of Lying and Equivocating

Research shows that virtually everyone hints, lies, and equivocates for a variety of reasons. Explore the ethical legitimacy of your lies and equivocations by following these directions:

1. For a two-day period, keep track of:
   a. Your hints, lies, and equivocations.
   b. Your reason for taking one of these approaches in each situation.
   c. The positive and negative consequences (for you and the other person) of avoiding self-disclosure.

2. Based on your analysis of the information collected in Step 1, identify the ethical legitimacy of each type of nondisclosing communication. Are any sorts of deception justifiable? Which sorts are not? How would you feel if you discovered the other person had not been straightforward with you under similar circumstances?

receiver—or one who chooses not to respond to them. If this does happen, you still have the choice to be more direct. If the costs of a straightforward message seem too high, you can withdraw without risk.

It's easy to see why people choose hints, equivocations, and white lies instead of complete self-disclosure. These strategies provide a way to manage difficult situations that is easier than the alternatives for both the speaker and the receiver of the message. In this sense, successful liars, equivocators, and hinters can be said to possess a certain kind of communicative competence. On the other hand, there are certainly times when honesty is the right approach, even if it's painful. At times like these, evaders could be viewed as lacking the competence or the integrity to handle a situation most effectively.

Are hints, benign lies, and equivocations an ethical alternative to self-disclosure? Some of the examples in these pages suggest the answer is a qualified "yes." Many social scientists and philosophers agree. Some argue that the morality of a speaker's *motives* for lying ought to be judged, not the deceptive act itself.[96] Others ask whether the *effects* of a lie will be worth the deception. Ethicist Sissela Bok offers some circumstances where deception may be justified: doing good, avoiding harm, and protecting a larger truth.[97] Perhaps the right questions to ask, then, are whether an indirect message is truly in the interests of the receiver, and whether this sort of evasion is the only effective way to behave. Bok suggests another way to check the justifiability of a lie: Imagine how others would respond if they knew what you were really thinking or feeling. Would they accept your reasons for not disclosing?

Summary

An interpersonal relationship is one in which two or more people meet one another's social needs to a greater or lesser degree. We form these relationships for a variety of reasons. Some of these reasons are rather straightforward (e.g., proximity, appearance, rewards) while others involve what can informally be called "chemistry" (e.g., similarity, mutual self-disclosure, reciprocal attraction).

Communication can be considered interpersonal according to either the context or the quality of interaction. Qualitatively interpersonal communication can occur both face-to-face and in mediated relationships. Communication in relationships consists of both content and relational messages. Explicit relational messages are termed *metacommunication.*

Some communication theorists suggest that intimate relationships pass through a series of stages, each of which is characterized by a unique mode of communication. These stages fall into three broad phases: coming together, relational maintenance, and coming apart. Although the movement within and between these stages does follow recognizable patterns, the amount and direction of movement are not predetermined. Some relationships move steadily toward termination, whereas others shift backward and forward as the partners redefine their desires for intimacy and distance.

Other theorists take a dialectical view, arguing that the same series of opposing desires operate throughout the entire span of relationships. These dialectical drives include autonomy versus connection, predictability versus novelty, and openness versus privacy. Since these opposing forces are inevitable, the challenge is to develop strategies for dealing with them that provide relational satisfaction.

Intimacy is a powerful need for most people. Intimacy can be created and expressed in a variety of ways: physically, emotionally, intellectually, and through shared activities. The notion of levels of intimacy has varied according to historical period, culture, and gender. Along with the desire for closeness, a need for distance is equally important. These opposing drives lead to conflicting communication behavior at different stages in people's lives and their relationships. The challenge is to communicate in a way that strikes a balance between intimacy and distance.

Self-disclosure is the process of deliberately revealing significant information about oneself that would not normally be known. The breadth and depth of self-disclosure can be described by the social penetration model. The Johari Window model reveals an individual's open, blind, hidden, and unknown areas. Complete self-disclosure is not common, nor is it always desirable. The chapter listed several guidelines to help determine when it is and is not appropriate. The chapter concluded by describing three widely used alternatives to self-disclosure: lies, equivocation, and hints. It discussed the conditions under which these alternatives can be appropriate.

Key Terms

affinity The degree to which people like or appreciate one another. As with all relational messages, affinity is usually expressed nonverbally. *p. 202*

altruistic lies Deception intended to be unmalicious, or even helpful, to the person to whom it is told. *p. 223*

breadth (of self-disclosure) The range of topics about which an individual discloses. See also *Depth.* *p. 217*

content message A message that communicates information about the subject being discussed. See also *Relational message.* *p. 202*

contextually interpersonal communication Any communication that occurs between two individuals. See also *Qualitatively interpersonal communication.* *p. 200*

control The social need to influence others. *p. 202*

depth (of self-disclosure) The level of personal information a person reveals on a particular topic. See also *Breadth.* *p. 217*

developmental models (of relational maintenance) These models propose that the nature of communication is different in various stages of interpersonal relationships. *p. 204*

dialectical model (of relational maintenance) A model claiming that, throughout their lifetime, people in virtually all interpersonal relationships must deal with equally important, simultaneous, and opposing forces such as connection and autonomy, predictability and novelty, and openness versus privacy. *p. 209*

dialectical tensions Inherent conflicts that arise when two opposing or incompatible forces exist simultaneously. *p. 209*

equivocal language Language with more than one likely interpretation. *p. 225*

immediacy The degree of interest and attraction we feel toward and communicate to others. As with all relational messages, immediacy is usually expressed nonverbally. *p. 202*

intimacy A state of closeness between two (or sometimes more) people. Intimacy can be manifested in several ways: physically, intellectually, emotionally, and via shared activities. *p. 212*

Johari Window A model that describes the relationship between self-disclosure and self-awareness. *p. 218*

metacommunication Messages (usually relational) that refer to other messages; communication about communication. *p. 203*

qualitatively interpersonal communication Interaction in which people treat one another as unique individuals, regardless of the context in which the interaction occurs or the number of people involved. Contrasted with impersonal communication. See also *Contextually interpersonal communication*. *p. 200*

relational message A message that expresses the social relationship between two or more individuals. *p. 202*

respect The degree to which we hold others in esteem. *p. 202*

self-disclosure The process of deliberately revealing information about oneself that is significant and that would not normally be known by others. *p. 215*

social penetration model A model describing how intimacy can be achieved via the breadth and depth of self-disclosure. *p. 217*

Case Study Questions

Review the case study on pages 192–193 and then answer the following questions in light of what you learned in this chapter.

1. Where would you place your relationship with Hideki on the personal-impersonal continuum? What types of intimacy does it contain?

2. What role might culture (yours and his) play in the concerns you have about your relationship with Hideki?

3. Which relational stage (pages 204–208) would you say captures your relationship with Hideki? Give reasons for your answer.

4. What dialectical tensions (pages 209–211) operate in your relationship with Hideki? What strategies (pages 211–212) could you use to manage those tensions?

5. What characteristics of self-disclosure (pages 215–216) and guidelines (pages 221–223) could you use to help decide whether and how to address your concerns about the relationship with Hideki? Are any alternatives to self-disclosure (pages 223–227) appropriate in this situation?

Activities

1. **Interpersonal Communication: Context and Quality**

   1. Examine your interpersonal relationships in a contextual sense by making two lists. The first should contain all the two-person relationships in which you have participated during the past week. The second should contain all your relationships that have occurred in small-group and public contexts. Are there any important differences that distinguish dyadic interaction from communication with a larger number of people?

   2. Now make a second set of two lists. The first one should describe all of your relationships that are interpersonal in a qualitative sense, and the second should describe all the two-person relationships that are more impersonal. Are you satisfied with the number of qualitatively interpersonal relationships you have identified?

3. Compare the lists you developed in Steps 1 and 2. See what useful information each one contains. What do your conclusions tell you about the difference between contextual and qualitative definitions of interpersonal communication?

2. **Identifying Relational Messages** To complete this exercise, you will need the help of a partner with whom you communicate on an ongoing basis.

1. Pick three recent exchanges between you and your partner. Although any exchanges will do, the most interesting ones will be those in which you sensed that something significant (positive or negative) was going on that wasn't expressed overtly.

2. For each exchange, identify both the content and relational messages that you were expressing. Identify relational messages in terms of dimensions such as affinity, respect, immediacy, and/or control.

3. Explain the concept of relational messages to your partner, and ask him or her to identify the relational messages received from you during the same exchanges. How closely does your partner's perception match your analysis of the relational messages?

4. Now identify the relational messages you interpreted your partner as sending during the three exchanges.

5. Ask your partner to describe the relational messages he or she believed were sent to you on these occasions. How closely did your interpretation match your partner's explanation?

Based on your analysis of these three exchanges, answer the following questions:

1. What significant kinds of relational messages are exchanged in your relationship?

2. How accurate are you in decoding your partner's relational messages? How accurate is your partner in decoding your relational messages?

3. What lessons have you learned from this exercise that can improve the quality of your relationship?

3. **Your I.Q. (Intimacy Quotient)** Answer the following questions as you think about your relationship with a person important in your life.

1. What is the level of physical intimacy in your relationship?

2. What intellectual intimacy do you share?

3. How emotionally intimate are you? Is your emotional intimacy deeper in some ways than in others?

4. Has your intimacy level changed over time? If so, in what ways?

After answering these questions, ask yourself how satisfied you are with the amount of intimacy in this relationship. Identify any changes you would like to occur, and describe the steps you could take to make them happen.

4. **Striking a Balance Between Intimacy and Distance** Choose an important interpersonal relationship with someone you encounter on a frequent, regular basis. You might choose a friend, family member, or romantic partner.

For at least a week, chart how your communication with this relational partner reflects your desire for either intimacy or distance. Use a seven-point scale, in which behavior seeking high intimacy receives a 7, whereas behavior seeking to avoid physical, intellectual, and/or emotional contact receives a 1. Use ratings from 2 through 6 to reflect intermediate stages. Record at least one rating per day, making more detailed entries if your desire for intimacy or distance changes during that period.

After charting your communication, reflect on what the results tell you about your personal desire for intimacy and distance. Consider the following questions:

1. Which state—intimacy or distance—seemed most desirable for you?

2. To the degree that you seek intimacy, which variety or varieties are most important to you: intellectual, emotional, and/or physical?

CHAPTER 8

Improving Interpersonal Relationships

Chapter Outline

YOU SHOULD UNDERSTAND:

1. The role of communication climate in interpersonal relationships.
2. Types of messages that contribute to confirming and disconfirming climates.
3. The unavoidable but potentially problematic role of conflict in interpersonal relationships.
4. Characteristics of nonassertive, directly aggressive, passive-aggressive, indirect, and assertive communications.
5. The influence of culture and gender on conflict styles.
6. The differences between win–lose, lose–lose, compromising, and win–win approaches to conflict resolution.

YOU SHOULD BE ABLE TO:

1. Identify disconfirming messages and replace them with confirming ones, using the Gibb categories of supportive communication.
2. Describe the degree to which you use nonassertive, directly aggressive, passive-aggressive, indirect, and assertive messages and choose more satisfying responses as necessary.
3. Compose and deliver an assertive message, using the behavior-interpretation-feeling-consequence-intention format.
4. Apply the win–win approach to an interpersonal conflict.

No matter how satisfying your relationships, there are almost certainly ways they could be better. At times even the best of friends, the closest of families, and the most productive coworkers become dissatisfied. Sometimes the people involved are unhappy with each other. At other times, one person's problem is unrelated to the relationship. In either case, there's a desire to communicate in a way that makes matters better.

The ideas in this chapter can help you improve the important relationships in your life. We'll begin by talking about the factors that make communication "climates" either positive or negative. Next we'll focus on methods for understanding and resolving interpersonal conflicts.

Communication Climates in Interpersonal Relationships

Personal relationships are a lot like the weather. Some are fair and warm, whereas others are stormy and cold; some are polluted, and others healthy. Some relationships have stable climates, whereas others change dramatically—calm one moment and turbulent the next. You can't measure the interpersonal climate by looking at a thermometer or glancing at the sky, but it's there nonetheless. Every relationship has a feeling, a pervasive mood that colors the interactions of the participants. The term **communication**

climate refers to the emotional tone of a relationship. A climate doesn't involve specific activities as much as the way people feel about each other as they carry out those activities. Consider two communication classes, for example. Both meet for the same length of time and follow the same syllabus. It's easy to imagine how one of these classes might be a friendly, comfortable place to learn, whereas the other might be cold and tense— even hostile. The same principle holds for families, coworkers, and other relationships: Communication climates are a function more of the way people feel about one another than of the tasks they perform.

CULTURAL IDIOM
on the other hand:
from the other point of view

Confirming and Disconfirming Messages

What makes some climates positive and others negative? A short but accurate answer is that the *communication climate is determined by the degree to which people see themselves as valued*. When we believe others view us as important, we are likely to feel good about our relationship. On the other hand, the relational climate suffers when we think others don't appreciate or care about us.

Messages that show you are valued have been called **confirming responses**.[1] In one form or another, confirming responses say "you exist," "you matter," "you're important." Actually, it's an oversimplification to talk about one type of confirming message. In truth, confirming communication occurs on three increasingly positive levels:[2]

> Communication climate is determined by the degree to which people see themselves as valued.

- *Recognition* The most fundamental act of confirmation is to recognize the other person. Recognition seems easy and obvious, and yet there are many times when we do not respond to others on this basic level. Failure to write or visit a friend is a common example. So is failure to return a phone message. Avoiding eye contact and not approaching someone you know on campus, at a party, or on the street can send a negative message. Of course, this lack of recognition may simply be an oversight. You might not notice your friend, or the pressures of work and school might prevent you from staying in touch. Nonetheless, if the other person *perceives* you as avoiding contact, the message has the effect of being disconfirming.

- *Acknowledgment* Acknowledging the ideas and feelings of others is a stronger form of confirmation. Listening is probably the most common form of acknowledgment. Of course, counterfeit listening—ambushing, stage hogging, pseudolistening, and so on—has the opposite effect of acknowledgment. More active acknowledgment includes asking questions, paraphrasing, and reflecting. Not surprisingly, employees give high ratings to managers who solicit their suggestions—even when the managers don't accept every suggestion.[3] As you read in Chapter 5, reflecting the speaker's thoughts and feelings can be a powerful way to offer support when others have problems.

- *Endorsement* Whereas acknowledgment means you are interested in another's ideas, endorsement means that you agree with them. It's easy to see why endorsement is the strongest type of confirming message, because it communicates the highest form of valuing. The most obvious form of endorsement is agreeing. Fortunately, it isn't necessary to agree completely with another person in order to endorse her or his message. You can probably find something in the message that you endorse. "I can see why you were so angry," you might reply to a friend, even if you don't approve

of his or her outburst. Of course, outright praise is a strong form of endorsement and one you can use surprisingly often after you look for opportunities to compliment others. Nonverbal endorsement can also enhance the quality of a relational climate. For example, women rate men who agree with them as more physically attractive than those who fail to do so.[4]

It's hard to overstate the importance of confirming messages. For instance, a positive climate is the best predictor of marital satisfaction.[5] Satisfied couples have a 5:1 ratio of positive to negative statements, whereas the ratio for dissatisfied partners is 1:1.[6] Positive, confirming messages are just as important in families. For example, the satisfaction that siblings feel with one another drops sharply as aggressive, disconfirming messages increase.[7] Confirmation is just as important in the classroom, where motivation and learning increase when teachers demonstrate a genuine interest and concern for students.[8]

> Satisfied couples have a 5:1 ratio of positive to negative statements, whereas the ratio for dissatisfied partners is 1:1.

In contrast to confirming communication, messages that deny the value of others have been labeled **disconfirming responses**. These show a lack of regard for the other person by either disputing or ignoring some important part of that person's message.[9] *Disagreement* can certainly be disconfirming, especially if it goes beyond disputing the other person's ideas and attacks the speaker personally. However, disagreement is not the most damaging kind of disconfirmation. It may be tough to hear someone say, "I don't think that's a good idea," but a personal attack like "You're crazy" is even tougher to hear. Far worse than disagreements are responses that *ignore* others' ideas—or even their existence.

Table 8-1 lists a number of deliberate tactics that have been used to create distance in an undesired relationship. It's easy to see how each of them is inherently disconfirming.

As you read in Chapter 7, every message has a relational dimension along with its content. This means that, whether or not we are aware of the fact, we send and receive confirming and disconfirming messages virtually whenever we communicate. Serious conversations about our relationships may not be common, but we convey our attitudes

Understanding Communication Technology

Can You Hear Me Now?

Thanks to technology, people have never been more connected—or more alienated.

I have traveled 36 hours to a conference on robotic technology in central Japan. The grand ballroom is Wi-Fi enabled, and the speaker is using the Web for his presentation. Laptops are open, fingers are flying. But the audience is not listening. Most seem to be doing their e-mail, downloading files, surfing the Web or looking for a cartoon to illustrate an upcoming presentation. Every once in a while audience members give the speaker some attention, lowering their laptop screens in a kind of digital curtsy.

In the hallway outside the plenary session attendees are on their phones or using laptops and pdas to check their e-mail. Clusters of people chat with each other, making dinner plans, "networking" in that old sense of the term—the sense that implies sharing a meal. But at this conference it is clear that what people mostly want from public space is to be alone with their personal networks. It is good to come together physically, but it is more important to stay tethered to the people who define one's virtual identity, the identity that counts.

We live in techno-enthusiastic times, and we are most likely to celebrate our gadgets. Certainly the advertising that sells us our devices has us working from beautiful, remote locations that signal our status. We are connected, tethered, so important that our physical presence is no longer required. There is much talk of new efficiencies; we can work from anywhere and all the time. But tethered life is complex; it is helpful to measure our thrilling new networks against what they may be doing to us as people.

Sherry Turkle

TABLE 8-1 Distancing Tactics

TACTIC	DESCRIPTION
Avoidance	Evading the other person.
Deception	Lying to or misleading the other person.
Degrading	Treating the other person with disrespect.
Detachment	Acting emotionally uninterested in the other person.
Discounting	Disregarding or minimizing importance of what the other person says.
Humoring	Not taking the other person seriously.
Impersonality	Treating the other person like a stranger; interacting with her or him as a role rather than a unique individual.
Inattention	Not paying attention to the other person.
Nonimmediacy	Displaying verbal or nonverbal clues that minimize interest, closeness, or availability.
Reserve	Being unusually quiet and uncommunicative.
Restraint	Curtailing normal social behaviors.
Restrict topics	Limiting conversation to less personal topics.
Shorten interaction	Ending conversations as quickly as possible.

Adapted from J. A. Hess, "Distance Regulation in Personal Relationships: The Development of a Conceptual Model and a Test of Representational Validity." *Journal of Social and Personal Relationships* 19 (2002): 663–683.

about one another even when we talk about everyday matters. In other words, it isn't *what* we communicate about that shapes a relational climate so much as *how* we speak and act toward one another.

It's important to note that disconfirming messages, like virtually every other kind of communication, are a matter of perception. Communicators are likely to downplay the significance of a message that is potentially hurtful, but intentionally so.[10] On the other hand, even messages that aren't intended to devalue the other person can be interpreted as disconfirming. Your failure to return a phone call or respond to the letter of an out-of-town friend might simply be the result of a busy schedule, but if the other person views the lack of contact as a sign that you don't value the relationship, the effect can be powerful.

How Communication Climates Develop

As soon as two people start to communicate, a relational climate begins to develop. If the messages are confirming, the climate is likely to be a positive one. If they disconfirm one another, the climate is likely to be hostile, cold, or defensive.

Verbal messages certainly contribute to the tone of a relationship, but many climate-shaping messages are nonverbal. The very act of approaching others is confirming, whereas avoiding them can be disconfirming. Smiles or frowns, the presence or absence of eye contact, tone of voice, the use of personal space—all these and other cues send messages about how the parties feel toward one another.

CULTURAL IDIOM

what goes around comes around:
expect to be treated the way you treat others

hold on:
wait

After a climate is formed, it can take on a life of its own and grow in a self-perpetuating **spiral**: a reciprocating communication pattern in which each person's message reinforces the other's.[11] In positive spirals, one partner's confirming message leads to a similar response from the other person. This positive reaction leads the first person to be even more reinforcing. Negative spirals are just as powerful, though they leave the partners feeling worse about themselves and each other. Research shows how spirals operate in relationships to reinforce the principle that "what goes around comes around." In one study of married couples, each spouse's response in conflict situations was similar to the other's statement.[12] Conciliatory statements (for example, supporting, accepting responsibilities, agreeing) were likely to be followed by conciliatory responses. Confrontational acts (such as criticism, hostile questions, and fault finding) were likely to trigger aggressive responses. The same pattern held for other kinds of messages: Avoidance begat avoidance, analysis begat analysis, and so on.

Escalatory conflict spirals are the most visible way that disconfirming messages reinforce one another.[13] One attack leads to another until a skirmish escalates into a full-fledged battle. Although they are less obvious, **avoidance spirals** can also be destructive.[14] Rather than fighting, the parties slowly lessen their dependence on one another, withdraw, and become less invested in the relationship.

Spirals rarely go on indefinitely. Most relationships pass through cycles of progression and regression. If the spiral is negative, partners may find the exchange growing so unpleasant that they switch from negative to positive messages without discussing the matter. In other cases they may engage in metacommunication. "Hold on," one might say. "This is getting us nowhere." In some cases, however, partners pass the "point of no return," leading to the breakup of a relationship. Even positive spirals have their limit: Even the best relationships go through periods of conflict and withdrawal, although a combination of time and communication skills can eventually bring the partners back into greater harmony.

Creating Positive Communication Climates

It's easy to see how disconfirming messages can pollute a communication climate. But what are some alternative ways of communicating that encourage positive relationships? The work of Jack Gibb gives a picture of what kinds of messages lead to both positive and negative spirals.[15]

After observing groups for several years, Gibb was able to isolate six types of defense-arousing communication and six contrasting behaviors that seemed to reduce the level of threat and defensiveness. The **Gibb categories** are listed in Table 8-2. Using the supportive types of communication and avoiding the defensive ones will increase the odds of creating and maintaining positive communication climates in your relationships.

Evaluation Versus Description   The first type of defense-provoking behavior Gibb noted is **evaluative communication**. Most people become irritated at judgmental statements, which are likely to be interpreted as indicating a lack of regard. Evaluative language has often been described as **"you" language** because most such statements contain an accusatory use of that word. For example,

- You don't know what you're talking about.
- You're not doing your best.
- You smoke too much.

TABLE 8-2   The Gibb Categories of Defensive and Supportive Behaviors

DEFENSIVE BEHAVIORS	SUPPORTIVE BEHAVIORS
1. Evaluation	1. Description
2. Control	2. Problem Orientation
3. Strategy	3. Spontaneity
4. Neutrality	4. Empathy
5. Superiority	5. Equality
6. Certainty	6. Provisionalism

Unlike evaluative "you" language, **descriptive communication** focuses on the speaker's thoughts and feelings instead of judging the listener. One form of descriptive communication is **"I" language**.[16] Instead of putting the emphasis on judging another's behavior, the descriptive speaker explains the personal effect of the other's action. For instance, instead of saying "You talk too much," a descriptive communicator would say, "When you don't give me a chance to say what's on my mind, I get frustrated." Notice that statements such as this include an account of the other person's behavior plus an explanation of its effect on the speaker and a description of the speaker's feelings.

Control Versus Problem Orientation   A second defense-provoking message involves some attempt to control the other person. A **controlling** message occurs when a sender seems to be imposing a solution on the receiver with little regard for the receiver's needs or interests. The control can range from relatively small matters (where to eat dinner or what television show to watch) to large ones (whether to remain in a relationship or how to spend a large sum of money).

Whatever the situation, people who act in controlling ways create a defensive climate. Researchers have found that the communication of abusive couples was characterized by opposition to one another's viewpoints.[17] The unspoken message such behavior communicates is "I know what's best for you, and if you do as I say, we'll get along."

By contrast, in **problem orientation**, communicators focus on finding a solution that satisfies both their needs and those of the others involved. The goal here isn't to

Source: © Reprinted by special permission of North America Syndicate.

"win" at the expense of your partner but rather to work out some arrangement in which everybody feels like a winner. The sidebar "A Comparison of Dialogue and Debate" shows several important differences between controlling and problem-oriented communication. The last section of this chapter has a great deal to say about "win–win" problem solving as a way to find problem-oriented solutions.

Strategy Versus Spontaneity   The third communication behavior that Gibb identified as creating a poor communication climate is **strategy**. A more accurate term to describe this type of behavior is *manipulation*. Manipulation explains why most people detest coworkers who are unfriendly with peers while acting friendly and helpful to the boss.[18] One of the surest ways to make people defensive is to get caught trying to manipulate them. Nobody likes to be a guinea pig or a sucker, and even well-meant manipulation can cause bad feelings.

Spontaneity is the label Gibb used as a contrast to strategy. A better term might be *honesty*. Despite the misleading label, spontaneous communication needn't be blurted out as soon as an idea comes to you. You might want to plan the wording of your message carefully so that you can express yourself clearly. The important thing is to be honest. A straightforward message may not always get what you want, but in the long run it's likely to pay dividends in a positive relational climate.

Neutrality Versus Empathy   Gibb used the term **neutrality** to describe a fourth behavior that arouses defensiveness. Probably a more descriptive term would be *indifference*. A neutral attitude is disconfirming because it communicates a lack of concern for the welfare of another and implies that the other person isn't very important to you.

The damaging effects of neutrality become apparent when you consider the hostility that most people have for the large, impersonal organizations with which they have to deal: "They think of me as a number instead of a person"; "I felt as if I were being handled by computers and not human beings." These two common statements reflect reactions to being handled in an indifferent way.

> Having empathy means accepting another's feelings, putting yourself in another's place.

Empathy is an approach that confirms the other person. Having empathy means accepting another's feelings, putting yourself in another's place. This doesn't mean you need to agree with that person. Gibb noted the importance of nonverbal messages in communicating empathy. He found that facial and bodily expressions of concern are often more important to the receiver than the words used.

Superiority Versus Equality   **Superiority** is a fifth type of communication that creates a defensive climate. When it seems that people believe they are better than we are, a defensive response is likely.

We often meet people who possess knowledge or talents greater than ours. But your own experiences will tell you that it isn't necessary for these people to project an attitude of superiority. Gibb found ample evidence that many who have superior skills and talents are capable of conveying an attitude of **equality**. Such people communicate that, although they may have greater talent in certain areas, they see others as having just as much worth as human beings.

Certainty Versus Provisionalism   **Certainty** is a style of communication that is considered dogmatic and unyielding. Messages that suggest the speaker's mind is already made up are likely to generate defensiveness.

Invitation to Insight

A Comparison of Dialogue and Debate

People will always have disagreements. The way they handle them both creates and reflects relational climates. The following list contrasts the very different types of communication that characterize dialogue and debate. As you review them, consider how dialogue confirms the other person, even in the face of disagreement, whereas debate is fundamentally disconfirming.

- Dialogue is collaborative: Two or more sides work together toward common understanding.
  Debate is oppositional: Two sides oppose each other and attempt to prove each other wrong.

- In dialogue, finding common ground is the goal.
  In debate, winning is the goal.

- Dialogue enlarges and possibly changes the participants' points of view.
  Debate affirms the participants' own points of view.

- Dialogue reveals assumptions for reevaluation.
  Debate defends assumptions as truth.

- Dialogue causes introspection about one's own position.
  Debaters critique the others' positions.

- Dialogue opens the possibility of reaching a better solution than any of the original ones.
  Debate defends one's own positions as the best and excludes other positions.

- Dialogue involves a genuine concern for the other person and seeks not to alienate or offend.
  Debate involves countering the other position without focusing on feelings or relationships and often belittles or deprecates the other position.

In contrast to dogmatic communication is **provisionalism**, in which people may have strong opinions but are willing to acknowledge that they don't have a corner on the truth and will change their stand if another position seems more reasonable.

There is no guarantee that using Gibb's supportive, confirming approach to communication will build a positive climate. But the chances for a constructive relationship will be greatest when communication consists of the kind of supportive approach described here. Besides boosting the odds of getting a positive response from others, supportive communication can leave you feeling better in a variety of ways: more in control of your relationships, more comfortable, and more positive toward others.

CULTURAL IDIOM

boosting the odds of:
increasing the chances of success

to wind up in:
to end up being in

open the door to:
remove barriers to

Managing Interpersonal Conflict

Even the most supportive communication climate won't guarantee complete harmony. Regardless of what we may wish for or dream about, a conflict-free world just doesn't exist. Even the best communicators, the luckiest people, are bound to wind up in situations when their needs don't match the needs of others. Money, time, power, sex, humor, aesthetic taste, as well as a thousand other issues, arise and keep us from living in a state of perpetual agreement.

For many people the inevitability of conflict is a depressing fact. They think that the existence of ongoing conflict means that there's little chance for happy relationships with others. Effective communicators know differently, however. They realize that although it's impossible to *eliminate* conflict, there are ways to *manage* it effectively. And those effective communicators know the subject of this chapter—that managing conflict skillfully can open the door to healthier, stronger, and more satisfying relationships.

The Nature of Conflict

Whatever form it may take, every interpersonal **conflict** involves an *expressed struggle between at least two interdependent parties who perceive incompatible goals, scarce resources, and interference from the other parties in achieving their goals.*[19] A closer look at the various parts of this definition helps to develop a clearer idea of how conflicts operate.

Expressed Struggle   A conflict doesn't exist unless both parties know that some disagreement exists. You may be upset for months because a neighbor's loud stereo keeps you from getting to sleep at night, but no conflict exists between the two of you until the neighbor learns about your problem. Of course, the expressed struggle doesn't have to be verbal. You can show your displeasure with somebody without saying a word. Giving a dirty look, using the silent treatment, and avoiding the other person are all ways of expressing yourself. But one way or another, both parties must know that a problem exists before they're in conflict.

Perceived Incompatible Goals   Conflicts often look as if one party's gain will be another's loss. For instance, consider the neighbor whose music keeps you awake at night. Does somebody have to lose? A neighbor who turns down the noise loses the enjoyment of hearing the music at full volume, but if the neighbor keeps the volume up, then you're still awake and unhappy.

But the goals in this situation really aren't completely incompatible—solutions do exist that allow both parties to get what they want. For instance, you could achieve peace and quiet by closing your windows and getting the neighbor to do the same. You might use a pair of earplugs. Or perhaps the neighbor could get a set of headphones and listen to the music at full volume without bothering anyone. If any of these solutions proves workable, then the conflict disappears.

Unfortunately, people often fail to see mutually satisfying answers to their problems. And as long as they *perceive* their goals to be mutually exclusive, they create a self-fulfilling prophecy in which the conflict is very real.

Perceived Scarce Resources   In a conflict, people believe there isn't enough of some resource to go around. The most obvious example of a scarce resource is money—a cause of many conflicts. If a person asks for a raise in pay and the boss would rather keep the money or use it to expand the business, then the two parties are in conflict.

Time is another scarce commodity. As authors, we are constantly in the middle of struggles about how to use the limited time we have to spend. Should we work on this book? Visit with our partners? Spend time with our kids? Enjoy the luxury of being alone? With only twenty-four hours in a day we're bound to end up in conflicts with our families, editors, students, and friends—all of whom want more of our time than we have available to give.

Interdependence   However antagonistic they might feel toward each other, the parties in a conflict are usually dependent on each other. The welfare and satisfaction of one depend on the actions of another. If this weren't true, then even in the face of scarce resources and incompatible goals there would be no need for conflict. Interdependence exists between conflicting nations, social groups, organizations, friends, and lovers. In each case, if the two parties didn't need each other to solve the problem, both would go their separate ways. In fact, many conflicts go unresolved because the parties fail to understand their interdependence. One of the first steps toward resolving a conflict is to take the attitude that "we're in this together."

CULTURAL IDIOM
dirty look:
facial expression indicating displeasure

Styles of Expressing Conflict

Communication scholars have identified a wide range of ways communicators handle conflicts.[23] Table 8-3 describes five ways people can act when their needs are not met. Each one has very different characteristics.

Nonassertion   Nonassertion is the inability or unwillingness to express thoughts or feelings in a conflict. Sometimes nonassertion comes from a lack of confidence. At other times, people lack the awareness or skill to use a more direct means of expression.

Sometimes people know how to communicate in a straightforward way but choose to behave nonassertively. For example, women are less likely to clearly refuse an unwanted request for physical intimacy from a dating partner whom they would like to see in the future than from one whom they don't want to see again.[24]

Nonassertion is a surprisingly common way of dealing with conflicts. One survey examined the conflict level of husbands and wives in normal "nondistressed" marriages. Over a five-day period, spouses reported that their partner engaged in an average of thirteen behaviors that were "displeasurable" to them but that they had only *one* confrontation during the same period.[25]

Nonassertion can take a variety of forms. One is *avoidance*—either physical (steering clear of a friend after having an argument) or conversational (changing the topic, joking, or denying that a problem exists). People who avoid conflicts usually believe it's easier to put up with the status quo than to face the problem head-on and try to solve it. *Accommodation* is another type of nonassertive response. Accommodators deal with conflict by giving in, putting the other's needs ahead of their own.

CULTURAL IDIOM
steering clear of:
avoiding

to face the problem head-on:
to confront the problem directly

TABLE 8-3   Individual Styles of Conflict

	NONASSERTIVE	DIRECTLY AGGRESSIVE	PASSIVE-AGGRESSIVE	INDIRECT	ASSERTIVE
APPROACH TO OTHERS	I'm not okay, you're okay.	I'm okay, you're not okay.	I'm okay, you're not okay.	I'm okay, you're not okay. (But I'll let you think you are.)	I'm okay, you're okay.
DECISION MAKING	Lets others choose.	Chooses for others. They know it.	Chooses for others. They don't know it.	Chooses for others. They don't know it.	Chooses for self.
SELF-SUFFICIENCY	Low.	High or low.	Looks high but usually low.	High or low.	Usually high.
BEHAVIOR IN PROBLEM SITUATIONS	Flees; gives in.	Outright attack.	Concealed attack.	Strategic, oblique.	Direct confrontation.
RESPONSE OF OTHERS	Disrespect, guilt, anger, frustration.	Hurt, defensiveness, humiliation.	Confusion, frustration, feelings of manipulation.	Unknowing compliance or resistance.	Mutual respect.
SUCCESS PATTERN	Succeeds by luck or charity of others.	Beats out others.	Wins by manipulation.	Gains unwitting compliance of others.	Attempts "win–win" solutions.

Adapted with permission from *The Assertive Woman* © 1970, 1987, 1997, and 2000, by Stanlee Phelps and Nancy Austin, San Luis Obispo, CA: Impact, 1975, p. 11; and Gerald Piaget, American Orthopsychiatric Association, 1975. Further reproduction prohibited.

Despite the obvious drawbacks of nonassertion, there are situations when accommodating or avoiding is a sensible approach. Avoidance may be the best course if a conflict is minor and short-lived. For example, you might let a friend's annoying grumpiness pass without saying anything, knowing that he is having one of his rare bad days. Likewise, you might not complain to a neighbor whose lawn sprinklers occasionally hit your newly washed car. You may also reasonably choose to keep quiet if the conflict occurs in an unimportant relationship, as with an acquaintance whose language you find offensive but whom you don't see often. Finally, you might choose to keep quiet if the risk of speaking up is too great: getting fired from a job you can't afford to lose, being humiliated in public, or even risking physical harm.

> There are situations when accommodating or avoiding is a sensible approach.

Direct Aggression   Whereas nonasserters avoid conflicts, communicators who use direct aggression embrace them. A **directly aggressive message** confronts the other person in a way that attacks his or her position—and even the dignity of the receiver. Many directly aggressive responses are easy to spot: "You don't know what you're talking about." "That was a stupid thing to do." "What's the matter with you?" Other forms of direct aggression come more from nonverbal messages than from words. It's easy to imagine a hostile way of expressing statements like "What is it now?" or "I need some peace and quiet."

Verbal aggressiveness may get you what you want in the short run. Yelling "Shut up" might stop the other person from talking, and saying "Get it yourself" may save you from some exertion, but the relational damage of this approach probably isn't worth the cost. Direct aggression can be hurtful, and the consequences for the relationship can be long-lasting.[26]

Passive Aggression   **Passive aggression** is far more subtle than its directly aggressive cousin. It occurs when a communicator expresses hostility in an obscure way. Psychologist George Bach terms this behavior "crazymaking"[27] and identifies several varieties. For example, "pseudoaccommodators" pretend to agree with you ("I'll be on time from now on") but don't comply with your request for change. "Guiltmakers" try to gain control by making you feel responsible for their choices: "I really should be studying, but I'll give you a ride." "Jokers" use humor as a weapon and then hide behind the complaint ("Where's your sense of humor?") when you object. "Trivial tyrannizers" do small things to drive you crazy instead of confronting you with their complaints: "forgetting" to take phone messages, playing the music too loud, and so on. "Withholders" punish their partners by keeping back something valuable, such as courtesy, affection, or humor.

Indirect Communication   The clearest communication is not necessarily the best approach. **Indirect communication** conveys a message in a roundabout manner, in order to save face for the recipient.[28] Although indirect communication lacks the clarity of an aggressive or assertive message, it involves more initiative than nonassertion. It also has none of the hostility of passive-aggressive crazymaking. The goal is to get what you want without arousing the hostility of the other person. Consider the case of the neighbor's annoying dog. One indirect approach would be to strike up a friendly conversation with the owners and ask if anything you are doing is too noisy for them, hoping they would get the hint.

@Work

Dealing with Sexual Harassment

Sexual harassment takes many forms. It may arise between members of the same sex or between men and women. It can be a blatant sexual overture, or any verbal or nonverbal behavior that creates a "hostile work environment." The harasser can be a supervisor, peer, subordinate, or even someone outside the organization.

Thanks to enlightened company policies and government legislation, targets of sexual harassment have legal remedies. While formal complaints are an assertive and powerful way to protect a target's rights, they can be time-consuming, and those lodging the complaints sometimes experience depression, ridicule, isolation, and reprisal.[20]

As Chapter 1 explained, competent communication involves picking the most effective approach. Here are several options to consider if you or someone you care about experiences harassment:[21]

1. *Consider dismissing the incident.* This nonassertive approach is only appropriate if you truly believe that the remark or behavior is trivial. Dismissing incidents that you believe are important can result in self-blame and diminished self-esteem. Even worse, it can lead to repetition of the offensive behavior.

2. *Tell the harasser to stop.* Assertively tell the harasser early that the behavior is unwelcome, and insist that it stop immediately. Your statement should be firm, but it doesn't have to be angry.

Remember that many words or deeds that make you uncomfortable may not be deliberately hostile remarks.

3. *Write a personal letter to the harasser.* A written statement may help the harasser to understand what behavior you find offensive. Just as important, it can show that you take the problem seriously. Detail specifics about what happened, what behavior you want stopped, and how you felt. You may want to include a copy of your organization's sexual harassment policy. Keep a record of when you delivered your message.

4. *Ask a trusted third party to intervene.* This indirect approach can sometimes boost the odds of persuading the harasser to stop. The person you choose should be someone who you are convinced understands your discomfort and supports your opinion. Also, be sure this intermediary is someone the harasser respects and trusts.

5. *Use company channels.* Report the situation to your supervisor, personnel office, or a committee that has been set up to consider harassment complaints.

6. *File a legal complaint.* If all else fails or the incident is egregious, you may file a complaint with the federal Equal Employment Opportunity Commission or with your state agency. You have the right to obtain the services of an attorney regarding your legal options.[22]

Because it saves face for the other party, indirect communication is often kinder than blunt honesty. If your guests are staying too long, it's probably kinder to yawn and hint about your big day tomorrow than to bluntly ask them to leave. Likewise, if you're not interested in going out with someone who has asked you for a date, it may be more compassionate to claim that you're busy than to say "I'm not interested in seeing you."

At other times we communicate indirectly in order to protect ourselves. You might, for example, test the waters by hinting instead of directly asking the boss for a raise, or by letting your partner know indirectly that you could use some affection, instead of asking outright. At times like these, an oblique approach may get the message across while softening the blow of a negative response.

The advantages of protecting oneself and saving face for others help explain why indirect communication is the most common way people make requests.[29] The risk of an indirect message, of course, is that the other party will misunderstand you or fail to get the message at all. There are also times when the importance of an idea is so great that hinting lacks the necessary punch. When clarity and directness are your goals, an assertive approach is in order.

Assertion **Assertive** people handle conflicts by expressing their needs, thoughts, and feelings clearly and directly but without judging others or dictating to them. They have the

> Because it saves face for the other party, indirect communication is often kinder than blunt honesty.

CULTURAL IDIOM

test the waters:
try

softening the blow of:
easing the effect of

punch:
force or effectiveness

attitude that most of the time it is possible to resolve problems to everyone's satisfaction. Possessing this attitude and the skills to bring it about doesn't guarantee that assertive communicators will always get what they want, but it does give them the best chance of doing so. An additional benefit of such an approach is that whether or not it satisfies a particular need, it maintains the self-respect of both the assertors and those with whom they interact. As a result, people who manage their conflicts assertively may experience feelings of discomfort while they are working through the problem. They usually feel better about themselves and each other afterward—quite a change from the outcomes of nonassertiveness or aggression.

At first glance, assertiveness seems like the most ethical communication style to use when you are faced with a conflict. The matter might not be so clear, however. Find out for yourself by following these steps.

1. Decide for yourself whether it is ever justifiable to use each of the other conflict styles: nonassertion, direct aggression, passive aggression, and indirect communication. Support your position on each style with examples from your own experience.

2. Explain your answer to classmates who disagree, and listen to their arguments.

3. After hearing positions that differ from yours, work with your classmates to develop a code of ethics for expressing conflict messages.

Characteristics of an Assertive Message

Knowing *about* assertive messages isn't the same as being able to express them. The next few pages will describe a method for communicating assertively. It works for a variety of messages: your hopes, problems, complaints, and appreciations. Besides giving you a way to express yourself directly, this format also makes it easier for others to understand you. A complete assertive message has five parts:

1. Behavioral Description   As you learned in Chapter 4, a behavioral description is an objective picture of the behavior in question, without any judging or editorializing. Put in terms of Gibb's categories, it uses descriptive rather than evaluative language. Notice the difference between a behavioral description and an evaluative judgment:

- *Behavioral description*: "You asked me to tell you what I really thought about your idea, and then when I gave it to you, you told me I was too critical."

- *Evaluative judgment*: "Don't be so touchy! It's hypocritical to ask for my opinion and then get mad when I give it to you."

Judgmental words like "touchy" and "hypocritical" invite a defensive reaction. The target of your accusation can reply "I'm not touchy or hypocritical!" It's harder to argue with the facts stated in an objective, behavioral description. Furthermore, the neutral language reduces the chances of a defensive reaction.

2. Your Interpretation of the Other Person's Behavior   This part is where you can use the perception-checking skill outlined in Chapter 3 (pages 79–81). Remember that a complete perception check includes two possible interpretations of the behavior: "Maybe you think I don't care because it took me two days to call you back. Is that it, or is there something else?"

Whether you offer just one interpretation or two, as described in Chapter 4, the key is to label your hunches as such instead of suggesting that you are positive about what the other person's behavior means.

3. A Description of Your Feelings   Expressing your feelings adds a new dimension to a message. For example, consider the difference between these two responses:

- "When you kiss me and nibble on my ear while we're watching television *[behavior]*, I think you probably want to make love *[interpretation]*, and *I feel excited.*"

- "When you kiss me and nibble on my ear while we're watching television *[behavior]*, I think you probably want to make love *[interpretation]*, and *I feel disgusted.*"

Likewise, adding feelings to the situation we have been examining makes the assertive message clearer:

- "When you said I was too critical after you asked me for my honest opinion *[behavior]*, it seemed to me that you really didn't want to hear a critical remark *[interpretation]*, and *I felt stupid for being honest [feeling].*"

4. A Description of the Consequences   A consequence statement explains what happens as a result of the behavior you have described, your interpretation, and the ensuing feeling. There are three kinds of consequences: What happens to you, the speaker ("When you tease me, I avoid you"), what happens to the target of the message ("When you drink too much, you start to drive dangerously"), or what happens to others ("When you play the radio so loud, it wakes up the baby").

5. A Statement of Your Intentions   Intention statements are the final element in the assertive format. They can communicate three kinds of messages:

- *Where you stand on an issue*: "I want you to know how much this bothers me." Or "I want you to know how much I appreciate your support."

- *Requests of others*: "I'd like to know whether you are angry." Or "I hope you'll come again."

- *Descriptions of how you plan to act in the future*: "Don't expect me ever to lend you anything again."

In our ongoing example, adding an intention statement would complete the assertive message:

- "When you said I was too critical after you asked me for my honest opinion *[behavior]*, it seemed to me that you really didn't want to hear a critical remark *[interpretation]*. That made me feel stupid for being honest *[feeling]*. Now I'm not sure whether I should tell you what I'm really thinking the next time you ask *[consequence]*. *I'd like to get it clear right now: Do you really want me to tell you what I think or not [intention]?*"

Before you try to deliver messages using the assertive format outlined here, there are a few points to remember. First, it isn't necessary or even wise always to put the elements in the order described here. As you can see from reviewing the examples on the preceding pages, it's sometimes best to begin by stating your feelings. In other cases, you can start by sharing your intentions or interpretations or by describing consequences.

You also ought to word your message in a way that suits your style of speaking. Instead of saying "I interpret your behavior to mean," you might choose to say "I think . . ." or "It seems to me . . ." or perhaps "I get the idea. . . ." In the same way, you can express your intentions by saying "I hope you'll understand (or do) . . ." or perhaps "I wish you would. . . ." It's important that you get your message across, but you should do it in a way that sounds and feels genuine to you.

Realize that there are some cases in which you can combine two elements in a single phrase. For instance, the statement ". . . and ever since then I've been wanting to talk to you" expresses both a consequence and an intention. In the same way, saying ". . . and after you said that, I felt confused" expresses a consequence and a feeling. Whether you combine elements or state them separately, the important point is to be sure that each one is present in your statement.

> In communication, as in many other activities, patience and persistence are essential.

Finally, you need to realize that it isn't always possible to deliver messages such as the ones here all at one time, wrapped up in neat paragraphs. It will often be necessary to repeat or restate one part many times before your receiver truly understands what you're saying. As you've already read, there are many types of psychological and physical noise that make it difficult for us to understand each other. Just remember: You haven't communicated successfully until the receiver of your message understands everything you've said. In communication, as in many other activities, patience and persistence are essential.

Gender and Conflict Style

The "Men Are from Mars, Women Are from Venus" theory of conflict has strong intuitive appeal, and a body of research seems to support it. Studies of children from preschool to early adolescence have shown that boys typically try to get their way by ordering one another around: "Lie down." "Get off my steps." "Gimme your arm." By contrast, girls are more likely to make proposals beginning with the word "let's": "Let's go find some." "Let's move *these* out *first*."[30] Whereas boys tell each other what role to take in pretend play ("Come on, be a doctor"), girls more commonly ask each other what role they want ("Will you be the patient for a few minutes?") or make a joint proposal ("We can both be doctors"). Furthermore, boys often make demands without offering an explanation ("Look, I want the wire cutters right now"). By contrast, girls often give reasons for their suggestions ("We gotta *clean* 'em first . . . 'cause they got germs"). When girls do have conflicts and disagreements, they are more likely to handle them via indirect aggression such as excluding someone from peer groups and complaining to others.[31]

Biology explains some differences between the way men and women deal with conflict. During disagreements, men tend to experience greater physiological arousal than women, which comes in the form of increased heart rate and blood pressure. Psychologist John Gottman explains the evolutionary basis for these differences. As hunters, Neolithic men needed to stay physiologically aroused and vigilant. By contrast,

> women had the opposite sort of role, in terms of survival of the species. Those women reproduced more effectively who had the milk-let-down reflex, which only happens when oxytocin is secreted in the brain . . . as any woman knows who's been breast-feeding, you have to be able to calm down and relax. But oxytocin is also the hormone of affiliation. So women have developed this sort of social order, caring for one another, helping one another, and affiliating, that also allows them to really calm down . . . it's one of nature's jokes. Women can calm down, men can't.[32]

Differences like these often persist into adulthood. For example, women are more likely than men to use indirect strategies instead of confronting conflict head-on. They are also more likely to compromise and give in to maintain relational harmony. Men, by contrast, are more likely to use aggression to get their way.[33] After a relational conflict begins, men are often more likely than women to withdraw if they become uncomfortable or fail to get their way.

Gender differences that appear in face-to-face communication also persist online. In conflicts, women using mediated communication are less likely than men to argue. Female messages are more supportive and rapport building, more empathetic, and use a more cooperative tone.[34] They use less powerful language and apologize more.[35] These differences are powerful enough that experimental subjects can infer the gender of their conversational partners from the language used in mediated exchanges.[36]

> Gender differences that appear in face-to-face communication also persist online.

Gottman suggests that whether conflicts are handled constructively or destructively lies mostly in the hands of women. He states, "It's women who matter here, because we find that 80 percent of the time women are the ones in our culture who raise issues."[37] He asserts that when women use critical, negative, or accusatory approaches, the stage is set for destructive conflict. Once the man's physiological arousal sets in, it's very hard to reverse. Although it sounds unfair to put responsibility on the women for managing disagreements more gently, that may be a small price to pay for preventing a destructive conflict that both people regret.

In contrast with the "Men Are from Mars, Women Are from Venus" view of conflict, a growing body of research suggests that the differences in how the two sexes handle conflict are rather small, and not at all representative of the stereotypical picture of aggressive men and passive women.[38] Where differences between the sexes do occur, they can sometimes be exactly the opposite of sex-role stereotypes. For example, when the actual conflict behaviors of both sexes are observed, women turn out to be more assertive than men about expressing their ideas and feelings, and men are more likely to withdraw from discussion.[39]

In other cases, people may *think* that there are greater differences in male and female ways of handling conflicts than actually occur.[40] People who assume that men are aggressive and women are accommodating may notice behavior that fits these stereotypes ("See how much he bosses her around? A typical man!"). On the other hand, behavior that doesn't fit these preconceived ideas (accommodating men, pushy women) goes unnoticed.

What, then, can we conclude about the influence of gender on conflict? Research has demonstrated that there are, indeed, some small but measurable differences in the two sexes. But, while men and women may have characteristically different conflict styles, the individual style of each communicator is more important than his or her sex in shaping the way he or she handles conflict.

Conflict in Mediated Communication

Mediated communication has changed the nature of interpersonal conflict. Disagreements handled via texting, chatting, e-mail, and blogging can unfold differently than those that play out in person. Some of the characteristics of mediated communication described in Chapter 2 are especially important during conflicts.

Delay   The asynchronous nature of most mediated channels means that communicators aren't obliged to respond immediately to one another.

The inherent delays in mediated conflicts present both benefits and risks. On the upside, the chance to cool down and think carefully before replying can prevent aggressive blow-ups.[41] On the other hand, it's easy to avoid responding to an e-mail, text, or IM. When you do reply, there's the temptation to craft insults and jabs that can make matters worse.

Disinhibition   The absence of face-to-face contact can make it easy to respond aggressively, without considering the consequences until it's too late. In person it's harder to overlook the impact of a hostile approach. Remember that communication is irreversible: It's no more possible to retract a message that's been delivered than it is to "unsqueeze" a tube of toothpaste.

> It's no more possible to retract a message that's been delivered than it is to "unsqueeze" a tube of toothpaste.

Permanence   Because e-mails and text messages come in written form, there's a permanent "transcript" that doesn't exist when communicators deal with conflict face-to-face. This record can help clarify misperceptions and faulty memories. On the other hand, the permanent documents that chronicle a conflict can stir up emotions that make it hard to forgive and forget.

If mediated communication seems to be making a conflict worse, you may want to consider shifting to a face-to-face approach. Although mediated conflict may feel easier at the time, it may create more lasting damage to the relationship.

Cultural Influences on Conflict

The ways in which people communicate during conflicts vary widely from one culture to another. The kind of rational, straight-talking, calm yet assertive approach that characterizes European American disagreements is not the norm in other cultures.[42] For example, in traditional African American culture, conflict is characterized by a greater tolerance for expressions of intense emotions than is the rational, calm model taught in mainstream U.S. culture.[43] Ethnicity isn't the only factor that shapes a communicator's preferred conflict style: The degree of assimilation also plays an important role. For example, Latino Americans with strong cultural identities tend to seek accommodation and compromise more than those with weaker cultural ties.[44]

Not surprisingly, people from different regions often manage conflict quite differently. In individualistic cultures like that of the United States, the goals, rights, and needs of each person are considered important, and most people would agree that it is an individual's right to stand up for himself or herself. By contrast, collectivist cultures (more common in Latin America and Asia) consider the concerns of the group to be more important than those of any individual. In these cultures, the kind of assertive behavior that might seem perfectly appropriate to an American or Canadian would seem rude and insensitive.

Another factor that distinguishes the assertiveness that is so valued by most native English speakers and northern Europeans from other cultures is the difference between high- and low-context cultural styles.[45] Low-context cultures like that of the United States place a premium on being direct and literal. By contrast, high-context cultures like that of Japan value self-restraint and avoid confrontation. Communicators in these cultures derive meaning from a variety of unspoken rules, such as the context, social conventions, and hints. Preserving and honoring the face of the other person are prime goals, and communicators go to great lengths to avoid any communication that might risk embarrassing a conversational partner. For this reason, what seems like "beating around the bush" to an American would be polite to an Asian. In Japan, for example, even a simple request like "close the door" would be too straightforward.[46] A more indirect statement like "it is somewhat cold today" would be more appropriate. To take a more important example, Japanese are reluctant to simply say "no" to a request. A more likely answer would be "Let me think about it for a while," which anyone familiar with Japanese culture would recognize as a refusal. When indirect communication is a cultural norm, it is unreasonable to expect more straightforward approaches to succeed.

It isn't necessary to look at Eastern Asian cultures to encounter cultural differences in conflict. The style of some other familiar cultures differs in important ways from the northern European and North American norm. These cultures see verbal disputes as a form of intimacy and even a game. Americans visiting Greece, for example, often think they are witnessing an argument when they are overhearing a friendly conversation.[47] A comparative study of American and Italian nursery school children showed that one of the Italian children's favorite pastimes was a kind of heated debating that Italians call *discussione*, which Americans would regard as arguing. Likewise, research has shown that working-class Jewish speakers of eastern European origin used arguments as a means of being sociable.

Within the United States, the ethnic background of communicators also plays a role in their ideas about conflict. When African American, Mexican American, and white American college students were asked about their views regarding conflict, some important differences emerged.[48] For example, white Americans seem more willing to accept conflict as a natural part of relationships, whereas Mexican Americans describe the short- and long-term dangers of disagreeing. Whites' willingness to experience conflicts may be part of their individualistic, low-context communication style of speaking directly and avoiding uncertainty. It's not surprising that people from more collective, high-context cultures that emphasize harmony among people with close relationships tend to handle conflicts in less direct ways. With differences like these, it's easy to imagine how two friends, lovers, or fellow workers from different cultural backgrounds might have trouble finding a conflict style that is comfortable for them both.

CULTURAL IDIOM

preserving and honoring the face:
protecting and respecting the other's dignity

"beating around the bush":
approaching something in an indirect way

Low-context cultures like that of the United States place a premium on being direct and literal.

Critical Thinking Probe

Valuing Diversity In Conflict Styles

The preceding section made it clear that conflict styles are shaped by social, technological, and cultural influences. Choose a conflict style different from yours—by virtue of gender, technology use, and/or culture—and identify the assumptions on which it is based. Next, suggest how people with different styles can adapt their assumptions and behaviors to communicate in a more satisfying manner.

Methods for Conflict Resolution

No matter what the relational style, gender, or culture of the participants, every conflict is a struggle to have one's goals met. Sometimes that struggle succeeds, and at other times it fails. In the remainder of this chapter we'll look at various approaches to resolving conflicts and see which ones are most promising.

Win–Lose   **Win–lose** conflicts are ones in which one party achieves its goal at the expense of the other. People resort to this method of resolving disputes when they perceive a situation as being an "either-or" one: Either I get what I want, or you get your way. The most clear-cut examples of win–lose situations are certain games, such as baseball or poker, in which the rules require a winner and a loser. Some interpersonal issues seem to fit into this win–lose framework: two coworkers seeking a promotion to the same job, for instance, or a couple who disagree on how to spend their limited money.

Power is the distinguishing characteristic in win–lose problem solving, because it is necessary to defeat an opponent to get what you want. The most obvious kind of power is physical. Some parents threaten their children with warnings such as "Stop misbehaving, or I'll send you to your room." Adults who use physical power to deal with each other usually aren't so blunt, but the legal system is the implied threat: "Follow the rules, or we'll lock you up."

Real or implied force isn't the only kind of power used in conflicts. People who rely on authority of many types engage in win–lose methods without ever threatening physical coercion. In most jobs, supervisors have the potential to use authority in the assignment of working hours, job promotions, desirable or undesirable tasks, and, of course, in the power to fire an unsatisfactory employee. Teachers can use the power of grades to coerce students to act in desired ways.

Even the usually admired democratic principle of majority rule is a win–lose method of resolving conflicts. However fair it may be, this system results in one group getting its way and another group being unsatisfied.

There are some circumstances when win–lose problem solving may be necessary, such as when there are truly scarce resources and where only one party can achieve satisfaction. For instance, if two suitors want to marry the same person, only one can succeed. And to return to an earlier example, it's often true that only one

"It's not enough that we succeed. Cats must also fail."

Source: Cartoonbank 115108

applicant can be hired for a job. But don't be too willing to assume that your conflicts are necessarily win–lose: As you'll soon read, many situations that seem to require a loser can be resolved to everyone's satisfaction.

There is a second kind of situation when win–lose is the best method. Even when cooperation is possible, if the other person insists on trying to defeat you, then the most logical response might be to defend yourself by fighting back. "It takes two to tango," the old cliché goes, and it also often takes two to cooperate.

A final and much less frequent justification for trying to defeat another person occurs when the other person is clearly behaving in a wrong manner and when defeating that person is the only way to stop the wrongful behavior. Few people would deny the importance of restraining a person who is deliberately harming others even if the aggressor's freedom is sacrificed in the process. Forcing wrongdoers to behave themselves is dangerous because of the wide difference in opinion between people about who is wrong and who is right. Given this difference, it would seem justifiable only in the most extreme circumstances to coerce others into behaving as we think they should.

Lose–Lose   In **lose–lose problem solving**, neither side is satisfied with the outcome. Although the name of this approach is so discouraging that it's hard to imagine how anyone could willingly use it, in truth lose–lose is a fairly common way to handle conflicts. In many instances the parties will both strive to be winners, but as a result of the struggle, both end up losers. On the international scene many wars illustrate this sad point. A nation that gains military victory at the cost of thousands of lives, large amounts of resources, and a damaged national consciousness hasn't truly won much. On an interpersonal level the same principle holds true. Most of us have seen battles of pride in which both parties strike out and both suffer.

Compromise   Unlike lose–lose outcomes, a **compromise** gives both parties at least some of what they wanted, though both sacrifice part of their goals. People usually settle for compromises when they see partial satisfaction as the best they can hope for. Although a compromise may be better than losing everything, this approach hardly seems to deserve the positive image it has with some people. In his valuable book on conflict resolution, management consultant Albert Filley makes an interesting observation about our attitudes toward this approach.[49] Why is it, he asks, that if someone says, "I will compromise my values," we view the action unfavorably, yet we talk admiringly about parties in a conflict who compromise to reach a solution? Although compromises may be the best obtainable result in some conflicts, it's important to realize that both people in a dispute can often work together to find much better solutions. In such cases *compromise* is a negative word.

Most of us are surrounded by the results of bad compromises. Consider a common example: the conflict between one person's desire to smoke cigarettes and another's need to breathe clean air. The win–lose outcomes of this conflict are obvious: Either the smoker abstains, or the nonsmoker gets polluted lungs—neither very satisfying. But a compromise in which the smoker gets to enjoy only a rare cigarette or must retreat outdoors and in which the nonsmoker still must inhale some fumes or feel like an ogre is hardly better. Both sides have lost a considerable amount of both comfort and goodwill. Of course, the costs involved in other compromises are even greater. For example, if a divorced couple compromise on child care by haggling over custody and then finally grudgingly agree to split the time with their children, it's hard to say that anybody has won.

CULTURAL IDIOM

"it takes two to tango":
it takes two people to shape a relationship

haggling over:
arguing about

Win–Win   In **win–win problem solving**, the goal is to find a solution that satisfies the needs of everyone involved. Not only do the parties avoid trying to win at the other's expense, they also believe that by working together it is possible to find a solution that allows both to reach their goals.

Some compromises approach this win–win ideal. You and the seller might settle on a price for a used car that is between what the seller was asking and what you wanted to pay. Although neither of you got everything you wanted, the outcome would still leave both of you satisfied. Likewise, you and your companion might agree to see a film that is the second choice for both of you in order to spend an evening together. As long as everyone is satisfied with an outcome, it's accurate to describe it as a win–win solution.

> Although a win–win approach sounds ideal, it is not always possible, or even appropriate.

Although a win–win approach sounds ideal, it is not always possible, or even appropriate. Table 8-4 suggests some factors to consider when deciding which approach to take when facing a conflict. There will certainly be times when compromising is the most sensible approach. You will even encounter instances when pushing for your own solution is reasonable. Even more surprisingly, you will probably discover that there are times when it makes sense to willingly accept the loser's role.

Steps in Win–Win Problem Solving

Although win–win problem solving is often the most desirable approach to managing conflicts, it is also one of the hardest to achieve. In spite of the challenge, it is definitely possible to become better at resolving conflicts. The following pages outline a method to increase your chances of being able to handle your conflicts in a win–win manner, so that both you and others have your needs met. As you learn to use this approach, you should find that more and more of your conflicts end up with win–win solutions. And even when total satisfaction isn't possible, this approach can preserve a positive relational climate.[50]

TABLE 8-4   Choosing the Most Appropriate Method of Conflict Resolution

1. Consider deferring to the other person:
   - When you discover you are wrong
   - When the issue is more important to the other person than it is to you
   - To let others learn by making their own mistakes
   - When the long-term cost of winning may not be worth the short-term gains

2. Consider compromising:
   - When there is not enough time to seek a win–win outcome
   - When the issue is not important enough to negotiate at length
   - When the other person is not willing to seek a win–win outcome

3. Consider competing:
   - When the issue is important and the other person will take advantage of your noncompetitive approach

4. Consider cooperating:
   - When the issue is too important for a compromise
   - When a long-term relationship between you and the other person is important
   - When the other person is willing to cooperate

As it is presented here, win–win problem solving is a highly structured activity. After you have practiced the approach a number of times, this style of managing conflict will become almost second nature to you. You'll then be able to approach your conflicts without the need to follow the step-by-step approach. But for the time being, try to be patient, and trust the value of the following pattern. As you read on, imagine yourself applying it to a problem that's bothering you now.

Identify Your Problem and Unmet Needs   Before you speak out, it's important to realize that the problem that is causing conflict is yours. Whether you want to return an un-satisfactory piece of merchandise, complain to noisy neighbors because your sleep is being disturbed, or request a change in working conditions from your employer, the problem is yours. Why? Because in each case *you* are the person who is dissatisfied. You are the one who has paid for the defective article; the merchant who sold it to you has the use of your good money. You are the one who is losing sleep as a result of your neighbors' activities; they are content to go on as before. You, not your boss, are the one who is unhappy with your working conditions.

Realizing that the problem is yours will make a big difference when the time comes to approach your partner. Instead of feeling and acting in an evaluative way, you'll be

CULTURAL IDIOM
second nature:
easy and natural

CULTURAL IDIOM

rolling in:
possessing large amounts of

frame of mind:
mood, mental state

to "jump":
to attack

more likely to share your problem in a descriptive way, which will not only be more accurate but also will reduce the chance of a defensive reaction.

After you realize that the problem is yours, the next step is to identify the unmet needs that leave you feeling dissatisfied. Sometimes a relational need underlies the content of the issue at hand. Consider these cases:

- A friend hasn't returned some money you lent long ago. Your apparent need in this situation might be to get the cash back. But a little thought will probably show that this isn't the only, or even the main, thing you want. Even if you were rolling in money, you'd probably want the loan repaid because of your most important need: *to avoid feeling victimized by your friend's taking advantage of you.*

- Someone you care about who lives in a distant city has failed to respond to several letters. Your apparent need may be to get answers to the questions you've written about, but it's likely that there's another, more fundamental need: *the reassurance that you're still important enough to deserve a response.*

As you'll soon see, the ability to identify your real needs plays a key role in solving interpersonal problems. For now, the point to remember is that before you voice your problem to your partner, you ought to be clear about which of your needs aren't being met.

Make a Date   Unconstructive fights often start because the initiator confronts a partner who isn't ready. There are many times when a person isn't in the right frame of mind to face a conflict: perhaps owing to fatigue, being in too much of a hurry to take the necessary time, upset over another problem, or not feeling well. At times like these, it's unfair to "jump" a person without notice and expect to get full attention for your problem. If you do persist, you'll probably have an ugly fight on your hands.

After you have a clear idea of the problem, approach your partner with a request to try to solve it. For example: "Something's been bothering me. Can we talk about it?" If the answer is "yes," then you're ready to go further. If it isn't the right time to confront your partner, find a time that's agreeable to both of you.

Describe Your Problem and Needs   Your partner can't possibly meet your needs without knowing why you're upset and what you want. Therefore, it's up to you to describe your problem as specifically as possible. When you do so, it's important to use terms that aren't overly vague or abstract. Recall our discussion of behavioral descriptions in Chapter 4 when clarifying your problem and needs.

Partner Checks Back   After you've shared your problem and described what you need, it's important to make sure that your partner has understood what you've said. As you can remember from the discussion of listening in Chapter 5, there's a good chance— especially in a stressful conflict situation—of your words being misinterpreted.

Solicit Partner's Needs   After you've made your position clear, it's time to find out what your partner needs in order to feel satisfied about this issue. There are two reasons why it's important to discover your partner's needs. First, it's fair. After all, the other person has just as much right as you to feel satisfied, and if you expect help in meeting your needs, then it's reasonable that you behave in the same way. Second, just as an unhappy partner will make it hard for you to become satisfied, a happy one will be more likely to cooperate in letting you reach your goals. Thus, it is in your own self-interest to discover and meet your partner's needs.

You can learn about your partner's needs simply by asking about them: "Now I've told you what I want and why. Tell me what you need to feel okay about this." After your partner begins to talk, your job is to use the listening skills discussed earlier in this book to make sure you understand.

Check Your Understanding of Partner's Needs   Paraphrase or ask questions about your partner's needs until you're certain you understand them. The surest way to accomplish this is to use the paraphrasing skills you learned in Chapter 5.

Negotiate a Solution   Now that you and your partner understand each other's needs, the goal becomes finding a way to meet them. This is done by trying to develop as many potential solutions as possible and then evaluating them to decide which one best meets the needs of both. The following steps can help communicators develop a mutually satisfying solution.

> You can learn about your partner's needs simply by asking about them.

1. **Identify and Define the Conflict.** We've discussed this process in the preceding pages. It consists of discovering each person's problem and needs, setting the stage for meeting all of them.

2. **Generate a Number of Possible Solutions.** In this step the partners work together to think of as many means as possible to reach their stated ends. The key word here is *quantity*: It's important to generate as many ideas as you can think of without worrying about which ones are good or bad. Write down every thought that comes up, no matter how unworkable; sometimes a far-fetched idea will lead to a more workable one.

3. **Evaluate the Alternative Solutions.** This is the time to talk about which solutions will work and which ones won't. It's important for all concerned to be honest about their willingness to accept an idea. If a solution is going to work, everyone involved has to support it.

4. **Decide on the Best Solution.** Now that you've looked at all the alternatives, pick the one that looks best to everyone. It's important to be sure everybody understands the solution and is willing to try it out. Remember: Your decision doesn't have to be final, but it should look potentially successful.

Follow Up on the Solution   You can't be sure the solution will work until you try it out. After you've tested it for a while, it's a good idea to set aside some time to talk over how things are going. You may find that you need to make some changes or even rethink the whole problem. The idea is to keep on top of the problem, to keep using creativity to solve it.

Win–win solutions aren't always possible. There will be times when even the best-intentioned people simply won't be able to find a way of meeting all their needs. In cases like this, the process of negotiation has to include some compromising. But even then the preceding steps haven't been wasted. The genuine desire to learn what the other person wants and to try to satisfy those desires will build a climate of goodwill that can help you find the best solution to the present problem and also improve your relationship in the future.

CULTURAL IDIOM
to keep on top of:
to be in control of

Summary

This chapter explored several factors that help make interpersonal relationships satisfying or unsatisfying. We began by defining *communication climate* as the emotional tone of a relationship as it is expressed in the messages being sent and received. We examined factors that contribute to positive and negative climates, learning that the underlying factor is the degree to which a person feels valued by others. We examined types of confirming and disconfirming messages, and then looked in detail at Gibb's categories of defensiveness-arousing and supportive behaviors.

The second half of the chapter dealt with interpersonal conflict. We saw that conflict is a fact of life in every relationship and that the way conflicts are handled plays a major role in the quality of a relationship. There are five ways people can behave when faced with a conflict: nonassertive, directly aggressive, passive-aggressive, indirect, and assertive. Each of these approaches can be appropriate at times, but the chapter focused on assertive communication skills because of their value and novelty for most communicators. We saw that conflict styles are affected by both gender and culture.

There are four outcomes to conflicts: win–lose, lose–lose, compromise, and win–win. Win–win outcomes are often possible, if the parties possess the proper attitudes and skills. The final section of the chapter outlined the steps in win–win problem solving.

Key Terms

assertive communication A style of communicating that directly expresses the sender's needs, thoughts, or feelings, delivered in a way that does not attack the receiver's dignity. *p. 247*

avoidance spiral A communication spiral in which the parties slowly reduce their dependence on one another, withdraw, and become less invested in the relationship. *p. 240*

certainty Messages that dogmatically imply that the speaker's position is correct and that the other person's ideas are not worth considering. Likely to generate a defensive response. *p. 242*

communication climate The emotional tone of a relationship as it is expressed in the messages that the partners send and receive. *p. 236*

compromise An approach to conflict resolution in which both parties attain at least part of what they seek through self-sacrifice. *p. 255*

confirming responses A message that expresses respect and valuing of the other person. *p. 237*

conflict An expressed struggle between at least two interdependent parties who perceive incompatible goals, scarce rewards, and interference from the other party in achieving their goals. *p. 244*

controlling communication Messages in which the sender tries to impose some sort of outcome on the receiver, usually resulting in a defensive reaction. *p. 241*

description In terms of communication climate, a statement in which the speaker describes his/her position. See also *Evaluative communication*. *p. 241*

direct aggression An expression of the sender's thoughts or feelings or both that attacks the position and dignity of the receiver. *p. 246*

disconfirming response A message that expresses a lack of caring or respect for another person. *p. 238*

empathy The ability to project oneself into another person's point of view, so as to experience the other's thoughts and feelings. *p. 242*

equality When communicators show that they believe others have just as much worth as human beings. *p. 242*

escalatory spiral A reciprocal pattern of communication in which messages, either confirming or disconfirming, between two or more communicators reinforce one another. *p. 240*

evaluative communication Messages in which the sender judges the receiver in some way, usually resulting in a defensive response. See also *"You" language*. *p. 241*

Gibb categories Six sets of contrasting styles of verbal and nonverbal behavior. Each set describes a communication style that is likely to arouse defensiveness and a contrasting style that is likely to prevent or reduce it. Developed by Jack Gibb. *p. 240*

"I" language Language that describes the speaker's position without evaluating others. Synonymous with *Descriptive communication*. *p. 241*

indirect communication Hinting at a message instead of expressing thoughts and feelings directly. See also *Assertive communication; Passive aggression*. *p. 247*

lose–lose problem solving An approach to conflict resolution in which neither party achieves its goals. *p. 255*

neutrality A defense-arousing behavior in which the sender expresses indifference toward a receiver. *p. 242*

nonassertion The inability or unwillingness to express one's thoughts or feelings when necessary. *p. 245*

passive aggression An indirect expression of aggression, delivered in a way that allows the sender to maintain a facade of kindness. *p. 247*

problem orientation A supportive style of communication in which the communicators focus on working together to solve their problems instead of trying to impose their own solutions on one another. *p. 241*

provisionalism A supportive style of communication in which the sender expresses a willingness to consider the other person's position. *p. 243*

spiral Reciprocal communication pattern in which each person's message reinforces the other's. *p. 240*

spontaneity Supportive communication behavior in which the sender expresses a message without any attempt to manipulate the receiver. *p. 242*

strategy A defense-arousing style of communication in which the sender tries to manipulate or trick a receiver; also, the general term for any type of plan, as in the plan for a persuasive speech. *p. 242*

superiority A type of communication that suggests one person is better than the other. *p. 242*

win–lose problem solving An approach to conflict resolution in which one party reaches its goal at the expense of the other. *p. 254*

win–win problem solving An approach to conflict resolution in which the parties work together to satisfy all their goals. *p. 256*

"You" language Language that judges another person, increasing the likelihood of a defensive reaction. See also *Evaluative communication*. *p. 241*

Case Study Questions

Review the case study found on pages 192–193 and then answer the following questions in light of what you have learned in this chapter.

1. What weather-related adjectives would you use to describe the communication climate in your relationship with Hideki? What kinds of confirming communication described by Gibb (pages 240–243) might improve this climate?

2. How would you describe Hideki's style of handling concerns about your partnership (pages 245–248)? How would you describe the style you might choose for dealing with your concerns?

3. Describe how you might choose an assertive, win–win approach to addressing your concerns with Hideki (pages 248–250). Might your approach be different if your partner were from the United States instead of Japan?

Activities

1. **Your Confirming and Disconfirming Messages** You can gain an understanding of how confirming and disconfirming messages create communication spirals by trying the following exercise.

   1. Identify the communication climate of an important personal relationship. Using weather metaphors (sunny, gloomy, calm) may help.

   2. Describe several confirming or disconfirming messages that have helped create and maintain the climate. Be sure to identify both verbal and nonverbal messages.

   3. Show how the messages you have identified have created either escalatory or deescalatory conflict spirals. Describe how these spirals reach limits and what events cause them to stabilize or reverse.

   4. Describe what you can do to either maintain the existing climate (if positive) or change it (if negative). Again, list both verbal and nonverbal behaviors.

2. **Constructing Supportive Messages** This exercise will give you practice in sending confirming messages that exhibit Gibb's categories of supportive behavior. You will find that you can communicate in a constructive way—even in conflict situations.

   1. Begin by recalling at least two situations in which you found yourself in an escalatory conflict spiral.

2. Using the Gibb categories, identify your defense-arousing messages, both verbal and nonverbal.

3. Now reconstruct the situations, writing a script in which you replace the defense-arousing behaviors with the supportive alternatives outlined by Gibb.

4. If it seems appropriate, you may choose to approach the other people in each of the situations you have described here and attempt to replay the exchange. Otherwise, describe how you could use the supportive approach you developed in Step 3 in future exchanges.

3. **Constructing Assertive Messages** Develop your skill at expressing assertive messages by composing responses for each of the following situations:

1. A neighbor's barking dog is keeping you awake at night.

2. A friend hasn't repaid the twenty dollars she borrowed two weeks ago.

3. Your boss made what sounded like a sarcastic remark about the way you put school before work.

4. An out-of-town friend phones at the last minute to cancel the weekend you planned to spend together.

Now develop two assertive messages you could send to a real person in your life. Discuss how you could express these messages in a way that is appropriate for the situation and that fits your personal style.

4. **Problem Solving in Your Life**

1. Recall as many conflicts as possible that you have had in one relationship. Identify which approach best characterizes each one: win–lose, lose–lose, compromise, or win–win.

2. For each conflict, describe the consequences (for both you and the other person) of this approach.

3. Based on your analysis, decide for yourself how successful you and your partner are at managing conflicts. Describe any differences in approach that would result in more satisfying outcomes. Discuss what steps you and your partner could take to make these changes.

For Further Exploration

For more resources about improving interpersonal relationships, see the *Understanding Human Communication* website at www.oup.com/us/uhc11. There you will find a variety of resources: a list of books and articles, links to descriptions of feature films and television shows at the *Now Playing* website, study aids, and a self-test to check your understanding of the material in this chapter.

MEDIA ROOM

For more film and television suggestions, see *Now Playing* at the *Understanding Human Communication* website at www.oup.com/us/uhc11.

Confirming and Disconfirming Communication Climates

Four Christmases (2008, Rated R)

Orlando "Brad" McVie (Vince Vaughn) and his girlfriend, Kate (Reese Witherspoon), are a happily unmarried couple who would do anything to avoid spending Christmas with their families. When Brad and Kate's holiday flight to Fiji is canceled, they have no choice but to hunker down with the relatives for the holidays. Because each family has separated through divorce, they end up visiting four different families on Christmas Day. Each family scene reveals a painfully disconfirming communication climate rife with unresolved family conflict, making clear why Brad and Kate avoided revisiting their pasts.

Changeling (2008, Rated R)

In 1928, single mother Christine Collins (Angelina Jolie) reports that the child returned to her by police is not her missing son. Collins's assertion ignites a major conflict with the Los Angeles Police Department, which is more concerned with getting positive press coverage than uncovering the truth. Replete with frustrating and hopeless scenes of manipulative and disconfirming communication, this film highlights the challenges of women in history who have refused to back down from conflict with those in power.

Antwone Fisher (2002, Rated R)

In *Antwone Fisher*, the namesake character (Derek Luke) lands in the office of Navy psychiatrist Jerome Davenport (Denzel Washington) after fighting with fellow sailors. As he grows to trust Davenport, Antwone reveals the harsh details of his life: He was abandoned at birth by his imprisoned mother, never knew his father, and was raised by a cruel foster family. Davenport's support helps nurture Antowne's feelings of self-worth. The film, based on a true story, is a moving example of how being ignored is the ultimate form of disconfirmation, and how confirmation and the love of people who care can heal major wounds.

Two and a Half Men (2003– , Rated TV-14)

In the darkly amusing television series *Two and a Half Men*, brothers Charlie (Charlie Sheen) and Alan (Jon Cryer) share a household with their cold, domineering mother Evelyn (Holland Taylor) and Alan's son Jake (Angus T. Jones). Much of the humorous banter revolves around disconfirmation, as all the characters except Jake discount and degrade one another.

Managing Conflict

Defiance (2008, Rated R)

Set in Belarus during World War II, this gripping film focuses on two brothers, Tuvia (Daniel Craig) and Zus (Liev Schreiber), who choose different paths to save their community from the Nazis. After struggling bitterly through most of the saga, the brothers reconcile their ongoing conflict by striking a compromise that allows them to meet the twin goals of fighting the enemy while preserving their community.

PART FOUR

Communication in Groups

Food Bank Task Force

For the last three years you have been a volunteer at the local food bank, which distributes meals to less-fortunate neighbors in your community. Until now, the food bank has managed to meet the community's needs with donations from local businesses, but an influx of poor and hungry residents makes it necessary to raise at least $20,000 to balance the coming year's budget.

Impressed with your dedication and aware of the skills you've developed in your communication class, the food bank's director has asked you to organize a committee to develop three to five realistic options for raising the necessary funds. This is a big responsibility—more than you've ever had before. You try to pass along the job of chairing the committee, but the director expresses confidence in you and implores you to accept this important job. "Remember," she says, "several volunteers have already signed up for the committee, so you won't have to go out and recruit anybody. And you don't have to actually raise the money. What we need from your committee is a list of options that the board of directors can choose to raise the $20,000. Just be sure that the approaches you present will work, and that our volunteers will support them."

With a nervous lump in your throat, you agree to chair the committee. Your first step is to review the list of people who have signed up to work with you. Grace Smith is a long-time volunteer. She is independently wealthy, a longtime supporter of the food bank, has plenty of free time, and an endless amount of energy. At first you thought she should chair the group, but the director diplomatically reminded you that Grace is both a chatterbox and somewhat disorganized. Over the years you have thought that Grace is at least as interested in socializing as helping needy community members. Todd McManus is a self-made man—a local restaurant owner who built his business from scratch; he has good ties to the business community. He is smart and dedicated, but he is very opinionated and has little patience with people he calls "time wasters." His passion is helping disadvantaged people become self-supporting. Todd is single and has a reputation as a Romeo who is always on the lookout for attractive women. Mikako Sato is a third-year economics student from Japan who is studying at the local university. She is a practicing Buddhist with a strong social conscience. You know she is extremely smart, but she is very quiet and avoids confrontation at almost any cost. Carlos Soares is a well-known musician who immigrated to this country from Portugal as a young man. He is passionate about the arts, and loves to perform. You suspect he will try to steer the group toward some sort of concert.

Your committee has four weeks to develop a set of recommendations for the food bank's board of directors. The director has told you that the committee members are ready to get started as soon as they receive direction from you.

Read the questions and activities on pages 297 (Chapter 9) and 322 (Chapter 10) to complete this case study.

Sooner or later, we all belong to groups. Whether you're on the job, a part of a volunteer initiative like the food bank task force, on an athletic team, with your family, or in any other group, understanding the dynamics of group communication can make the difference between success and failure.

After studying Chapters 9 and 10, you will understand better

- The stages that every task-oriented group must face and how to work through them effectively.
- How the goals of individual members can either help or hinder the group's success.
- The kinds of power and influence held by official leaders and other group members.
- How to create conditions that lead to satisfying communication that helps get the group's job done.

Communicating in Groups

Chapter Outline

After studying the material in this chapter . . .

How important are groups?

You can answer this question for yourself by trying a simple experiment. Start by thinking of all the groups you belong to now and have belonged to in the past: the family you grew up with, the classes you have attended, the companies you have worked for, the teams you have played on, the many social groups you have been a member of—the list is a long one. Now, one by one, imagine that you had never belonged to each of these groups. Start with the less important ones, and the results aren't too dramatic, but very soon you will begin to see that a great deal of the information you have learned, the benefits you have gained—even your very identity have all come from group membership.

On the job, groups are the setting in which most work takes place. In one survey, 75 percent of the professionals surveyed reported that they "always" or "often" worked in teams.[1] In the growing multimedia field, the ability to work effectively as a team has been identified as the top nontechnical job skill.[2] When negotiating is conducted by teams instead of individuals, the results are better for everyone involved.[3]

This doesn't mean that every group experience is a good one. Some are vaguely unrewarding, rather like eating food that has no taste and gives no nourishment. And others are downright miserable. Sometimes it is easy to see why a group succeeds or fails, but in other cases matters aren't so clear.[4]

> In one survey, 75 percent of the professionals surveyed reported that they "always" or "often" worked in teams.

This chapter will help you understand better the nature of group communication. It will start by explaining just what a group is—because not every collection of people qualifies. It will go on to examine the reasons why people form groups and then look at several types of groups. Finally, it will conclude by looking at some common characteristics all groups share.

The Nature of Groups

Before we go any further, we need to clarify some fundamental qualities that define groups, and look at the ways in which members can communicate.

What Is a Group?

Imagine that you are taking a test on group communication. Which of the following would you identify as groups?

- A crowd of onlookers gawking at a burning building
- Several passengers at an airline ticket counter discussing their hopes to find space on a crowded flight
- An army battalion

Because all these situations seem to involve groups, your experience as a canny test taker probably tells you that a commonsense answer will get you in trouble here—and you're right. When social scientists talk about *groups*, they use the word in a special way that excludes each of the preceding examples.

What are we talking about when we use the word *group*? For our purposes a **group** consists of a *small collection of people who interact with each other, usually face-to-face, over*

Invitation to Insight

The Power of Small Groups

What do the Communist Party, Alcoholics Anonymous, and evangelical Christians all have in common? They adopted and refined the technique of organizing in small cells to achieve change. This is the fascinating theme of Malcolm Gladwell's *New Yorker* article, "The Cellular Church."

Gladwell uses the story of Rick Warren's Saddleback Church in Orange County, California, to make this theme come alive. For those of you not familiar with Rick Warren, he is the author of *The Purpose-Driven Life* (23 million copies sold so far and it is just getting started) and founder of the Saddleback Church, an evangelical Christian church with 20,000 members in its congregation and the hub of a global network of 1,100 other evangelical Christian churches.

Gladwell focuses on a core challenge confronting any voluntary organization—how to make it scalable. On the one hand, many voluntary organizations want to grow so they need to have low barriers to entry. But if they grow too fast or too big, they begin to lose the sense of community and identity that is necessary to retain members. He notes that "historically, churches have sacrificed size for community" but this changed back in the 1970s and 1980s when the evangelical movement began to build megachurches. It turns out the cellular model has been key to the success of megachurches—cells helped them to solve the scalability challenge.

What are these cells? Gladwell observes that they are "exclusive, tightly knit groups of six or seven who meet in one another's homes during the week to worship and pray." It turns out, at least 40 million Americans now participate in a religious cell of this type. This is also the organizational model that led to the early success of the Communist Party and the continuing success of Alcoholics Anonymous and its many spin-offs.

John Hagel

THE FAR SIDE ® BY GARY LARSON

The Far Side® by Gary Larson © 1987 FarWorks, Inc. All Rights Reserved. The Far Side® and the Larson® signature are registered trademarks of FarWorks, Inc. Used with permission.

© 1987 FarWorks, Inc. All Rights Reserved/Dist. by Creators Syndicate

"And so you just threw everything together? ... Matthews, a posse is something you have to *organize*."

time in order to reach goals. A closer examination of this definition will show why none of the collections of people described in the preceding quiz qualifies as a group.

Interaction Without interaction, a collection of people isn't a group. Consider, for example, the onlookers at a fire. Though they all occupy the same area at a given time, they have virtually nothing to do with each other. Of course, if they should begin interacting—working together to give first aid or to rescue victims, for example—the situation would change. This requirement of interaction highlights the difference between true groups and collections of individuals who merely co-act—simultaneously engaging in a similar activity without communicating with one another. For example, students who passively listen to a lecture don't technically constitute a group until they begin to exchange messages—verbal and nonverbal—with each other and their instructor. (This explains why some students feel isolated even though they spend so much time on a crowded campus. Despite being surrounded by others, they really don't belong to any groups.)

Interdependence In groups, members don't just interact: Their members are *interdependent*.[5] The behavior of one person affects all the others in what can be called a "ripple effect."[6] Consider your own experience in family and work groups: When one member behaves poorly, his or her actions shape the way the entire group functions. The ripple effect can be positive as well as negative: Beneficial actions by some members help everyone.

Time A collection of people who interact for a short while doesn't qualify as a group. As you'll soon read, groups who work together for any length of time begin to take on characteristics that aren't present in temporary aggregations. There are some occasions when a collection of individuals pulls together to tackle a goal quite quickly. A stirring example of this phenomenon occurred on September 11, 2001, when a group of passengers on United Airlines flight 93 banded together in a matter of minutes to thwart the efforts of hijackers who were attempting to crash the plane into the White House. Despite examples of ad hoc groups like this, most groups work together long enough to develop a sense of identity and history that shapes their ongoing effectiveness.

Size Our definition of *groups* included the word *small*. Most experts in the field set the lower limit of group size at three members.[7] This decision isn't arbitrary, because there are some significant differences between two- and three-person communication. For example, the only ways two people can resolve a conflict are to change one another's minds, give in, or compromise; in a larger group, however, there's a possibility of members forming alliances either to put increased pressure on dissenting members or to outvote them.

There is less agreement about when a group stops being small.[8] Though no expert would call a five hundred–member army battalion a group in our sense of the word (it would be labeled an organization), most experts are reluctant to set an arbitrary upper limit. Probably the best description of smallness is the ability for each member to be able to know and react to every other member. It's sufficient to say that our focus in these pages will be on collections of people ranging in size from three to around twenty.

As the reading on page 269 shows, bigger usually isn't better. Research suggests that the optimal size for a group is the smallest number of people capable of performing the task at hand effectively.[9] This definition makes it clear that there is no magic number or formula for choosing the best group size. The optimal number will change according to the task, as well as contextual factors such as politics, legal requirements, and institutional norms.[10] But generally speaking, as a group becomes larger, it is harder to schedule meetings, the members have less access to important information, and they have fewer chances to participate—three ingredients in a recipe for dissatisfaction.

> The optimal size for a group is the smallest number of people capable of performing the task at hand effectively.

Goals   Group membership isn't always voluntary, as some family members and most prison inmates will testify. But whether or not people choose to join groups, they usually hope to achieve one or more goals. At first the goal-related nature of group membership seems simple and obvious. In truth, however, there are several types of goals, which we will examine in the following pages.

Virtual and Face-to-Face Groups

The explosion of communication technologies has led to the growth of **virtual groups**—teams who interact with one another through mediated channels, without meeting face-to-face. With computers, webcams, and Internet connections, members of a virtual group can swap ideas as easily as if they were in the same room.[11] It can take a while for virtual groups to work out relating to one another online, but initial problems are usually resolved within a short time.[12]

Despite the lack of personal contact between members, virtual teams actually can be superior to face-to-face teams in at least two ways. First, getting together is fast and easy. A virtual team can meet whenever necessary, even if the members are widely separated. This ease of interaction isn't just useful in the business world. For most groups of students working on class projects, finding a convenient time to meet can be a major headache. Virtual groups don't face the same challenges.

A second advantage of virtual teams is the leveling of the status differences that can get in the way of effective group functioning. When people connect via computer networks, rank is much less prominent than when groups meet face-to-face.[13] This "leveling" effect also reduces gender differences, equalizing the contributions of men and women far more than occurs in face-to-face groups.[14]

Goals of Groups and Their Members

We can talk about two types of goals when we examine groups. The first type involves **individual goals**—the motives of individual members—whereas the second involves **group goals**—the outcome the group seeks to accomplish.

their own interests ahead of the group's is especially great when there is less need for interdependence. John Krakauer captures this situation clearly in his account of a team of climbers seeking to reach the peak of Mount Everest:

> There were more than fifty people camped on the Col that night, huddled in shelters pitched side by side, yet an odd feeling of isolation hung in the air. We were a team in name only, I'd sadly come to realize. Although in a few hours we would leave camp as a group, we would ascend as individuals, linked to one another by neither rope nor any deep sense of loyalty. Each client was in it for himself or herself, pretty much. And I was no different: I sincerely hoped Doug got to the top, for instance, yet I would do everything in my power to keep pushing on if he turned around.[19]

Characteristics of Groups

Whatever their function, all groups have certain characteristics in common. Understanding these characteristics is a first step to behaving more effectively in your own groups.

Rules and Norms

Many groups have formal **rules**—explicit, officially stated guidelines that govern what the group is supposed to do and how the members should behave. In a classroom, these rules include how absences will be treated, whether papers must be typed, and so on. Alongside the official rules, an equally powerful set of standards also operates, often without being discussed. Sociologists call these unstated rules **norms**. Norms are shared values, beliefs, behaviors, and procedures that govern a group's operation. For instance, you probably won't find a description of what jokes are and aren't acceptable in the bylaws of any groups you belong to, yet you can almost certainly describe the unstated code if you think about it. Is sexual humor acceptable? How much, and what types? What about religious jokes? How much kidding of other group members is proper? Matters such as these vary from one group to another, according to the norms of each one.[20]

There are three categories of group norms: social, procedural, and task. **Social norms** govern the relationship of members to each other. How honest and direct will members be with one another? What emotions will and won't be expressed, and in what ways? Matters such as these are handled by the establishment of social norms, usually implicit ones. **Procedural norms** outline how the group should operate. Will the group make decisions by accepting the vote of the majority, or will the members keep talking until consensus is reached? Will one person run meetings, or will discussion be leaderless? **Task norms** focus on how the job itself should be handled. For example, a key task norm is "Does the job have to be done perfectly, or will members settle for an adequate, if imperfect, solution?" The answer to this question results in a task-related norm. All groups have social norms, whereas problem-solving, learning, and growth groups also have procedural and task norms.

Table 9-1 lists some typical rules and norms that operate in familiar groups. It is important to realize that the actual rules and norms that govern a group don't always match the idealized ones that embody cultural standards. Consider the matter of punctuality, for example. A cultural norm in our society is that meetings should begin at the scheduled time, yet some groups soon generate the usually unstated agreement that the real business won't commence until ten or so minutes later. On a more serious level, one cultural norm is that other people should be treated politely and with respect, but in some groups failure to listen, sarcasm, and even outright hostility make the principle of civility a sham.

It is important to understand a group's norms. Following them is one way to gain acceptance into the group, and sometimes recognizing norms that cause problems can be a way to help the group operate more effectively. For instance, in some groups a norm is to discourage new ideas by criticism, sarcasm, or indifference. Pointing this out to members might be a way to change the unwritten rules and thereby improve the group's work.

TABLE 9-1 Typical Rules and Norms in Two Types of Groups

FAMILY

RULES (EXPLICIT)

- If you don't do the chores, you don't get your allowance.
- If you're going to be more than a half-hour late, phone home so the others don't worry about you.
- If the gas gauge reads "empty," fill up the tank before bringing the car home.
- Don't make plans for Sunday nights. That's time for the family to spend together.
- Daniel gets to watch *Sesame Street* from 5 to 6 P.M.

NORMS (UNSTATED)

- When Dad is in a bad mood, don't bring up problems.
- Don't talk about Sheila's divorce.
- It's okay to tease Lupe about being short, but don't make comments about Shana's complexion.
- As long as the kids don't get in trouble, the parents won't ask detailed questions about what they do with their friends.
- At family gatherings, try to change the subject when Uncle Max brings up politics.

ON-THE-JOB MEETINGS

RULES (EXPLICIT)

- Regular meetings are held every Monday morning at 9 A.M.
- The job of keeping minutes rotates from person to person.
- Meetings last no more than an hour.
- Don't leave the meetings to take phone calls except in emergencies.

NORMS (UNSTATED)

- Use first names.
- It's okay to question the boss's ideas, but if she doesn't concede after the first remark, don't continue to object.
- Tell jokes at the beginning of the meeting, but avoid sexual or ethnic topics.
- It's okay to talk about "gut feelings," but back them up with hard facts.
- Don't act upset when your ideas aren't accepted, even if you're unhappy.

If norms are rarely stated, how is it possible to identify them? There are two sets of clues that can help you pin down norms. First, look for behaviors that occur often.[21] For instance, notice what time meetings begin. Observe the amount of work members are willing to contribute to the group. See what kinds of humor are and aren't used. Habitual behaviors like these suggest the unspoken rules that the group lives by. Second, look for clues that members are being punished for violating norms. Most punishments are subtle, of course: pained expressions from other members when a speaker talks too much, no laughter following an inappropriate joke, and so on.

Roles

Whereas norms define acceptable group standards, **roles** define patterns of behavior expected of members. Just like norms, some roles are officially recognized. These **formal roles** are assigned by an organization or group partly to establish order. Formal roles usually come with a label, such as "assistant coach," "treasurer," or "customer service representative." Unlike these formal classifications, **informal roles** (sometimes called "functional roles") are rarely acknowledged by the group.[22] Table 9-2 lists some of the

TABLE 9-2   Functional Roles of Group Members

TASK ROLES	TYPICAL BEHAVIORS	EXAMPLES
1. Initiator/Contributor	Contributes ideas and suggestions; proposes solutions and decisions; proposes new ideas or states old ones in a novel fashion.	"How about taking a different approach to this chore? Suppose we . . ."
2. Information Seeker	Asks for clarification of comments in terms of their factual adequacy; asks for information or facts relevant to the problem; suggests information is needed before making decisions.	"Do you think the others will go for this?" "How much would the plan cost us?" "Does anybody know if those dates are available?"
3. Information Giver	Offers facts or generalizations that may relate to the group's task.	"I bet Chris would know the answer to that." "*Newsweek* ran an article on that a couple of months ago. It said . . ."
4. Opinion Seeker	Asks for clarification of opinions made by other members of the group and asks how people in the group feel.	"Does anyone else have an idea about this?" "That's an interesting idea, Ruth. How long would it take to get started?"
5. Opinion Giver	States beliefs or opinions having to do with suggestions made; indicates what the group's attitude should be.	"I think we ought to go with the second plan. It fits the conditions we face in the Concord plant best. . . ."
6. Elaborator/Clarifier	Elaborates ideas and other contributions; offers rationales for suggestions; tries to deduce how an idea or suggestion would work if adopted by the group.	"If we followed Lee's suggestion, each of us would need to make three calls." "Let's see . . . at thirty-five cents per brochure, the total cost would be $525.00."
7. Coordinator	Clarifies the relationships among information, opinions, and ideas or suggests an integration of the information, opinions, and ideas of subgroups.	"John, you seem most concerned with potential problems. Mary sounds confident that they can all be solved. Why don't you list the problems one at a time, John, and Mary can respond to each one."

TABLE 9-2 Functional Roles of Group Members (continued)

TASK ROLES	TYPICAL BEHAVIORS	EXAMPLES
8. Diagnostician	Indicates what the problems are.	"But you're missing the main thing, I think. The problem is that we can't afford . . ."
9. Orienter/Summarizer	Summarizes what has taken place; points out departures from agreed-on goals; tries to bring the group back to the central issues; raises questions about the direction in which the group is heading.	"Let's take stock of where we are. Helen and John take the position that we should act now. Bill says, 'Wait.' Rusty isn't sure. Can we set that aside for a moment and come back to it after we . . ."
10. Energizer	Prods the group to action.	"Come on, guys. We've been wasting time. Let's get down to business."
11. Procedure Developer	Handles routine tasks such as seating arrangements, obtaining equipment, and handing out pertinent papers.	"I'll volunteer to see that the forms are printed and distributed." "I'd be happy to check on which of those dates are free."
12. Secretary	Keeps notes on the group's progress.	"Just for the record, I'll put these decisions in the memo and get copies to everyone in the group."
13. Evaluator/Critic	Constructively analyzes group's accomplishments according to some set of standards; checks to see that consensus has been reached.	"Look, we said we only had two weeks, and this proposal will take at least three. Does that mean that it's out of the running, or do we need to change our original guidelines?"

SOCIAL/MAINTENANCE ROLES

1. Supporter/Encourager	Praises, agrees with, and accepts the contributions of others; offers warmth, solidarity, and recognition.	"I really like that idea, John." "Priscilla's suggestion sounds good to me. Could we discuss it further?"
2. Harmonizer Reliever	Reconciles disagreements; mediates differences; reduces tensions by giving group members a chance to explore their differences.	"I don't think you two are as far apart as you think. Henry, are you saying _____ ? Benson, you seem to be saying _____ . Is that what you mean?"
3. Tension	Jokes or in some other way reduces the formality of the situation; relaxes the group members.	"Let's take a break . . . maybe have a drink." "You're a tough cookie, Bob. I'm glad you're on our side!"
4. Conciliator	Offers new options when his or her own ideas are involved in a conflict; willing to admit errors so as to maintain group cohesion.	"Looks like our solution is halfway between you and me, John. Can we look at the middle ground?"
5. Gatekeeper	Keeps communication channels open; encourages and facilitates interaction from those members who are usually silent.	"Susan, you haven't said anything about this yet. I know you've been studying the problem. What do you think about _____?"
6. Feeling Expresser	Makes explicit the feelings, moods, and relationships in the group; shares own feelings with others.	"I'm really glad we cleared things up today." "I'm just about worn out. Could we call it a day and start fresh tomorrow?"
7. Follower	Goes along with the movement of the group passively, accepting the ideas of others, sometimes serving as an audience.	"I agree. Yes, I see what you mean. If that's what the group wants to do, I'll go along."

most common informal roles in task-oriented groups. As the list shows, informal roles describe the functions members can fill rather than their formal positions. You can probably think of many groups in which members occupy functional roles. For example, you can probably think of many groups in which some members were clearly leaders and others followers.

Informal roles are not formally assigned to members. In fact, they are rarely even recognized as existing. Many of the roles may be filled by more than one member, and some of them may be filled by different people at different times. The important fact is that, at crucial times, the necessary informal roles must be filled by someone.

> The ideal ratio is 2:1, with task-related behavior dominating.

Notice that the informal roles listed in Table 9-2 fall into two categories: task and maintenance. **Task roles** help the group accomplish its goals, and **social roles** (also called "maintenance roles") help the relationships among the members run smoothly. Not all roles are constructive. Table 9-3 lists several **dysfunctional roles** that prevent a group from working effectively. Research suggests that the presence of positive social roles and the absence of dysfunctional ones are key ingredients in the effectiveness of groups.[23]

What is the optimal balance between task and social functions? According to Robert Bales, one of the earliest and most influential researchers in the area, the ideal ratio is 2:1, with task-related behavior dominating.[24] This ratio allows the group to get its work done while at the same time taking care of the personal needs and concerns of the members.

Role Emergence   We said earlier that most group members aren't aware of the existence of informal roles. You will rarely find members saying things like "You ask most of the questions, I'll give opinions, and she can be the summarizer." Yet it's fairly obvious that over time certain members do begin to fulfill specific roles. How does this process occur?

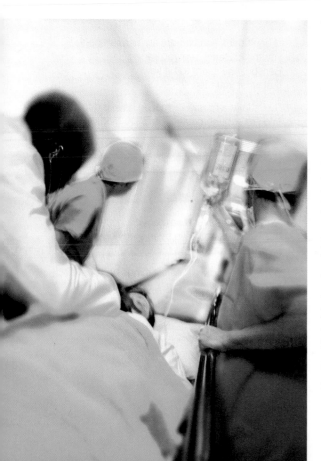

There are two answers to this question. One factor in role differentiation is the personal characteristics of each member. But by themselves, personal skills and traits aren't enough to earn a member acceptance as possessor of a role, especially in newly formed groups where no formal leader exists. The process of role emergence has been studied extensively by communication scholar Ernest Bormann, who identified a predictable series of stages groups go through in role designation.[25] (Remember that this process is almost never discussed and is rarely performed consciously.)

At first, members will make bids for certain roles. A particularly analytical communicator might audition for the role of critic by pointing out flaws in a proposal, for example. In order for this role to "take," the group members must endorse the bid by acknowledging and accepting it verbally and nonverbally—giving the would-be critic their attention and making positive comments about the observations. If the group does not support the first few initial bids, a sensitive member is likely to try another role.

Role-Related Problems and Solutions   Groups can suffer from at least three role-related problems. The first occurs when one

TABLE 9-3 Dysfunctional Roles of Group Members

DYSFUNCTIONAL ROLES	TYPICAL BEHAVIORS	EXAMPLES
1. Blocker	Interferes with progress by rejecting ideas or taking a negative stand on any and all issues; refuses to cooperate.	"Wait a minute! That's not right! That idea is absurd." "You can talk all day, but my mind is made up."
2. Aggressor	Struggles for status by deflating the status of others; boasts, criticizes.	"Wow, that's really swell! You turkeys have botched things again." "Your constant bickering is responsible for this mess. Let me tell you how you ought to do it."
3. Deserter	Withdraws in some way; remains indifferent, aloof, sometimes formal; daydreams; wanders from the subject, engages in irrelevant side conversations.	"I suppose that's right . . . I really don't care."
4. Dominator	Interrupts and embarks on long monologues; is authoritative; tries to monopolize the group's time.	"Bill, you're just off base. What we should do is this. First . . ."
5. Recognition Seeker	Attempts to gain attention in an exaggerated manner; usually boasts about past accomplishments; relates irrelevant personal experiences, usually in an attempt to gain sympathy.	"That reminds me of a guy I used to know . . ." "Let me tell you how I handled old Marris . . ."
6. Joker	Displays a lack of involvement in the group through inappropriate humor, horseplay, or cynicism.	"Why try to convince these guys? Let's just get the mob to snuff them out." "Hey, Carla, wanna be my roommate at the sales conference?"
7. Cynic	Discounts chances for group's success.	"Sure, we could try that idea, but it probably won't solve the problem. Nothing we've tried so far has worked."

Source: "Functional Roles of Group Members" and "Dysfunctional Roles of Group Members," adapted from *Groups in Context: Leadership and Participation in Decision-Making Groups* by Gerald Wilson and Michael Hanna, pp. 144–146. © 1986. Reprinted by permission of McGraw-Hill Companies, Inc.

or more important informal roles—either task or social—go unfilled. For instance, there may be no information giver to provide vital knowledge or no harmonizer to smooth things over when members disagree.

There are other cases when the problem isn't an absence of candidates to fill certain roles, but rather an overabundance of them. This situation can lead to unstated competition between members, which gets in the way of group effectiveness. You have probably seen groups in which two people both want to be the tension-relieving comedian. In such cases, the problem arises when the members become more concerned with occupying their pet position than with getting the group's job done.

Even when there's no competition over roles, a group's effectiveness can be threatened when one or more members suffer from "role fixation"—acting out a specific role whether or not the situation requires it.[26] As you learned in Chapter 1, a key ingredient of communication competence is flexibility—the ability to choose the right behavior for a given situation. Members who always take the same role—even a constructive one—lack competence, and they hinder the group. As in other areas of life, too much of

CULTURAL IDIOM

occupying their pet position: playing their favorite

CULTURAL IDIOM

just the ticket:
the right thing

a good thing can be a problem. You can overcome the potential role-related problems by following these guidelines:

- Look for unfilled roles. When a group seems to be experiencing problems, use the list in Table 9-2 as a kind of checklist to diagnose what roles might be unfilled.

- Make sure unfilled roles are filled. After you have identified unfilled roles, you may be able to help the group by filling them yourself. If key facts are missing, take the role of information seeker and try to dig them out. If nobody is keeping track of the group's work, offer to play secretary and take notes. Even if you are not suited by skill or temperament to a job, you can often encourage others to fill it.

- Avoid role fixation. Don't fall into familiar roles if they aren't needed. You may be a world-class coordinator or critic, but these talents will only annoy others if you use them when they aren't needed. In most cases your natural inclination to be a supporter might be just the ticket to help a group succeed, but if you find yourself in a group where the members don't need or want this sort of support, your encouragement might become a nuisance.

- Avoid dysfunctional roles. Some of these roles can be personally gratifying, especially when you are frustrated with a group, but they do nothing to help the group succeed, and they can damage your reputation as a team player. Nobody needs a blocker, a joker, or any other of the dysfunctional roles listed in Table 9-3. Resist the temptation to indulge yourself by taking on any of them.

Critical Thinking Probe

Functional and Dysfunctional Roles

Identify the functional and dysfunctional roles in an established group. You might analyze a group to which you belong (e.g., an athletic team or class group), a group who can be observed (e.g., city council, faculty, senate), or even a fictional group. How do the roles in the group you are analyzing contribute to the group's success (or lack of it)? How might members take on different roles to make the group more effective?

Patterns of Interaction

In interpersonal and public speaking settings, information exchange is relatively uncomplicated, taking basically two routes: either between the two individuals in an interpersonal dyad or between the speaker and the audience in a public speaking situation. In groups, however, things aren't so simple. The mathematical formula that identifies the number of possible interactions between individuals is

$$\frac{N(N-1)}{2}$$

where N equals the number of members in a group. Thus, in even a relatively small five-member group, there are ten possible combinations of two-person conversations and seventy-five possible multiperson interactions. Besides the sheer quantity of information exchanged, the more complex structure of groups affects the flow of information in other ways, too.

A look at Figure 9-1 (usually called a **sociogram**) will suggest the number and complexity of interactions that can occur in a group. Arrows connecting members indicate remarks shared between them. Two-headed arrows represent two-way conversations, whereas one-headed arrows represent remarks that did not arouse a response. Arrows directed to the center of the circle indicate remarks made to the group as a whole. A network analysis of this sort can reveal both the amount of participation by each member and the recipients of every member's remarks.

In the group pictured in Figure 9-1, person E appears to be connected to the group only through a relationship with person A; E never addressed any other members, nor did they address E. Also notice that person A is the most active and best-connected member. A addressed remarks to the group as a whole and to every other member and was the object of remarks from three individuals as well.

Sociograms don't tell the whole story, because they do not indicate the quality of the messages being exchanged. Nonetheless, they are a useful tool in diagnosing group communication.

Physical arrangement influences communication in groups. It's obviously easier to interact with someone you can see well. Lack of visibility isn't a serious problem in dyadic settings, but it can be troublesome in groups. For example, group members seated in a circle are more likely to talk with persons across from them than with those on either side.[27] Different things happen when members are seated in rectangular arrangements. Research with twelve-person juries showed that those sitting at either end of rectangular tables participated more in discussions and were viewed by other members as having more influence on the decision-making process.[28] Rectangular seating patterns have other consequences as well. Research conducted on six-person groups seated at rectangular tables showed that as distance between two persons increased, other members perceived them as being less friendly, less talkative, and less acquainted with each other.[29]

If group members always stayed together and shared every piece of information with one another, their interaction would resemble the pattern in Figure 9-2—what communication theorists have called an **all-channel network**. But not all groups meet

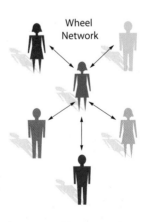

FIGURE 9-1 Patterns of Interaction in a Five-Person Group

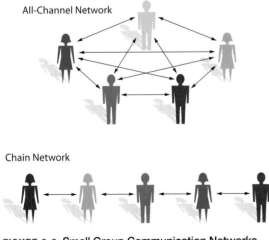

FIGURE 9-2 Small Group Communication Networks

face-to-face. The crew who waits tables and prepares the food at a restaurant and the group of nurses, aids, and technicians who staff an eight- or ten-hour hospital shift rarely sit down together to discuss their work. When group members aren't in immediate contact with one another, information can flow through a variety of other networks (see Figure 9-2). Some follow a **chain network**, moving sequentially from one member to another. Chains are an efficient way to deliver simple verbal messages or to circulate written information when members can't manage to attend a meeting at one time. You might use this approach to route an important message to members of a team at work, asking each person to initial a memo and pass it along to the next person on a routing slip. Chain networks are not very reliable for lengthy or complex verbal messages, because the content of the message can change as it passes from one person to another.

Another communication pattern is the **wheel network**, in which one person acts as a clearinghouse, receiving and relaying messages to all other members. Like chains, wheel networks are sometimes a practical choice, especially if one member is available to communicate with others all or most of the time. In a class group, you might use a wheel network if one of your members is usually near a telephone. This person can become the informational hub who keeps track of messages and people. Groups sometimes use wheel networks when relationships are strained between two or more members. In cases like this, the central member can serve as a mediator or facilitator who manages messages as they flow between others.

The success of a wheel network depends heavily on the skill of the **gatekeeper**—the person through whom information flows. If he or she is a skilled communicator, these mediated messages may help the group function effectively. But if the gatekeeper consciously or unconsciously distorts messages to suit personal goals or plays members off against one another, the group is likely to suffer.

Decision-Making Methods

Another way to classify groups is according to the approach they use to make decisions. There are several approaches a group can use to make decisions. We'll look at each of them now, examining their advantages and disadvantages.[30]

Consensus   **Consensus** occurs when all members of a group support a decision. The advantages of consensus are obvious: Full participation can increase the quality of the decision as well as the commitment of the members to support it. Consensus is especially important in decisions on critical or complex matters; in such cases, methods using less input can diminish the quality of or enthusiasm for a decision. Despite its advantages, consensus also has its disadvantages. It takes a great deal of time, which makes it unsuitable for emergencies. In addition, it is often very frustrating: Emotions can run high on important matters, and patience in the face of such pressures is difficult. Because of the need to deal with these emotional pressures, consensus calls for more communication skill than do other decision-making approaches. As with many things in life, consensus has high rewards, which come at a proportionately high cost.

> Consensus calls for more communication skill than do other decision-making approaches.

Majority Control   A naive belief of many people (perhaps coming from overzealous high school civics teachers) is that the democratic method of majority rule is always superior. This method does have its advantages in matters where the support of all members isn't necessary, but in more important matters it is risky. Remember that even if a 51

Source: DILBERT: © by Scott Adams/Dist. by United Feature Syndicate, Inc.

percent majority of the members favors a plan, 49 percent might still oppose it—hardly sweeping support for any decision that needs the support of all members in order to work.

Besides producing unhappy members, decisions made under majority rule often are of a quality inferior to that of decisions hashed out by a group until the members reach consensus.[31] Under majority rule, members who recognize that they are outvoted often participate less, and the deliberations usually end after a majority opinion has formed—even though minority viewpoints might be worthwhile.

Expert Opinion   Sometimes one group member will be defined as an expert and, as such, will be given the power to make decisions. This method can work well when that person's judgment is truly superior. For example, if a group of friends is backpacking in the wilderness, and one becomes injured, it would probably be foolish to argue with the advice of a doctor in the group. In most cases, however, matters aren't so simple. Who is the expert? There is often disagreement on this question. Sometimes a member might think he or she is the best qualified to make a decision, but others will disagree. In a case like this, the group probably won't support that person's advice, even if it is sound.

Minority Control   Sometimes a few members of a group will decide matters. This approach works well with noncritical questions that would waste the whole group's time. In the form of a committee, a minority of members also can study an issue in greater detail than can the entire group. When an issue is so important that it needs the support of everyone, it's best at least to have the committee report its findings for the approval of all members.

Authority Rule   Authority rule is the approach most often used by autocratic leaders. Though it sounds dictatorial, there are times when such an approach has its advantages. This method is quick: There are cases when there simply isn't time for a group to decide what to do. The approach is also perfectly acceptable with routine matters that don't require discussion in order to gain approval. When overused, however, this approach causes problems. Much of the time group decisions are of higher quality and gain more support

CULTURAL IDIOM
hashed out:
discussed thoroughly

CULTURAL IDIOM

wishy-washy:
lacking decisiveness

buy-in:
support

holdouts:
those who refuse to participate
until they receive a satisfactory
contract offer

from members than those made by an individual. Thus, failure to consult with members can lead to a decrease of effectiveness even when the leader's decision is a reasonable one.

Which of these decision-making approaches is best? The answer can vary from one culture to another. In Japan, consensus is highly valued. British and Dutch business-people also value the "team must be aboard" approach. On the other hand, German, French, and Spanish communicators depend more on the decision of a strong leader and view a desire for consensus as somewhat wishy-washy.[32]

Culture notwithstanding, the most effective approach in a given situation depends on the circumstances:

- **The type of decision** Some decisions can best be made by an expert, whereas others will benefit from involving the entire group.

- **The importance of the decision** If the decision is relatively unimportant, it's probably not worth involving all members of the group. By contrast, critical decisions probably require the participation, and ideally the buy-in, of all members.

- **Time available** If time is short, it may not be possible to assemble the entire group for deliberations.[33]

When choosing a decision-making approach, weigh the pros and cons of each before you decide which one has the best chance of success in the situation your group is facing.

Cultural Influences on Group Communication

In past generations, most groups in the United States and Canada were ethnically and culturally homogenous. People could expect to work, study, and play with others who were fundamentally similar to themselves. Social forces have changed society dramatically. Over the next decade, former minority groups will account for more than half of the population in California, Hawaii, New Mexico, and Texas and almost 50 percent in

Understanding Diversity

Baseball in Japan and the USA

The concept and practice of group harmony, or *wa*, is what most dramatically differentiates Japanese baseball from the American game. It is the connecting thread running through all Japanese life and sports. While "Let It All Hang Out" and "Do Your Own Thing" are mottoes of contemporary American society, the Japanese have their own credo in the well-worn proverb, "The Nail That Sticks Up Shall Be Hammered Down." It is practically a national slogan.

Holdouts, for example, are rare in Japan. A player usually takes what the club deigns to give him and that's that. Demanding more money is evidence that a player is putting his own interests before those of the team.

In the pressure-cooker world of U.S. pro sports, temper outbursts are considered acceptable, and at times even regarded as a salutary show of spirit. In Japan, however, a player's behavior is often considered as important as his batting average. Batting slumps are usually accompanied by embarrassed smiles. Temper tantrums—along with practical joking, bickering, complaining, and other norms of American clubhouse life—are viewed in Japan as unwelcome incursions into the team's collective peace of mind.

When [Tokyo] Giants top pitcher Takashi Nishimoto ignored the instructions of a coach in practice one summer day in 1985, the coach punched him between the eyes. Nishimoto was also forced to apologize and pay a one hundred thousand–yen fine for insubordination.

Moreover, untoward behavior is also seen as a sign of character weakness and a "small heart," as well as being detrimental to the team's image overall. In Japan, a "real man" is one who keeps his emotions to himself and thinks of others' feelings.

Robert Whiting
You Gotta Have Wa

other states, including New York, New Jersey, and Maryland.[34] Changes like these make it more and more likely that we will find ourselves in groups with people from backgrounds different than ours.

Fortunately, the growing body of research about communicating across diversity offers encouraging news about what happens when people from different backgrounds get together. While homogenous groups may be more cohesive,[35] diverse groups often develop better solutions to problems[36] and enjoy themselves more while working together.[37]

One ingredient in working effectively in diverse groups is understanding the often subtle cultural factors that shape communication. After surveying over 160,000 members of organizations in sixty countries, Geert Hofstede identified five cultural forces that shape the attitudes and behaviors of groups and individuals.[38] We will examine each of them in the following pages.

> One ingredient in working effectively in diverse groups is understanding the often subtle cultural factors that shape communication.

Individualism Versus Collectivism

Some cultures value the individual, whereas others value the group. As Table 9-4 shows, the United States is one of the world's more individualistic societies, along with Canada, Australia, and Britain. By contrast, Latin American and Asian societies are generally more collectivistic.

Members of **individualistic** cultures view their primary responsibility as being to themselves, whereas members of **collectivistic** societies feel loyalties and obligations to the groups of which they are members: the family, the community, the organization they work for, and their working teams. Members of individualistic societies gain most of their identity and self-esteem from their own accomplishments, whereas members of collectivistic societies are identified with the groups to which they belong. Individualistic cultures are also characterized by self-reliance and competition, whereas collectivistic cultures are more attentive to and concerned with the opinions of significant others.[39] Individualistic and collectivistic cultures have very different approaches to communication. For example, individualistic cultures are relatively tolerant of conflicts, using a direct, solution-oriented approach. By contrast, members of collectivistic cultures are less direct, often placing a greater emphasis on harmony.[40]

It's easy to see how a culture's individualistic or collectivistic orientation can affect group communication. Members of collectivistic cultures are more likely to be team players, whereas members of individualistic ones are far more likely to produce and reward stars. As members of highly individualistic cultures, Americans and Canadians often need to control their desires to dominate group discussions and to "win" in problem-solving situations. Consensus may be a desirable outcome, but it doesn't always come easily to individualists. By contrast, members of collectivistic cultures need to consider speaking out—even if it means disagreeing—when it is in the best interests of the group.

Power Distance

Some cultures accept differences in power and status, whereas others accept them grudgingly, if at all. Most members of U.S. and Canadian cultures are firm believers in the principle of equality, which means that the notion that some people are entitled to greater power or privilege doesn't come easily. In other cultures, status differences are accepted as a fact of life.[41] **Power distance** refers to the degree to which members are

TABLE 9-4 Cultural Values in Selected Countries

(Countries ranked lower on each list are closer to the mean)	
INDIVIDUALISTIC	**COLLECTIVISTIC**
U.S.A.	Venezuela
Australia	Taiwan
Great Britain	Mexico
Canada	Philippines
LOW POWER DISTANCE	**HIGH POWER DISTANCE**
Israel	Philippines
New Zealand	Mexico
Germany	India
U.S.A.	France
LOW UNCERTAINTY AVOIDANCE	**HIGH UNCERTAINTY AVOIDANCE**
Singapore	Greece
India	Japan
Philippines	Peru
U.S.A.	Mexico
HIGH TASK ORIENTATION	**HIGH SOCIAL ORIENTATION**
Japan	Sweden
Austria	Norway
Italy	Chile
Mexico	Portugal
LONG-TERM FOCUS	**SHORT-TERM FOCUS**
China (includes Hong Kong and Taiwan)	Pakistan
Japan	Canada
South Korea	Great Britain
Brazil	U.S.A.
India	Australia

Source: Based on research summarized in G. Hofstede, *Culture and Organizations: Software of the Mind* (New York: McGraw-Hill, 1997).

willing to accept a difference in power and status between members of a group. In a culture with a high power distance, group members might willingly subordinate themselves to a leader—especially one whose title comes from socially accepted sources such as age, experience, training, or status. By contrast, members of cultures where low power distance is the norm would probably be less likely to feel that groups need a leader, or that people who occupy that role automatically deserve unquestioning obedience. Supervisors, bosses, teachers, and so on certainly have the respect of the members they lead in cultures where low power distance is the norm—but mostly because they earn it. In low power distance cultures, group members expect leaders to be more considerate of their interests and needs. "After all," they assume, "we're basically equal."

Uncertainty Avoidance

Some cultures accept—and even welcome—risk, uncertainty, and change.[42] Others, characterized by **uncertainty avoidance**, are uncomfortable with these unavoidable trends. Instead, they favor stability and tradition. Geography offers no clue to a culture's tolerance of uncertainty. Countries whose members tend to avoid surprises include Greece, Portugal, Turkey, Mexico, and Israel. Among those who are more comfortable with change are Denmark, Hong Kong, Ireland, and India.

It should come as no surprise that uncertainty avoidance affects the way members of groups communicate. People who avoid uncertainty are uncomfortable with ambiguous tasks and reluctant to take risks. They worry more about the future, are more loyal to employers, and accept seniority as the basis for leadership. They view conflict as undesirable and are also less willing to compromise when disagreements arise. By contrast, members of groups who come from cultures with a higher tolerance for uncertainty are more willing to take risks, more accepting of change, and more willing to break rules for pragmatic reasons. They accept conflict as natural and are willing to compromise when disagreements occur.

Task Versus Social Orientation

Groups in societies with a strong task orientation (Japan, Austria, and Switzerland are examples) focus heavily on getting the job done. By contrast, groups in societies with a high degree of social orientation (including the Scandinavian countries, Chile, Portugal, and Thailand) are more likely to be concerned about the feelings of members and their smooth functioning as a team. When compared to other countries, the United States falls slightly toward the task-oriented end of the spectrum, and Canada is almost exactly in the middle, balanced between task and social concerns.[43]

Task-oriented societies are characterized by a focus on making the team more competent through training and the use of up-to-date methods. In task-oriented societies members are highly concerned with individual success: advancing to more responsible jobs, better training, and so on. By contrast, groups in socially oriented societies focus more on collective concerns: cooperative problem solving, a friendly atmosphere, and good physical working conditions. Members may still be interested in solving the problem at hand, but they are reluctant to do so if the personal costs to members—in stress and hard feelings—may be high.

Short- Versus Long-Term Orientation

Members of some cultures look for quick payoffs, whereas members of other cultures are willing to defer gratification in pursuit of long-range goals. The willingness to work hard today for a future payoff is especially common in East Asian cultures, including China, Japan, and South Korea. Western industrialized cultures are much more focused on short-term results.

As long as all group members share the same orientation toward payoffs, the chances for harmony are good. When some people push for a quick fix, while others urge patience, conflicts are likely to arise.

It's easy to see how a society's orientation toward short- or long-term goals, task or social aspects of groups, uncertainty, individuality, and power distance can make a tremendous difference in how a group operates. Whether the group is an athletic team, a military unit, a working group, or a family, the principle is the same. Cultural values shape what groups communicate about and how they interact. Cultural differences don't account for every difference in group functioning, of course, but they do provide a common set of assumptions that exerts a subtle yet powerful effect on communication.

CULTURAL IDIOM

payoffs:
rewards

Leadership and Power in Groups

"What are you, a leader or a follower?" we're asked, and we know which position is the better one. Even in groups without designated leaders, some members are more influential than others, and those who aren't out front at least some of the time are likely to feel frustrated.

The following pages will focus on how communication operates to establish influence. We will begin by looking at sources of power in groups, showing that not all influence rests with the person who is nominally in charge. We will then take a look at the communication behaviors that work best when one communicator is designated as the leader—or wants to acquire that role.

Power in Groups

We can begin by defining **power** as the ability to influence others. A few examples show that influence can appear in many forms.[44]

- In a tense meeting, apartment dwellers are arguing over crowded parking and late-night noise. One tenant cracks a joke and lightens up the tense atmosphere.

- A project team at work is trying to come up with a new way to attract customers. The youngest member, fresh from a college advertising class, suggests a winning idea.

- Workers are upset after the boss passes over a popular colleague and hires a newcomer for a management position. Despite their anger, they accept the decision after the colleague persuades them that she is not interested in a career move anyhow.

- A teacher motivates students to meet a deadline by awarding bonus points for projects that are turned in early and deducting points for ones turned in late.

These examples suggest that power comes in a variety of forms. We will examine each of them now.

Legitimate Power   Sometimes the ability to influence others comes from **legitimate power** (sometimes called *position power*). Legitimate power arises from the title one holds—supervisor, parent, or professor, for example.

Social scientists use the term **nominal leader** to label the person who is officially designated as being in charge of a group. Realize, however, that not all legitimate power resides with nominal leaders. The men and women with orange caps and vests who direct traffic at road repair sites are unlikely to be in charge of the project, yet they possess legitimate power in the eyes of motorists, who stop and start at their command.

Even in groups who begin with no official leader, members can acquire legitimate power by the acknowledgment of others. Juries elect forepersons, and committees elect chairpersons. Teams choose a captain. Negotiating groups elect spokespeople. The subject of leadership emergence has been studied extensively.[45] Researchers have discovered several communicator characteristics that members who emerge as leaders possess: They speak up in group discussions without dominating others, they demonstrate their competence on the subject being discussed, they observe group norms, and they have the support of other influential members.

Coercive Power   **Coercive power** comes from the threat or actual imposition of unpleasant consequences. In school, at home, on the job, and in many other settings we sometimes do what others tell us, not because of respect for the wisdom of their decisions but because the results of not obeying would be unpleasant.

There appears to be a gender difference in the use of coercive power in mediated work groups. Among same-sex groups, men use argumentative, challenging and abusive language most often.[46] In mixed-sex groups, women are more likely than men to drop out of the conversation rather than defend their ideas.[47]

There are three reasons why coercion usually isn't the most effective type of power. First, it's likely to create a negative communication climate, because nobody likes to be threatened. Second, it can produce what has been called a "boomerang effect" in which a member who is threatened with punishment resists by doing exactly what the other members don't want. Third, coercion alone may tell others what *not* to do, but it doesn't tell them what you *do* want them to do. Telling an unproductive member, "If you can't contribute useful information, we'll kick you out of the group" doesn't offer much advice about what would count as "useful information."

Social scientists say that coercion has the best chance of success when it involves denial of an expected reward rather than the imposition of a negative consequence.[48] For example, canceling an upcoming vacation of a working group who doesn't meet its deadline is better than reducing employees' salaries. Even under circumstances like this, however, coercion alone is not as effective as the next kind of power, which involves rewards.

Reward Power   **Reward power** exists when others are influenced by the granting or promise of desirable consequences. Rewards come in a variety of forms. The most obvious are material reinforcers: money, awards, and so on. Other rewards can be social in nature. The praise of someone you respect can be a powerful motivator. Even spending time with people you like can be reinforcing.

Rewards don't come only from the official leader of a group. The goodwill of other members can sometimes be even more valuable. In a class group, for example, having your fellow students think highly of you might be a more powerful reward than the grade you could receive from the instructor. In fact, subordinates sometimes can reward nominal leaders just as much as the other way around. A boss might work hard to accommodate employees in order to keep them happy, for example.

Expert Power   **Expert power** exists when we are influenced by people because of what we believe they know or can do. For example, when a medical emergency occurs, most group members would gladly let a doctor, nurse, or paramedic make decisions because of that person's obvious knowledge. In groups it isn't sufficient to be an expert: The other members have to view you as one. This means that it is important to make your qualifications known if you want others to give your opinions extra weight.

Information Power   As its name implies, **information power** comes from a member's knowledge that he or she can help the group reach its goal. Not all useful information comes from experts with special credentials. For instance, a fundraising group seeking donations from local businesses might profit from the knowledge that one member has about which merchants are hospitable to the group's cause. Likewise, a class group working on a term project might benefit from the knowledge of one student who has taken other classes from the instructor who will be grading their work.

Referent Power   Referent power comes from the respect, liking, and trust others have for a member. If you have high referent power, you may be able to persuade others to follow your lead because they believe in you or because they are willing to do you a favor.

> Members acquire referent power by behaving in ways others in the group admire and by being genuinely likable.

Members acquire referent power by behaving in ways others in the group admire and by being genuinely likable. The kinds of confirming communication behaviors described in Chapter 8 can go a long way toward boosting referent power. Listening to others' ideas, honoring their contributions, and taking a win–win approach to meeting their needs lead to liking and respect.

After our look at various ways members can influence one another, three important characteristics of power in groups become clearer.[49]

- **Power Is Group Centered.** Power isn't something an individual possesses. Instead, it is conferred by the group. You may be an expert on the subject being considered, but if the other members don't think you are qualified to talk, you won't have expert power. You might try to reward other people by praising their contributions, but if they don't value your compliments, then all the praise in the world won't influence them.

- **Power Is Distributed Among Group Members.** Power rarely belongs to just one person. Even when a group has an official leader, other members usually have the power to affect what happens. This influence can be positive, coming from information, expertise, or social reinforcement. It can also be negative, coming from punishing behaviors such as criticizing or withholding the contributions that the group needs to succeed. You can appreciate how power is distributed among members by considering the effect just one member can have by not showing up for meetings or failing to carry out his or her part of the job.

- **Power Isn't an Either-Or Concept.** It's incorrect to assume that power is something that members either possess or lack. Rather, it is a matter of degree. Instead of talking about someone as "powerful" or "powerless," it's more accurate to talk about how much influence he or she exerts.

By now you can see that power is available to every member of a group. Table 9-5 outlines ways of acquiring the various types of power we have just examined.

What Makes Leaders Effective?

Even though power is distributed among members of a group, it is still important to explore the special role played by the nominal leader. In the next few pages we will describe the communication-related factors that contribute to leader effectiveness.

Trait Analysis   Over two thousand years ago, Aristotle proclaimed, "From the hour of their birth some are marked out for subjugation, and others for command."[50] This is a radical expression of **trait theories of leadership**, sometimes labeled as the "great man" (or "great woman") approach. Social scientists began their studies of leader effectiveness by conducting literally hundreds of studies that compared leaders to nonleaders. The results of all this research were mixed. Yet, as Table 9-6 shows, a number of distinguishing characteristics did emerge in several categories.

The majority of these categories involved social skills. For example, leaders talk more often and more fluently and are regarded as more popular, cooperative, and socially skillful.[51] Leaders also possess goal-related skills that help groups perform their tasks. They are somewhat more intelligent, possess more task-relevant information, and are more dependable than other members. Just as important, leaders want the role and act in ways that will help them achieve it. Finally, physical appearance seems to play

TABLE 9-5 Methods for Acquiring Power in Small Groups

Power isn't the only goal to seek in a group. Sometimes being a follower is a comfortable and legitimate role to play. But when you do seek power, the following methods outline specific ways to shape the way others behave and the decisions they make.

LEGITIMATE AUTHORITY

1. Become an authority figure. If possible, get yourself appointed or elected to a position of leadership. Do so by following Steps 2–5.

2. Speak up without dominating others. Power comes from visibility, but don't antagonize others by shutting them out.

3. Demonstrate competence on the subject. Enhance legitimate authority by demonstrating information and expertise power.

4. Follow group norms. Show that you respect the group's customs.

5. Gain support of other members. Don't try to carve out authority on your own. Gain the visible support of other influential members.

INFORMATION POWER

1. Provide useful but scarce or restricted information. Show others that you possess information that isn't available elsewhere.

2. Be certain the information is accurate. One piece of mistaken information can waste the group's time, lead to bad decisions, and destroy your credibility. Check your facts before speaking up.

EXPERT POWER

1. Make sure members are aware of your qualifications. Let others know that you have expertise in the area being discussed.

2. Don't act superior. You will squander your authority if you imply your expertise makes you superior to others. Use your knowledge for the good of the group, not ego building.

REWARD AND COERCIVE POWER

1. Try to use rewards as a first resort and punishment as a last resort. People respond better to pleasant consequences than unpleasant ones, so take a positive approach first.

2. Make rewards and punishments clear in advance. Let people know your expectations and their consequences. Don't surprise them.

3. Be generous with praise. Let others know that you recognize their desirable behavior.

REFERENT POWER

1. Enhance your attractiveness to group members. Do whatever you can to gain the liking and respect of other members without compromising your principles.

2. Learn effective presentation skills. Present your ideas clearly and effectively in order to boost your credibility.

Adapted from J. Dan Rothwell, *In Mixed Company: Small Group Communication*, 3rd ed. (Fort Worth, TX: Harcourt Brace, 1998), pp. 252–272. Reprinted with permission of Wadsworth, an imprint of the Wadsworth Group, a division of Thomson Learning. Fax 800-730-2215.

a role in leadership. As a rule, leaders tend to be slightly taller, heavier, and physically more attractive than other members. They also seem to possess greater athletic ability and stamina.

Despite these general findings, trait theories have limited practical value. Later research has shown that many other factors are important in determining leader success and that not everyone who possesses these traits becomes a leader. Organizational researchers Warren Bennis and Burt Nanus interviewed ninety American leaders, including

TABLE 9-6 Some Traits Associated with Leaders

FACTOR NO.	FACTORS APPEARING IN THREE OR MORE STUDIES	FREQUENCY
1	Social and interpersonal skills	16
2	Technical skills	18
3	Administrative skills	12
4	Leadership effectiveness and achievement	15
5	Social nearness, friendliness	18
6	Intellectual skills	11
7	Maintaining cohesive work group	9
8	Maintaining coordination and teamwork	7
9	Task motivation and application	17
10	General impression	12
11	Group task supportiveness	17
12	Maintaining standards of performance	5
13	Willingness to assume responsibility	10
14	Emotional balance and control	15
15	Informal group control	4
16	Nurturant behavior	4
17	Ethical conduct, personal integrity	10
18	Communication, verbality	6
19	Ascendance, dominance, decisiveness	11
20	Physical energy	6
21	Experience and activity	4
22	Mature, cultured	3
23	Courage, daring	4
24	Aloof, distant	3
25	Creative, independent	5
26	Conforming	5

Reprinted with permission of The Free Press, a division of Macmillan, Inc., from *Stodgill's Handbook of Leadership*, rev. ed., by Bernard M. Bass. Copyright © 1974, 1981 by The Free Press.

Ray Kroc, the founder of McDonald's; professional football coach John Robinson; and John H. Johnson, publisher of *Ebony*. Their analysis led to the conclusion that the principle that "leaders must be charismatic" is a myth.

> Some are, most aren't. Among the ninety there were a few—but damned few—who probably correspond to our fantasies of some "divine inspiration," that "grace under stress" we associated with J.F.K. or the beguiling capacity to spellbind for which we remember Churchill. Our leaders were all "too human"; they were short and tall, articulate and inarticulate, dressed for success and dressed for failure, and there was virtually nothing in terms of physical appearance, personality, or style that set them apart from their followers. Our guess is that it operates in the other direction; that is, charisma is the result of effective leadership, not the other way around, and that those who are good at it are granted a certain amount of respect and even awe by their followers, which increases the bond of attraction between them.[52]

Leadership Style   As researchers began to realize that traits aren't the key to effective leadership, they began to look in other areas. Some scholars theorized that good leadership is a matter of communication style—the way leaders deal with members. Three basic approaches were identified. The first approach was an **authoritarian leadership style** that relied on legitimate, coercive, and reward power to influence others. The second approach was a **democratic leadership style**, which invited other members to share in decision making. The third approach was the **laissez-faire leadership style**, in which the leader gave up the power to dictate, transforming the group into a leaderless collection of equals. Early research suggested that the democratic style produced the highest-quality results,[53] but later research showed that matters weren't so simple.[54] For instance, groups with autocratic leaders proved more productive under stressful conditions, but democratically led groups did better when the situation was nonstressful.[55]

> Groups with autocratic leaders proved more productive under stressful conditions, but democratically led groups did better when the situation was nonstressful.

Research showed that there is some merit to the styles approach. One extensive study of more than twelve thousand managers showed that a democratic approach to leadership correlated highly with success. Effective managers usually sought the advice and opinions of their subordinates, whereas average or unsuccessful ones were more authoritarian and less concerned with the welfare or ideas of the people who reported to them.[56] Despite this fact, a democratic approach isn't always the best one. For example, an autocratic approach gets the job done much more quickly, which can be essential in situations where time is of the essence.

Some researchers have focused on leadership style from a different perspective. Robert R. Blake and Jane S. Mouton developed an approach based on the relationship between the designated leader's concern with the task and with the relationships among members.[57] Their **Leadership Grid** consists of a two-dimensional model pictured in Figure 9-3. The horizontal axis measures the leader's concern for production. This involves a focus on accomplishing the organizational task, with efficiency being the main concern. The vertical axis measures the leader's concern for people's feelings and ideas. Blake and Mouton suggest that the most effective leader is the one who adopts a 9,9 style—showing high concern for both task and relationships.

Situational Approaches   Most contemporary scholars are convinced that the best style of leadership varies from one set of circumstances to another.[58] In an effort to pin down which approach works best in a given situation, psychologist Fred Fiedler attempted to find out when a task-oriented approach was most effective and when a more

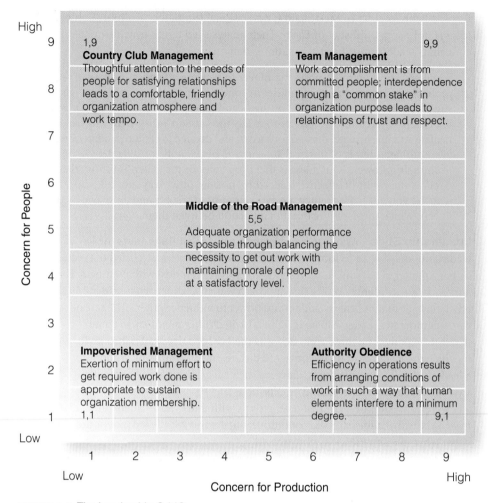

FIGURE 9-3 The Leadership Grid®

Source: The Leadership Grid® Figure from *Leadership Dilemmas–Grid Solutions*, by Robert R. Blake and Anne Adams McCanse (Houston: Gulf Publishing Co.), p. 29. Copyright © 1991 by Scientific Methods, Inc. Reproduced by permission of the owners.

relationship-oriented approach was most effective.[59] From his research, Fiedler developed a situational theory of leadership. Although the complete theory is too complex to describe here, the general conclusion of **situational leadership** is that a leader's style should change with the circumstances. A task-oriented approach works best when conditions are either highly favorable (good leader-member relations, strong leader power, and clear task structure) or highly unfavorable (poor leader-member relations, weak leader power, and an ambiguous task), whereas a more relationship-oriented approach is appropriate in moderately favorable or moderately unfavorable conditions.

> A leader's style should change with the circumstances.

More recently, some social scientists have suggested that a leader's focus on task or relational issues should vary according to the readiness of the group being led (see Figure 9-4).[60] Readiness involves the members' level of motivation, willingness to take responsibility, and the amount of knowledge and experience they have in a given

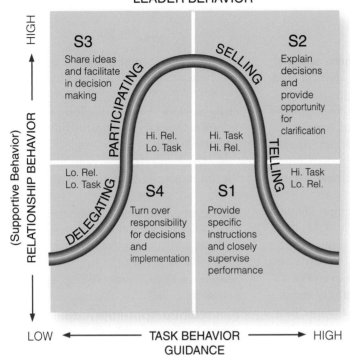

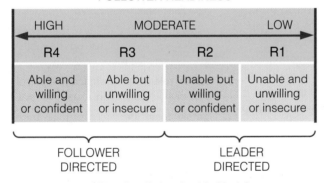

FIGURE 9-4 Hersey and Blanchard's Leadership Model

Source: "Situational Leadership Behavior." From *Management of Organizational Behavior*, 8th edition, © 2001. Adapted/reprinted with permission of Center for Leadership Studies, Escondido, CA 92025. All Rights Reserved.

situation. For example, a new, inexperienced group would need more task-related direction, whereas a more experienced group might require more social support and less instruction about how to do the job. A well-seasoned group could probably handle the job well without much supervision at all. This approach suggests that, because an employee's readiness changes from one job to another, the best way to lead should vary as well.

Summary

Groups play an important role in many areas of our lives—families, education, employment, and friendships, to name a few. Groups possess several characteristics that distinguish them from other communication contexts. They involve interaction and interdependence over time among a small number of participants with the purpose of achieving one or more goals. Groups have their own goals, as do individual members. Member goals fall into two categories: task related and social. Sometimes individual and group goals are compatible, and sometimes they conflict.

Groups can be put into several classifications—learning, growth, problem solving, and social. All these types of groups share certain characteristics: the existence of group norms, individual roles for members, patterns of interaction that are shaped by the group's structure, and the choice of one or more ways of reaching decisions.

Groups don't work in a vacuum. The culture in which they work influences the way members communicate with one another. The chapter examined five ways in which culture influences interaction: individualism versus collectivism, power distance, uncertainty avoidance, task versus social orientation, and short- versus long-term goals.

Many naive observers of groups confuse the concepts of leader and leadership. We defined *leadership* as the ability to influence the behavior of other members through the use of one or more types of power—legitimate, coercive, reward, expert, information, or referent. We saw that many nominal leaders share their power with other members. Leadership has been examined from many perspectives—trait analysis, leadership style, and situational variables.

Key Terms

all-channel network A communication network pattern in which group members are always together and share all information with one another. *p. 281*

CULTURAL IDIOM

work in a vacuum:
function as if there are no other individuals or influences

authoritarian leadership style A leadership style in which the designated leader uses legitimate, coercive, and reward power to dictate the group's actions. *p. 293*

chain network A communication network in which information passes sequentially from one member to another. *p. 282*

coercive power The power to influence others by the threat or imposition of unpleasant consequences. *p. 289*

collectivistic orientation A cultural orientation focusing on loyalties and obligations to the group, which may include the family, the community, the organization, and work teams. *p. 285*

consensus Agreement between group members about a decision. *p. 282*

democratic leadership style A style in which the nominal leader invites the group's participation in decision making. *p. 293*

dysfunctional roles Individual roles played by group members that inhibit the group's effective operation. See also *Functional roles*. *p. 278*

expert power The ability to influence others by virtue of one's perceived expertise on the subject in question. See also *Information power*. *p. 289*

formal role A role assigned to a person by group members or an organization, usually to establish order. *p. 276*

gatekeepers Producers of mass messages, who determine what messages will be delivered to consumers, how those messages will be constructed, and when they will be delivered. *p. 282*

group A small collection of people whose members interact with each other, usually face to face, over time in order to reach goals. *p. 269*

group goals Goals that a group collectively seeks to accomplish. See also *Individual goals*. *p. 271*

hidden agendas Individual goals that group members are unwilling to reveal. *p. 273*

individual goals Individual motives for joining a group. *p. 271*

individualistic orientation A cultural orientation focusing on the value and welfare of individual members, as opposed to a concern for the group as a whole. See also *Collectivistic orientation*. *p. 285*

informal roles Roles usually not explicitly recognized by a group that describe functions of group members, rather than their positions. Sometimes called "functional roles." See also *Formal role. p. 276*

information power The ability to influence others by virtue of the otherwise obscure information one possesses. See also *Expert power. p. 289*

laissez-faire leadership style A style in which the designated leader gives up his or her formal role, transforming the group into a loose collection of individuals. *p. 293*

Leadership Grid A two-dimensional model that identifies leadership styles as a combination of concern for people and the task at hand. *p. 293*

legitimate power The ability to influence a group owing to one's position in a group. See also *Nominal leader. p. 288*

nominal leader The person who is identified by title as the leader of a group. *p. 288*

norms Shared values, beliefs, behaviors, and procedures that govern a group's operation. *p. 274*

power The ability to influence others' thoughts and/or actions. *p. 288*

power distance The degree to which members are willing to accept a difference in power and status between members of a group. *p. 285*

procedural norms Norms that describe rules for the group's operation. *p. 274*

referent power The ability to influence others by virtue of the degree to which one is liked or respected. *p. 290*

reward power The ability to influence others by the granting or promising of desirable consequences. *p. 289*

roles The patterns of behavior expected of group members. *p. 276*

rule Explicit, officially stated guideline that governs group functions and member behavior. *p. 274*

situational leadership A theory that argues that the most effective leadership style varies according to leader-member relations, the nominal leader's power, and the task structure. *p. 294*

social norms Group norms that govern the way members relate to one another. See also *Task norms. p. 274*

social orientation Individual goals that involve affiliation, influence, and esteem of others. *p. 272*

social roles Emotional roles concerned with maintaining smooth personal relationships among group members. Also termed *maintenance functions.* See also *Task functions. p. 278*

sociogram Graphic representation of the interaction patterns in a group. *p. 280*

task norms Group norms that govern the way members handle the job at hand. See also *Social norms. p. 274*

task orientation A cultural orientation that focuses heavily on getting the job done. *p. 272*

task roles Roles group members take on in order to help solve a problem. See also *Social roles. p. 278*

trait theories of leadership The belief that it is possible to identify leaders by personal traits, such as intelligence, appearance, or sociability. *p. 290*

uncertainty avoidance A cultural orientation signified by the degree to which members welcome risk, uncertainty, and change. *p. 286*

virtual groups People who interact with one another via mediated channels, without meeting face-to-face. *p. 271*

wheel network A communication network in which a gatekeeper regulates the flow of information from all other members. *p. 282*

Case Study Questions

Review the case study on pages 264–265 and answer the following questions in light of what you have learned in this chapter.

1. What can you speculate are the individual goals of group members? Which of these goals do you expect members will share, and which might operate as hidden agendas? How might those individual goals help or hinder the group from achieving its goal? What can you do to increase the chances that individual goals don't interfere with the group's goal?

2. What procedural and task norms will help this group be successful? What social norms would interfere with the group's success?

3. Given the group's task, which of the functional roles described on pages 276–278 do you think are most important to the success of your group? What role-related problems might occur if the roles you listed remain unfilled?

4. How might the cultural background of members affect the group's communication?

5. What types of power (described on pages 288–290) can you expect group members to have and use? How could those types of power affect the success of the group, for better or worse?

6. Choose either the styles or situational approach to leadership on pages 293–295 and describe how you would use your chosen style to be an effective leader.

Resources   For many tasks, groups possess a greater collection of resources than do most individuals. Sometimes the resources are physical. For example, three or four people can put up a tent or dig a ditch better than a lone person. Pooled resources can also lead to qualitatively better solutions. Think, for instance, about times when you have studied with other students for a test, and you discussed and learned material you otherwise might have overlooked if not for the group. Groups not only have more resources than individuals, but also through interaction among the members they are better able to mobilize them.

Accuracy   Another benefit of group work is the increased likelihood of catching errors. At one time or another, we all make stupid mistakes, like the man who built a boat in his basement and then wasn't able to get it out the door. Working in a group increases the chance that foolish errors like this won't slip by. Sometimes, of course, mistakes aren't so obvious, which makes groups even more valuable as an error-checking mechanism. Another side to the error-detecting story is the risk that group members will support each other in a bad idea. We'll discuss this problem later in this chapter when we focus on conformity.

Commitment   Besides coming up with superior solutions, groups also generate a higher commitment to carrying them out. Members are most likely to accept solutions they have helped create, and they will work harder to carry out those solutions. This fact has led to the principle of **participative decision making**, in which people contribute to the decisions that will affect them. This is an especially important principle for those in authority, such as supervisors, teachers, and parents. As professors, we have seen the difference between the sullen compliance of students who have been forced to accept a policy with which they disagree and the much more willing cooperation of students when they help develop such a policy.

When to Use Groups for Problem Solving

Despite their advantages, groups aren't always the best way to solve a problem. Many jobs can be tackled more quickly and easily—even more efficiently—by one or more people working independently. Answering the following questions will help you decide when to solve a problem using a group and when to tackle it alone.[5]

Is the Job Beyond the Capacity of One Person?   Some jobs are simply too big for one person to manage. They may call for more information than a single person possesses or can gather. For example, a group of friends planning a large New Year's party will probably have a better event if they pool their ideas than if one person tries to think of everything. Some jobs also require more time and energy than one person can spare.

Putting on the New Year's party could involve a variety of tasks: inviting the guests, hiring a band, finding a place large enough to hold the party, buying food and drinks, and so on. It's both unrealistic and unfair to expect one or two people to do all this work.

Are Individuals' Tasks Interdependent?   Remember that a group is more than a collection of individuals working side by side. The best tasks for groups are ones where the individuals can help one another in some way. Think of a group of disgruntled renters considering how to protest unfair landlords. In order to get anywhere, they realize that they have to assign areas of responsibility to each member: researching the law, getting new members, publicizing their complaints, and so on. It's easy to see that these jobs are all interdependent: Getting new members, for example, will require publicity; and publicizing complaints will involve showing how the renters' legal rights are being violated.

Even when everyone is working on the same job, there can be interdependence if different members fulfill the various functional roles described in Chapter 9. Some people might be better at task-related roles like information giving, diagnosing, and summarizing. Others might contribute by filling social roles such as harmonizing, supporting, or relieving tension. People working independently simply don't have the breadth of resources to fill all these functions.

Is There More Than One Decision or Solution?   Groups are best suited to tackling problems that have no single, cut-and-dried answer: What's the best way to boost membership in a campus organization? How can funds be raised for a charity? What topic should the group choose for a class project? Gaining the perspectives of every member boosts the odds of finding high-quality answers to questions like these.

By contrast, a problem with only one solution won't take full advantage of a group's talents. For example, phoning merchants to get price quotes and looking up a series of books in the library don't require much creative thinking. Jobs like these can be handled by one or two people working alone. Of course, it may take a group meeting to decide how to divide the work to get the job done most efficiently.

> A problem with only one solution won't take full advantage of a group's talents.

Is There Potential for Disagreement?   Tackling a problem as a group is essential if you need the support of everyone involved. Consider a group of friends planning a vacation trip. Letting one or two people choose the destination, schedule, and budget would be asking for trouble, because their decisions would almost certainly disappoint at least some of the people who weren't consulted. It would be far smarter to involve everyone in the most important decisions, even if doing so took more time. After the key decisions were settled, it might be fine to delegate relatively minor issues to one or two people.

Group Problem-Solving Strategies and Formats

Groups meet to solve problems in a variety of settings and for a wide range of reasons. The formats they use are also varied. Some groups meet before an audience to address a problem. The onlookers may be involved in, and affected by, the topic under discussion, like the citizens who attend a typical city council meeting or voters who attend a candidates' debate. In other cases, the audience members are simply interested spectators, as occurs in televised discussions such as *Meet the Press* and *Face the Nation*.

Problem-Solving Formats

This list of problem-solving formats and approaches is not exhaustive, but it provides a sense of how a group's structure can shape its ability to come up with high-quality solutions.

Breakout Groups   When the number of members is too large for effective discussion, **breakout groups** can be used to maximize effective participation. In this approach, subgroups (usually consisting of five to seven members) simultaneously address an issue and then report back to the group at large. The best ideas of each breakout group are then assembled to form a high-quality decision.

CULTURAL IDIOM

cut-and-dried:
the usual thing

boosts the odds of:
increases the chances of success

Problem Census   **Problem census** works especially well when some members are more vocal than others, because it equalizes participation. Members use a separate card to list each of their ideas. The leader collects all cards and reads them to the group one by one, posting each on a board visible to everyone. Because the name of the person who contributed each item isn't listed, issues are separated from personalities. As similar items are read, the leader posts and arranges them in clusters. After all items are read and posted, the leader and members consolidate similar items into a number of ideas that the group needs to address.

Focus Group   **Focus groups** are used as a market research tool to enable sponsoring organizations to learn how potential users or the public at large regards a new product or idea. Unlike other groups discussed here, focus groups don't include decision makers or other members who claim any expertise on a subject. Instead, their comments are used by decision makers to figure out how people in the wider world might react to ideas.

Parliamentary Procedure   Problem-solving meetings can follow a variety of formats. A session that uses **parliamentary procedure** observes specific rules about how topics may be discussed and decisions made. The standard reference book for parliamentary procedure is the revised edition of *Robert's Rules of Order*. Although the parliamentary rules may seem stilted and cumbersome, when well used, they do keep a discussion on track and protect the rights of the minority against domination by the majority.

Panel Discussion   Another common problem-solving format is the **panel discussion**, in which the participants talk over the topic informally, much as they would in an ordinary conversation. A leader (called a "moderator," in public discussions) may help the discussion along by encouraging the comments of some members, cutting off overly talkative ones, and seeking consensus when the time comes for making a decision.

TABLE 10-1   Some Communication Factors Associated with Group Productivity

The group contains the smallest number of members necessary to accomplish its goals.

Members care about and agree with the group's goals.

Members are clear about and accept their roles, which match the abilities of each member.

Group norms encourage high performance, quality, success, and innovation.

The group members have sufficient time together to develop a mature working unit and accomplish its goals.

The group is highly cohesive and cooperative.

The group spends time defining and discussing problems it must solve and decisions it must make.

Periods of conflict are frequent but brief, and the group has effective strategies for dealing with conflict.

The group has an open communication structure in which all members may participate.

The group gets, gives, and uses feedback about its effectiveness.

Adapted from research summarized in S. A. Wheelan, D. Murphy, E. Tsumaura, and S. F. Kline, "Member Perceptions of Internal Group Dynamics and Productivity." *Small Group Research* 29 (1998): 371–393.

Symposium   In a **symposium** the participants divide the topic in a manner that allows each member to deliver in-depth information without interruption. Although this format lends itself to good explanations of each person's decision, the one-person-at-a-time nature of a symposium won't lead to a group decision. The contributions of the members must be followed by the give-and-take of an open discussion.

CULTURAL IDIOM
the give-and-take:
sharing

Forum   A **forum** allows nonmembers to add their opinions to the group's deliberations before the group makes a decision. This approach is commonly used by public agencies to encourage the participation of citizens in the decisions that affect them.

Solving Problems in Virtual Groups

Over more than two decades, researchers have investigated the advantages and disadvantages of computer-mediated meetings as compared to face-to-face interaction.[7] Studies suggest that computer conferencing does have several advantages. Most obviously, it's much easier to schedule and meet online, because members don't need to travel any farther than their computers. Asynchronous meetings are especially convenient, because group members can log on at their convenience, independent of other participants. Furthermore, computer-mediated sessions encourage more balanced participation: Members who might have kept quiet in face-to-face sessions are more comfortable "speaking out" online. Also, online meetings generate a permanent record of the proceedings, which can be convenient.

Despite their advantages, computer-mediated groups aren't a panacea. The lack of nonverbal cues makes it difficult to convey and understand members' emotions and attitudes. Mediated meetings may be more convenient, but groups working at a distance take more time to reach decisions than those who meet face-to-face. Because typing

---

@Work

Setting Up a Virtual Group

Setting up communication for a virtual group is easy. For multiway telephone conference calls, ask your phone company for instructions. For computer-mediated interaction, services like Google Groups (http://www.groups.google.com) provide a surprising array of free services that let you create and host your own virtual team. In any of over forty languages, you and your groupmates can exchange messages in real time or asynchronously, collaborate on shared files, link to web pages, vote and poll one another, and schedule events and reminders on a group calendar.

Here are a few guidelines to help make your virtual group most effective:[6]

1. Seek input from all team members. Despite the leveling effect of communicating online, some members of virtual groups may hold back from participating. Make sure to solicit information and opinions from quiet members.

2. Strive for "face time," especially during the group's formation. Virtual teams are most cohesive, trusting, and successful when members have had a chance to spend time together in person, especially during the group's development.

3. Be mindful of time zone differences. When members of a virtual team are dispersed across time zones, it's especially important to schedule meetings so no members are inconvenienced.

4. Consider using "back channels." Use telephone, personal e-mail, and instant messaging to confer directly with one or more team members when you need to deal with issues and relationships personally in a way that will save the group time and effort.

5. Double check the technology. Make sure in advance of meetings that all the technology on which your team relies is working. It can be frustrating and discouraging to waste meeting time dealing with glitches.

takes more time and effort than speaking, messages conveyed via computer can lack the detail of spoken ones. In some cases, members may not even bother to type out a message online that they would have shared in person. Finally, the string of separate messages that is generated in a computerized medium can be hard to track, sort out, and synthesize in a meaningful way.

Research comparing the quality of decisions made by face-to-face and online groups is mixed. Some studies have found no significant differences. Others have found that computer-mediated groups generate more ideas than people meeting in person, although they take longer to reach agreement on which are best.[8] The growing body of research suggests that certain types of mediated communication work better than others. For example, asynchronous groups seem to make better decisions than those functioning in a "chat" mode.[9] Groups who have special decision-support software perform better than ones operating without this advantage.[10] Having a moderator also improves the effectiveness of online groups.[11]

What use does this information have for groups who want to decide how to meet? Perhaps the most valuable lesson is that online meetings should not replace face-to-face ones, but they can be a *supplement* to in-person sessions. Combining the two forms of interaction can help groups operate both efficiently and effectively.[12]

Approaches and Stages in Problem Solving

Groups may have the potential to solve problems effectively, but they don't always live up to this potential. What makes some groups succeed and others fail? Researchers spent much of the twentieth century asking this question. Two useful answers emerged from their work.

A Structured Problem-Solving Approach

Although we often pride ourselves on facing problems rationally, social scientists have discovered that logic and reason usually play little part in the way we make decisions.[13] The tendency to use nonrational approaches is unfortunate, because research shows that, to a great degree, a group's effectiveness is determined by whether or not it approaches a problem rationally and systematically.[14] Just as a poor blueprint or a shaky foundation can weaken a house, groups can fail by skipping one or more of the necessary steps in solving a problem.

> A structured procedure produces better results than "no pattern" discussions.

As early as 1910, John Dewey introduced his famous "reflective thinking" method as a systematic approach to solving problems.[15] Since then, other experts have suggested modifications of Dewey's approach. Some emphasize answering key questions, whereas others seek "ideal solutions" that meet the needs of all members. Research comparing various methods has clearly shown that, although no single approach is best for all situations, a structured procedure produces better results than "no pattern" discussions.[16]

The following problem-solving model contains the elements common to most structured approaches developed in the last century:

1. Identify the problem
   a. Determine the group's goals
   b. Determine individual members' goals

2. Analyze the problem
   a. Word the problem as a broad, open question
   b. Identify criteria for success
   c. Gather relevant information
   d. Identify supporting and restraining forces

3. Develop creative solutions through brainstorming or the nominal group technique
   a. Avoid criticism at this stage
   b. Encourage "freewheeling" ideas
   c. Develop a large number of ideas
   d. Combine two or more individual ideas

4. Evaluate the solutions by asking which solution:
   a. will best produce the desired changes
   b. is most achievable
   c. contains the fewest serious disadvantages

5. Implement the plan
   a. Identify specific tasks
   b. Determine necessary resources
   c. Define individual responsibilities
   d. Provide for emergencies

6. Follow up on the solution
   a. Meet to evaluate progress
   b. Revise approach as necessary

CULTURAL IDIOM

freewheeling:
unrestricted thinking

dire straits:
extremely difficult situation

Identify the Problem   Sometimes a group's problem is easy to identify. The crew of a sinking ship, for example, doesn't need to conduct a discussion to understand that its goal is to avoid drowning or being eaten by a large fish.

There are many times, however, when the problems facing a group aren't so clear. As an example, think of an athletic team stuck deep in last place well into the season. At first the problem seems obvious: an inability to win any games. But a closer look at the situation might show that there are unmet goals—and thus other problems. For instance, individual members may have goals that aren't tied directly to winning: making friends, receiving acknowledgment as good athletes, not to mention the simple goal of having fun—of playing in the recreational sense of the word. You can probably see that if the coach or team members took a simplistic view of the situation, looking only at the team's win–loss record, player errors, training methods, and so on, some important problems would probably go overlooked. In this situation, the team's performance could probably be best improved by working on the basic problems—the frustration of the players about having their personal needs unmet. What's the moral here? That the way to start understanding a group's problem is to identify the concerns of each member.

What about groups who don't have problems? Several friends planning a surprise birthday party and a family deciding where to go for its vacation don't seem to be in the dire straits of a losing athletic team: They simply want to have fun. In cases like these, it may be helpful to substitute the word *challenge* for the more gloomy word *problem*. However we express it, the same principle applies to all task-oriented groups: The best

B.C.

Source: By permission of John L. Hart and Creators Syndicate, Inc.

place to start work is to identify what each member seeks as a result of belonging to the group.

Analyze the Problem   After you have identified the general nature of the problem facing the group, you are ready to look at the problem in more detail. There are several steps you can follow to accomplish this important job.

Word the Problem as a Broad, Open Question   If you have ever seen a formal debate, you know that the issue under discussion is worded as a proposition: "The United States should reduce its foreign aid expenditures," for example. Many problem-solving groups define their task in much the same way. "We ought to spend our vacation in the mountains," suggests one family member. The problem with phrasing problems as propositions is that such wording invites people to take sides. Though this approach is fine for formal debates (which are contests rather like football or card games), premature side taking creates unnecessary conflict in most problem-solving groups.

> State the problem as an open question that encourages exploratory thinking.

A far better approach is to state the problem as an open question that encourages exploratory thinking. Asking "Should we vacation in the mountains or at the beach?" still forces members to choose sides. A far better approach involves asking a question to help define the general goals that came out during the problem-identification stage: "What do we want our vacation to accomplish?" (that is, "relaxation," "adventure," "low cost," and so on).

Notice that this question is truly exploratory. It encourages the family members to work cooperatively, not forcing them to make a choice and then defend it. This absence of an either-or situation boosts the odds that members will listen openly to one another rather than listening selectively in defense of their own positions. There is even a chance that the cooperative, exploratory climate that comes from wording the question most broadly will help the family arrive at consensus about where to vacation, eliminating the need to discuss the matter any further.

Identify Criteria for Success   Phrasing the challenge as an open-ended question will help the group identify the criteria for a successful solution. Imagine that a neighborhood task force asks the question "How can we create a safer environment?" Developing an answer calls for clarifying what would count as the desired outcome. Fewer incidents reported to police? Less graffiti? More people on the street at night? Knowing what members want puts a group on the road to achieving its goal.

Gather Relevant Information   Groups often need to know important facts before they can make decisions or even understand the problem. We remember one group of students who determined to do well on a class presentation. One of their goals, then, was "to get an A grade." They knew that, to do so, they would have to present a topic that interested both the instructor and the students in the audience. Their first job, then, was to do a bit of background research to find out what subjects would be well received. They interviewed the instructor, asking what topics had been successes and failures in previous semesters. They tested some possible subjects on a few classmates and noted their reactions. From this research they were able to modify their original question—"How can we choose and develop a topic that will earn us an A grade?"—into a more specific one—"How can we choose and develop a topic that contains humor, action, and lots of information (to demonstrate our research skills to the instructor) and that contains practical information that will improve the audience's social life, academic standing, or financial condition?"

CULTURAL IDIOM

damper on:
something that reduces or restricts

Identify Supporting and Restraining Forces   After members understand what they are seeking, the next step is to see what forces stand between the group and its goals. One useful tool for this approach is the **force field analysis**—a list of the forces that help and hinder the group.[17] By returning to our earlier example of the troubled team, we can see how the force field operates. Suppose the team defined its problem-question as "How can we (1) have more fun and (2) grow closer as friends?"

One restraining force in Area 1 was clearly the team's losing record. But, more interestingly, discussion revealed that another damper on enjoyment came from the coach's obsession with winning and his infectiously gloomy behavior when the team failed. The main restraining force in Area 2 proved to be the lack of socializing among team members in nongame situations. The helping forces in Area 1 included the sense of humor possessed by several members and the confession by most players that winning wasn't nearly as important to them as everyone had suspected. The helping force in Area 2 was the desire of all team members to become better friends. In addition, the fact that members shared many interests was an important plus.

> It's important to realize that most problems have many impelling and restraining forces.

It's important to realize that most problems have many impelling and restraining forces, all of which need to be identified during this stage. This may call for another round of research. After the force field is laid out, the group is ready to move on to the next step—namely, deciding how to strengthen the impelling forces and weaken the restraining ones.

Develop Creative Solutions   After the group has set up a list of criteria for success, the next job is to develop a number of ways to reach its goal. Considering more than one solution is important, because the first solution may not be the best one. During this development stage, creativity is essential.[18] The biggest danger is the tendency of members to defend their own idea and criticize others'. This kind of behavior leads to two problems. First, evaluative criticism almost guarantees a defensive reaction from members whose ideas have been attacked. Second, evaluative criticism stifles creativity. People who have just heard an idea rebuked—however politely—will find it hard even to think of more alternatives, let alone share them openly and risk possible criticism. The following strategies can keep groups creative and maintain a positive climate.

Brainstorm   Probably the best-known strategy for encouraging creativity and avoiding the dangers just described is **brainstorming**.[19] There are four important rules connected with this strategy:

1. *Criticism Is Forbidden.* As we have already said, nothing will stop the flow of ideas more quickly than negative evaluation.
2. *"Freewheeling" Is Encouraged.* Sometimes even the most outlandish ideas prove workable, and even an impractical suggestion might trigger a workable idea.

3. *Quantity Is Sought.* The more ideas generated, the better the chance of coming up with a good one.

4. *Combination and Improvement Are Desirable.* Members are encouraged to "piggyback" by modifying ideas already suggested and to combine previous suggestions.

Although brainstorming is a popular creativity booster, it isn't a guaranteed strategy for developing novel and high-quality ideas. In some experiments, individuals working alone were able to come up with a greater number of high-quality ideas than were small groups.[20] Nevertheless, brainstorming can help a group tap its creative potential.

Use the Nominal Group Technique   Because people in groups often can't resist the tendency to criticize one another's ideas, the **nominal group technique** was developed to let members brainstorm ideas without being attacked. As the following steps show, the pattern involves alternating cycles of individual work followed by discussion.

1. Each member works alone to develop a list of possible solutions.

2. In round-robin fashion, each member in turn offers one item from his or her list. The item is listed on a chart visible to everyone. Other members may ask questions to clarify an idea, but no evaluation is allowed during this step.

3. Each member privately ranks his or her choice of the ideas in order, from most preferable (five points) to least preferable (one point). The rankings are collected, and the top ideas are retained as the most promising solutions.

4. A free discussion of the top ideas is held. At this point critical thinking (though not personal criticism) is encouraged. The group continues to discuss until a decision is reached, either by majority vote or consensus.

Evaluate Possible Solutions   After it has listed possible solutions, the group can evaluate the usefulness of each. One good way of identifying the most workable solutions is to ask three questions.

1. *Will This Proposal Produce the Desired Changes?* One way to find out is to see whether it successfully overcomes the restraining forces in your force field analysis.

2. *Can the Proposal Be Implemented by the Group?* Can the members strengthen supporting forces and weaken restraining ones? Can they influence others to do so? If not, the plan isn't a good one.

3. *Does the Proposal Contain Any Serious Disadvantages?* Sometimes the cost of achieving a goal is too great. For example, one way to raise money for a group is to rob a bank. Although this plan might be workable, it causes more problems than it solves.

Implement the Plan   Everyone who makes New Year's resolutions knows the difference between making a decision and carrying it out. There are several important steps in developing and implementing a plan of action.

1. *Identify Specific Tasks to Be Accomplished.* What needs to be done? Even a relatively simple job usually involves several steps. Now is the time to anticipate all the tasks facing the group. Remember everything now, and you will avoid a last-minute rush later.

2. *Determine Necessary Resources.* Identify the equipment, material, and other resources the group will need in order to get the job done.

3. *Define Individual Responsibilities.* Who will do what? Do all the members know their jobs? The safest plan here is to put everyone's duties in writing, including the due date. This might sound compulsive, but experience shows that it increases the chance of having jobs done on time.

4. *Provide for Emergencies.* Murphy's Law states, "Whatever can go wrong, will." Anyone experienced in group work knows the truth of this law. People forget or welsh on their obligations, get sick, or quit. Machinery breaks down. (One corollary of Murphy's Law is "The copying machine will be out of order whenever it's most needed.") Whenever possible, you ought to develop contingency plans to cover foreseeable problems. Probably the single best suggestion we can give here is to plan on having all work done well ahead of the deadline, knowing that, even with last-minute problems, your time cushion will allow you to finish on time.

CULTURAL IDIOM

welsh on:
fail to fulfill

time cushion:
extra time allowance

Follow Up on the Solution   Even the best plans usually require some modifications after they're put into practice. You can improve the group's effectiveness and minimize disappointment by following two steps.

1. *Meet Periodically to Evaluate Progress.* Follow-up meetings should be part of virtually every good plan. The best time to schedule these meetings is as you put the group's plan to work. At that time, a good leader or member will suggest: "Let's get together in a week (or a few days or a month, depending on the nature of the task). We can see how things are going and take care of any problems."

2. *Revise the Group's Approach as Necessary.* These follow-up meetings will often go beyond simply congratulating everyone for coming up with a good solution. Problems are bound to arise, and these periodic meetings, in which the key players are present, are the place to solve them.

Although these steps provide a useful outline for solving problems, they are most valuable as a general set of guidelines and not as a precise formula that every group should follow. As Table 10-2 suggests, certain parts of the model may need emphasis depending on the nature of the specific problem; the general approach will give virtually any group a useful way to consider and solve a problem.

Despite its advantages, the rational, systematic problem-solving approach isn't perfect. The old computer saying "Garbage in, garbage out" applies here: If the group doesn't possess creative talent, a rational and systematic approach to solving problems won't do much good. Despite this, the rational approach does increase the odds that a group can solve problems successfully. Following the guidelines—even imperfectly— will help members analyze the problem, come up with solutions, and carry them out better than they could without a plan.

TABLE 10-2 Adapting Problem-Solving Methods to Special Circumstances

CIRCUMSTANCES	METHOD
Members have strong feelings about the problem.	Consider allowing a period of emotional ventilation before systematic problem solving.
Task difficulty is high.	Follow the structure of the problem-solving method carefully.
Many possible solutions.	Emphasize brainstorming.
High level of member acceptance required.	Carefully define needs of all members, and seek solutions that satisfy all needs.
High level of technical quality required.	Emphasize evaluation of ideas; consider inviting outside experts.

Source: Adapted from "Adapting Problem-Solving Methods," *Effective Group Discussion*, 10th ed., John Brilhart and Gloria Galanes, p. 291. Copyright © 2001. Reprinted by permission of McGraw-Hill Companies, Inc.

CULTURAL IDIOM

sizing up:
assessing

Developmental Stages in Problem-Solving Groups

When it comes to solving problems in groups, research shows that the shortest distance to a solution isn't always a straight line. Communication scholar Aubrey Fisher analyzed tape recordings of problem-solving groups and discovered that many successful groups seem to follow a four-stage process when arriving at a decision.[21] As you read about his findings, visualize how they have applied to problem-solving groups in your experience.

In the **orientation stage**, members approach the problem and one another tentatively. In some groups people may not know one another well, and even in ones where they are well acquainted they may not know one another's position on the issue at hand. For these reasons, people are reluctant to take a stand during the orientation stage. Rather than state their own position clearly and unambiguously, they test out possible ideas cautiously and rather politely. There is little disagreement. This cautiousness doesn't mean that members agree with one another; rather, they are sizing up the situation before asserting themselves. The orientation stage can be viewed as a calm before the storm.

After members understand the problem and become acquainted, a successful group enters the **conflict stage**. During this stage, members take strong positions and defend them against those who oppose their viewpoint. Coalitions are likely to form, and the discussion may become polarized. The conflict needn't be personal: It can focus on the issues at hand while preserving the members' respect for one another. Even when the climate does grow contentious, conflict seems to be a necessary stage in group development. The give-and-take of discussion tests the quality of ideas, and weaker ones may suffer a well-deserved death here.[22]

> Conflict seems to be a necessary stage in group development.

After a period of conflict, effective groups move to an **emergence stage**. One idea might emerge as the best one, or the group might combine the best parts of several plans into a new solution. As they approach consensus, members back off from their dogmatic positions. Statements become more tentative again: "I guess that's a pretty good idea," "I can see why you think that way."

Finally, an effective group reaches the **reinforcement stage**. At this point not only do members accept the group's decision, they also endorse it. Whereas members used evidence to back up differing positions in the conflict stage, now they find evidence that will support the decision. Even if members disagree with the outcome, they do not voice their concerns. There is an unspoken drive toward consensus and harmony.

Ongoing groups can expect to move through this four-stage process with each new issue, so that their interaction takes on a cyclic pattern (see Figure 10-1). In fact, a group who deals with several issues at once might find itself in a different stage for each problem. In one series of studies, nearly 50 percent of the problem-solving groups examined followed this pattern.[23] The same research showed that a smaller percentage of groups (about 30 percent) didn't follow a cyclical pattern. Instead, they skipped the preliminary phases and focused on the solution.

What is the significance of the findings? They tell us that, like children growing toward adulthood, many groups can expect to pass through phases. Knowing that these phases are natural and predictable can be reassuring. It can help curb your impatience when the group is feeling its way through an orientation stage. It can also help you feel less threatened when the inevitable and necessary conflicts take place. Understanding the nature of emergence and reinforcement can help you know when it is time to stop arguing and seek consensus.

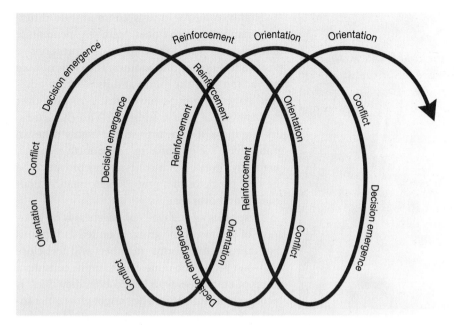

FIGURE 10-1 Cyclical Stages in an Ongoing Problem-Solving Group. *Source:* From John K. Brilhart, Gloria J. Galanes, and Katherine Adams, *Effective Group Discussion*, 10th ed. (New York: McGraw-Hill, 2001), p. 289.

Maintaining Positive Relationships

The task-related advice in the preceding pages will be little help if the members of a group don't get along. We therefore need to look at some ways to maintain good relationships among members. Many of the principles described earlier in this book apply here. Because these principles are so important, we will review them here.

Basic Skills

Groups are most effective when members feel good about one another.[24] Probably the most important ingredient in good personal relationships is mutual respect, and the best way to demonstrate respect for the other person is to listen carefully. A more natural tendency, of course, is to assume you understand the other members' positions and to interrupt or ignore them. Even if you are right, however, this tendency can create a residue of ill feelings. On the other hand, careful listening can at least improve the communication climate—and you may even learn something from your groupmates.

Groups are bound to disagree sooner or later. When they do, the win–win problem-solving methods outlined in Chapter 8 boost the odds of solving the immediate issue in the most constructive way.[25] As you read in Chapter 9, taking votes and letting the majority rule can often leave a sizable minority whose unhappiness can haunt the group's future work. Consensus is harder to reach in the short term but far more beneficial in the long term.

Building Cohesiveness

Cohesiveness can be defined as the degree to which members feel connected with and committed to their group. You might think of cohesiveness as the glue that bonds individuals together, giving them a collective sense of identity.

CULTURAL IDIOM
boost the odds of:
increase the chances of success

Highly cohesive groups communicate differently than less cohesive ones. Members spend more time interacting, and there are more expressions of positive feelings for one another. They report more satisfaction with the group and its work. In addition, cohesive groups have greater control over the behavior of their members.[26] With characteristics like these, it's no surprise that highly cohesive groups have the potential to be productive. In fact, one study revealed that cohesiveness proved to be the best predictor of a group's performance, both initially and over time.[27]

Despite its advantages, cohesiveness is no guarantee of success: If the group is united in supporting unproductive norms, members will feel close but won't get the job done. For example, consider a group of employees who have a boss they think is incompetent and unfair. They might grow quite cohesive in their opposition to the perceived tyranny, spending hours after (or during) work swapping complaints. They might even organize protests, work slowdowns, grievances to their union, or mass resignations. All these responses would boost cohesiveness, but they would not necessarily make the company more successful nor help the employees.

Research has disclosed a curvilinear relationship between cohesiveness and productivity: Up to a certain point, productivity increases as group members become a unified team. Beyond this point, however, the mutual attraction members feel for one another begins to interfere with the group's efficient functioning. Members may enjoy one another's company, but this enjoyment can keep them from focusing on the job at hand.

The goal, then, is to boost cohesiveness in a way that also helps get the job done. There are eight factors that can bring about these goals.

1. **Shared or Compatible Goals** People draw closer when they share a similar aim or when their goals can be mutually satisfied. For example, members of a conservation group might have little in common until a part of the countryside they all value is threatened by development. Some members might value the land because of its beauty; others, because it provides a place to hunt or fish; and still others, because the nearby scenery increases the value of their property, but as long as their goals are compatible, this collection of individuals will find that a bond exists that draws them together.

2. **Progress Toward Goals** While a group is making progress, members feel highly cohesive; when progress stops, cohesiveness decreases. All other things being equal, players on an athletic team feel closest when the team is winning. During extended losing streaks, it is likely that players will feel less positive about the team and less willing to identify themselves as members of the group.

3. **Shared Norms and Values** Although successful groups will tolerate and even thrive on some differences in members' attitudes and behavior, wide variation in the group's definition of what actions or beliefs are proper will reduce cohesiveness. If enough members hold different ideas of what behavior is acceptable, the group is

likely to break up. Disagreements over values or norms can fall into many areas, such as humor, finance, degree of candor, and proportion of time allotted to work and play.

CULTURAL IDIOM
bickering:
quarreling

4. **Lack of Perceived Threat Between Members** Cohesive group members see no threat to their status, dignity, and material or emotional well-being. When such interpersonal threats do occur, they can be very destructive. Often competition arises within groups, and as a result members feel threatened. Sometimes there is a struggle over who will be the nominal leader. At other times, members view others as wanting to take over a functional role (problem solver, information giver, and so on), either through competition or criticism. Sometimes the threat is real, and sometimes it's only imagined, but in either case the group must neutralize it or face the consequences of reduced cohesiveness.

5. **Interdependence of Members** Groups become cohesive when their needs can be satisfied only with the help of other members. When a job can be done just as well by one person alone, the need for membership decreases. This factor explains the reason for food cooperatives, neighborhood yard sales, and community political campaigns. All these activities enable the participants to reach their goal more successfully than if they acted alone.

6. **Threat from Outside the Group** When members perceive a threat to the group's existence or image (groups have self-concepts, just as individuals do), they grow closer together. Almost everyone knows of a family whose members seem to fight constantly among themselves—until an outsider criticizes one of them. At this point, the internal bickering stops, and for the moment the group unites against its common enemy. The same principle often works on a larger scale when nations bind up their internal differences in the face of external aggression.

7. **Mutual Attraction and Friendship** This factor is somewhat circular because friendship and mutual attraction often are a result of the points just listed, yet groups often do become close simply because the members like each other. Social groups are a good example of a type of group that stays together because its members enjoy one another's company.

8. **Shared Group Experiences** When members have been through some unusual or trying experience, they draw together. This explains why soldiers who have been in combat together often feel close and stay in touch for years after; it also accounts for the ordeal of fraternity pledging and other initiations. Many societies have rituals that all members share, thus increasing the group's cohesiveness.

Critical Thinking Probe

The Pros and Cons of Cohesiveness

1. Based on the information on pages 315–317 of this chapter and your own experiences, give examples of groups who meet each of the following descriptions:
   a. A level of cohesiveness so low that it interferes with productivity
   b. An optimal level of cohesiveness
   c. A level of cohesiveness so high that it interferes with productivity
2. For your answers to a and c, offer advice on how the level of cohesiveness could be adjusted to improve productivity.
3. Are there ever situations where maximizing cohesiveness is more important than maximizing productivity? Explain your answer, supporting it with examples.

Overcoming Dangers in Group Discussion

Even groups with the best of intentions often find themselves unable to reach satisfying decisions. At other times, they make decisions that later prove to be wrong. Though there's no foolproof method of guaranteeing high-quality group work, there are several dangers to avoid.

Information Underload and Overload

Information underload occurs when a group lacks information necessary to operate effectively. Sometimes the underload results from overlooking parts of a problem. We know of one group who scheduled a fund-raising auction without considering what other events might attract potential donors. They later found that their event was scheduled opposite an important football game, resulting in a loss of sorely needed funds. In other cases, groups suffer from underload because they simply don't conduct enough research. For example, a group of partners starting a new business has to be aware of all the startup costs to avoid going bankrupt in the first months of operation. Overlooking one or two important items can make the difference between success and failure.

Sometimes groups can suffer from too much information. **Information overload** occurs when the rate or complexity of material is too great to manage. Having an abundance of information might seem like a blessing, but anyone who has tried to do conscientious library research has become aware of the paralysis that can result from being overwhelmed by an avalanche of books, magazine and newspaper articles, reviews, films, and research studies. When too much information exists, it is hard to sort out the essential from the unessential information. Group expert J. Dan Rothwell offers several tips for coping with information overload.[28] First, specialize whenever possible. Try to parcel out areas of responsibility instead of expecting each member to explore every angle of the topic. Second, be selective: Take a quick look at each piece of information to see whether it has real value for your task. If it doesn't, move on to examine more promising material. Third, limit your search. Information specialists have discovered that there is often a curvilinear relationship between the amount of information a group possesses and the quality of its decision. After a certain point, gathering more material can slow you down without contributing to the quality of your group's decisions.

> After a certain point, gathering more material can slow you down without contributing to the quality of your group's decisions.

Unequal Participation

The value of involving group members in making decisions—especially decisions that affect them—is great.[29] When people participate, their loyalty to the group increases. (Your own experience will probably show that most group dropouts were quiet and withdrawn.) Broad-based participation has a second advantage: It increases the amount of resources focused on the problem. As a result, the quality of the group's decisions goes up. Finally, participation increases members' loyalty to the decisions that they played a part in making.

The key to effective participation is balance. Domination by a few vocal members can reduce a group's ability to solve a problem effectively. Research shows that the proposal receiving the largest number of favorable comments is usually the one chosen even if it isn't the best one.[30] Furthermore, ideas of high-status members (who aren't always talkers) are given more consideration than those of lower-status members.[31] The moral to this story? Don't assume that quantity of speech or the status of the speaker automatically defines the quality of an idea. Instead, seek out and seriously consider the ideas of quieter members.

Not all participation is helpful, of course. It's better to remain quiet than to act out the dysfunctional roles described in Chapter 9—cynic, aggressor, dominator, and so on. Likewise, the comments of a member who is uninformed can waste time. Finally, downright ignorant or mistaken input can distract a group.

Source: © Original Artist. Reproduction rights obtainable from www.CartoonStock.com

You can encourage the useful contributions of quiet members in a variety of ways. First, keep the group small. In groups with three or four members, participation is roughly equal, but after size increases to between five and eight, there is a dramatic gap between the contributions of members.[32] Even in a large group you can increase the contributions of quiet members by soliciting their opinions. This approach may seem obvious, but in their enthusiasm to speak out, more verbal communicators can overlook the people who don't speak up. When normally reticent members do offer information, reinforce their contributions. It isn't necessary to go overboard by gushing about a quiet person's brilliant remark, but a word of thanks and an acknowledgment of the value of an idea increase the odds that the contributor will speak up again in the future. Another strategy is to assign specific tasks to normally quiet members. The need to report on these tasks guarantees that they will speak up. A final strategy is to use the nominal group technique, described in Chapter 9, to guarantee that the ideas of all members are heard.

Different strategies can help when the problem is one or more members talking too much—especially when their remarks aren't helpful. If the talkative member is at all sensitive, withholding reinforcement can deliver a diplomatic hint that it may be time to listen more and speak less. A lack of response to an idea or suggestion can work as a hint to cut back on speaking. Don't confuse lack of reinforcement with punishment, however: Attacking a member for dominating the group is likely to trigger a defensive reaction and cause more harm than good. If the talkative member doesn't respond to subtle hints, politely expressing a desire to hear from other members can be effective. The next stage in this series of escalating strategies for dealing with dominating members is to question the relevancy of remarks that are apparently off the wall: "I'm confused about what last Saturday's party has to do with the job we have to do today. Am I missing something?"

CULTURAL IDIOM

to go overboard:
to do so much as to be excessive

gushing about:
being overly enthusiastic

off the wall:
unconventional, ridiculous

Balancing participation in group discussions can involve stifling some members and urging others to speak up when they would prefer to be silent. Explore the ethical justification for these actions by answering the following questions.

1. Are there any circumstances when it is legitimate to place quiet group members in the position of speaking up when they would rather remain quiet? When does it become unreasonable to urge quiet members to participate?

2. Does discouraging talkative members ever violate the principles of free speech and tolerance for others' opinions? Describe when it is and is not appropriate to limit a member's contributions.

After developing your ethical guidelines, consider how willing you would feel if they were applied to you.

CULTURAL IDIOM

rock the boat:
disturb a stable condition

Pressure to Conform

There's a strong tendency for group members to go along with the crowd, which often results in bad decisions. A classic study by Solomon Asch illustrated this point. College students were shown three lines of different lengths and asked to identify which of them matched a fourth line. Although the correct answer was obvious, the experiment was a setup: Asch had instructed all but one member of the experimental groups to vote for the wrong line. As a result, fully one-third of the uninformed subjects ignored their own good judgment and voted with the majority. If simple tasks like this one generate such conformity, it is easy to see that following the (sometimes mistaken) crowd is even more likely in the much more complex and ambiguous tasks that most groups face.

Even when there's no overt pressure to follow the majority, more subtle influences motivate members—especially in highly cohesive groups—to keep quiet rather than voice any thoughts that deviate from what appears to be the consensus. "Why rock the boat if I'm the only dissenter?" members think. "And if everybody else feels the same way, they're probably right."

With no dissent, the group begins to take on a feeling of invulnerability: an unquestioning belief that its ideas are correct and even morally right. As its position solidifies, outsiders who disagree can be viewed as the enemy, disloyal to what is obviously the only legitimate viewpoint. Social scientists use the term **groupthink** to describe a group's collective striving for unanimity that discourages realistic appraisals of alternatives to its chosen decision.[33] Groupthink has led to a number of disasters, including the United States' botched Bay of Pigs invasion of Cuba in the 1960s, the *Challenger* space shuttle disaster in 1986, and the corporate culture that led to the downfall of energy giant Enron in 2001.

Several group practices can discourage this troublesome force.[34] A first step is to recognize the problem of groupthink as it begins to manifest itself. If agreement comes quickly and easily, the group may be avoiding the tough but necessary search for alternatives. Beyond vigilance, a second step to discourage groupthink is to

THE FAR SIDE®   BY GARY LARSON

Laboratory peer pressure

minimize status differences. If the group has a nominal leader, he or she must be careful not to use various types of power that come with the position to intimidate members. A third step involves developing a group norm that legitimizes disagreement. After members recognize that questioning one another's positions doesn't signal personal animosity or disloyalty, a constructive exchange of ideas can lead to top-quality solutions. Sometimes it can be helpful to designate a person or subgroup as "devil's advocate" who reminds the others about the dangers of groupthink and challenges the trend toward consensus.

CULTURAL IDIOM

devil's advocate:
one who argues against a widely held view in order to clarify issues

Summary

Despite the bad reputation of groups in some quarters, research shows that they are often the most effective setting for problem solving. They command greater resources, both quantitatively and qualitatively, than do either individuals or collections of people working in isolation; their work can result in greater accuracy; and the participative nature of the solutions they produce generates greater commitment from members.

Groups aren't always the best forum for solving problems. They should be used when the problem is beyond the capacity of one person to solve, when tasks are interdependent, when there is more than one desired solution or decision, and when the agreement of all members is essential.

Groups use a wide variety of discussion formats when solving problems. Some use parliamentary procedure to govern decision-making procedures. Others use moderated panel discussions, symposia, or forums. The best format depends on the nature of the problem and the characteristics of the group.

Since face-to-face meetings can be time-consuming and difficult to arrange, computer-mediated communication can be a good alternative for some group tasks. Some group work can be handled via computer or teleconferencing, where members communicate in real time over digital networks. Other tasks can be handled via asynchronous discussions, in which members exchange messages at their convenience. Mediated meetings provide a record of discussion and they can make it easier for normally quiet members to participate, but they can take more time and they lack the nonverbal richness of face-to-face conversation. Given the pros and cons of mediated meetings, smart communicators should give thoughtful consideration about when to use this approach.

Groups stand the best chance of developing effective solutions to problems if they begin their work by identifying the problem, avoiding the mistake of failing to recognize the hidden needs of individual members. Their next step is to analyze the problem, including identification of forces both favoring and blocking progress. Only at this point should the group begin to develop possible solutions, taking care not to stifle creativity by evaluating any of them prematurely. During the implementation phase of the solution, the group should monitor the situation carefully and make any necessary changes in its plan.

Most groups can expect to move through several stages as they solve a problem. The first of these stages is orientation, during which the members get an initial sense of one another's positions. The conflict stage is characterized by partisanship and open debate over the merits of contending ideas. In the emergence stage, the group begins to move toward choosing a single solution. In the reinforcement stage, members endorse the group's decision.

Groups who pay attention only to the task dimension of their interaction risk strains in the relationships among members. Many of these interpersonal problems can be avoided by using the skills described in Chapter 8 as well as by following the guidelines in this chapter for building group cohesiveness and encouraging participation.

Smart members will avoid some common dangers that threaten a group's effectiveness. They will make sure to get the information they need, without succumbing to overload. They will make sure that participation is equal by encouraging the contributions of quiet members and keeping more talkative people on track. They will guard against groupthink by minimizing pressure on members to conform for the sake of harmony or approval.

After studying the material in this chapter . . .

YOU SHOULD UNDERSTAND:

1. The importance of defining a clear speech purpose.
2. The differences among a general purpose, a specific purpose, and a thesis.
3. The necessity of analyzing a speaking situation.
4. The difference between facilitative and debilitative stage fright.
5. The reasons for debilitative stage fright.
6. The differences among the various types of speech delivery.
7. The visual and auditory aspects of delivery.

YOU SHOULD BE ABLE TO:

1. Choose an effective speaking topic.
2. Formulate a purpose statement and thesis statement that will help you develop that topic.
3. Analyze both the audience and occasion in any speaking situation.
4. Gather information on your chosen topic from a variety of sources.
5. Overcome debilitative stage fright.
6. Choose the most effective type of delivery for a particular speech.

CULTURAL IDIOM

toast:
the speech given before a drink to honor someone

Even if you never took a course in which speech giving was required, you would almost certainly face the challenge of giving a speech at some point. It might be a job-related presentation, or something more personal, such as the wedding toast or a eulogy for a lost friend. You might improve the world as you appeal for a civic-improvement project in your hometown or try to persuade listeners to deal more effectively with global problems like war, religious strife, or environmental threats.

Despite the potential benefits of effective speeches, many people view the prospect of standing before an audience with the same enthusiasm they have for a trip to the dentist or the tax auditor. In fact, giving a speech seems to be one of the most anxiety-producing things we can do: *The Book of Lists* claims that Americans fear public speaking more than they do insects, heights, accidents, and even death.[1]

There's no guarantee that the following chapters will make you love the idea of giving speeches, but we can promise that the information these chapters contain will give you the tools to design and deliver remarks that will be clear, interesting, and effective. And it's very likely that, as your skill grows, your confidence will too. This chapter will deal with your first steps in that process, through careful speech planning.

Getting Started

Your first tasks are generally choosing a topic, determining your purpose, and finding information.

Choosing Your Topic

The first question many student speakers face is "What should I talk about?" When you need to choose a topic, you should try to pick one that is right for you, your audience, and the situation. You should try to choose a topic that interests you, and you should try to decide on your topic as early as possible. Those who wait until the last possible moment usually find that they don't have enough time to complete the speech and practice it.

Defining Your Purpose

No one gives a speech—or expresses *any* kind of message—without having a reason to do so. Your first step in focusing your speech is to formulate a clear and precise statement of that purpose.

Writing a Purpose Statement

Your **purpose statement** should be expressed in the form of a complete sentence that describes exactly what you want your speech to accomplish. It should include your **general purpose**, which might be to inform, persuade, or entertain. Beyond that, though, there are three criteria for an effective purpose statement:

1. **A Purpose Statement Should Be Result-Oriented.** Having a *result orientation* means that your purpose is focused on the outcome you want to accomplish with your audience members. For example, if you were giving an informative talk on the high cost of college, this would be an inadequate purpose statement:

   My purpose is to tell my audience about high college costs.

   As that statement is worded, your purpose is "to tell" an audience something, which suggests that the speech could be successful even if no one listened! A result-oriented purpose statement should refer to the response you want from your audience: It should tell what the audience members will know or be able to do after listening to your speech.

2. **A Purpose Statement Should Be Specific.** To be effective, a purpose statement should be worded specifically, with enough details so that you would be able to measure or test your audience, after your speech, to see if you had achieved your purpose. In the example given earlier, simply "knowing about high college costs" is too vague; you need something more specific, such as:

   After listening to my speech, my audience will be able to reduce college costs.

   This is an improvement, but it can be made still better by applying a third criterion:

3. **A Purpose Statement Should Be Realistic.** It's fine to be ambitious, but you need to design a purpose that has a reasonable chance of success. You can appreciate the importance of having a realistic goal by looking at some unrealistic ones, such as "My purpose is to convince my audience to make federal budget deficits illegal." Unless your audience happens to be a joint session of Congress, it won't have the power to change U.S. fiscal policy. But any audience can write its congressional representatives or sign a petition. In your speech on college costs, it would be impossible for your audience members to change the entire structure of college financing. So a better purpose statement for this speech might sound something like this:

   After listening to my speech, my audience will be able to list four simple steps to lower their college expenses.

Consider the following sets of purpose statements:

LESS EFFECTIVE	MORE EFFECTIVE
To talk about professional wrestling (not receiver-oriented)	After listening to my speech, my audience will understand that kids who imitate professional wrestlers can be seriously hurt.
To tell my audience about textbook prices (not specific)	After my speech, the audience will be able to list five ways to save money on textbooks.

You probably won't include your purpose statement word-for-word in your actual speech. Rather than being aimed at your listeners, a specific purpose statement usually is a tool to keep you focused on your goal as you plan your speech.

Stating Your Thesis

After you have defined the purpose, you are ready to start planning what is arguably the most important sentence in your entire speech. The **thesis statement** tells your listeners the central idea of your speech. It is the one idea that you want your audience to remember after it has forgotten everything else you had to say. The thesis statement for a speech about winning in small claims court might be worded like this:

Arguing a case on your own in small claims court is a simple, five-step process that can give you the same results you would achieve with a lawyer.

> The thesis statement tells your listeners the central idea of your speech.

Unlike your purpose statement, your thesis statement is almost always delivered directly to your audience. The thesis statement is usually formulated later in the speech-making process, after you have done some research on your topic. The progression from topic to purpose to thesis is, therefore, another focusing process, as you can see in the following example:

Topic: Organ donation

Specific Purpose: After listening to my speech, audience members will recognize the importance of organ donation and will sign an organ donor's card for themselves.

Thesis: Because not enough of us choose to become organ donors, thousands of us needlessly die every year. You can help prevent this needless dying.

Analyzing the Speaking Situation

There are two components to analyze in any speaking situation: the audience and the occasion. To be successful, every choice you make in putting together your speech—your purpose, topic, and all the material you use to develop your speech—must be appropriate to both of these components.

The Listener: Audience Analysis

Audience analysis involves identifying and adapting your remarks to the most pertinent characteristics of your listeners.

Audience Purpose   Just as you have a purpose for speaking, audience members have a reason for gathering. Sometimes virtually all the members of your audience will have the same, obvious goal. Expectant parents at a natural childbirth class are all seeking a healthy delivery, and people attending an investment seminar are looking for ways to increase their net worth.

There are other times, however, when audience purpose can't be so easily defined. In some instances, different listeners will have different goals, some of which might not be apparent to the speaker. Consider a church congregation, for example. Whereas most members might listen to a sermon with the hope of applying religious principles to their lives, a few might be interested in being entertained or in merely appearing pious. In the same way, the listeners in your speech class probably have a variety of motives for attending. Becoming aware of as many of these motives as possible will help you predict what will interest them. Observing audience demographics helps you make that prediction.

Demographics   **Demographics** are characteristics of your audience that can be categorized, such as cultural differences, age, gender, group membership, number of people, and so on. Demographic characteristics might affect your speech planning in a number of ways.[2] For example:

"I'll tell you what this election is about. It's about homework, and pitiful allowances, and having to clean your room. It's also about candy, and ice cream, and staying up late."

Source: The New Yorker. ALL RIGHTS RESERVED.
http://www.cartoonbank.com

1. **Cultural Diversity.** Do audience members differ in terms of race, religion, or national origin? The guideline here might be *Do not exclude or offend any portion of your audience on the basis of cultural differences.* If there is a dominant cultural group represented, you might decide to speak to it, but remember that the point is to analyze, not stereotype, your audience. If you talk down to any segment of your listeners, you have probably stereotyped them.

2. **Gender.** While masculine and feminine stereotypes are declining, it is still important to think about how gender can affect the way you choose and approach a topic. Every speech teacher has a horror story about a student getting up in front of a class composed primarily, but not entirely, of men and speaking on a subject such as "Picking Up Babes."

3. **Age.** Our interests vary and change with our age. These differences may run relatively deep; our approach to literature, films, finance, health, and long-term success may change dramatically over just a few years, perhaps from graphic novels to serious literature, from punk to classical music, or from hip-hop to epic poetry.

4. **Group Membership.** Groups generally form around shared interests among the members. By examining the groups to which they belong, you can surmise audience members' political leanings (Young Republicans, College Democrats, Campus Reform Party), religious beliefs (CYO, Hillel, or Muslim Students' Association), or occupation (Bartenders Union or National Communication Association). Group membership is often an important consideration in college classes. Consider the difference between a "typical" college day class and one that meets in the evening. At many colleges the evening students are generally older and tend to belong to civic groups, church clubs, and the local chamber of commerce. Daytime students are more likely to belong to sororities and fraternities, sports clubs, and social action groups.

CULTURAL IDIOM
talk down to:
speak in a condescending way
"Picking Up Babes":
offensive term for making the acquaintance of women or girls with sexual purposes in mind

CULTURAL IDIOM
stuffy:
impersonal, not relating to the
audience

5. **Number of People.** Topic appropriateness varies with the size of an audience. With a small audience you can be less formal and more intimate—you can, for example, talk more about your own inner feelings and personal experiences. If you gave a speech before five people as impersonally as if they were a standing-room-only crowd in a lecture hall, they would probably find you stuffy. On the other hand, if you talked to three hundred people about your unhappy childhood, you'd probably make them uncomfortable.

You have to decide which demographics of your audience are important for a particular speech. For example, when Syrena Rexroat, a student at Northwood University in Michigan, gave a speech on how boys fall behind in elementary and secondary education, she knew gender was an important demographic. She adapted to her female audience members in this way:

> Before we go any further with this issue we must understand that this is not an issue of attacking a girl's education or women in general. This is about analyzing our education system, recognizing where there are flaws, and then doing what we need to do as a country to fix them.[3]

These five demographic characteristics are important examples, but the list goes on. Other demographic characteristics that might be important in a college classroom include:

- educational level
- economic status
- hometown
- year in school
- major subject
- ethnic background

A final factor to consider in audience analysis concerns members' attitudes, beliefs, and values.

Ethical Challenge

Adapting to Speaking Situations

How much adaptation is ethical? How far would you go to be effective with an audience? Try the following exercise with your classmates.

1. Prepare, in advance, three index cards: one with a possible topic for a speech, one with a possible audience, and one with a possible occasion.
2. Form groups of four members each. Mark the back of each card with "A" for "audience," "T" for "topic," or "O" for "occasion," and turn the cards face down.
3. Take one card from each of the other members.
4. Turn the cards over. For each set, decide which characteristics of the audience, topic, and occasion would most likely affect the way the speech was developed.
5. Discuss the adaptation that would be necessary in each situation and the role ethics would play in determining how far you would go.

Attitudes, Beliefs, and Values   Audience members' feelings about you, your subject, and your intentions for them are central issues in audience analysis. One way to approach these issues is through a consideration of attitudes, beliefs, and values.[4] Attitudes, beliefs, and values reside in human consciousness like layers of an onion. **Attitudes** lie closest to the surface. They reflect a predisposition to view you or your topic in a favorable or unfavorable way. **Beliefs** lie a little deeper, and deal with the truth of something. **Values** are deeply rooted feelings about a concept's inherent worth or worthiness. You can begin to appreciate the usefulness of these concepts by considering an example. Suppose you were a dentist trying to persuade a group of patients to floss their teeth more often. Consider how audience analysis would help you design the most promising approach:

Attitudes. How do your listeners feel about the importance of dental hygiene? If they recognize its importance, you can proceed confidently, knowing they'll probably want to hear what you have to say. On the other hand, if they are vaguely disgusted by even thinking about the topic, you will need to begin by making them want to listen.

Beliefs. Does your audience accept the relationship between regular flossing and dental health? Or do you need to inform them about the consequences of neglecting this daily ritual?

Values. Which underlying values matter most to your listeners: Health? Attractiveness? Career success? The approach you'll use will depend on the answer to these questions.

Figure 11-1 shows the relationship among attitudes, beliefs, and values. Experts in audience analysis, such as professional speechwriters, often try to concentrate on values. As one team of researchers pointed out, "Values have the advantage of being comparatively small in number, and owing to their abstract nature, are more likely to be shared by large numbers of people."[5] Stable American values include the ideas of good citizenship, the work ethic, tolerance of political views, individualism, and justice for all. Kashif Powell, a student at Morehouse College, appealed to his audience's values when he wanted to make the point that the diamond industry often funds terrorists:

> Attitudes, beliefs, and values reside in human consciousness like layers of an onion.

> We as a nation and as an international community invest in gems and jewels whose production costs individuals their lives. . . . And we do this to show we care. There is something fundamentally wrong with this picture.[6]

Kashif pointed out that one value—saving lives—was more important than another—giving someone a diamond to prove that you love them. You can often make an inference about audience members' attitudes by recognizing the beliefs and values they are likely to hold. In this example, Kashif knew that his audience valued human life, which would lead to a belief that people ought to do what they can to save lives, which would lead to the attitude that personal actions to help in this regard, even if indirect, are the proper thing to do.

The analysis of hidden psychological states can be extremely helpful in audience analysis. For example, a group of religious fundamentalists might hold the value of "obeying God's word." This might lead to the belief—based on their religious training—that women are not meant to perform the same functions in society as men. This, in turn, might lead to the attitude that women ought not to pursue careers as firefighters, police officers, or construction workers.

You can also make a judgment about one attitude your audience members hold based on your knowledge of other attitudes they hold. If your audience is made up of undergraduates who have a positive

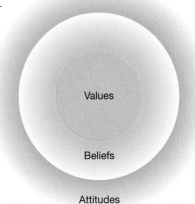

FIGURE 11-1 Structure of Values, Beliefs, and Attitudes

attitude toward liberation movements, it is a good bet they also have a positive attitude toward civil rights and ecology. If they have a negative attitude toward collegiate sports, they may also have a negative attitude toward fraternities and sororities. This should not only suggest some appropriate topics for each audience but should also suggest ways that those topics could be developed.

Critical Thinking Probe

Attitudes, Beliefs, and Values

Find a persuasive appeal in an advertisement, newspaper editorial, or another source. Identify an attitude, belief, or value that the source of the message is appealing to. Explain why you have identified the appeal the way you have (i.e., why it is an attitude or belief rather than a value, etc.). Explain why, in your opinion, this appeal is or is not effective.

The Occasion

The second phase in analyzing a speaking situation focuses on the occasion. The occasion of a speech is determined by the circumstances surrounding it. Three of these circumstances are time, place, and audience expectations.

Time   Your speech occupies an interval of time that is surrounded by other events. For example, other speeches might be presented before or after yours, or comments might be made that set a certain tone or mood. External events such as elections, the start of a new semester, or even the weather can color the occasion in one way or the other. The date on which you give your speech might have some historical significance. If that historical significance relates in some way to your topic, you can use it to help build audience interest.

> Your speech occupies an interval of time that is surrounded by other events.

The time available for your speech is also an essential consideration. You should choose a topic that is broad enough to say something worthwhile but brief enough to fit your limits. "Wealth," for example, might be an inherently interesting topic to some college students, but it would be difficult to cover such a broad topic in a ten-minute speech and still say anything significant. However, a topic like "How to Make Extra Money in Your Spare Time" could conceivably be covered in ten minutes in enough depth to make it worthwhile. All speeches have limits, whether they are explicitly stated or not. If you are invited to say a few words, and you present a few volumes, you might not be invited back.

Place   Your speech also occupies a physical space. The beauty or squalor of your surroundings and the noise or stuffiness of the room should all be taken into consideration. These physical surroundings can be referred to in your speech if appropriate. If you were talking about world poverty, for example, you could compare your surroundings to those that might be found in a poorer country.

Audience Expectations   Finally, your speech is surrounded by audience expectations. A speech presented in a college class, for example, is usually expected to reflect a high level of thought and intelligence. This doesn't necessarily mean that it has to be boring or humorless; wit and humor are, after all, indicative of intelligence. But it does mean that you have to put a little more effort into your presentation than if you were discussing the same subject with friends over coffee.

@Work

Sample Analysis of a Speaking Situation

Audience: Employees in the Production Department of my company

Situation: Training session on sexual harassment

Management has realized that our company is at risk of being slapped with a harassment lawsuit. The most likely offenders are several "good old boys" who have worked in the Production Department a long time. They are really nice guys, and I know they view their jokes and comments as good-natured fun and not harassment. On the other hand, several female employees have complained about being offended by these men.

One of my duties as an intern in the Human Resources Department of my company is to share the latest information on sexual harassment with employees. My bosses know that this topic has been covered in my classes, and they decided I should pass it along.

Purpose: After I am finished speaking, I want audience members to view sexual harassment as a legitimate concern and to be careful to avoid communicating in a way that might be perceived as harassing.

Analysis: This is a tricky situation for me: First of all, these guys will be a captive audience, forced to listen to a subject that they find annoying. Also, I am younger than anyone in my audience, and I'm a woman. In fact, I've been the target of some of the behavior I'm being asked to discourage! There's a strong risk that the men who are the target of my remarks won't take me seriously, so I have to change their attitude about the subject and me.

I know that scolding and threatening these men would be a big mistake. Even if they didn't object out loud, they would probably regard me as some sort of chip-on-the-shoulder feminist and consider the advice I offered as "politically correct" and out of touch with the way the real world operates.

To avoid this sort of negative reaction, I need to separate myself from the law that they dislike, taking the position of sharing with them "here's what I've learned about how it works." I might even give them a few examples of harassment suits that I think were frivolous, so we can agree that some people are much too sensitive. That common ground will help put us on the same side. Then I can emphasize that they don't have to agree with the law to follow it. I'll tell stories of people like them who suffered as targets of harassment suits, pointing out that even an unfair accusation of harassment could make all of our lives miserable. My basic argument will be that potentially harassing behavior "isn't worth it."

I also hope to use my age and gender as advantages. A couple of the men have told me that they have daughters my age. I could ask the group to imagine how they would feel if their daughters were the targets of suggestive comments and sexual jokes. I'll tell them that I know how angry and protective my dad would feel, and I'll tell them that I know that, as good fathers, they'd feel the same way. I could also ask them to think about how they would feel if their wives, sisters, or mothers were the targets of jokes that made those women feel uncomfortable.

I don't think any speech will totally reverse attitudes that were built over these men's lifetimes, but I do think that getting on their side will be much more effective than labeling them as insensitive sexist pigs and threatening them with lawsuits.

When you are considering the occasion of your speech, it pays to remember that every occasion is unique. Although there are obvious differences among the occasions of a college class, a church sermon, and a bachelor party "roast," there are also many subtle differences that will apply only to the circumstances of each unique event.

Gathering Information

This discussion about planning a speech purpose and analyzing the speech situation makes it apparent that it takes time, interest, and knowledge to develop a topic well. Setting aside a block of time to reflect on your own ideas is essential. However, you will also need to gather information from outside sources.

By this time you are probably familiar with both Web searches and library research as forms of gathering information. Sometimes, however, speakers overlook interviewing, personal observation, and survey research as equally effective methods of gathering information. Let's review all these methods here and perhaps provide a new perspective on one or more of them.

CULTURAL IDIOM

bachelor party:
a men-only gathering of the groom and his friends just prior to his wedding

roast:
an entertaining program where the guest of honor is teased in an affectionate manner

Web Research

The ease of search engines like Google and Yahoo has made them the popular favorite for speech research. But students are sometimes so grateful for finding a website dealing with their topic that they forget to evaluate it. Like any other written sources you would use, the website should be accurate and rational. Beyond that, there are three specific criteria that you can use to evaluate the quality of a website:

1. **Credibility.** Anyone can establish a website, so it is important to evaluate where your information is coming from. Who wrote the page? Anonymous sources should not be used. If the sources *are* listed, are their credentials listed? What institution publishes the document? Remember that a handsome site design doesn't guarantee high-quality information, but misspellings and grammatical mistakes are good signs of low quality.

2. **Objectivity.** What opinions (if any) are expressed by the author? The domain names .edu, .gov, .org, or .net are generally preferable to .com because if the page is a mask for advertising, the information might be biased.

3. **Currency.** When was the page produced? When was it updated? How up-to-date are the links? If any of the links are dead, the information might not be current.

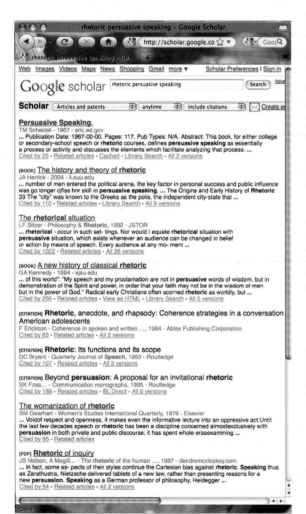

For some special search engines, like Google Scholar, the criteria of credibility, objectivity, and currency will be practically guaranteed. However, these guidelines are especially important when accessing information from Wikipedia, the popular online encyclopedia. Because anyone can edit a Wikipedia article at any time, many professors forbid the use of it as a primary resource. Others allow Wikipedia to be used for general information and inspiration. Most will allow its use when articles have references to external sources (whether online or not) and the student reads the references and checks whether they really do support what the article says.

However you use the Web, remember that it is a good addition to, but *not* a substitute for, library research. Library experts help you make sense of and determine the validity of the information you find. And a library can be a great environment for concentration, a place of quiet with minimum distractions that is rare in our media age.

Library Research

Libraries, like people, tend to be unique. Although many of your library's resources will be available online through your school's website, it can be extremely rewarding to get to know your library in person, to see what kind of special collections and services it offers, and just to find out where everything is. There are, however, a few resources that are common to most libraries, including the library catalog, reference works, periodicals, nonprint materials, and databases.

The Library Catalog　The library catalog is an ancient and noble information-storing device. Once housed in long rows of oak drawers, today's catalogs are computerized, but they remain your key to all the books and other materials in the library. Each work is filed according to subject, author, and title, so you can look for general topics as well as for specific books and authors.

Reference Works   Reference works will also be listed in the library catalog. There are wonders there that could turn you into an information maven for life. There are encyclopedias galore, even specialized ones such as *The Historical Dictionary of American Slang* and *The Encyclopedia of American History*; there are statistical compilations such as *The World Almanac, Facts on File*, and *The Guinness Book of World Records*; you can find out *Who's Who in America* or even *Who Was Who*. You can collect a lot of facts in a short time in the reference room. Reference works are good for uncovering basic information, definitions, descriptions, and sources for further investigation.

Periodicals   Magazines, journals, and newspapers are good resources for finding recently published material on interesting topics. Specialized indexes such as *Psychological Abstracts* can be used to find articles in specific fields, and newspaper indexes such as *The New York Times Index* can be used to find online newspaper articles. Periodicals are a good source of high-interest, up-to-date information on your topic.

Nonprint Materials   Most libraries are also treasuries of nonprint and audiovisual materials. Films, records, tapes, and videotapes can be used not only as research tools but also as aids during your presentation. Your library probably has an orientation program that will acquaint you with what it has to offer in the way of nonprint materials.

Databases   Libraries have access to databases that are not available to home users without hefty subscription fees. **Databases** are computerized collections of highly credible information from a wide variety of sources. One popular collection of databases is Lexis-Nexis, which contains millions of articles from news services, magazines, scholarly journals, conference papers, books, law journals, and other sources. Other popular databases include ProQuest, Factiva, and Academic Search Premier, and there are dozens of specialized databases, such as Communication and Mass Media Complete.

Database searches are slightly different from Web searches; they generally don't respond well to long strings of terms or searches worded as questions. With databases it is best to use one or two key terms with a connector such as AND, OR, or NOT.[7] Once you learn this technique and a few other rules (perhaps with a librarian's help), you will be able to locate dozens of citations on your topic in just a few minutes. After you have located the items you want, you can read or print out abstracts or whole articles.

> Libraries have access to databases that are not available to home users without hefty subscription fees.

Interviewing

The information-gathering interview allows you to view your topic from an expert's perspective, to take advantage of that expert's experience, research, and thought. You can also use an interview to stimulate your own thinking. Often the interview will save you hours of Internet or library research and allow you to present ideas that you could not have uncovered any other way. And because the interview is an interaction with an expert, many ideas that otherwise might be unclear can become more understandable through questions and answers. Interviews can be conducted face-to-face, by telephone, or by e-mail. If you do use an interview for research, you might want to read the section on that type of interview in the Appendix.

Survey Research

One advantage of **survey research**—the distribution of questionnaires for people to respond to—is that it can give you up-to-date answers concerning "the way things are" for a specific audience. For example, if you handed out questionnaires a week or so before presenting a speech on the possible dangers of body piercing, you could present information like this in your speech:

> *According to a survey I conducted last week, 90 percent of the students in this class believe that body piercing is basically safe. Only 10 percent are familiar with the scarring and injury that can result from this practice. Two of you, in fact, have experienced serious infections from body piercing: one from a pierced tongue and one from a simple pierced ear.*

That statement would be of immediate interest to your audience members because *they* were the ones who were surveyed. Another advantage of conducting your own survey is that it is one of the best ways to find out about your audience: It is, in fact, *the* best way to collect the demographic data mentioned earlier. The one disadvantage of conducting your own survey is that, if it is used as evidence, it might not have as much credibility as published evidence found in the library. But the advantages seem to outweigh the disadvantages of survey research in public speaking.

> Remember that it is the quality rather than the quantity of the research that is most important.

No matter how you gather your information, remember that it is the *quality* rather than the quantity of the research that is most important. The key is to determine carefully what type of research will answer the questions you need to have answered. Sometimes only one type of research will be necessary; at other times every type mentioned here will have to be used.

The preliminary tasks of analyzing the audience and gathering information are a great help in minimizing the anxiety of actually giving a speech. We'll look at that form of anxiety more closely now.

Managing Communication Apprehension

The terror that strikes the hearts of so many beginning speakers is commonly known as *stage fright* or *speech anxiety* and is called *communication apprehension* by communication scholars.[8] Whatever term you choose, the important point to realize is that fear about speaking can be managed in a way that works for you rather than against you.

Facilitative and Debilitative Communication Apprehension

Although communication apprehension is a very real problem for many speakers, it is definitely a problem that can be overcome. Interestingly enough, the first step in feeling less apprehensive about speaking is to realize that a certain amount of nervousness is not only natural but also facilitative. That is, **facilitative communication apprehension** is a factor that can help improve your performance. Just as totally relaxed actors or musicians aren't likely to perform at the top of their potential, speakers think more rapidly and express themselves more energetically when their level of tension is moderate.

It is only when the level of anxiety is intense that it becomes **debilitative**, inhibiting effective self-expression. Intense fear causes trouble in two ways. First, the strong emotion keeps you from thinking clearly.[9] This has been shown to be a problem even in the preparation process: Students who are highly anxious about giving a speech will find the preliminary steps, including research and organization, to be more difficult.[10]

Second, intense fear leads to an urge to do something, anything, to make the problem go away. This urge to escape often causes a speaker to speed up delivery, which results in a rapid, almost machine-gun style. As you can imagine, this boost in speaking rate leads to even more mistakes, which only add to the speaker's anxiety. Thus, a relatively small amount of nervousness can begin to feed on itself until it grows into a serious problem.

Sources of Debilitative Communication Apprehension

Before we describe how to manage debilitative communication apprehension, let's consider why people are afflicted with the problem in the first place.[11]

Previous Negative Experience   People often feel apprehensive about speech giving because of unpleasant past experiences. Most of us are uncomfortable doing *anything* in public, especially if it is a form of performance in which our talents and abilities are being evaluated. An unpleasant experience in one type of performance can cause you to expect that a future similar situation will also be unpleasant.[12] These expectations can be realized through the self-fulfilling prophecies discussed in Chapter 3. A traumatic failure at an earlier speech and low self-esteem from critical parents during childhood are common examples of experiences that can cause later communication apprehension.

You might object to the idea that past experiences cause communication apprehension. After all, not everyone who has bungled a speech or had critical parents is debilitated in the future. To understand why some people are affected more strongly than others by past experiences, we need to consider another cause of communication apprehension.

Irrational Thinking   Cognitive psychologists argue that it is not events that cause people to feel nervous but rather the beliefs they have about those events. Certain irrational beliefs leave people feeling unnecessarily apprehensive. Psychologist Albert Ellis lists several such beliefs, or examples of **irrational thinking**, which we will call "fallacies" because of their illogical nature.[13]

1. **Catastrophic failure.** People who succumb to the **fallacy of catastrophic failure** operate on the assumption that if something bad can happen, it probably will. Their thoughts before a speech resemble these:

   "As soon as I stand up to speak, I'll forget everything I wanted to say."

   "Everyone will think my ideas are stupid."

   "Somebody will probably laugh at me."

   Although it is naive to imagine that all your speeches will be totally successful, it is equally naive to assume they will all fail miserably. One way to escape the fallacy of catastrophic failure is to take a more realistic look at the situation. Would your audience members really hoot you off the stage? Will they really think your ideas are stupid? Even if you did forget your remarks for a moment, would the results be a genuine disaster? It helps to remember that nervousness is more apparent to the speaker than to the audience.[14] Beginning public speakers, when congratulated for their poise during a speech, are apt to say, "Are you kidding? I was dying up there."

2. **Perfection.** Speakers who succumb to the **fallacy of perfection** expect themselves to behave flawlessly. Whereas such a standard of perfection might serve as a target and a source of inspiration (like the desire to make a hole in one while golfing), it is totally unrealistic to expect that you will write and deliver a perfect speech—especially as a beginner. It helps to remember that audiences don't expect you to be perfect.

Audiences don't expect you to be perfect.

CULTURAL IDIOM

flashy:
showy, gaudy

Practicing the Speech

A smooth and natural delivery is the result of extensive practice. Get to know your material until you feel comfortable with your presentation. One way to do that is to go through some or all of the following steps:

1. First, present the speech to yourself. "Talk through" the entire speech, including your examples and forms of support. Don't skip through parts of your speech as you practice by saying "This is where I present my statistics" or "This is where I explain about photosynthesis." Make sure you know how you plan to present your statistics and explanations.

2. Tape-record the speech, and listen to it. Because we hear our own voices partially through our cranial bone structure, we are sometimes surprised at what we sound like to others. Videotaping has been proven to be an especially effective tool for rehearsals, giving you an idea of what you look like, as well as sound like.[17]

3. Present the speech in front of a small group of friends or relatives.[18]

4. Present the speech to at least one listener in the room in which you will present the final speech (or, if that room is not available, a similar room).

In each of these steps, critique your speech according to the guidelines that follow.

Guidelines for Delivery

Let's examine some nonverbal aspects of presenting a speech. As you read in Chapter 6, nonverbal behavior can change, or even contradict, the meaning of the words a speaker utters. If audience members want to interpret how you feel about something, they are likely to trust your nonverbal communication more than the words you speak. If you tell them, "It's great to be here today," but you stand before them slouched over with your hands in your pockets and an expression on your face like you're about to be shot, they are likely to discount what you say. This might cause your audience members to react negatively to your speech, and their negative reaction might make you even more nervous. This cycle of speaker and audience reinforcing each other's feelings can work for you, though, if you approach a subject with genuine enthusiasm. Enthusiasm is shown through both the visual and auditory aspects of your delivery.

Visual Aspects of Delivery

Visual aspects of delivery include appearance, movement, posture, facial expression, and eye contact.

Appearance   Appearance is not a presentation variable as much as a preparation variable. Some communication consultants suggest new clothes, new glasses, and new hairstyles for their clients. In case you consider any of these, be forewarned that you should be attractive to your audience but not flashy. Research suggests that audiences like speakers who are similar to them, but they prefer the similarity to be shown conservatively.[19] Speakers, it seems, are perceived to be more credible when they look businesslike.

Movement   The way you walk to the front of your audience will express your confidence and enthusiasm. And after you begin speaking, nervous energy can cause your body to shake and twitch, and that can be distressing both to you and to your audience. One way to control involuntary movement is to move voluntarily when you feel the need to move. Don't feel that you have to stand in one spot or that all your gestures need to be carefully planned. Simply get involved in your message, and let your involvement create the motivation for your movement. That way, when you move, you will emphasize what you are saying in the same way you would emphasize it if you were talking to a group of friends.

Movement can also help you maintain contact with all members of your audience. Those closest to you will feel the greatest contact. This creates what is known as the "action zone" in the typical classroom, within the area of the front and center of the room. Movement enables you to extend this action zone, to include in it people who would otherwise remain uninvolved. Without overdoing it, you should feel free to move toward, away, or from side to side in front of your audience.

> Move with the understanding that it will add to the meaning of the words you use.

Remember: Move with the understanding that it will add to the meaning of the words you use. It is difficult to bang your fist on a podium or take a step without conveying emphasis. Make the emphasis natural by allowing your message to create your motivation to move.

Posture   Generally speaking, good posture means standing with your spine relatively straight, your shoulders relatively squared off, and your feet angled out to keep your body from falling over sideways. In other words, rather than standing at military attention, you should be comfortably erect.

Good posture can help you control nervousness by allowing your breathing apparatus to work properly; when your brain receives enough oxygen, it's easier for you to think clearly. Good posture also increases your audience contact because the audience members will feel that you are interested enough in them to stand formally, yet relaxed enough to be at ease with them.

Facial Expression   The expression on your face can be more meaningful to an audience than the words you say. Try it yourself with a mirror. Say, "You're a terrific audience," for example, with a smirk, with a warm smile, with a deadpan expression, and then with a scowl. It just doesn't mean the same thing. But, don't try to fake it. Like your movement, your facial expressions will reflect your genuine involvement with your message.

Eye Contact   Eye contact is perhaps the most important nonverbal facet of delivery. Eye contact not only increases your direct contact with your audience but also can be used to help you control your nervousness. Direct eye contact is a form of reality testing. The most frightening aspect of speaking is the unknown. How will the audience react? What will it think? Direct eye contact allows you to test your perception of your audience as you speak. Usually, especially in a college class, you will find that your audience is more "with" you than you think. By deliberately establishing contact with any apparently bored audience members, you might find that they are interested, they just aren't showing that interest because they don't think anyone is looking.

To maintain eye contact, you could try to meet the eyes of each member of your audience squarely at least once during any given presentation. After you have made definite eye contact, move on to another audience member. You can learn to do this quickly, so you can visually latch on to every member of a good-sized class in a relatively short time.

The characteristics of appearance, movement, posture, facial expression, and eye contact are visual, nonverbal facets of delivery. Now consider the auditory nonverbal messages that you might send during a presentation.

CULTURAL IDIOM
squared off:
evenly aligned
deadpan:
an expressionless face
squarely:
directly

"And now a correction: Portions of last night's story on diving mules which were read with an air of ironic detachment should actually have been presented with earnest concern."

Auditory Aspects of Delivery

As you read in Chapter 6, your paralanguage—the way you use your voice—says a good deal about you, especially about your sincerity and enthusiasm. In addition, using your voice well can help you control your nervousness. It's another cycle: Controlling your vocal characteristics will decrease your nervousness, which will enable you to control your voice even more. But this cycle can also work in the opposite direction. If your voice is out of control, your nerves will probably be in the same state. Controlling your voice is mostly a matter of recognizing and using appropriate volume, rate, pitch, and articulation.

Volume   The loudness of your voice is determined by the amount of air you push past the vocal folds in your throat. The key to controlling volume, then, is controlling the amount of air you use. The key to determining the right volume is audience contact. Your delivery should be loud enough so that your audience members can hear everything you say but not so loud that they feel you are talking to someone in the next room. Too much volume is seldom the problem for beginning speakers. Usually they either are not loud enough or have a tendency to fade off at the end of a thought. Sometimes, when they lose faith in an idea in midsentence, they compromise by mumbling the end of the sentence so that it isn't quite coherent.

Rate   There is a range of personal differences in speaking speed, or **rate**. Daniel Webster, for example, is said to have spoken at around 90 words per minute, whereas one actor who is known for his fast-talking commercials speaks at about 250. Normal speaking speed, however, is between 120 and 150 words per minute. If you talk much more slowly than that, you may tend to lull your audience to sleep. Faster speaking rates are stereotypically associated with speaker competence,[20] but if you speak too rapidly, you will tend to be unintelligible. Once again, your involvement in your message is the key to achieving an effective rate.

Pitch   The highness or lowness of your voice—**pitch**—is controlled by the frequency at which your vocal folds vibrate as you push air through them. Because taut vocal folds vibrate at a greater frequency, pitch is influenced by muscular tension. This explains why nervous speakers have a tendency occasionally to "squeak," whereas relaxed speakers seem to be more in control. Pitch will tend to follow rate and volume. As you speed up or become louder, your pitch will have a tendency to rise. If your range in pitch is too narrow, your voice will have a singsong quality. If it is too wide, you may sound overly dramatic. You should control your pitch so that your listeners believe you are talking with them rather than performing in front of them. Once again, your involvement in your message should take care of this naturally for you.

When considering volume, rate, and pitch, keep emphasis in mind. Remember that a change in volume, pitch, or rate will result in emphasis. If you pause or speed up, your rate will suggest emphasis. Words you whisper or scream will be emphasized by their volume.

> A change in volume, pitch, or rate will result in emphasis.

Articulation   The final auditory nonverbal behavior, articulation, is perhaps the most important. For our purposes here, **articulation** means pronouncing all the parts of all the necessary words and nothing else.

It is not our purpose to condemn regional or ethnic dialects within this discussion. It is true that a considerable amount of research suggests that regional dialects can cause negative impressions,[21] but our purpose here is to suggest careful, not standardized, articulation. Incorrect articulation is usually nothing more than careless articulation. It is caused by (1) leaving off parts of words (deletion), (2) replacing parts of words (substitution), (3) adding parts to words (addition), or (4) overlapping two or more words (slurring).

Deletion   The most common mistake in articulation is **deletion**, or leaving off part of a word. As you are thinking the complete word, it is often difficult to recognize that you are saying only part of it. The most common deletions occur at the ends of words, especially -*ing* words. *Going, doing,* and *stopping* become *goin', doin',* and *stoppin'*. Parts of words can be left off in the middle, too, as in *terr'iss* for *terrorist, Innernet* for *Internet,* and *asst* for *asked.*

Substitution   **Substitution** takes place when you replace part of a word with an incorrect sound. The ending -*th* is often replaced at the end of a word with a single *t*, as when *with* becomes *wit*. The *th-* sound is also a problem at the beginning of words, as *this, that,* and *those* have a tendency to become *dis, dat,* and *dose*. (This tendency is especially prevalent in many parts of the northeastern United States.)

Understanding Diversity

A Compendium of American Dialects

The following is a short glossary of examples of regionalized pronunciation (with apologies to all residents who find them exaggerated).

Appalachian Hill Country
Bile To bring water to 212 degrees
Cowcumber Vittle you make pickles out of
Hern Not his'n
Tard Exhausted

Bawlamerese (Spoken around Baltimore)
Arn What you do with an arnin board
Blow Opposite of above
Pleece Two or more po-leece
Torst Tourist

Boston
Back The outer covering of a tree trunk
Had licka Hard liquor
Moa Opposite of less
Pahk To leave your car somewhere, as in "Pahk the cah in Haavaad Yahd"

NooYorkese
Huh Opposite of him
Mel pew? May I help you?
Reg you la caw fee Coffee with milk and sugar
Pock A place with trees and muggers

Philadelphia
Fluffya The name of the city
Mayan Opposite of yours
Pork A wooded recreational area
Tail What you use to dry off with after a shower

Southern
Abode A plank of wood
Bidness Such as, "MistahCottah'spaynutbidness"
Shurf Local law enforcement officer
Watt The color of the Watt House in Wushinton

Texas
Ah stay Iced tea
Bayer A beverage made from hops
Pars A town in Texas. Also, the capital of France
Awful Tar Famous tall structure in Pars, France

Other interesting regionalisms can be found at the Slanguisticswebsite, www.slanguage.com.

Addition   The articulation problem of **addition** is caused by adding extra parts to words, such as *incentative* instead of *incentive, athalete* instead of *athlete,* and *orientated* instead of *oriented.* Sometimes this type of addition is caused by incorrect word choice, as when *irregardless* is used for *regardless.*

Another type of addition is the use of "tag questions," such as *you know?* or *you see?* or *right?* at the end of sentences. To have every other sentence punctuated with one of these barely audible superfluous phrases can be annoying.

Probably the worst type of addition, or at least the most common, is the use of *uh* and *anda* between words. *Anda* is often stuck between two words when and isn't even needed. If you find yourself doing that, you might want just to pause or swallow instead.[22]

Slurring   **Slurring** is caused by trying to say two or more words at once—or at least overlapping the end of one word with the beginning of the next. Word pairs ending with *of* are the worst offenders in this category. *Sort of* becomes *sorta, kind of* becomes *kinda,* and *because of* becomes *becausa.* Word combinations ending with to are often slurred, as when *want to* becomes *wanna.* Sometimes even more than two words are blended together, as when *that is the way* becomes *thatsaway.* Careful articulation means using your lips, teeth, tongue, and jaw to bite off your words, cleanly and separately, one at a time.

Sample Speech

Matthew Wozny, currently a student at Harvard University, was assigned this speech by his Latin instructor in the spring of 2010, while he was still a senior at Regis High School in New York City. He was asked to speak at Language Night, when prospective freshmen and their parents arrived to hear about the various languages that the school had to offer.

Matthew defined his purpose as follows:

After listening to this speech, prospective freshmen will be able to make an informed choice about whether or not they want to study Latin at the high school level.

He worded his thesis statement this way:

The benefits of studying Latin far outweigh the fact that few people speak it.

When asked how he went about analyzing his audience, Matthew responded as follows:

I first spoke with classmates and asked them why they had chosen Latin. Some said because they didn't have to speak it; others said they had studied some of it in grammar school; still others said they were enamored of its erudite/scholarly appearance. My next move was to ask my close friends taking other languages (French, German, Chinese, and Spanish) why they had *not* taken Latin. It turned out the primary reason was that, to their mind, Latin is a dead and unspoken language (incidentally the same thinking I had made upon listening to the Latin speech when I was an incoming freshman).[23]

After analyzing his audience, Matthew realized that he had to adapt his comments for both parents and young students. Moreover, there would be both students and parents who were leaning toward other languages and might therefore be less interested in hearing what he had to say.

In his analysis of occasion, Matthew reasoned that he would have to be brief—in fact, he was asked to speak for no more than four minutes. This was important, because his audience would be sitting through presentations about Spanish, French, German, and Chinese by both students and faculty. Also, the event was partially festive; refreshments were served and everyone socialized before the presentations. Therefore, he could afford to be relatively informal.

Matthew gathered information from his textbooks, from Web searches, and from interviewing his instructor and his classmates.

Matthew decided to deliver his speech from manuscript, at least partially to maintain his time limits. He practiced it until his delivery was smooth enough that he felt he was talking with, rather than talking at, his audience. He practiced alone, and then in front of classmates, and then in front of his parents. During the speech, he wished he had also practiced in the actual auditorium, where he would be using a microphone:

> The public address system created an echo effect to my words. As I was delivering the speech, half the time I was considering what I should do to adjust. I tried moving the microphone back a bit; didn't work. I tried moving myself back as much as I could. Nothing. I tried speaking more slowly. This allowed me to gauge my audience's reaction to this travesty, but it did not solve my crisis-at-hand. I tried speaking more quietly, and that might have worked, but I couldn't keep it up—I'm used to having to project to an audience without the aid of a microphone.[24]

In the end, Matthew controlled both his nervousness and the impact of his speech by overcoming what was essentially irrational thinking: The audience could hear his speech perfectly, in spite of the slight echo effect.

Sample Speech   # Why Study Latin?   **Matthew Wozny**

1   Good evening everyone. My name is Matthew Wozny. I am a senior at this wonderful school, and I have been studying Latin for four years now.

2   Precisely four years ago I sat just as you are sitting, nervous about yet ready to make the big leap to high school. Coming into this evening four years ago, I was unsure about the language to which I would commit myself for three years. I sat troubled: one language stood out. That language, Latin, lusciously lovely (note the clever use of alliteration), was the only one that was not spoken, the only one that was . . . dead. No doubt you are all considering this presumption as you prepare to make your purposeful decision.

3   But, Latin is hardly a dead language. In fact, you will be pleased to hear that it's even the official (spoken and written) language of expansive and populous Vatican City. To be sure, I have never heard a word of Latin spoken on the street. If I gaze downward onto the sidewalk and locate a misplaced penny, nickel, quarter, or dime, however, I'll be sure to see the Latin "E Pluribus Unum," or "Out of Many, One," inscribed on the coin. I need only look above me, moreover, to find the mottos of institutions embossed above their doorways. To put it another way, one does not have to look far to find Latin perceptibly piercing everyday life. It might interest my audience to know that Regis' motto "Deo et Patriae," meaning "For God and for Country," is Latin. So, too, is Harvard College's motto "Veritas," which translates as "Truth."

A simple greeting, concisely identifying himself and showing an appreciation for Regis High School.

Comment to prospective freshmen reflects his analysis of this part of his audience; he knows they'll identify with the way he felt four years earlier. Pointing out the alliteration was strictly for the parents.

Simple but elegant examples were chosen to appeal to students. His research here consisted of just looking around at where Latin appears in everyday life.

4 While one studies, or should study, a language to gain access to its culture, when I had to make the fateful decision, I couldn't have cared less. It didn't matter to me that Latin is the language of scholarship; the language of Western history; of Virgil, arguably the world's greatest poet; of Cicero, arguably the world's greatest orator; of Caesar, arguably the greatest strategic mind of all time; or the language of tremendous insights into the human condition. About all this I couldn't have cared less. The practicality, the usefulness of a language—only that influenced my choice.

> Pointing out that Latin permits access to one of history's great cultures was aimed at parents; admitting that he cared little for this point before high school is for the students. Here, his research consisted of a quick review of his Latin textbooks.

5 It is no secret that the majority of English vocabulary—over sixty percent, in fact—derives from Latin. Indeed, even the legal terms of which some of you—forgive me, I mean most of you (you are incoming Regis students, after all)—will be learning in law school are Latin words. Latin's presence in the English language makes it inevitable that studying Latin vocabulary—and I can attest to this—greatly expands one's English vocabulary (and, if you plan to be a polyglot, the vocabulary of every Romance language). In addition, the complex Latin grammar inculcates a profound understanding of English grammar into the student. Both skills, I furtively add, comprise precisely two of three sections on the SAT.

> A practical consideration: Studying Latin improves English skills, especially those that are tested on the SAT. The comment on law school is directed toward parents; Regis's reputation for producing successful law students is well known.

6 Choosing Latin has been undoubtedly the second-best decision I have made (the first, of course, was accepting the invitation to attend Regis!), yet I suppose all I can offer you are my assurances. I promise you it's not difficult (I repeat, you are incoming Regians, after all). Its practicalities undoubtedly outweigh the small fact that very few people speak it. And, finally, perhaps most important, Latin, I assure you, will never be as boring as I suspect my speech might have been. Thank you.

> The final tribute to Regis High School is for both parents and kids, as is the modest disclaimer. Matthew states his thesis explicitly here.

Summary

This chapter dealt with your first tasks in preparing a speech: choosing and developing a topic. Some guidelines for choosing a topic include these: Look for a topic early and stick with it, choose a topic you find interesting, and choose a topic you already know something about.

One of your tasks is to understand your purpose so that you can stick to it as you prepare your speech. General purposes include entertaining, informing, and persuading. Specific purposes are expressed in the form of purpose statements, which must be result-oriented, specific, and realistic.

Your next task is to formulate a thesis statement, which tells what the central idea of your speech is. Another early task is to analyze the speaking situation, including the audience and the occasion. When analyzing your audience, you should consider the audience purpose, demographics, attitudes, beliefs, and values. When analyzing the occasion, you should consider the time (and date) your speech will take place, the time available, the location, and audience expectations.

Although much of your speech will be based on personal reflection about your own ideas and experiences, it is usually necessary to gather some information from outside sources. Techniques for doing so include interviewing and surveys, as well as Internet and library research.

Carefully considering each of these preliminary tasks will enable you to avoid debilitative (as opposed to facilitative) communication apprehension. Sources of debilitative communication apprehension include irrational thinking, which might include a belief in one or more of the following fallacies: the fallacy of catastrophic failure (something is going to ruin this presentation), the fallacy of perfection (a good speaker never does anything wrong), the fallacy of absolute approval (everyone has to like you), and the fallacy of overgeneralization (you always mess up speeches). There are several methods of overcoming communication apprehension. The first is to remember that nervousness is natural, and use it to your advantage. The others include being rational, receiver-oriented, positive, and prepared.

There are four types of delivery: extemporaneous, impromptu, manuscript, and memorized. In each type, the speaker must be concerned with both visual and auditory aspects of the presentation. Visual aspects include appearance, movement, posture, facial expression, and eye contact. Auditory aspects include volume, rate, pitch, and articulation. The four most common articulation problems are deletion, substitution, addition, and slurring of word sounds.

Throughout all these preliminary tasks you will be organizing information and choosing supporting material. These processes will be discussed in the next chapter.

Key Terms

addition The articulation error that involves adding extra parts to words. *p. 346*

articulation The process of pronouncing all the necessary parts of a word. *p. 345*

attitude Predisposition to respond to an idea, person, or thing favorably or unfavorably. *p. 333*

audience analysis A consideration of characteristics including the type, goals, demographics, beliefs, attitudes, and values of listeners. *p. 330*

belief An underlying conviction about the truth of an idea, often based on cultural training. *p. 333*

database A computerized collection of information that can be searched in a variety of ways to locate information that the user is seeking. *p. 337*

debilitative communication apprehension Intense level of anxiety about speaking before an audience, resulting in poor performance. *p. 338*

deletion Articulation error that involves leaving off parts of words. *p. 345*

demographics Audience characteristics that can be analyzed statistically, such as age, gender, education, and group membership. *p. 331*

extemporaneous speech A speech that is planned in advance but presented in a direct, conversational manner. *p. 341*

facilitative communication apprehension A moderate level of anxiety about speaking before an audience that helps improve the speaker's performance. *p. 338*

fallacy of approval The irrational belief that it is vital to win the approval of virtually every person a communicator deals with. *p. 340*

fallacy of catastrophic failure The irrational belief that the worst possible outcome will probably occur. *p. 339*

fallacy of overgeneralization Irrational beliefs in which (1) conclusions (usually negative) are based on limited evidence or (2) communicators exaggerate their shortcomings. *p. 340*

fallacy of perfection The irrational belief that a worthwhile communicator should be able to handle every situation with complete confidence and skill. *p. 339*

general purpose One of three basic ways a speaker seeks to affect an audience: to entertain, inform, or persuade. *p. 329*

impromptu speech A speech given "off the top of one's head," without preparation. *p. 341*

irrational thinking Beliefs that have no basis in reality or logic; one source of debilitative communication apprehension. *p. 339*

manuscript speech A speech that is read word for word from a prepared text. *p. 341*

memorized speech A speech learned and delivered by rote without a written text. *p. 341*

pitch The highness or lowness of one's voice. *p. 344*

purpose statement A complete sentence that describes precisely what a speaker wants to accomplish. *p. 329*

rate The speed at which a speaker utters words. *p. 344*

slurring The articulation error that involves overlapping the end of one word with the beginning of the next. *p. 346*

specific purpose The precise effect that the speaker wants to have on an audience. Expressed in the form of a purpose statement. *p. 329*

substitution The articulation error that involves replacing part of a word with an incorrect sound. *p. 345*

survey research Information gathering in which the responses of a sample of a population are collected to disclose information about the larger group. *p. 338*

thesis statement A complete sentence describing the central idea of a speech. *p. 330*

value A deeply rooted belief about a concept's inherent worth. *p. 333*

visualization Technique for behavior rehearsal (for example, for a speech) that involves imagining the successful completion of the task. *p. 340*

Case Study Questions

Instructions: Reread the case study on pages 324–325 to answer the following questions in light of what you have learned in this chapter.

1. What audiences will you target for your presentations marketing your school?

2. What will be your specific purpose for each audience?

3. How will the situational factors listed on pages 330–335 shape how you design and present each message?

4. For each of the audiences you identified, what type of delivery (see page 341) would be most effective for your presentation?

5. How can you use the visual and vocal aspects of delivery described on pages 342–346 to make your delivery most effective?

Activities

1. **Formulating Purpose Statements** Write a specific purpose statement for each of the following speeches:

   1. An after-dinner speech at an awards banquet in which you will honor a team who has a winning, but not championship, record. (You pick the team. For example: "After listening to my speech, my audience members will appreciate the individual sacrifices made by the members of the chess team.")

   2. A classroom speech in which you explain how to do something. (Again, you choose the topic: "After listening to my speech, my audience members will know at least three ways to maximize their comfort and convenience on an economy class flight.")

   3. A campaign speech in which you support the candidate of your choice. (For example, "After listening to my speech, my audience members will consider voting for Alexandra Rodman in order to clean up student government.")

   Answer the following questions about each of the purpose statements you make up: Is it result-oriented? Is it precise? Is it attainable?

2. **Formulating Thesis Statements** Turn each of the following purpose statements into a statement that expresses a possible thesis. For example, if you had a purpose statement such as this:

   After listening to my speech, my audience will recognize the primary advantages and disadvantages of home teeth bleaching.

   you might turn it into a thesis statement such as this:

   Home bleaching your teeth can significantly improve your appearance, but watch out for injury to the gums and damaged teeth.

   1. At the end of my speech, the audience members will be willing to sign my petition supporting the local needle exchange program for drug addicts.

   2. After listening to my speech, the audience members will be able to list five disadvantages of tattoos.

   3. During my speech on the trials and tribulations of writing a research paper, the audience members will show their interest by paying attention and their amusement by occasionally laughing.

3. **Gathering Information** Break up into groups of eight or fewer. Select a topic of your own choosing or one of the following:

   1. Who came up with the idea of latitude and longitude lines, and how do they work?

   2. College athletes are exploited by the schools they play for.

   3. Our jury system does not work.

   4. U.S. schools are not safe.

   5. What are the steps in the design and construction of the Macy's Thanksgiving Day parade balloons?

   6. What do modern-day witches believe?

   7. What does it mean to be innumerate, and how many people suffer from this problem?

   Assign each member of your group a different research source:

   1. Internet search engine

   2. Library catalog

   3. Reference works

   4. Periodicals

   5. Databases

   6. Talk to a librarian.

   7. Talk to a professor.

   8. Conduct a survey of your other class members.

   During the next class period, report back to the class on which research sources were most productive.

4. **Communication Apprehension: A Personal Analysis** To analyze your own reaction to communication apprehension, think back to your last public speech, and rate yourself on how rational, receiver-oriented, positive, and prepared you were. How did these attributes affect your anxiety level?

5. **Types of Delivery** Identify at least one speech you have seen presented using the four types of delivery: extemporaneous, impromptu, manuscript, or memorized. For this speech, decide whether the type of delivery was effective for the topic, speaker, and

situation. Explain why or why not. If the speech was not effective, suggest a more appropriate type.

6. **Articulation Exercises** Tongue twisters can be used to practice careful articulation out loud. Try these two classics:

  I. She sells seashells down by the seashore.

  2. Peter Piper picked a peck of pickled peppers.

Now make up some of your own and try them out. Make twisters for both consonant sounds ("Frank's friendly face flushed furiously") and vowel sounds ("Oliver oiled the old annoying oddity").

For Further Exploration

For more resources about preliminary considerations in planning a speech, see the *Understanding Human Communication* website at www.oup.com/us/uhc11. There you will find a variety of resources: a list of books and articles, links to descriptions of feature films and television shows at the Now Playing website, study aids, and a self-test to check your understanding of the material in this chapter.

MEDIA ROOM

For more resources about communication in film and television, see *Now Playing* at the *Understanding Human Communication* website at www.oup.com/us/uhc11.

Managing Communication Apprehension

Anchorman: The Legend of Ron Burgundy (2004, Rated PG-13)
Many films and television shows depict speakers and performers struggling to manage their anxiety. Sometimes poignant and sometimes amusing, these scenes illustrate both the challenges of facing an audience with confidence, and strategies for doing so. In *Anchorman: The Legend of Ron Burgundy*, the namesake character (Will Ferrell) and Veronica Corningstone (Christina Applegate) are romantically involved news reporters whose relationship, disputes, and competition for the top anchor spot make for some nerve-racking (and very amusing) presentations on camera. In her effort to replace the slick Ron as lead anchor, Veronica overcomes her communication apprehension and excels in her first broadcast as lead anchor.

Raise Your Voice (2000, Rated PG)
This film tells the story of how talented teenager Terri Fletcher (Hillary Duff) develops a debilitating case of communication apprehension that prevents her from performing after her brother's death. The film shows how her new friend Jay helps her regain the confidence to face audiences again.

Analyzing the Speaking Situation

Election (1999, Rated R)
In this dark comedy, ultra-ambitious Tracy Flick (Reese Witherspoon) finds herself running for high school class president against a dumb "jock" and his oddball sister. The film includes a classic campaign assembly scene showcasing the candidates' different speech competencies and composure levels.

Four Weddings and a Funeral (1995, Rated PG)
In this film boyish Charles (Hugh Grant) delivers coy, charming, and amusing toasts at several weddings. One of Charles's friends tries unsuccessfully to copy this speaking style, embarrassing himself in front of the guests. These contrasting performances demonstrate the importance of choosing a speaking style that suits your personality.

40 Inspirational Speeches in 2 Minutes (2010, available at http://www.youtube.com/ watch?v=d6wRkzCW5qI)
The YouTube mashup entitled *40 Inspirational Speeches in 2 Minutes* is perhaps the best condensed version of movie scenes in which characters have to analyze their audience and occasion to fulfill their objective. These clips are fun and, in their own way, inspirational.

Organization and Support

Chapter Outline

After studying the material in this chapter . . .

Knowing what you are talking about and *communicating* that knowledge aren't the same thing. It's frustrating to realize you aren't expressing your thoughts clearly, and it's equally unpleasant to know that a speaker has something worth saying, yet be unable to figure out just what it is because the material is too jumbled to understand. In the following pages, you will learn methods of organizing and supporting your thoughts effectively.

Structuring Your Speech

Being clear to your audience isn't the only benefit of good organization: Structuring a message effectively will help you refine your own ideas and construct more-persuasive messages.

A good speech is like a good building: Both grow from a careful plan. In Chapter 11 you began this planning by formulating a purpose, analyzing your audience, and conducting research. You apply that information to the structure of the speech through outlining. Like any other plan, a speech outline is the framework on which your message is built. It contains your main ideas and shows how they relate to one another and your thesis. Virtually every speech outline ought to follow the basic structure outlined in Figure 12-1.

This **basic speech structure** demonstrates the old aphorism for speakers: "Tell what you're going to say, say it, and then tell what you said." Although this structure sounds redundant, the research on listening cited in Chapter 5 demonstrates that receivers forget much of what they hear. The clear, repetitive nature of the basic speech structure reduces the potential for memory loss, because audiences have a tendency to listen more carefully during the beginning and ending of a speech.[1] Your outline will reflect this basic speech structure.

Introduction

   I. Attention-getter
   II. Preview

Body

   I.
   II.
   III. } Three to five
   IV. main points
   V.

Conclusion

   I. Review
   II. Final remarks

FIGURE 12-1 Basic Speech Structure

Outlines come in all shapes and sizes, but the three types that are most important to us here are working outlines, formal outlines, and speaking notes.

Your Working Outline

A **working outline** is a construction tool used to map out your speech. The working outline will probably follow the basic speech structure, but only in rough form. It is for your eyes only and you'll probably create several drafts as you refine your ideas. As your ideas solidify, your outline will change accordingly, becoming more polished as you go along.

Your Formal Outline

A **formal outline** such as the one shown on page 357 uses a consistent format and set of symbols to identify the structure of ideas.

A formal outline serves several purposes. In simplified form, it can be displayed as a visual aid or distributed as a handout. It can also serve as a record of a speech that was delivered; many organizations send outlines to members who miss meetings at which presentations were given. Finally, in speech classes, instructors often use speech outlines to analyze student speeches. When one is used for that purpose, it is usually a full-sentence outline and includes the purpose, the thesis and topic, and/or title. Most instructors also require a bibliography of sources at the end of the outline. The bibliography should include full research citations, the correct form for which can be found in any style guide, such as *The Craft of Research*, by Wayne Booth et al.[2] There are at least six standard bibliographic styles. Whichever style you use, you should be consistent in form and remember the two primary functions of a bibliographic citation: to demonstrate the credibility of your source and to enable the readers—in this case your professor or your fellow students—to find the source if they want to check its accuracy or explore your topic in more detail.

> Another person should be able to understand the basic ideas included in your speech by reading the formal outline.

Another person should be able to understand the basic ideas included in your speech by reading the formal outline. In fact, that's one test of the effectiveness of your outline. See if the outline on page 357 passes this test for you.

Your Speaking Notes

Like your working outline, your speaking notes are for your use only, so the format is up to you. Many teachers suggest that speaking notes should be in the form of a brief keyword outline, with just enough information listed to jog your memory but not enough to get lost in.

Many teachers also suggest that you fit your notes on one side of one three-by-five-inch note card. Other teachers recommend that you also have your introduction and conclusion on note cards, and still others recommend that your longer quotations be written out on note cards. Your notes for a speech on the gas consumption crisis (see sample outline, page 357) might look like the ones in Figure 12-2.

Principles of Outlining

Over the years, a series of rules or principles for the construction of outlines has evolved. These rules are based on the use of the standard symbols and format discussed next.

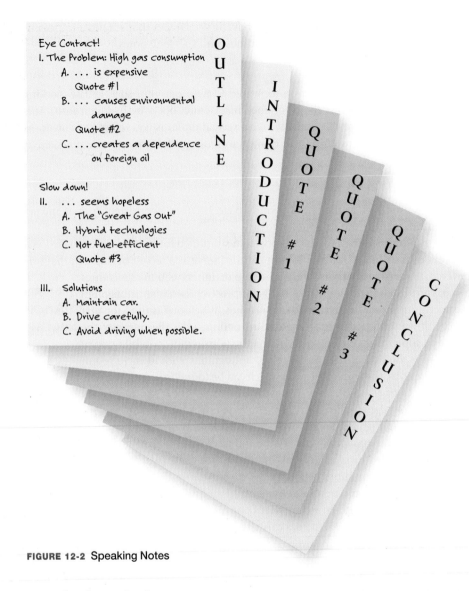

FIGURE 12-2 Speaking Notes

Standard Symbols

A speech outline generally uses the following symbols:

I. Main point (roman numeral)
  A. Subpoint (capital letter)
    1. Sub-subpoint (standard number)
      a. Sub-subsubpoint (lowercase letter)

In the examples in this chapter, the major divisions of the speech—introduction, body, and conclusion—are not given symbols. They are listed by name, and the roman numerals for their main points begin anew in each division. An alternative form is to list these major divisions with roman numerals, main points with capital letters, and so on.

SPEECH OUTLINE

The following outline is based on a speech by Neal Stewart of Kansas State University.[3]

Title: "The Gas Consumption Crisis"

General purpose: To persuade

Specific purpose: After listening to my speech, audience members will take a few simple steps to help alleviate the gas consumption crisis.

Thesis: Our nation's high gasoline consumption is dangerous, and we don't seem to care.

INTRODUCTION

I. Attention-Getter: The TV movie *Oil Storm* predicted a future of $8-a-gallon gasoline.
II. Thesis statement
III. Preview of main points

BODY

I. High gasoline consumption is dangerous.
  A. High gas consumption is expensive.
    1. It hits working-poor families the hardest.
    2. It drives up the cost of everything else.
  B. High gas consumption causes environmental damage.
  C. High gas consumption creates a dependence on foreign oil, leaving us in a precarious political position.
II. High gasoline consumption seems hopeless.
  A. The "Great Gas Out" was an attempt at a boycott, but . . .
    1. It failed because people needed to get to work.
    2. It failed because "armchair activism" is seldom effective.
  B. Hybrid technologies are the best answer, but . . .
    1. Hybrid cars are expensive.
    2. Hybrid cars are in limited production.
  C. We know how to be fuel-efficient, but . . .
    1. We don't carpool.
    2. We speed.
    3. We buy gas-guzzling SUVs.

III. High gasoline consumption requires real-world solutions.
  A. It helps to prepare and maintain your car.
    1. Keep tires properly inflated.
    2. Keep your engine properly tuned up.
    3. Keep excess weight out of the car.
  B. It helps to drive more carefully.
    1. Don't speed.
    2. Use cruise control on highway.
    3. Avoid aggressive driving.
  C. It helps to avoid driving whenever possible.
    1. Use mass transit.
    2. Walk whenever possible.
    3. Bike whenever possible.

CONCLUSION

I. Review of main points
II. Final remarks: "Let's change our behaviors now, so we can keep the *Oil Storm* scenario where it belongs—in Hollywood."

BIBLIOGRAPHY

Laura Bell, "When Gasoline Prices Rise," *Oil and Gas Journal*, May 21, 2010, p. 15.

Deron Lovass and Gal Luft, "From Gas Crisis to Cure," Tompaine.com. Accessed April 27, 2010. Available at http://www.tompaine.com/articles/2006/04/27/from_gas_crisis_to_cure.php.

Michael Milstein, "Even as Gas Prices Rise, We're Fueling Up," *The Oregonian*, April 20, 2010, p. A01.

Steven Mufson and Jon Cohen, "Tipping-Point Shock: Confounding the Experts, A Poll Finds Prices Must Go Way Higher to Alter Driving," *The Washington Post*, May 24, 2010, p. D01.

Steven Oberbeck, "Gasoline Prices: Utahns Feel Sting Like Rest of Nation," *The Salt Lake Tribune*, online, April 23, 2010.

"Tips to Improve Your Gas Mileage," U.S. Department of Energy, online. Accessed July 2, 2010. Available at http://www.fueleconomy.gov/feg/driveHabits.shtml.

"We Were Warned: Out of Gas," CNN Classroom Edition, online, June 19, 2010. Available at http://www.cnn.com/2007/EDUCATION/06/12/cnnpce.out.of.gas/.

Tom Whipple, "The Peak Oil Crisis: Week 12," *Falls Church News-Press*, online, May 3, 2010.

Standard Format

In the sample outlines in this chapter, notice that each symbol is indented a number of spaces from the symbol above it. Besides keeping the outline neat, the indentation of different-order ideas is actually the key to the technique of outlining; it enables you to coordinate and order ideas in the form in which they are most comprehensible to the human mind. If the standard format is used in your working outline, it will help you create a well-organized speech. If it is used in speaking notes, it will help you remember everything you want to say.

Proper outline form is based on a few rules and guidelines, the first of which is the rule of division.

The Rule of Division

In formal outlines main points and subpoints always represent a division of a whole. Because it is impossible to divide something into fewer than two parts, you always have at least two main points for every topic. Then, if your main points are divided, you will always have at least two subpoints, and so on. Thus, the rule for formal outlines is: Never a "I" without a "II," never an "A" without a "B," and so on.

Three to five is considered to be the ideal number of main points. It is also considered best to divide those main points into three to five subpoints, when necessary and possible. If you were speaking on the topic of the gas consumption crisis, you might divide the body of your topic as shown in the sample outline on page 357.

The Rule of Parallel Wording

Your main points should be worded in a similar, or "parallel," manner. For example, if you are developing a speech against capital punishment, your main points might look like this:

I. Capital punishment is not effective: It is not a deterrent to crime.
II. Capital punishment is not constitutional: It does not comply with the Eighth Amendment.
III. Capital punishment is not civilized: It does not allow for a reverence for life.

Whenever possible, subpoints should also be worded in a parallel manner. For your points to be worded in a parallel manner, they should each contain one, and only one, idea. (After all, they can't really be parallel if one is longer or contains more ideas than the others.) This will enable you to completely develop one idea before moving on to another one in your speech. If you were discussing cures for indigestion, your topic might be divided incorrectly if your main points looked like this:

I. "Preventive cures" help you before eating.
II. "Participation cures" help you during and after eating.

You might actually have three ideas there and thus three main points:

I. Prevention cures (before eating)
II. Participation cures (during eating)
III. Postparticipation cures (after eating)

Organizing Your Outline into a Logical Pattern

An outline should reflect a logical order for your points. You might arrange them from newest to oldest, largest to smallest, best to worst, or in a number of other ways that follow. The organizing pattern you choose ought to be the one that best develops your thesis.

Time Patterns

Arrangement according to **time patterns**, or chronology, is one of the most common patterns of organization. The period of time could be anything from centuries to seconds. In a speech on airline food, a time pattern might look like this:

  I. Early airline food: a gourmet treat
 II. The middle period: institutional food at thirty thousand feet
III. Today's airline food: the passenger starves

Arranging points according to the steps that make up a process is another form of time patterning. The topic "Recording a Hit Song" might use this type of patterning:

  I. Find an agent
 II. Record the demo CD
III. Promote the song

Time patterns are also the basis of **climax patterns**, which are used to create suspense. For example, if you wanted to create suspense in a speech about military intervention, you could chronologically trace the steps that eventually led us into Vietnam, Afghanistan, or Iraq in such a way that you build up your audience's curiosity. If you told of these steps through the eyes of a soldier who entered military service right before one of those wars, you would be building suspense as your audience wonders what will become of that soldier.

The climax pattern can also be reversed. When it is, it is called *anticlimactic* organization. If you started your military intervention speech by telling the audience that you were going to explain why a specific soldier was killed in a specific war, and then you went on to explain the things that caused that soldier to become involved in that war, you would be using anticlimactic organization. This pattern is helpful when you have an essentially uninterested audience, and you need to build interest early in your speech to get the audience to listen to the rest of it.

> The organizing pattern you choose ought to be the one that best develops your thesis.

Space Patterns

Space patterns are organized according to area. The area could be stated in terms of continents or centimeters or anything in between. If you were discussing the Great Lakes, for example, you could arrange them from west to east:

  I. Superior
 II. Michigan
III. Huron
 IV. Erie
  V. Ontario

Topic Patterns

A topical arrangement or **topic pattern** is based on types or categories. These categories could be either well known or original; both have their advantages. For example, a division of college students according to well-known categories might look like this:

I. Freshmen

II. Sophomores

III. Juniors

IV. Seniors

Well-known categories are advantageous because audiences quickly understand them. But familiarity also has its disadvantages. One disadvantage is the "Oh, this again" syndrome. If the members of an audience feel they have nothing new to learn about the components of your topic, they might not listen to you. To avoid this, you could invent original categories that freshen up your topic by suggesting an original analysis. For example, original categories for "college students" might look like this:

I. Grinds—students who go to every class and read every assignment before it is due.

II. Renaissance students—students who find a satisfying balance of scholarly and social pursuits.

III. Burnouts—students who have a difficult time finding the classroom, let alone doing the work.

Understanding Diversity

Nontraditional Patterns of Organization

In addition to the traditional patterns usually taught in public speaking classes, researchers are looking at other organizational patterns commonly used by women and ethnic speakers. For example, Cheryl Jorgenson-Earp is exploring a number of alternative patterns that women have used historically. She argues that many speakers are uncomfortable with the standard organization patterns because of cultural backgrounds or personal inclinations. As alternatives, she proposes several less direct and more "organic" patterns that provide a clear structure for a speech but have a less linear form.

One of these is the Wave pattern. In this pattern the speaker uses repetitions and variations of themes and ideas. The major points of the speech come at the crest of the wave. The speaker follows these with a variety of examples leading up to another crest, where she repeats the theme or makes another major point.

Perhaps the most famous speech that illustrates this pattern is the Reverend Martin Luther King Jr.'s "I Have a Dream." King used this memorable line as the crest of a wave that he followed with examples of what he saw in his dream; then he repeated the line. He ended with a "peak" conclusion that emerged from the final wave in the speech—repetition and variation on the phrase "Let freedom ring."

An excerpt from Sojourner Truth's "Ain't I a Woman?" speech also illustrates this pattern.

That man over there says that women need to be helped into carriages, and lifted over ditches, and to have the best place everywhere. Nobody ever helps me into carriages, or over mud-puddles, or gives me any best place!

And ain't I a woman?

Look at me! Look at my arm! I have ploughed and planted, and gathered into barns, and no man could head me!

And ain't I a woman?

I could work as much and eat as much as a man—when I could get it—and bear the lash as well!

And ain't I a woman?

I have borne thirteen children and seen them most all sold off to slavery, and when I cried out with my mother's grief, none but Jesus heard me!

And ain't I a woman?

Clella Jaffe, *Public Speaking: Concepts and Skills for a Diverse Society*, 5th ed., (c) 2007. Reprinted with permission of Wadsworth, an imprint of the Wadsworth Group, a division of Thomson Learning.

Sometimes topics are arranged in the order that will be easiest for your audience to remember. To return to our Great Lakes example, the names of the lakes could be arranged so their first letters spell the word "HOMES." Words used in this way are known as mnemonics. Carol Koehler, a professor of communication and medicine, uses the mnemonic "CARE" to describe the characteristics of a caring doctor:

C stands for *concentrate*. Physicians should hear with their eyes and ears . . .

A stands for *acknowledge*. Show them that you are listening . . .

R stands for *response*. Clarify issues by asking questions, providing periodic recaps . . .

E stands for *exercise emotional control*. When your "hot buttons" are pushed . . .[4]

Problem-Solution Patterns

The **problem-solution pattern**, as you might guess from its no-nonsense name, describes what's wrong and proposes a way to make things better. It is usually (but not always) divisible into two distinct parts, as in this example:

I. The Problem: Addiction (which could then be broken down into addiction to cigarettes, alcohol, prescribed drugs, and street drugs)
II. The Solution: A national addiction institute (which would study the root causes of addiction in the same way that the National Cancer Institute studies the root causes of cancer)

We will discuss this pattern in more detail in Chapter 14.

Cause-Effect Patterns

Cause-effect patterns are similar to problem-solution patterns in that they are basically two-part patterns: First you discuss something that happened, then you discuss its effects.

A variation of this pattern reverses the order and presents the effects first and then the causes. Persuasive speeches often have effect-cause or cause-effect as the first two main points. Elizabeth Hallum, a student at Arizona State University, organized the first two points of a speech on "workplace revenge"[5] like this:

I. The effects of the problem
   A. Lost productivity
   B. Costs of sabotage
II. The causes of the problem
   A. Employees feeling alienated
   B. Employers' light treatment of incidents of revenge

The third main point in this type of persuasive speech is often "solutions," and the fourth main point is often "the desired audience behavior." Elizabeth's final points were:

III. Solutions: Support the National Employee Rights Institute
IV. Desired Audience Response: Log on to *www.disgruntled.com*.

Cause-effect and problem-solution patterns are often combined in various arrangements. Chapter 14 has more to say about the organization of persuasive speeches.

Using Transitions

Transitions keep your message moving forward. They perform the following functions:

They tell how the introduction relates to the body of the speech.

They tell how one main point relates to the next main point.

They tell how your subpoints relate to the points they are part of.

They tell how your supporting points relate to the points they support.

Transitions, to be effective, should refer to the previous point and to the upcoming point, showing how they relate to one another and to the thesis. They usually sound something like this:

"Like [previous point], another important consideration in [topic] is [upcoming point]."

"But _____ isn't the only thing we have to worry about. _____ is even more potentially dangerous."

"Yes, the problem is obvious. But what are the solutions? Well, one possible solution is . . ."

Sometimes a transition includes an internal review (a restatement of preceding points), an internal preview (a look ahead to upcoming points), or both:

"So far we've discussed _____ , _____ , and _____ . Our next points are _____ , _____ , and _____ ."

You can find several examples of transitions in the sample speech at the end of this chapter.

Beginning and Ending the Speech

The **introduction** and **conclusion** of a speech are vitally important, although they usually will occupy less than 20 percent of your speaking time. Listeners form their impression of a speaker early, and they remember what they hear last; it is, therefore, vital to make those few moments at the beginning and end of your speech work to your advantage.

The Introduction

There are four functions of the speech introduction. It serves to capture the audience's attention, preview the main points, set the mood and tone of the speech, and demonstrate the importance of the topic.

Capturing Attention   There are several ways to capture an audience's attention. The following discussion shows how some of these ways might be used in a speech entitled "Communication Between Plants and Humans."

Refer to the Audience   The technique of referring to the audience is especially effective if it is complimentary: "Julio's speech last week about how animals communicate was so interesting that I decided to explore a related topic: Whether people can communicate with plants!"

Refer to the Occasion   A reference to the occasion could allude to the event of your speech, as in "Even though the focus of this course is *human* communication, it seems appropriate to talk about whether humans can communicate with plants."

"I'd like to thank all those who made it possible for me to be here tonight."

Source: Reprinted with permission from John Callahan/Levin Represents.

Refer to the Relationship Between the Audience and the Subject "My topic, 'Communicating with Plants,' ties right in with our study of human communication. We can gain several insights into our communication with one another by examining our interactions with our little green friends."

Refer to Something Familiar to the Audience The technique of referring to something familiar to the audience is especially effective if you are discussing a topic that might seem new or strange to that audience. For example, "See that lilac bush outside the window? At this very moment it might be reacting to the joys and anxieties that you are experiencing in this classroom."

Cite a Startling Fact or Opinion A statement that surprises audience members is bound to make them sit up and listen. If the audience members think they've heard it all before about plant-human communication, you might mention, "There is now actual scientific evidence that plants appreciate human company, kind words, and classical music."

Ask a Question A rhetorical question causes your audience to think rather than to answer out loud. "Have you ever wondered why some people seem able to grow beautiful, healthy plants effortlessly, whereas others couldn't make a weed grow in the best soil?" This question is designed to make the audience respond mentally, "Yeah, why is that?"

Tell an Anecdote A personal story perks up audience interest because it shows the human side of what might otherwise be dry, boring information. "The other night, while taking a walk in the country, I happened on a small garden that was rich with lush vegetation. But it wasn't the lushness of the vegetation that caught my eye at first. There, in the middle of the garden, was a man who was talking quite animatedly to a giant sunflower."

Use a Quotation   Quotable quotes sometimes have a precise, memorable wording that would be difficult for you to say as well. Also, they allow you to borrow from the credibility of the quoted source. For example, "Thorne Bacon, the naturalist, recently said about the possibility of plants and humans communicating, 'Personally, I cannot imagine a world so dull, so satiated, that it should reject out of hand arresting new ideas which may be as old as the first amino acid in the chain of life on earth.'"

Tell a Joke   If you happen to know or can find a joke that is appropriate to your subject and occasion, it can help you build audience interest: "We once worried about people who talked to plants, but that's no longer the case. Now we only worry if the plants talk back." Be sure, though, that the joke is appropriate to the audience, as well as to the occasion and to you as a speaker.

Previewing Main Points   After you capture the attention of the audience, an effective introduction will almost always state the speaker's thesis and give the listeners an idea of the upcoming main points. Katherine Graham, the former publisher of the *Washington Post*, addressed a group of businessmen and their wives in this way:

> I am delighted to be here. It is a privilege to address you. And I am especially glad the rules have been bent for tonight, allowing so many of you to bring along your husbands. I think it's nice for them to get out once in a while and see how the other half lives. Gentlemen, we welcome you.
>
> Actually, I have other reasons for appreciating this chance to talk with you tonight. It gives me an opportunity to address some current questions about the press and its responsibilities—whom we are responsible to, what we are responsible for, and generally how responsible our performance has been.[6]

Thus, Ms. Graham previewed her main points:

1. To explain whom the press is responsible to
2. To explain what the press is responsible for
3. To explain how responsible the press has been

Sometimes your preview of main points will be even more straightforward:

"I have three points to discuss: They are _____ , _____ , and _____ ."

Sometimes you will not want to refer directly to your main points in your introduction. Your reasons for not doing so might be based on a plan calling for suspense, humorous effect, or stalling for time to win over a hostile audience. In that case, you might preview only your thesis:

"I am going to say a few words about _____ ."

"Did you ever wonder about _____ ?"

"_____ is one of the most important issues facing us today."

Setting the Mood and Tone of Your Speech   Notice, in the example just given, how Katherine Graham began her speech by joking with her audience. She was a powerful woman speaking before an all-male organization; the only women in the audience were the members' wives. That is why Ms. Graham felt it necessary to put her audience members at ease by joking with them about women's traditional role in society. By beginning in this manner, she assured the men that she would not berate them for the sexist bylaws of their organization. She also showed them that she was going to approach her topic with wit and intelligence. Thus, she set the mood and tone for her entire speech. Imagine how different that mood and tone would have been if she had begun this way:

> Before I start today, I would just like to say that I would never have accepted your invitation to speak here had I known that your organization does not accept women as members. Just where do you Cro-Magnons get off, excluding more than half the human race from your little club?

Demonstrating the Importance of Your Topic to Your Audience   Your audience members will listen to you more carefully if your speech relates to them as individuals. Based on your audience analysis, you should state directly *why* your topic is of importance to your audience members. This importance should be related as closely as possible to their specific needs at that specific time. For example, Stephanie Hamilton, a student at North Dakota State University, presented a speech about loopholes in the justice system when crimes of violence occur on cruise ships. After telling the story of a rape aboard ship, she established the importance of her topic this way:

> Each year, millions of people take to the seas on cruises. Many of us have taken cruises of our own or plan to take one someday and practically everyone knows at least someone who has taken a cruise. Even if we will never take a cruise, we are a part of society and a possible target for crime. If someone were found guilty of a crime, would we want them free? That is exactly what is happening without laws of recourse in place for our protection. We don't need to let our family, friends, neighbors or ourselves be taken advantage of and never given justice.[7]

> You should state directly why your topic is of importance to your audience members.

The Conclusion

The conclusion, like the introduction, is an especially important part of your speech. The conclusion has three essential functions: to restate the thesis, to review your main points, and to provide a memorable final remark.

You can review your thesis either by repeating it or by paraphrasing it. Or you might devise a striking summary statement for your conclusion to help your audience remember your thesis. Grant Anderson, a student at Minnesota State University, gave a speech against the policy of rejecting blood donations from homosexuals. He ended his conclusion with this statement: "The gay community still has a whole host of issues to contend with, but together all of us can all take a step forward by recognizing this unjust and discriminatory measure. So stand up and raise whatever arm they poke you in to draw blood and say 'Blood is Blood' no matter who you are."[8] Grant's statement was concise but memorable.

Your main points can also be reviewed artistically. For example, first look back at that example of an introduction by Katherine Graham, then read her conclusion to that speech:

> So instead of seeking flat and absolute answers to the kinds of problems I have discussed tonight, what we should be trying to foster is respect for one another's conception of where duty lies, and understanding of the real worlds in which we try to do our best. And we should be hoping for the energy and sense to keep on arguing and questioning, because there is no better sign that our society is healthy and strong.

Let's take a closer look at how and why this conclusion was effective. Ms. Graham posed three questions in her introduction. She dealt with those questions in her speech and reminded her audience, in her conclusion, that she had answered the questions.

PREVIEW (FROM INTRODUCTION OF SPEECH)	REVIEW (FROM CONCLUSION)
1. To whom is the press responsible?	1. To its own conception of where its duty lies
2. What is the press responsible for?	2. For doing its best in the "real world"
3. How responsible has the press been?	3. It has done its best

You can make your final remarks most effective by avoiding the following mistakes:

Do Not End Abruptly   Make sure that your conclusion accomplishes everything it is supposed to accomplish. Develop it fully. You might want to use signposts such as "Finally . . . ," "In conclusion . . . ," or "To sum up what I've been talking about here . . ." to let your audience know that you have reached the conclusion of the speech.

Don't Ramble Either   Prepare a definite conclusion, and never, never end by mumbling something like "Well, I guess that's about all I wanted to say . . ."

Don't Introduce New Points   The worst kind of rambling is "Oh, yes, and something I forgot to mention is . . ."

Don't Apologize   Don't say, "I'm sorry I didn't have more time to research this subject" or any of those sad songs. They will only highlight the possible weaknesses of your speech, and there's a good chance those weaknesses were far more apparent to you than to your audience. It's best to end strong. You can use any of the attention-getters suggested for the introduction to make the conclusion memorable. In fact, one kind of effective closing is to refer to the attention-getter you used in your introduction and remind your audience how it applies to the points you made in your speech.

CULTURAL IDIOM

sad songs:
statements meant to elicit sympathy

@Work

Organizing Business Presentations

When top business executives plan an important speech, they often call in a communication consultant to help organize their remarks. Even though they are experts, executives are so close to the topic of their message that they may have difficulty arranging their ideas so others will understand or be motivated by them.

Consultants stress how important organization and message structure are in giving presentations. Seminar leader and corporate trainer T. Stephen Eggleston sums up the basic approach: "Any presentation . . . regardless of complexity . . . should consist of the same four basic parts: an opening, body, summary and closing."[9]

Ethel Cook, a Massachusetts consultant, is very specific about how much time should be spent on each section of a speech. "In timing your presentation," she says, "an ideal breakdown would be:

Opening - 10 to 20 percent
Body - 65 to 75 percent
Closing - 10 to 20 percent."[10]

Within the body of a presentation, business coach Vadim Kotelnikov gives his clients a step-by-step procedure to organize their ideas. "List all the points you plan to cover," he advises. "Group them in sections and put your list of sections in the order that best achieves your objectives. Begin with the most important topics."[11]

Toastmasters International, an organization that runs training programs for business professionals, suggests alternative organizational patterns:

To organize your ideas into an effective proposal, use an approach developed in the field of journalism—the "inverted pyramid." In the "inverted pyramid" format, the most important information is given in the first few paragraphs. As you present the pitch, the information becomes less and less crucial. This way, your presentation can be cut short, yet remain effective.[12]

While each consultant may offer specific tips, all agree that clear organization is essential when a business speaker wants his or her ideas to be understood and appreciated.

Supporting Material

It is important to organize ideas clearly and logically. But clarity and logic by themselves won't guarantee that you'll interest, enlighten, or persuade others; these results call for the use of supporting materials. These materials—the facts and information that back up and prove your ideas and opinions—are the flesh that fills out the skeleton of your speech.

Functions of Supporting Material

There are four functions of supporting material.

To Clarify As explained in Chapter 4, people of different backgrounds tend to attach different meanings to words. Supporting material can help you overcome this potential source of confusion by helping you clarify key terms and ideas. For example, when Ed Rubinstein, the economics analyst at the *National Review*, spoke at Hillsdale College in Michigan on "The Economics of Crime," he needed to clarify what he meant by a "career criminal." He used supporting material in this way:

> The career criminal, according to James Q. Wilson, was long ago identified as: "typically an impulsive young man who grew up in a discordant family where one or both parents had a criminal record, discipline was erratic, and human relations were cold and unpredictable. He had a low IQ and poor verbal skills. His behavioral problems appeared early, often by age eight, and included dishonesty and aggressiveness. Even in kindergarten or first grade he was disruptive, defiant, and badly behaved. He had few friends and was not emotionally close to those associates with whom he began stealing and assaulting."[13]

To Make Interesting A second function of support is to make an idea interesting or to catch your audience's attention. For example, Buey Ruet, a student at the University of Nebraska Omaha, started his speech on "Sudan's Forgotten War" this way:

> Twelve years ago, a woman by the name of Workinsh Admasu opened a letter, which required her eight- and thirteen-year-old boys to immediately report to military training camp. Three weeks after basic training the boys, along with another 300,000 eight- to fourteen-year-olds, strapped on AK 47s that were half their body weight and headed off to fight in Sudan's Civil War. . . . I am here today to persuade you to take action against the genocide that has claimed the lives of millions of southern black Africans. If you are wondering why I care about this topic so much, that eight-year-old boy was me. My thirteen-year-old brother and I were forced to experience things that no other child should ever have to experience.[14]

To Make Memorable A third function of supporting materials, related to the preceding one, is to make a point memorable. We have already mentioned the importance of "memorable" statements in a speech conclusion; use of supporting material in the introduction and body of the speech provides another way to help your audience retain important information. When Chris Griesinger of Eastern Michigan University spoke about the importance of pain management, he wanted his audience to remember the severity of the problem, so he used the following as supporting material:

> Every year the National Committee on Treatment of Intractable Pain receives letters from people sharing their stories of loved ones who died in pain. One letter reads, "I lost my mother to cancer. Her pain was so horrid that she lost her mind and ate her bottom lip completely off from clenching her top teeth so tightly. My thirteen-year-old sister and I watched this for six weeks."[15]

To Prove   Finally, supporting material can be used as evidence, to prove the truth of what you are saying. If you were giving a speech on what is known as the immigration crisis, you might want to point out that concerns about immigration are nothing new. The following could be used to prove that point:

> A prominent American once said, about immigrants, "Few of their children in the country learn English. . . . The signs in our streets have inscriptions in both languages. . . . Unless the stream of their importation could be turned they will soon so outnumber us that all the advantages we have will not be able to preserve our language, and even our government will become precarious." This sentiment did not emerge from the rancorous debate over the immigration bill defeated not long ago in the Senate. It was not the lament of some guest of Lou Dobbs or a Republican candidate intent on wooing bedrock conservative votes. Guess again. Voicing this grievance was Benjamin Franklin. And the language so vexing to him was the German spoken by new arrivals to Pennsylvania in the 1750s, a wave of immigrants whom Franklin viewed as the "most stupid of their nation."[16]

Types of Supporting Material

As you may have noted, each function of support could be fulfilled by several different types of material. Let's take a look at these different types of supporting material.

Definitions   It's a good idea to give your audience members definitions of your key terms, especially if those terms are unfamiliar to them or are being used in an unusual way. A good definition is simple and concise. When Elizabeth Hobbs, a student at Truman State University in Missouri, gave a speech on U.S. torture policy, she needed to define a key term, "extraordinary rendition":

> Give your audience members definitions of your key terms, especially if those terms are unfamiliar to them.

> "Extraordinary rendition" is the phrase used by the CIA to describe the U.S. practice of secretly sending terrorist suspects to countries where torture is routine.[17]

Examples   An **example** is a specific case that is used to demonstrate a general idea. Examples can be either factual or hypothetical, personal or borrowed. In Elizabeth Hobbs's speech on U.S. torture policy, she used the following example:

> He was kidnapped while making a business trip to Macedonia. To be transported to a secret prison in Afghanistan, he was beaten, his underwear was forcibly removed and he was put into a diaper, and chained spread eagle inside the plane. In Afghanistan he was beaten, interrogated and put into solitary confinement. To get out, he started a hunger strike, but after 37 days without food, a feeding tube was forced through his nose and into his stomach. Nearly five months later he was released, with no explanation of his imprisonment.
>
> Does this sound like Chile under the Pinochet regime? Prisoner abuse in Uzbekistan? A Russian gulag? It wasn't. This is a story of a victim of America's War on Terror.[18]

Hypothetical examples can often be more powerful than factual examples, because hypothetical examples ask audience members to imagine something—thus causing them to become active participants in the thought. Stephanie Wideman of the University of West Florida used a hypothetical example to start off her speech on oil prices:

> The year is 2020. One day you are asked not to come into work, not because of a holiday, but instead because there is not enough energy available to power your office. You see, it is not that the power is out, but that they are out of power.[19]

Statistics   Statistics are numbers that are arranged or organized to show that a fact or principle is true for a large percentage of cases. Statistics are actually collections of examples, which is why they are often more effective as proof than are isolated examples. Here's the way a newspaper columnist used statistics to prove a point about gun violence:

> I had coffee the other day with Marian Wright Edelman, president of the Children's Defense Fund, and she mentioned that since the murders of Robert Kennedy and the Rev. Martin Luther King Jr. in 1968, well over a million Americans have been killed by firearms in the United States. That's more than the combined U.S. combat deaths in all the wars in all of American history. "We're losing eight children and teenagers a day to gun violence," she said. "As far as young people are concerned, we lose the equivalent of the massacre at Virginia Tech about every four days."[20]

Because statistics can be powerful proof, you have certain rules to follow when using them. You should make sure that they make sense and that they come from a credible source. You should also cite the source of the statistic when you use it. A final rule is based on effectiveness rather than ethics. You should reduce the statistic to a concrete image if possible. For example, $1 billion in $100 bills would be about the same height as a sixty-story building. Using concrete images such as this will make your statistics more than "just numbers" when you use them. For example, one observer expressed the idea of Bill Gates's wealth this way:

> Examine Bill Gates' wealth compared to yours: Consider the average American of reasonable but modest wealth. Perhaps he has a net worth of $100,000. Mr. Gates' worth is 400,000 times larger. Which means that if something costs $100,000 to him, to Bill it's as though it costs 25 cents. So for example, you might think a new Lamborghini Diablo would cost $250,000, but in Bill Gates dollars that's 63 cents.[21]

> You should reduce the statistic to a concrete image if possible. For example, $1 billion in $100 bills would be about the same height as a sixty-story building.

Analogies/Comparison-Contrast   We use **analogies**, or comparisons, all the time, often in the form of figures of speech, such as similes and metaphors. A simile is a direct comparison that usually uses *like* or *as*, whereas a metaphor is an implied comparison that does not use *like* or *as*. So if you said that the rush of refugees from a war-torn country was "like a tidal wave," you would be using a simile. If you used the expression "a tidal wave of refugees," you would be using a metaphor.

Source: DILBERT: Scott Adams, Inc./Dist. by United Feature Syndicate, Inc.

Analogies are extended metaphors. They can be used to compare or contrast an unknown concept with a known one. For example, here's how one writer made her point against separate Academy Awards for men and women:

> Many hours into the 82nd Academy Awards ceremony this Sunday, the Oscar for best actor will go to Morgan Freeman, Jeff Bridges, George Clooney, Colin Firth or Jeremy Renner. Suppose, however, that the Academy of Motion Picture Arts and Sciences presented separate honors for best white actor and best non-white actor, and that Mr. Freeman was prohibited from competing against the likes of Mr. Clooney and Mr. Bridges. Surely, the academy would be derided as intolerant and out of touch; public outcry would swiftly ensure that Oscar nominations never again fell along racial lines.
>
> Why, then, is it considered acceptable to segregate nominations by sex, offering different Oscars for best actor and best actress?[22]

Anecdotes   An **anecdote** is a brief story with a point, often (but not always) based on personal experience. (The word *anecdote* comes from the Greek, meaning "unpublished item.") Ronald Reagan was famous for his use of anecdotes. In his farewell address, when he wanted to make the point that America stood as a symbol of freedom to people in other lands, he used the following anecdote:

> It was back in the early eighties, at the height of the boat people, and a sailor was hard at work on the carrier *Midway*, which was patrolling the South China sea. The sailor, like most American servicemen, was young, smart and fiercely observant. The crew spied on the horizon a leaky little boat—and crammed inside were refugees from Indochina hoping to get to America. The *Midway* sent a small launch to bring them to the ship, and safety. As the refugees made their way through the choppy seas, one spied the sailor on deck, and stood up and called out to him. He yelled, "Hello American Sailor—Hello Freedom Man."
>
> A small moment with a big meaning, a moment the sailor, who wrote it in a letter, couldn't get out of his mind. And when I saw it, neither could I. [23]

Quotation/Testimony   Using a familiar, artistically stated saying will enable you to take advantage of someone else's memorable wording. For example, if you were giving a speech on personal integrity, you might quote Mark Twain, who said, "Always do right. This will gratify some people, and astonish the rest." A quotation like that fits Alexander Pope's definition of "true wit": "What was often thought, but ne'er so well expressed."

You can also use quotations as **testimony**, to prove a point by using the support of someone who is more authoritative or experienced on the subject than you are. When Rajiv Khanna, a student at Newman University in Kansas, wanted to prove that the distortion of history was a serious problem, he used testimony this way:

> Eugene Genovese, Professor Emeritus of History at Emory University, states in the July 11 issue of the *Chronicle of Higher Education*, "The distortion of history remains a serious problem to the academic community and the country at large." He continues, "As individuals who are history-making animals, we remain rooted in the past, and we are shaped by our society's version of its history."[24]

Sometimes testimony can be paraphrased. For example, when one business executive was talking on the subject of diversity, he used a conversation he had with Jesse Jackson Sr., an African American leader, as testimony:

> At one point in our conversation, Jesse talked about the stages of advancement toward a society where diversity is fully valued. He said the first stage was emancipation—the end of slavery. The second stage was the right to vote and the third stage was the political power to actively participate in government—to be part of city hall, the Governor's

office and Capitol Hill. Jesse was clearly focused, though, on the fourth stage—which he described as the ability to participate fully in the prosperity that this nation enjoys. In other words, economic power.[25]

Have you ever "stretched" supporting material to help it conform to a point you were trying to make? (An example might be citing an "expert" for an idea of your own when discussing a social issue with a friend.) How far can you stretch the facts without stepping onto thin ethical ice?

Styles of Support: Narration and Citation

Most of the forms of support discussed in the preceding section could be presented in either of two ways: through narration or through citation. **Narration** involves telling a story with your information. You put it in the form of a small drama, with a beginning, middle, and end. For example, Evan McCarley of the University of Mississippi narrated the following example in his speech on the importance of drug courts:

> Oakland contractor Josef Corbin has a lot to be proud of. Last year his firm, Corbin Building Inc., posted revenue of over 3 million dollars after funding dozens of urban restoration projects. His company was ranked as one of the 800 fastest-growing companies in the country, all due to what his friends call his motivation for success. Unfortunately, until 1996 Corbin used this motivation to rob and steal on the streets of San Francisco to support a heroin and cocaine habit. But when he was charged with possession in 1996, Josef was given the option to participate in a state drug court, a program targeted at those recently charged with drug use, possession, or distribution. The drug court offers offenders free drug treatment, therapy, employment, education, and weekly meetings with a judge, parole officer and other accused drug offenders.[26]

Understanding Communication Technology

Plagiarism in a Digital Age

Some experts believe that the Web is redefining how students understand the concept of authorship and originality. After all, the Internet is the home of file sharing that allows us to download music, movies, and TV programs without payment. Google and Wikipedia are our main portals to random free information, also. It all seems to belong to us, residing on our computer as it does. Information wants to be free.

According to one expert on the topic, "Now we have a whole generation of students who've grown up with information that just seems to be hanging out there in cyberspace and doesn't seem to have an author. It's possible to believe this information is just out there for anyone to take."[27]

Other experts beg to differ. They say students are fully aware of what plagiarism is, online or off, and they know it's cheating. It's just that it's so easy to copy and paste online material, and students like to save time wherever they can.

Public speaking instructors are on the front lines of those fighting plagiarism, because it's so important for successful student speakers to speak from the heart, in their own words and with their own voice. Plus, citing research enhances credibility. Plagiarism in public speaking isn't just cheating, it's ineffective.

The general rule for the digital age is: Thou shalt not cut and paste into a final draft—not for a paper, and not for a speech. Cutting and pasting is fine for research, but everything that's cut and pasted should be placed in a separate "research" file, complete with a full citation for the website you found it in. Then switch to your "draft" file to put everything in your own words, and go back to the research file to find the attribution information when you need to cite facts and ideas that you got from those sources.

Citation, unlike narration, is a simple statement of the facts. Citation is shorter and more precise than narration, in the sense that the source is carefully stated. Citation will always include such phrases as "According to the July 25, 2010, edition of *Time* magazine," or "As Mr. Smith made clear in an interview last April 24." Evan McCarley cited statistics later in his speech on drug courts:

> Fortunately, Corbin's story, as reported in the May 30th *San Francisco Chronicle*, is not unique, since there are currently over 300 drug courts operating in 21 states, turning first-time and repeat offenders into successful citizens with a 70% success rate.[28]

Some forms of support, such as anecdotes, are inherently more likely to be expressed as narration. Statistics, on the other hand, are nearly always cited rather than narrated. However, when you are using examples, quotation/testimony, definitions, and analogies, you often have a choice.

Sample Speech

The sample speech for this chapter was presented by Delisa Shepherd, a student in Professor Dan Flickstein's Introduction to Public Speaking class at Brooklyn College of the City University of New York, during the spring semester of 2010. The assignment was for an informative speech of three to five minutes. This was her first speech in the class, and she chose as her topic the educational value of graphic novels. She had recently taken an English class called The Graphic Novel, and while she was choosing a topic for this speech one of books from that class caught her eye and inspired her.

She organized her ideas according to a simple topical pattern.

Her supporting material was taken from an article she found in a library database, online reference works such as the *Encyclopedia Britannica* and the *Merriam-Webster Dictionary*, graphic novels from her own bookshelf, and her own experience. Delisa lists the following three works on her bibliography:

Bibliography

Carter, James Bucky. "Going Graphic." *Educational Leadership*, March 2009: 68–72. EBSCO Host. Web. 16 Nov. 2009.

"Comic Strip." *Encyclopedia Britannica*. Encyclopedia Britannica, 2010. Web. 12 Mar. 2010 <http://search.eb.com/eb/article-278938>.

Spiegelman, Art. *Maus: A Survivor's Tale*. New York: Pantheon, 1986. Print.

Delisa presented the speech from the outline shown below. Some comments about her organization and support appear on the right side of the page.

Delisa Shepherd   Prof. Flickstein

Speech 3   2/23/10

Comics in the Classroom: The Educational Value of Graphic Novels

Purpose: After listening to my speech, my audience will appreciate how graphic novels can and are being used as learning materials.

Introduction

I. When I told friends and family that I'd be reading graphic novels for an English class last semester I received mixed reactions, but all were surprised that I was reading comics for class.

Attention-getter begins introduction.

II. Many Americans believe that comics are only good for entertaining and don't understand how they could be used for academic purposes.

She involves her audience by appealing to their desire to learn.

III. We are beginning to see that there are graphic novels that possess just as much literary merit as their picture-less counterparts.

IV. In this speech I want to show you that comics aren't just entertaining, they can also be educational.

Thesis statement; previews main point

Transition: Let's begin with looking at the way Americans perceive comics.

This transition moves her audience to her first main point.

Body

I. Americans tend to view comics as kid stuff or a quick laugh.

A. This way of thinking is understandable.

Notice the parallel wording in these subpoints. Definition used as support.

1. The very word *comic*, coming from the Greek *komikos*, which means "of or pertaining to comedy," denotes something meant to entertain, not educate. (Merriam-Webster)

2. American exposure to and knowledge of comics tends to be limited to the funny pages, Superman, Archie, and the like.

Transition: So we don't really expect much from them.

B. This way of thinking is largely American.

Encyclopedia articles used as support.

1. In other countries comics are way more popular. (Encyclopedia Britannica)

2. Perhaps the most notable example is Japan. (Encyclopedia Britannica)

a. Manga, Japanese comics, are popular both in and outside Japan. (Encyclopedia Britannica)

b. Manga has a wide variety of subjects and target age groups. (Encyclopedia Britannica)

C. Our way of thinking is slowly but surely changing.

Transition: Now that our views are shifting in the right direction, let's talk about what makes some graphic novels worthy to be called "learning material."

Transition to her second subpoint.

II. My experience with using graphic novels, specifically Art Spiegelman's *Maus*, has shown me that they can be just as useful as regular novels.

Graphic novel examples used as support.

A. In this tale of the Holocaust, the author utilizes anthropomorphism, a literary technique where animals behave as humans.

1. This technique can be found in many novels, such as *Alice in Wonderland*.

2. The Jews were portrayed as mice because the Nazis thought of them as vermin.

B. The pictures themselves utilize symbolism and motif.

1. In the frame on the handout, the characters are trying to escape Poland without being caught by the Nazis.

2. You may or may not have noticed that the roads form a swastika, which symbolizes them not being able to escape the Germans and foreshadows their eventual capture.

Transition: So it's obvious that comics can bring something to the table as far as substance goes, but it's also becoming clear that they can be a real asset in the classroom.

Transition to her third subpoint.

III. In his article "Going Graphic," James B. Carter, assistant professor of English education at the University of Texas at El Paso, makes a case for the use of comics as a learning aide.

Journal article cited as support.

    A. Carter explains that comics appeal to readers who are more visual, such as boys.

    B. Research shows comics often act as a gateway to more reading and more varied reading.

Conclusion

I. We used to look at comics as we do many things, from a fixed angle, not taking the time to see and understand the whole picture.

She restates her thesis and reviews her main points.

II. Thanks in part to great works like *Maus* and the people who support them, we are widening our gaze.

III. I hope I've at least shown you how versatile comics can be, and that you won't judge a comic by its cover.

She leaves her audience with memorable final remarks.

Summary

This chapter dealt with speech organization and supporting material. Speech organization is a process that begins with the formulation of a thesis statement to express the central idea of a speech. The thesis is established in the introduction, developed in the body, and reviewed in the conclusion of a structured speech. The introduction will also gain the audience's attention, preview the main points, set the mood and tone of the speech, and demonstrate the importance of the topic to the audience. The conclusion will review your thesis and/or main points and supply the audience with a memory aid.

Organizing the body of the speech will begin with a list of points you might want to make. These points are then organized according to the principles of outlining. They are divided, coordinated, and placed in a logical order. Transitions from point to point help make this order apparent to your audience. Organization follows a pattern, such as time, space, topic, problem-solution, cause-effect, motivated sequence, or climax arrangements.

Supporting materials are the facts and information you use to back up what you say. Supporting material has four purposes: to clarify, to make interesting, to make memorable, and to prove.

Types of support include *definitions* of key terms; *examples*, which can be real or hypothetical; *statistics*, which show that a fact or principle is true for a large percentage of cases; *analogies*, which compare or contrast an unknown or unfamiliar concept with a known or familiar one; *anecdotes*, which add a lively, personal touch; and *quotations and testimony*, which are used for memorable wording as well as ideas from a well-known or authoritative source. Any piece of support might combine two or more of these types. Support may be narrated (told in story form) or cited (stated briefly).

Key Terms

analogy Extended comparison that can be used as supporting material in a speech. *p. 369*

anecdote A brief personal story used to illustrate or support a point in a speech. *p. 370*

basic speech structure The division of a speech into introduction, body, and conclusion. *p. 354*

cause-effect pattern Organizing plan for a speech that demonstrates how one or more events result in another event or events. *p. 361*

citation Brief statement of supporting material in a speech. *p. 372*

climax pattern Organizing plan for a speech that builds ideas to the point of maximum interest or tension. *p. 359*

conclusion (of a speech) The final structural unit of a speech, in which the main points are reviewed and final remarks are made to motivate the audience to act or help listeners remember key ideas. *p. 362*

example A specific case that is used to demonstrate a general idea. *p. 368*

formal outline A consistent format and set of symbols used to identify the structure of ideas. *p. 355*

hypothetical example Example that asks an audience to imagine an object or event. *p. 368*

introduction (of a speech) The first structural unit of a speech, in which the speaker captures the audience's attention and previews the main points to be covered. *p. 362*

narration Presentation of speech supporting material as a story with a beginning, middle, and end. *p. 371*

problem-solution pattern Organizing pattern for a speech that describes an unsatisfactory state of affairs and then proposes a plan to remedy the problem. *p. 361*

space pattern Organizing plan in a speech that arranges points according to their physical location. *p. 359*

statistic Numbers arranged or organized to show how a fact or principle is true for a large percentage of cases. *p. 369*

testimony Supporting material that proves or illustrates a point by citing an authoritative source. *p. 370*

time pattern Organizing plan for a speech based on chronology. *p. 359*

topic pattern Organizing plan for a speech that arranges points according to logical types or categories. *p. 360*

transition Phrase that connects ideas in a speech by showing how one relates to the other. *p. 362*

working outline Constantly changing organizational aid used in planning a speech. *p. 355*

After studying the material in this chapter . . .

YOU SHOULD UNDERSTAND:

1. The difference between an informative and a persuasive speech topic.
2. The importance of having a specific informative purpose.
3. The importance of creating information hunger.
4. The importance of using clear language.
5. The importance of generating audience involvement.
6. The functions and types of visual aids.

YOU SHOULD BE ABLE TO:

1. Formulate an effective informative purpose statement.
2. Create information hunger by stressing the relevance of your material to your listeners' needs.
3. Use the strategies outlined in this chapter to organize unfamiliar information in an understandable manner.
4. Emphasize important points in your speech.
5. Generate audience involvement.
6. Use visual aids effectively.

CULTURAL IDIOM

rain down on:
fall like rain, overwhelm

Some people call it the age of information. But others call it the age of information glut, data smog, and clutter. There are, in fact, a hundred names for it, but they all deal with the same idea: there is just too much information around.

Social scientists tell us that the information glut leads to **information overload**, which is a form of psychological stress that occurs when people become confused and have trouble sorting through all the information that is available to them.[1] Some experts use another term, **information anxiety**, for the same phenomenon.

Because of this, the informative speaker's responsibility is not just to provide new information. Informative speaking—when it's done effectively—seeks to relieve information overload by turning information into **knowledge** for an audience. Information is the raw materials, the contradicting facts and competing claims that rain down on public consciousness. Knowledge is what you get when you are able to make sense of and use those raw materials. Effective public speakers filter information into knowledge by reaching small audiences with messages tailored for them, in an environment in which they can see if the audience is "getting it." If they aren't, the speaker can adjust the message and work with the audience until they do.

Informative speaking goes on all around you: in your professors' lectures or in a mechanic's explanation of how to keep your car from breaking down. You engage in this type of speaking frequently whether you realize it or not. Sometimes it is formal, as when you give a report in class. At other times, it is more casual, as when you tell a friend how to prepare your favorite dish. The main objective of this chapter is to give you the skills you need to enhance all of your informative speaking.

Types of Informative Speaking

There are several types of informative speaking. The primary types have to do with the content and purpose of the speech.

By Content

Informative speeches are generally categorized according to their content, including the following types:

Speeches About Objects   This type of informative speech is about anything that is tangible (that is, capable of being seen or touched). Speeches about objects might include an appreciation of the Grand Canyon (or any other natural wonder) or a demonstration of the newest technological gadget (or any other product).

Speeches About Processes   A process is any series of actions that leads to a specific result. If you spoke on the process of aging, the process of learning to juggle, or the process of breaking into the accounting business, you would be giving this type of speech.

Speeches About Events   You would be giving this type of informative speech if your topic dealt with anything notable that happened, was happening, or might happen: the U.S. invasion of Iraq, an upcoming film festival, or the prospects of your favorite baseball team winning the national championship.

Speeches About Concepts   Concepts include intangible ideas, such as beliefs, theories, ideas, and principles. If you gave an informative speech about postmodernism, vegetarianism, or any other "ism," you would be giving this type of speech. Other topics would include everything from New Age religions to theories about extraterrestrial life to rules for making millions of dollars.

By Purpose

We also distinguish among types of informative speeches depending upon the speaker's purpose. We ask, "Does the speaker seek to describe, explain, or instruct?"

Descriptions   A speech of **description** is the most straightforward type of informative speech. You might introduce a new product to a group of customers, or you might describe what a career in nursing would be like. Whatever its topic, a descriptive speech uses details to create a "word picture" of the essential factors that make that thing what it is.

Explanations   **Explanations** clarify ideas and concepts that are already known but not understood by an audience. For example, your audience members might already know that a U.S. national debt exists, but they might be baffled by the reasons why it has become so large. Explanations often deal with the question of *why*. Why do we have a national debt? Why do we have to wait until the age of twenty-one to drink legally? Why did tuition need to be increased this semester?

Instructions   Instructions teach something to the audience in a logical, step-by-step manner. They are the basis of training programs and orientations. They often deal with the question of *how to*. This type of speech sometimes features a demonstration or a visual aid. Thus, if you were giving instructions on "The Perfect Golf Swing," you might demonstrate with your own club. For instructions on "How to Perform CPR," you could use a volunteer or a dummy.

> These types of informative speeches aren't mutually exclusive.

These types of informative speeches aren't mutually exclusive. There is considerable overlap, as when you give a speech about objects that has the purpose of explaining them. Still, even this imperfect categorization demonstrates how wide a range of informative topics is available. One final distinction we need to make, however, is the difference between an informative and a persuasive speech topic.

Informative Versus Persuasive Topics

There are many similarities between an informative and a persuasive speech. In an informative speech, for example, you are constantly trying to "persuade" your audience to listen, understand, and remember. In a persuasive speech, you "inform" your audience about your arguments, your evidence, and so on. However, two basic characteristics differentiate an informative topic from a persuasive topic.

An Informative Topic Tends to Be Noncontroversial

In an informative speech, you generally do not present information that your audience is likely to disagree with. Again, this is a matter of degree. For example, you might want to give a purely informative talk on traditional Chinese medicine, simply describing what its practitioners believe and do. By contrast, a talk either boosting or criticizing traditional Chinese medicine would clearly be persuasive.

The noncontroversial nature of informative speaking does not mean that your speech topic should be uninteresting to your audience, but rather that your approach to it should not engender conflict. You could speak about the animal rights movement, for example, by explaining the points of view of both sides in an interesting but objective manner.

Understanding Diversity

How Culture Affects Information

Cultural background is always a part of informative speaking, although it's not always easy to spot. Sometimes this is because of ethnocentrism, the belief in the inherent superiority of one's own ethnic group or culture. According to communication scholars Larry Samovar and Richard Porter, ethnocentrism is exemplified by what is taught in schools.

Each culture, whether consciously or unconsciously, tends to glorify its historical, scientific, and artistic accomplishments and frequently to minimize the accomplishments of other cultures. In this way, schools in all cultures, whether they intend to or not, teach ethnocentrism. For instance, the next time you look at a world map, notice that the United States is prominently located in the center—unless, of course, you are looking at a Chinese or Russian map. Many students in the United States, if asked to identify the great books of the world, would likely produce a list of books mainly by Western, white, male authors. This attitude of subtle ethnocentrism, or the reinforcing of the values, beliefs, and prejudices of the culture, is not a uniquely American phenomenon. Studying only the Koran in Iranian schools or only the Old Testament in Israeli classrooms is also a quiet form of ethnocentrism.

From Larry Samovar and Richard Porter, *Communication Between Cultures*, 5th ed., © 2010. Reprinted with permission of Wadsworth, an imprint of the Wadsworth Group, a division of Cengage Learning.

The Informative Speaker Does Not Intend to Change Audience Attitudes

The informative speaker does seek a response (such as attention and interest) from the listener and does try to make the topic important to the audience. But the speaker's primary intent is not to change attitudes or to make the audience members *feel* differently about the topic. For example, an informative speaker might explain how a microwave oven works but will not try to "sell" a specific brand of oven to the audience.

The speaker's intent is best expressed in a specific informative purpose statement, which brings us to the first of our techniques of informative speaking.

Techniques of Informative Speaking

The techniques of informative speaking are based on a number of principles of human communication in general, and public speaking specifically, that we have discussed in earlier chapters. The most important principles to apply to informative speaking include those that help an audience understand and care about your speech. Let's look at the way these principles apply to specific techniques.

"I know so much that I don't know where to begin."

Source: © The New Yorker Collection 1987 James Stevenson from cartoonbank .com. All Rights Reserved.

Create Information Hunger

An effective informative speech creates **information hunger**: a reason for your audience members to want to listen to and learn from your speech. To do so, you can use the analysis of communication functions discussed in Chapter 1 as a guide. You read there that communication of all types helps us meet our physical needs, identity needs, social needs, and practical needs. In informative speaking, you could tap into your audience members' physical needs by relating your topic to their survival or to the improvement of their living conditions. If you gave a speech on food (eating it, cooking it, or shopping for it), you would be dealing with that basic need. In the same way, you could appeal to identity needs by showing your audience members how to be respected—or simply by showing them that you respect them. You could relate to social needs by showing them how your topic could help them be well liked. Finally, you can relate your topic to practical audience needs by telling your audience members how to succeed in their courses, their job search, or their quest for the perfect outfit.

Think about informative messages you receive, either from your professors or from other speakers. How closely do they connect with your needs? Can you provide an example of how even apparently unconnected topics can be linked to your needs by effective speakers?

Critical Thinking Probe

Audience Needs and Information Hunger

Make It Easy to Listen

Remember the complex nature of listening discussed in Chapter 5 and make it easy for your audience members to hear, pay attention, understand, and remember. This means first that you should speak clearly and with enough volume to be heard by all your listeners. It also means that as you put your speech together you should take into consideration those techniques that recognize the way human beings process information. For example:

Limit the Amount of Information You Present   Remember that you probably won't have enough time to transmit all your research to your audience in one sitting. It's better to make careful choices about the three to five main ideas you want to get across and then develop those ideas fully. Remember, too much information leads to overload, anxiety, and a lack of attention on the part of your audience.

Use Familiar Information to Increase Understanding of the Unfamiliar   Move your audience members from information that you can assume, on the basis of your audience analysis, that they know about to your newer information. For example, if you are giving a speech about how the stock market works, you could compare the daily activity of a broker with that of a salesperson in a retail store, or you could compare the idea of capital growth (a new concept to some listeners) with interest earned in a savings account (a more familiar concept).

Use Simple Information to Build Up Understanding of Complex Information   Just as you move your audience members from the familiar to the unfamiliar, you can move them from the simple to the complex. An average college audience, for example, can understand the complexities of genetic modification if you begin with the concept of inherited characteristics.

Use Clear, Simple Language

Another technique for effective informative speaking is to use clear language—which means using precise, simple wording and avoiding jargon. Dictionaries and thesauri are handy tools for picking precise vocabulary. The online dictionary.com and the "thesaurus" function that can be found under the "tools/language" tab of most word processing programs can be consulted easily as you plan your speech. You should remember, though, that picking the right word, the most precise word, seldom means using a word that is unfamiliar to your audience. In fact, just the opposite is true. Important ideas do not have to sound complicated. Along with simple vocabulary, you should also strive toward simple syntax by using direct, short sentence structure. For example, Christine Zani of the University of Wisconsin-Eau Claire began her informative speech on the history of forensics competition like this:

> Four years ago, when I attended my very first speech team meeting, I had no idea what to expect. I had never competed or traveled before, and I was pretty sure Forensics had

something to do with that CSI show. But, I became hooked, and having no under-standing of what competitive speech even was, I began what has now been a four-year journey to try to piece together the conglomerate history of an activity that has—since its birth—attracted some of the best young minds in the country.

This is one of the oldest intercollegiate activities in America. It has engaged thou-sands of competitors, boasts an impressive list of distinguished alumni, requires a con-siderable amount of time, and has significantly impacted the lives of its participants and the world around it.[2]

Each idea within that description of forensics is stated directly, using simple, clear language.

Define a Specific Informative Purpose

As Chapter 11 explained, any speech must be based on a purpose statement that is audience-oriented, precise, and attainable. When you are preparing an informative speech, it is especially important to define in advance, for yourself, a clear informative purpose. An **informative purpose statement** will generally be worded to stress audience knowledge, ability, or both:

> After listening to my speech, my audience will be able to recall the three most important questions to ask when shopping for a digital video recorder.
>
> After listening to my speech, my audience will be able to identify the four basic principles of aerodynamics.
>
> After listening to my speech, my audience will be able to discuss the idea of modernism.

Notice that in each of these purpose statements a specific verb such as *to recall*, *to identify*, or *to discuss* points out what the audience will be able to do after hearing the speech. Other key verbs for informative purpose statements include these:

Accomplish	Choose	Explain	Name	Recognize
Analyze	Contrast	Integrate	Operate	Review
Apply	Describe	List	Perform	Summarize

A clear purpose statement will lead to a clear thesis statement. As you remember from Chapter 11 a thesis statement presents the central idea of your speech. Sometimes your thesis statement for an informative speech will just preview the central idea:

> Digital video recorders have so many features that it is difficult for the uninformed consumer to make a choice.
>
> Understanding the laws of aerodynamics could help save your life some day.
>
> Every effective form of storytelling conforms to the rules of dramatic structure.

At other times, the thesis statement for an informative speech will delineate the main points of that speech:

> When shopping for a digital video recorder, the informed consumer seeks to balance price, dependability, and user friendliness.
>
> The four basic principles of aerodynamics—lift, thrust, drag, and gravity—make it clear how an airplane flies.
>
> Five components of dramatic structure—conflict, rising tension, climax, resolution, and denouement—are found in every effective form of storytelling.

Setting a clear informative purpose will help keep you focused as you prepare and present your speech.

CULTURAL IDIOM
ironclad:
mandatory

Use a Clear Organization and Structure

Because of the way humans process information (that is, in a limited number of chunks at any one time),[3] organization is extremely important in an informative speech. Rules for structure may be mere suggestions for other types of speeches, but for informative speeches they are ironclad.

Chapter 12 discusses some of these rules:

Limit your speech to three to five main points.

Divide, coordinate, and order those main points.

Use a strong introduction that previews your ideas.

Use a conclusion that reviews your ideas and makes them memorable.

Use transitions, internal summaries, and internal previews.

The repetition that is inherent in strong organization will help your audience members understand and remember those points. This will be especially true if you use a well-organized introduction, body, and conclusion.

The Introduction   The following principles of organization from Chapter 12 become especially important in the introduction of an informative speech:

1. Establish the importance of your topic to your audience.

2. Preview the thesis, the one central idea you want your audience to remember.

3. Preview your main points.

For example, Katelyn Wood of Illinois State University began her speech on the Arab news channel al-Jazeera with the following introduction:

Regardless of positive or negative observations from the U.S., al-Jazeera is one of the most influential institutions in the world; in fact, it's ranked number 5 in Forbes' most recognizable brand names—just behind Apple and Starbucks. And with al-Jazeera International pushing to gain more popularity with American audiences as the non-Western perspective on international relations, it is imperative to gain a better understanding of this incredibly powerful force in world media that has not only given voice to liberal Arab reformers, but radical extremists as well. To do so we'll first look at the history of al-Jazeera, next, understand exactly what the channel covers, before finally looking at some of its setbacks.[4]

The Body   In the body of an informative speech, the following organizational principles take on special importance:

1. Limit your division of main points to three to five subpoints.

2. Use transitions, internal summaries, and internal previews.

3. Order your points in the way that they will be most easy to understand and remember.

Katelyn Wood followed these principles for organizing her ideas on al-Jazeera. She introduced her first two subpoints—on the ownership and target audience of the news channel—this way:

An October 19, 2006, report from the *Arkansas Gazette* explained that one year after it was launched in 1996, President Clinton described the network as a beacon of democracy, but most Americans hadn't heard of the channel until after 9/11 when it broadcast videos of Osama bin Laden defending the attacks. With such contradictory publicity surrounding al-Jazeera, it is important to understand the history of the channel by looking at both its owner and target audience.

The Conclusion   Organizational principles are also important in the conclusion of an informative speech:

1. Review your main points.
2. Remind your audience members of the importance of your topic to them.
3. Provide your audience with a memory aid.

For example, here is the way Katelyn Wood concluded her speech on al-Jazeera:

> Today we have looked at the history of al-Jazeera, what the channel covers, as well as some problems with the network. While journalists working for the station continue to be accused of working for an organization that has an anti-American agenda, it is important to question the validity of the skeptics. Could it be that our culture is punishing a network simply because it has portrayed Western culture from the outside? Regardless, perhaps American media has a few lessons to learn.

Use Supporting Material Effectively

Another technique for effective informative speaking has to do with the supporting material discussed in Chapter 12. Three of the purposes of support (to clarify, to make interesting, and to make memorable) are essential to informative speaking. Therefore, you should be careful to support your thesis in every way possible. Notice the way in which Katelyn Wood uses solid supporting material in the preceding examples.

Visual aids can grab your audience members' attention and keep them attuned to your topic throughout your speech. Katelyn might have used one or two PowerPoint slides to show what an al-Jazeera broadcast looks like, to increase audience comprehension.

You should also try to briefly explain where your supporting material came from. These **vocal citations** build the credibility of your explanations and increase audience trust in the accuracy of what you are saying. For example, when Kerry Konda of Northern State University in South Dakota gave a speech on posttraumatic stress disorder, he used the following vocal citation:

> On March 1, 2006, the *Journal of the American Medical Association* published a report on a study conducted by Charles Hoge, Jennifer Auchterlonie, and Charles Milliken which found 1 in 5 soldiers returning from Iraq and Afghanistan suffered from posttraumatic stress disorder, a statistic that rivals the Vietnam experience.[5]

By telling concisely and simply where his information came from, Kerry reassured his audience that his statistics were credible.

Emphasize Important Points

One specific principle of informative speaking is to stress the important points in your speech through repetition and the use of signposts.

Repetition   Repetition is one of the age-old rules of learning. Human beings are more likely to comprehend information that is stated more than once. This is especially true in a speaking situation, because, unlike a written paper, your audience members cannot go back to reread something they have missed. If their minds have wandered the first time you say something, they just might pick it up the second time.

Of course, simply repeating something in the same words might bore the audience members who actually are paying attention, so effective speakers learn to say the same thing in more than one way. Kathy Levine, a student at Oregon State University, used this technique in her speech on contaminated dental water:

> The problem of dirty dental water is widespread. In a nationwide *20/20* investigation, the water used in approximately 90% of dental offices is dirtier than the water found in public toilets. This means that 9 out of 10 dental offices are using dirty water on their patients.[6]

Redundancy can be effective when you use it to emphasize important points.[7] It is ineffective only when (1) you are redundant with obvious, trivial, or boring points or (2) you run an important point into the ground. There is no sure rule for making certain you have not overemphasized a point. You just have to use your best judgment to make sure that you have stated the point enough that your audience members get it without repeating it so often that they want to give it back.

> Redundancy can be effective when you use it to emphasize important points.

Signposts   Another way to emphasize important material is by using **signposts**: words or phrases that emphasize the importance of what you are about to say. You can state, simply enough, "What I'm about to say is important," or you can use some variation of that statement: "But listen to this . . . ," or "The most important thing to remember is . . . ," or "The three keys to this situation are . . . ," and so on.

Generate Audience Involvement

The final technique for effective informative speaking is to get your audience involved in your speech. **Audience involvement** is the level of commitment and attention that listeners devote to a speech. Educational psychologists have long known that the best way to teach people something is to have them do it; social psychologists have added to this rule by proving, in many studies, that involvement in a message increases audience comprehension of, and agreement with, that message.

There are many ways to encourage audience involvement in your speech. One way is by following the rules for good delivery by maintaining enthusiasm, energy, eye contact, and so on. Other ways include personalizing your speech, using audience participation, using volunteers, and having a question-and-answer period.

Personalize Your Speech   One way to encourage audience involvement is to give audience members a human being to connect to. In other words, don't be afraid to be yourself and to inject a little of your own personality into the speech. If you happen to be good at storytelling, make a narration part of your speech. If humor is a personal strength, be funny. If you feel passion about your topic, show it. Certainly if you have any experience that relates to your topic, use it.

Use Audience Participation   **Audience participation**, having your listeners actually do something during your speech, is another way to increase their involvement in your message. For example, if you were giving a demonstration on isometric exercises (which don't require too much room for movement), you could have the entire audience stand up and do one or two sample exercises. If you were explaining how to fill out a federal income-tax form, you could give each class member a sample form to fill out as you explain it. Outlines and checklists can be used in a similar manner for just about any speech.

Here's how one student organization used audience participation to demonstrate the various restrictions that were once placed on voting rights:

> Voting is something that a lot of us may take for granted. Today, the only requirements for voting are that you are a U.S. citizen aged 18 or older who has lived in the same place for at least 30 days—and that you have registered. But it hasn't always been that way. Americans have had to struggle for the right to vote. I'd like to illustrate this by asking everyone to please stand.
>
> [Wait, prod class to stand.]
>
> I'm going to ask some questions. If you answer no to any question, please sit down.
>
> Do you have five extra dollars in your pocket right now? If not, sit down. Up until 1964, poll taxes existed in many states.
>
> Have you resided at the same address for at least one year? If not, sit down. Residency requirements of more than 30 days weren't abolished until 1970.
>
> Are you white? If not, sit down. The 15th Amendment gave non-whites the right to vote in 1870 but many states didn't enforce it until the late 1960s.
>
> Are you male? If not, sit down. The 19th Amendment only gave women the right to vote in 1920.
>
> Do you own a home? If not, sit down. Through the mid-1800s only property owners could vote.
>
> Are you Protestant? If not, sit down. That's right. Religious requirements existed in the early days throughout the country.[8]

Use Volunteers   If the action you are demonstrating is too expensive or intricate to allow all the class members to take part, you can select one or two volunteers from the audience to help you out. You will increase the psychological involvement of all the members, because they will tend to identify with the volunteers.

Have a Question-and-Answer Period   One way to increase audience involvement that is nearly always appropriate if time allows is to answer questions at the end of your speech. You should encourage your audience to ask questions. Solicit questions and be patient waiting for the first one. Often no one wants to ask the first question. When the questions do start coming, the following suggestions might increase your effectiveness in answering them:

1. Listen to the substance of the question. Don't zero in on irrelevant details; listen for the big picture—the basic, overall question that is being asked. If you are not really sure what the substance of a question is, ask the questioner to paraphrase it. Don't be afraid to let the questioners do their share of the work.

2. Paraphrase confusing questions. Use the active listening skills described in Chapter 5. You can paraphrase the question in just a few words: "If I understand your question, you are asking _____ . Is that right?"

3. Avoid defensive reactions to questions. Even if the questioner seems to be calling you a liar or stupid or biased, try to listen to the substance of the question and not to the possible personality attack.

Rubes®   **By Leigh Rubin**

"In order to adequately demonstrate just how many ways there are to skin a cat, I'll need a volunteer from the audience."

Source: "Rubes" by Leigh Rubin. By permission of Leigh Rubin and Creators Syndicate.

4. Answer the question as briefly as possible. Then check the questioner's comprehension of your answer. Sometimes you can simply check his or her nonverbal response—if he or she seems at all confused, you can ask, "Does that answer your question?"

FIG. 13-1 Model: Cutaway Human Eye

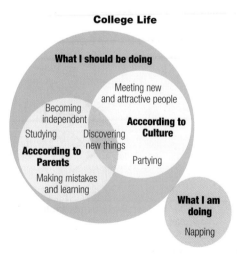

FIG. 13-2 Venn Diagram

Using Visual Aids

Visual aids are graphic devices used in a speech to illustrate or support ideas. While they can be used in any type of speech, they are especially important in informative speeches. For example, they can be extremely useful when you want to show how things look (photos of your trek to Nepal or the effects of malnutrition) or how things work (a demonstration of a new ski binding, a diagram of how seawater is made drinkable). Visual aids can also show how things relate to one another (a graph showing the relationships among gender, education, and income).

Types of Visual Aids

There is a wide variety of types of visual aids. The most common types include the following.

Objects and Models Sometimes the most effective visual aid is the actual thing you are talking about. This is true when the thing you are talking about is portable enough to carry and simple enough to use during a demonstration before an audience: a piece of sports equipment such as a lacrosse racket or a small piece of weight-training equipment. **Models** such as the one shown in Figure 13-1 are scaled representations of the object you are discussing and are used when that object is too large (the new campus arts complex) or too small (a DNA molecule) or simply don't exist any more (a *Tyrannosaurus rex*).

Diagrams A **diagram** is any kind of line drawing that shows the most important properties of an object. Diagrams do not try to show everything but just those parts of a thing that the audience most needs to be aware of and understand. Blueprints and architectural plans are common types of diagrams, as are maps and organizational charts. A diagram is most appropriate when you need to simplify a complex object or phenomenon and make it more understandable to the audience. Figure 13-2 shows different perceptions of college life in the form of a Venn diagram, which uses overlapping circles to show all the expectations that belong in a particular set.

Word and Number Charts   **Word charts** and **number charts** are visual depictions of key facts or statistics. Shown visually, these facts and numbers will be understood and retained better than if you just talked about them. Many speakers arrange the main points of their speech, often in outline form, as a word chart. Other speakers list their main statistics. Figure 13-3 shows a word chart listing the components of critical thinking.

Pie Charts   **Pie charts** are shaped as circles with wedges cut into them. They are used to show divisions of any whole: where your tax dollars go, the percentage of the population involved in various occupations, and so on. Pie charts are often made up of percentages that add up to 100 percent. Usually, the wedges of the pie are organized from largest to smallest. The pie chart in Figure 13-4 represents college student preferences in movie genres.

Bar and Column Charts   **Bar charts**, such as the one shown in Figure 13-5, compare two or more values by stretching them out in the form of horizontal rectangles. **Column charts**, such as the one shown in Figure 13-6, perform the same function as bar charts but use vertical rectangles.

> CRITICAL THINKING
>
> Reasoning
> Making judgments
>   and decisions
> Problem solving

FIG. 13-3 Word Chart: Critical Thinking

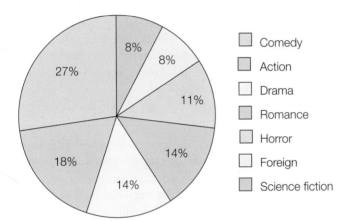

FIG. 13-4 Pie Chart: College Student Preferences in Movie Genres

Comedy
Action
Drama
Romance
Horror
Foreign
Science fiction

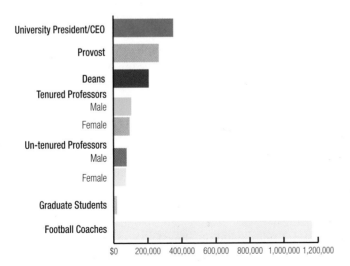

FIG. 13-5 Bar Chart: Academic Salaries

Email	100%
SMS texting	96%
Social networking sites (e.g., Facebook, MySpace)	94%
Instant messaging	86%
Blogging	82%
VOIP telephone services (e.g., Skype)	65%

FIG. 13-6 Column Chart: Social Media Use by College Students

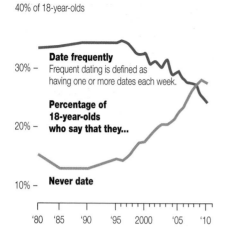

40% of 18-year-olds

Date frequently
Frequent dating is defined as
having one or more dates each week.

**Percentage of
18-year-olds
who say that they...**

30% –

20% –

10% – **Never date**

'80   '85   '90   '95   2000   '05   '10

FIG. 13-7 Line Chart: The Demise of Dating

Line Charts

A **line chart** maps out the direction of a moving point; it is ideally suited for showing changes over time. The time element is usually placed on the horizontal axis so that the line visually represents the trend over time. Trends in dating habits among eighteen-year-olds, for example, are represented by the line chart in Figure 13-7.

Media for the Presentation of Visual Aids

Obviously, many types and variations of visual aids can be used in any speech. And a variety of materials can be used to present these aids.

Chalkboards, Whiteboards, and Polymer Marking Surfaces   The major advantage of these write-as-you-go media is their spontaneity. With them you can create your visual aid as you speak, including items generated from audience responses. Along with the odor of whiteboard markers and the squeaking of chalk, a major disadvantage of these media is the difficulty of preparing visual aids on them in advance, especially if several speeches are scheduled in the same room at the same hour.

Flip Pads and Poster Board   Flip pads are like oversized writing tablets attached to a portable easel. Flip pads enable you to combine the spontaneity of the chalkboard (you can write on them as you go) with a portability that enables you to prepare them in advance. If you plan to use your visuals more than once you can prepare them in advance on rigid poster board and display them on the same type of easel.

Despite their advantages, flip pads and poster boards are bulky, and preparing professional-looking exhibits on them requires a fair amount of artistic ability.

Handouts   The major advantage of handouts is that audience members can take away the information they contain after your speech. For this reason, handouts are excellent memory and reference aids. The major disadvantage is that they are distracting when handed out during a speech: First, there is the distraction of passing them out, and second, there is the distraction of having them in front of the audience members while you have gone on to something else. It's best, therefore, to pass them out at the end of the speech.

Projectors   When your audience is too large to view handheld images, projectors are an ideal tool. *Overhead projectors* use transparencies—large, clear sheets of acetate—to cast an image on a screen. Most copy shops can transform ordinary pages into transparencies for a modest fee. If you have enough time to take a photograph of your visual aid with slide film, you can use a *slide projector* for an especially effective presentation. *Computer projectors* allow you to use a screen image directly from a computer screen, making them the most direct way to use computer software presentations.

Other Electronic Media   A wide range of other electronic media are available as presentation aids. Audio aids such as tape recordings and CDs can supply information that could not be presented any other way (comparing musical styles, for example, or demonstrating the differences in the sounds of gas and diesel engines), but in most cases you should use them sparingly. Remember that your presentation already relies heavily on your audience's sense of hearing; it's better to use a visual aid, if possible, than to overwork the audio.

Of course, there are audiovisual aids, including films, DVDs, and sound-on-slide. These should also be used sparingly, however, because they allow audience members to receive information passively, thus relieving them of the responsibility of becoming active participants in the presentation. The general rule when using these media is *Don't let them get in the way of the direct, person-to-person contact that is the primary advantage of public speaking.*

Rules for Using Visual Aids

It's easy to see that each type of visual aid and each medium for its presentation has its own advantages and disadvantages. No matter which type you use, however, there are a few rules to follow.

Simplicity Keep your visual aids simple. Your goal is to clarify, not confuse. Use only key words or phrases, not sentences. The "rule of seven" states that each exhibit you use should contain no more than seven lines of text, each with no more than seven words. Keep all printing horizontal. Omit all nonessential details.

Size Visual aids should be large enough for your entire audience to see them at one time but portable enough for you to get them out of the way when they no longer pertain to the point you are making.

Attractiveness Visual aids should be visually interesting and as neat as possible. If you don't have the necessary skills—either artistic or computer—try to get help from a friend or at the computer or audiovisual center on your campus.

Appropriateness Visuals must be appropriate to all the components of the speaking situation—you, your audience, and your topic—and they must emphasize the point you are trying to make. Don't make the mistake of using a visual aid that looks good but has only a weak link to the point you want to make—such as showing a map of a city transit system while talking about the condition of the individual cars.

Reliability You must be in control of your visual aid at all times. Test all electronic media (projectors, computers, and so on) in advance, preferably in the room where you will speak. Just to be safe, have nonelectronic backups ready in case of disaster. Be conservative when you choose demonstrations: Wild animals, chemical reactions, and gimmicks meant to shock a crowd can often backfire.

When it comes time for you to use the visual aid, remember one more point: Talk to your audience, not to your visual aid. Some speakers become so wrapped up in their props that they turn their backs on their audience and sacrifice all their eye contact.

Using PowerPoint

Several specialized programs exist just to produce visual aids. The most popular of these programs is Microsoft's PowerPoint®. In its simplest form, PowerPoint lets you build an effective slide show out of your basic outline. You can choose color-coordinated backgrounds and consistent formatting that match the tone and purpose of your presentation. PowerPoint contains a clip art library that allows you to choose images to accompany your words. It allows you to import images from outside sources and to build your own charts. To use PowerPoint, you can enter the program by clicking on the button for "Blank Presentation" or you can activate PowerPoint's "Wizard" function. Either way, the program will walk you through the stages of creating a slide show. It will, for example, show you a gallery of layout styles, and ask you which type you would like.

From this point on it is basically point, click, and follow directions. PowerPoint allows you to choose from several combinations of charts, text, and clip art. These visuals, like any type of computer-generated visual, can then be run directly from a computer

CULTURAL IDIOM

gimmicks:
clever means of drawing attention

wrapped up in:
giving all one's attention to something

projector, printed onto overhead transparencies, converted to 35mm slides at any photo shop or simply printed out in handout form. (See pages 392–393 for a discussion of the pros and cons of various presentation media.) Advanced uses of the program produce multimedia presentations with animated slide, sound, and video elements.

If you would like to learn more about using PowerPoint, there are several Web-based tutorial programs, which you can find easily by keying "PowerPoint" into your favorite search engine.

@Work

The Pros and Cons of PowerPoint

PowerPoint is by far the most popular form of work presentation today. In fact, as one expert points out, "Today there are great tracts of corporate America where to appear at a meeting without PowerPoint would be unwelcome and vaguely pretentious, like wearing no shoes."[9]

The Pros

The advantages of PowerPoint are well known. Proponents say that PowerPoint slides can focus the attention of audience members on important information at the appropriate time. They also help listeners appreciate the relationship between different pieces of information. By doing so, they make the logical structure of an argument more transparent.

Some experts think the primary advantage of PowerPoint is that it forces otherwise befuddled speakers to organize their thoughts in advance. Most, however, insist that its primary benefit is in providing two channels of information rather than just one. This gives audiences a visual source of information that is a more efficient way to learn than just by listening. One psychology professor puts it this way: "We are visual creatures. Visual things stay put, whereas sounds fade. If you zone out for 30 seconds—and who doesn't?—it is nice to be able to glance up on the screen and see what you missed."[10]

The Cons

For all its popularity, PowerPoint has been receiving some bad press lately, being featured in articles with such downbeat titles as "PowerPoint Is Evil"[11] and "Does PowerPoint Make You Stupid?"[12] But the statement that truly put the anti-PowerPoint argument on the map was a twenty-three-page pamphlet with a less dramatic title, *The Cognitive Style of Power Point*,[13] because it was authored by Edward R. Tufte, the well-respected author of several influential books on the effective design of visual aids.

According to Tufte, the use of low-content PowerPoint slides trivializes important information. It encourages oversimplification by asking the presenter to summarize key concepts in as few words as possible—the ever-present bullet points.

Tufte also insists that PowerPoint makes it easier for a speaker to hide lies and logical fallacies. When dazzling slides are used, the audience stays respectfully still and a speaker can quickly move past gross generalizations, imprecise logic, superficial reasoning, and misleading conclusions.

Perhaps most seriously, opponents of PowerPoint say that it is an enemy of interaction, that it interferes with the spontaneous give-and-take that is so important in effective public speaking. One expert summarized this effect by saying, "Instead of human contact, we are given human display."[14]

The Middle Ground?

PowerPoint proponents say that it is just a tool, one that can be used effectively or ineffectively. They are the first to admit that a poorly done PowerPoint presentation can be boring and ineffective, such as the infamous "triple delivery," in which precisely the same text is seen on the screen, spoken aloud, and printed on the handout in front of you. One proponent insists, "Tufte is correct in that most talks are horrible and most PowerPoint slides are bad—but that's not PowerPoint's fault. Most writing is awful, too, but I don't go railing against pencils or chalk."[15]

PowerPoint proponents say that PowerPoint should not be allowed to overpower a presentation—it should be just one element of a speech, not the whole thing. They point out that even before the advent of the personal computer, some people argued that speeches with visual aids stressed format over content. PowerPoint just makes it extremely easy to stress impressive format over less-than-impressive content, but that's a tendency that the effective speaker recognizes and works against. Thus, proponents say, the arguments for and against PowerPoint are really the arguments for and against visual aids. These arguments are merely accentuated now that they apply to one of the most influential media technologies of our day. Opponents shake their heads sadly at this explanation and insist that every technology changes the humans that use it in some way, and sometimes those changes are subtle and dangerous.

  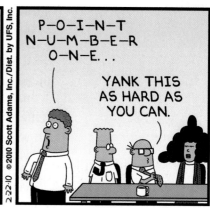

After reviewing "The Pros and Cons of PowerPoint" on page 394, would you say that PowerPoint is a benefit or detriment to effective public speaking? What forms of support would you use to back up your argument?

Critical Thinking Probe

The Effects of PowerPoint

Sample Speech

The sample speech for this chapter was presented by Robert Whittley, a student at Western Kentucky University, where he was coached by Ben Robin. Robert competed with this speech at forensics tournaments during the spring of 2010. He won four regular-season tournaments with it and went to the quarterfinals at the National Forensics Association Tournament.

Robert chose to speak on the skin disease vitiligo. He was originally attracted to this topic because of an interest in Michael Jackson:

> Michael Jackson was demonized for most of his career, particularly because of his race adaptation—and I saw this as a means to hopefully set the record straight about him.[16]

As Robert developed his speech, he realized that vitiligo also led to some higher-order thoughts about the impact of race in today's society. This led to the following thesis statement:

> Vitiligo is an often-misunderstood disease that offers us valuable insight into our conception of race.

This, in turn, led to a two-pronged purpose statement:

> After listening to my speech, my audience will understand vitiligo as a disease and will understand how it offers insights into our conception of race.

His informative organization can be seen in the following outline. (Parenthetical numbers refer to paragraphs in the speech.)

Introduction

I. Attention-getter: Michael Jackson seemed to transform himself from black to white. (1–4)

II. Statement of thesis. (5)

III. Preview of main points creates information hunger by establishing the widespread nature of this disease. (6)

Body

I. What is vitiligo? (7–8)

Vitiligo is defined as a loss of melanin within the epidermis, causing white patches of depigmentation. (8)

Vitiligo can be treated in several ways. (9–11)

Transition to next main point. (12)

II. How does it affect those who have it? (12-18)

Some face discrimination. (12–15)

Some suffer from depression. (16)

Some suffer from a loss of identity. (17–18)

Transition to final main point. (19)

III. What are the cultural and societal implications of this disease? (19–24)

Colorism is an unconscious prejudice against blackness. (19–21)

Michael Jackson personified this prejudice. (22–24)

Conclusion (25)

I. Review of main points. (25)

II. Final remarks: Michael Jackson serves as a symbol of hope for African Americans, vitiligo victims, or anyone who is uniquely different. (25)

Sample Speech **Black or White** **Robert L. Whittley**

1 During the late 1970s, the music and dancing talent of one "Bad" individual "Thrilled" America. [Show Visual Aid 1] Michael Jackson was one of the most influential entertainers of all time, having broken over eleven national music records. However, over the course of his three-decade career, he received his fair share of controversy.

High-impact introduction catches audience attention. The slides focus that attention. Robert believed that relating his topic to Michael Jackson would create information hunger in his audience.

2 Yes, part of this scrutiny surfaced due to his legal troubles. However, a significant amount of public scorn centered on Jackson's dramatic transformation from black to white. [Show Visual Aid 2] And while he crooned "It Doesn't Matter," the truth is, it did, as many fans and critics not so subtly argued that Michael bleached his skin on purpose, in order to be "white."

VISUAL AID 1

3 According to the official autopsy report, released on February 9, 2010, Michael Jackson was definitely the victim of the skin disease vitiligo, a condition in which the immune system attacks the melanin in human skin, causing a loss of pigmentation.

A clear and concise definition of "vitiligo."

4 And it's not just Michael Jackson. According to the World Health Organization, vitiligo affects 2 to 4 percent of the global population, or 248 million people. To put that in perspective, 248 million people is roughly 80 percent of all the men, women, and children in the United States.

5 A more comprehensive evaluation of vitiligo, which is completely unknown by most and misunderstood by many more, promises to help us better understand this disease as well as offer insight into the hidden prejudices that still lurk behind our conception of race.

6 To do this, we will learn exactly what vitiligo is. Next, we will delve into the lives of individuals living with the condition. Finally, we will critically examine some of the cultural and societal implications derived from a disease that even that most famous man in the world couldn't get his fans to understand.

VISUAL AID 2

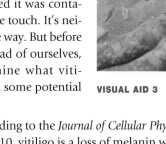

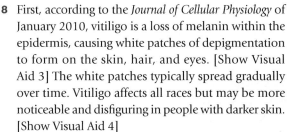

VISUAL AID 3

7 In the past, vitiligo was thought to be caused by demonic possession and many feared it was contagious to the touch. It's neither, by the way. But before we get ahead of ourselves, let's examine what vitiligo is, and some potential treatments.

8 First, according to the *Journal of Cellular Physiology* of January 2010, vitiligo is a loss of melanin within the epidermis, causing white patches of depigmentation to form on the skin, hair, and eyes. [Show Visual Aid 3] The white patches typically spread gradually over time. Vitiligo affects all races but may be more noticeable and disfiguring in people with darker skin. [Show Visual Aid 4]

9 Currently there is no cure for vitiligo. However, according to the *Journal of Dermatology* of February 2010, there have been new findings in treatment. A twice-daily applied tacrolimus ointment, similar to a facial cream, is being made available to patients, and studies show promising results that can begin after only three months. The ointment works as a makeup to both hide the signs of vitiligo and slow down the spread.

VISUAL AID 4

Statistics, grounded in a comparison, establish the widespread nature of this disease.

Statement of thesis.

Preview of main points; their presentation on a word chart helps the audience organize them in their mind.

Preview of first main point.

Here Robert describes vitiligo in a way that builds on his earlier definition.

Robert builds the credibility of his idea by concisely citing its authoritative source.

10   According to the *Springer London Ultraviolet Phototherapy Journal* of January 2010, one of the most effective treatments for vitiligo is commonly known as PUVA, the oral administration of psoralen, a drug that reacts with UV light to cause skin to darken. PUVA is usually used after poor response to topical treatments. While PUVA typically yields better results, it isn't a perfect solution, because it may cause nausea and itching, and it darkens all skin, not just the white patches.

> Again, he carefully cites the source of his information.

11   If both ointment and PUVA fail to yield the desired results, a last option for many is chemical depigmentation, or bleaching, to make all skin the same tone and complexion. Michael Jackson sought out this treatment as a last option.

12   Michael Jackson's prominent use of the sparkling glove was an iconic feature of his performance. But music scholars believe that it was being used to cover emerging white patches on his hand. However, vitiligo has affected people in more ways than clothing, namely through issues with social class and identity.

> Transition to next main point.

13   Some vitiligo victims take full advantage of their light skin. According to the *New York Times* on January 19, 2010, skin tone plays a powerful role in who gets hired, convicted, or elected. Luke Davis knows this all too well.

> Development of next subpoint.

14   The *Daily Mail Journal Online*, last updated July 24, 2009, explains that Luke was born dark skinned, but when he was eleven, white blotches appeared on his skin. As a young child growing up in a mostly white orphanage, Davis always prayed for white skin. Some thirty years later, he openly confesses that it is one of the best things that could have happened to him.

> This human story increases human interest, making it easier for his audience to listen.

15   Davis credits his light skin for his well-paying job. In fact, his boss later confessed that he was glad he hired Davis because he couldn't stand the thought of hiring a black man. Davis claims that as a white man he no longer has to deal with racism or discrimination.

16   However, many experience a profoundly different scenario here in the States. The *Quarterly Journal of Fundamentals of Mental Health* of Fall 2010 suggests that vitiligo patients experience a high prevalence of depression, reporting that 75 percent found their disfigurement moderately or severely intolerable.

> Evidence and statistics.

17   MSNBC's *Health Today* of August 25, 2009, shares Darcel Vludt's story. She started seeing blotches of depigmented skin at the age of five. Her family often took trips to the beach, and while she was there, other kids would poke fun at her. She was often called a Dalmatian, and other children were afraid to touch her for fear of catching the disease.

> Another example helps develop the next subpoint.

18   Today, at twenty-three, Darcel's skin no longer holds remnants of the dark completion from her youth, which has brought about new issues, specifically a lost sense of identity. [Show Visual Aid 5] Her father works for the UN in Africa, and there are always puzzled faces when the two are together. In America, when she goes into black dance clubs, other patrons often give her hurtful looks, as if to say, "You don't belong here."

VISUAL AID 5

19   Michael Jackson changed the way we think, act, and live through his powerful lyrics. Similarly, studying vitiligo may yield important insights into some of the lingering effects of colorism and MJ's legacy.

> Transition to final main point.

20 The previously cited *New York Times* article describes "colorism" as an unconscious prejudice against not blacks but blackness itself. Our brains, shaped by culture and history, create caste hierarchies that privilege those who are whiter and punish those who are darker.

> Definition, carefully worded in clear, plain language.

21 Clearly, attitudes towards colorism have progressed as a result of discussion and civil rights. But these attitudes haven't been completely corrected if vitiligo allows dark-skinned individuals to "live as a white person" and simultaneously receive scrutiny from the "black" community. These observations suggest that race and skin color are synonymous for some. Furthermore, historical, familial, and cultural connections can be severed simply by altering skin pigmentation. [Return to Visual Aid 1]

22 An Alternet.org article on July 9, 2009, a few days after his death, went so far as to suggest that Jackson should not be considered a black icon, because he bleached his skin and tried so hard to not be black. These misunderstandings surrounding his disease extend beyond his legacy. The *Boston Globe* of June 28, 2009, states that Michael Jackson lived at the poles of black pride and insecurity. For African Americans, Jackson's struggles with acceptance in a predominantly white world mirrored their own.

23 Michael Jackson is the perverse personification of the "double consciousness" that W. E. B. DuBois described over a century ago in *The Souls of Black Folk*. He wrote that "double consciousness" is this sense of always looking at oneself through the eyes of others, of measuring one's soul by the tape of a world that looks on in amused contempt and pity.

> Clear definition of "double consciousness."

24 Simply put, how can Michael Jackson, a white man, personify black struggle? But Michael Jackson did not forsake his roots or reject his race. In fact, the knowledge of his vitiligo may further propel him as a hopeful figure for anyone who faces oppression due to skin color.

> Review of main points.

25 So today, we've defined vitiligo, explored the lives of those with it, and examined implications surrounding how we conceptualize race. Michael Jackson was a person at the center of much public awe, distaste, and aversion. However strange, he will continue to serve as a symbol of hope for African Americans, vitiligo victims, or anyone who is uniquely different . . . which at least on some level includes all of us.

> Final remarks.

Summary

This chapter classified informative speaking based on content (speeches about objects, processes, events, and concepts) and purpose (descriptions, explanations, and instructions). Next, it discussed the differences between informative and persuasive speaking. It then suggested techniques for effective informative speaking. These techniques include using a specific informative purpose that stresses audience knowledge and/or ability, creating information hunger by tapping into audience needs, and making it easy to listen by limiting the amount of information you present, using familiar information to increase understanding of the unfamiliar, and using simple information to build up understanding of complex information. Other techniques include emphasizing important points through repetition and signposts; using clear organization and structure; using effective supporting materials, including visual aids; using clear language (language that uses precise, simple vocabulary and avoids jargon); and involving the audience through audience participation, the use of volunteers, and a question-and-answer period.

Key Terms

audience involvement Level of commitment and attention that listeners devote to a speech. *p. 388*

audience participation Listener activity during speech; technique to increase audience involvement. *p. 388*

bar chart Visual aid that compares two or more values by showing them as elongated horizontal rectangles. *p. 391*

column chart Visual aid that compares two or more values by showing them as elongated vertical rectangles. *p. 391*

description Type of speech that uses details to create a "word picture" of the essential factors that make that thing what it is. *p. 381*

diagram A line drawing that shows the most important components of an object. *p. 390*

explanations Speeches or presentations that clarify ideas and concepts already known but not understood by an audience. *p. 381*

information anxiety Psychological stress that occurs when dealing with too much information. *p. 360*

information hunger Audience desire, created by a speaker, to learn information. *p. 383*

Information overload Decline in efficiency that occurs when the rate of complexity of material is too great to manage. *p. 380*

informative purpose statement A complete statement of the objective of a speech, worded to stress audience knowledge and/or ability. *p. 385*

instructions Remarks that teach something to an audience in a logical, step-by-step manner. *p. 382*

knowledge Understanding acquired by making sense of the raw material of information. *p. 380*

line chart Visual aid consisting of a grid that maps out the direction of a trend by plotting a series of points. *p. 392*

model (in speeches and presentations) Replica of an object being discussed. Usually used when it would be difficult or impossible to use the actual object. *p. 390*

number chart Visual aid that lists numbers in tabular form in order to clarify information. *p. 391*

pie chart A visual aid that divides a circle into wedges, representing percentages of the whole. *p. 391*

signpost A phrase that emphasizes the importance of upcoming material in a speech. *p. 388*

visual aids Graphic devices used in a speech to illustrate or support ideas. *p. 390*

vocal citation A simple, concise, spoken statement of the source of your evidence. *p. 387*

word chart Visual aid that lists words or terms in tabular form in order to clarify information. *p. 391*

Case Study Questions

Instructions: Reread the case study on pages 324–325 to answer the following questions in light of what you have learned in this chapter.

1. Describe how you can use the techniques of informative speaking listed on pages 383–390 to improve the effectiveness of your presentation marketing your school.

2. What can you do to generate audience involvement?

3. Describe any visual aids you could use in the speech you are designing, and explain how you can use the guidelines discussed in this chapter to make them most effective.

Activities

1. **Informative Purpose Statements** For practice in defining informative speech purposes, reword the following statements so that they specifically point out what the audience will be able to do after hearing the speech.

   1. My talk today is about building a wood deck.

   2. My purpose is to tell you about vintage car restoration.

   3. I am going to talk about toilet training.

   4. I'd like to talk to you today about sexist language.

   5. There are six basic types of machines.

   6. The two sides of the brain have different functions.

   7. Do you realize that many of you are sleep deprived?

2. **Effective Repetition** Create a list of three statements, or use the three that follow. Restate each of these ideas in three different ways.

   1. The magazine *Modern Maturity* has a circulation of more than twenty million readers.

   2. Before buying a used car, you should have it checked out by an independent mechanic.

   3. One hundred thousand pounds of dandelions are imported into the United States annually for medical purposes.

3. **Using Clear Language** For practice in using clear language, select an article from any issue of a professional journal in your major field. Using the suggestions in this chapter, rewrite a paragraph from the article so that it will be clear and interesting to the layperson.

4. **Inventing Visual Aids** Take any sample speech. Analyze it for where visual aids might be effective. Describe the visual aids that you think will work best. Compare the visuals you devise with those of your classmates.

For Further Exploration

For more resources about informative speaking, see the *Understanding Human Communication* website at www.oup.com/us/uhc11. You will find a variety of material: a list of books and articles, links to descriptions of feature films and television shows at the *Now Playing* website, study aids, and a self-test to check your understanding of the material in this chapter.

MEDIA ROOM

For more resources about communication in film and television, see *Now Playing* at the *Understanding Human Communication* website at www.oup.com/us/uhc11.

Techniques of Informative Speaking

Freedom Writers (2007, Rated PG-13)
Films about inspiring teachers have captivated audiences for decades. Regardless of the time or setting, these master teachers present information in ways that not only informs, but also entertains and empowers students. In *Freedom Writers*, young teacher Erin Gruwell (Hilary Swank) motivates her at-risk students to apply themselves and pursue goals they previously thought were impossible. By connecting her subject matter to the students' personal concerns, Gruwell creates a hunger for learning.

The History Boys (2006, Rated R)
This film shows how the quirky faculty and headmaster at Cutlers' Grammar School in Britain inspire their overachieving yet immature students with their very different teaching styles. One teacher offers a diet of historical facts and figures, another spouts poetry, and a third challenges students with questions about knowledge versus truth and grades versus learning.

Mona Lisa Smile (2003, Rated PG-13)
Free-spirited art professor Katherine Watson (Julia Roberts) leads conservative 1950s Wellesley female students to question their traditional gender roles. While teaching them to appreciate art, Watson both connects and clashes with the young women as they struggle with the repressive norms of their midcentury upbringing and their longing for intellectual and personal freedom.

Matilda (1996, Rated G)
In *Matilda*, a young girl (Mara Wilson) learns from a unique teacher named Miss Honey. Despite the discouragement and verbal abuse of Matilda's crabby parents (Rhea Perlman and Danny DeVito), sweet Miss Honey cultivates her student's intellect with words of encouragement and a love of learning.

Mr. Holland's Opus (1995, Rated PG)
Glenn Holland (Richard Dreyfuss) initially takes a job teaching high school music as a way to pay the rent while he strives to compose his own masterpiece. As time goes on, Holland finds ways to share his passion for music, and in so doing transforms both his own life and those of his students.

Boston Public (2000–2004, Not Rated)
The television series *Boston Public* follows the professional and personal lives of ten faculty members at fictional Winslow High School. The dramatic series examines the teachers' lives as they handle trouble-making students, irate parents, and administrative challenges. Comparing the unique classroom style of each teacher provides a useful way to explore effective and ineffective approaches to informative speaking.

After studying the material in this chapter . . .

YOU SHOULD UNDERSTAND:

1. The characteristics of persuasion and the ethical questions involved.
2. The differences among questions of fact, value, and policy.
3. The difference between the goals of convincing and actuating.
4. The difference between direct and indirect approaches.
5. The importance of setting a clear persuasive purpose.
6. The basic idea of persuasive structure.
7. The importance of analyzing and adapting to your audience.
8. The components of personal credibility.

YOU SHOULD BE ABLE TO:

1. Formulate an effective persuasive strategy to convince or actuate an audience.
2. Formulate your persuasive strategy based on ethical guidelines.
3. Bolster your credibility as a speaker by enhancing your competence, character, and charisma.
4. Build persuasive arguments through audience analysis, solid evidence, and careful reasoning.
5. Organize a persuasive speech for greatest audience effect.

How persuasion works and how to accomplish it successfully are complex topics. Our understanding of persuasion begins with classical wisdom and extends to the latest psychological research. We begin by looking at what we really mean by the term.

Characteristics of Persuasion

Persuasion is the process of motivating someone, through communication, to change a particular belief, attitude, or behavior. Implicit in this definition are several characteristics of persuasion.

Persuasion Is Not Coercive

Persuasion is not the same thing as coercion. If you held a gun to someone's head and said, "Do this, or I'll shoot," you would be acting coercively. Besides being illegal, this approach would be ineffective. As soon as the authorities came and took you away, the person would stop following your demands.

The failure of coercion to achieve lasting results is also apparent in less dramatic circumstances. Children whose parents are coercive often rebel as soon as they can; students who perform from fear of an instructor's threats rarely appreciate the subject matter; and employees who work for abusive and demanding employers are often unproductive and eager to switch jobs as soon as possible. Persuasion, on the other hand, makes a listener *want* to think or act differently.

Persuasion Is Usually Incremental

Attitudes do not normally change instantly or dramatically. Persuasion is a process. When it is successful, it generally succeeds over time, in increments, and usually small increments at that. The realistic speaker, therefore, establishes goals and expectations that reflect this characteristic of persuasion.

Communication scientists explain this characteristic of persuasion through **social judgment theory**.[1] This theory tells us that when members of an audience hear a persuasive appeal, they compare it to opinions that they already hold. The preexisting opinion is called an **anchor**, but around this anchor there exist what are called **latitudes of acceptance**, **latitudes of rejection**, and **latitudes of noncommitment**. A diagram of any opinion, therefore, might look something like Figure 14-1.

People who care very strongly about a particular point of view will have a very narrow latitude of noncommitment. People who care less strongly will have a wider latitude of noncommitment. Research suggests that audience members simply will not respond to appeals that fall within their latitude of rejection. This means that persuasion in the real world takes place in a series of small movements. One persuasive speech may be but a single step in an overall persuasive campaign. The best example of this is the various communications that take place during the months of a political campaign. Candidates watch the opinion polls carefully, adjusting their appeals to the latitudes of acceptance and noncommitment of the uncommitted voters.

Public speakers who heed the principle of social judgment theory tend to seek realistic, if modest, goals in their speeches. For example, if you were hoping to change audience views on the pro-life/pro-choice question, social judgment theory suggests that the first step would be to consider a range of arguments such as this:

Abortion is a sin.

Abortion should be absolutely illegal.

Abortion should be allowed only in cases of rape and incest.

A woman should be required to have her husband's permission to have an abortion.

A girl under the age of eighteen should be required to have a parent's permission before she has an abortion.

Abortion should be allowed during the first three months of pregnancy.

A girl under the age of eighteen should not be required to have a parent's permission before she has an abortion.

A woman should not be required to have her husband's permission to have an abortion.

Abortion is a woman's personal decision.

Abortion should be discouraged but legal.

Abortion should be available anytime to anyone.

Abortion should be considered simply a form of birth control.

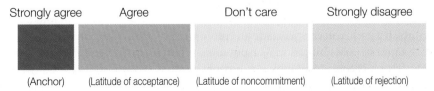

Strongly agree	Agree	Don't care	Strongly disagree
(Anchor)	(Latitude of acceptance)	(Latitude of noncommitment)	(Latitude of rejection)

FIGURE 14-1 Latitudes of Acceptance, Rejection, and Noncommitment

You could then arrange these positions on a continuum, and estimate how listeners would react to each one. The statement that best represented the listeners' point of view would be their anchor. Other items that might also seem reasonable to them would make up their latitude of acceptance. Opinions that they would reject would make up their latitude of rejection. Those statements that are left would be the listeners' latitude of noncommitment.

Social judgment theory suggests that the best chance of changing audience attitudes would come by presenting an argument based on a position that fell somewhere within the listeners' latitude of noncommitment—even if this isn't the position that you ultimately wanted them to accept. If you pushed too hard by arguing a position in your audience's latitude of rejection, your appeals would probably backfire, making your audience *more* opposed to you than before.

Persuasion Is Interactive

The transactional model of communication described in Chapter 1 makes it clear that persuasion is not something you do *to* audience members but rather something you do *with* them. This mutual activity is best seen in an argument between two people, in which an openness to opposing arguments is essential to resolution. As one observer has pointed out,

> Arguments are not won by shouting down opponents. They are won by changing opponents' minds—something that can happen only if we give opposing arguments a respectful hearing and still persuade their advocates that there is something wrong with those arguments. In the course of this activity, we may well decide that there is something wrong with our own.[2]

Even in public communication, both speaker and audience are active. This might be manifested in the speaker taking an audience survey *before* a speech, a sensitivity to audience reactions *during* a speech, or an open-minded question-and-answer period *after* a speech.

Persuasion Can Be Ethical

Even when they understand the difference between persuasion and coercion, some people are still uncomfortable with the idea of persuasive speaking. They see it as the work of high-pressure hucksters: salespeople with their feet stuck in the door, unscrupulous politicians taking advantage of beleaguered taxpayers, and so on. Indeed, many of the principles we are about to discuss have been used by unethical speakers for unethical purposes, but that is not what all—or even most—persuasion is about. Ethical persuasion plays a necessary and worthwhile role in everyone's life.

It is through ethical persuasion that we influence others' lives in worthwhile ways. The person who says, "I do not want to influence other people," is really saying, "I do not want to get involved with other people," and that is an abandonment of one's responsibilities as a human being. Look at the good you can accomplish through persuasion: You can convince a loved one to give up smoking or to not keep a firearm in the house; you can get members of your community to conserve energy or to join together to refurbish a park; you can persuade an employer to hire you for a job where your own talents, interests, and abilities will be put to their best use.

Persuasion is considered ethical if it conforms to accepted standards. But what are the standards today? If your plan is selfish and not in the best interest of your audience members, but you are honest about your motives—is that ethical? If your plan is in

CULTURAL IDIOM

backfire:
produce a result opposite of the one intended

high-pressure hucksters:
aggressive and persistent salespeople

the best interest of your audience members, yet you lie to them to get them to accept the plan—is that ethical? Philosophers and rhetoricians have argued for centuries over questions like these.

There are many ways to define **ethical persuasion**.[3] For our purpose, we will consider it as *communication in the best interest of the audience that does not depend on false or misleading information to change an audience's attitude or behavior.* The best way to appreciate the value of this simple definition is to consider the many strategies listed in Table 14-1 that do not fit it. For example, faking enthusiasm about a speech topic, plagiarizing material from another source and passing it off as your own, and making up statistics to support your case are clearly unethical.

Besides being wrong on moral grounds, unethical attempts at persuasion have a major practical disadvantage: If your deception is uncovered, your credibility will suffer. If, for example, prospective buyers uncover your attempt to withhold a structural flaw in the condominium you are trying to sell, they will probably suspect that the property has other hidden problems. Likewise, if your speech instructor suspects that you are lifting material from other sources without giving credit, your entire presentation will be suspect. One unethical act can cast doubt on future truthful statements. Thus, for pragmatic as well as moral reasons, honesty really is the best policy.

CULTURAL IDIOM
lifting material:
using another's words or ideas
as one's own

TABLE 14-1   Unethical Communication Behaviors

1. Committing Plagiarism
   a. Claiming someone else's ideas as your own
   b. Quoting without citing the source

2. Relaying False Information
   a. Deliberate lying
   b. Ignorant misstatement
   c. Deliberate distortion and suppression of material
   d. Fallacious reasoning to misrepresent truth

3. Withholding Information; Suppression
   a. About self (speaker); not disclosing private motives or special interests
   b. About speech purpose
   c. About sources (not revealing sources; plagiarism)
   d. About evidence; omission of certain evidence (card stacking)
   e. About opposing arguments; presenting only one side

4. Appearing to Be What One Is Not; Insincerity
   a. In words, saying what one does not mean or believe
   b. In delivery (for example, feigning enthusiasm)

5. Using Emotional Appeals to Hinder Truth
   a. Using emotional appeals as a substitute or cover-up for lack of sound reasoning and valid evidence
   b. Failing to use balanced appeals

Adapted from Mary Klaaren Andersen, "An Analysis of the Treatment of Ethos in Selected Speech Communication Textbooks" (unpublished dissertation, University of Michigan, 1979), pp. 244–247.

Ethical Challenge

Analyzing
Communication
Behaviors

Read Table 14-1 carefully. The behaviors listed there are presented in what some (but certainly not all) communication experts would describe as "most serious to least serious" ethical faults. Do you agree or disagree with the order of this list? Explain your answer, and whether you would change the order of any of these behaviors or not. Are there any other behaviors that you would add to this list?

Categorizing Types of Persuasion

There are several ways to categorize the types of persuasive attempts you will make as a speaker. What kinds of subjects will you focus on? What results will you be seeking? How will you go about getting those results? In the following pages we will look at each of these questions.

By Types of Proposition

Persuasive topics fall into one of three categories, depending on the type of thesis statement (referred to as a "proposition" in persuasion) that you are advancing. The three categories are propositions of fact, propositions of value, and propositions of policy.

Propositions of Fact   Some persuasive messages focus on **propositions of fact**: issues in which there are two or more sides about conflicting information, where listeners are required to choose the truth for themselves. Some questions of fact are these:

> The Bush administration did/did not mislead the American public about the reasons for going to war in Iraq.
>
> Windmills are/are not a practical way for the private homeowner to create clean energy.
>
> Bottled water is/is not healthier for you than tap water.

These examples show that many questions of fact can't be settled with a simple "yes" or "no" or with an objective piece of information. Rather, they are open to debate, and answering them requires careful examination and interpretation of evidence, usually collected from a variety of sources. That's why it is possible to debate questions of fact, and that's why these propositions form the basis of persuasive speeches and not informative ones.

Propositions of Value   **Propositions of value** go beyond issues of truth or falsity and explore the worth of some idea, person, or object. Propositions of value include the following:

> Cheerleaders are/are not just as valuable as the athletes on the field.
>
> The United States is/is not justified in attacking countries that harbor terrorist organizations.
>
> The use of laboratory animals for scientific experiments is/is not cruel and immoral.

In order to deal with most propositions of value, you will have to explore certain propositions of fact. For example, you won't be able to debate whether the experimental use of animals in research is immoral—a proposition of value—until you have dealt with propositions of fact such as how many animals are used in experiments and whether experts believe they actually suffer.

Propositions of Policy   **Propositions of policy** go one step beyond questions of fact or value: They recommend a specific course of action (a "policy"). Some questions of policy are these:

> The United States should/should not create a guest worker program that allows immigrants to enter the country legally on a temporary basis to fill jobs that employers say would otherwise go unfilled.

> The Electoral College should/should not be abolished.

> Genetic engineering of plants and livestock is/is not an appropriate way to increase the food supply.

Looking at persuasion according to the type of proposition is a convenient way to generate topics for a persuasive speech, because each type of proposition suggests different topics. Selected topics could also be handled differently depending on how they are approached. For example, a campaign speech could be approached as a proposition of fact ("Candidate X has done more for this community than the opponent"), a proposition of value ("Candidate X is a better person than the opponent"), or a proposition of policy ("We should get out and vote for Candidate X"). Remember, however, that a fully developed persuasive speech is likely to contain all three types of propositions. If you were preparing a speech advocating that college athletes should be paid in cash for their talents (a proposition of policy), you might want to first prove that the practice is already widespread (a proposition of fact) and that it is unfair to athletes from other schools (a proposition of value).

By Desired Outcome

We can also categorize persuasion according to two major outcomes: convincing and actuating.

Convincing   When you set about to **convince** an audience, you want to change the way its members think. When we say that convincing an audience changes the way its members think, we do not mean that you have to swing them from one belief or attitude to a completely different one. Sometimes audience members will already think the way you want them to, but they will not be firmly enough committed to that way of thinking. When that is the case, you reinforce, or strengthen, their opinions. For example, if your audience already believed that the federal budget should be balanced but did not consider the idea important, your job would be to reinforce members' current beliefs. Reinforcing is still a type of change, however, because you are causing an audience to adhere more strongly to a belief or attitude. In other cases, a speech to convince will begin to shift attitudes without bringing about a total change of thinking. For example, an effective speech to convince might get a group of skeptics to consider the possibility that bilingual education is/isn't a good idea.

> Sometimes audience members will already think the way you want them to, but they will not be firmly enough committed to that way of thinking.

Actuating   When you set about to **actuate** an audience, you want to move its members to a specific behavior. Whereas a speech to convince might move an audience to action, it won't be any specific action that you have recommended. In a speech to actuate, you do recommend that specific action.

There are two types of action you can ask for—adoption or discontinuance. The former asks an audience to engage in a new behavior; the latter asks an audience to stop behaving in an established way. If you gave a speech for a political candidate and then

asked for contributions to that candidate's campaign, you would be asking your audience to adopt a new behavior. If you gave a speech against smoking and then asked your audience members to sign a pledge to quit, you would be asking them to discontinue an established behavior.

By Directness of Approach

We can also categorize persuasion according to the directness of approach employed by the speaker.

Direct Persuasion   In **direct persuasion** the speaker will make his or her purpose clear, usually by stating it outright early in the speech. This is the best strategy to use with a friendly audience, especially when you are asking for a response that the audience is reasonably likely to give you. Direct persuasion is the kind we hear in most academic situations. Eugene Nemirovskiy, a student at Glendale Community College in California, used direct persuasion in his speech about America's mental health care system. Part of his introduction announced his intention to persuade in this way:

> The Virginia Tech shooter, Seung-Hui Cho, was released from a psychiatric hospital and ordered by the court to go to an outpatient treatment center. He never received care and no one enforced the court order. In Brooklyn, this past June, Esmin Green keeled over and died on the floor of a psychiatric emergency-room while she waited for help. She waited for more than 24 hours. . . . In fixing health care we've forgotten mental health-care. There's no parallel thing happening in other healthcare fields. People are not languishing or being neglected in cardiology wards across America. . . . In order to cure our mental health care systems we must first uncover what needs to be fixed, then, second, why the problems occur, and finally offer some viable solutions.[4]

Indirect Persuasion   **Indirect persuasion** disguises or deemphasizes the speaker's persuasive purpose in some way. The question "Is a season ticket to the symphony worth the money?" (when you intend to prove that it is) is based on indirect persuasion, as is any strategy that does not express the speaker's purpose at the outset.

Indirect persuasion is sometimes easy to spot. A television commercial that shows us attractive young men and women romping in the surf on a beautiful day and then flashes the product name on the screen is pretty indisputably indirect persuasion. Political oratory also is sometimes indirect persuasion, and it is sometimes more difficult to identify as such. A political hopeful might be ostensibly speaking on some great social issue when the real persuasive message is "Please—remember my name, and vote for me in the next election."

In public speaking, indirect persuasion is usually disguised as informative speaking, but this approach isn't necessarily unethical. In fact, it is probably the best approach to use when your audience is hostile to either you or your topic. It is also often necessary to use the indirect approach to get a hearing from listeners who would tune you out if you took a more direct approach. Under such circumstances, you might want to ease into your speech slowly.[5] You might take some time to make your audience feel good about you or the social action you are advocating. If you are speaking in favor of your candidacy for city council, but you are in favor of a tax increase and your audience is not, you might talk for a while about the benefits that a well-financed city council

CULTURAL IDIOM
tune you out:
stop listening

can provide to the community. You might even want to change your desired audience response. Rather than trying to get audience members to rush out to vote for you, you might want them simply to read a policy statement that you have written or become more informed on a particular issue. The one thing you cannot do in this instance is to begin by saying "My appearance here today has nothing to do with my candidacy for city council." That would be a false statement. It is more than indirect; it is untrue and therefore unethical.

The test of the ethics of an indirect approach would be whether you would express your persuasive purpose directly if asked to do so. In other words, if someone in the audience stopped you and asked, "Don't you want us to vote for you for city council?" You would admit to it rather than deny your true purpose, if you were ethical.

Find a current political speech in a newspaper such as the *New York Times*, or on the Internet. Which type of persuasive strategy is used in the speech: direct or indirect? Is the strategy used effectively? Why or why not?

Critical Thinking Probe

Direct or Indirect Persuasion?

Creating the Persuasive Message

Persuasive speaking has been defined as "reason-giving discourse." Its principal technique, therefore, involves proposing claims and then backing those claims up with reasons that are true. Preparing an effective persuasive speech isn't easy, but it can be made easier by observing a few simple rules. These include the following: Set a clear, persuasive purpose; structure the message carefully; use solid evidence; and avoid fallacies.

Set a Clear, Persuasive Purpose

Remember that your objective in a persuasive speech is to move the audience to a specific, attainable attitude or behavior. In a speech to convince, the purpose statement will probably stress an attitude:

After listening to my speech, my audience members will agree that steps should be taken to save whales from extinction.

In a speech to actuate, the purpose statement will stress behavior:

After listening to my speech, my audience members will sign my petition.

As Chapter 11 explained, your purpose statement should always be specific, attainable, and worded from the audience's point of view. "The purpose of my speech is to save the whales" is not a purpose statement that has been carefully thought out. Your audience members wouldn't be able to jump into the ocean and save the whales, even if your speech motivated them into a frenzy. They might, however, be able to support a specific piece of legislation.

A clear, specific purpose statement will help you stay on track throughout all the stages of preparation of your persuasive speech. Because the main purpose of your speech is to have an effect on your audience, you have a continual test that you can use for every idea, every piece of evidence, and every organizational structure that you think of using. The question you ask is "Will this help me to get the audience members to think/feel/behave in the manner I have described in my purpose statement?" If the answer is "yes," you forge ahead.

Structure the Message Carefully

A sample structure of the body of a persuasive speech is outlined in Figure 14-2. With this structure, if your objective is to convince, you concentrate on the first two components: establishing the problem and describing the solution. If your objective is to actuate, you add the third component, describing the desired audience reaction.

There are, of course, other structures for persuasive speeches. This one can be used as a basic model, however, because it is easily applied to most persuasive topics.

Describe the Problem   In order to convince an audience that something needs to be changed, you have to show members that a problem exists. After all, if your listeners don't recognize the problem, they won't find your arguments for a solution very important. An effective description of the problem will answer two questions, either directly or indirectly.

What Is the Nature of the Problem?   Your audience members might not recognize that the topic you are discussing is a problem at all, so your first task is to convince them that there is something wrong with the present state of affairs. For example, if your thesis were "This town needs a shelter for homeless families," you would need to show that there are, indeed, homeless families and that the plight of these homeless families is serious.

> Your first task is to convince them that there is something wrong with the present state of affairs.

Your approach to defining your problem will depend largely on your audience analysis, as discussed in Chapter 11. If your prespeech analysis shows that your audience may not feel sympathetic to your topic, you will need to explain why your topic is, indeed, a problem that your audience should recognize. In a speech about the plight of the homeless, you might need to establish that most homeless people are not lazy, able-bodied drifters who choose to panhandle and steal instead of work. You could cite respected authorities, give examples, and maybe even show photographs to demonstrate that some homeless people are hardworking but unlucky parents and innocent children who lack shelter owing to forces beyond their control.

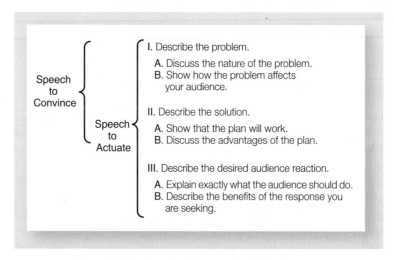

FIGURE 14-2 Sample Structure for a Persuasive Speech

How Does the Problem Affect Your Audience?   It's not enough to prove that a problem exists. Your next challenge is to show your listeners that the problem affects them in some way. This is relatively easy in some cases: the high cost of tuition, the lack of convenient parking near campus, the quality of food in the student center. In other cases, you will need to spell out the impact to your listeners more clearly. Hope Stallings, a student at Berry College in Georgia, presented a speech on deferred prosecution agreements for large corporations. She connected this topic to her audience in the following way:

> What do Morgan Stanley, Wachovia, Fannie Mae, Merrill Lynch, and AIG all have in common? You might say that they all contributed to the credit crisis in September, and according to the *Washington Post* of March 5, 2009, the ensuing $787 billion government bailout of big business. And you'd be right—partially. You see, these corporations have something else in common. In the past five years, each has been indicted on criminal charges like fraud. Never heard about the trials or verdict? That's because in spite of their fraudulent behavior, these corporations never went to court. They avoided the media spotlight, investor scrutiny, and public outrage by entering into deferred prosecution agreements. The *Record* of July 21, 2008, explains that deferred prosecution agreements allow corporations to avoid criminal convictions by paying a small fine out of court. In other words, these companies paid our government to ensure that we remain ignorant, and we have, right up to the collapse of our economy and our personal financial security.[6]

The problem section of a persuasive speech is often broken up into segments discussing the cause and the effect of the problem. (The sample speech at the end of this chapter is an example of this type of organization.)

Describe the Solution   Your next step in persuading your audience members is to convince them that there is an answer to the problem you have just introduced. To describe your solution, you should answer two questions:

Will the Solution Work?   A skeptical audience might agree with the desirability of your solution but still not believe that it has a chance of succeeding. In the homeless speech discussed previously, you would need to prove that the establishment of a shelter can help unlucky families get back on their feet—especially if your audience analysis shows that some listeners might view such a shelter as a way of coddling people who are too lazy to work.

What Advantages Will Result from Your Solution?   You need to describe in specific terms how your solution will lead to the desired changes. This is the step where you will paint a vivid picture of the benefits of your proposal. In the speech proposing a shelter for homeless families, the benefits you describe would probably include these:

1. Families will have a safe place to stay, free of the danger of living on the street.

2. Parents will have the resources that will help them find jobs: an address, telephone, clothes washers, and showers.

3. The police won't have to apply antivagrancy laws (such as prohibitions against sleeping in cars) to people who aren't the intended target of those laws.

4. The community (including your listeners) won't need to feel guilty about ignoring the plight of unfortunate citizens.

Describe the Desired Audience Response   When you want to go beyond simply a strategy to convince your audience members and use a strategy to actuate them to follow your solution, you need to describe exactly what you want them to do. This action step, like the previous ones, should answer two questions:

CULTURAL IDIOM

get back on their feet:
return to a financially stable lifestyle

paint a . . . picture:
describe in detail

What Can the Audience Do to Put Your Solution into Action?   Make the behavior you are asking your audience members to adopt as clear and simple as possible for them. If you want them to vote in a referendum, tell them when and where to go to vote and how to go about registering, if necessary (some activists even provide transportation). If you're asking them to support a legislative change, don't expect them to write their congressional representative. *You* write the letter or draft a petition, and ask them to sign it. If you're asking for a donation, pass the hat at the conclusion of your speech, or give audience members a stamped, addressed envelope and simple forms that they can return easily.

What Are the Direct Rewards of This Response?   Your solution might be important to society, but your audience members will be most likely to adopt it if you can show that they will get a personal payoff. Show that supporting legislation to reduce acid rain will produce a wide range of benefits, from reduced lung damage to healthier forests to longer life for their car's paint. Explain that saying "no" to a second drink before driving will not only save lives but also help your listeners avoid expensive court costs, keep their insurance rates low, and prevent personal humiliation. Show how helping to establish and staff a homeless shelter can lead to personal feelings of satisfaction and provide an impressive demonstration of community service on a job-seeking résumé.

Adapt the Model Persuasive Structure   Describing the problem and the solution makes up the basic structure for any persuasive speech. However, you don't have to analyze too many successful persuasive speeches to realize that the best of them do far more than the basic minimum. In one adaptation of the basic model, the speaker will combine the solution with the desired audience response. Another adaptation is known as the Motivated Sequence.

Motivated Sequence   The **Motivated Sequence** was proposed by a scholar named Alan Monroe in the 1930s.[7] In this persuasive pattern the problem is broken down into an attention step and a need step, and the solution is broken down into a satisfaction step, a visualization step, and an action step. In a speech on "Canine Liberation,"[8] the motivated sequence might break down like this:

I. The attention step draws attention to your subject. ("Cheers for the urban guerillas of New York City, the dauntless men and women who let their dogs loose in the parks!")

II. The need step establishes the problem. ("In this country, we tend to think that freedom for dogs encourages bad behavior. Nothing could be further from the truth. Freedom actually improves a dog's conduct.")

III. The satisfaction step proposes a solution. ("The time has come for New York and other American cities to unleash their dogs.")

IV. The visualization step describes the results of the solution. ("In the splendid cities of Europe, well-mannered dogs are accepted almost everywhere as a normal part of life.")

V. The action step is a direct appeal for the audience to do something. ("Demand that parts of Central Park become leash-free. Dog lovers of New York, unite!")

Use Solid Evidence

All the forms of support discussed in Chapter 12 can be used to back up your persuasive arguments.[9] Your objective here is not to find supporting material that just clarifies your ideas, but rather to find the perfect example, statistic, definition, analogy, anecdote, or testimony to establish the truth of your claim in the mind of this specific audience.

You choose **evidence** that strongly supports your claim, and you should feel free to use **emotional evidence**, which is supporting material that evokes audience feelings such as fear, anger, sympathy, pride, or reverence. Emotional evidence is an ethical fault only when it is used to obscure the truth (see Table 14-1, page 407). It is ethical, however, to use emotion to give impact to a truth.

Whatever type of evidence you use, you should cite your sources carefully. It is important that your audience knows that your sources are credible, unbiased, and current. If you are quoting the source of an interview, give a full statement of the source's credentials:

> *According to Sean Wilentz, Dayton–Stockton Professor of History, Director of American Studies at Princeton University, and the author of several books on this topic . . .*

If the currency of the interview is important, you might add, "I spoke to Professor Wilentz just last week . . . " If you are quoting an article, give a quick statement of the author's credentials and the full date and title of the magazine:

> *According to Professor Sean Wilentz of Princeton University, in an article in the April 21, 2006,* Rolling Stone Magazine . . .

You do not need to give the title of the article (although you may, if it helps in any way) or the page number. If you are quoting from a book, include a quick statement of the author's credentials:

> *According to Professor Sean Wilentz of Princeton University, in his book* The Rise of American Democracy . . .

You don't need to include the copyright date unless it's important to authenticate the currency of the quotation, and you don't have to mention the publisher or city of publication unless it's relevant to your topic. Generally, if you're unsure about how to cite your sources in a speech, you should err in the direction of too much information rather than too little.

Carefully cited sources are part of a well-reasoned argument. This brings us to our next step in creating a persuasive message.

> Whatever type of evidence you use, you should cite your sources carefully.

Avoid Fallacies

A **fallacy** (from the Latin word meaning "false") is an error in logic. Although the original meaning of the term implied purposeful deception, most logical fallacies are not recognized as such by those who use them. Scholars have devoted lives and volumes to the description of various types of logical fallacies.[10] Here are some of the most common ones to keep in mind when building your persuasive argument:[11]

Attack on the Person Instead of the Argument (*Ad Hominem*)   In an *ad hominem* **fallacy** the speaker attacks the integrity of a person in order to weaken the argument. At its most crude level, an *ad hominem* argument is easy to detect. "How can you believe that fat slob?" is hardly persuasive. It takes critical thinking to catch more subtle *ad hominem* arguments, however. Consider this one: "All this talk about 'family values' is hypocritical. Take Senator _____ , who made a speech about the 'sanctity of marriage' last year. Now it turns out he was having an affair with his secretary, and his wife is suing him for divorce." Although the senator certainly does seem to be a hypocrite, his behavior doesn't necessarily weaken the merits of family values.

Reduction to the Absurd (*Reductio Ad Absurdum*)

A *reductio ad absurdum* fallacy unfairly attacks an argument by extending it to such extreme lengths that it looks ridiculous. "If we allow developers to build homes in one section of this area, soon we will have no open spaces left. Fresh air and wildlife will be a thing of the past." "If we allow the administration to raise tuition this year, soon they will be raising it every year, and before we know it only the wealthiest students will be able to go to school here." This extension of reasoning doesn't make any sense: Developing one area doesn't necessarily mean that other areas have to be developed, and one tuition increase doesn't mean that others will occur. Any of these policies might be unwise or unfair, but the *ad absurdum* reasoning doesn't prove it.

Either-Or

An **either-or fallacy** sets up false alternatives, suggesting that if the inferior one must be rejected, then the other must be accepted. An angry citizen used either-or thinking to support a proposed city ordinance: "Either we outlaw alcohol in city parks, or there will be no way to get rid of drunks." This reasoning overlooks the possibility that there may be other ways to control public drunkenness besides banning all alcoholic beverages. The old saying "America, love it or leave it" provides another example of either-or reasoning. For instance, when an Asian-born college professor pointed out examples of lingering discrimination in the United States, some suggested that if she didn't like her adopted country she should return to her native home—ignoring that it is possible to admire a country and still envision ways to make it a better place.

False Cause (*Post Hoc Ergo Propter Hoc*)

A *post hoc* fallacy mistakenly assumes that one event causes another because they occur sequentially. An old (and not especially funny) joke illustrates the *post hoc* fallacy. Mac approaches Jack and asks, "Hey, why are you snapping your fingers?" Jack replies, "To keep the elephants away." Mac is incredulous: "What are you talking about? There aren't any elephants within a thousand miles of here." Jack smiles and keeps on snapping: "I know. Works pretty well, doesn't it?"

> When considering endorsements and claims, it's smart to ask yourself whether the source is qualified to make them.

In real life, *post hoc* fallacies aren't always so easy to detect. For example, one critic of education pointed out that the increase in sexual promiscuity among adolescents began about the same time as prayer in public schools was prohibited by the courts. A causal link in this case may exist: Decreased emphasis on spirituality could contribute to promiscuity. But it would take evidence to establish a *definite* connection between the two phenomena.

Appeal to Authority (*Argumentum Ad Verecundiam*)

An *argumentum ad verecundiam* fallacy involves relying on the testimony of someone who is not an authority in the case being argued. Relying on experts is not a fallacy, of course. A movie star might be just the right person to offer advice on how to seem more glamorous, and a professional athlete could be the best person to comment on what it takes to succeed in organized sports. But an *ad verecundiam* fallacy occurs when the movie star promotes a political candidate or the athlete tells us why we should buy a certain kind of automobile. When considering endorsements and claims, it's smart to ask yourself whether the source is qualified to make them.

Bandwagon Appeal (*Argumentum Ad Populum*)

An *argumentum ad populum* fallacy is based on the often dubious notion that, just because many people favor an idea, you should, too. Sometimes, of course, the mass appeal of an idea can be a sign of its merit. If most of your friends have enjoyed a film or a new book, there is probably a good chance that you will, too. But in other cases widespread acceptance of an idea is

Understanding Diversity

Cultural Differences in Persuasion

Different individuals have a tendency to view persuasion differently, and often these differences are based on cultural background. Even the ability to recognize logical argument is, to a certain extent, culturally determined. Not all cultures use logic in the same way that the European-American culture does. The influence of the dominant culture is seen even in the way we talk about argumentation. When we talk about "defending" ideas and "attacking our opponent's position" we are using male-oriented militaristic/aggressive terms. Logic is also based on a trust in objective reality, on information that is verifiable through our senses. As one researcher points out, such a perspective can be culturally influenced:

> Western culture assumes a reality that is materialist and limited to comprehension via the five senses. African

culture assumes a reality that is both material and spiritual viewed as one and the same.[12]

The way logic is viewed differs between Eastern and Western hemisphere cultures, also. As Samovar and Porter point out:

> Westerners discover truth by active searching and the application of Aristotelian modes of reasoning. On the contrary, many Easterners wait patiently, and if truth is to be known it will make itself apparent.[13]

It is because of cultural differences such as these that speech experts have always recommended a blending of logical and emotional evidence.

no guarantee of its validity. In the face of almost universal belief to the contrary, Galileo reasoned accurately that the earth is not the center of the universe, and he suffered for his convictions. The lesson here is simple to comprehend but often difficult to follow: When faced with an idea, don't just follow the crowd. Consider the facts carefully and make up your own mind.

CULTURAL IDIOM
follow the crowd:
do what the majority does

Adapting to the Audience

It is important to know as much as possible about your audience for a persuasive speech. For one thing, you should appeal to the values of your audience whenever possible, even if they are not *your* strongest values. This advice does not mean you should pretend to believe in something. According to our definition of *ethical persuasion*, pretense is against the rules. It does mean, however, that you have to stress those values that are felt most forcefully by the members of your audience.[14]

> It is important to know as much as possible about your audience for a persuasive speech.

In addition, you should analyze your audience carefully to predict the type of response you will get. Sometimes you have to pick out one part of your audience—a **target audience**, the subgroup you must persuade to reach your goal—and aim your speech mostly at those members. Some of your audience members might be so opposed to what you are advocating that you have no hope of reaching them. Still others might already agree with you, so they do not need to be persuaded. A middle portion of your audience members might be undecided or uncommitted, and they would be the most productive target for your appeals.

Of course, you need not ignore that portion of your audience who does not fit your target. For example, if you were giving a speech against smoking, your target might be the smokers in your class. Your main purpose would be to get them to quit, but at the same time, you could convince the nonsmokers not to start and to use their influence to help their smoking friends quit.

All of the methods of audience analysis described in Chapter 11—surveys, observation, interviews, and research—are valuable in collecting information about your audience for a persuasive speech.

CULTURAL IDIOM

on the other hand:
from the other point of view

Establish Common Ground

It helps to stress as many similarities as possible between yourself and your audience members. This technique helps prove that you understand them: If not, why should they listen to you? Also, if you share a lot of common ground, it shows you agree on many things; therefore, it should be easy to settle one disagreement—the one related to the attitude or behavior you would like them to change.

The manager of public affairs for *Playboy* magazine gave a good demonstration of establishing common ground when he reminded a group of Southern Baptists that they shared some important values with him:

> I am sure we are all aware of the seeming incongruity of a representative of *Playboy* magazine speaking to an assemblage of representatives of the Southern Baptist convention. I was intrigued by the invitation when it came last fall, though I was not surprised. I am grateful for your genuine and warm hospitality, and I am flattered (although again not surprised) by the implication that I would have something to say that could have meaning to you people. Both *Playboy* and the Baptists have indeed been considering many of the same issues and ethical problems; and even if we have not arrived at the same conclusions, I am impressed and gratified by your openness and willingness to listen to our views.[15]

Organize According to the Expected Response

It is much easier to get an audience to agree with you if the members have already agreed with you on a previous point. Therefore, you should arrange your points in a persuasive speech so you develop a "yes" response. In effect, you get your audience into the habit of agreeing with you. For example, if you were giving a speech on the donation of body organs, you might begin by asking the audience members if they would like to be able to get a kidney if they needed one. Then you might ask them if they would like to have a major role in curbing tragic and needless dying. The presumed response to both questions is "yes." It is only when you have built a pattern of "yes" responses that you would ask the audience to sign organ donor cards.

An example of a speaker who was careful to organize material according to expected audience response was the late Robert Kennedy. Kennedy, when speaking on civil rights before a group of South Africans who believed in racial discrimination, arranged his ideas so that he spoke first on values that he and his audience shared—values like independence and freedom.[16]

If audience members are already basically in agreement with you, you can organize your material to reinforce their attitudes quickly and then spend most of your time convincing them to take a specific course of action. If, on the other hand, they are hostile to your ideas, you have to spend more time getting the first "yes" out of them.

Neutralize Potential Hostility

One of the trickier problems in audience adaptation occurs when you face an audience hostile to you or your ideas. Hostile audiences are those who have a significant number of members who feel adversely about you, your topic, or the speech situation. Members of a hostile audience could range from unfriendly to violent. Two guidelines for handling this type of audience are (1) show that you understand their point of view and (2) if possible, use appropriate humor. A good example of a speaker who observed these guidelines was First Lady and literacy activist Barbara Bush when she was invited to speak at the commencement exercises at Wellesley College in 1990. After the invitation

was announced, 150 graduating seniors at the prestigious women's college signed a petition in protest. They wrote, in part:

> We are outraged by this choice and feel it is important to make ourselves heard immediately. Wellesley teaches us that we will be rewarded on the basis of our own work, not on that of a spouse. To honor Barbara Bush as a commencement speaker is to honor a woman who has gained recognition through the achievements of her husband.[17]

Mrs. Bush decided to honor her speaking obligation, knowing that these 150 students and others who shared their view would be in the audience of 5,000 people. Mrs. Bush diffused most of this hostility by presenting a speech that stressed that everyone should follow her personal dream and be tolerant of the dreams of others:

> For over fifty years, it was said that the winner of Wellesley's annual hoop race would be the first to get married. Now they say the winner will be the first to become a C.E.O. Both of these stereotypes show too little tolerance. . . . So I offer you today a new legend: the winner of the hoop race will be the first to realize her dream, not society's dream, her own personal dream.[18]

Ethical Challenge

Adapting to a Hostile Audience

How far would you go in adapting to a hostile audience? What forms would that adaptation take? Discuss this question with your classmates, using a specific speech situation as an example. You can make up the speech situation or choose one of the following:

1. Speaking before a group of advertising executives about your firm belief that there should be heavy governmental penalties for false or deceptive advertising
2. Speaking before a group of Catholic bishops about your belief in reproductive choice
3. Speaking before a group of animal rights advocates about advances in interspecies (animal to human) organ transplants

Building Credibility as a Speaker

Credibility refers to the believability of a speaker. Credibility isn't an objective quality; rather, it is a perception in the minds of the audience. In a class such as the one you're taking now, students often wonder how they can build their credibility. After all, the members of the class tend to know each other well by the time the speech assignments roll around. This familiarity illustrates why it's important to earn a good reputation before you speak, through your class comments and the general attitude you've shown.

It is also possible for credibility to change during a speaking event. In fact, researchers speak in terms of initial credibility (what you have when you first get up to speak), derived credibility (what you acquire while speaking), and terminal credibility (what you have after you finish speaking). It is not uncommon for a student with low initial credibility to earn increased credibility while speaking and to finish with much higher terminal credibility.

Without credibility, you won't be able to convince your listeners that your ideas are worth accepting even if your material is outstanding. On the other hand, if you can develop a high degree of credibility in the eyes of your listeners, they will be likely to open up to ideas they wouldn't otherwise accept. Members of an audience form judgments about the credibility of a speaker based on their perception of many characteristics, the most important of which might be called the "Three Cs" of credibility: competence, character, and charisma.[19]

CULTURAL IDIOM
roll around:
occur, arrive

Competence

Competence refers to the speaker's expertise on the topic. Sometimes this competence can come from personal experience that will lead your audience to regard you as an authority on the topic you are discussing. If everyone in the audience knows you've earned big profits in the stock market, they will probably take your investment advice seriously. If you say that you lost twenty-five pounds from a diet-and-exercise program, most audience members will be likely to respect your opinions on weight loss.

The other way to be seen as competent is to be well prepared for speaking. A speech that is well researched, organized, and presented will greatly increase the audience's perception of the speaker's competence. Your personal credibility will therefore be enhanced by the credibility of your evidence, including the sources you cite, the examples you choose, the way you present statistics, the quality of your visual aids, and the precision of your language.

Character

Competence is the first component of being believed by an audience. The second is being trusted, which is a matter of character. *Character* involves the audience's perception of at least two ingredients: honesty and impartiality. You should try to find ways to talk about yourself (without boasting, of course) that demonstrate your integrity. You might describe how much time you spent researching the subject or demonstrate your open-mindedness by telling your audience that you changed your mind after your investigation. For example, if you were giving a speech arguing against a proposed tax cut in your community, you might begin this way:

> You might say I'm an expert on the municipal services of this town. As a lifelong resident, I owe a debt to its schools and recreation programs. I've been protected by its police and firefighters and served by its hospitals, roads, and sanitation crews.
>
> I'm also a taxpayer who's on a tight budget. When I first heard about the tax cut that's been proposed, I liked the idea. But then I did some in-depth investigation into the possible effects, not just to my tax bill but to the quality of life of our entire community. I looked into our municipal expenses and into the expenses of similar communities where tax cuts have been mandated by law.

Charisma

Charisma is spoken about in the popular press as an almost indefinable, mystical quality. Even the dictionary defines it as "a special quality of leadership that captures the popular imagination and inspires unswerving allegiance and devotion." Luckily, communication scholars favor a more down-to-earth definition. For them, charisma is the audience's perception of two factors: the speaker's enthusiasm and likability. Whatever the definition, history and research have both shown us that audiences are more likely to be persuaded by a charismatic speaker than by a less charismatic one who delivers the same information.

Enthusiasm is sometimes called "dynamism" by communication scholars. Your enthusiasm will mostly be perceived from how you deliver your remarks, not from what you say. The nonverbal parts of your speech will show far better than your words that you believe in what you are saying. Is your voice animated and sincere? Do your gestures reflect your enthusiasm? Do your facial expression and eye contact show you care about your audience?

You can boost your likability by showing that you like and respect your audience. Insincere flattery will probably boomerang, but if you can find a way to give your listeners a genuine compliment, they'll be more receptive to your ideas.

CULTURAL IDIOM
down-to-earth:
practical

boomerang:
create a negative effect

@Work

Persuasion Skills in the World of Sales

The skills you develop while learning to prepare persuasive speeches are generalizable to a number of important skills in the world of work. The advice of business consultant George Rodriguez makes it clear that the process of developing a successful sales plan is very much like the planning involved in building a persuasive speech.

"A sales plan is basically your strategic and tactical plan for achieving your marketing objectives," Rodriguez explains. "It is a step-by-step and detailed process that will show how you will acquire new business; and how you will gain more business from your existing customer base."[20]

The process of audience analysis is as important in sales-plan development as it is in persuasive speaking. "The first step is to clearly identify your target markets," Rodriquez says. "Who are more likely to buy your product? The more defined your target market, the better. Your target market can be defined as high-income men ages 30–60 who love to buy the latest electronic gadgets; or mothers with babies 0–12 months old living in urban areas."

And don't forget the guideline that persuasion is interactive. "Prospects are more likely to purchase if you can talk to them about solving their problems," Rodriguez points out.

Rodriguez is far from alone in pointing out the importance of thinking in terms of problems and solutions. Business consultant Barbara Sanfilippo advises her clients to "Prepare, prepare, and plan your calls. Today's customers and prospects have very little time to waste. They want solutions. A sales consultant who demonstrates a keen understanding of customers' needs and shows up prepared will earn the business."[21] Sanfilippo suggests reviewing the customer's website and interviewing key people in advance of the meeting.

Sanfilippo also points out the importance of building credibility: "How can you stand out from the pack of sales professionals and consultants all offering similar services?" she asks rhetorically. "Establish Credibility and Differentiate!"

But George Rodriguez probably has the last word in how valuable training in persuasive speaking is to the sales professional. Before you make that first sales call, he says, "You may want to take courses on how to improve your confidence and presentation skills."

Building your personal credibility through a recognition of the roles of competence, character, and charisma is an important component of your persuasive strategy. When combined with a careful consideration of audience adaptation, persuasive structure, and persuasive purpose, it will enable you to formulate the most effective strategy possible.

Sample Speech

The sample speech for this chapter was presented by Katie Donovan, a student and member of the forensics team at Rice University in Houston, Texas. She was coached by David Worth and became a finalist in several speech tournaments during the spring of 2010. She also qualified for the American Forensic Association's National Individual Events Tournament of Excellence and won her team's Speaker of the Year Award with this speech.

Katie's topic is based on a proposition of policy that led to the following thesis statement:

We should reduce our use of plastic shopping bags.

Her purpose statement could be stated as follows:

After listening to my speech, audience members will reduce their use of single-use plastic shopping bags and consider other long-term solutions to this problem.

Katie was drawn to this topic by a small story on the BBC about India passing regulations to cut down on plastic bag use after a devastating 2009 flood in Mumbai. She explains, "I had never realized just how much damage these bags could do and figured few other people knew the extent of the harms, either."[22]

In fact, as a dedicated speech competitor, Katie's advice to beginning speakers is as follows:

> The more you care about your topic the better the speech will be, no matter how long you spend preparing for it. The speeches that win are the speeches where the speakers have an obvious passion for the problem they are discussing.[23]

Katie did her research in her campus library. She learned about one researcher, Dr. Susan Selke, in a magazine article, and contacted her by e-mail. Soon Katie and Selke were maintaining a correspondence, and Selke was supplying her with insights into the topic and was able to help direct her research.

Katie begins with an indirect persuasive approach to avoid an "oh this again" reaction on the part of her audience. She moves rather quickly, however, into a direct approach. She definitely wants to actuate a specific audience behavior.

Katie carefully organized her speech in a problem-cause-solutions format, arranging her points for persuasive impact. Her persuasive organization can be seen in the following outline. (Parenthetical numbers refer to paragraphs in the speech.)

Introduction (1–4)

  I. Attention-getter (1–3)
 II. Statement of thesis (4)
III. Preview of main points (4)

Body (5–21)

   I. Plastic shopping bags continue to be a major environmental problem. (5–10)
     A. Plastic bags are not regenerative. (6)
     B. Plastic bags are not biodegradable. (7)
     C. Plastic bags clog oceans and endanger wildlife. (8)
     D. Plastic bags clog drainage systems and endanger humans. (9–10)
     Transition to second main point (11)
  II. This problem exists because of a number of reasons. (12–14)
     A. Stores use plastic bags because they are popular and low-cost. (12)
     B. Shopper use plastic bags out of apathy. (13)
       1. Shoppers aren't reminded of alternatives by stores. (14)
       2. Shoppers use them out of habit. (14)
       3. Shoppers forget that the bags are dangerous. (14)
III. Solutions can be found on the federal, local, and individual levels. (15–18)
     A. On the federal level, support the Bag Reduction Act. (16)
     B. On the local level, push your local leaders for a bag ban. (17)
     C. On the personal level, bring reusable bags when you go shopping. (18)

Conclusion (22–25)

  I. Review of main points (22)
 II. Restatement of thesis (23)
III. Final remarks (24)

As you read Katie's speech, notice how she expands on this outline as she develops her argument point by point.

Bagging It: The Problem's Not Solved   **Katie Donovan**

1   They congregate in our oceans, countryside, and cities. There are enough in America that, if each were worth one dollar, we could pay off California's $26 billion budget deficit. They are only useful for about an hour, and they get used at a rate of one million a minute. And, according to the *Montreal Gazette* of July 11, 2009, they killed one thousand people during Mumbai's last monsoon season.

The attention-getter is in the form of an intriguing riddle (an indirect approach). It uses current headlines (California's budget deficit), statistics, and a startling statement of fact (about the Mumbai monsoons).

2   What are they? The single-use disposable plastic shopping bag. Keep America Beautiful's annual report of 2009 explains that, though America's overall litter is decreasing, these bags account for 42 percent of all road litter, an increase of 165 percent in less than a decade.

More well-sourced statistics used as evidence.

3   You've heard this before. In fact, in public speaking, we like to talk about *new* problems. Audiences don't like to listen to old topics. But that's the problem: We dismiss these issues because they are old, forgetting that they are not solved. The simple problem of the single-use disposable shopping bag shouldn't be worsening. But it is, and this forces us to once again address the issue.

Here Katie seeks to establish common ground with her audience while also overcoming possible audience objections to this topic.

4   So, to help us get a handle on what the United Nations Environment Program referred to in June of 2009 as "the litter that should be banned or phased out rapidly everywhere," we will examine the problems caused by the disposable shopping bag, investigate why this predicament persists, and develop some solutions so that we can get our groceries guilt-free.

Statement of thesis and preview of main points.

5   The problem with "bagging it" stems from plastic's biggest drawback: the difficulties of disposal. Put simply, they aren't regenerative recyclables and they're lethal to humans and animals alike.

Preview of first main point. The following paragraphs contain effective evidence supporting the importance of her topic.

6   While regenerative materials like aluminum can be processed into the same item over and over, plastic degrades with each recycling phase and becomes unusable. As a result, the recycling process yields lower-quality plastic, costs more than making new bags, and requires almost as much energy as the initial production.

First subpoint.

7   Additionally, the bags just aren't green. In my personal interview with Dr. Susan Selke on November 3, 2009, this associate director of Michigan State University's School of Packaging confirmed that, despite the plastic industry's attempts to convince the public otherwise, there is no such thing as biodegradable plastic. Plastic bags will take one thousand years to decompose on their own, meaning that those bags you see by the side of the road will outlast you, and your children, and thirty-eight more generations.

Second subpoint, backed up with a highly credible personal interview and statistics presented as a personal and concrete example.

8   But the bags do more than just take up space in landfills. Millions of bags simply never make it to a trash can or recycling center. The Australian government's Department of Environment and Heritage concluded last year that there are 46,000 pieces of plastic in every square mile of ocean on the planet. The Algalita Marine Research Center found in September of 2009 that every year 100,000 whales, seals, turtles, and fish are choked, strangled, or starved by plastic bags.

Third subpoint, again backed up with high-impact concrete statistics.

9   And they don't affect just animals. The bags clog drainage systems worldwide, causing widespread flooding on every continent. The rains of Mumbai's monsoon season were only able to kill so many people because these bags overran the sewer system. And, according to a Florida Department of Environmental Protection's report released February 1, 2010, Tallahassee, a city of less than 200,000 people, permanently employs three flush trucks and over two dozen employees solely to keep the storm drains and ditches free of plastic bags.

Fourth subpoint, backed up with examples.

10 Worse, these plastics that sit in our gutters are effective conduits for hydrophobic poisons like DDT and polychlorinated biphenyl. Research from the National Toxicology Program published in November 2009 confirms that these chemicals cause cancer, brain damage, and birth defects. Clearly, single-use disposable shopping bags are lethal.

More evidence, and a review of this first main point.

11 Now that we've seen the harms of the shopping bag, we can examine the causes of this problem. There are two reasons for the continued presence of these bags at the checkout: industrial apathy and individual ignorance.

Transition to second main point.

12 Since plastic bags first became an option in 1977, stores have provided the bags as a service. The idea for a convenient, disposable tote to hold your purchases sold itself. Today, a plastic grocery bag costs a single cent. Thus, stores don't see a reason to limit this service.

First subpoint.

13 But this problem has a second cause: individual apathy. *The Guardian* of February 4, 2010, explains that 45 percent of shoppers have a reusable bag, but only 12 percent of those shoppers use the bag more than twice. That means that in a room of one hundred people, fewer than six regularly bring a reusable shopping bag.

Second subpoint.

14 This apathy has three causes: commercial indifference, habit, and forgetfulness. Stores don't regularly mention reusable bags to their customers, so the issue stays out of mind. Even shoppers who are aware of the problem routinely forget and simply use the bags right there at checkout. But worse, a vast majority of people falsely believe that the bags they use aren't harmful, or that their individual use doesn't change anything. Because of this industrial apathy and individual ignorance, the *Marine Pollution Bulletin*, published in August of 2009, approximates that one trillion plastic bags are used globally each year.

Three sub-subpoints.

15 Now that we know why the problems persist, we can take action to end our dependence on shopping bags. Solutions can be found on the federal, local, and individual levels.

Transition to final main point includes a review of the last point and a preview of the next.

16 First, contact your congressional representative and tell them you support the bag tax in House Resolution 2091: the Bag Reduction Act. This act allows the IRS to levy an excise tax on companies that offer disposable shopping bags. This program can't solve everything, but it's been proven that making it more expensive to offer single-use bags decreases their use. For example, the *Belfast Telegraph* of February 2, 2010, reports that Ireland implemented a bag tax equivalent to 20 U.S. cents per bag in March of 2002 and has since seen a 95 percent reduction in the use of plastic bags. This act helps challenge the widespread use of cheap single-use shopping bags by simply making it more expensive for stores to offer them.

Katie organizes the subpoints in these next three paragraphs according to expected response. Federal and local solutions might seem too difficult or unproductive; the personal solution, however, is easy and guaranteed to have an impact.

17 Second, push your local leaders for a bag ban. A growing number of U.S. cities including San Francisco, Oakland, Los Angeles, Portland, Madison, Brownsville, Washington DC, Westport, and Boston have already implemented or are considering a bag ban. According to the *China Daily* of May 26, 2009, China's outright ban on the production, sale, and possession of plastic bags as of June, 2010, has already cut the use of 40 billion bags. However, the movement here is small and faces immense opposition from the plastics industry, making your vocal support crucial for America to start seeing a real decrease in our disposable-bag consumption.

18 Finally, instead of waiting for lawmakers, you can make a direct impact yourself. Bring reusable bags when you go shopping. Yes, this solution is ridiculously simple. So there's no reason not to do it. But most people simply aren't making this choice.

19   And if you think using paper bags to cut down on your plastic use is the solution, according to the U.S. Department of Agriculture's website, updated daily, those supposedly eco-friendly paper sacks annually consume enough trees in the U.S. to hold 1 million metric tons of carbon, the equivalent of shutting down an entire coal-fired power plant for a whole year. The answer to plastic bags isn't paper, so our best option as individuals is to turn to reusable bags.

Here she refutes a counterpoint that she predicts some audience members will be asking themselves.

20   But remember, movements only become effective when people get on the bandwagon, so pick up a reusable bag and use it. Stores like Target and CVS will even reward your efforts with a discount on your purchase.

Here her appeal becomes extremely direct.

21   By acting to tax, ban, and simply stop using single-use disposable shopping bags, we can finally put an end to this embarrassingly old problem.

22   Today, we've examined the problems brought on by single-use disposable shopping bags, identified the industrial and individual causes that keep these bags around, before finally turning to the solutions available on a federal, local, and individual level.

Review of main points.

23   We've all heard that we are supposed to use reusable bags, but the truth is that after years of talking about it, few of us are actually doing it. Florida's Department of Environmental Protection said it best when they warned Florida's legislature that these bags "have terrible consequences in a throwaway society—yet there are simple, readily available ways to reduce our dependence."

She restates her thesis to remind her audience about the relevance and currency of her topic.

24   We may not be able to pay off California's budget deficit in plastic bags, and we can't bring back the lives lost in the Mumbai flooding, but by no longer using single-use disposable shopping bags we can help to end the harms done to our forests, oceans, wildlife, and fellow humans. And that is pretty convenient.

Her final remarks leave the audience with a strong appeal for her desired action.

Summary

Persuasion—the act of moving someone, through communication, toward a belief, attitude, or behavior—can be both worthwhile and ethical. Ethical persuasion requires that the speaker be sincere and honest and avoid such behaviors as plagiarism. It also requires that the persuasion be in the best interest of the audience.

Persuasion can be categorized according to the type of proposition (fact, value, or policy), outcome (convincing or actuating), or approach (direct or indirect). A persuasive strategy is put into effect through the use of several techniques. These include setting a specific, clear persuasive purpose, structuring the message carefully, using solid evidence (including emotional evidence), using careful reasoning, adapting to the audience, and building credibility as a speaker.

A typical structure for a speech to convince requires you to explain what the problem is and then propose a solution. For a speech to actuate, you also have to ask for a desired audience response. The basic three-pronged structure can be adapted to more elaborate persuasive plans, but the basic components will remain a part of any persuasive strategy. For each of these components, you need to analyze the arguments your audience will have against accepting what you say and then answer those arguments.

In adapting to your audience, you should establish common ground, organize your speech in such a way that you can expect a "yes" response along each step of your persuasive plan, and take special care with a hostile audience. In building credibility, you should keep in mind the audience's perception of your competence, character, and charisma.

Key Terms

actuate To move members of an audience toward a specific behavior. *p. 409*

ad hominem **fallacy** Fallacious argument that attacks the integrity of a person to weaken his or her position. *p. 415*

anchor The position supported by audience members before a persuasion attempt. *p. 405*

argumentum ad populum **fallacy** Fallacious reasoning based on the dubious notion that because many people favor an idea, you should, too. *p. 416*

argumentum ad verecundiam **fallacy** Fallacious reasoning that tries to support a belief by relying on the testimony of someone who is not an authority on the issue being argued. *p. 416*

convincing A speech goal that aims at changing audience members' beliefs, values, or attitudes. *p. 409*

credibility The believability of a speaker or other source of information. *p. 419*

direct persuasion Persuasion that does not try to hide or disguise the speaker's persuasive purpose. *p. 410*

either-or fallacy Fallacious reasoning that sets up false alternatives, suggesting that if the inferior one must be rejected, then the other must be accepted. *p. 416*

emotional evidence Evidence that arouses emotional reactions in an audience. *p. 415*

ethical persuasion Persuasion in an audience's best interest that does not depend on false or misleading information to induce change in that audience. *p. 407*

evidence Material used to prove a point, such as testimony, statistics, and examples. *p. 415*

fallacy An error in logic. *p. 415*

indirect persuasion Persuasion that disguises or deemphasizes the speaker's persuasive goal. *p. 410*

latitude of acceptance In social judgment theory, statements that a receiver would not reject. *p. 405*

latitude of noncommitment In social judgment theory, statements that a receiver would not care strongly about one way or another. *p. 405*

latitude of rejection In social judgment theory, statements that a receiver could not possibly accept. *p. 405*

Motivated Sequence A five-step plan used in persuasive speaking; also known as "Monroe's Motivated Sequence." *p. 414*

persuasion The act of motivating a listener, through communication, to change a particular belief, attitude, value, or behavior. *p. 404*

post hoc **fallacy** Fallacious reasoning that mistakenly assumes that one event causes another because they occur sequentially. *p. 416*

proposition of fact Claim bearing on issue in which there are two or more sides of conflicting factual evidence. *p. 408*

proposition of policy Claim bearing on issue that involves adopting or rejecting a specific course of action. *p. 409*

proposition of value Claim bearing on issue involving the worth of some idea, person, or object. *p. 408*

reductio ad absurdum **fallacy** Fallacious reasoning that unfairly attacks an argument by extending it to such extreme lengths that it looks ridiculous. *p. 416*

social judgment theory Explanation of attitude change that posits that opinions will change only in small increments and only when the target opinions lie within the receiver's latitudes of acceptance and noncommitment. *p. 405*

target audience That part of an audience that must be influenced in order to achieve a persuasive goal. *p. 417*

Case Study Questions

Instructions: Reread the case study on pages 324–325 to answer the following questions in light of what you have learned in this chapter.

1. What type of proposition, outcome, and approach would you use in your presentation marketing your school? (See pages 408–411 to answer.)

2. What can you say to establish common ground with your audience? What techniques can you employ if you will be facing a hostile audience?

3. How can you boost your credibility with your audience by using the strategies on pages 419–421?

4. How can you make your presentation most effective and ethical by adhering to the characteristics on pages 406–407?

Activities

1. **Audience Latitudes of Acceptance** To better understand the concept of latitudes of acceptance, rejection, and noncommitment, formulate a list of perspectives on a topic of your choice. This list should contain eight to ten statements that represent a variety of attitudes, such as the list pertaining to the pro-life/pro-choice issue on page 405. Arrange this list from your own point of view, from most acceptable to least acceptable. Then circle the single statement that best represents your own point of view. This will be your

"anchor." Underline those items that also seem reasonable. These make up your latitude of acceptance on this issue. Then cross out the numbers in front of any items that express opinions that you cannot accept. These make up your latitude of rejection. Those statements that are left would be your latitude of noncommitment. Do you agree that someone seeking to persuade you on this issue would do best by advancing propositions that fall within this latitude of noncommitment?

2. **Personal Persuasion** When was the last time you changed your attitude about something after discussing it with someone? In your opinion, was this persuasion interactive? Not coercive? Incremental? Ethical? Explain your answer.

3. **Propositions of Fact, Value, and Policy** Which of the following are propositions of fact, propositions of value, and propositions of policy?

   1. "Three Strikes" laws that put felons away for life after their third conviction are/are not fair.

   2. Elder care should/should not be the responsibility of government.

   3. The mercury in dental fillings is/is not healthy for the dental patient.

   4. Congressional pay raises should/should not be delayed until an election has intervened.

   5. Third-party candidates strengthen/weaken American democracy.

   6. National medical insurance should/should not be provided to all citizens of the United States.

   7. Elderly people who are wealthy do/do not receive too many Social Security benefits.

   8. Tobacco advertising should/should not be banned from all media.

   9. Domestic violence is/is not on the rise.

   10. Pit bulls are/are not dangerous animals.

4. **Structuring Persuasive Speeches** For practice in structuring persuasive speeches, choose one of the following topics, and provide a full-sentence outline that conforms to the outline in Figure 14-2, page 412.

   It should/should not be more difficult to purchase a handgun.

   Public relations messages that appear in news reports should/should not be labeled as advertising.

   Newspaper recycling is/is not important for the environment.

   Police should/should not be required to carry nonlethal weapons only.

   Parole should/should not be abolished.

   The capital of the United States should/should not be moved to a more central location.

   We should/should not ban capital punishment.

   Bilingual education should/should not be offered in all schools in which students speak English as a second language.

5. **Find the Fallacy** Test your ability to detect shaky reasoning by identifying which fallacy is exhibited in each of the following statements.

   a. *ad hominem*   d. *post hoc*

   b. *ad absurdum*   e. *ad verecundiam*

   c. either-or   f. *ad populum*

   _____ 1. Some companies claim to be in favor of protecting the environment, but you can't trust them. Businesses exist to make a profit, and the cost of saving the earth is just another expense to be cut.

   _____ 2. Take it from me, imported cars are much better than domestics. I used to buy only American, but the cars made here are all junk.

   _____ 3. Rap music ought to be boycotted. After all, the number of assaults on police officers went up right after rap became popular.

   _____ 4. Carpooling to cut down on the parking problem is a stupid idea. Look around—nobody carpools!

   _____ 5. I know that staying in the sun can cause cancer, but if I start worrying about every environmental risk I'll have to stay inside a bomb shelter breathing filtered air, never drive a car or ride my bike, and I won't be able to eat anything.

   _____ 6. The biblical account of creation is just another fairy tale. You can't seriously consider the arguments of those Bible-thumping, know-nothing fundamentalists, can you?

6. **The Credibility of Persuaders** Identify someone who tries to persuade you via public speaking or mass communication. This person might be a politician, a teacher, a member of the clergy, a coach, a boss, or anyone else. Analyze this person's credibility in terms of the three dimensions discussed in the chapter. Which dimension is most important in terms of this person's effectiveness?

Employment Strategies

In a perfect world, the person with the best qualifications will get a job. In reality, the person who knows the most about getting hired often gets the desired position. Though job-getting skills are no substitute for qualifications after the actual work begins, they are necessary if you are going to be hired in the first place. The following guidelines will boost the odds of your getting the job you deserve.

Cultivate Personal Networks

Everybody belongs to personal networks—interlocking relationships linked by communication. Yours probably include friends, family, school, and community. Beyond the everyday value of communicating with these people, career-related **networking** is

> The person who knows the most about getting hired often gets the desired position.

the strategic process of deliberately meeting people and maintaining contacts that result in information, advice, and leads that enhance one's career. Rich networks provide the kind of social capital described in the "@Work" box on page 228 of Chapter 7.

Once you think about it, the potential value of networking is obvious. If you're looking for a job, personal contacts can tell you about positions that may not even be public yet. When many candidates seek the same job, people you know can put in a good word for you with potential employers, and also give you tips on how to pursue the position you're seeking.

The number of jobs found through networking is staggering. It exceeds the number of those that come from Web searches, headhunters, or other formal means.[1] Some research suggests that less than 10 percent of job seekers find employment by using the Internet.[2] One study of over 150,000 jobs found that more people were hired by referrals than by any other source.[3] Another survey conducted by global resources company DBM revealed that 75 percent of job seekers obtained their current positions through personal networking.[4] The reverse is also true: Most employers find good employees through their personal networks.[5]

Networking Strategies   Here are some tips that will enhance your networking skills.[6]

1. **View Everyone as a Networking Prospect** Besides the people in your immediate everyday networks, you have access to a wealth of other contacts: Former coworkers, neighbors and schoolmates, people you've met at social and community events, professional people whose services you have used . . . the list can be quite long and diverse.

2. **Seek Referrals** Each contact in your immediate network has connections to people you don't already know and who might be able to help you. Social scientists examined the "six degrees of separation" hypothesis by studying over 45,000 messages exchanged in over 150 countries. They discovered that the average number of links separating any two people in the world is indeed a half-dozen.[7] You can take advantage of this principle by only seeking people removed from your personal network by just one degree: If you ask ten people for referrals and each of them knows ten others who might be able to help, you have the potential of support from one hundred information givers.

3. **Show Appreciation** The best way to repay people who help you is by expressing gratitude for their help. Beyond a sincere thank-you, take the time to let your contacts know when their help has made a difference in your career advancement. Besides being the right thing to do, your expressions of thanks will distinguish you as the kind of person worth helping again in the future.

Networking on the Web   In addition to personal networking, there are plenty of on-line websites where job seekers can make themselves known to prospective employers. It can't hurt to join at least a few professional networking sites and set up a basic profile. Many business professionals maintain a presence on these six sites, and sometimes more.

LinkedIn (www.linkedin.com) has about 75 million members across the globe, and its website represents over 150 industries. There is no charge to become a basic member, but there are more advanced networking tools available for a membership fee. On LinkedIn, members create their own profile page, including information about work experience and education, and then create connections to people they know. Through a network of connections that already exist, users can ask for referrals, introductions, and business opportunities. LinkedIn is a way to get to know people who may be able to help you professionally, through people you already know.

Ecademy (ecademy.com) does not report membership numbers, so it is impos-sible to say how many users it has, but it is a well-known site amongst professional networkers. Basic membership is free, and users have the option to upgrade to two more advanced networking levels for a fee. Through Ecademy, users learn about networking events and can even arrange one-on-one meetings with other members. Members cre-ate a profile page and can then send messages to other members, depending on each person's membership level. Higher levels offer greater access to users. There is a space for blog postings, ratings of businesses, and personal testimonials.

Xing (xing.com) reports about 6 million members, mainly in Europe and China. Although this site does not have a blogging feature, it allows members to create a profile page, join groups, send messages to other members, and learn about offline events. A free basic membership on Xing will allow you to have an online presence if someone performs an online search of your name, but you will need to pay for more advanced features on the site.

Ryze (ryze.com) is a professional networking site with roughly five hundred thou-sand members. Similar to the sites already mentioned, a paid membership gets you more options but is not required to join and have a basic profile. Ryze boasts over one thousand groups you can join once you are a member. There are no blogs, but the ability to join the network groups is the highlight of this site.

> You should be mindful of how information posted on Facebook will be regarded by people with whom you deal professionally.

Plaxo (plaxo.com) has 15 million members and counting. It offers users a free membership that allows them to show off what they are do-ing online by linking other websites and services to their profile. For ex-ample, your Plaxo profile can link to your Flickr account to show off your photos, and even announce "new updates" anytime you post on an-other linked website. As with most other sites, a paid upgrade will allow you to explore more networking tools on the site, but is not necessary.

Facebook (www.facebook.com) is the world's largest social networking site, but it shouldn't be a primary tool for career-related communication. As you'll read elsewhere in this appendix (pages A-15–A-18), you should be mindful of how information posted there will be regarded by people with whom you deal professionally.

Conduct Informational Interviews

Sooner or later your networking and personal research are likely to point you toward people whose knowledge, experience, and contacts could shape your career. These may be people you already know, but whom you suddenly view in a new way: a successful neighbor or relative, for example. In other cases, you may casually meet someone who you realize could be a great career asset, perhaps at a social event, or even as a seatmate on the train or plane. Finally, you may read or hear about a total stranger whose perspective could transform your career.

Goals of Informational Interviews   Regardless of the source, with a little initiative and planning you can approach these contacts and request an **informational interview**: a structured meeting in which you seek answers from a source whose knowledge can help enhance your success.

The best informational interview has three goals:

1. To *conduct research* that helps you understand a job, organization, or field
2. To *be remembered favorably* by the person you are interviewing (so he or she may mention you to others who can also advance your career)
3. To *gain referrals* to other people who might also be willing to help you

Contacting Interviewees   Unless you know a prospective interviewee well, the best approach is usually to make your first contact in writing, either via e-mail or a "snail mail" letter. A phone call might be easier, but it runs at least two risks. First, you may miss the person and be forced to leave a voice mail message that can either be too short to explain yourself or too long to hold your recipient's attention. Even if the potential interviewee answers your call, you may have caught him or her at a bad time. With a letter, you can carefully edit your introduction until it's just right, and assume that the recipient will read it whenever he or she is ready.

In your written message, you should do the following (see Figure A-1):

- Introduce yourself.
- Explain your reason for the interview (emphasizing that you're seeking information, not asking for a job).
- Identify the amount of time your questions are likely to take. (Don't ask for more than one hour. The shorter amount of time you request, the better are your odds of being seen.)
- State a range of dates when you are available to meet. Be as flexible as possible.
- Promise that you'll follow up with a phone call to schedule an appointment.

Questions to Ask   More than any other factor, the questions you ask and the way you ask them will determine the success or failure of an interview. Truly good questions rarely come spontaneously, even to the best of interviewers.

The first thing to realize is that a career-related informational interview is ultimately about *you*, and not the person you're talking with. Fascinating as it might be, dwelling on the life story of the person you're interviewing isn't likely to help advance your career. Instead, probe your interviewee for information that will help you succeed. You can appreciate the difference by comparing these types of questions:

Focused on interviewee (less effective): "Did you go to graduate school? Where? Why?"

Focused on you (better): "Do you think it would be helpful for me to go to graduate school? Where? Why?" (Or "Why not?")

Focused on interviewee (less effective): "What was your first job?"

Focused on you (better): "What kinds of jobs do you think would be good for me in the early stages of my career?"

TO: Roland Sanchez
FROM: Andrew Kao
SUBJECT: Seeking your advice
DATE: February 18, 2011

Dear Mr. Sanchez:

As an aspiring entrepreneur, I read with interest the recent article in the *Washington Post* about your success in growing NX solutions from scratch to an internationally renowned consulting firm.

I am currently in my final year as an International Business major in the University of Maryland's Robert H. Smith School of Business. I'll receive my Bachelor of Science degree next December. If things continue to go well, that degree should be awarded with honors.

My purpose in writing is to seek your advice about career paths after I graduate. I'm fascinated with the idea of a career similar to yours, and want to approach that goal in the best way. Several options seem possible, including graduate school, employment with a large firm, or seeking a spot in a small but promising firm where I may be able to have a bigger impact.

I would be most grateful for the chance to meet with you and gain the benefit of your experience. All of my classes are in the morning, so I could be available most any afternoon.

I will call your office next week hoping to set up an appointment. In the meantime, I'll be looking forward to hearing from you via e-mail or phone.

Thanks in advance for any help you can offer. I look forward to benefiting from your advice.

Sincerely,

Andrew Kao

FIGURE A1-1 Letter Seeking Informational Interview

Focused on interviewee (less effective): "What do you think helped you become successful in your career?"

Focused on you (better): "What lessons have you learned in your career that you think could help me become as successful as you are?"

Don't fall into the trap of making this a journalistic interview. If you've told your interviewee up front that you're seeking career advice, it will be clear that you are the focus of this conversation.

Once you're clear about the topics you want to cover, you can design questions that will get the information you're seeking. There are a number of question types, each of which has its own uses.

1. **Factual Versus Opinion** As their name implies, **factual questions** are usually straightforward requests for information: "What are the three fastest-growing companies in this field?" or "What's the average entry-level salary in this field?" By contrast, **opinion questions** ask for the interviewer's evaluation: "What parts of the country do you think will offer the best chance for advancement in the next few years?" or "How important do you think it is to be bilingual?" When planning an interview, ask yourself whether you're more interested in facts or opinions and plan your questions accordingly.

2. **Open Versus Closed Questions** **Closed questions** call for a specific, usually concise answer: "Do you think I should rent or lease?" or "Is the code for that software open source or proprietary?"

   By contrast, **open questions** invite the interviewee to reply in whatever way he or she chooses: "What do you think about the risks of working for an Internet start-up company?" or "Why did you say that accounting is a must-take course?"

   Developing good open questions takes time and thought. Questions that are poorly worded or ones that are too broad or too narrow to get the information you seek can be a waste of time. A good list of open-ended questions can help in several ways. First, you will almost certainly have enough lengthy responses to fill the allotted time, soothing a common fear of inexperienced interviewers. Your open questions, inviting comment as they do, will also make your subject feel more comfortable. Second, the way in which your subject chooses to answer your open questions will tell you more about him or her than you could probably learn by asking only morerestrictive closed questions, which can be answered in a few words.

3. **Direct Versus Indirect Questions** Most of the time the best way to get information is to ask a **direct question**. There are times, however, when a subject won't be willing to give a candid response. This sort of situation usually occurs when a straightforward reply would be embarrassing or risky. For instance, you probably wouldn't want to ask questions like, "What's your salary?" or "Do you ever have to compromise your ethical standards?"

   At times like these it's wise to seek information by using **indirect questions**, which do not directly request the information you are seeking. Instead of the direct questions above, you could ask, "In today's dollars, what kind of salary might I expect if I ever held a position like yours?" or "Are there any ethical dilemmas that come with this kind of job?"

4. **Primary Versus Secondary Questions** Sometimes you'll need to ask only an initial, primary question to get the fact or opinion you need in a given content area. But more often you will need to follow up your first question with others to give you all the information you need. These follow-ups are called secondary questions.

   Primary Question: "In your opinion, who are the best people for me to ask about careers in the financial planning field?"

   Secondary Questions: "How could I meet them?" "Do you think they'd be willing to help?" "How could each one help me?"

Sometimes an interviewer can follow up with secondary responses that aren't really questions. Simple **probes**—interjections, silences, and other brief remarks—can open up or direct an interviewee and uncover useful information.

Interviewer: "What **traits** are you looking for in a new employee?"

Respondent: "Flexibility is the most important thing for us."

Interviewer: "Flexibility?"

Respondent: "Yes. Things change so rapidly in our organization that we need people who can adapt to whatever happens next."

It can be smart to develop a list of secondary questions to each primary one. In many cases, however, the best follow-ups will occur to you during the interview, depending on how the respondent answers your first question. As you ask and probe, be sure each secondary question you ask helps achieve your goal. It's easy to wind up taking an interesting digression, only to discover that you didn't get the information you were after.

5. **Neutral Versus Leading** A **neutral question** gives the interviewee a chance to respond without any influence from the interviewer. By contrast, a **leading question** is one in which the interviewer—either directly or indirectly—signals the desired answer. A few examples illustrate the difference between these two types of questions:

NEUTRAL QUESTION	LEADING QUESTION
"What do you think about my idea?"	"I've worked very hard on this idea, and I'm proud of it. What do you think?"
"Do you think sexism is a problem in this industry?"	"What examples of sexism have you seen in this industry?"

6. **Hypothetical** A **hypothetical question** seeks a response by proposing a "what-if" situation. "If your own son or daughter were considering the career I've asked you about, what would you say?"

Hypothetical questions can encourage interviewees to offer information they wouldn't volunteer if asked directly. For instance, your interviewee might not be comfortable criticizing specific organizations in your field, but you could get the information you're seeking by asking, "If you had to rank the top five or six nonprofits in this community, what would the list look like?"

After the Informational Interview Good manners call for sending a note of thanks to the interviewer who has taken time to give you advice and information. Such a note can also be strategically saavy: It serves as a tangible reminder of you, and it provides a written record of your name and contact information. It can be smart to keep your contact alive by sending follow-up messages letting your interviewee know how you have put his or her advice to good use. If the interviewee has referred you to other people, be sure to let him or her know the results of your conversations with those people.

The Selection Interview

For many people the short time spent facing a potential employer is the most important interview of a lifetime. A **selection interview** may occur when you are being considered for employment, but it may also occur when you are being evaluated for promotion or reassignment. In an academic setting, selection interviews are often part of the process of being chosen for an award, a scholarship, or admission to a graduate program. Being chosen for the position you seek depends on making a good impression on the person or people who can hire you, and your interviewing skills can make the difference between receiving a job offer and being an also-ran.

Preparing for the Interview

A good interview begins long before you sit down to face the other person. There are several steps you can take to boost your chances for success.

CULTURAL IDIOM

to wind up:
to bring to an end, to finish

an also-ran:
an unsuccessful applicant

Background Research   Displaying your knowledge of an organization in an interview is a terrific way to show potential employers that you are a motivated and savvy person. Along with what you've learned from informational interviews, diligent Web browsing can reveal a wealth of information about a prospective employer and the field in which you want to work. (See the "Web Research" section on page 336 in Chapter 11 for details on searching tools and strategies.)

Most business firms, government agencies, and nonprofit agencies have websites that will help you understand their mission. If you're lucky, those websites will also contain the names of people you'll want to know about and possibly refer to during an interview.

Beyond an organization's own website, you can almost certainly find what others have published about the places where you might want to work. In your search engine, type the name of the organization and/or key people who work there. You are likely to be pleased and surprised at what you learn.

Create a Résumé   No matter how extensive and supportive your network, sooner or later you will need a résumé to provide a snapshot of your professional strengths and interests. For guidelines on the various types of résumés, type "create résumé" into your favorite search engine. Figure A-2 illustrates a common format for this document.

Along with a print version of your résumé, it's smart to have a digital version posted on a Web-based job bank, sometimes called an online job board. Some popular sites include Dice (dice.com), Monster (monster.com), and Computer Jobs (computerjobs.com).

When posting your résumé online, there are several important steps to take to ensure that it displays correctly. A flawed résumé can do more harm than good.

- Create your document in a word processing program, but save the final version as a PDF file.

- If you are e-mailing a résumé, include it as an attachment. Do not paste the résumé in the body of your e-mail, because the formatting may not transfer properly.

- Be aware that once you post or e-mail your résumé, there is no guarantee of where it may be sent or copied. You may want to protect your privacy by including your e-mail address but not your home address or phone number.

Prepare for Likely Questions   Regardless of the organization and job, most interviewers have similar concerns, which they explore with similar questions. Here are some of the most common ones, with commentary on how you can prepare to answer them.

1. **Tell me something about yourself.**
   This broad, opening question gives you a chance to describe what qualities you possess that can help the employer (e.g., enthusiastic, motivated, entrepreneurial). Be sure to keep your answer focused on the job for which you're applying—this isn't a time to talk about your hobbies, family, or pet peeves.

2. **What makes you think you're qualified to work for this company?**
   This question may sound like an attack, but it really is another way of asking "How can you help us?" It gives you another chance to show how your skills and interests fit with the company's goals.

CAMILLA DORANTES

E-mail: camilla.dorantes@connectmail.net   Phone: 223-242-3554

SUMMARY OF QUALIFICATIONS

- Academic background in political and economic dimensions of environmental policy
- Experience working in commercial and nonprofit organizations related to sustainability
- Strong work ethic and ability to work independently as necessary

EDUCATION

Current: University of Southern California
> Graduating (Bachelor of Science degree) in May 2013
> Major in Global Studies, Pacific Rim Studies Emphasis

Fall 2010: Tokyo International Studies University (Fulbright Junior Scholar)

> Japanese language program, ethnographic study of contemporary Japanese culture

RELATED EXPERIENCE

**December 2010–February 2011: Undergraduate Research Fellow,
University of Southern California**
> In Asia, analyzed the effectiveness of committees designed to create international
> environmental policy. Interviewed officials from municipal government, business, and
> nonprofit sectors in Japan, China, and Singapore.

**January 2010– present: Correspondent, Environmental Policy blog
(http://greenpolicy.org)**
> Published dispatches on insights gained from travels in Asia for the award-winning
> website.

**September 2009–October 2009: Assistant Coordinator, International
Environmental Treaty, West Coast**
> Assisted in coordinating media and fundraising events to educate public and recruited
> volunteers for this campaign to promote and protect environmental rights around the
> world.

**March 2009–May 2009: International Green Research Intern, Southern
California World Trade Center**
> Conducted individualized, in-depth sales and marketing research for the Trade Center's
> members.

January 2009–March 2009: Intern, Greenpeace San Diego
> Conducted research to identify immediate environmental threats across California; helped
> develop funding proposals for major donors.

LANGUAGES

> Fluency in Spanish
> Competence in Japanese

FIGURE A-2 Sample Résumé Format

3. **What accomplishments have given you the most satisfaction?**
The accomplishments you choose needn't be directly related to former employment, but they should demonstrate qualities that would help you be successful in the job for which you're interviewing. Your accomplishments might demonstrate creativity, perseverance in the face of obstacles, self-control, or dependability.

4. **Why do you want to work for us?**
As the research cited in Table A-1 shows, employers are impressed by candidates who have done their homework about the organization. This question offers you the chance to demonstrate your knowledge of the employer's organization and to show how your talents fit with its goals.

5. **What college subjects did you like most and least?**
Whatever your answer, show how your preferences about schoolwork relate to the job for which you are applying. Sometimes the connection between college courses and a job is obvious. At other times, though, you can show how apparently unrelated subjects do illustrate your readiness for a job. For example, you might say, "I really enjoyed cultural anthropology courses because they showed me the importance of understanding different cultures. I think that those courses would help me a lot in relating to your overseas customers and suppliers."

6. **Where do you see yourself in five years?**
This familiar question is really asking "How ambitious are you?" "How well do your plans fit with this company's goals?" "How realistic are you?" If you have studied the industry and the company, your answer will reflect an understanding of the workplace realities and a sense of personal planning that should impress an employer.

7. **What major problems have you faced, and how have you dealt with them?**
The specific problems aren't as important as the way you responded to them. What (admirable) qualities did you demonstrate as you grappled with the problems you have chosen to describe? Perseverance? Calmness? Creativity? You may even choose to describe a problem you didn't handle well, to show what you learned from the experience that can help you in the future.

8. **What are your greatest strengths and weaknesses?**
The "strength" question offers another chance to sell yourself. As you choose an answer, identify qualities that apply to employment. "I'm a pretty good athlete" isn't a persuasive answer, unless you can show how your athletic skill is job related. For instance, you might talk about being a team player, having competitive drive, or having the ability to work hard and not quit in the face of adversity.

   Whatever answer you give to the "weakness" question, try to show how your awareness of your flaws makes you a desirable person to hire. There are four ways to respond to this question:

   - *Discuss a weakness that can also be viewed as a strength.*
     "When I'm involved in a big project I tend to work too hard, and I can wear myself out."

   - *Discuss a weakness that is not related to the job at hand, and end your answer with a strength that is related to the job.*
     (for a job in sales) "I'm not very interested in accounting. I'd much rather work with people selling a product I believe in."
     (for a job in accounting) "I'm not great at sales and marketing. I'm at my best working with numbers and talking to people about them."

   - *Discuss a weakness the interviewer already knows about from your résumé, application, or the interview.*

TABLE A-1   Communication Behaviors of Successful and Unsuccessful Interviewees

	UNSUCCESSFUL INTERVIEWEES	SUCCESSFUL INTERVIEWEES
Statements about the position	Had only vague ideas of what they wanted to do; changed "ideal job" up to six times during the interview.	Specific and consistent about the position they wanted; were able to tell why they wanted the position.
Use of company name	Rarely used the company name.	Referred to the company by name four times as often as unsuccessful interviewees.
Knowledge about company and position	Made it clear that they were using the interview to learn about the company and what it offered.	Made it clear that they had researched the company; referred to specific brochures, journals, or people who had given them information.
Level of interest, enthusiasm	Responded neutrally to interviewer's statements: "Okay," "I see." Indicated reservations about company or location.	Expressed approval of information provided by the interviewer nonverbally and verbally: "That's great!" Explicitly indicated desire to work for this particular company.
Picking up on interviewer's clues	Gave vague or negative answers even when a positive answer was clearly desired ("How are your math skills?").	Answered positively and confidently—and backed up the claim with a specific example of "problem solving" or "toughness."
Use of industry terms and technical jargon	Used almost no technical jargon.	Used technical jargon: "point of purchase display," "NCR charge," "two-column approach," "direct mail."
Use of specifics in answers	Gave short answers—ten words or fewer, sometimes only one word; did not elaborate. Gave general responses: "Fairly well."	Supported claims with specific personal experiences, comparisons, statistics, statements of teachers and employers.
Questions asked by interviewee	Asked a small number of general questions.	Asked specific questions based on knowledge of the industry and the company. Personalized questions: "What would my duties be?"
Control of time and topics	Interviewee talked 37 percent of the interview time, initiated 36 percent of the comments.	Interviewee talked 55 percent of the total time, initiated subjects 56 percent of the time.

Based on research reported by Lois J. Einhorn, "An Inner View of the Job Interview: An Investigation of Successful Communicative Behaviors." *Communication Education* 30 (July 1981): 217–228.

"I don't have a lot of experience in multimedia design at this early stage of my career. But my experience in other kinds of computer programming and my internship in graphic arts have convinced me that I can learn quickly."

■ *Discuss a weakness you have been working to remedy.*
"I know being bilingual is important for this job. That's why I've enrolled in a Spanish course."

9. **What are your salary requirements?**

Your answer should be based on knowledge of the prevailing compensation rates in the industry and geography in question. Shooting too high can knock you out of consideration, whereas shooting too low can cost you dearly. Give your answer naming a salary range and backing up your numbers: "Based on the research I've done about compensation in this area, I'd expect to start somewhere between $35,000 and $38,500." As you give your answer, watch the interviewer. If he or she seems to respond favorably, you're in good shape. If you notice signs of disapproval, follow up: ". . . depending, of course, on fringe benefits and how quickly I could expect to be promoted. However, salary isn't the most important criterion for me in choosing a job, and I won't necessarily accept the highest offer I get. I'm interested in going somewhere where I can get good experience and use my talents to make a real contribution." It's important to know your "bottom line" for compensation in advance so you don't end up accepting an offer at a salary you can't afford to take.

Dress for Success   First impressions can make or break an interview. Research shows that many interviewers form their opinions about applicants within the first four minutes of conversation.[8] Physical attractiveness is a major influence on how applicants are rated, so it makes sense to do everything possible to look your best. The basic rules apply, no matter what the job or company: Be well groomed and neatly dressed.

The proper style of clothing can vary from one type of job or organization to another. A good rule of thumb is to come dressed as you would for the first day of work. When in doubt it's best to dress formally and conservatively. It's unlikely that an employer will think less of you for being overdressed, but looking too casual can be taken as a sign that you don't take the job or the interview seriously.

Come Prepared   Come to the interview with materials that will help the employer learn more about why you are ready, willing, and able to do the job. Bring extra copies of your résumé. Come prepared to take notes: You'll need something to write on and a pen or pencil. If appropriate, bring copies of your past work: reports you've helped prepare, performance reviews by former employers, drawings or designs you have created in work or school, letters of commendation, and so on. Besides demonstrating your qualifications, items like these demonstrate that you know how to sell yourself. Bring along the names, addresses, and phone numbers of any references you haven't listed in your résumé.

Know When and Where to Go   Don't risk sabotaging the interview before it begins by showing up late. Be sure you're clear about the time and location of the meeting. Research parking or public transportation to be sure you aren't held up by delays. There's virtually no good excuse for showing up late. Even if the interviewer is forgiving, a bad start is likely to shake your confidence and impair your performance.

Managing Your Anxiety   Feeling anxious about an employment interview is understandable. After all, the stakes are high—especially if you really want the job.

Managing your feelings in interviews calls for the same approach described in the "Managing Communication Apprehension" section of Chapter 11 (see pages 338–341). Realize that a certain amount of anxiety is understandable. If you can reframe those feelings as *excitement* about the prospect of holding a great job, the feelings can even work to your advantage.

If feelings of anxiety get out of hand, consider whether you are indulging yourself with any of the fallacies of catastrophic failure or perfection. Following the guidelines on pages 339–340 can help shrink your concerns and give you ways of managing them.

CULTURAL IDIOM
bottom line:
minimum requirements
rule of thumb:
practical plan of action

During the Interview

There are several things you can do as an interviewee to make the interview a success.

Follow the Interviewer's Lead   Let the interviewer set the emotional tone of the session. Along with topics and verbal style, pay attention to the kinds of nonverbal cues described in Chapter 6: the interviewer's posture, gestures, vocal qualities, and so on. If he or she is informal, you can loosen up and be yourself, but if he or she is formal and proper, you should act the same way. A great deal depends on the personal chemistry between interviewer and applicant, so try to match the interviewer's style without becoming phony. If the tone of the interview doesn't fit well with you, this may be a signal that you won't feel comfortable with this company. It may be smart to see whether the interviewer's approach represents the whole company, either by asking for a tour or speaking with other employees on your own. This desire to learn about the company shows that you are a thinking person who takes the job seriously, so your curiosity isn't likely to offend the interviewer.

Keep Your Answers Brief   It's easy to rattle on in an interview, either out of enthusiasm, a desire to show off your knowledge, or nervousness, but in most cases long answers are not a good idea. The interviewer probably has lots of ground to cover, and long-winded answers won't help this task. A good rule of thumb is to keep your responses under two minutes.

Keep on the Subject   It is sometimes tempting to go overboard with your answers, sidetracking the discussion into areas that won't help the interviewer. It's often a good idea to ask the interviewer whether your answers are being helpful and then to adjust them accordingly.

Be Ready for Behavioral Interviews   Most sophisticated employers realize that past performance can be the best predictor of future behavior. For that reason, there is an increasing trend toward **behavioral interviews**—sessions that explore specifics of the applicant's past performance as it relates to the job at hand. Typical behavioral questions include the following:

> Describe a time you needed to work as part of a team.
>
> Tell me about a time when you had to think on your feet to handle a challenging situation.
>
> Describe a time when you were faced with an ethical dilemma, and discuss how you handled it.

Your challenge, when faced with behavioral questions, is to answer in a way that shows the prospective employer how your past performance demonstrates your ability to handle the job you are now seeking. One format for constructing such answers has three parts:

1. Offer specific examples of a situation, and how you handled it.
2. Show the result of your behavior.
3. Draw a connection between the incident you've described and the job you are seeking.

Here are some examples of good answers to behavioral questions:

Q: Give an example of a time when you were faced with an overwhelming amount of work.

A: Last year I was chairperson of the committee that organized a triathlon to raise money for a friend who had enormous medical bills after being in a car accident. When I took

CULTURAL IDIOM

the personal chemistry:
how two people get along with or react to each other

to rattle on:
to utter responses that are excessively wordy

ground to cover:
topics to discuss

long-winded:
speaking for a long time

go overboard:
do so much as to be excessive

on the job, I had no idea how big it was: logistics, publicity, fund-raising, legal—it was huge. And some of the people who originally offered to help backed out halfway through the planning. At first I tried to do everything myself, but after a while I realized that this was not going to work. So I wound up recruiting more people, and my job turned out to be supporting and encouraging them rather than doing it all. If I'm lucky enough to get this job, that's the approach I'd take as a manager.

Q: Tell me about a time when you had to work with someone you didn't like, or someone who didn't like you.

A: A very talented teammate in my Marketing class term project kept making somewhat sexist jokes, even after I told him they made me uncomfortable. Changing teams wasn't possible, and I figured complaining to the professor would jeopardize our success on the project. So I did my best to act professionally, even in the face of those jokes. We got the job done, and received an outstanding evaluation, so I guess my discomfort was worth it. What I learned from this experience is that we don't always get to choose the people we work with, and that sometimes you have to put the job ahead of personal feelings.

> The selection interview is also a chance for you to learn whether the job and organization are right for you.

Be Prepared to Ask Questions of Your Own   Besides answering the employer's questions, the selection interview is also a chance for you to learn whether the job and organization are right for you. In this sense, both the potential boss and the prospective employee are interviewing one another.

Near the end of the interview, you'll probably be asked if you have any questions. It might seem as if you know all the important facts about the job, but a look at the following list suggests that a question or two can produce some useful information, as well as show the interviewer that you are also realistically assessing the fit between yourself and the organization:

1. Why is this position open now? How often has it been filled in the past five years? What have been the primary reasons for people leaving it in the past?

2. What is the biggest problem facing your staff now? How have past and current employees had trouble solving this problem?

3. What are the primary results you would like to see me produce?

4. How would you describe the management style I could expect from my supervisors?

5. Where could a person go who is successful in this position? Within what time frame?

Follow Up After the Interview   Follow up your interview with a note of thanks to the interviewer. (Many candidates don't take this step, which will make your response especially impressive.) Express your appreciation for the chance to get acquainted with the company, and let the interviewer know that the interview left you excited about the chance of becoming associated with it.

Most employment advisors agree that this is one situation where a handwritten message can be appropriate. Whether your thank-you message is handwritten or computer-generated, be sure to have a literate proofreader review it, as a mistake here can damage your prospects. One job seeker ruined her chances of employment by mentioning the "report" (instead of "rapport") that she felt with the interviewer.

Interviewing and the Law

Most laws governing what topics can and can't be covered in job interviews boil down to two simple principles: First, questions may not be aimed at discriminating on the basis of race, color, religion, gender, sexual orientation, disabilities, national origin, or age. Second, questions must be related to what the U.S. government's Equal Employment Opportunity Commission (EEOC) calls *bona fide occupational qualifications*. In other words, prospective employers may only ask about topics that are related to the job at hand. Another basic principle is that employers should ask the same job-related questions of all candidates. For example, if an interviewer asks whether one candidate has international experience, he or she should ask all others the same question.

These principles help distinguish between legal and illegal questions:

ILLEGAL	LEGAL
Were you born in Latin America?	Fluency in Spanish is an important part of this job. Are you fluent in that language?
If you don't mind my asking, how did you get that limp?	Being on your feet for several hours per day is part of this job. Do you have any physical conditions that would make it hard to do that?
Do you have any children at home?	Are you able to work occasional nights and weekends?
Please tell me about any political clubs or organizations to which you belong.	Tell me about any job-related organizations you belong to that you think will enhance your ability to do this job.

Despite the law, there is a good chance that interviewers will ask illegal questions. This will probably have more to do with being uninformed than malicious. Still, when faced with a question that's not legal, you will need to know how to respond. There are several options:

1. *Answer without objecting.* Answer the question, even though you know it is probably unlawful: "No, I'm not married. But I'm engaged." Recognize, though, that this could open the door for other illegal questions—and perhaps even discrimination in hiring decisions.

2. *Seek explanation.* Ask the interviewer firmly and respectfully to explain why this question is related to the job: "I'm having a hard time seeing how my marital status relates to my ability to do this job. Can you explain?"

3. *Redirect.* Shift the focus of the interview away from a question that isn't job related and toward the requirements of the position itself: "What you've said so far suggests that age is not as important for this position as knowledge of accounting. Can you tell me more about the kinds of accounting that are part of this job?"

4. *Refuse.* Explain politely but firmly that you will not provide the information requested: "I'd rather not talk about my religion. That's a very private and personal matter for me."

5. *Withdrawal.* End the interview immediately and leave, stating your reasons firmly but professionally: "I'm very uncomfortable with these questions about my personal life, and I don't see a good fit between me and this organization. Thank you for your time."

There's no absolutely correct way to handle illegal questions. The option you choose will depend on several factors: the likely intent of the interviewer, the nature of the questions, and, of course, your desire for the job—and finally, your "gut level" of comfort with the whole situation.

Communicating for Career Advancement

Careful, strategic communication (or its absence) can enhance (or damage) your career, from before you begin looking for a job until the day you retire. In the remaining pages, you'll read tips on how to manage the way others regard you, and how to handle yourself in ways that distinguish you as the kind of capable person who is an asset to any organization.

Managing Your Professional Identity

The "@Work" box in Chapter 3 (page 86) describes the importance of managing your identity on the job. That sort of identity management extends into cyberspace and deserves special consideration.

You almost certainly have an online identity. If someone plugged your name into a search engine like Google, at least a few hits would probably surface. The information that shows up about you in cyberspace is more than a curiosity or ego-booster: It can either enhance or damage your career prospects.

> According to the *New York Times*, 70 percent of U.S. recruiters report having rejected job candidates because of personal information online.

By now you probably have been warned about the risks of posting potentially embarrassing information about yourself online, especially if you're looking for a job. According to the *New York Times*, 70 percent of U.S. recruiters report having rejected job candidates because of personal information online.[9] (If you need a reminder about the perils of exposing your personal life in cyberspace, reread the story of ill-fated intern Kevin Colvin, on page 50.)

Despite cautionary tales, it's worth detailing the dimensions of your online identity that can either enhance or damage your chances of getting a job or getting promoted. According to the creators of ClaimID, a service designed to help users control their online identities, web-based information that can shape your career success falls into one of four categories.[10] Each calls for different management strategies.

Constructing a Personal Website

Designing your own site can give you the personal creative touches that a predesigned site can't offer. If getting a job is your goal, your personal website should be focused on maintaining a professional image. You can include hobbies and interests unrelated to your skills and industry, but they should not be the focus of your site. The best way to make sure people can find your site is to choose a domain name that captures your complete real name. If your name is not available, make sure at least your complete last name is included in your domain name.

An important part of your personal website is your photo. Most employers are not allowed to request a photo with your résumé submission; however, appearance does matter to them. Help employers find out that you look like an excellent future employee by posting your photo on the homepage of your site. Make sure you don't confuse a nice appearance with being attractive. Overt attempts at appearing attractive can come across as too sexual or tacky. Physical attractiveness is not as important as looking put-together. Choose an outfit that shows you can work with clients outside the workplace and will represent the company well. Save personal photos for your password-protected social networking sites, and include only one or two professional photos on your website that is open to the public.

Once you create your website, you may want to monitor its success. Google Trends is a program you can download for free that can monitor your personal and business websites. Google Trends can show you two important pieces of information: how often a set of keywords, either your name or your company's name, appears on the Web, and also how frequently people search for it. Using a tool called "Hot Searches," you can see how often people search for your company over a span of time.

Information by You, About Yourself   This category includes social networking profiles and personal websites you have created and intentionally posted where anybody can view them. (See the box on page A-16 for more information about constructing your own website.) It may also include a detailed résumé, or information you've entered into a job-search site such as Monster.com or LinkedIn.com.

Self-authored information gives you a chance to promote yourself in ways that go beyond the one- or two-page résumé you bring to a job interview. If you've contributed to a worthy project, participated in volunteer work, or won any awards, create a place online that features these accomplishments and interests.

When posting information about yourself online, be sure to consider how it will look to viewers. You may be proud of your membership in the National Rifle Association or Planned Parenthood, but a prospective employer might not find your affiliations so admirable. Political philosophy, religious affiliations, and even your musical preferences may all be better kept private, or at least behind a secure firewall where only the people you know and trust will see them.

Information by Others About You   This category includes everything viewable online that anyone has ever said about you. Some websites are organized specifically to capture comments about individuals. Students can rate their professors (www.ratemyprofessor.com), friends can rate one another (www.ratemyeverything.net), and you can rate the attractiveness of strangers (www.hotornot.com). Commentary on these sites can be insensitive, unfair, and even blatantly false, but it can damage your reputation nonetheless. Even if your name isn't listed on a dedicated website, searchers may find random posts about you by typing your name into a simple search. One waitress was shocked to find that a customer's review of the restaurant where she worked mentioned her by name as having a bad attitude.

If you think your online reputation has been unfairly damaged, you can seek help from firms to protect your image. For example, reputationdefender.com will monitor your online identity and contact offending websites, asking them to remove unflattering information. Of course, a far less extensive and burdensome approach is to minimize the chances of reputation damage by being on your best public behavior.

Information about you can also come from belonging to groups that post membership information online for unrestricted viewing. You may not have intended for inquiring minds to know that you belong to Yahoo's Mysticism and Witchcraft Interest Group or Meetup.com's Obsessive Compulsive Support Group, but unless you're careful, that information can become public. One employee learned the hard way that group membership isn't necessarily private when she sent an e-mail to her boss from her Yahoo account. The boss was surprised to find, underneath his reply confirmation, the message "Shelly has just posted a comment on the Pregnant Career Women's Message Board."

Information by You, Not About You   This category includes anything that you have created online that isn't self-referential. It can include text-based material, such as school projects and your reviews of music or films. It can also include nontextual information such as your art or music portfolio. This sort of information can showcase your talents in ways that are likely to impress current or potential employers or clients.

You can steer potential readers to this sort of material by compiling it all in a single place online. You don't have to be a Web designer to pull this off: Resources like Google's blogspot.com are free and easy to use.

Once your online showcase is set up, you can reference it in your résumé and other job-seeking materials. Beyond this, you can steer Web surfers to your blog by including your full name in the blog's URL and title. This approach insures that searchers will find it when they type your name into their search engine.

Along with potentially career-enhancing material, there's a risk that you may have posted material that will reflect poorly on you. Almost any griping, complaining, gossiping, or bad-mouthing can come back to haunt you, even if it was justified.

Information About You, Not by You   This category involves material that turns up in a search when others' names are identical or similar to yours. Nobody is likely to confuse you with the John or Jane Doe who is currently doing research in Antarctica; but sometimes mistaken identity can be less obvious. One job seeker Googled herself out of curiosity, only to find that the first hit was the Facebook page of another person with the same name. She clicked the link and was taken to a personal profile loaded with immature comments.

If a search of your name generates potentially damaging hits of people who are unrelated to you, consider distinguishing yourself by including your middle name or middle initial on your résumé and all other information you post where online seekers might find it.

If you discover incorrect or potentially damaging information about yourself online, you might consider seeking professional help to set the record straight. Services that help people take back control of their online identity include Naymz.com, Ziki.com, Wink.com, and ClaimID.

Distinguishing Yourself on the Job

Once you're on the job, distinguishing yourself from the pack can be a challenge. It can be hard to figure out which behaviors cast you in a positive light, and which might give the impression you are a self-promoting "suck-up." Here are a few guidelines that will serve you well.

Communicate in a Principled Manner   Communicating with integrity isn't always easy. Management can favor business practices that put the company before the customers that it serves, and even reward employees who support ethical transgressions.[11] The culture in some organizations favors bad-mouthing, competing, and "working the system." One employee recalls how her colleagues joked about ways to be the least productive while getting paid the most.

> Principled communication means following your own set of ethics rather than relying on the approval of others.

Principled communication means following your own set of ethics rather than relying on the approval of others. You don't need to explicitly state that you don't like what's being said, or chastise coworkers for bad behavior. You can simply lead by example. A good policy is to avoid any type of communication that you will not feel good about later, and try not to say anything about anyone that you would not say in his or her presence.

World-renowned leadership consultant Steven Covey emphasizes that principled communication is not as difficult as it seems:

> Correct principles are like compasses: They are always pointing the way. And if we know how to read them, we won't get lost, confused, or fooled by conflicting voices and values. Principles such as fairness, equity, justice, integrity, honesty, and trust are not invented by us: They are the laws of the universe that pertain to human relationships and organizations. They are part of the human condition, consciousness, and conscience.[12]

Taking the high road may seem to have short-term costs, but the long-term benefits justify this approach. Covey explains the long-term benefits of principled communication this way:

> People instinctively trust those whose personalities are founded upon correct principles. We have evidence of this in our long-term relationships. We learn that technique is relatively unimportant compared to trust, which is the result of our trustworthiness over time. When trust is high, we communicate easily, effortlessly, instantaneously. We can make mistakes, and others will still capture our meaning. But when trust is low, communication is exhausting, time-consuming, ineffective, and inordinately difficult.[13]

Use Gossip Wisely   Malicious gossip is another behavior that may provide short-term satisfaction, but which can damage your career. Besides reflecting character defects,[14] gossiping can mark you as untrustworthy.

In addition to making a bad impression, gossip can be hurtful. "Gossip is high stakes," says Sam Chapman, the CEO of Empower, the public relations agency that banned gossip. "It's emotionally lethal. It's leading to suicides." He urges executives to make it clear that they don't engage in gossip, and says that their employees will follow the example.

Avoiding malicious talk doesn't mean all gossip is bad. In fact, researchers have found that certain types of workplace gossip can help people unite during struggles, form positive alliances, and engage in healthy competition. For example, when workers gossip about someone who got fired, they learn what happens to people who break the rules, and it may motivate employees to work harder or create greater loyalties to their company.[15]

One key to identifying benign or even helpful gossip lies in its intention. If your juicy information is helpful to others, it may be worth sharing. Are personnel changes coming? Have you heard something important about a new policy? As long as you aren't breaking a promise to keep the information confidential, it may be worth sharing.

Along with usefulness, a second criterion for "good" gossip is its tone. One executive proposed this test: Before you start talking, stop and ask yourself, "Is it kind?"[16] Stories and information spread through word of mouth don't always have to be negative or malicious. If someone at work received an award, completed a major project, or even lost weight, go ahead and spread the word. People who speak kindly of others get noticed.

> One executive proposed this test: Before you start talking, stop and ask yourself, "Is it kind?"

In sum, it's unrealistic to avoid talking about other people; just make sure, when you do, that you aren't casting a shadow upon your own character by denigrating the target of your story.

Exceed Others' Expectations   Bare-minimum performance may not get you fired, but neither will it get you noticed. One method for standing out is to do more than what's required by your job description.[17]

Positively exceeding expectations may mean

- finishing a job ahead of schedule;
- providing more information than was requested;
- doing a better job than others anticipated.

The ways in which you can go above and beyond depend a lot on the type of organization where you work. If you're not sure what you could be doing, consider volunteering to serve on a committee, offering to help orient a new employee, showing up to work on a weekend or after hours (if it's allowed), offering to deliver a presentation, or tackling a job that keeps getting delayed due to other work demands. The few minutes or hours jobs like this take will be well worth the reputation it earns you.

Greet People   Most career-minded individuals have been advised to learn names as a method of standing out. While learning names is an important networking tool, a simple hello can also have a powerful impact.[18] Greet people even if you don't know their names.

If you can't remember someone's name, you can always say, "This is really embarrassing because I know who you are, but I've forgotten your name." Everyone forgets names, but few people risk their own embarrassment by asking. Making it a priority to reach out to others will in turn help them remember you.

Sweat the Small Stuff   You may have heard the phrase *Don't Sweat the Small Stuff*. In fact, making a good impression requires paying attention to every detail.

Situations where details seem unimportant are exactly the situations you can use to stand out from the average employee. A common faux pas committed by new employees is thinking that mediated messages don't require the same etiquette as face-to-face interactions. Even if you are just shooting your boss a quick reply or confirmation, make sure you have a salutation, body, and closing, and always use proper grammar, spelling, and punctuation. Using "I" instead of "i" and "you" instead of "u" is imperative to any business correspondence, no matter how casual. In a world of text messaging, we are so accustomed to shortcutting our communication that we rarely realize the bad impression it makes at work. Take a moment to compose e-mails that sound articulate, professional, and respectful.

Besides making sure the work you do is impeccable, pay attention to the way you present yourself in career-related contexts. Casual use of slang and profanity risks offending others. It's smart to heed advice from the *Wall Street Journal*: "Tiny missteps may derail your career. You appear unpolished when you talk like an adolescent, or curse at colleagues."[19]

> Don't be a "nodder." Nodders fake understanding when they really don't.

How you look can be just as important as what you say. No one wants to hire or promote someone they fear won't represent the company well. One executive recruiter warns, "Outdated clothes, frayed cuffs, messy hair, scuffed shoes or excess cleavage also signal poor judgment."[20]

Behaving professionally can distinguish you from the pack. A now-successful businesswoman recalls that her big break came when the boss chose her to accompany him to an important trade show. When she asked why he chose her instead of others with more experience, he replied that she was the only employee who he knew wouldn't embarrass the company.

Ask Questions   Don't be a "nodder." Nodders fake understanding when they really don't.[21] When you aren't sure about an idea, assignment, or procedure, ask for clarification. To justify your request for clarification, consider prefacing questions with something like "I really want to understand what you're saying . . . " or "I want to make sure I get this right."

Summary

Beyond professional qualifications, strategic planning and effective communication can enhance your career. Developing relationships, knowing what to do in an interview, and distinguishing yourself at work can provide an edge in a competitive, demanding workplace.

Developing relationships with people who can help you is integral to success. You can develop and maintain personal networks by viewing everyone as a networking prospect, seeking referrals, and showing appreciation whenever you receive help. Making a name for yourself online through professional websites is equally important. Conducting informational interviews with those who have experience, expertise, and contacts can enhance your career prospects.

Selection interviews can be a critically important part of career advancement. Before an interview, conduct background research, create an impressive résumé, and prepare for questions that the interviewer is likely to ask. During the interview make sure to let the interviewer take the lead. Keep your answers brief and on topic, and be prepared for the interviewer to ask you to demonstrate a skill or respond to a specific situation. Don't forget to plan questions to ask the interviewer at the end.

Managing your professional identity can create the desired impression. Online information about you speaks volumes to others. It is important to monitor and control information about yourself that others create, as well as what you create and post yourself.

Getting ahead isn't always about seeking a new place of employment. You can receive a promotion or reassignment by distinguishing yourself at your current workplace. Get noticed by communicating in a principled manner. Exceed the expectations of your superiors, get to know people at work, and pay attention to details. Asking questions instead of assuming can help you perform in a way that shows initiative. In sum, being qualified for a job or promotion isn't enough: Help others help you by standing out in a way that makes you a desirable employee in whom they would want to invest.

Key Terms

behavioral interview Session that explores specifics of the applicant's past performance as it relates to the job at hand. *p. A-13*

closed question Interview question that can be answered in a few words. *p. A-6*

direct question Interview question that makes a straightforward request for information. *p. A-6*

factual question Interview question that investigates matters of fact. See also *Opinion question.* *p. A-6*

hypothetical question Seeks a response by proposing a "what-if" situation. *p. A-7*

indirect question Interview question that does not directly request the information being sought. See also *Direct question.* *p. A-6*

informational interview Interview intended to collect facts and opinions from the respondent. *p. A-4*

leading question A question in which the interviewer—either directly or indirectly—signals the desired answer. *p. A-7*

networking The strategic process of deliberately meeting people and maintaining contacts that results in information, advice, and leads that enhance one's career. *p. A-2*

neutral question A question that gives the interviewee a chance to respond without any influence from the interviewer. *p. A-7*

open question Interview question that requires the interviewee to respond in detail. See also *Closed question.* *p. A-6*

opinion question Interview question seeking the interviewee's opinion. See also *Factual question.* *p. A-6*

probe An interjection, silence, or brief remark designed to open up or direct an interviewee. *p. A-6*

selection interview Interview in which a candidate is evaluated for a new position—either initial employment, promotion, or reassignment. *p. A-7*

NOTES

CHAPTER 1

1. For an in-depth look at this topic, see S. B. Cunningham, "Intrapersonal Communication: A Review and Critique," in S. Deetz, ed., *Communication Yearbook* 15 (Newbury Park, CA: Sage, 1992).

2. L. Wheeler and J. Nelek, "Sex Differences in Social Participation." *Journal of Personality and Social Psychology* 35 (1977): 742–754.

3. J. John, "The Distribution of Free-Forming Small Group Size." *American Sociological Review* 18 (1953): 569–570.

4. R. Verderber, A. Elder, and E. Weiler, "A Study of Communication Time Usage among College Students" (unpublished study, University of Cincinnati, 1976).

5. For a summary of the link between social support and health, see S. Duck, "Staying Healthy . . . with a Little Help from Our Friends?" in *Human Relationships*, 2nd ed. (Newbury Park, CA: Sage, 1992).

6. S. Cohen, W. J. Doyle, D. P. Skoner, B. S. Rabin, and J. M. Gwaltney, "Social Ties and Susceptibility to the Common Cold." *Journal of the American Medical Association* 277 (1997): 1940–1944.

7. Three articles in *Journal of the American Medical Association* 267 (January 22/29, 1992) focus on the link between psychosocial influences and coronary heart disease: R. B. Case, A. J. Moss, N. Case, M. McDermott, and S. Eberly, "Living Alone after Myocardial Infarction" (pp. 515–519); R. B. Williams, J. C. Barefoot, R. M. Calif, T. L. Haney, W. B. Saunders, D. B. Pryon, M. A. Hlatky, I. C. Siegler, and D. B. Mark, "Prognostic Importance of Social and Economic Resources among Medically Treated Patients with Angiographically Documented Coronary Artery Disease" (pp. 520–524); and R. Ruberman, "Psychosocial Influences on Mortality of Patients with Coronary Heart Disease" (pp. 559–560).

8. J. Stewart, *Bridges, Not Walls: A Book about Interpersonal Communication*, 9th ed. (New York: McGraw-Hill, 2004), p. 11.

9. R. Shattuck, *The Forbidden Experiment: The Story of the Wild Boy of Aveyron* (New York: Farrar, Straus & Giroux, 1980), p. 37.

10. For a fascinating account of Genie's story, see R. Rymer, *Genie: An Abused Child's Flight from Silence* (New York: HarperCollins, 1993). Linguist Susan Curtiss provides a more specialized account of the case in her book *Genie: A Psycholinguistic Study of a Modern-Day "Wild Child"* (San Diego: Academic Press, 1977).

11. R. B. Rubin, E. M. Perse, and C. A. Barbato, "Conceptualization and Measurement of Interpersonal Communication Motives." *Human Communication Research* 14 (1988): 602–628.

12. W. Goldschmidt, *The Human Career: The Self in the Symbolic World* (Cambridge, MA: Basil Blackmun, 1990).

13. *Job Outlook 2004, National Association of Colleges and Employers.* Report at http://www.jobweb.com/joboutlook/2004outlook/.

14. M. S. Peterson, "Personnel Interviewers' Perceptions of the Importance and Adequacy of Applicants' Communication Skills." *Communication Education* 46 (1997): 287–291.

15. M. W. Martin and C. M. Anderson, "Roommate Similarity: Are Roommates Who Are Similar in Their Communication Traits More Satisfied?" *Communication Research Reports* 12 (1995): 46–52.

16. E. Kirchler, "Marital Happiness and Interaction in Everyday Surroundings: A Time-Sample Diary Approach for Couples." *Journal of Social and Personal Relationships* 5 (1988): 375–382.

17. R. B. Rubin and E. E. Graham, "Communication Correlates of College Success: An Exploratory Investigation." *Communication Education* 37 (1988): 14–27.

18. R. L. Duran and L. Kelly, "The Influence of Communicative Competence on Perceived Task, Social and Physical Attraction." *Communication Quarterly* 36 (1988): 41–49.

19. C. E. Shannon and W. Weaver, *The Mathematical Theory of Communication* (Urbana: University of Illinois Press, 1949).

20. See, for example, M. Dunne and S. H. Ng, "Simultaneous Speech in Small Group Conversation: All-Together-Now and One-at-a-Time?" *Journal of Language and Social Psychology* 13 (1994): 45–71.

21. The issue of intentionality has been a matter of debate by communication theorists. For a sample of the arguments on both sides, see J. O. Greene, ed., *Message Production: Advances in Communication Theory* (New York: Erlbaum, 1997); M. T. Motley, "On Whether One Can(not) Communicate: An Examination via Traditional Communication Postulates." *Western Journal of Speech Communication* 54 (1990): 1–20; J. B. Bavelas, "Behaving and Communicating: A Reply to Motley." *Western Journal of Speech Communication* 54 (1990): 593–602; and J. Stewart, "A Postmodern Look at Traditional Communication Postulates." *Western Journal of Speech Communication* 55 (1991): 354–379.

22. K. J. Gergen, *The Saturated Self: Dilemmas of Identity in Contemporary Life* (New York: Basic Books, 1991), p. 158.

23. T. P. Mottet and V. P. Richmond, "Student Nonverbal Communication and Its Influence on Teachers and Teaching: A Review of Literature," in J. L. Chesebro and J. C. McCroskey, eds., *Communication for Teachers* (Needham Heights, MA: Allyn & Bacon, 2001).

24. M. Dainton and L. Stafford, "The Dark Side of 'Normal' Family Interaction," in B. H. Spitzberg and W. R. Cupach, eds., *The Dark Side of Interpersonal Communication* (Hillsdale, NJ: Erlbaum, 1993).

25. For a thorough review of this topic, see B. H. Spitzberg and W. R. Cupach, *Handbook of Interpersonal Competence Research* (New York: Springer-Verlag, 1989).

26. See J. M. Wiemann, J. Takai, H. Ota, and M. Wiemann, "A Relational Model of Communication Competence," in B. Kovacic, ed., *Emerging Theories of Human Communication* (Albany: SUNY Press, 1997). These goals, and the strategies used to achieve them, needn't be conscious. See G. M. Fitzsimons and J. A. Bargh, "Thinking of You: Nonconscious Pursuit of Interpersonal Goals

Associated with Relationship Partners." *Journal of Personality and Social Psychology* 84 (2003): 148–164.

27. For a review of the research citing the importance of flexibility, see M. M. Martin and C. M. Anderson, "The Cognitive Flexibility Scale: Three Validity Studies." *Communication Reports* 11 (1998): 1–9.

28. For a discussion of the trait versus state assessments of communication, see D. A. Infante, A. S. Rancer, and D. F. Womack, *Building Communication Theory*, 3rd ed. (Prospect Heights, IL: Waveland Press, 1996), pp. 159–160. For a specific discussion of trait versus state definitions of communication competence, see W. R. Cupach and B. H. Spitzberg, "Trait versus State: A Comparison of Dispositional and Situational Measures of Interpersonal Communication Competence." *Western Journal of Speech Communication* 47 (1983): 364–379.

29. B. R. Burleson and W. Samter, "A Social Skills Approach to Relationship Maintenance," in D. Canary and L. Stafford, eds., *Communication and Relationship Maintenance* (San Diego: Academic Press, 1994), p. 12.

30. L. K. Guerrero, P. A. Andersen, P. F. Jorgensen, B. H. Spitzberg, and S. V. Eloy. "Coping with the Green-Eyed Monster: Conceptualizing and Measuring Communicative Responses to Romantic Jealousy." *Western Journal of Communication* 59 (1995): 270–304.

31. See B. J. O'Keefe, "The Logic of Message Design: Individual Differences in Reasoning about Communication." *Communication Monographs* 55 (1988): 80–103.

32. See, for example, A. D. Heisel, J. C. McCroskey, and V. P. Richmond, "Testing Theoretical Relationships and Nonrelationships of Genetically-Based Predictors: Getting Started with Communibiology." *Communication Research Reports* 16 (1999): 1–9; and J. C. McCroskey and K. J. Beatty, "The Communibiological Perspective: Implications for Communication in Instruction." *Communication Education* 49 (2000): 1–6.

33. S. L. Kline and B. L. Clinton, "Developments in Children's Persuasive Message Practices." *Communication Education* 47 (1998): 120–136.

34. M. A. de Turck and G. R. Miller, "Training Observers to Detect Deception: Effects of Self-Monitoring and Rehearsal." *Human Communication Research* 16 (1990): 603–620.

35. R. B. Rubin, E. E. Graham, and J. T. Mignerey, "A Longitudinal Study of College Students' Communication Competence." *Communication Education* 39 (1990): 1–14.

36. See, for example, R. Martin, "Relational Cognition Complexity and Relational Communication in Personal Relationships." *Communication Monographs* 59 (1992): 150–163; D. W. Stacks and M. A. Murphy, "Conversational Sensitivity: Further Validation and Extension." *Communication Reports* 6 (1993): 18–24; and A. L. Vangelisti and S. M. Draughton, "The Nature and Correlates of Conversational Sensitivity." *Human Communication Research* 14 (1987): 167–202.

37. Research summarized in D. E. Hamachek, *Encounters with the Self*, 2nd ed. (Fort Worth, TX: Holt, Rinehart and Winston, 1987), p. 8. See also J. A. Daly, A. L. Vangelisti, and S. M. Daughton, "The Nature and Correlates of Conversational Sensitivity," in M. V. Redmond, ed., *Interpersonal Communication: Readings in Theory and Research* (Fort Worth, TX: Harcourt Brace, 1995).

38. D. A. Dunning and J. Kruger, *Journal of Personality and Social Psychology* (December 1999).

39. Adapted from the work of R. P. Hart as reported by M. L. Knapp in *Interpersonal Communication and Human Relationships* (Boston: Allyn & Bacon, 1984), pp. 342–344. See also R. P. Hart and

D. M. Burks, "Rhetorical Sensitivity and Social Interaction." *Speech Monographs* 39 (1972): 75–91; and R. P. Hart, R. E. Carlson, and W. F. Eadie, "Attitudes toward Communication and the Assessment of Rhetorical Sensitivity." *Communication Monographs* 47 (1980): 1–22.

40. Adapted from J. C. McCroskey and L. R. Wheeless, *Introduction to Human Communication* (Boston: Allyn & Bacon, 1976), pp. 3–10.

41. J. L. Smith, W. Ickes, and S. Hodges (eds.), *Managing Interpersonal Sensitivity: Knowing When—and When Not—to Understand Others* (Hauppauge, NY: Nova Science Publishers, 2010).

42. W. B. Pearce and K. A. Pearce, "Extending the Theory of the Coordinated Management of Meaning (CMM) through a Community Dialogue Process." *Communication Theory* 10 (2000): 405–423. See also E. M. Griffin, *A First Look at Communication Theory*, 5th ed. (New York: McGraw-Hill, 2003), pp. 66–81.

43. J. A. M. Meerloo, *Conversation and Communication* (Madison, CT: International Universities Press, 1952), p. 91.

44. For a detailed rationale of the position argued in this section, see G. H. Stamp and M. L. Knapp, "The Construct of Intent in Interpersonal Communication." *Quarterly Journal of Speech* 76 (1990): 282–299. See also J. Stewart, "A Postmodern Look at Traditional Communication Postulates." *Western Journal of Speech Communication* 55 (1991): 354–379.

45. For a thorough discussion of communication difficulties, see N. Coupland, H. Giles, and J. M. Wiemann, eds., *"Miscommunication" and Problematic Talk* (Newbury Park, CA: Sage, 1991).

46. J. C. McCroskey and L. R. Wheeless, *Introduction to Human Communication* (Boston: Allyn & Bacon, 1976), p. 5.

CHAPTER 2

1. I. Jenks, "Living on the Future Edge." Presentation handout, 21st Century Fluency Project (Kelowna], B.C., Canada: The Info Savvy Group, 2009).

2. United Nations Cyberschoolbus. Retrieved February 2, 2010, from http://www.un.org/Pubs/CyberSchoolBus/aboutus.html.

3. Aristotle, *On Rhetoric: A Theory of Civic Discourse*, trans. George A. Kennedy (New York: Oxford University Press, 1991).

4. See, for example, J. D. Peters, J. Durham, and P. Simonson, *Mass Communication and American Social Thought: Key Texts: 1919–1968* (Lanham, MD: Rowman and Littlefield, 1997).

5. R. L. Heath and J. Bryant, *Human Communication Theory and Research* (Hillsdale, NJ: Lawrence Erlbaum Associates, 2000).

6. Ibid.

7. A. Kohut, S. Keeter, C. Doherty, R. Suro, and G. Escobar, "America's Immigration Quandary." Pew Research Center, 2006. Retrieved January 17, 2009, from http://people-press.org/report/ ?pageid=1050.

8. U.S. Census Bureau, "State & County QuickFacts." Retrieved January 17, 2009, from http://quickfacts.census.gov.

9. Statistics Canada/Statistoqe Canada. Retrieved January 12, 2009, from http://www12.statcan.ca/english/census01/home/Index .cfm.

10. J. S. Passel and D. Cohn, "U.S. Population Projections: 2005–2050." Pew Research Center, 2008. Retrieved January 15, 2009, from http://pewsocialtrends.org/pubs/703/population -projections-united-states.

11. 2008 Census Bureau, http://quickfacts.census.gov/qfd/ states/00000.html.

12. *Directory of Foreign Firms Operating in the U.S.*, 18th ed. (Millis, MA: Uniworld, 2005).

13. 2007 Annual Report, General Electric Co. Retrieved January 10, 2009, from http://www.companythumbs.com/ReportByCompanyG100.asp?lc=G&arYear=2007.

14. Institute of International Education, Open Doors Report (2009). Retrieved January 10, 2009, from http://opendoors.iienetwork.org/?p=150649.

15. A. P. Carnevale and R. A. Frye, *Crossing the Great Divide: Can We Achieve Equity When Generation Y Goes to College?* (Princeton, NJ: Educational Testing Services, 2000).

16. Grunwald Associates National Study, reported at the September 27, 2007, Millenials Conference, New York City.

17. China Internet Watch (February 26, 2009), "Tencent's QZone Shows Great Social Networking Potential." Retrieved January 10, 2010, from http://www.chinainternetwatch.com/13/tencent-qzone-200-million-users/.

18. Press Release: Russia Has World's Most Engaged Social Networking Audience: Com.score, Inc., May 2009.

19. I. Davis, "Plot Your Course for the New World." *The Financial Times*, January 13, 2006.

20. A. L. Kroeber and C. Kluckhohn, *Culture: A Critical Review of Concepts and Definitions.* Harvard University, Peabody Museum of American Archeology and Ethnology Papers 47 (1952).

21. L. A. Samovar and R. E. Porter, *Communication Between Cultures*, 6th ed. (Belmont, CA: Wadsworth, 2007).

22. M. J. Collier, "Communication Competence Problematics in Ethnic Relationships." *Communication Monographs* 63 (1996): 314–336.

23. W. B. Gudykunst and Y. Matsumoto, "Cross-Cultural Variability of Communication in Personal Relationships," in W. B. Gudykunst, S. Ting-Toomey, and T. Nishida, eds., *Communication in Personal Relationships Across Cultures* (Newbury Park, CA: Sage, 1996), pp. 19–56.

24. E. T. Hall, *Beyond Culture* (New York: Doubleday, 1959).

25. L. Leets, "Explaining Perceptions of Racist Speech." *Communication Research* 28 (1991): 676–706, and L. Leets, "Disentangling Perceptions of Subtle Racist Speech: A Cultural Perspective." *Journal of Language and Social Psychology* 22 (1993): 1–24.

26. H. C. Triandis, *Individualism and Collectivism* (Boulder, CO: Westview, 1995).

27. P. A. Andersen, *Nonverbal Communication: Forms and Functions* (Palo Alto, CA: Mayfield, 1999).

28. G. Hofstede, *Culture's Consequences: Comparing Values, Behaviors, Institutions, and Organizations Across Nations*, 2nd ed. (Thousand Oaks, CA: Sage, 1993).

29. D. A. Cai and E. L. Fink, "Conflict Style Differences Between Individualists and Collectivists." *Communication Monographs* 69 (2002): 67–87.

30. See, for example, G. Moss, K. Kubacki, M. Hersh, and R. Gunn, "Knowledge Management in Higher Education: A Comparison of Individualistic and Collectivist Cultures." *European Journal of Education* 42 (2007): 377–394.

31. Hofstede, *Culture's Consequences.*

32. A. Cohen, "One Nation, Many Cultures: A Cross-Cultural Study of the Relationship Between Personal Cultural Values and Commitment in the Workplace to In-Role Performance and Organizational Citizenship Behavior." *Cross-Cultural Research: The Journal of Comparative Social Science* 41 (2007): 273–300.

33. Hofstede, *Culture's Consequences.*

34. L. A. Arasaratnam, "Further Testing of a New Model of Intercultural Communication Competence." *Communication Research Reports* 23 (2006): 93–99.

35. T. F. Pettigrew and L. R. Tropp, "Does Intergroup Contact Reduce Prejudice? Recent Meta-Analytic Findings," in S. Oskamp, ed., *Reducing Prejudice and Discrimination: Social Psychological Perspectives* (Mahwah, NJ: Erlbaum, 2000), pp. 93–114.

36. T. F. Pettigrew and L. R Tropp, "A Meta-Analytic Test of Intergroup Contact Theory." *Journal of Personality and Social Psychology* 90 (May 2006): 751–783.

37. J. W. Kassing, "Development of the Intercultural Willingness to Communicate Scale." *Communication Research Reports* 14 (1997): 399–407.

38. Y. Amichai-Hamburger and K. Y. A. McKenna, "The Contact Hypothesis Reconsidered: Interacting via the Internet." *Journal of Computer-Mediated Communication* 11 (2006). Retrieved February 2, 2010, from http://jcmc.indiana.edu/vol11/issue3/amichai-hamburger.html.

39. P. Iyer, *The Lady and the Monk: Four Seasons in Kyoto* (New York: Vintage, 1990): 129–130.

40. Ibid, pp. 220–221.

41. R. Steves, "Culture Shock." *Europe Through the Back Door Newsletter* 50 (May–September, 1996): 9.

42. M. S. Kim, J. E. Hunter, A. Miyahara, A. M. Horvath, M. Bresnahan, and H. Yoon, "Individual- vs. Culture-Level Dimensions of Individualism and Collectivism: Effects on Preferred Conversational Styles." *Communication Monographs* 63 (1996): 28–49.

43. C. R. Berger, "Beyond Initial Interactions: Uncertainty, Understanding, and the Development of Interpersonal Relationships," in H. Giles and R. St. Clair, eds., *Language and Social Psychology* (Oxford, England: Blackwell, 1979).

44. L. J. Carrell, "Diversity in the Communication Curriculum: Impact on Student Empathy." *Communication Education* 46 (1997): 234–244.

45. P. B. O'Sullivan, "Masspersonal Communication: Rethinking the Mass-Interpersonal Divide." Paper presented at the annual meeting of the International Communication Association, New York, May 25, 2009. Retrieved online from http://www.allacademic.com/meta/p14277_index.html.

46. A. Lenhart, M. Madden, and A. Smith, "Teens and Social Media." *Pew Internet & American Life Project* (December 2007). Retrieved January 16, 2010, from http://www.pewinternet.org/Reports/2007/Teens-and-Social-Media/1-Summary-of-Findings.aspx?r=1.

47. S. Johnson, "How Twitter Will Change the Way We Live." *Time* online (June 5, 2009).

48. K. S. Surinder and R. B. Cooper, "Exploring the Core Concepts of Media Richness Theory: The Impact of Cue Multiplicity and Feedback Immediacy on Decision Quality." *Journal of Management Information Systems* 20 (2003): 263–299.

49. P. M. Leonardi, J. W. Treem, and M. H. Jackson, "The Connectivity Paradox: Using Technology to Both Decrease and Increase Perceptions of Distance in Distributed Work Arrangements." *Journal of Applied Communication Research* 38 (2010): 85–105.

50. A. Lenhart and K. Purcell, "Social Media and Young Adults." *Pew Internet & American Life Project* (February 2010). Retrieved February 22, 2010, from http://pewinternet.org/Reports/2010/Social-Media-and-Young-Adults.

51. M. Prensky, "Mobile Phone Imagination—Using Devices Kids Love for the Education." Vodafone *Receiver* (December 5, 2005). Retrieved April 22, 2010, from http://www.receiver.vodafone.com/14/index.html.

52. "Census Bureau: Texting Grows Among Americans." NPR *Morning Edition* (December 17, 2009). Retrieved from http://www.npr.org/templates/story/story.php?storyId=121549494.

53. Lenhart and Purcell, "Social Media"; "Portrait of a Twitter User: Status Update Demographics." *Pew Internet & American Life Project* (October 21, 2009). Retrieved from http://pewinternet.org/Infographics/Twitter-demographics—Fall-2009.aspx.

54. "Online Activities 2000–2009." *Pew Internet & American Life Project* (December 2009): 4. Retrieved January 10, 2010, from http://www.pewinternet.org/Trend-Data/Online-Activities-20002009.aspx.

55. Lenhart, Madden, and Smith, "Teens and Social Media."

56. W. J. Severin and J. W. Tankard, *Communication Theories: Origins, Methods, and Uses in the Mass Media,* 4th ed. (New York: Longman, 1997): 197–214.

57. T. E. Ruggiero, "Uses and Gratifications Theory in the 21st Century." *Mass Communication & Society* 3 (2000): 3–37. For a somewhat different categorization of uses and gratifications, see A. N. Joinson, "'Looking at,' 'Looking up' or 'Keeping up with' People? Motives and Uses of Facebook," in *Proceedings of the 26th Annual SIGCHI Conference on Human Factors in Computing Systems* (Florence, Italy, April 5–10 2008), ACM, New York, (pp. 1027–1036).

58. R. H. Lengel and R. L. Daft, "The Selection of Communication Media as an Executive Skill." *Academy of Management Executive* 2 (1988): 225–232.

59. A. Lenhart, "Teens and Sexting." *Pew Internet & American Life Project* (December 2009): 4. Retrieved January 10, 2009 from http://www.pewinternet.org/Reports/2009/Teens-and-Sexting.aspx.

60. MTV-AP Digital Abuse Study, Executive Summary (2009). Available at http://www.athinline.org/MTV-AP_Digital_Abuse_Study_Executive_Summary.pdf.

61. News release from WLWT, NBC affiliate in Cinncinati, Ohio. Retrieved March 6, 2009, from http://www.wlwt.com/health/18873648/detail.html.

62. M. Bauerlein, "Why Gen-Y Johnny Can't Read Nonverbal Cues." *Wall Street Journal* (September 4, 2009). Retrieved from http://online.wsj.com/article/SB10001424052970203863204574348493483201758.html.

63. S. A. Watts, "Evaluative Feedback: Perspectives on Media Effects." *Journal of Computer-Mediated Communication* 12 (2007). Retrieved January 29, 2010 from http://jcmc.indiana.edu/vol12/issue2/watts.html. See also A. K. Turnage, "Email Behaviors and Organizational Conflict." *Journal of Computer-Mediated Communication* 13(1) (2007), article 3. Retrieved January 16, 2009, from http://jcmc.indiana.edu/vol13/issue1/turnage.html.

64. M. L. Ybarra and K. J. Mitchell, "Prevalence and Frequency of Internet Harassment Instigation: Implications for Adolescent Health." *Journal of Adolescent Health* 41(2) (August 2007): 189–195.

65. 2007 Executive Research Summary "Teens and Cyberbullying," produced by the National Crime Prevention Council. Retrieved January 19, 2010, from http://www.ncpc.org.

66. S. E. Caplan, "A Social Skill Account of Problematic Internet Use." *Journal of Communication* 55 (2005): 721–736; H. Schiffrin, A. Edelman, M. Falkenstein, and C. Stewart, "Associations Among Computer-Mediated Communication, Relationships, and Well-being." *Cyberpsychology, Behavior, and Social Networking* 13 (2010): 1–14; C. M. Morrison and H. Gore, "The Relationship Between Excessive Internet Use and Depression: A Questionnaire-Based Study of 1,319 Young People and Adults." *Psychopathology* 43 (2010): 121–126.

67. Ibid. (Caplan 2005).

68. C. Ko, J. Yen, C. Chen, S. Chen, and C. Yen, "Proposed Diagnostic Criteria of Internet Addiction for Adolescents." *The Journal of Nervous and Mental Disease* 11 (2005): 728–733.

69. K. Young, *Caught in the Net: How to Recognize the Signs of Internet Addiction and a Winning Strategy for Recovery* (Wiley, 1998).

70. See, for example, "Teens Creating Content." Pew Internet & American Life Project. Retrieved February 2, 2010, from http://www.pewinternet.org/Reports/2007/Teens-and-Social-Media/3-Teens-creating-content/18-Videos-are-not-restricted-as-often-as-photos.aspx?r=1.

71. D. L. Strayer, F. A. Drews, D. J. Crouch, and W. A. Johnston, "Why Do Cell Phone Conversations Interfere with Driving?" in W. R. Walker and D. Herrmann, eds., *Cognitive Technology: Transforming Thought and Society* (Jefferson, NC: McFarland & Company Inc., 2005), pp. 51–68.

72. J. T. Cohen and J. D. Graham, "A Revised Economic Analysis of Restrictions on the Use of Cell Phones while Driving." *Harvard Center for Risk Analysis* 23 (2003): 5–17.

73. D. L. Strayer and F. A. Drew, "Profiles in Driver Distraction: Effects of Cell Phone Conversations on Younger and Older Drivers." *Human Factors* 46 (Winter 2004): 640–649.

74. Nationwide Mutual Insurance Company, 2007 Report. Retrieved January 10, 2010, from http://www.nationwide.com/newsroom/nationwide-fights-dwd.jsp.

75. Study conducted by Virginia Tech Transportation Institute, 2009. Cited by Virginia Tech News. Retrieved January 10, 2009, from http://www.vtnews.vt.edu/story.php?relyear=2009&itemno=571.

CHAPTER 3

1. D. Hamachek, *Encounters with the Self*, 3rd ed. (Fort Worth, TX: Holt, Rinehart and Winston, 1992), pp. 5–8. See also J. D. Campbell and L. F. Lavallee, "Who Am I? The Role of Self-Concept Confusion in Understanding the Behavior of People with Low Self-Esteem," in R. F. Baumeister, ed., *Self-Esteem: The Puzzle of Low Self-Regard* (New York: Plenum Press, 1993), pp. 3–20.

2. R. F. Baumeister, *The Cultural Animal: Human Nature, Meaning, and Social Life* (New York: Oxford University Press, 2005); and R. F. Baumeister, J. D. Campbell, J. I. Krueger, and K. D. Vohs, "Does High Self-Esteem Cause Better Performance, Interpersonal Success, Happiness, or Healthier Lifestyles?" *Psychological Science in the Public Interest* 4 (2003), 1–44.

3. K. D. Vohs and T. F. Heatherton, "Ego Threats Elicit Different Social Comparison Process Among High and Low Self-Esteem People: Implications for Interpersonal Perceptions." *Social Cognition* 22 (2004): 168–191.

4. Arthur W. Combs and Donald Snygg, *Individual Behavior*, rev. ed. (New York: Harper & Row, 1959), p. 134.

5. See also J. Keltikangas, "The Stability of Self-Concept During Adolescence and Early Adulthood: A Six-Year Follow-Up Study." *Journal of General Psychology* 117 (1990): 361–369.

6. K. N. Kubric and R. M. Chory, "Exposure to Television Makeover Programs and Perceptions of Self." *Communication Research Reports* 24 (2007): 283–291.

7. P. N. Myers and F. A. Biocca, "The Elastic Body Image: The Effect of Television Advertising and Programming on Body Image

Distortions in Young Women." *Journal of Communication* 42 (1992): 108–134.

8. V. DeMunk, *Culture, Self, and Meaning* (Prospect Heights, IL: Waveland, 2000).

9. H. Giles and P. Johnson, " 'Ethnolinguistic Identity Theory': A Social Psychological Approach to Language Maintenance." *International Journal of Sociology of Language* 68 (1987): 69–99.

10. S. P. Banks, "Achieving 'Unmarkedness' in Organizational Discourse: A Praxis Perspective on Ethnolinguistic Identity." *Journal of Language and Social Psychology* 6 (1982): 171–190.

11. T. M. Singelis and W. J. Brown, "Culture, Self, and Collectivist Communication." *Human Communication Research* 21 (1995): 354–389. See also H. R. Markus and S. Kitayama, "A Collective Fear of the Collective: Implications for Selves and Theories of Selves." *Personality and Social Psychology* 20 (1994): 568–579.

12. J. Servaes, "Cultural Identity and Modes of Communication," in J. A. Anderson, ed., *Communication Yearbook* 12 (Newbury Park, CA: Sage, 1989), p. 396.

13. A. Bharti, "The Self in Hindu Thought and Action," in *Culture and Self: Asian and Western Perspectives* (New York: Tavistock, 1985).

14. W. B. Gudykunst and S. Ting-Toomey, *Culture and Interpersonal Communication* (Newbury Park, CA: Sage, 1988).

15. L. A. Samovar, R. E. Porter, and E. R. McDaniel, *Communication Between Cultures*, 7th ed. (Boston, MA: Cengage, 2007), p. 91.

16. D. Klopf, "Cross-Cultural Apprehension Research: A Summary of Pacific Basin Studies," in J. Daly and J. McCroskey, eds., *Avoiding Communication: Shyness, Reticence, and Communication Apprehension* (Beverly Hills, CA: Sage, 1984).

17. S. Ting-Toomey, "A Face-Negotiation Theory," in Y. Kim and W. Gudykunst, eds., *Theory in Interpersonal Communication* (Newbury Park, CA: Sage, 1988).

18. T. M. Steinfatt, "Personality and Communication: Classical Approaches," in J. C. McCroskey and J. A. Daly, eds., *Personality and Interpersonal Communication* (Newbury Park, CA: Sage, 1987), p. 42.

19. G. W. Allport and H. W. Odbert, "Trait Names, a Psychological Study." *Psychological Monographs* 47 (1936).

20. J. Kagan, *Unstable Ideas: Temperament, Cognition, and Self* (Cambridge, MA: Harvard University Press, 1989).

21. J. C. McCroskey and V. Richmond, *The Quiet Ones: Communication Apprehension and Shyness* (Dubuque, IA: Gorsuch Scarisbrick, 1980). See also T. J. Bouchard, D. T. Lykken, M. McGue, and N. L. Segal, "Sources of Human Psychological Differences—The Minnesota Study of Twins Reared Apart," *Science* 250 (October 12, 1990): 223–228.

22. P. D. MacIntyre and K. A. Thivierge, "The Effects of Speaker Personality on Anticipated Reactions to Public Speaking." *Communication Research Reports* 12 (1995): 125–133.

23. J. Kolligan Jr., "Perceived Fraudulence as a Dimension of Perceived Incompetence," in R. J. Sternberg and J. Kolligen Jr., eds., *Competence Considered* (New Haven, CT: Yale University Press, 1990).

24. B. J. Zimmerman, A. Bandura, and M. Martinez-Pons, "Self-Motivation for Academic Attainment: The Role of Self-Efficacy Beliefs and Personal Goal Setting." *American Educational Research Journal* 29 (1992): 663–676.

25. G. Downey and S. I. Feldman, "Implications of Rejection Sensitivity for Intimate Relationships." *Journal of Personality and Social Psychology* 70 (1996): 1327–1343.

26. C. L. Kleinke, T. R. Peterson, and T. R. Rutledge, "Effects of Self-Generated Facial Expressions on Mood." *Journal of Personality and Social Psychology* 74 (1998): 272–279.

27. J. G. Holmes, "Interpersonal Expectations as the Building Blocks of Social Cognition: An Interdependence Theory Perspective." *Personal Relationships* 9 (2002): 1–26.

28. Robert Rosenthal and Lenore Jacobson, *Pygmalion in the Classroom* (New York: Holt, Rinehart and Winston, 1968).

29. For a detailed discussion of how self-fulfilling prophecies operate in relationships, see P. Watzlawick, "Self-Fulfilling Prophecies," in J. O'Brien and P. Kollock, eds., *The Production of Reality*, 3rd ed. (Thousand Oaks, CA: Pine Forge Press, 2005), pp. 382–394.

30. W. James, *The Letters of William James*, ed. H. James (Boston, 1920), p. 462.

31. P. M. Neidenthal, M. Brauer, J. B. Halberstadt, and A. H. Innes-Ker, "When Did Her Smile Drop? Facial Mimicry and the Influences of Emotional State on the Detection of Change in Emotional Expression." *Cognition and Emotion* 15 (2001): 853–864.

32. C. N. Macrae and G. V. Bodenhausen, "Social Cognition: Categorical Person Perception." *British Journal of Psychology* 92 (2001): 239–256.

33. W. Matthys and P. Cohen-Kettenis, "Boys' and Girls' Perceptions of Peers in Middle Childhood: Differences and Similarities." *Journal of Genetic Psychology* 155 (1994): 15–24.

34. J. Heisler and S. Crabill, "Who Are 'stinkybug' and 'packerfan4'? Email Pseudonyms and Participants' Perceptions of Demography, Productivity, and Personality." *Journal of Computer-Mediated Communication* 12 (2006), article 6. Retrieved from http://jcmc.indiana.edu/vol12/issue1/heisler.html.

35. V. Manusov, M. R. Winchatz, and L. M. Manning, "Acting Out Our Minds: Incorporating Behavior into Models of Stereotype-Based Expectancies for Cross-Cultural Interactions." *Communication Monographs* 64 (1997): 119–139.

36. V. Manusov, "It Depends on Your Perspective: Effects of Stance and Beliefs About Intent on Person Perception." *Western Journal of Communication* 5 (1993): 27–41.

37. C. L. M. Shaw, "Personal Narrative: Revealing Self and Reflecting Other." *Human Communication Research* 24 (1997): 302–319.

38. P. M. Sias, "Constructing Perceptions of Differential Treatment: An Analysis of Coworkers' Discourse." *Communication Monographs* 63 (1996): 171–187.

39. J. M. Martz, J. Verette, X. B. Arriaga, L. F. Slovik, C. L. Cox, and C. E. Rusbult, "Positive Illusion in Close Relationships." *Personal Relationships* 5 (1998): 159–181.

40. J. C. Pearson, "Positive Distortion: 'The Most Beautiful Woman in the World,' " in K. M. Galvin and P. J. Cooper, eds., *Making Connections: Readings in Relational Communication*, 2nd ed. (Los Angeles: Roxbury, 2000), p. 186.

41. Summarized in D. E. Hamachek, *Encounters with Others* (New York: Holt, Rinehart and Winston, 1982), pp. 23–30.

42. J. Willis and A. Todorov, "First Impressions: Making Up Your Mind After a 100-Ms Exposure to a Face." *Psychological Science* 17 (2006): 592–598.

43. T. D. Nelson, "Ageism: Prejudice Against Our Featured Future Self." *Journal of Social Issues* 61 (2005): 207–221.

44. S. E. Zenmore, S. T. Fiske, and H. J. Kim, "Gender Stereotypes and the Dynamics of Social Interaction," in T. Eckes and H. M. Trautner, eds., *The Developmental Social Psychology of Gender* (Mahwah, NJ: Erlbaum, 2000), pp. 207–241.

45. M. Allen, "Methodological Considerations When Examining a Gendered World," in D. J. Canary and K. Dindia, eds., *Handbook of Sex Differences and Similarities in Communication* (Mahwah, NJ: Erlbaum, 1998), pp. 427–444.

46. B. Allen, " 'Diversity' and Organizational Communication." *Journal of Applied Communication Research* 23 (1995): 143–155. See also R. Buttny, "Reported Speech in Talking Race on Campus." *Human Communication Research* 23 (1997): 477–506.

47. For a review of these perceptual biases, see D. Hamachek, *Encounters with the Self*, 3rd ed. (Fort Worth, TX: Harcourt Brace Jovanovich, 1992). See also T. N. Bradbury and F. D. Fincham, "Attributions in Marriage: Review and Critique." *Psychological Bulletin* 107 (1990): 3–33. For information on the self-serving bias, see J. Shepperd, W. Malone, and K. Sweeny, "Exploring Causes of the Self-Serving Bias." *Social and Personality Psychology Compass* 2/2 (2008): 895–908.

48. B. Sypher and H. E. Sypher, "Seeing Ourselves as Others See Us." *Communication Research* 11 (January 1984): 97–115.

49. Reported by D. Myers, "The Inflated Self." *Psychology Today* 14 (May 1980): 16.

50. See, for example, D. E. Kanouse and L. R. Hanson, "Negativity in Evaluations," in E. E. Jones, D. E. Kanouse, H. H. Kelley, R. E. Nisbett, S. Valins, and B. Weiner, eds., *Attribution: Perceiving the Causes of Behavior* (Morristown, NJ: General Learning Press, 1972).

51. C. I. Marek, M. B. Wanzer, and J. L. Knapp, "An Exploratory Investigation of the Relationship Between Roommates' First Impressions and Subsequent Communication Patterns." *Communication Research Reports* 21 (2004): 210–220.

52. See, for example, Penny Baron, "Self-Esteem, Ingratiation, and Evaluation of Unknown Others." *Journal of Personality and Social Psychology* 30 (1974): 104–109; and Elaine Walster, "The Effect of Self-Esteem on Romantic Liking." *Journal of Experimental and Social Psychology* 1 (1965): 184–197.

53. P. A. Mongeau and C. M. Carey, "Who's Wooing Whom II? An Experimental Investigation of Date-Initiation and Expectancy Violation." *Western Journal of Communication* 60 (1996): 195–213.

54. See, for example, J. B. Walther, D. C. DeAndrea, and S. T. Tong, "Computer-Mediated Communication Versus Vocal Communication in the Amelioration of Stereotypes: A Replication with Three Theoretical Models." Paper presented at the annual meeting of the National Communication Association, Chicago, IL (November 2009).

55. J. B. Walther, "Impression Development in Computer-Mediated Interaction." *Western Journal of Communication* 57 (1993): 381–398.

56. A. J. Gill, J. Oberlander, and E. Austin, "Rating Email Personality at Zero Acquaintance." *Personality and Individual Differences* 40 (2005): 497–507.

57. J. B. Walther, T. Loh, and L. Granka, "Let Me Count the Ways: The Interchange of Verbal and Nonverbal Cues in Computer-Mediated and Face-to-Face Affinity." *Journal of Language and Social Psychology* 24 (2005): 36–65.

58. M. Lea and R. Spears, "Paralanguage and Social Perception in Computer-Mediated Communication." *Journal of Organizational Computing* 2 (1992): 321–341.

59. J. B. Walther and L. C. Tidwell, "Nonverbal Cues in Computer-Mediated Communication, and the Effect of Chronemics on Relational Communication." *Journal of Organizational Computing* 5 (1995): 355–378.

60. J. W. Bagby, "A Cross-Cultural Study of Perceptual Predominance in Binocular Rivalry." *Journal of Abnormal and Social Psychology* 54 (1957): 331–334.

61. H. Giles, N. Coupland, and J. M. Wiemann, " 'Talk Is Cheap . . .' but 'My Word Is My Bond': Beliefs About Talk," in K. Bolton and H. Kwok, eds., *Sociolinguistics Today: International Perspectives* (London: Routledge & Kegan Paul, 1992).

62. M. J. Collier, "Rule Violations in Intercultural/Ethnic Advisement Contexts." Paper presented at the annual meeting of the Western Speech Communication Association, Tucson, AZ, 1986.

63. P. Andersen, M. Lustig, and J. Anderson, "Changes in Latitude, Changes in Attitude: The Relationship Between Climate, Latitude, and Interpersonal Communication Predispositions." Paper presented at the annual convention of the Speech Communication Association, Boston, 1987. P. Andersen, M. Lustig, and J. Andersen, "Regional Patterns of Communication in the United States: Empirical Tests." Paper presented at the annual convention of the Speech Communication Association, New Orleans, 1988.

64. J. B. Stiff, J. P. Dillard, L. Somera, H. Kim, and C. Sleight, "Empathy, Communication, and Prosocial Behavior." *Communication Monographs* 55 (1988): 198–213.

65. D. Goleman, *Emotional Intelligence: Why It Can Matter More Than I.Q.* (New York: Bantam, 1995).

66. R. Lennon and N. Eisenberg, "Gender and Age Differences in Empathy and Sympathy," in N. Eisenberg and J. Strayer, eds., *Empathy and Its Development* (Cambridge, England: Cambridge University Press, 1987).

67. T. Adler, "Look at Duration, Depth in Research on Emotion." *APA Monitor* (October 1990): 10.

68. N. D. Feshbach, "Parental Empathy and Child Adjustment/Maladjustment," in N. Eisenberg and J. Strayer, eds., *Empathy and Its Development* (Cambridge, England: Cambridge University Press, 1987).

69. T. R. Peterson and C. C. Horton, "Rooted in the Soil: How Understanding the Perspectives of Landowners Can Enhance the Management of Environmental Disputes." *Quarterly Journal of Speech* 81 (1995): 139–166.

70. C. M. Shaw and R. Edwards, "Self-Concepts and Self-Presentation of Males and Females: Similarities and Differences." *Communication Reports* 10 (1997): 56–62.

71. E. Goffman, *The Presentation of Self in Everyday Life* (Garden City, NY: Doubleday, 1959), and *Relations in Public* (New York: Basic Books, 1971).

72. W. R. Cupach and S. Metts, *Facework* (Thousand Oaks, CA: Sage, 1994). See also P. Brown and S. C. Levinson, *Politeness: Some Universals in Language Usage* (Cambridge, England: Cambridge University Press, 1987).

73. W. F. Sharkey, H. S. Park, and R. K. Kim, "Intentional Self Embarrassment." *Communication Studies* 55 (2004): 379–399.

74. C. M. Scotton, "The Negotiation of Identities in Conversation: A Theory of Markedness and Code Choice." *International Journal of Sociological Linguistics* 44 (1983): 119–125.

75. J. Stewart and C. Logan, *Together: Communicating Interpersonally*, 5th ed. (New York: McGraw-Hill, 1998), p. 120.

76. M. R. Leary and R. M. Kowalski, "Impression Management: A Literature Review and Two-Component Model." *Psychological Bulletin* 107 (1990): 34–47.

77. V. Brightman, A. Segal, P. Werther, and J. Steiner, "Ethological Study of Facial Expression in Response to Taste Stimuli." *Journal of Dental Research* 54 (1975): 141.

78. N. Chovil, "Social Determinants of Facial Displays." *Journal of Nonverbal Behavior* 15 (1991): 141–154.

79. Leary and Kowalski, "Impression Management."

80. P. Fleming and A. Sturdy, " 'Just Be Yourself!': Towards Neo-Normative Control in Organisations?" *Employee Relations* 31(2009): 569–583.

81. B. R. Ragins, "Disclosure Disconnects: Antecedents and Consequences of Disclosing Invisible Stigmas Across Life Domains." *Academy of Management Review* 33 (2008): 194–215.

82. B. R. Ragins, R. Singh, and J. M. Cornwell, "Making the Invisible Visible: Fear and Disclosure of Sexual Orientation at Work." *Journal of Applied Psychology* 92 (2007): 1103–1118.

83. J. E. Pachankis, "The Psychological Implications of Concealing a Stigma: A Cognitive-Affective-Behavioral Model." *Psychological Bulletin* 133 (2007): 328–345.

84. M. Snyder, "Self-Monitoring Processes," in L. Berkowitz, ed., *Advances in Experimental Social Psychology* (New York: Academic Press, 1979), and "The Many Me's of the Self-Monitor." *Psychology Today* (March 1983): 34f.

85. The following discussion is based on material in D. Hamachek, *Encounters with the Self*, 3rd ed. (Fort Worth, TX: Holt, Rinehart and Winston, 1992), pp. 24–26.

86. L. M. Coleman and B. M. DePaulo, "Uncovering the Human Spirit: Moving Beyond Disability and 'Missed' Communications," in N. Coupland, H. Giles, and J. M. Wiemann, eds., *"Miscommunication" and Problematic Talk* (Newbury Park, CA: Sage, 1991), pp. 61–84.

87. J. B. Walther, "Computer-Mediated Communication: Impersonal, Interpersonal, and Hyperpersonal Interaction." *Communication Research* 23 (1996): 3–43.

88. J. T. Hancock and P. J. Durham, "Impression Formation in Computer-Mediated Communication Revisited: An Analysis of the Breadth and Intensity of Impressions." *Communication Research* 28 (2001): 325–347.

89. J. R. Suler, "Identity Management in Cyberspace." *Journal of Applied Psychoanalytic Studies* 4 (2002): 455–459.

90. J. L. Gibbs, N. B. Ellison, and R. D. Heino, "Self-Presentation in Online Personals: The Role of Anticipated Future Interaction, Self-Disclosure, and Perceived Success in Internet Dating." *Communication Research* 33 (2006): 1–26.

91. See, for example, D. Chandler, "Personal Home Pages and the Construction of Identities on the Web." http://www.aber.ac.uk/~dgc/webident.html. Accessed May 8, 2006.

92. C. Toma, J. Hancock, and N. Ellison, "Separating Fact from Fiction: An Examination of Deceptive Self-Presentation in Online Dating Profiles." *Personality and Social Psychology Bulletin* 34 (2008): 1023–1036.

CHAPTER 4

1. W. S. Y. Wang, "Language and Derivative Systems," in W. S. Y. Wang, ed., *Human Communication: Language and Its Psychobiological Basis* (San Francisco: Freeman, 1982), p. 36.

2. O. Sacks, *Seeing Voices: A Journey into the World of the Deaf* (Berkeley: University of California Press, 1989), p. 17.

3. Adapted from J. O'Brien and P. Kollock, *The Production of Reality*, 3rd ed. (Thousand Oaks, CA: Pine Forge Press, 2001), p. 66.

4. M. Henneberger, "Misunderstanding of Word Embarrasses Washington's New Mayor." *New York Times* (January 29, 1999). Online at http://www.nyt.com

5. C. K. Ogden and I. A. Richards, *The Meaning of Meaning* (New York: Harcourt Brace, 1923), p. 11.

6. S. Duck, "Maintenance as a Shared Meaning System," in D. J. Caharg and L. Stafford, eds., *Communication and Relational Maintenance* (San Diego: Academic Press, 1993).

7. D. Crystal, *Language and the Internet* (Cambridge, England: Cambridge University Press, 2001).

8. W. B. Pearce and V. Cronen, *Communication, Action, and Meaning* (New York: Praeger, 1980). See also J. K. Barge, "Articulating CMM as a Practical Theory." *Human Systems: The Journal of Systemic Consultation and Management* 15 (2004): 193–204, and E. M. Griffin, *A First Look at Communication Theory*, 6th ed. (New York: McGraw-Hill, 2006).

9. Genesis 2:19. This biblical reference was noted by D. C. Mader, "The Politically Correct Textbook: Trends in Publishers' Guidelines for the Representation of Marginalized Groups." Paper presented at the annual convention of the Eastern Communication Association, Portland, ME, May 1992.

10. J. L. Cotton, B. S. O'Neill, and A. Griffin, "The 'Name Game': Affective and Hiring Reactions to First Names." *Journal of Managerial Psychology* 23(2008): 18–39.

11. J. L. Brunning, N. K. Polinko, J. I. Zerbst, and J. T. Buckingham, "The Effect on Expected Job Success of the Connotative Meanings of Names and Nicknames." *Journal of Social Psychology* 140 (2000), 197–201.

12. B. Coffey and P. A. McLaughlin, "Do Masculine Names Help Female Lawyers Become Judges? Evidence from South Carolina." *American Law and Economics Review* 11 (2009): 112–133.

13. G. W. Smith, "The Political Impact of Name Sounds." *Communication Monographs* 65 (1998): 154–172.

14. R. G. Fryer and S. D. Levitt, "The Causes and Consequences of Distinctively Black Names." *Quarterly Journal of Economics* 119 (2004): 767–805.

15. C. A. VanLear, "Testing a Cyclical Model of Communicative Openness in Relationship Development." *Communication Monographs* 58 (1991): 337–361.

16. T. Varadarajan, "Big Names, Big Battles." *New York Times* (July 26, 1999). Online at http://aolsvc.aol.com/computercenter/internet/index.adp.

17. D. H. Naftulin, J. E. Ware Jr., and F. A. Donnelly, "The Doctor Fox Lecture: A Paradigm of Educational Seduction." *Journal of Medical Education* 48 (July 1973): 630–635. See also C. T. Cory, ed., "Bafflegab Pays." *Psychology Today* 13 (May 1980): 12, and H. W. Marsh and J. E. Ware Jr., "Effects of Expressiveness, Content Coverage, and Incentive on Multidimensional Student Rating Scales: New Interpretations of the 'Dr. Fox' Effect." *Journal of Educational Psychology* 74 (1982): 126–134.

18. J. S. Armstrong, "Unintelligible Management Research and Academic Prestige." *Interfaces* 10 (1980): 80–86.

19. For a summary of research on this subject, see J. J. Bradac, "Language Attitudes and Impression Formation," in H. Giles and W. P. Robinson, eds., *The Handbook of Language and Social Psychology* (Chichester, England: Wiley, 1990), pp. 387–412.

20. H. Giles and P. F. Poseland, *Speech Style and Social Evaluation* (New York: Academic Press, 1975).

21. C. Miller and K. Swift, *Words and Women* (New York: Harper-Collins, 1991) p. 27.

22. For a discussion of racist language, see H. A. Bosmajian, *The Language of Oppression* (Lanham, MD: University Press of America, 1983).

23. Mader, "The Politically Correct Textbook," p. 5.

24. S. L. Kirkland, J. Greenberg, and T. Pysczynski, "Further Evidence of the Deleterious Effects of Overheard Derogatory Ethnic Labels: Derogation Beyond the Target." *Personality and Social Psychology Bulletin* 12 (1987): 216–227.

25. For a review of the relationship between power and language, see J. Liska, "Dominance-Seeking Language Strategies: Please Eat the Floor, Dogbreath, or I'll Rip Your Lungs Out, O.K.?" in S. A. Deetz, ed., *Communication Yearbook* 15 (Newbury Park, CA: Sage, 1992). See also N. A. Burrell and R. J. Koper, "The Efficacy of Powerful/Powerless Language on Persuasiveness/Credibility: A Meta-Analytic Review," in R. W. Preiss and M. Allen, eds., *Prospects and Precautions in the Use of Meta-Analysis* (Dubuque, IA: Brown & Benchmark, 1994).

26. L. A. Hosman, "The Evaluative Consequences of Hedges, Hesitations, and Intensifiers: Powerful and Powerless Speech Styles." *Human Communication Research* 15 (1989): 383–406. L. A. Hosman and S. A. Siltanen, "Powerful and Powerless Language Forms: Their Consequences for Impression Formation, Attributions of Control of Self and Control of Others, Cognitive Responses, and Message Memory." *Journal of Language and Social Psychology*, 25 (2006): 33–46.

27. S. H. Ng and J. J. Bradac, *Power in Language: Verbal Communication and Social Influence* (Newbury Park, CA: Sage, 1993). See also S. A. Reid and S. H. Ng, "Language, Power, and Intergroup Relations." *Journal of Social Issues* 55 (1999): 119–139.

28. S. Parton, S. A. Siltanen, L. A. Hosman, and J. Langenderfer, "Employment Interview Outcomes and Speech Style Effects." *Journal of Language and Social Psychology* 21 (2002): 144–161.

29. A. El-Alayli, C. J. Myers, T. L. Petersen, and A. L. Lystad, " 'I Don't Mean to Sound Arrogant, but . . . ': The Effects of Using Disclaimers on Person Perception." *Personality and Social Psychology Bulletin* 34, 130–143.

30. D. Tannen, *Talking from 9 to 5* (New York: Morrow, 1994), p. 101.

31. D. Geddes, "Sex Roles in Management: The Impact of Varying Power of Speech Style on Union Members' Perception of Satisfaction and Effectiveness." *Journal of Psychology* 126 (1992): 589–607.

32. L. A. Samovar and R. E. Porter, *Communication Between Cultures*, 3rd ed. (Belmont, CA: Wadsworth ITP, 1998), pp. 58–59.

33. H. Giles, J. Coupland, and N. Coupland, eds., *Contexts of Accommodation: Developments in Applied Sociolinguistics* (Cambridge, England: Cambridge University Press, 1991).

34. See, for example, R. A. Bell and J. G. Healey, "Idiomatic Communication and Interpersonal Solidarity in Friends' Relational Cultures." *Human Communication Research* 18 (1992): 307–335, and R. A. Bell, N. Buerkel-Rothfuss, and K. E. Gore, "Did You Bring the Yarmulke for the Cabbage Patch Kid?: The Idiomatic Communication of Young Lovers." *Human Communication Research* 14 (1987): 47–67.

35. J. Cassell and D. Tversky, "The Language of Online Intercultural Community Formation." *Journal of Computer-Mediated Communication* 10 (2005): Article 2.

36. "OMG: IM Slang Is Invading Everyday English." NPR *Weekend Edition*, February 18, 2006. Online at http://www.npr.org/templates/story/story.php?storyId=5221618.

37. A. Maass, D. Salvi, L. Arcuri, and G. R. Semin, "Language Use in Intergroup Context." *Journal of Personality and Social Psychology* 57 (1989): 981–993.

38. M. Wiener and A. Mehrabian, *A Language within Language* (New York: Appleton-Century-Crofts, 1968).

39. E. S. Kubanyu, D. C. Richard, G. B. Bower, and M. Y. Muraoka, "Impact of Assertive and Accusatory Communication of Distress and Anger: A Verbal Component Analysis." *Aggressive Behavior* 18 (1992): 337–347.

40. T. L. Scott, "Teens Before Their Time." *Time* (November 27, 2000): 22.

41. M. T. Motley and H. M. Reeder, "Unwanted Escalation of Sexual Intimacy: Male and Female Perceptions of Connotations and Relational Consequences of Resistance Messages." *Communication Monographs* 62 (1995): 356–382.

42. T. Wallstein, "Measuring the Vague Meanings of Probability Terms." *Journal of Experimental Psychology: General* 115 (1986): 348–365.

43. T. Labov, "Social and Language Boundaries Among Adolescents." *American Speech* 4 (1992): 339–366.

44. UCLA Slang. Retrieved October 24, 2001, from http://www.cs.rpi.edu/~kennyz/doc/humor/slang.humor.

45. M. Kakutani, "Computer Slang Scoffs at Wetware." *Santa Barbara News-Press* (July 2, 2000): D1.

46. M. Myer and C. Fleming, "Silicon Screenings." *Newsweek* (August 15, 1994): 63.

47. S. I. Hayakawa, *Language in Thought and Action* (New York: Harcourt Brace, 1964).

48. E. M. Eisenberg, "Ambiguity as Strategy in Organizational Communication." *Communication Monographs* 51 (1984): 227–242, and E. M. Eisenberg and M. G. Witten, "Reconsidering Openness in Organizational Communication." *Academy of Management Review* 12 (1987): 418–426.

49. J. K. Alberts, "An Analysis of Couples' Conversational Complaints." *Communication Monographs* 55 (1988): 184–197.

50. B. Streisand, Crystal Award speech delivered at the Crystal Awards, Women in Film luncheon, 1992.

51. B. Morrison, "What You Won't Hear the Pilot Say." *USA Today* (September 26, 2000): A1.

52. E. M. Eisenberg, ed., *Strategic Ambiguities: Essays on Communication, Organization and Identity* (Thousand Oaks, CA: Sage, 2007).

53. For detailed discussions of the relationship between gender and communication, see D. J. Canary and T. M. Emmers-Sommer, *Sex and Gender Differences in Personal Relationships* (New York: Guilford, 1997); J. Wood, *Gendered Lives: Communication, Gender, and Culture* (Belmont, CA: Wadsworth, 1994); and J. C. Pearson, *Gender and Communication*, 2nd ed. (Madison, WI: Brown & Benchmark, 1994).

54. See, for example, A. Haas and M. A. Sherman, "Reported Topics of Conversation Among Same-Sex Adults." *Communication Quarterly* 30 (1982): 332–342.

55. R. A. Clark, "A Comparison of Topics and Objectives in a Cross Section of Young Men's and Women's Everyday Conversations," in D. J. Canary and K. Dindia, eds., *Sex Differences and Similarities in Communication: Critical Essays and Empirical Investigations of Sex and Gender in Interaction* (Mahwah, NJ: Erlbaum, 1998).

56. J. T. Wood, *Gendered Lives: Communication, Gender, and Culture*, 4th ed. (Belmont, CA: Wadsworth, 2001), p. 141.

57. M. A. Sherman and A. Haas, "Man to Man, Woman to Woman." *Psychology Today* 17 (June 1984): 72–73.

58. A. Haas and M. A. Sherman, "Conversational Topic as a Function of Role and Gender." *Psychological Reports* 51 (1982): 453–454.

59. M. R. Mehl, S. Vazire, N. Ramírez-Esparza, R. B. Slatcher, and J. W. Pennebaker, "Are Women Really More Talkative Than Men?" *Science* 317 (July 2007): 82.

60. For a summary of research on the difference between male and female conversational behavior, see H. Giles and R. L. Street Jr., "Communication Characteristics and Behavior," in M. L. Knapp and G. R. Miller, eds., *Handbook of Interpersonal Communication* (Beverly Hills, CA: Sage, 1985): 205–261, and A. Kohn, "Girl Talk, Guy Talk," *Psychology Today* 22 (February 1988): 65–66.

61. A. B. Fox, D. Bukatko, M. Hallahan, and M. Crawford, "The Medium Makes a Difference: Gender Similarities and Differences in Instant Messaging." *Journal of Language and Social Psychology* 26 (2007): 389–397.

62. L. L. Carli, "Gender, Language, and Influence." *Journal of Personality and Social Psychology* 59 (1990): 941–951.

63. D. J. Canary and K. S. Hause, "Is There Any Reason to Research Sex Differences in Communication?" *Communication Quarterly* 41 (1993): 129–144.

64. C. J. Zahn, "The Bases for Differing Evaluations of Male and Female Speech: Evidence from Ratings of Transcribed Conversation." *Communication Monographs* 56 (1989): 59–74. See also L. M. Grob, R. A. Meyers, and R. Schuh, "Powerful? Powerless Language Use in Group Interactions: Sex Differences or Similarities?" *Communication Quarterly* 45 (1997): 282–303.

65. J. T. Wood and K. Dindia, "What's the Difference? A Dialogue About Differences and Similarities Between Women and Men," in D. J. Canary and K. Dindia, eds., *Sex Differences and Similarities in Communication: Critical Essays and Empirical Investigations of Sex and Gender in Interaction* (Mahwah, NJ: Erlbaum, 1998).

66. D. L. Rubin, K. Greene, and D. Schneider, "Adopting Gender-Inclusive Language Reforms: Diachronic and Synchronic Variation." *Journal of Language and Social Psychology* 13 (1994): 91–114.

67. D. S. Geddes, "Sex Roles in Management: The Impact of Varying Power of Speech Style on Union Members' Perception of Satisfaction and Effectiveness." *Journal of Psychology* 126 (1992): 589–607.

68. For a thorough discussion of the challenges involved in translation from one language to another, see L. A. Samovar, R. E. Porter, and E. R. McDaniel, *Communication Between Cultures*, 7th ed. (Boston: Cengage, 2010), pp. 149–154.

69. N. Sugimoto, "'Excuse Me' and 'I'm Sorry': Apologetic Behaviors of Americans and Japanese." Paper presented at the Conference on Communication in Japan and the United States, California State University, Fullerton, CA, March 1991.

70. A summary of how verbal style varies across cultures can be found in Chapter 5 of W. B. Gudykunst and S. Ting-Toomey, *Culture and Interpersonal Communication* (Newbury Park, CA: Sage, 1988).

71. M. Morris, *Saying and Meaning in Puerto Rico: Some Problems in the Ethnology of Discourse* (Oxford, England: Pergamon, 1981).

72. L. Leets and H. Giles, "Words as Weapons—When Do They Wound?" *Human Communication Research* 24 (1997): 260–301, and L. Leets, "When Words Wound: Another Look at Racist Speech." Paper presented at the annual conference of the International Communication Association, San Francisco, May 1999.

73. A. Almaney and A. Alwan, *Communicating with the Arabs* (Prospect Heights, IL: Waveland, 1982).

74. K. Basso, "To Give Up on Words: Silence in Western Apache Culture." *Southern Journal of Anthropology* 26 (1970): 213–230.

75. J. Yum, "The Practice of Uye-ri in Interpersonal Relationships in Korea," in D. Kincaid, ed., *Communication Theory from Eastern and Western Perspectives* (New York: Academic Press, 1987).

76. For a summary of scholarship supporting the notion of linguistic determinism, see L. Boroditsky, "Lost in Translation." *Wall Street Journal Online* (July 23, 2010). Retrieved August 11, 2010 from http://online.wsj.com/article/NA_WSJ_PUB:SB10001424052748703467304575383131592767868.html.

77. L. Martin and G. Pullum, *The Great Eskimo Vocabulary Hoax* (Chicago: University of Chicago Press, 1991).

78. H. Giles and A. Franklyn-Stokes, "Communicator Characteristics," in M. K. Asante and W. B. Gudykunst, eds., *Handbook of International and Intercultural Communication* (Newbury Park, CA: Sage, 1989).

79. L. Sinclair, "A Word in Your Ear," in *Ways of Mankind* (Boston: Beacon Press, 1954).

80. B. Whorf, "The Relation of Habitual Thought and Behavior to Language," in J. B. Carrol, ed., *Language, Thought, and Reality* (Cambridge, MA: MIT Press, 1956). See also Harry Hoijer, "The Sapir-Whorf Hypothesis," in Larry A. Samovar and Richard E. Porter, eds., *Intercultural Communication: A Reader*, 7th ed. (Belmont, CA: Wadsworth, 1994), pp. 194–200.

81. N. Postman, *Crazy Talk, Stupid Talk* (New York: Delta, 1976), p. 122.

82. Ibid., pp. 123–124.

CHAPTER 5

1. R. Emanuel, J. Adams, K. Baker, E. K. Daufin, C. Ellington, E. Fitts, J. Himsel, L. Holladay, and D. Okeowo, "How College Students Spend Their Time Communicating." *International Journal of Listening* 22 (2008): 13–28.

2. Research summarized in A. D. Wolvin and C. G. Coakley, "A Survey of the Status of Listening Training in Some Fortune 500 Corporations." *Communication Education* 40 (1991): 152–164.

3. M. L. Beall, J. Gill-Rosier, J. Tate, and A. Matten, "State of the Context: Listening in Education." *International Journal of Listening* 22 (2008): 123–132.

4. J. Davis, A. Foley, N. Crigger, and M. C. Brannigan, "Healthcare and Listening: A Relationship for Caring." *International Journal of Listening* 22 (2008): 168–175; J. Davis, C. R. Thompson, A. Foley, C. D. Bond, and J. DeWitt, "An Examination of Listening Concepts in the Healthcare Context: Differences Among Nurses, Physicians, and Administrators." *International Journal of Listening* 22 (2008): 152–167.

5. D. C. Schnapp, "Listening in Context: Religion and Spirituality." *International Journal of Listening* 22 (2008): 133–140.

6. J. Flynn, T. Valikoski, and J. Grau, "Listening in the Business Context: Reviewing the State of Research." *International Journal of Listening* 22 (2008): 141–151.

7. S. Covey, *The Seven Habits of Highly Effective People* (New York: Simon & Schuster, 1989).

8. B. D. Sypher, R. N. Bostrom, and J. H. Seibert, "Listening Communication Abilities and Success at Work." *Journal of Business Communication* 26 (1989): 293–303.

9. K. W. Hawkins and B. P. Fullion, "Perceived Communication Skill Needs for Work Groups." *Communication Research Reports* 16 (1999): 167–174.

10. S. D. Johnson and C. Bechler, "Examining the Relationship Between Listening Effectiveness and Leadership Emergence." *Small Group Research* 29 (1998): 452–471.

11. J. Franzen, "The Listener." *The New Yorker* (October 6, 2003): 85.

12. A. L. Vangelisti, "Couples' Communication Problems: The Counselor's Perspective." *Journal of Applied Communication Research* 22 (1994): 106–126.

13. A. D. Wolvin, "Meeting the Communication Needs of the Adult Learner." *Communication Education* 33 (1984): 267–271.

14. K. J. Prage and D. Buhrmester, "Intimacy and Need Fulfillment in Couple Relationships." *Journal of Social and Personal Relationships* 15 (1998): 435–469.

15. K. K. Hjalone and L. L. Pecchioni, "Relational Listening: A Grounded Theoretical Model." *Communication Reports* 14 (2001): 59–71.

16. W. G. Powers and P. L. Witt, "Expanding the Theoretical Framework of Communication Fidelity." *Communication Quarterly* 56 (2008): 247–267; M. Fitch-Hauser, W. G. Powers, K. O'Brien, and S. Hanson, "Extending the Conceptualization of Listening Fidelity." *International Journal of Listening* 21 (2007): 81–91; W. G. Powers and G. D. Bodie, "Listening Fidelity: Seeking Congruence Between Cognitions of the Listener and the Sender." *International Journal of Listening* 17 (2003): 19–31.

17. R. G. Nichols, "Factors in Listening Comprehension." *Speech Monographs* 15 (1948): 154–163.

18. M. Imhof, "In the Eye of the Beholder: Children's Perception of Good and Poor Listening Behavior." *International Journal of Listening* 16 (2002): 40–57.

19. M. H. Lewis and N. L. Reinsch Jr., "Listening in Organizational Environments." *Journal of Business Communication* 25 (1988): 49–67.

20. T. L. Thomas and T. R. Levine, "Disentangling Listening and Verbal Recall: Related but Separate Constructs?" *Human Communication Research* 21 (1994): 103–127.

21. Nichols, "Factors in Listening Comprehension."

22. N. Cowan and A. M. AuBuchon, "Short-Term Memory Loss Over Time Without Retroactive Stimulus Interference." *Psychonomic Bulletin and Review* 15 (2008): 230–235.

23. J. Brownell, "Perceptions of Effective Listeners: A Management Study." *Journal of Business Communication* 27 (1990): 401–415.

24. N. Spinks and B. Wells, "Improving Listening Power: The Payoff." *Bulletin of the Association for Business Communication* 54 (1991): 75–77.

25. Reported by R. Nichols and L. Stevens, "Listening to People." *Harvard Business Review* 35 (September–October 1957): 85–92.

26. W. Winter, A. Ferreira, and N. Bowers, "Decision-Making in Married and Unrelated Couples." *Family Process* 12 (1973): 83–94.

27. E. Langer, *Mindfulness* (Reading, MA: Addison-Wesley, 1990).

28. J. K. Burgoon, C. R. Berger, and V. R. Waldron, "Mindfulness and Interpersonal Communication." *Journal of Social Issues* 56 (2000): 105–127. Langer, *Mindfulness*, p. 90.

29. R. G. Nichols, "Listening Is a Ten-Part Skill." *Nation's Business* 75 (September 1987): 40.

30. A. L. Vangelisti, M. L. Knapp, and J. A. Daly, "Conversational Narcissism." *Communication Monographs* 57 (1990): 251–274.

31. K. B. McComb and F. M. Jablin, "Verbal Correlates of Interviewer Empathic Listening and Employment Interview Outcomes." *Communication Monographs* 51 (1984): 367.

32. "Info Stupidity." *New Scientist* 186 (April 30, 2005): 6–7.

33. L. Lin, "Breadth-Biased Versus Focused Cognitive Control in Media Multitasking Behaviors." *Proceedings of the National Academy of Sciences* 106 (September 15, 2009): 15521–15522. http://www.pnas.org/content/106/37/15521.full.pdf

34. E. Ophir, C. Nass, and A. Wagner, "Cognitive Control in Media Multitaskers." *Proceedings of the National Academy of Sciences* 106 (2009): 15583–15587.

35. J. Hansen, *24/7: How Cell Phones and the Internet Change the Way We Live, Work, and Play* (New York: Praeger, 2007). See also J. W. Turner and N. L. Reinsch, "The Business Communicator as Presence Allocator: Multicommunicating, Equivocality, and Status at Work." *Journal of Business Communication* 44 (2007): 36–58.

36. R. Drullman and G. F. Smoorenburg, "Audio-Visual Perception of Compressed Speech by Profoundly Hearing-Impaired Subjects." *Audiology* 36 (1997): 165–177.

37. "Listen to This: Hearing Problems Can Stress Relationships." Available at http://www.energizer.com/livehealthy/#listentothis (2008). See also D. N. Shafer, "Hearing Loss Hinders Relationships." *ASHA Leader* 12 (2007): 5–7.

38. N. Kline, *Time to Think: Listening to Ignite the Human Mind* (London: Ward Lock, 1999), p. 21.

39. A. Mulac, J. M. Wiemann, S. J. Widenmann, and T. W. Gibson, "Male/Female Language Differences and Effects in Same-Sex and Mixed-Sex Dyads: The Gender-Linked Language Effect." *Communication Monographs* 55 (1988): 315–335.

40. C. Kiewitz, J. B. Weaver III, B. Brosius, and G. Weimann, "Cultural Differences in Listening Styles Preferences: A Comparison of Young Adults in Germany, Israel, and the United States." *International Journal of Public Opinion Research* 9 (1997): 233–248.

41. L. L. Barker and K. W. Watson, *Listen Up* (New York: St. Martin's Press, 2000).

42. J. L. Chesebro, "The Relationship Between Listening Styles and Conversational Sensitivity." *Communication Research Reports* 16 (1999): 233–238.

43. K. W. Watson, L. L. Barker, and J. B. Weaver, "The Listening Styles Profile" (New Orleans: SPECTRA, 1995).

44. For a brief summary of ancient rhetoric, see E. Griffin, *A First Look at Communication Theory*, 4th ed. (New York: McGraw-Hill, 2000).

45. R. Remer and P. De Mesquita, "Teaching and Learning the Skills of Interpersonal Confrontation," in D. Cahn, ed., *Intimates in Conflict: A Communication Perspective* (Norwood, NJ: Erlbaum, 1991), p. 242.

46. Adapted from D. A. Infante, *Arguing Constructively* (Prospect Heights, IL: Waveland, 1988), pp. 71–75.

47. J. Sprague and D. Stuart, *The Speaker's Handbook*, 3rd ed. (Fort Worth, TX: Harcourt Brace Jovanovich, 1992), p. 172.

48. For a detailed look at empathic listening, see S. Spacapan and S. Oskamp, *Helping and Being Helped: Naturalistic Studies* (Newbury Park, CA: Sage, 1992).

49. See research cited in B. Burleson, "Comforting Messages: Their Significance and Effects," in J. A. Daly and J. M. Wiemann, eds., *Communicating Strategically: Strategies in Interpersonal Communication* (Hillside, NJ: Erlbaum, 1990).

50. For a summary of research on online support groups, see J. B. Walther and S. Boyd, "Attraction to Computer-Mediated Social Support," in C. A. Lin and D. Atkin, eds., *Communication Technology and Society: Audience Adoption and Uses* (Cresskill, NJ: Hampton Press, 2002).

51. M. Tanis, "Online Support Groups," in A. Joinson, K. McKenna, T. Postmes, and U. Reips, eds., *The Oxford Handbook of Internet Psychology* (Oxford, UK: Oxford University Press, 2007).

52. For a comprehensive discussion of gender similarities and differences in social support, see B. R. Burleson, "Psychological Mediators of Sex Differences in Emotional Support: A Reflection on the Mosaic." *Communication Reports* 15 (Winter 2002): 71–79.

53. J. B. Weaver and M. D. Kirtley, "Listening Styles and Empathy." *Southern Communication Journal* 60 (1995): 131–140.

54. C. E. Currona, J. A. Suhr, and R. MacFarlane, "Interpersonal Transactions and the Psychological Sense of Support," in S. Duck, ed., *Personal Relationships and Social Support* (London: Sage, 1990).

55. D. J. Goldsmith and K. Fitch, "The Normative Context of Advice as Social Support." *Human Communication Research* 23 (1997): 454–476.

56. D. J. Goldsmith and K. Fitch, "The Normative Context of Advice as Social Support." *Human Communication Research* 23 (1997): 454–476. See also D. J. Goldsmith and E. L. MacGeorge, "The Impact of Politeness and Relationship on Perceived Quality of Advice About a Problem." *Human Communication Research* 26 (2000): 234–263. See also B. R. Burleson, "Social Support," in M. L. Knapp and J. A. Daly, eds., *Handbook of Interpersonal Communication*, 3rd ed. (Thousand Oaks, CA: Sage, 2002).

57. D. Goldsmith, "The Sequential Placement of Advice." Paper presented at the annual convention of the Speech Communication Association, New Orleans, November 1994.

58. B. Burleson, "What Counts as Effective Emotional Support?", in M. T. Motley, ed., *Studies in Applied Interpersonal Communication* (Thousand Oaks, CA: Sage, 2008).

59. D. Goldsmith, "Soliciting Advice: The Role of Sequential Placement in Mitigating Face Threat." *Communication Monographs* 67 (2000): 1–19.

60. E. L. MacGeorge, B. Feng, and E. R. Thompson, " 'Good' and 'Bad' Advice: How to Advise More Effectively," in M. T. Motley, ed., *Studies in Applied Interpersonal Communication* (Thousand Oaks, CA: Sage, 2008).

61. D. J. Goldsmith and E. L. MacGeorge, "The Impact of Politeness and Relationship on Perceived Quality of Advice About a Problem." *Human Communication Research* 26 (2000): 234–263. See also N. Miczo and J. K. Burgoon, "Facework and Nonverbal Behavior in Social Support Interactions Within Romantic Dyads," in M. T. Motley, ed., *Studies in Applied Interpersonal Communication* (Thousand Oaks, CA: Sage, 2008).

62. See, for example, L. Pearlin and M. McCall, "Occupational Stress and Marital Support: A Description of Microprocesses," in J. Eckenrode and S. Gore, eds., *Stress Between Work and Family* (New York: Plenum, 1990).

63. D. Hample, "Anti-comforting Messages," in K. M. Galvin and P. J. Cooper, eds., *Making Connections: Readings in Relational Communication*, 4th ed. (Los Angeles, CA: Roxbury, 2006).

64. M. Davidowitz and R. D. Myricm, "Responding to the Bereaved: An Analysis of 'Helping' Statements." *Death Education* 8 (1984): 1–10. See also H. L. Servaty-Seib and B. R. Burleson, "Bereaved Adolescents' Evaluations of the Helpfulness of Support-Intended Statements." *Journal of Social and Personal Relationships* 24 (2008): 207–223.

65. "Helping Adults, Children Cope with Grief." *Washington Post* (September 13, 2001). Online at http://www.washingtonpost.com/wp-dyn/articles/A23679-2001Sep13.html.

66. Adapted from B. R. Burleson, "Comforting Messages: Features, Functions, and Outcomes," in J. A. Daly and J. M. Wiemann, eds., *Strategic Interpersonal Communication* (Hillsdale, NJ: Erlbaum, 1994), p. 140.

67. J. M. Gottman, *The Marriage Clinic: A Scientifically-Based Marital Therapy* (New York: Norton, 1999), p. 10.

68. T. Lewis and V. Manusov, "Listening to Another's Distress in Everyday Relationships." *Communication Quarterly* 57 (2009): 282–301.

69. L. A. Hosman, "The Evaluational Consequences of Topic Reciprocity and Self-Disclosure Reciprocity." *Communication Monographs* 54 (1987): 420–435.

70. R. A. Clark and J. G. Delia, "Individuals' Preferences for Friends' Approaches to Providing Support in Distressing Situations." *Communication Reports* 10 (1997): 115–121.

71. See, for example, R. Silver and C. Wortman, "Coping with Undesirable Life Events," in J. Garber and M. Seligman, eds., *Human Helplessness: Theory and Applications* (New York: Academic Press, 1981), pp. 279–340, and C. R. Young, D. E. Giles, and M. C. Plantz, "Natural Networks: Help-Giving and Help-Seeking in Two Rural Communities." *American Journal of Community Psychology* 10 (1982): 457–469.

72. Clark and Delia, "Individuals' Preferences."

73. Burleson, "Comforting Messages."

74. R. W. Young and C. M. Cates, "Emotional and Directive Listening in Peer Mentoring." *International Journal of Listening* 18 (2004): 21–33.

CHAPTER 6

1. For a survey of the issues surrounding the definition of nonverbal communication, see M. Knapp and J. A. Hall, *Nonverbal Communication in Human Interaction*, 6th ed. (Belmont, CA: Wadsworth, 2010), Chapter 1.

2. C. F. Keating, "Why and How the Silent Self Speaks Volumes," in V. Manusov and M. L. Patterson, eds., *The SAGE Handbook of Nonverbal Communication* (Thousand Oaks, CA: Sage, 2006).

3. F. Manusov, "Perceiving Nonverbal Messages: Effects of Immediacy and Encoded Intent on Receiver Judgments." *Western Journal of Speech Communication* 55 (Summer 1991): 235–253.

4. For a discussion of intentionality, see M. L. Knapp, *Nonverbal Communication in Human Interaction*, pp. 9–12.

5. M. T. Palmer and K. B. Simmons, "Communicating Intentions Through Nonverbal Behaviors: Conscious and Nonconscious Encoding of Liking." *Human Communication Research* 22 (1995): 128–160.

6. A. R. Dennis, S. T. Kinney, and Y. T. Hung, "Gender Differences in the Effects of Media Richness." *Small Group Research* 30 (1999): 405–437.

7. See S. W. Smith, "Perceptual Processing of Nonverbal Relational Messages," in D. E. Hewes, ed., *The Cognitive Bases of Interpersonal Communication* (Hillsdale, NJ: Erlbaum, 1994).

8. J. Burgeon, D. Buller, J. Hale, and M. de Turck, "Relational Messages Associated with Nonverbal Behaviors." *Human Communication Research* 10 (Spring 1984): 351–378.

9. G. Y. Lim and M. E. Roloff, "Attributing Sexual Consent." *Journal of Applied Communication Research* 27 (1999): 1–23.

10. "Safeway Clerks Object to 'Service with a Smile.'" *San Francisco Chronicle* (September 2, 1998).

11. D. Druckmann, R. M. Rozelle, and J. C. Baxter, *Nonverbal Communication: Survey, Theory, and Research* (Newbury Park, CA: Sage, 1982).

12. M. T. Motley and C. T. Camden, "Facial Expression of Emotion: A Comparison of Posed Expressions versus Spontaneous Expressions in an Interpersonal Communication Setting." *Western Journal of Speech Communication* 52 (Winter 1988): 1–22.

13. See, for example, R. Rosenthal, J. A. Hall, M. R. D. Matteg, P. L. Rogers, and D. Archer, *Sensitivity to Nonverbal Communication: The PONS Test* (Baltimore, MD: Johns Hopkins University Press, 1979).

14. J. A. Hall, "Gender, Gender Roles, and Nonverbal Communication Skills," in R. Rosenthal, ed., *Skill in Nonverbal Communication: Individual Differences* (Cambridge, MA: Oelgeschlager, Gunn, and Hain, 1979), pp. 32–67.

15. Research supporting these claims is cited in J. K. Burgoon and G. D. Hoobler, "Nonverbal Signals," in M. L. Knapp and J. A. Daly, eds., *Handbook of Interpersonal Communication*, 3rd ed. (Thousand Oaks, CA: Sage, 2002).

16. S. E. Jones and C. D. LeBaron, "Research on the Relationship between Verbal and Nonverbal Communication: Emerging Interactions." *Journal of Communication* 52 (2002): 499–521.

17. P. Ekman and W. Friesen, *Unmasking the Face* (New York: Prentice Hall, 1975).

18. R. Birdwhistell, *Kinesics and Context* (Philadelphia: University of Pennsylvania Press, 1970): Chapter 9.

19. P. Ekman, W. V. Friesen, and J. Baer, "The International Language of Gestures." *Psychology Today* 18 (May 1984): 64–69.

20. E. Hall, *The Hidden Dimension* (Garden City, NY: Anchor Books, 1969).

21. Ibid.

22. D. L. Rubin, "'Nobody Play by the Rule He Know': Ethnic Interference in Classroom Questioning Events," in Y. Y. Kim, ed., *Interethnic Communication: Recent Research* (Newbury Park, CA: Sage, 1986).

23. A. M. Warnecke, R. D. Masters, and G. Kempter, "The Roots of Nationalism: Nonverbal Behavior and Xenophobia." *Ethnology and Sociobiology* 13 (1992): 267–282.

24. S. Weitz, ed., *Nonverbal Communication: Readings with Commentary* (New York: Oxford University Press, 1974).

25. For a comparison of Japanese and Arab nonverbal communication norms, see D. G. Leathers, *Successful Nonverbal Communication* (New York: Macmillan, 1986), pp. 258–261.

26. M. Booth-Butterfield and F. Jordan, "'Act Like Us': Communication Adaptation among Racially Homogeneous and Heterogeneous Groups." Paper presented at the Speech Communication Association meeting, New Orleans, 1988.

27. B. P. Rourke, *Nonverbal Learning Disabilities: The Syndrome and the Model* (New York: Guilford Press, 1989).

28. E. S. Fudge, "Nonverbal Learning Disorder Syndrome?" Retrieved from http://www.nldontheweb.org/fudge.htm.

29. J. A. Hall, "Male and Female Nonverbal Behavior," in A. W. Siegman and S. Feldstein, eds., *Multichannel Integrations of Nonverbal Behavior* (Hillsdale, NJ: Erlbaum, 1985); J. A. Hall, "Women's and Men's Nonverbal Communication," in V. Manusov and M. L. Patterson, eds., *The SAGE Handbook of Nonverbal Communication* (Thousand Oaks, CA: Sage, 2006).

30. J. A. Hall, J. D. Carter, and T. G. Horgan, "Status Roles and Recall of Nonverbal Cues." *Journal of Nonverbal Behavior* 25 (2001): 79–100.

31. For a comprehensive summary of male-female differences and similarities in nonverbal communication, see P. A. Andersen, *Nonverbal Communication: Forms and Functions* (Mountain View, CA: Mayfield, 1999), p. 107. For a detailed summary of similarities and differences, see D. J. Canary and T. M. Emmers-Sommer, *Sex and Gender Differences in Personal Relationships* (New York: Guilford, 1997).

32. Andersen, *Nonverbal Communication*, p. 107.

33. E. S. Cross and E. A. Franz, "Talking Hands: Observation of Bimanual Gestures as a Facilitative Working Memory Mechanism." Paper presented at the Cognitive Neuroscience Society 10th Annual Meeting, New York, March 30–April 1, 2003.

34. Hall, *The Hidden Dimension*.

35. C. R. Kleinke, "Compliance to Requests Made by Gazing and Touching Experimenters in Field Settings." *Journal of Experimental Social Psychology* 13 (1977): 218–233.

36. M. F. Argyle, F. Alkema, and R. Gilmour, "The Communication of Friendly and Hostile Attitudes: Verbal and Nonverbal Signals." *European Journal of Social Psychology* 1 (1971): 385–402.

37. D. B. Buller and J. K. Burgoon, "Deception: Strategic and Nonstrategic Communication," in J. Daly and J. M. Wiemann, eds., *Interpersonal Communication* (Hillsdale, NJ: Erlbaum, 1994).

38. J. K. Burgoon, D. B. Buller, L. K. Guerrero, and C. M. Feldman, "Interpersonal Deception: VI. Effects on Preinteractional and International Factors on Deceiver and Observer Perceptions of Deception Success." *Communication Studies* 45 (1994): 263–280, and J. K. Burgoon, D. B. Buller, and L. K. Guerrero, "Interpersonal Deception: IX. Effects of Social Skill and Nonverbal Communication on Deception Success and Detection Accuracy." *Journal of Language and Social Psychology* 14 (1995): 289–311.

39. R. G. Riggio and H. S. Freeman, "Individual Differences and Cues to Deception." *Journal of Personality and Social Psychology* 45 (1983): 899–915.

40. A. Vrij, "Nonverbal Communication and Deception," in V. Manusov and M. L. Patterson, eds., *The SAGE Handbook of Nonverbal Communication* (Thousand Oaks, CA: Sage, 2006).

41. B. M. DePaulo, J. J. Lindsay, B. E. Malone, L. Muhlenbruck, K. Charlton, and H. Cooper, "Cues to Deception." *Psychological Bulletin* 129 (2003): 74–118, and A. Vrig, K. Edward, K. P. Roberts, and R. Bull, "Detecting Deceit Via Analysis of Verbal and Nonverbal Behavior." *Journal of Nonverbal Behavior* 24 (2000): 239–263.

42. N. E. Dunbar, A. Ramirez Jr., and J. K. Burgoon, "The Effects of Participation on the Ability to Judge Deceit." *Communication Reports* 16 (2003): 23–33.

43. A. Vrig, L. Akehurst, S. Soukara, and R. Bull, "Detecting Deceit via Analyses of Verbal and Nonverbal Behavior in Children and Adults." *Human Communication Research* 30 (2004): 8–41.

44. M. G. Millar and K. U. Millar, "The Effects of Suspicion on the Recall of Cues to Make Veracity Judgments." *Communication Reports* 11 (1998): 57–64.

45. S. A. McCornack and M. R. Parks, "What Women Know That Men Don't: Sex Differences in Determining the Truth behind Deceptive Messages." *Journal of Social and Personal Relationships* 7 (1990): 107–118.

46. S. A. McCornack and T. R. Levine, "When Lovers Become Leery: The Relationship between Suspicion and Accuracy in Detecting Deception." *Communication Monographs* 7 (1990): 219–230.

47. M. A. deTurck, "Training Observers to Detect Spontaneous Deception: Effects of Gender." *Communication Reports* 4 (1991): 81–89.

48. S. Leal and A. Vrij, "Blinking During and After Lying." *Journal of Nonverbal Behavior* 32 (2008): 187–194.

49. S. Porter and L. Ten Brinke, "Reading Between the Lies: Identifying Concealed and Falsified Emotions in Universal Facial Expressions." *Psychological Science* 19 (2008): 508.

50. P. Ekman and M. O'Sullivan, "Who Can Catch a Liar?" *American Psychologist* 46 (1991): 913–920. See also S. Porter and L. ten Brinke, "The Truth About Lies: What Works in Detecting High-Stakes Deception?" *Legal and Criminological Psychology* 15 (2010): 57–75.

51. R. E. Maurer and J. H. Tindall, "Effect of Postural Congruence on Client's Perception of Counselor Empathy." *Journal of Counseling Psychology* 30 (1983): 158–163.

52. V. Manusov, "Reacting to Changes in Nonverbal Behaviors: Relational Satisfaction and Adaptation Patterns in Romantic Dyads." *Human Communication Research* 21 (1995): 456–477.

53. M. B. Myers, D. Templer, and R. Brown, "Coping Ability of Women Who Become Victims of Rape." *Journal of Consulting and Clinical Psychology* 52 (1984): 73–78. See also C. Rubenstein, "Body Language That Speaks to Muggers." *Psychology Today* 20 (August 1980): 20, and J. Meer, "Profile of a Victim." *Psychology Today* 24 (May 1984): 76.

54. J. M. Iverson, "How to Get to the Cafeteria: Gesture and Speech in Blind and Sighted Children's Spatial Descriptions." *Developmental Psychology* 35 (1999): 1132–1142.

55. P. Ekman, *Telling Lies: Clues to Deceit in the Marketplace, Politics, and Marriage* (New York: Norton, 1985), pp. 109–110.

56. W. Donaghy and B. F. Dooley, "Head Movement, Gender, and Deceptive Communication." *Communication Reports* 7 (1994): 67–75.

57. P. Ekman and W. V. Friesen, "Nonverbal Behavior and Psychopathology," in R. J. Friedman and M. N. Katz, eds., *The Psychology of Depression: Contemporary Theory and Research* (Washington, DC: J. Winston, 1974).

58. R. Sutton and A. Rafaeli, "Untangling the Relationship between Displayed Emotions and Organizational Sales: The Case of Convenience Stores." *Academy of Management Journal* 31 (1988): 463.

59. D. Matsumoto, "Culture and Nonverbal Behavior," in V. Manusov and M. L. Patterson, eds., *The SAGE Handbook of Nonverbal Communication* (Thousand Oaks, CA: Sage, 2006).

60. P. Edman, W. V. Friesen, and P. Ellsworth, *Emotion in the Human Face: Guidelines for Research and an Integration of Findings* (Elmsford, NY: Pergamon, 1972).

61. C. L. Kleinke, "Gaze and Eye Contact: A Research Review." *Psychological Bulletin* 100 (1986): 78–100.

62. J. A. Starkweather, "Vocal Communication of Personality and Human Feeling." *Journal of Communication* II (1961): 69, and K. R. Scherer, J. Koiwunaki, and R. Rosenthal, "Minimal Cues in the Vocal Communication of Affect: Judging Emotions from Content-Masked Speech." *Journal of Psycholinguistic Speech* I (1972): 269–285. See also F. S. Cox and C. Olney, "Vocalic Communication of Relational Messages." Paper delivered at the annual meeting of the Speech Communication Association, Denver, 1985.

63. K. L. Burns and E. G. Beier, "Significance of Vocal and Visual Channels for the Decoding of Emotional Meaning." *Journal of Communication* 23 (1973): 118–130. See also T. G. Hegstrom, "Message Impact: What Percentage Is Nonverbal?" *Western Journal of Speech Communication* 43 (1979): 134–143, and E. M. McMahan, "Nonverbal Communication as a Function of Attribution in Impression Formation." *Communication Monographs* 43 (1976): 287–294.

64. A. Mehrabian and M. Weiner, "Decoding of Inconsistent Communications." *Journal of Personality and Social Psychology* 6 (1967): 109–114.

65. D. Buller and K. Aune, "The Effects of Speech Rate Similarity on Compliance: Application of Communication Accommodation Theory." *Western Journal of Communication* 56 (1992): 37–53. See also D. Buller, B. A. LePoire, K. Aune, and S. V. Eloy, "Social Perceptions as Mediators of the Effect of Speech Rate Similarity on Compliance." *Human Communication Research* 19 (1992): 286–311, and J. Francis and R. Wales, "Speech a la Mode: Prosodic Cues, Message Interpretation, and Impression Formation." *Journal of Language and Social Psychology* 13 (1994): 34–44.

66. C. E. Kimble and S. D. Seidel, "Vocal Signs of Confidence." *Journal of Nonverbal Behavior* 15 (1991): 99–105.

67. K. J. Tusing and J. P. Dillard, "The Sounds of Dominance: Vocal Precursors of Perceived Dominance during Interpersonal Influence." *Human Communication Research* 26 (2000): 148–171.

68. M. Zuckerman and R. E. Driver, "What Sounds Beautiful Is Good: The Vocal Attractiveness Stereotype." *Journal of Nonverbal Behavior* 13 (1989): 67–82.

69. M. Hosoda and E. Stone-Romero, "The Effects of Foreign Accents on Employment-Related Decisions." *Journal of Managerial Psychology* 25 (2010): 113–132.

70. For a summary, see M. L. Knapp and J. A. Hall, *Nonverbal Communication in Human Interaction*, 3rd ed. (New York: Holt, Rinehart and Winston, 1992), pp. 93–132. See also W. Hensley, "Why Does the Best Looking Person in the Room Always Seem to Be Surrounded by Admirers?" *Psychological Reports* 70 (1992): 457–469.

71. L. K. Guerrero and M. L. Hecht, *The Nonverbal Communication Reader: Classic and Contemporary Readings*, 3rd ed. (Long Grove, IL: Waveland Press, 2008).

72. N. Yee and J. N. Bailenson, "A Method for Longitudinal Behavioral Data Collection in Second Life." *Presence* 17 (2008): 594–596.

73. V. Ritts, M. L. Patterson, and M. E. Tubbs, "Expectations, Impressions, and Judgments of Physically Attractive Students: A Review." *Review of Educational Research* 62 (1992): 413–426.

74. K. F. Abdala, M. L. Knapp, and K. E. Theune, "Interaction Appearance Theory: Changing Perceptions of Physical Attractiveness through Social Interaction." *Communication Theory* 12 (2002): 8–40.

75. L. Bickman, "The Social Power of a Uniform." *Journal of Applied Social Psychology* 4 (1974): 47–61.

76. S. G. Lawrence and M. Watson, "Getting Others to Help: The Effectiveness of Professional Uniforms in Charitable Fund Raising." *Journal of Applied Communication Research* 19 (1991): 170–185.

77. L. Bickman, "Social Roles and Uniforms: Clothes Make the Person." *Psychology Today* 7 (April 1974): 48–51.

78. L. E. Temple and K. R. Loewen, "Perceptions of Power: First Impressions of a Woman Wearing a Jacket." *Perceptual and Motor Skills* 76 (1993): 339–348.

79. T. F. Hoult, "Experimental Measurement of Clothing as a Factor in Some Social Ratings of Selected American Men." *American Sociological Review* 19 (1954): 326–327.

80. S. Hart, T. Field, M. Hernandez-Reif, and B. Lundy, "Preschoolers' Cognitive Performance Improves Following Massage." *Early Child Development and Care* 143 (1998): 59–64. For more about the role

of touch in relationships, see D. Keltner, *Born to Be Good: The Science of a Meaningful Life* (New York: Norton, 2009), pp. 173–198.

81. A. Montagu, *Touching: The Human Significance of the Skin* (New York: Harper & Row, 1972), p. 93.

82. L. J. Yarrow, "Research in Dimension of Early Maternal Care." *Merrill-Palmer Quarterly* 9 (1963): 101–122.

83. E. Hall, "Touch, Status, and Gender at Professional Meetings." *Journal of Nonverbal Behavior* 20 (1996): 23–44.

84. See, for example, C.Segrin, "The Effects of Nonverbal Behavior on Outcomes of Compliance Gaining Attempts." *Communication Studies* 11 (1993): 169–187.

85. C. R. Kleinke, "Compliance to Requests Made by Gazing and Touching Experimenters in Field Settings." *Journal of Experimental Social Psychology* 13 (1977): 218–223.

86. F. N. Willis and H. K. Hamm, "The Use of Interpersonal Touch in Securing Compliance." *Journal of Nonverbal Behavior* 5 (1980): 49–55.

87. A. H. Crusco and C. G. Wetzel, "The Midas Touch: Effects of Interpersonal Touch on Restaurant Tipping." *Personality and Social Psychology Bulletin* 10 (1984): 512–517.

88. N. Gueguen and M. Vion, "The Effect of a Practitioner's Touch on a Patient's Medication Compliance." *Psychology, Health and Medicine* 14 (2009): 689–694.

89. Segrin, "Effects of Nonverbal Behavior."

90. J. Hornik, "Effects of Physical Contact on Customers' Shopping Time and Behavior." *Marketing Letters* 3 (1992): 49–55.

91. D. E. Smith, J. A. Gier, and F. N. Willis, "Interpersonal Touch and Compliance with a Marketing Request." *Basic and Applied Social Psychology* 3 (1982): 35–38.

92. T. Field, D. Lasko, P. Mundy, T. Henteleff, S. Kabat, S. Talpins, and M. Dowling, "Brief Report: Autistic Children's Attentiveness and Responsivity Improve After Touch Therapy." *Journal of Autism and Developmental Disorders* 27 (1997): 333–338.

93. M.W. Kraus, C. Huang, and D. Keltner, "Tactile Communication, Cooperation, and Performance: An Ethological Study of the NBA." *Emotion* (in press).

94. Y. K. Chan, "Density, Crowding, and Factors Intervening in Their Relationship: Evidence from a Hyper-Dense Metropolis." *Social-Indicators-Research* 48 (1999): 103–124.

95. Hall, *The Hidden Dimension*, pp. 113–130.

96. M. Hackman and K. Walker, "Instructional Communication in the Televised Classroom: The Effects of System Design and Teacher Immediacy." *Communication Education* 39 (1990): 196–206. See also J. C. McCroskey and V. P. Richmond, "Increasing Teacher Influence through Immediacy," in V. P. Richmond and J. C. McCroskey, eds., *Power in the Classroom: Communication, Control, and Concern* (Hillsdale, NJ: Erlbaum, 1992).

97. C. Conlee, J. Olvera, and N. Vagim, "The Relationships Among Physician Nonverbal Immediacy and Measures of Patient Satisfaction with Physician Care." *Communication Reports* 6 (1993): 25–33.

98. A. Mehrabian, *Public Places and Personal Spaces: The Psychology of Work, Play, and Living Environments.* (New York: Basic Books, 1976), p. 69.

99. E. Sadalla, "Identity and Symbolism in Housing." *Environment and Behavior* 19 (1987): 569–587.

100. A. H. Maslow and N. L. Mintz, "Effects of Esthetic Surroundings." *Journal of Psychology* 41 (1956): 247–254.

101. R. Sommer, *Personal Space: The Behavioral Basis of Design.* (Englewood Cliffs, NJ: Prentice-Hall,1969) p. 78.

102. Sommer, *Personal Space*, p. 35.

103. D. I. Ballard and D. R. Seibold, "Time Orientation and Temporal Variation across Work Groups: Implications for Group and Organizational Communication." *Western Journal of Communication* 64 (2000): 218–242.

104. R. Levine, *A Geography of Time: The Temporal Misadventures of a Social Psychologist* (New York: Basic Books, 1997).

105. See, for example, O. W. Hill, R. A. Block, and S. E. Buggie, "Culture and Beliefs about Time: Comparisons among Black Americans, Black Africans, and White Americans." *Journal of Psychology* 134 (2000): 443–457.

106. R. Levine and E. Wolff, "Social Time: The Heartbeat of Culture." *Psychology Today* 19 (March 1985): 28–35. See also R. Levine, "Waiting Is a Power Game." *Psychology Today* 21 (April 1987): 24–33.

107. J. K. Burgoon, D. B. Buller, and W. G. Woodall, *Nonverbal Communication* (New York: McGraw-Hill, 1996) p. 148.

CHAPTER 7

1. D. Byrne, "An Overview (and Underview) of Research and Theory within the Attraction Paradigm." *Journal of Social and Personal Relationships* 14 (1997): 417–431.

2. E. Hatfield and S. Sprecher, *Mirror, Mirror: The Importance of Looks in Everyday Life* (Albany: State University of New York Press, 1986).

3. E. Walster, E. Aronson, D. Abrahams, and L. Rottmann, "Importance of Physical Attractiveness in Dating Behavior." *Journal of Personality and Social Psychology* 4 (1966): 508–516.

4. E. Berscheid and E. H. Walster, *Interpersonal Attraction*, 2nd ed. (Reading, MA: Addison-Wesley, 1978).

5. K. F. Albada, "Interaction Appearance Theory: Changing Perceptions of Physical Attractiveness through Social Interaction." *Communication Theory* 12 (2002): 8–41.

6. D. Hamachek, *Encounters with Others: Interpersonal Relationships and You* (New York: Holt, Rinehart and Winston, 1982).

7. See, for example, D. Byrne, "An Overview (and Underview) of Research and Theory within the Attraction Paradigm." *Journal of Social and Personal Relationships* 14 (1997): 417–431. For a discussion of some ways in which similarity does not enhance relational longevity, see M. N. Shiota and R. W. Levenson, "Birds of a Feather Don't Always Fly Farthest: Similarity in Big Five Personality Predicts More Negative Marital Satisfaction Trajectories in Long-Term Marriages." *Psychology and Aging* 22 (2007): 667–675.

8. S. Luo and E. Klohnen, "Assortive Mating and Marital Quality in Newlyweds: A Couple-Centered Approach." *Journal of Personality and Social Psychology* 88 (2005): 304–326. See also D. M. Amodio and C. J. Showers, "Similarity Breeds Liking Revisited: The Moderating Role of Commitment." *Journal of Social and Personal Relationships* 22 (2005): 817–836.

9. F. E. Aboud and M. J. Mendelson, "Determinants of Friendship Selection and Quality: Developmental Perspectives," in W. M. Bukowski and A. F. Newcomb, eds., *The Company They Keep: Friendship in Childhood and Adolescence* (New York: Cambridge University Press, 1998), pp. 87–112.

10. B. R. Burleson and W. Samter, "Similarity in the Communication Skills of Young Adults: Foundations of Attraction, Friendship, and Relationship Satisfaction." *Communication Reports* 9 (1996): 127–139.

11. L. Heatherington, V. Escudero, and M. L. Friedlander, "Couple Interaction During Problem Discussions: Toward an Integrative Methodology." *Journal of Family Communication* 5 (2005): 191–207.

12. S. Specher, "Insiders' Perspectives on Reasons for Attraction to a Close Other." *Social Psychology Quarterly* 61 (1998): 287–300.

13. E. Aronson, *The Social Animal*, 9th ed. (New York: Worth/Freeman, 2008). See Chapter 9: Liking, Loving, and Interpersonal Sensitivity.

14. K. Dindia, "Self-Disclosure Research: Knowledge Through Meta-Analysis," in M. Allen and R. W. Preiss, eds., *Interpersonal Communication Research: Advances Through Meta-Analysis* (Mahwah, NJ: Erlbaum, 2002), pp. 169–185.

15. C. Flora, "Close Quarters." *Psychology Today* 37 (January/February 2004): 15–16.

16. C. Haythornthwaite, M. M. Kazmer, and J. Robbins, "Community Development Among Distance Learners: Temporal and Technological Dimensions." *Journal of Computer-Mediated Communication* 6 (2000): Issue 1, Article 2. Retrieved from http://jcmc.indiana.edu/vol6/issue1/haythornthwaite.html.

17. See, for example, M. E. Roloff, *Interpersonal Communication: The Social Exchange Approach* (Beverly Hills, CA: Sage, 1981).

18. For a discussion of the characteristics of impersonal and interpersonal communication, see A. P. Bochner, "The Functions of Human Communication in Interpersonal Bonding," in C. C. Arnold and J. W. Bowers, eds., *Handbook of Rhetorical and Communication Theory* (Boston: Allyn and Bacon, 1984), p. 550; S. Trenholm and A. Jensen, *Interpersonal Communication* (Belmont, CA: Wadsworth, 1987), p. 37; and J. Stewart, K. E. Zediker, and S. Witteborn, *Together: Communicating Interpersonally: A Social Construction Approach* (New York: Oxford University Press, 2007).

19. K. O'Toole, "Study Takes Early Look at Social Consequences of Net Use." Stanford Online Report. Accessed online February 16, 2000, at http://www.stanford.edu/dept/news/report/news/february16/internetsurvey-216.html.

20. R. T. Craig, "Issue Forum Introduction: Mobile Media and Communication: What Are the Important Questions?" *Communication Monographs* 74 (2007): 386.

21. R. Kraut, M. Patterson, V. Lundmark, S. Kiesler, T. Mukophadhyay, and W. Scherlis, "Internet Paradox: A Social Technology That Reduces Social Involvement and Psychological Well-Being?" *American Psychologist* 53 (1998): 1017–1031.

22. M. Daum, "The Age of Friendaholism." *Los Angeles Times* (March 7, 2009): B 13. For an extensive critique of false intimacy in social networking sites, see W. Deresiewicz, "Faux Friendship." *The Chronicle of Higher Education* (December 6, 2009). Retrieved June 8, 2010, from http://chronicle.com/article/The-End-of-Solitude/3708/.

23. See J. B. Walther, "Computer-Mediated Communication: Impersonal, Interpersonal, and Hyperpersonal Interaction." *Communication Research* 23 (1996): 3–43.

24. B. G. Chenault, "Developing Personal and Emotional Relationships via Computer-Mediated Communication." *CMC Magazine*. Accessed online May 1998 at http://www.december.com/cmc/mag/1998/may/chenref.html.

25. "Pew Internet and American Life Project." Pew Charitable Trusts (May 2000). http://www.pewinternet.org.

26. L. Rainie and J. Anderson, "The Future of the Internet III: How Experts See It." Pew Internet and American Life Project (Washington, DC, 2008).

27. B. Wellman, A. Smith, A. Wells, and T. Kennedy, "Networked Families." Pew Internet and American Life Project (Washington, DC, 2008).

28. UCLA Center for Communication Policy, "Surveying the Digital Future." Accessed online October 25, 2000, at www.ccp.ucla.edu.

29. D. Tannen, *Newsweek* (May 16, 1994): 41.

30. H. Reingold, *The Virtual Community* (New York: Addison-Wesley, 1993). See also P. Wallace, *The Psychology of the Internet* (Cambridge, MA: Cambridge University Press, 1999).

31. J. B. Walther, "Computer-Mediated Communication: Impersonal, Interpersonal, and Hyper-Personal Interaction." *Communication Research* 23 (1996): 3–43.

32. See J. P. Dillard, D. H. Solomon, and M. T. Palmer, "Structuring the Concept of Relational Communication." *Communication Monographs* 66 (1999): 46–55.

33. T. S. Lim and J. W. Bowers, "Facework: Solidarity, Approbation, and Tact." *Human Communication Research* 17 (1991): 415–450.

34. J. R. Frei and P. R. Shaver, "Respect in Close Relationships: Prototype, Definition, Self-Report Assessment, and Initial Correlates." *Personal Relationships* 9 (2002): 121–139.

35. See C. M. Rossiter Jr., "Instruction in Metacommunication." *Central States Speech Journal* 25 (1974): 36–42, and W. W. Wilmot, "Metacommunication: A Reexamination and Extension," in *Communication Yearbook* 4 (New Brunswick, NJ: Transaction Books, 1980).

36. M. L. Knapp and A. L. Vangelisti, *Interpersonal Communication and Human Relationships*, 6th ed. (Boston: Allyn and Bacon, 2009).

37. D. J. Canary and L. Stafford, eds., *Communication and Relational Maintenance* (San Diego: Academic Press, 1994). See also J. Lee, "Effective Maintenance Communication in Superior-Subordinate Relationships." *Western Journal of Communication* 62 (1998): 181–208.

38. B. W. Scharlott and W. G. Christ, "Overcoming Relationship-Initiation Barriers: The Impact of a Computer-Dating System on Sex Role, Shyness, and Appearance Inhibitions." *Computers in Human Behavior* 11 (1995):191–204.

39. J. H. Tolhuizen, "Communication Strategies for Intensifying Dating Relationships: Identification, Use and Structure." *Journal of Social and Personal Relationships* 6 (1989): 413–434.

40. L. K. Guerrero and P. A. Andersen, "The Waxing and Waning of Relational Intimacy: Touch as a Function of Relational Stage, Gender and Touch Avoidance." *Journal of Social and Personal Relationships* 8 (1991): 147–165.

41. L. A. Baxter, "Symbols of Relationship Identity in Relationship Culture." *Journal of Social and Personal Relationships* 4 (1987): 261–280.

42. C. J. Bruess and J. C. Pearson, "Like Sands through the Hour Glass: These Are the Rituals Functioning in Day-to-Day Married Lives." Paper delivered at the Speech Communication Association convention, San Antonio, TX, November 1995.

43. H. Giles and P. F. Poseland, *Speech Style and Social Evaluation* (London: Academic Press, 1975).

44. M. Roloff, C. A. Janiszewski, M. A. McGrath, C. S. Burns, and L. A. Manrai, "Acquiring Resources from Intimates: When Obligation Substitutes for Persuasion." *Human Communication Research* 14 (1988): 364–396.

45. J. K. Burgoon, R. Parrott, B. A. LePoire, D. L. Kelley, J. B. Walther, and D. Perry, "Maintaining and Restoring Privacy through Different Types of Relationships." *Journal of Social and Personal Relationships* 6 (1989): 131–158.

46. J. A. Courtright, F. E. Millar, L. E. Rogers, and D. Bagarozzi, "Interaction Dynamics of Relational Negotiation: Reconciliation versus Termination of Distressed Relationships." *Western Journal of Speech Communication* 54 (1990): 429–453.

47. D. M. Battaglia, F. D. Richard, D. L. Datteri, and C. G. Lord, "Breaking Up Is (Relatively) Easy to Do: A Script for the Dissolution of Close Relationships." *Journal of Social and Personal Relationships* 15 (1998): 829–845.

48. See, for example, L. A. Baxter and B. M. Montgomery, "A Guide to Dialectical Approaches to Studying Personal Relationships," in B. M. Montgomery and L. A. Baxter, eds., *Dialectical Approaches to Studying Personal Relationships* (New York: Erlbaum, 1998), and L. A. Ebert and S. W. Duck, "Rethinking Satisfaction in Personal Relationships from a Dialectical Perspective," in R. J. Sternberg and M. Hojjatr, eds., *Satisfaction in Close Relationships* (New York: Guilford, 1997).

49. Summarized by L. A. Baxter, "A Dialogic Approach to Relationship Maintenance," in D. J. Canary and L. Stafford, eds., *Communication and Relational Maintenance* (San Diego: Academic Press, 1994).

50. D. Morris, *Intimate Behavior*, New York: Kodansha Globe, 1971, pp. 21–29.

51. D. Barry, *Dave Barry Turns 40* (New York: Fawcett, 1990), p. 47.

52. C. A. VanLear, "Testing a Cyclical Model of Communicative Openness in Relationship Development." *Communication Monographs* 58 (1991): 337–361.

53. Adapted from L. A. Baxter and B. M. Montgomery, "A Guide to Dialectical Approaches to Studying Personal Relationships," in B. M. Montgomery and L. A. Baxter, eds, *Dialectical Approaches to Studying Persnal Relationships*. pp. 1–16.

54. L. M. Register and T. B. Henley, "The Phenomenology of Intimacy." *Journal of Social and Personal Relationships* 9 (1992): 467–481.

55. D. Morris, *Intimate Behavior* (New York: Bantam, 1973), p. 7.

56. K. Floyd, "Meanings for Closeness and Intimacy in Friendship." *Journal of Social and Personal Relationships* 13 (1996): 85–107.

57. L. A. Baxter, "A Dialogic Approach to Relationship Maintenance," in D. Canar and L. Stafford, eds., *Communication and Relational Maintenance* (San Diego: Academic Press, 1994).

58. J. T. Wood and C. C. Inman, "In a Different Mode: Masculine Styles of Communicating Closeness." *Applied Communication Research* 21 (1993): 279–295.

59. See, for example, K. Dindia and M. Allen, "Sex Differences in Self-Disclosure: A Meta-Analysis." *Psychological Bulletin* 112 (1992): 106–124; I. and P. Backlund, *Exploring GenderSpeak* (New York: McGraw-Hill, 1994), p. 219; and J. C. Pearson, L. H. Turner, and W. Todd-Mancillas, *Gender and Communication*, 2nd ed. (Dubuque, IA: W. C. Brown, 1991), pp. 170–171.

60. See, for example, K. Floyd, "Gender and Closeness among Friends and Siblings." *Journal of Psychology* 129 (1995): 193–202, and K. Floyd, "Communicating Closeness among Siblings: An Application of the Gendered Closeness Perspective." *Communication Research Reports* 13 (1996): 27–34.

61. E. L. MacGeorge, A. R. Graves, B. Feng, S. J. Gillihan, and B. R. Burleson, "The Myth of Gender Cultures: Similarities Outweigh Differences in Men's and Women's Provision of and Responses to Supportive Communication." *Sex Roles* 50 (2004): 143–175.

62. C. Inman, "Friendships among Men: Closeness in the Doing," in J. T. Wood, ed., *Gendered Relationships* (Mountain View, CA: 1996). See also S. Swain, "Covert Intimacy in Men's Friendships: Closeness in Men's Friendships," in B. J. Risman and P. Schwartz, eds., *Gender in Intimate Relationships: A Microstructural Approach* (Belmont, CA: Wadsworth, 1989).

63. C. K. Reissman, *Divorce Talk: Women and Men Make Sense of Personal Relationships* (New Brunswick: Rutgers University Press, 1990).

64. For a useful survey of cultural differences in interpersonal communication, see W. B. Gudykunst, S. Ting-Toomey, and T. Nishida, eds., *Communication in Personal Relationships Across Cultures* (Thousand Oaks, CA: Sage, 1996).

65. M. Argyle and M. Henderson, "The Rules of Relationships," in S. Duck and D. Perlman, eds., *Understanding Personal Relationships* (Beverly Hills, CA: Sage, 1985).

66. W. B. Gudykunst, "The Influence of Cultural Variability on Perceptions of Communication Behavior Associated with Relationship Terms." *Human Communication Research* 13 (1986): 147–166.

67. H. C. Triandis, *Culture and Social Behavior* (New York: McGraw-Hill, 1994), p. 230.

68. C. W. Franklin, "'Hey Home—Yo Bro.' Friendship among Black Men," in P. M. Nardir, ed., *Men's Friendships* (Newbury Park, CA: Sage, 1992).

69. L. B. Rosenfeld and W. L. Kendrick, "Choosing to Be Open: Subjective Reasons for Self-Disclosing." *Western Journal of Speech Communication* 48 (Fall 1984): 326–343.

70. I. Altman and D. A. Taylor, *Social Penetration: The Development of Interpersonal Relationships* (New York: Holt, Rinehart and Winston, 1973).

71. J. Luft, *Of Human Interaction* (Palo Alto, CA: National Press, 1969).

72. W. B. Gudykunst and S. Ting-Toomey, *Culture and Interpersonal Communication* (Newbury Park, CA: Sage, 1988), pp. 197–198, S. Ting-Toomey, "A Comparative Analysis of the Communicative Dimensions of Love, Self-Disclosure, Maintenance, Ambivalence, and Conflict in Three Cultures: France, Japan, and the United States." Paper presented at the International Communication Association convention, Montreal, 1987.

73. S. Duck and D. E. Miell, "Charting the Development of Personal Relationships," in R. Gilmour and S. Duck, eds., *Studying Interpersonal Interaction* (Hillsdale, NJ: Erlbaum, 1991).

74. S. Duck, "Some Evident Truths About Conversations in Everyday Relationships: All Communications Are Not Created Equal." *Human Communication Research* 18 (1991): 228–267.

75. J. C. Pearson, *Communication in the Family*, 2nd ed. (Needham, MA: Allyn & Bacon, 1993), pp. 292–296.

76. Summarized in J. Pearson, *Communication in the Family* (New York: Harper & Row, 1989), pp. 252–257.

77. E. M. Eisenberg and M. G. Witten, "Reconsidering Openness in Organizational Communication." *Academy of Management Review* 12 (1987): 418–428.

78. L. B. Rosenfeld and J. R. Gilbert, "The Measurement of Cohesion and Its Relationship to Dimensions of Self-Disclosure in Classroom Settings." *Small Group Behavior* 20 (1989): 291–301.

79. J. A. Jaksa and M. Pritchard, *Communication Ethics: Methods of Analysis*, 2nd ed. (Belmont, CA: Wadsworth, 1994), pp. 65–66.

80. D. O'Hair and M. J. Cody, "Interpersonal Deception: The Dark Side of Interpersonal Communication?" in B. H. Spitzberg and W. R. Cupach, eds., *The Dark Side of Interpersonal Communication* (Hillsdale, NJ: Erlbaum, 1993).

81. M. E. Kaplar and A. K. Gordon, "The Enigma of Altruistic Lying: Perspective Differences in What Motivates and Justifies Lie

Telling Within Romantic Relationships." *Personal Relationships* 11 (2004).

82. R. E. Turner, C. Edgley, and G. Olmstead, "Information Control in Conversation: Honesty Is Not Always the Best Policy." *Kansas Journal of Sociology* 11 (1975): 69–89.

83. K. L. Bell and B. M. DePaulo, "Liking and Lying." *Basic and Applied Social Psychology* 18 (1996): 243–266.

84. R. S. Feldman, J. A. Forrest, and B. R. Happ, "Self-Presentation and Verbal Deception: Do Self-Presenters Lie More?" *Basic and Applied Social Psychology* 24 (2002): 163–170.

85. S. A. McCornack and T. R. Levine, "When Lies Are Uncovered: Emotional and Relational Outcomes of Discovered Deception." *Communication Monographs* 57 (1990): 119–138.

86. See M. A. Hamilton and P. J. Mineo, "A Framework for Understanding Equivocation." *Journal of Language and Social Psychology* 17 (1998): 3–35.

87. S. Metts, W. R. Cupach, and T. T. Imahori, "Perceptions of Sexual Compliance-Resisting Messages in Three Types of Cross-Sex Relationships." *Western Journal of Communication* 56 (1992): 1–17.

88. J. B. Bavelas, A. Black, N. Chovil, and J. Mullett, *Equivocal Communication* (Newbury Park, CA: Sage, 1990), p. 171.

89. Ibid.

90. See, for example, W. P. Robinson, A. Shepherd, and J. Heywood, "Truth, Equivocation/Concealment, and Lies in Job Applications and Doctor-Patient Communication." *Journal of Language & Social Psychology* 17 (1998): 149–164.

91. Several of the following examples were offered by M. T. Motley, "Mindfulness in Solving Communicators' Dilemmas." *Communication Monographs* 59 (1992): 306–314.

92. D. B. Buller and J. K. Burgoon, "Deception," in *Communicating Strategically: Strategies in Interpersonal Communication* (Hillsdale, NJ: Erlbaum, 1994).

93. S. Bok, *Lying: Moral Choice in Public and Private Life* (New York: Pantheon, 1978).

94. For a summary of the link between social capital and career success, see V. Krebs, "Social Capital: The Key to Success for the 21st Century Organization." *International Association for Human Resources Journal* 12 (2008): 38–42. See also S. E. Seibert, M. L. Kraimer, and R. C. Liden, "A Social Capital Theory of Career Success." *Academy of Management Journal* 44 (2001): 219–237.

95. M. S. Granovetter, "The Strength of Weak Ties." *American Journal of Sociology* 78 (1973): 1360–80.

96. N. B. Ellison, C. Steinfield, and C. Lampe, "The Benefits of Facebook 'Friends': Social Capital and College Students' Use of Online Social Network Sites." *Journal of Computer-Mediated Communication* 12(4) (2007): Article 1. http://jcmc.indiana.edu/vol12/issue4/ellison.html.

97. C. Steinfield, J. M. DiMicco, N. B. Ellison, and C. Lampe, "Bowling Online: Social Networking and Social Capital Within the Organization." Proceedings of the Fourth International Conference on Communities and Technologies (University Park, PA, June 25–27, 2009), New York, NY, 245–254.

CHAPTER 8

1. K. N. L. Cissna and E. Seiburg, "Patterns of Interactional Confirmation and Disconfirmation," in M. V. Redmond, ed., *Interpersonal Communication: Readings in Theory and Research* (Fort Worth, TX: Harcourt Brace, 1995).

2. Ibid.

3. M. W. Allen, "Communication Concepts Related to Perceived Organizational Support." *Western Journal of Communication* 59 (1995): 326–346.

4. B. Bower, "Nice Guys Look Better in Women's Eyes." *Science News* (March 18, 1995): 165.

5. See, for example, J. Veroff, E. Douvan, T. L. Orbuch, and L. K. Acitelli, "Happiness in Stable Marriages: The Early Years," in T. N. Bradbury, ed., *The Development Course of Marital Dysfunction* (New York: Cambridge University Press, 1999), pp. 152–179.

6. D. J. Canary and T. M. Emmers-Sommer, *Sex and Gender Differences in Personal Relationships* (New York: Guilford, 1997).

7. J. J. Teven, M. M. Martin, and N. C. Neupauer, "Sibling Relationships: Verbally Aggressive Messages and Their Effect on Relational Satisfaction." *Communication Reports* 11 (1998): 179–186.

8. K. Ellis, "The Impact of Perceived Teacher Confirmation on Receiver Apprehension, Motivation, and Learning." *Communication Education* 53 (2004): 1–20.

9. For a discussion of reactions to disconfirming responses, see A. L. Vangelisti and L. P. Crumley, "Reactions to Messages That Hurt: The Influence of Relational Contexts." *Communication Monographs* 64 (1998): 173–196. See also L. M. Cortina, V. J. Magley, J. H. Williams, and R. D. Langhout, "Incivility in the Workplace: Incidence and Impact." *Journal of Occupational Health Psychology* 6 (2001): 64–80.

10. A. L. Vangelisti, "Messages That Hurt," in W. R. Cupach and B. H. Spitzberg, eds., *The Dark Side of Interpersonal Communication* (Hillsdale, NJ: Erlbaum, 1994).

11. See W. W. Wilmot, *Dyadic Communication* (New York: Random House, 1987), pp. 149–158, and L. M. Andersson and C. M. Pearson, "Tit for Tat? The Spiraling Effect of Incivility in the Workplace." *Academy of Management Review* 24 (1999): 452–471. See also L. N. Olson and D. O. Braithwaite, "'If You Hit Me Again, I'll Hit You Back': Conflict Management Strategies of Individuals Experiencing Aggression during Conflicts." *Communication Studies* 55 (2004): 271–286.

12. C. Burggraf and A. L. Sillars, "A Critical Examination of Sex Differences in Marital Communication." *Communication Monographs* 54 (1987): 276–294. See also D. A. Newton and J. K. Burgoon, "The Use and Consequences of Verbal Strategies during Interpersonal Disagreements." *Human Communication Research* 16 (1990): 477–518.

13. W. W. Wilmot and J. L. Hocker, *Interpersonal Conflict*, 7th ed. (New York: McGraw-Hill, 2007), pp. 21–22.

14. Ibid., pp. 23–24.

15. J. Gibb, "Defensive Communication." *Journal of Communication* 11 (1961): 141–148. See also W. F. Eadie, "Defensive Communication Revisited: A Critical Examination of Gibb's Theory." *Southern Speech Communication Journal* 47 (1982): 163–177.

16. For a review of research supporting the effectiveness of "I" language, see R. F. Proctor II and J. R. Wilcox, "An Exploratory Analysis of Responses to Owned Messages in Interpersonal Communication." *Et Cetera: A Review of General Semantics* 50 (1993): 201–220. See also R. F. Proctor II, "Responsibility or Egocentrism?: The Paradox of Owned Messages." *Speech Association of Minnesota Journal* 16 (1989): 59–60.

17. T. C. Sabourin and G. H. Stamp, "Communication and the Experience of Dialectical Tensions in Family Life: An Examination of Abusive and Nonabusive Families." *Communication Monographs* 62 (1995): 213–243.

18. R. Vonk, "The Slime Effect: Suspicion and Dislike of Likeable Behavior Toward Superiors." *Journal of Personality and Social Psychology* 74 (1998): 849–864.

19. A. L. Sillars, "Interpersonal Conflict," in C. Berger, M. Roloff, and D. R. Roskos-Ewoldsen, eds., *Handbook of Communication Science*, 2nd ed. (Thousand Oaks, CA: Sage, 2009), pp. 273–289.

20. New Mexico Commission on the Status of Women, *Dealing with Sexual Harassment* (2002). Retrieved June 17, 2010, from http://www.womenscommission.state.nm.us/Publications/sexhbrochre.pdf.

21. Adapted from R. B. Adler and J. M. Elmhorst, *Communicating at Work: Principles and Practices for Business and the Professions*, 10th ed. (New York: McGraw-Hill, 2010), pp. 118–119.

22. For information on filing a formal complaint, see http://www.eeoc.gov/laws/types/sexual_harassment.cfm.

23. See, for example, L. A. Baxter, W. W. Wilmot, C. A. Simmons, and A. Swartz, "Ways of Doing Conflict: A Folk Taxonomy of Conflict Events in Personal Relationships," in P. J. Kalbfleisch, ed., *Interpersonal Communication: Evolving Interpersonal Relationships* (Hillsdale, NJ: Erlbaum, 1993).

24. P. J. Lannutti and J. I. Monahan, "'Not Now, Maybe Later': The Influence of Relationship Type, Request Persistence, and Alcohol Consumption on Women's Refusal Strategies." *Communication Studies* 55 (2004): 362–377.

25. G. R. Birchler, R. L. Weiss, and J. P. Vincent, "Multimethod Analysis of Social Reinforcement Exchange Between Maritally Distressed and Nondistressed Spouse and Stranger Dyads." *Journal of Personality and Social Psychology* 31 (1975): 349–360.

26. J. R. Meyer, "Effect of Verbal Aggressiveness on the Perceived Importance of Secondary Goals in Messages." *Communication Studies* 55 (2004): 168–184.

27. G. R. Bach and H. Goldberg, *Creative Aggression* (Garden City, NY: Doubleday, 1974).

28. See K. Kellermann and B. C. Shea, "Threats, Suggestions, Hints, and Promises: Gaining Compliance Efficiently and Politely." *Communication Quarterly* 44 (1996): 145–465.

29. J. Jordan and M. E. Roloff, "Acquiring Assistance from Others: The Effect of Indirect Requests and Relational Intimacy on Verbal Compliance." *Human Communication Research* 16 (1990): 519–555.

30. Research summarized by D. Tannen in *You Just Don't Understand: Women and Men in Conversation* (New York: William Morrow, 1989), pp. 152–157, 162–165.

31. N. Crick, "Relational and Overt Forms of Peer Victimization: A Multiinformant Approach." *Journal of Consulting and Clinical Psychology* 66 (1998): 337–347.

32. J. Gottman, Interview with *Edge*: "The Mathematics of Love" (May 14, 2004). Retrieved on June 23, 2010, from http://www.edge.org/documents/archive/edge159.html.

33. The information in this paragraph is drawn from research summarized by J. T. Wood in *Gendered Lives*, 6th ed. (Belmont, CA: Wadsworth, 2005).

34. S. Herring, "Gender and Democracy in Computer-Mediated Communication." *Electronic Journal of Communication* 3 (1993): 1–17.

35. V. Savicki, M. Kelley, and D. Lingenfelter, "Gender and Group Composition in Small Task Groups Using Computer-Mediated Communication." *Computers in Human Behavior* 12 (1996): 209–224.

36. S. Yates, "Gender, Identity, and CMC." *Journal of Computer Assisted Learning* 13 (1997): 281–290. See also S. Yates, "Gender, Language and CMC for Education." *Learning and Instruction* 11 (2001): 21–34.

37. Ibid.

38. B. M. Gayle, R. W. Preiss, and M. A. Allen, "Embedded Gender Expectations: A Covariate Analysis of Conflict Situations and Issues." *Communication Research Reports* 15 (1998): 379–387.

39. D. J. Canary and T. M. Emmers-Sommer, *Sex and Gender Differences in Personal Relationships* (New York: Guilford Press, 1997).

40. M. Allen, "Methodological Considerations When Examining a Gendered World," in D. J. Canary and K. Dindia, eds., *Handbook of Sex Differences and Similarities in Communication* (Mahwah, NJ: Erlbaum, 1998), pp. 427–444.

41. University of Colorado Conflict Research Consortium, "Shuttle Diplomacy/Mediated Communication." Boulder, Colorado: International Online Training Program on Intractable Conflict. Retrieved online June 16, 2010, at http://www.colorado.edu/conflict/peace/treatment/shuttle.htm.

42. For a more detailed discussion of culture, conflict, and context, see W. B. Gudykunst and S. Ting-Toomey, *Culture and Interpersonal Communication* (Newbury Park, CA: Sage, 1988), pp. 153–160.

43. B. L. Speicher, "Interethnic Conflict: Attribution and Cultural Ignorance." *Howard Journal of Communications* 5 (1995): 195–213.

44. S. Ting-Toomey, K. K. Yee-Jung, R. B. Shapiro, W. Garcia, and T. Wright, "Ethnic Identity Salience and Conflict Styles in Four Ethnic Groups: African Americans, Asian Americans, European Americans, and Latino Americans." Paper presented at the annual conference of the Speech Communication Association, New Orleans, November 1994.

45. See, for example, S. Ting-Toomey, "Rhetorical Sensitivity Style in Three Cultures: France, Japan, and the United States." *Central States Speech Journal* 39 (1988): 28–36.

46. K. Okabe, "Indirect Speech Acts of the Japanese," in L. Kincaid, ed., *Communication Theory: Eastern and Western Perspectives* (San Diego: Academic Press, 1987), pp. 127–136.

47. The following research is summarized in Tannen, *You Just Don't Understand*, p. 160.

48. M. J. Collier, "Communication Competence Problematics in Ethnic Relationships." *Communication Monographs, 63* (1996): 314–336.

49. A. C. Filley, *Interpersonal Conflict Resolution* (Glenview, IL: Scott Foresman, 1975), p. 23.

50. For a brief discussion of constructive problem solving, see A. Gallo, "The Right Way to Fight." *Harvard Business Review* (May 11, 2009). Retrieved June 16, 2010, from http://blogs.hbr.org/hmu/2010/05/the-right-way-to-fight.html.

CHAPTER 9

1. M. V. Redmond, "A Plan for the Successful Use of Teams in Design Education." *Journal of Architectural Education* 17 (May 1986): 27–49.

2. "Professional Occupations in Multimedia." *California Occupational Guide, Number 2006* (Sacramento, CA: California State Employment Division, 1995), p. 4. See also "A Labor Market Analysis of the Interactive Digital Media Industry: Opportunities in Multimedia." (San Francisco: Reagan & Associates, 1997), pp. 15–29.

3. L. Thompson, E. Peterson, and S. E. Brodt, "Team Negotiation: An Examination of Integrative and Distributive Bargaining." *Journal of Personality and Social Psychology* 70 (1996): 66–78.

4. For a more detailed discussion of the advantages and disadvantages of working in groups, see S. A. Beebe and J. T. Masterson, *Communicating in Small Groups: Principles and Practices*, 9th ed. (Needham Heights: Allyn & Bacon, 2003).

5. E. A. Marby, "The Systems Metaphor in Group Communication," in L. R. Frey, ed., *Handbook of Group Communication Theory and Research* (Thousand Oaks, CA: Sage, 1999).

6. J. D. Rothwell, *In Mixed Company: Small Group Communication*, 5th ed. (Belmont, CA: Wadsworth, 2004), pp. 29–31.

7. "Is Your Team Too Big? Too Small? What's the Right Number?" Published June 14, 2006, in Knowledge@Wharton. Retrieved January 26, 2009, from Knowledge@Wharton, http://knowledge.wharton.upenn.edu/article.cfm?articleid=1501.

8. See, for example, J. R. Katzenbach and D. K. Smith, "The Discipline of Teams." *Harvard Business Review* 86 (March–April 1993): 111–120.

9. J. Hackman, "The Design of Work Teams," in J. Lorsch, ed., *Handbook of Organizational Behavior* (Englewood Cliffs, NJ: Prentice Hall, 1987), pp. 315–342.

10. Rothwell, *In Mixed Company*, pp. 42–47.

11. See, for example, A. Powell, G. Piccoli, and B. Ives, "Virtual Teams: A Review of Current Literature and Directions for Future Research." *ACM SIGMIS Database* 35 (2004): 6–16. See also J. B. Walther and N. Bazarova, "Validation and Application of Electronic Propinquity Theory to Computer-Mediated Communication in Groups." *Communication Research* 35 (2008): 622–645.

12. B. J. Alge, C. Wiethoff, and H. J. Klein, "When Does the Medium Matter? Knowledge-Building Experiences and Opportunities in Decision-Making Teams." *Organizational Behavior and Human Decision Processes* 91 (2003): 26–37. See also E. V. Hobman, P. Bordia, B. Irmer, and A. Chang, "The Expression of Conflict in Computer-Mediated and Face-To-Face Groups." *Small Group Research* 33(2002): 439–465.

13. S. L. Herndon, "Theory and Practice: Implications for the Implementation of Communication Technology in Organizations." *Journal of Business Communication* 34 (January 1997): 121–129.

14. D. M. Anderson and C. J. Haddad, "Gender, Voice and Learning in Online Course Environments." *Journal of Asynchronous Learning Networks* 9 (2005): 3–14.

15. For a discussion of the relationship between individual and group goals, see L. Frey, "Individuals in Groups," in L. R. Frey and J. K. Barge, eds., *Managing Group Life: Communicating in Decision-Making Groups* (Boston: Houghton Mifflin, 1997).

16. See, for example, P. Michelman, "How Will You Make Your Team a *Team*?" in *Managing Teams for High Performance* (Cambridge, MA: Harvard Management Press, 2007).

17. Ibid.

18. C. E. Larson and F. M. J. LaFasto, *Teamwork: What Must Go Right, What Can Go Wrong* (Thousand Oaks, CA: Sage, 1989).

19. J. Krakauer, *Into Thin Air* (New York: Anchor, 1997), pp. 212–213.

20. See D. Scheerhorn and P. Geist, "Social Dynamics in Groups," in Frey and Barge, *Managing Group Life*.

21. S. B. Shimanoff, "Group Interaction via Communication Rules," in R. S. Cathcart and L. A. Samovar, eds., *Small Group Communication: A Reader*, 5th ed. (Dubuque, IA: W. C. Brown, 1988), pp. 50–64.

22. D. S. Gouran, R. Y. Hirokawa, K. M. Julian, and G. B. Leatham, "The Evolution and Current Status of the Functional Perspective on Communication in Decision-Making and Problem-Solving Groups," in S. A. Deetz, ed., *Communication Yearbook* 16 (Newbury Park, CA: Sage, 1992). See also G. M. Wittenbaum, A. B.

Hollingshead, P. B. Paulus, R. Y. Hirokawa, D. G. Ancona, R. S. Peterson, K. A. Jehn, and K. Yoon, "The Functional Perspective as a Lens for Understanding Groups." *Small Group Research* 35 (2004): 17–43.

23. M. E. Mayer, "Behaviors Leading to More Effective Decisions in Small Groups Embedded in Organizations." *Communication Reports* 11 (1998): 123–132.

24. R. F. Bales and P. L. Strodbeck, "Phases in Group Problem Solving." *Journal of Abnormal and Social Psychology* 46 (1951): 485–495.

25. E. Bormann, *Small Group Communication: Theory and Practice* (New York: Harper & Row, 1990).

26. N. Postman, *Crazy Talk, Stupid Talk* (New York: Dell, 1976).

27. B. Steinzor, "The Spatial Factor in Face-to-Face Discussion Groups." *Journal of Abnormal and Social Psychology* 45 (1950): 522–555.

28. P. L. Strodtbeck and L. H. Hook, "The Social Dimensions of a Twelve-Man Jury Table." *Sociometry* 24 (1961): 397–415.

29. N. F. Russo, "Connotations of Seating Arrangements." *Cornell Journal of Social Relations* 2 (1967): 37–44.

30. Adapted from D. W. Johnson and F. P. Johnson, *Joining Together: Group Theory and Group Skills*, 10th ed. (Boston: Allyn and Bacon, 2003).

31. R. Hastle, *Inside the Jury* (Cambridge, MA: Harvard University Press, 1983).

32. B. Day, "The Art of Conducting International Business." *Advertising Age* (October 6, 1990): 48.

33. Adapted from R. B. Adler and J. M. Elmhorst, *Communicating at Work: Principles and Practices for Business and the Professions*, 8th ed. (New York: McGraw-Hill, 2005), p. 269.

34. Population Reference Bureau, "The Changing American Pie, 1999 and 2025." Retrieved October 13, 2004, from http://www.prb.org/AmeristatTemplate.cfm?Section=RaceandEthnicity&template=/ContentManagement/ContentDisplay.cfm&ContentID=2743.

35. S. G. Barsade and D. E. Gibson, "Group Emotion: A View from Top and Bottom," in D. H. Gruenfeld, ed., *Composition* (Greenwich, CT: JAI Press, 1998). See also K. Y. Williams and C. A. O'Reilly, "Demography and Diversity in Organizations: A Review of 40 Years of Research," in B. Staw and R. Sutton, eds., *Research in Organizational Behavior* 20 (1998): 77–140.

36. Williams and O'Reilly, "Demography and Diversity in Organizations."

37. S. B. Paletz, K. Peng, M. Erez, and C. Maslach, "Ethnic Composition and Its Differential Impact on Group Processes in Diverse Teams." *Small Group Research* 35 (2004): 128–157.

38. G. Hofstede, *Cultures and Organizations: Software of the Mind* (New York: McGraw-Hill, 1997), p. 158.

39. See H. C. Triandis, R. Bontempo, M. Villareal, M. Asai, and N. Lucca, "Individualism and Collectivism: Cross-Cultural Perspectives of Self-Ingroup Relationships." *Journal of Personality and Social Psychology* 54 (1988): 323–338.

40. Research supporting these differences is summarized in S. Ting-Toomey, "Identity and Interpersonal Bonding," in M. K. Asante and W. B. Gudykunst, eds., *Handbook of International and Intercultural Communication* (Newbury Park, CA: Sage, 1989), pp. 351–373.

41. Hofstede, *Cultures and Organizations*, pp. 65–109.

42. Ibid., pp. 110–147.

43. Ibid., pp. 189–210.

44. The following types of power are based on the categories developed by J. R. French and B. Raven, "The Basis of Social Power,"

in D. Cartright and A. Zander, eds., *Group Dynamics* (New York: Harper & Row, 1968), p. 565.

45. For a detailed discussion of leadership emergence, see E. G. G. Bormann and N. C. Bormann, *Effective Small Group Communication*, 6th ed. (New York: Pearson Custom Publishing, 1997).

46. V. Savicki, D. Lingenfelter, and M. Kelley, "Gender Language Style and Group Composition in Internet Discussion Groups." *Journal of Computer-Mediated Communication* 2 (1996). Retrieved April 1, 2010, from http://www.ascusc.org/jcmc/vol2/issue3/savicki .html.

47. J. Wolfe, "Why Do Women Feel Ignored? Gender Differences in Computer-Mediated Classroom Interactions." *Computers and Composition* 16(1999): 153–166.

48. C. Conrad, *Strategic Organizational Communication: An Integrated Perspective*, 2nd ed. (Fort Worth, TX: Holt, Rinehart and Winston, 1990), p. 139.

49. J. D. Rothwell, *In Mixed Company: Small Group Communication*, 5th ed. (Belmont, CA: Wadsworth, 2004), pp. 247–282.

50. Aristotle, *Politics* (New York: Oxford University Press, 1958), Book 7.

51. See B. L. Kelsey, "The Dynamics of Multicultural Groups." *Small Group Research* 29 (1998): 602–623.

52. W. Bennis and B. Nanus, *Leaders: The Strategies for Taking Charge* (New York: Harper & Row, 1985),.

53. K. Lewin, R. Lippitt, and R. K. White, "Patterns of Aggressive Behavior in Experimentally Created Social Climates." *Journal of Social Psychology* 10 (1939): 271–299.

54. G. Cheney, "Democracy in the Workplace: Theory and Practice from the Perspective of Communication." *Journal of Applied Communication Research* 23 (1995): 167–200.

55. L. L. Rosenbaum and W. B. Rosenbaum, "Morale and Productivity Consequences of Group Leadership Style, Stress, and Type of Task." *Journal of Applied Psychology* 55 (1971): 343–358.

56. J. Hall and S. Donnell, "Managerial Achievement: The Personal Side of Behavioral Theory." *Human Relations* 32 (1979): 77–101.

57. R. R. Blake and A. A. McCanse, *Leadership Dilemmas—Grid Solutions* (Houston: Gulf Publishing Co., 1991).

58. For a discussion of situational theories, see G. L. Wilson, *Groups in Context*, 6th ed. (New York: McGraw-Hill, 2002), pp. 190–194.

59. F. E. Fiedler, *A Theory of Leadership Effectiveness* (New York: McGraw-Hill, 1967).

60. P. Hersey and K. Blanchard, *Management of Organizational Behavior: Utilizing Human Resources*, 8th ed. (Upper Saddle River, NJ: Prentice Hall, 2001).

CHAPTER 10

1. L. Tuck, "Meeting Madness." *Presentations* (May 1995): 20.

2. C. Downs, D. M. Berg, and W. A. Linkugel, *The Organizational Communicator* (New York: Harper & Row, 1977), p. 127.

3. G. L. Wilson, *Groups in Context: Leadership and Participation in Small Groups* (New York: McGraw-Hill, 2005), 12–13.

4. See, for example, C. Pavitt, "Do Interacting Groups Perform Better Than Aggregates of Individuals?" *Human Communication Research* 29 (2003): 592–599, G. M. Wittenbaum, "Putting Communication into the Study of Group Memory," *Human Communication Research* 29 (2004): 616–623, and M. G. Frank, T. H. Feely, N. Paolantonio, and T. J. Servoss, "Individual and Small Group Accuracy in Judging Truthful and Deceptive Communication." *Group Decision and Negotiation* 13 (2004): 45–54.

5. R. B. Adler and J. M. Elmhorst, *Communicating at Work: Principles and Practices for Business and the Professions*, 10th ed. (New York: McGraw-Hill, 2010), pp. 278–279.

6. D. L. Duarte and N. T. Snyder, *Mastering Virtual Teams: Strategies, Tools and Techniques That Succeed,* 3rd ed. (San Francisco: Josey-Bass, 2006) and J. D. Rothwell, *In Mixed Company: Communicating in Small Groups and Teams*, 7th ed. (Boston: Wadsworth, 2010), pp. 378–380.

7. See, for example, D. P. Brandon and A. B. Hollingshead, "Characterizing Online Groups," in A. Joinson, K. McKenna, T. Postmes, and U. Reips, eds., *The Oxford Handbook of Internet Psychology* (New York: Oxford University Press, 2007). See also G. Hertel, S. Geister, and U. Konradt, "Managing Virtual Teams: A Review of Current Empirical Research." *Human Resource Management Review* 15 (2005): 69–95, and R. Benbunan-Fich, S. R. Hiltz, and M. Turoff, "A Comparative Content Analysis of Face-to-Face vs. Asynchronous Group Decision Making." *Decision Support Systems* 34 (2003): 457–469.

8. A. Powell, G. Piccoli, and B. Ives, "Virtual Teams: A Review of Current Literature and Directions for Future Research." *Data Base for Advances in Information Systems* 35 (2004): 6–36.

9. G. M. Johnson, "Synchronous and Asynchronous Text-Based CMC in Educational Contexts: A Review of Recent Research." *Tech Trends* 50 (2006): 46–53.

10. C. Lin, C. Standing, and Y. Liu, "A Model to Develop Effective Virtual Teams." *Decision Support Systems* 45 (2008): 1031–1045.

11. B. B. Baltes, M. W. Dickson, M. P. Sherman, C. C. Bauer, and J. S. LaGanke, "Computer-Mediated Communication and Group Decision Making: A Meta-Analysis." *Organizational Behavior and Human Decision Processes* (2002): 156–179.

12. K. Nowak, J. H. Watt, and J. B. Walther, "Computer Mediated Teamwork and the Efficiency Framework: Exploring the Influence of Synchrony and Cues on Media Satisfaction and Outcome Success." *Computers in Human Behavior* 25 (2009): 1108–1119.

13. M. Zey, ed., *Decision Making: Alternatives to Rational Choice Models* (Newbury Park, CA: Sage, 1992). For a discussion of how groups "muddle through" in organizational decision making, see H. Mintzberg and A. McHugh, "Strategy Formation in an Adhocracy." *Administrative Science Quarterly* 30 (1985): 160–197.

14. See, for example, A. L. Salazar, R. Y. Hirokawa, K. M. Propp, K. M. Julian, and G. B. Leatham, "In Search of True Causes: Examination of the Effect of Group Potential and Group Interaction on Decision Performance." *Human Communication Research* 20 (1994): 529–599.

15. J. Dewey, *How We Think* (New York: Heath, 1910).

16. M. S. Poole, "Procedures for Managing Meetings: Social and Technological Innovation," in R. A. Swanson and B. O. Knapp, eds., *Innovative Meeting Management* (Austin, TX: 3M Meeting Management Institute, 1991). See also M. S. Poole and M. E. Holmes, "Decision Development in Computer-Assisted Group Decision Making." *Human Communication Research* 22 (1995): 90–127.

17. K. Lewin, *Field Theory in Social Science* (New York: Harper & Row, 1951), pp. 30–59.

18. See S. Jarboe, "Group Communication and Creativity Processes," in L. R. Frey, ed., *Handbook of Group Communication Theory and Research* (Thousand Oaks, CA: Sage, 1999).

19. A. Osborn, *Applied Imagination* (New York: Scribner's, 1959).

20. See, for example, M. Diehl and W. Strobe, "Productivity Loss in Brainstorming Groups: Toward the Solution of a Riddle." *Journal of Personality and Social Psychology* 53 (1987): 497–509, and V.

Brown, M. Tumero, T. S. Larey, and P. B. Paulus, "Modeling Cognitive Interactions during Group Brainstorming." *Small Group Research* 29 (1998): 495–526.

21. B. A. Fisher, "Decision Emergence: Phases in Group Decision Making." *Speech Monographs* 37 (1970): 53–66.

22. C. R. Frantz and K. G. Jin, "The Structure of Group Conflict in a Collaborative Work Group during Information Systems Development." *Journal of Applied Communication Research* 23 (1995): 108–127.

23. M. Poole and J. Roth, "Decision Development in Small Groups IV: A Typology of Group Decision Paths." *Human Communication Research* 15 (1989): 323–356. Also, M. Poole and J. Roth, "Decision Development in Small Groups V: Test of a Contingency Model." *Human Communication Research* 15 (1989): 549–589.

24. S. A. Wheelan, D. Murphy, E. Tsumura, and S. F. Kline, "Member Perceptions of Internal Group Dynamics and Productivity." *Small Group Research* 29 (1998): 371–393.

25. S. M. Farmer and J. Roth, "Conflict-Handling Behavior in Work Groups: Effects of Group Structure, Decision Process, and Time." *Small Group Research* 29 (1998): 669–713.

26. B. Mullen and C. Cooper, "The Relation between Group Cohesiveness and Performance: An Integration." *Psychological Bulletin* 115 (1994): 210–227.

27. R. T. Keller, "Predictors of the Performance of Project Groups in R & D Organizations." *Academy of Management Journal* 29 (1986): 715–726. See also B. A. Welch, K. W. Mossholder, R. P. Stell, and N. Bennett, "Does Work Group Cohesiveness Affect Individuals' Performance and Organizational Commitment?" *Small Group Research* 29 (1998): 472–494.

28. Rothwell, *In Mixed Company*, 7th ed. (Boston: Wadsworth-Cengage, 2010), pp. 139–142.

29. M. E. Mayer, "Behaviors Leading to More Effective Decisions in Small Groups Embedded in Organizations." *Communication Reports* 11 (1998): 123–132.

30. L. R. Hoffman and N. R. F. Maier, "Valence in the Adoption of Solutions by Problem-Solving Groups: Concept, Method, and Results." *Journal of Abnormal and Social Psychology* 69 (1964): 264–271.

31. E. P. Torrence, "Some Consequences of Power Differences on Decision Making in Permanent and Temporary Three-Man Groups." *Research Studies, Washington State College* 22 (1954): 130–140.

32. R. F. Bales, F. L. Strodtbeck, T. M. Mills, and M. E. Roseborough, "Channels of Communication in Small Groups." *American Sociological Review* 16 (1951): 461–468.

33. I. Janis, *Groupthink: Psychological Studies of Policy Decisions and Fiascoes.* (Boston: Houghton Mifflin, 1982). See also R. S. Baron, "So Right It's Wrong: Groupthink and the Ubiquitous Nature of Polarized Group Decision Making," in M. P. Zanna, ed., *Advances in Experimental Social Psychology*, vol. 37 (San Diego: Elsevier Academic Press, 2005).

34. Adapted from Rothwell, *In Mixed Company*, pp. 223–226.

CHAPTER II

1. D. Wallenchinsky and A. Wallace, *The Book of Lists* (New York: Little, Brown, 1995).

2. For an example of how demographics have been taken into consideration in great speeches, see G. Stephens, "Frederick Douglass' Multiracial Abolitionism: 'Antagonistic Cooperation' and 'Redeemable Ideals' in the July 5 Speech." *Communication Studies* 48 (Fall 1997): 175–194. On July 5, 1852, Douglass gave a speech titled "What to the Slave Is the 4th of July," attacking the hypocrisy of Independence Day in a slaveholding republic. It was one of the greatest antislavery speeches ever given, and part of its success stemmed from the way Douglass sought common ground with his multiracial audience.

3. Syrena Rexroat, "Gender Educational Gap," in *Winning Orations, 2009*, Interstate Oratorical Association, 2009. Syrena was coached by Anderson Rapp.

4. For example, see J. E. Kopfman and S. Smith, "Understanding the Audiences of a Health Communication Campaign: A Discriminant Analysis of Potential Organ Donors Based on Intent to Donate." *Journal of Applied Communication Research* 24 (February 1996): 33–49.

5. R. K. Stutman and S. E. Newell, "Beliefs Versus Values: Silent Beliefs in Designing a Persuasive Message." *Western Journal of Speech Communication* 48, 4 (Fall 1984): 364.

6. Kashif J. Powell, "The Prettiest Justification for Genocide," in *Winning Orations, 2006* (Interstate Oratorical Association, 2006). Kashif was coached by Betsy McCann.

7. In information science parlance, these are referred to as Boolean terms.

8. Some recent literature specifically refers to Public Speaking Anxiety, or PSA. See, for example, G.D. Bodie, "A Racing Heart, Rattling Knees, and Ruminative Thoughts: Defining, Explaining, and Treating Public Speaking Anxiety." *Communication Education* 59, 1 (January 2010): 70–105.

9. See, for example, J. Borhis and M. Allen, "Meta-analysis of the Relationship between Communication Apprehension and Cognitive Performance." *Communication Education* 41, 1 (January 1992): 68–76.

10. J. A. Daly, A. L. Vangelisti, and D. J. Weber, "Speech Anxiety Affects How People Prepare Speeches: A Protocol Analysis of the Preparation Process of Speakers." *Communication Monographs* 62 (December 1995): 123–134.

11. Researchers generally agree that communication apprehension has three causes: genetics, social learning, and inadequate skills acquisition. See, for example, A. N. Finn, "Public Speaking: What Causes Some to Panic?" *Communication Currents* 4, 4 (2009): 1–2.

12. See, for example, C. R. Sawyer and R. R. Behnke, "Communication Apprehension and Implicit Memories of Public Speaking State Anxiety." *Communication Quarterly* 45, 3 (Summer 1997): 211–222.

13. Adapted from A. Ellis, *A New Guide to Rational Living* (North Hollywood, CA: Wilshire Books, 1977). G. M. Philips listed a different set of beliefs that he believed contributes to reticence. The beliefs are: (1) an exaggerated sense of self-importance. (Reticent people tend to see themselves as more important to others than others see them.) (2) Effective speakers are born, not made. (3) Skillful speaking is manipulative. (4) Speaking is not that important. (5) I can speak whenever I want to; I just choose not to. (6) It is better to be quiet and let people think you are a fool than prove it by talking (they assume they will be evaluated negatively). (7) What is wrong with me requires a (quick) cure. See J. A. Keaten, L. Kelly, and C. Finch, "Effectiveness of the Penn State Program in Changing Beliefs Associated with Reticence." *Communication Education* 49, 2 (April 2000): 134.

14. R. R. Behnke, C. R. Sawyer, and P. E. King, "The Communication of Public Speaking Anxiety." *Communication Education* 36 (April 1987): 138–141.

15. J.M. Honeycutt, C. W.Choi, and J. R. DeBerry, "Communication Apprehension and Imagined Interactions." *Communication Research Reports* 26, 2 (July 2009): 228–236.

16. R. R. Behnke and C. R. Sawyer, "Milestones of Anticipatory Public Speaking Anxiety." *Communication Education* 48, 2 (April 1999): 165.

17. J. S. Hinton and M. W. Kramer, "The Impact of Self-Directed Videotape Feedback on Students' Self-Reported Levels of Communication Competence and Apprehension." *Communication Education* 47, 2 (April 1998): 151–161. Significant increases in competency and decreases in apprehension were found using this method.

18. Research has confirmed that speeches practiced in front of other people tend to be more successful. See, for example, T. E. Smith and A. B. Frymier, "'Get 'Real': Does Practicing Speeches Before an Audience Improve Performance?" *Communication Quarterly* 54 (February 2006): 111–125.

19. See, for example, L. R. Rosenfeld and J. M. Civikly, *With Words Unspoken* (New York: Holt, Rinehart and Winston, 1976), p. 62. Also see S. Chaiken, "Communicator Physical Attractiveness and Persuasion." *Journal of Personality and Social Psychology* 37 (1979): 1387–1397.

20. A study demonstrating this stereotype is R. L. Street Jr. and R. M. Brady, "Speech Rate Acceptance Ranges as a Function of Evaluative Domain, Listener Speech Rate, and Communication Context." *Speech Monographs* 49 (December 1982): 290–308.

21. See, for example, A. Mulac and M. J. Rudd, "Effects of Selected American Regional Dialects upon Regional Audience Members." *Communication Monographs* 44 (1977): 184–195. Some research, however, suggests that nonstandard dialects do not have the detrimental effects on listeners that were once believed. See, for example, F. L. Johnson and R. Buttny, "White Listeners' Responses to 'Sounding Black' and 'Sounding White': The Effect of Message Content on Judgments about Language." *Communication Monographs* 49 (March 1982): 33–39.

22. V. Smith, S. A. Siltanen, and L. A. Hosman, "The Effects of Powerful and Powerless Speech Styles and Speaker Expertise on Impression Formation and Attitude Change." *Communication Research Reports* 15, 1 (Fall 1998): 27–35. In this study, a powerful speech style was defined as one without hedges and hesitations such as "uh" and "anda."

23. Matthew Wozny, correspondence with George Rodman, May 2010, concerning his speech presented at Regis Language Night, Regis High School, New York City, March 19, 2010.

24. Matthew Wozny correspondence with George Rodman, May 2010.

CHAPTER 12

1. See, for example, L. Stern, *The Structures and Strategies of Human Memory* (Homewood, IL: Dorsey Press, 1985). See also C. Turner, "Organizing Information: Principles and Practices." *Library Journal* (June 15, 1987).

2. W. C. Booth, G. C. Colomb, and J. M. Williams, *The Craft of Research* (Chicago: University of Chicago Press, 2003).

3. Neal Stewart, "Untitled," in *Winning Orations, 2006* (Interstate Oratorical Association, 2006). Neal was coached by Craig Brown, Bobby Imbody, and Erica Imbody. The outline and bibliography have been adapted for demonstration purposes.

4. C. Koehler, "Mending the Body by Lending an Ear: The Healing Power of Listening." *Vital Speeches of the Day* (June 15, 1998): 543.

5. Elizabeth Hallum, "Untitled," in *Winning Orations, 1998* (Interstate Oratorical Association, 1998), p. 4. Elizabeth was coached by Clark Olson.

6. K. Graham, "The Press and Its Responsibilities." *Vital Speeches of the Day* 42 (April 15, 1976).

7. Stephanie Hamilton, "Cruise Ship Violence," in *Winning Orations, 2000* (Interstate Oratorical Association, 2000), p. 92. Stephanie was coached by Angela Hatton.

8. Grant Anderson, "Don't Reject My Homoglobin," in *Winning Orations, 2009* (Interstate Oratorical Association, 2009), p. 33. Grant was coached by Leah White.

9. T. S. Eggleston, "The Key Steps to an Effective Presentation," http://www.the-eggman.com/writings/keystep1.html, accessed May 19, 2010.

10. E. Cook, "Making Business Presentations Work," www.businessknowhow.com/manage/presentation101.htm, accessed May 19, 2010.

11. V. Kotelnikov, "Effective Presentations," http://www.1000ventures.com/business_guide/crosscuttings/presentations_main.html, accessed May 19, 2010.

12. Toastmasters International, Inc.'s Communication and Leadership Program at www.toastmasters.org, accessed May 19, 2010.

13. E. Rubinstein, "The Economics of Crime: The Rational Criminal." *Vital Speeches of the Day* (October 15, 1995): 19.

14. Buey Ruet, "Sudan's Forgotten War," in *Winning Orations, 2006* (Interstate Oratorical Association, 2006), p. 49. Buey was coached by David Campbell.

15. Chris Griesinger, "Untitled," in *Winning Orations, 2006* (Interstate Oratorical Association, 2006), p. 37. Chris was coached by Ray Quiel.

16. K. C. Davis, "The Founding Immigrants." *New York Times*, online, (July 3, 2007).

17. Elizabeth Hobbs, "Untitled," in *Winning Orations, 2006* (Interstate Oratorical Association, 2006), p. 45. Elizabeth was coached by Kevin Minch and Kris Stroup.

18. Elizabeth Hobbs, "Untitled."

19. Stephanie Wideman, "Planning for Peak Oil: Legislation and Conservation," in *Winning Orations, 2006* (Interstate Oratorical Association, 2006), p. 7. Stephanie was coached by Brendan Kelly.

20. B. Herbert, "Hooked on Violence." *New York Times*, online, April 26, 2007.

21. D. Sheriff, "Bill Gates—Too Rich." Posted on CRTNET discussion group, April 1, 1998.

22. K. Elsesser, "And the Gender-Neutral Oscar Goes To . . . " *New York Times*, online, March 4, 2010.

23. R. Reagan, "President's Farewell Address to the American People." *Vital Speeches of the Day* (February 1, 1989): 226.

24. Rajiv Khanna, "Distortion of History," in *Winning Orations, 2000* (Interstate Oratorical Association, 2000), p. 46. Rajiv was coached by Alexis Hopkins.

25. R. C. Notebaert, "Leveraging Diversity: Adding Value to the Bottom Line." *Vital Speeches of the Day* (November 1, 1998): 47.

26. Evan McCarley, "On the Importance of Drug Courts," in *Winning Orations, 2009* (Interstate Oratorical Association, 2009), p. 36.

27. Teresa Fishman, director of the Center for Academic Integrity at Clemson University, quoted in T. Gabriel, "Plagiarism Lines Blur

for Students in Digital Age," *New York Times*, online, August 1, 2010.

28. Evan McCarley, "On the Importance of Drug Courts."

CHAPTER 13

1. See, for example, R. S. Wurman, *Information Anxiety 2* (Indianapolis: Que, 2000).

2. Christine Zani, "History of Forensics," informative speech presented at the annual tournament of the American Forensics Association, Spring 2007.

3. See K. D. Fransden and D. A. Clement, "The Functions of Human Communication in Informing: Communicating and Processing Information," in C. C. Arnold and J. W. Bowers, eds., *Handbook of Rhetorical and Communication Theory* (Boston: Allyn and Bacon, 1984), pp. 338–399.

4. Katelyn Wood, "Al-Jazeera," speech presented at the annual tournament of the American Forensics Association, Spring 2007. Katelyn won second place in Informative Speaking with this speech.

5. Kerry J. Konda, "The War at Home," in *Winning Orations, 2006* (Interstate Oratorical Association, 2006), p. 74. Kerry was coached by Kevin Sackreiter.

6. Kathy Levine, "The Dentist's Dirty Little Secret," in *Winning Orations, 2001* (Interstate Oratorical Association, 2001), p. 77. Kathy was coached by Trischa Goodnow.

7. J. T. Cacioppo and R. E. Petty, "Effects of Message Repetition and Position on Cognitive Response, Recall, and Persuasion." *Journal of Personality and Social Psychology* 37 (1979): 97–109.

8. Voter registration project, New York Public Interest Research Group, Brooklyn College chapter, 2004.

9. Ian Parker, "Absolute PowerPoint." *New Yorker* (May 28, 2001): 78.

10. Steven Pinker, a psychology professor at MIT, quoted in Laurence Zuckerman, "Words Go Right to the Brain, but Can They Stir the Heart?" *New York Times* (April 17, 1999), p. 9.

11. Edward Tufte, "PowerPoint is Evil: Power Corrupts. PowerPoint Corrupts Absolutely." *Wired* (September 2003). Available at http://www.wired.com/wired/archive/11.09/ppt2.html.

12. Tad Simons, "Does PowerPoint Make You Stupid?" *Presentations* (March 2004): 25.

13. Edward R. Tufte, *The Cognitive Style of PowerPoint* (Cheshire, CT: Graphics Press, 2003).

14. Parker, "Absolute PowerPoint," p. 86.

15. Don Norman, a design expert cited in Tad Simons, "Does PowerPoint Make You Stupid?"

16. Robert Whittley, personal correspondence with George Rodman, May, 2010.

CHAPTER 14

1. For an explanation of social judgment theory, see E. Griffin, *A First Look at Communication Theory*, 5th ed. (New York: McGraw-Hill, 2003).

2. C. Lasch, "Journalism, Publicity and the Lost Art of Argument." *Gannett Center Journal* (Spring 1990): 1–11.

3. See, for example, James A. Jaska and Michael S. Pritchard, *Communication Ethics: Methods of Analysis*, 2nd ed. (Wadsworth, 1994).

4. Eugene Nemirovskiy, "Mental Health Care: A Slow-Motion Train Wreck," won 1st place at the 2009 Arizona Interstate Oratory Contest, and placed in multiple final rounds in the southwest & in California during 2009.

5. Some research suggests that audiences may perceive a direct strategy as a threat to their freedom to form their own opinions. This perception hampers persuasion. See J. W. Brehm, *A Theory of Psychological Reactance* (New York: Academic Press, 1966).

6. Hope Stallings, "Prosecution Deferred is Justice Denied," *Winning Orations 2009*, Interstate Oratorical Association, 2009. Hope was coached by Randy Richardson and Melanie Conrad.

7. A. Monroe, *Principles and Types of Speech* (Glenview, IL: Scott, Foresman, 1935).

8. This example is adapted from Elizabeth Marshall Thomas, "Canine Liberation." *New York Times* (May 1, 1996), p. A19.

9. For an excellent review of the effects of evidence, see J. C. Reinard, "The Empirical Study of Persuasive Effects of Evidence: The Status after Fifty Years of Research." *Human Communication Research* (Fall 1988): 3–59.

10. There are, of course, other classifications of logical fallacies than those presented here. See, for example, B. Warnick and E. Inch, *Critical Thinking and Communication: The Use of Reason in Argument*, 2nd ed. (New York: Macmillan, 1994), pp. 137–161.

11. J. Sprague and D. Stuart, *The Speaker's Handbook*, 3rd ed. (Fort Worth, TX: Harcourt Brace Jovanovich, 1992), p. 172.

12. L. J. Myers, "The Nature of Pluralism and the African American Case." *Theory into Practice* 20 (1981): 3–4. Cited in Larry A. Samovar and Richard E. Porter, *Communication between Cultures*, 2nd ed. (New York: Wadsworth, 1995), p. 251.

13. Samovar and Porter, *Communication between Cultures*, pp. 154–155.

14. For an example of how one politician failed to adapt to his audience's attitudes, see M. J. Hostetler, "Gov. Al Smith Confronts the Catholic Question: The Rhetorical Legacy of the 1928 Campaign." *Communication Quarterly* 46, 1 (Winter 1998): 12–24. Smith was reluctant to discuss religion, attributed bigotry to anyone who brought it up, and was impatient with the whole issue. He lost the election. Many years later, John F. Kennedy dealt with "the Catholic question" more reasonably and won.

15. A. Mount, speech before the Southern Baptist Convention, in W. A. Linkugel, R. R. Allen, and R. Johannessen, eds., *Contemporary American Speeches*, 3rd ed. (Belmont, CA: Wadsworth, 1973).

16. H. J. Rudolf, "Robert F. Kennedy at Stellenbosch University." *Communication Quarterly* 31 (Summer 1983): 205–211.

17. Preface to Barbara Bush's speech, "Choices and Change," in O. Peterson, ed., *Representative American Speeches, 1990–1991* (New York: H. W. Wilson Co., 1991), p. 162.

18. B. Bush, "Choices and Change," speech presented to the graduating class of Wellesley College in Wellesley, MA, on June 1, 1990. Reprinted in Peterson, *Representative American Speeches, 1990–1991*, p. 166.

19. J. A. DeVito, *The Communication Handbook: A Dictionary* (New York: Harper & Row, 1986), pp. 84–86.

20. George Rodriguez, "How to Develop a Winning Sales Plan," www.powerhomebiz.com/062006/salesplan.htm.; Accessed July 26, 2010.

21. Barbara Sanfilippo, "Winning Sales Strategies of Top Performers," www.selfgrowth.com/articles/Sanfilippo2.html. Accessed May 15, 2010.

22. Katie Donovan, personal correspondence with George Rodman, May, 2010,2007.
23. Katie Donovan, personal correspondence.

APPENDIX

1. M. Granovetter, *Getting a Job: A Study of Contacts and Careers*, 2nd ed. (Chicago: University of Chicago Press, 1995).
2. R. N. Bolles, *What Color Is Your Parachute? A Practical Manual for Job-Hunters and Career-Changers 2009 edition.* (Berkeley, CA: Ten Speed Press, 2009), pp. 27–40.
3. W. Baker, *Achieving Success through Social Capital* (San Francisco: Josey-Bass, 2000), p. 10.
4. G. Crispin and M. Mehler, "Impact of the Internet on Source of Hires," Accessed August 9, 2010 at http://www.careerxroads.com/news/impactoftheinternet.doc.
5. M. S. Granovetter, "The Strength of Weak Ties," *American Journal of Sociology* 78 (1973), pp. 1360–80.
6. The information in this section is based on material in R.B. Adler and J.M. Elmhorst, *Communicating at Work: Principles and Practices for Business and the Professions*, 10th ed. (New York: McGraw-Hill, 2010), pp. 19–23.
7. P. S. Dodds, R. Muhamad, and D. J. Watts., "An Experimental Study of Search in Global Social Networks," *Science, 301* (2003), pp. 827–829.
8. M. Rabin and J. L. Schrag, "First Impressions Matter: A Model of Confirmatory Bias." *The Quarterly Journal of Economics 14* (1999): 37–82.
9. J. Rosen, "The End of Forgetting." *New York Times Magazine* (July 25, 2010), pp. 30–35.
10. M.C. Habib, "Managing Your Identity Online." *Net Connect*, 132 (2007): 2–4. Retrieved July 20, 2010 from Business Source Premier.
11. J. Kang, "Ethical Conflict and Job Satisfaction of Public Relations Practitioners." *Public Relations Review*, 36 (2010): 152–156.
12. S.R. Covey. "Principled Communication." Published: 2001 in *Executive Excellence*. Retrieved July 14, 2010 from Get Synergized: http://www.getsynergized.com/communication_covey.htm.
13. Ibid.
14. S. Farley, D. Timme, J. Hart, "On Coffee Talk and Break-Room Chatter: Perceptions of Women Who Gossip in the Workplace." *Journal of Social Psychology*, 150 (2010): 361–368.
15. J. Zaslow, "Before You Gossip, Ask Yourself This . . ." Published January 6, 2010 in *Moving On*. Retrieved July 10, 2010 from: http://online.wsj.com/article/SB10001424052748704160504574640111681307026.html.
16. Ibid.
17. "New Hires—Stand Out At Work." Published May 2010 in OfficePro. Retrieved July 10, 2010 from http://web.ebscohost.com.libproxy.sbcc.edu:2048/bsi/detail?vid=4&hid=9&sid=079bf30df37c-4ad6-897ec1626aa9bb49%40sessionmgr14&bdata=JnNpdGU9YnNpLWxpdmU%3d#db=buh&AN=50544049
18. Ibid.
19. J.S. Lublin,"The Keys to Unlocking Your Most Successful Career: Five Simple But Crucial Lessons Culled From Many Years of Offering Advice to Workers, Bosses and Job Seekers." Published: July 6, 2010 in the *Wall Street Journal*. Retrieved July 12, 2010 from http://online.wsj.com/article/SB10001424052748704293604575343322516508414.html.
20. Ibid.
21. S. Crescenzo, "What Kind of Communicator Are You?" *Communication World*, 27(2010):10–11.

GLOSSARY

Abstract language Language that lacks specificity or does not refer to observable behavior or other sensory data. See also *Behavioral description*.

Abstraction ladder A range of more- to less-abstract terms describing an event or object.

Action-oriented listening A listening style that is primarily concerned with accomplishing the task at hand.

Actuate To move members of an audience toward a specific behavior.

Ad hominem fallacy Fallacious argument that attacks the integrity of a person to weaken his or her position.

Addition The articulation error that involves adding extra parts to words.

Advising response Helping response in which the receiver offers suggestions about how the speaker should deal with a problem.

Affect blend The combination of two or more expressions, each showing a different emotion.

Affinity The degree to which people like or appreciate one another. As with all relational messages, affinity is usually expressed nonverbally.

All-channel network A communication network pattern in which group members are always together and share all information with one another.

Altruistic lies Deception intended to be unmalicious, or even helpful, to the person to whom it is told.

Ambushing A style in which the receiver listens carefully to gather information to use in an attack on the speaker.

Analogy Extended comparison that can be used as supporting material in a speech.

Analyzing statement A helping style in which the listener offers an interpretation of a speaker's message.

Anchor The position supported by audience members before a persuasion attempt.

Anecdote A brief personal story used to illustrate or support a point in a speech.

Argumentum ad populum fallacy Fallacious reasoning based on the dubious notion that because many people favor an idea, you should, too.

Argumentum ad verecundiam fallacy Fallacious reasoning that tries to support a belief by relying on the testimony of someone who is not an authority on the issue being argued.

Articulation The process of pronouncing all the necessary parts of a word.

Assertive communication A style of communicating that directly expresses the sender's needs, thoughts, or feelings, delivered in a way that does not attack the receiver's dignity.

Asynchronous communication Communication that occurs when there's a time gap between when a message is sent and when it is received.

Attending The process of focusing on certain stimuli from the environment.

Attitude Predisposition to respond to an idea, person, or thing favorably or unfavorably.

Attribution The process of attaching meaning.

Audience analysis A consideration of characteristics including the type, goals, demographics, beliefs, attitudes, and values of listeners.

Audience involvement Level of commitment and attention that listeners devote to a speech.

Audience participation Listener activity during speech; technique to increase audience involvement.

Authoritarian leadership style A leadership style in which the designated leader uses legitimate, coercive, and reward power to dictate the group's actions.

Avoidance spiral A communication spiral in which the parties slowly reduce their dependence on one another, withdraw, and become less invested in the relationship.

Bar chart Visual aid that compares two or more values by showing them as elongated horizontal rectangles.

Basic speech structure The division of a speech into introduction, body, and conclusion.

Behavioral description An account that refers only to observable phenomena.

Behavioral interview Session that explores specifics of the applicant's past performance as it relates to the job at hand.

Belief An underlying conviction about the truth of an idea, often based on cultural training.

Brainstorming A method for creatively generating ideas in groups by minimizing criticism and encouraging a large quantity of ideas without regard to their workability or ownership by individual members.

Breadth (of self-disclosure) The range of topics about which an individual discloses. See also *Depth*.

Breakout groups A strategy used when the number of members is too large for effective discussion. Subgroups simultaneously address an issue and then report back to the group at large.

Cause-effect pattern Organizing plan for a speech that demonstrates how one or more events result in another event or events.

Certainty Messages that dogmatically imply that the speaker's position is correct and that the other person's ideas are not worth considering. Likely to generate a defensive response.

Chain network A communication network in which information passes sequentially from one member to another.

Channel Medium through which a message passes from sender to receiver.

Chronemics The study of how humans use and structure time.

Citation Brief statement of supporting material in a speech.

Climax pattern Organizing plan for a speech that builds ideas to the point of maximum interest or tension.

Closed question Interview question that can be answered in a few words.

Coculture The perception of membership in a group that is part of an encompassing culture.

Coercive power The power to influence others by the threat or imposition of unpleasant consequences.

Cohesiveness The totality of forces that causes members to feel themselves part of a group and makes them want to remain in that group.

Collectivistic culture A culture where members focus on the welfare of the group as a whole, rather than a concern by individuals for their own success. See also *Individualistic orientation*.

Collectivistic orientation A cultural orientation focusing on loyalties and obligations to the group, which may include the family, the community, the organization, and work teams.

Column chart Visual aid that compares two or more values by showing them as elongated vertical rectangles.

Comforting A response style in which a listener reassures, supports, or distracts the person seeking help.

Communication The process of creating meaning through symbolic interaction.

Communication climate The emotional tone of a relationship as it is expressed in the messages that the partners send and receive.

Communication competence Ability to maintain a relationship on terms acceptable to all parties.

Compromise An approach to conflict resolution in which both parties attain at least part of what they seek through self-sacrifice.

Conclusion (of a speech) The final structural unit of a speech, in which the main points are reviewed and final remarks are made to motivate the audience to act or help listeners remember key ideas.

Confirming responses A message that expresses respect and valuing of the other person.

Conflict An expressed struggle between at least two interdependent parties who perceive incompatible goals, scarce rewards, and interference from the other party in achieving their goals.

Conflict stage A stage in problem-solving groups when members openly defend their positions and question those of others.

Consensus Agreement between group members about a decision.

Content message A message that communicates information about the subject being discussed. See also *Relational message*.

Content-oriented listening A listening style that focuses on the content of a message.

Contextually interpersonal communication Any communication that occurs between two individuals. See also *Qualitatively interpersonal communication*.

Control The social need to influence others.

Controlling communication Messages in which the sender tries to impose some sort of outcome on the receiver, usually resulting in a defensive reaction.

Convergence Accommodating one's speaking style to another person, who usually is desirable or has higher status.

Convincing A speech goal that aims at changing audience members' beliefs, values, or attitudes.

Coordination Interaction in which participants interact smoothly, with a high degree of satisfaction but without necessarily understanding one another well.

Counterfeit question A question that disguises the speaker's true motives, which do not include a genuine desire to understand the other person.

Credibility The believability of a speaker or other source of information.

Critical listening Listening in which the goal is to judge the quality or accuracy of the speaker's remarks.

Culture The language, values, beliefs, traditions, and customs people share and learn.

Database A computerized collection of information that can be searched in a variety of ways to locate information that the user is seeking.

Debilitative communication apprehension Intense level of anxiety about speaking before an audience, resulting in poor performance.

Decoding The process in which a receiver attaches meaning to a message.

Defensive listening A response style in which the receiver perceives a speaker's comments as an attack.

Deletion Articulation error that involves leaving off parts of words.

Democratic leadership style A style in which the nominal leader invites the group's participation in decision making.

Demographics Audience characteristics that can be analyzed statistically, such as age, gender, education, and group membership.

Depth (of self-disclosure) The level of personal information a person reveals on a particular topic. See also *Breadth*.

Description In terms of communication climate, a statement in which the speaker describes his/her position. See also *Evaluative communication*.

Developmental models (of relational maintenance) These models propose that the nature of communication is different in various stages of interpersonal relationships.

Diagram A line drawing that shows the most important components of an object.

Dialectical model (of relational maintenance) A model claiming that, throughout their lifetime, people in virtually all interpersonal relationships must deal with equally important, simultaneous, and opposing forces such as connection and autonomy, predictability and novelty, and openness versus privacy.

Dialectical tensions Inherent conflicts that arise when two opposing or incompatible forces exist simultaneously.

Direct aggression An expression of the sender's thoughts or feelings or both that attacks the position and dignity of the receiver.

Direct persuasion Persuasion that does not try to hide or disguise the speaker's persuasive purpose.

Direct question Interview question that makes a straightforward request for information. See also *Indirect question*.

Disconfirming response A message that expresses a lack of caring or respect for another person.

Disfluency A nonlinguistic verbalization. For example, *um, er, ah*.

Disinhibition The tendency to transmit messages without considering their consequences. See also *Flaming*.

Divergence A linguistic strategy in which speakers emphasize differences between their communicative style and others' in order to create distance.

Dyad A two-person unit.

Dyadic communication Two-person communication.

Dysfunctional roles Individual roles played by group members that inhibit the group's effective operation.

Either-or fallacy Fallacious reasoning that sets up false alternatives, suggesting that if the inferior one must be rejected, then the other must be accepted.

Emblems Deliberate nonverbal behaviors with precise meanings, known to virtually all members of a cultural group.

Emergence stage A stage in problem solving when the group moves from conflict toward a single solution.

Emotional evidence Evidence that arouses emotional reactions in an audience.

Emotive language Language that conveys the sender's attitude rather than simply offering an objective description.

Empathy The ability to project oneself into another person's point of view, so as to experience the other's thoughts and feelings.

Encoding The process of putting thoughts into symbols, most commonly words.

Environment Both the physical setting in which communication occurs and the personal perspectives of the parties involved.

Equality When communicators show that they believe others have just as much worth as human beings.

Equivocal language Language with more than one likely interpretation.

Equivocal words Words that have more than one dictionary definition.

Equivocation A vague statement that can be interpreted in more than one way.

Escalatory spiral A reciprocal pattern of communication in which messages, either confirming or disconfirming, between two or more communicators reinforce one another.

Ethical persuasion Persuasion in an audience's best interest that does not depend on false or misleading information to induce change in that audience.

Ethnocentrism The attitude that one's own culture is superior to others'. See also *Disinhibition*.

Euphemism A pleasant-sounding term used in place of a more direct but less pleasant one.

Evaluative communication Messages in which the sender judges the receiver in some way, usually resulting in a defensive response. See also *"You" language*.

Evidence Material used to prove a point, such as testimony, statistics, and examples.

Example A specific case that is used to demonstrate a general idea.

Expert power The ability to influence others by virtue of one's perceived expertise on the subject in question. See also *Information power*.

Explanations Speeches or presentations that clarify ideas and concepts already known but not understood by an audience.

Extemporaneous speech A speech that is planned in advance but presented in a direct, conversational manner.

Face The socially approved identity that a communicator tries to present.

Facework Verbal and nonverbal behavior designed to create and maintain a communicator's face and the face of others.

Facilitative communication apprehension A moderate level of anxiety about speaking before an audience that helps improve the speaker's performance.

Factual question Interview question that investigates matters of fact. See also *Opinion question*.

Factual statement A statement that can be verified as being true or false. See also *Inferential statement; Opinion statement*.

Fallacy An error in logic.

Fallacy of approval The irrational belief that it is vital to win the approval of virtually every person a communicator deals with.

Fallacy of catastrophic failure The irrational belief that the worst possible outcome will probably occur.

Fallacy of overgeneralization Irrational beliefs in which (1) conclusions (usually negative) are based on limited evidence or (2) communicators exaggerate their shortcomings.

Fallacy of perfection The irrational belief that a worthwhile communicator should be able to handle every situation with complete confidence and skill.

Feedback The discernible response of a receiver to a sender's message.

Flaming Sending angry and/or insulting e-mails, text messages, and website postings.

Focus group Used in market research by sponsoring organizations to survey potential users or the public at large regarding a new product or idea.

Force field analysis A method of problem analysis that identifies the forces contributing to resolution of the problem and the forces that inhibit its resolution.

Formal outline A consistent format and set of symbols used to identify the structure of ideas.

Formal role A role assigned to a person by group members or an organization, usually to establish order. See also *Informal roles*.

Forum A discussion format in which audience members are invited to add their comments to those of the official discussants.

Gatekeepers Producers of mass messages, who determine what messages will be delivered to consumers, how those messages will be constructed, and when they will be delivered.

General purpose One of three basic ways a speaker seeks to affect an audience: to entertain, inform, or persuade.

Gibb categories Six sets of contrasting styles of verbal and nonverbal behavior. Each set describes a communication style that is likely to arouse defensiveness and a contrasting style that is likely to prevent or reduce it. Developed by Jack Gibb.

Group A small collection of people whose members interact with each other, usually face to face, over time in order to reach goals.

Group goals Goals that a group collectively seeks to accomplish. See also *Individual goals*.

Groupthink A group's collective striving for unanimity that discourages realistic appraisals of alternatives to its chosen decision.

Haptics The study of touch.

Hearing The process wherein sound waves strike the eardrum and cause vibrations that are transmitted to the brain.

Hidden agendas Individual goals that group members are unwilling to reveal.

High-context culture A culture that avoids direct use of language to express information, especially about relational matters. Instead, members of the culture rely on the context of a message to convey meaning. See also *Low-context culture*.

Hypothetical example Example that asks an audience to imagine an object or event.

Hypothetical question Seeks a response by proposing a "what-if" situation.

"I" language Language that describes the speaker's position without evaluating others. Synonymous with *Descriptive communication*.

Identity management Strategies used by communicators to influence the way others view them.

Illustrators Nonverbal behaviors that accompany and support verbal messages.

Immediacy The degree of interest and attraction we feel toward and communicate to others. As with all relational messages, immediacy is usually expressed nonverbally.

Impromptu speech A speech given "off the top of one's head," without preparation.

Indirect communication Hinting at a message instead of expressing thoughts and feelings directly. See also *Assertive communication; Passive aggression*.

Indirect persuasion Persuasion that disguises or deemphasizes the speaker's persuasive goal.

Indirect question Interview question that does not directly request the information being sought. See also *Direct question*.

Individual goals Individual motives for joining a group. See also *Group goals*.

Individualistic culture A culture where members focus on the value and welfare of individual members, as opposed to a concern for the group as a whole.

Individualistic orientation A cultural orientation focusing on the value and welfare of individual members, as opposed to a concern for the group as a whole. See also *Collectivistic orientation*.

Inferential statement Conclusion arrived at from an interpretation of evidence. See also *Factual statement*.

Informal roles Roles usually not explicitly recognized by a group that describe functions of group members, rather than their positions. Sometimes called "functional roles." See also *Formal role*.

Information anxiety Psychological stress that occurs when dealing with too much information.

Information hunger Audience desire, created by a speaker, to learn information.

Information overload Decline in efficiency that occurs when the rate of complexity of material is too great to manage.

Information power The ability to influence others by virtue of the otherwise obscure information one possesses. See also *Expert power*.

Information underload Decline in efficiency that occurs when there is a shortage of the information that is necessary to operate effectively.

Informational interview Interview intended to collect facts and opinions from the respondent.

Informational listening Listening in which the goal is to receive accurately the same thoughts the speaker is trying to convey.

Informative purpose statement A complete statement of the objective of a speech, worded to stress audience knowledge and/or ability.

In-groups Groups with which we identify. See also *Out-groups*.

Insensitive listening Failure to recognize the thoughts or feelings that are not directly expressed by a speaker, instead accepting the speaker's words at face value.

Instructions Remarks that teach something to an audience in a logical, step-by-step manner.

Insulated listening A style in which the receiver ignores undesirable information.

Intergroup communication The interaction between members of different cocultures.

Interpersonal communication Communication in which the parties consider one another as unique individuals rather than as objects. It is characterized by minimal use of stereotyped labels; unique, idiosyncratic social rules; and a high degree of information exchange.

Interpretation The perceptual process of attaching meaning to stimuli that have previously been selected and organized.

Intimacy A state of closeness between two (or sometimes more) people. Intimacy can be manifested in several ways: physically, intellectually, emotionally, and via shared activities.

Intimate distance One of Hall's four distance zones, ranging from skin contact to eighteen inches.

Intrapersonal communication Communication that occurs within a single person.

Introduction (of a speech) The first structural unit of a speech, in which the speaker captures the audience's attention and previews the main points to be covered.

Irrational thinking Beliefs that have no basis in reality or logic; one source of debilitative communication apprehension.

Jargon The specialized vocabulary that is used as a kind of shorthand by people with common backgrounds and experience.

Johari Window A model that describes the relationship between self-disclosure and self-awareness.

Judging response A reaction in which the receiver evaluates the sender's message either favorably or unfavorably.

Kinesics The study of body movement, gesture, and posture.

Knowledge Understanding acquired by making sense of the raw material of information.

Laissez-faire leadership style A style in which the designated leader gives up his or her formal role, transforming the group into a loose collection of individuals.

Language A collection of symbols, governed by rules and used to convey messages between individuals.

Latitude of acceptance In social judgment theory, statements that a receiver would not reject.

Latitude of noncommitment In social judgment theory, statements that a receiver would not care strongly about one way or another.

Latitude of rejection In social judgment theory, statements that a receiver could not possibly accept.

Leadership grid A two-dimensional model that identifies leadership styles as a combination of concern for people and the task at hand.

Leading question A question in which the interviewer—either directly or indirectly—signals the desired answer.

Legitimate power The ability to influence a group owing to one's position in a group. See also *Nominal leader*.

Line chart Visual aid consisting of a grid that maps out the direction of a trend by plotting a series of points.

Linear communication model A characterization of communication as a one-way event in which a message flows from sender to receiver.

Linguistic intergroup bias The tendency to label people and behaviors in terms that reflect their in-group or out-group status.

Linguistic relativism A moderate form of linguistic determinism that argues that language exerts a strong influence on the perceptions of the people who speak it.

Listening Process wherein the brain reconstructs electrochemical impulses generated by hearing into representations of the original sound and gives them meaning.

Listening fidelity The degree of congruence between what a listener understands and what the message sender was attempting to communicate.

Lose–lose problem solving An approach to conflict resolution in which neither party achieves its goals.

Low-context culture A culture that relies heavily on language to make messages, especially of a relational nature, explicit. See also *High-context culture*.

Manipulators Movements in which one part of the body grooms, massages, rubs, holds, fidgets, pinches, picks, or otherwise manipulates another part.

Manuscript speech A speech that is read word for word from a prepared text.

Mass communication The transmission of messages to large, usually widespread audiences via broadcast means (such as radio and television), print (such as newspapers, magazines, and books), multimedia (such as CD-ROM, DVD, and the World Wide Web), and other forms of media such as recordings and movies.

Mediated communication Communication sent via a medium other than face-to-face interaction, e.g., telephone, e-mail, instant messaging. Can be both mass and personal.

Memorized speech A speech learned and delivered by rote without a written text.

Message A sender's planned and unplanned words and nonverbal behaviors.

Metacommunication Messages (usually relational) that refer to other messages; communication about communication.

Microexpressions Momentary expressions that reflect an emotional state.

Mindful listening Active, high-level information processing.

Mindless listening Passive, low-level information processing.

Model (in speeches and presentations) Replica of an object being discussed. Usually used when it would be difficult or impossible to use the actual object.

Monochronic The use of time that emphasizes punctuality, schedules, and completing one task at a time.

Motivated sequence A five-step plan used in persuasive speaking; also known as "Monroe's Motivated Sequence."

Narration Presentation of speech supporting material as a story with a beginning, middle, and end.

Narrative The stories people create and use to make sense of their personal worlds.

Networking The strategic process of deliberately meeting people and maintaining contacts that result in information, advice, and leads that enhance one's career.

Neutral question A question that gives the interviewee a chance to respond without any influence from the interviewer.

Neutrality A defense-arousing behavior in which the sender expresses indifference toward a receiver.

Noise External, physiological, and psychological distractions that interfere with the accurate transmission and reception of a message.

Nominal group technique Method for including the ideas of all group members in a problem-solving session.

Nominal leader The person who is identified by title as the leader of a group.

Nonassertion The inability or unwillingness to express one's thoughts or feelings when necessary.

Nonverbal communication Messages expressed by other than linguistic means.

Norms Shared values, beliefs, behaviors, and procedures that govern a group's operation.

Number chart Visual aid that lists numbers in tabular form in order to clarify information.

Open question Interview question that requires the interviewee to respond in detail. See also *Closed question*.

Opinion question Interview question seeking the interviewee's opinion. See also *Factual question*.

Opinion statement A statement based on the speaker's beliefs. See also *Factual statement*.

Organization The perceptual process of organizing stimuli into patterns.

Orientation stage A stage in problem-solving groups when members become familiar with one another's position and tentatively volunteer their own.

Out-groups Groups of people that we view as different from us. See also *In-groups*.

Panel discussion A discussion format in which participants consider a topic more or less conversationally, without formal procedural rules. Panel discussions may be facilitated by a moderator.

Paralanguage Nonlinguistic means of vocal expression: rate, pitch, tone, and so on.

Paraphrasing Feedback in which the receiver rewords the speaker's thoughts and feelings. Can be used to verify understanding, demonstrate empathy, and help others solve their problems.

Parliamentary procedure A problem-solving method in which specific rules govern the way issues may be discussed and decisions made.

Participative decision making Development of solutions with input by the people who will be affected.

Passive aggression An indirect expression of aggression, delivered in a way that allows the sender to maintain a facade of kindness.

People-oriented listening A listening style that is primarily concerned with creating and maintaining positive relationships.

Perceived self The person we believe ourselves to be in moments of candor. It may be identical with or different from the presenting and ideal selves.

Perception checking A three-part method for verifying the accuracy of interpretations, including a description of the sense data, two possible interpretations, and a request for confirmation of the interpretations.

Personal distance One of Hall's four distance zones, ranging from eighteen inches to four feet.

Persuasion The act of motivating a listener, through communication, to change a particular belief, attitude, value, or behavior.

Phonological rules Linguistic rules governing how sounds are combined to form words.

Pie chart A visual aid that divides a circle into wedges, representing percentages of the whole.

Pitch The highness or lowness of one's voice.

Polychronic The use of time that emphasizes flexible schedules in which multiple tasks are pursued at the same time.

Post hoc fallacy Fallacious reasoning that mistakenly assumes that one event causes another because they occur sequentially.

Power The ability to influence others' thoughts and/or actions.

Power distance The degree to which members are willing to accept a difference in power and status between members of a group.

Pragmatic rules Rules that govern how people use language in everyday interaction.

Prejudice An unfairly biased and intolerant attitude toward others who belong to an out-group.

Presenting self The image a person presents to others. It may be identical to or different from the perceived and ideal selves. See also Face.

Probe An interjection, silence, or brief remark designed to open up or direct an interviewee.

Problem census Used to equalize participation in groups when the goal is to identify important issues or problems. Members first put ideas on cards, which are then compiled by a leader to generate a comprehensive statement of the issue or problem.

Problem orientation A supportive style of communication in which the communicators focus on working together to solve their problems instead of trying to impose their own solutions on one another.

Problem-solution pattern Organizing pattern for a speech that describes an unsatisfactory state of affairs and then proposes a plan to remedy the problem.

Procedural norms Norms that describe rules for the group's operation.

Prompting Using silence and brief statements of encouragement to draw out a speaker.

Proposition of fact Claim bearing on issue in which there are two or more sides of conflicting factual evidence.

Proposition of policy Claim bearing on issue that involves adopting or rejecting a specific course of action.

Proposition of value Claim bearing on issue involving the worth of some idea, person, or object.

Provisionalism A supportive style of communication in which the sender expresses a willingness to consider the other person's position.

Proxemics The study of how people and animals use space.

Pseudolistening An imitation of true listening in which the receiver's mind is elsewhere.

Public communication Communication that occurs when a group becomes too large for all members to contribute. It is characterized by an unequal amount of speaking and by limited verbal feedback.

Public distance One of Hall's four distance zones, extending outward from twelve feet.

Purpose statement A complete sentence that describes precisely what a speaker wants to accomplish.

Qualitatively interpersonal communication Interaction in which people treat one another as unique individuals, regardless of the context in which the interaction occurs or the number of people involved. Contrasted with impersonal communication. See also Contextually interpersonal communication.

Questioning A style of helping in which the receiver seeks additional information from the sender. Some questioning responses are really disguised advice.

Rate The speed at which a speaker utters words.

Receiver One who notices and attends to a message.

Reductio ad absurdum fallacy Fallacious reasoning that unfairly attacks an argument by extending it to such extreme lengths that it looks ridiculous.

Referent power The ability to influence others by virtue of the degree to which one is liked or respected.

Reflected appraisal The influence of others on one's self-concept.

Reflecting Listening that helps the person speaking hear and think about the words just spoken.

Reinforcement stage A stage in problem-solving groups when members endorse the decision they have made.

Relational message A message that expresses the social relationship between two or more individuals.

Relative words Words that gain their meaning by comparison.

Remembering The act of recalling previously introduced information. Recall drops off in two phases: short- and long-term.

Residual message The part of a message a receiver can recall after short- and long-term memory loss.

Respect The degree to which we hold others in esteem.

Responding Providing observable feedback to another person's behavior or speech.

Reward power The ability to influence others by the granting or promising of desirable consequences.

Richness A term used to describe the abundance of nonverbal cues that add clarity to a verbal message.

Roles The patterns of behavior expected of group members.

Rule Explicit, officially stated guideline that governs group functions and member behavior.

Salience How much weight we attach to a particular person or phenomenon.

Sapir-Whorf hypothesis Theory that the structure of a language shapes the worldview of its users.

Selection The perceptual act of attending to some stimuli in the environment and ignoring others.

Selection interview Interview in which a candidate is evaluated for a new position—either initial employment, promotion, or reassignment.

Selective listening A listening style in which the receiver responds only to messages that interest him or her.

Self-concept The relatively stable set of perceptions each individual holds of himself or herself.

Self-disclosure The process of deliberately revealing information about oneself that is significant and that would not normally be known by others.

Self-esteem The part of the self-concept that involves evaluations of self-worth.

Self-fulfilling prophecy A prediction or expectation of an event that makes the outcome more likely to occur than would otherwise have been the case.

Self-serving bias The tendency to interpret and explain information in a way that casts the perceiver in the most favorable manner.

Semantic rules Rules that govern the meaning of language as opposed to its structure. See also *Syntactic rules*.

Sender The originator of a message.

Sex role The social orientation that governs behavior, in contrast to a person's biological gender.

Significant other A person whose opinion is important enough to affect one's self-concept strongly.

Signpost A phrase that emphasizes the importance of upcoming material in a speech.

Sincere question A question posed with the genuine desire to learn from another person. See also *Counterfeit question*.

Situational leadership A theory that argues that the most effective leadership style varies according to leader-member relations, the nominal leader's power, and the task structure.

Slang Language used by a group of people whose members belong to a similar coculture or other group.

Slurring The articulation error that involves overlapping the end of one word with the beginning of the next.

Small group communication Communication within a group of a size such that every member can participate actively with the other members.

Social distance One of Hall's distance zones, ranging from four to twelve feet.

Social judgment theory Explanation of attitude change that posits that opinions will change only in small increments and only when the target opinions lie within the receiver's latitudes of acceptance and noncommitment.

Social media Digital communication channels used primarily for personal reasons that allow for mediated interactions between one person and an infinite number of receivers for the purpose of information exchange and social interaction.

Social norms Group norms that govern the way members relate to one another. See also *Task norms*.

Social orientation Individual goals that involve affiliation, influence, and esteem of others.

Social penetration model A model describing how intimacy can be achieved via the breadth and depth of self-disclosure.

Social roles Emotional roles concerned with maintaining smooth personal relationships among group members. Also termed *maintenance functions*. See also *Task roles*.

Sociogram Graphic representation of the interaction patterns in a group.

Space pattern Organizing plan in a speech that arranges points according to their physical location.

Specific purpose The precise effect that the speaker wants to have on an audience. Expressed in the form of a purpose statement.

Spiral Reciprocal communication pattern in which each person's message reinforces the other's.

Spontaneity Supportive communication behavior in which the sender expresses a message without any attempt to manipulate the receiver.

Stage hogging A listening style in which the receiver is more concerned with making his or her own point than with understanding the speaker.

Statistic Numbers arranged or organized to show how a fact or principle is true for a large percentage of cases.

Stereotyping The perceptual process of applying exaggerated beliefs associated with a categorizing system.

Strategy A defense-arousing style of communication in which the sender tries to manipulate or trick a receiver; also, the general term for any type of plan, as in the plan for a persuasive speech.

Substitution The articulation error that involves replacing part of a word with an incorrect sound.

Superiority A type of communication that suggests one person is better than the other.

Supportive listening The reception approach to use when others seek help for personal dilemmas.

Survey research Information gathering in which the responses of a sample of a population are collected to disclose information about the larger group.

Symbol An arbitrary sign used to represent a thing, person, idea, event, or relationship in ways that make communication possible.

Sympathy Compassion for another's situation. See also *Empathy*.

Symposium A discussion format in which participants divide the topic in a manner that allows each member to deliver in-depth information without interruption.

Synchronous communication Communication that occurs in real time.

Syntactic rules Rules that govern the ways in which symbols can be arranged as opposed to the meanings of those symbols. See also *Semantic rules*.

Target audience That part of an audience that must be influenced in order to achieve a persuasive goal.

Task norms Group norms that govern the way members handle the job at hand. See also *Social norms*.

Task orientation A cultural orientation that focuses heavily on getting the job done.

Task roles Roles group members take on in order to help solve a problem. See also *Social roles*.

Territory Fixed space that an individual assumes some right to occupy.

Testimony Supporting material that proves or illustrates a point by citing an authoritative source.

Thesis statement A complete sentence describing the central idea of a speech.

Time pattern Organizing plan for a speech based on chronology.

Time-oriented listening A listening style that is primarily concerned with minimizing the time necessary to accomplish the task at hand.

Topic pattern Organizing plan for a speech that arranges points according to logical types or categories.

Trait theories of leadership The belief that it is possible to identify leaders by personal traits, such as intelligence, appearance, or sociability.

Transactional communication model A characterization of communication as the simultaneous sending and receiving of messages in an ongoing, irreversible process.

Transition Phrase that connects ideas in a speech by showing how one relates to the other.

Uncertainty avoidance The cultural tendency to seek stability and honor tradition instead of welcoming risk, uncertainty, and change.

Understanding The act of interpreting a message by following syntactic, semantic, and pragmatic rules.

Value A deeply rooted belief about a concept's inherent worth.

Virtual groups People who interact with one another via mediated channels, without meeting face-to-face.

Visual aids Graphic devices used in a speech to illustrate or support ideas.

Visualization Technique for behavior rehearsal (for example, for a speech) that involves imagining the successful completion of the task.

Vocal citation A simple, concise, spoken statement of the source of your evidence.

Web 2.0 A term used to describe how the Internet has evolved from a one-way medium into a "masspersonal" phenomenon.

Wheel network A communication network in which a gatekeeper regulates the flow of information from all other members.

Win–lose problem solving An approach to conflict resolution in which one party reaches its goal at the expense of the other.

Win–win problem solving An approach to conflict resolution in which the parties work together to satisfy all their goals.

Word chart Visual aid that lists words or terms in tabular form in order to clarify information.

Working outline Constantly changing organizational aid used in planning a speech.

"You" language Language that judges another person, increasing the likelihood of a defensive reaction. See also *Evaluative communication*.

CREDITS

INDEX

ting $8, and it was only the first day. PLUS he was horning in on our business.

"What do we do next?" asked Kyle.

"I could pound Neil," said Chuckie helpfully. He cracked his knuckles. "It would be so much fun, I wouldn't even charge. It would be on the house."

"Chuckie! You can't go around pounding people," Lucy said.

"Why not?" he asked.

"He's a grownup, for one thing," I said.

"It's against the law," said Kyle. "You could be arrested."

"Plus, it isn't nice. There are other ways to solve problems, you know," said Lucy.

"Maybe," said Chuckie. "But pounding has always worked for me. Anyway, what other ways are there?"

"Interrogation. Surveillance. Plans," I said. "To name a few."

"See, Chuckie, when it comes to plans, Willie's the expert," Kyle said. "He's probably already thought of a way to get Neil

to leave the cemetery alone. Right, Willie?"

"Uh . . . right!" Actually, I didn't have a plan. I had a headache. But maybe my head hurt because there was a plan in there. Any minute the plan would pop out. Then my headache would be gone. And La Malle would be history. And we would have solved the world's greatest case.

And best of all? *I'd* be the hero. Not Chuckie, the Wizard of Worm.

"So, Willie," said Chuckie. "How's the old plan coming along?"

"Great!" I said. "I have a brilliant idea that will make Mr. Briefcase turn in his blueprints." I didn't, of course. But my head sure hurt.

"What *is* it?" Chuckie asked.

"Well, I can't say right now," I said. "Because . . . it's complicated. It has a lot of parts."

"A lot of parts, huh?" said Chuckie. "Well, time is money. The more parts to your plan, the better for me. *Ka-ching!*"

At the cemetery, Big Voice was mowing the lawn. He turned off the mower and grinned at us.

"HELLO, WILLIE! I SEE YOU BROUGHT THE WHOLE TEAM. EVEN SCARFACE."

How did Big Voice know my name? How did he know Scarface? How did he know we were a team?

"LORAINE WILL LIKE IT THAT HER PARROT CAME TO VISIT. LORAINE'S A

NICE LADY," Big Voice yelled. He rolled the lawnmower into the shed and locked it up.

"YOU HAVE A LOT OF WORK TO DO, SO YOU PROBABLY WANT TO BE ALONE. I HAVE TO LEAVE NOW. BUT I'LL BE BACK."

How did Big Voice know we had work to do? What did he mean, he'd be back?

When we got to Loraine's grave, Scarface flew to her tombstone. "*Loraaaaine!*" she called. She started stroking the tombstone with her beak. "*Love ya, baby. Love ya, baby. Mwiiip!*"

Mwiiip is Scarface's kissing sound.

"Wow," I said. "Do you think Scarface *knows* this is Loraine's place?"

"*Mwiiip mwiiip mwiiip,*" smacked Scarface.

"It sure seems like it," Lucy said. "I wonder how she knows Loraine's . . . you know, under there?"

I shrugged. "Beats me."

Kyle crouched down and squinted at the tombstone. "Look what the stone says. 'Loraine Lamonde, *beloved* aunt of Neil.' What a joke. Neil's a dirty rat."

"*Neil's a dirty rat. Dirty rat dirty rat,*" said Scarface, returning to her perch on Kyle's shoulder.

"So, Willie," said Chuckie, grinning. "Don't you think you should tell us the plan now? That is, if you really have one."

"Yeah, Willie," said Lucy. "Tell us your plan."

"Okaaaaay," I said. Man, I really had to think fast. I *knew* the plan was in my head somewhere. I squeezed my head and thought. But it sure was hard to think with eight eyeballs staring at me.

Suddenly, Scarface swooped off Kyle's shoulder and flew into the hole in the tree. Kyle ran up to the tree and looked inside. "Hey, Scarface, come out of there."

"*Hellooooo,*" said Scarface in Loraine's exact voice.

"Cool! It's like the tree is talking," Chuckie said.

Yowzer! Suddenly, my head started hurting like crazy. Like it was full of something. Like something was going to pop.

"Don't worry, Kyle. Scarface will fly out when she's ready," said Lucy. "Maybe she likes it in there."

"*Loraaaaine,*" said Scarface in Loraine's exact voice.

My head started hurting even more.

"I guess," said Kyle.

"*Neil's a dirty rat. Dirty rat dirty rat,*" said Scarface in Loraine's exact voice . . . only spookier because of the tree echo. It sure sounded funny. Almost like a gho—

POP!

Ka-chinG!

I stood on a tree stump. "I'm ready to reveal The Plan," I announced.

"Take your time," said Chuckie. "Tick tick tick . . . *Ka-ching!*"

"*Ka-ching!*" repeated Scarface in Loraine's ghostly voice.

"Okay. Here's the first part. We write a letter to Neil and tell him to come to the cemetery. We sign it 'Loraine,'" I said.

"But Loraine's dead," said Kyle. "And maybe Neil doesn't believe in ghosts."

"*Woooo-ooooo,*" said Scarface from inside the hole.

Lucy said, "I think a letter's a great idea. Everybody kind of believes in ghosts . . . even when they say they don't. We just have to convince Neil that it's really from Loraine."

"We need some kind of evidence," I said, tapping my chin. "Something that proves it's from Loraine. But what?"

Kyle waved his hand. "Information *only Loraine would know!* You know her detective files, the ones she left in the attic? There's secret information about all kinds of people in there—I bet there's scoop on Neil!"

"Okay," I said. "Now we get to Part Two. That's the part where we smear something really stinky on the envelope. To make it seem like it's been handled by a dead body."

"Nice touch," said Chuckie. "What are you thinking of? Dog doo? Gunk from a gym locker? Stuff from the back of a garbage truck?"

"Better," I said. "We can scrape up something from under my bed."

"I told you Willie was brilliant," Lucy said to Chuckie.

"Now for Part Three. Just before Neil comes to the cemetery, we put Scarface in the tree hole."

"Why?" said Kyle.

"*Why?*" repeated Scarface in Loraine's exact voice, only echo-y.

"I get it!" said Lucy. "Because when Scarface is in there, she sounds like the ghost of Loraine. It'll scare the pants off Neil."

"I thought you were a dork," Chuckie said to me. "But you're almost as sneaky as me."

"Thank you," I said. "I guess."

We went back to headquarters. Then we opened Loraine's secret file. Aha! There it was. A folder for Neil Lamonde.

We read it.

"Wow. Loraine called Neil 'Jelly Belly' when he was a kid. He must have hated it. Let's use that!" said Lucy.

"And get this!" I said. "Loraine wrote, 'Jelly Belly cheats at Monopoly. He steals money from the bank. Anybody who cheats at a game will cheat in life. I'm going to keep an eye on my nephew.'"

"So he was kind of a Junior Slimeball, huh?" Kyle said. "And a klutz, too. Look." He pointed to a bunch of report cards. "He got F's in gym."

Lucy shook her head. "How can you even *get* an F in gym?"

"And he was a liar, too," I said, pointing to one of Loraine's entries. "It says here that he broke Loraine's lamp and then he said Scarface did it."

"Once a scumbag, always a scumbag, I guess," said Lucy.

"Maybe he wasn't totally rotten," said Chuckie. "Maybe he was trying to be nice. Maybe he was lonely."

"Yeah, right," said Lucy.

"Fat chance," I said, laughing. That Chuckie. Sometimes he could really be funny. But when I looked at him, he wasn't laughing. Huh?

"Maybe there's a copy of Loraine's will in the files somewhere. Maybe Neil's mentioned in it as an heir. Let's take a look under 'W' for 'Will,'" Lucy said.

There it was, under "W." Loraine's "Last Will and Testament."

"It says here that Neil inherited Loraine's house," I said.

"Then he sold it to us," Kyle said.

"And LOOK!" yelled Lucy. "He inherited the family cemetery, too. Oak Hill Cemetery! The article said it was 'privately owned.' That's because it's owned by Neil. And now he's moving his own dead relatives for a dumb shopping center."

"Well, one thing's for sure. I won't feel bad when we make Neil squirm. He deserves it. Let's write the letter," Kyle said.

Here's what we wrote:

Dear Jelly Belly,

I remember how you swiped money from the bank when we played Monopoly.

I remember when you broke my lamp. You said Scarface did it.

I remember your report cards. How could you get an F in gym?

See, Neil, I know lots of scummy things about you. And guess what? Now that I'm a ghost, I know even more! Every time you run a red light, I see it. Every time you lie, I hear it. Every time you cheat, I know it. You can pretty much say, I know all, I see all.

And I talk, too. Your dirty little secrets are NOT safe with me. You know what they say about "the silence of the grave?" It's a big, fat lie because DEAD GUYS TALK, and I'm a regular blabbermouth.

I like Oak Hill Cemetery, and right now I'm not resting in peace. If you build a shopping center here, it will be over my dead body.

Get it? Just a little cemetery humor.

It's time to talk. Meet me at my grave at 3:15 Monday . . . or else!

Your Old Aunt Blabbermouth,
Loraine

After that, we walked outside and released Chuckie. He walked away, alone.

"Call me crazy," I said. "But I had a really funny thought. Remember when Chuckie said Neil might have tried to be nice? That he was lonely? Do you think that's because the Chuckster is lonely, too?"

Kyle said, "He really doesn't have any friends. Who'd be friends with somebody that rotten?"

"Maybe he's not trying to scam us with his bodyguard service. Maybe he's lonely," I said. "But I still don't trust him."

"Yeah," said Lucy. "Some people have tarantulas for pets. They say the spider would never hurt them. That they're just misunderstood. That they're really furry and sweet. I'm glad—for the spiders—that somebody thinks they're cute. But I'd rather have a puppy."

We went to my house and into my bedroom. I knelt next to my bed and held my nose. Then I felt around until my hand sank into something gooey. *Spludge.* I pulled it out.

"What *is* that?" asked Lucy.

"I'm not sure what it *was.* Now it's a black-ish, softish, goopish something."

"And it REEKS!" said Kyle.

"It's perfect," we said together. We smeared it on the envelope and mailed the letter.

* 13 *

voice fRom the GRave

On Monday, we got everything ready at the cemetery. We put Scarface in the tree hole, along with some peanuts. With a bunch of peanuts, Scarface would stay put. We put a walkie-talkie in there, too, and taped the "talk" button down. We posted Chuckie at the gate. Then we went to the hill with the other walkie-talkie and binoculars. We were ready.

All we needed was Neil. Had he gotten the letter? Did he believe it? Would he come?

At 3:17 Neil drove up in his big black rich-guy car. He got out and looked over his shoulder. He pulled his hat low on his head and walked toward Loraine's grave.

I crossed my fingers. "So far so good," I said.

Neil got to Loraine's grave. "Hello?" we heard him say through the walkie-talkie. "Hello. Anybody here?"

"Come on, Scarface," whispered Kyle. "Say hello."

But Scarface didn't.

"Auntie," Neil said. "Are you here?" He waited, but Scarface still didn't talk. Neil threw up his arms. "This is dumb. It's just some kind of prank. There's no such thing as ghosts. I knew it." He spun around to leave.

"Come on, Scarface," whispered Kyle. "*Talk.*"

Neil started to walk away. Suddenly . . .

"*Hello. Hello. Hello hello hello,*" Scarface said.

Neil stopped dead in his tracks and looked around frantically. "W-w-who's there?"

"*Loraaaaine,*" said Scarface. "*Wooo-oooo.*"

Neil looked over his shoulder and skulked back to the grave. "Auntie?" he said.

"*I know something you don't know,*" Scarface sang, the way Chuckie had a few days ago.

"What?!"

"*I know something you don't know,*" Scarface sang again.